I AM WITH YOU ALWAYS

FATHER BENEDICT GROESCHEL, C.F.R.

I AM WITH YOU ALWAYS

A STUDY OF THE HISTORY AND MEANING OF

PERSONAL DEVOTION TO JESUS CHRIST

FOR CATHOLIC, ORTHODOX, AND PROTESTANT CHRISTIANS

IGNATIUS PRESS SAN FRANCISCO

Nihil Obstat: Monsignor Michael F. Hull, S.T.D.
Imprimatur: †The Most Reverend Dennis J. Sullivan, D.D.
Auxillary Bishop of the Archdiocese of New York
November 2, 2010

The *Nihil Obstat* and *Imprimatur* are official declaration that this book is free of doctrinal or moral error. There are no implications contained therein that those who have granted the *Nihil Obstat* and *Imprimatur* agree with the content, opinion or statements expressed.

Cover painting:
Annunciation by Father John Lynch

Father Benedict has explained that
in this painting, Father Lynch seeks to communicate
the dynamism of the Holy Spirit filling the Virgin
as she speaks with the archangel.
Although the painting is done in the classical style,
the artist has striven to present a quality
familiar to contemporary believers.

Cover design by Roxanne Mei Lum

ISBN 978-1-58617-257-2
Library of Congress Control Number 2010922768
Printed in the United States of America ♾

To Pope Benedict XVI
in gratitude for
his devotion to Christ
and his openness to all
Christians and all who believe in God

Contents

Acknowledgments

This book has been more than a decade in the making. So many people helped with it over the years that that I am afraid it is difficult not to leave someone out. I feel, however, that I must make the attempt to list as many as I can remember.

First of all I am deeply indebted to the team of personal editors whose help was indispensable: James Monti in the beginning chapters and Charles Pendergast throughout eight years of extraordinarily capable assistance. More recently John Collins has carefully helped with the completion of this book.

Dr. Ted Campbell of Southern Methodist University provided the initial inspiration for this work. As he has done for so many of my books, Fr. John Lynch provided a remarkable original painting for the cover, this time of the Annunciation, when the Son of God first came to be among us and to remain with us always. I am also very grateful to Dr. Timothy George of the Beeson School of Theology for his input on Evangelical spirituality. The exploration of Orthodox devotion was made possible by the staff of St. Vladimir's Seminary in Yonkers, New York, and their excellent library. I am indebted, as well, to the faculty of St. Nersess Armenian Seminary and particularly to Fr. Kerekin Karparian, pastor of St. Gregory Armenian Church in New Rochelle, New York, for their guidance on Armenian spirituality. Special thanks go to Fr. Michael Plekon for his advice and council on Eastern Christianity and to my co-worker Fr. Eugene Fulton, who is a Catholic priest of the Byzantine Rite. Finally, I am deeply grateful to the sisters and the staff of the Corrigan Memorial Library of St. Joseph's Seminary in Yonkers, New York.

We have carefully sought and obtained permission to cite many works and authors in this volume and we are grateful for all permissions we have received. Special mention must be made of the Classics of Western Spirituality series published by the Paulist Press and of my friend Richard Payne who guided this great publishing project. Finally I want to express my thanks to the Franciscan Friars of the Renewal, many of whom assisted me in various aspects of this project, and to the staff of Trinity Retreat, who provided much support and encouragement. My thanks go, as well, to David Burns and Helen Carbone.

I will always keep in my prayers those who assisted us in this very substantial project, which had to be done during the spare time of all involved, in between many other responsibilities.

Introduction

The Unique Qualities of Christianity

The study of the various religions of the world reveals that although they have much in common, each is unique. This is especially true of Christianity, which has at least three distinct characteristics. First, it is the religion of the God who suffers and dies, who assumes the full scope of the human condition with all its tragedies. Second, most of Christ's followers believe that Jesus Christ, risen from the dead, is still close to them. They believe that His voice is heard in the Scriptures and that His mysterious presence is experienced in the sacraments. Even the most unsacramental of Protestants acknowledge and respond to the presence of Jesus Christ and the Holy Spirit in very personal ways. Nothing in the practice of most sacramental Christians denies the personal experience of Christ apart from the sacraments, for example, in personal prayer. Quite the contrary is true. The medieval Catholic writer St. Bernard of Clairvaux speaks of three comings of Christ: at the Incarnation, at the Last Judgment, and His invisible presence among those who believe in Him.[1] Christ's words "Behold, I am with you always, to the close of the age" (Mt 28:20) are embraced wherever Christianity is taken seriously.

The belief in Christ's presence gives rise to Christianity's third unique characteristic: personal devotion to Christ—a response to Him as friend; a deeply felt sense of reverence, gratitude, trust, dedication, repentance for our faults; and ultimately an all-encompassing impulse to love and serve Him. This experience is properly called Christian devotion. One might object that this personal response is not lacking in the other monotheistic religions. That is true. Because the Son of God took on humanity, however, giving God a human face, Christians are capable of a very personal, intimate, and loving devotion to Him. This differs considerably from the relationship of a devout Jew or Muslim with the Lord in which the most profound experience of God is likely to be one of reverence and awe.

This book is about Christian devotion, its meaning and importance and its many varieties of expression. It is interesting to note

[1] See St. Bernard, Sermon "*In Adventu Domini*", in *The Liturgy of the Hours* (New York: Catholic Book Publishing, 1975), 1: 169–70.

that throughout its two-thousand-year-long history, devotion to Christ has been amazingly similar across the sadly divided branches of Christianity. This largely unrecognized similarity has been obscured by polemical battles over theology and the interpretation of history. In doing this study over several years, I have found very little explicit recognition of the essential unity of Christian devotion despite obvious similarities. With the coming of ecumenism in the twentieth century, there was some acknowledgment that "we worship the same God and follow the same Jesus Christ", but few realized that the best representatives of the various branches of Christianity loved their Founder in much the same way and expressed their devotion in similar terms, consciously and unconsciously borrowing from one another.

Doing the research for this volume has been a constant source of delight and amazement. In the last half century alone Orthodox iconography, or sacred art, permeated European Protestantism and brought a new flavor to all Europeans seeking to worship Christ. We have seen Protestant Pentecostals influencing Roman Catholic worship, while Catholic charismatics were seen in St. Peter's Basilica, with the Pope accepting their experiences enthusiastically. Spiritual writers of the Catholic tradition, like Thomas à Kempis, Francis de Sales, and Thomas Merton, are being accepted across the spectrum of Christian denominations. As we have said, in all these expressions the central focus is love for and devotion to Jesus Christ.

An Astounding Meeting

I became aware of the universality of Christian devotion when I attended an ecumenical meeting of Christian leaders at the invitation of Cardinal William Keeler of Baltimore. I was astounded to see on the program a lecture on the meaning and propriety of devotion to the Sacred Heart of Jesus, which was given by Dr. Ted Campbell, a noted Methodist theologian and historian and now professor at Southern Methodist University, Perkins School of Theology. Dr. Campbell drew fascinating parallels between the Sacred Heart and Protestant devotion to Christ.[2] My head was reeling when he mentioned that Thomas Goodwin, chaplain to Oliver Cromwell, a most un-Catholic person, had preached a three hours' sermon on the subject of the holy Heart of Jesus and His love for sinners. As I listened, I became aware of why I had felt at home when I had preached at Protestant services in the 1960s and 1970s, the heyday of ecumenism. Although a traditional Catholic, I have never felt out of place in either Orthodox churches or in most Christian denominations called Protestant. We all believe that Jesus Christ is somehow with us and that our response to His presence must be love—even though we express that

[2] See Ted A. Campbell, *The Religion of the Heart: A Study of European Religious Life in the Seventeenth and Eighteenth Centuries* (Columbia, S.C.: University of South Carolina Press, 1991).

love in different ways. Because of this I began the most interesting and revealing intellectual adventure of my life in writing this book.

Devotion—A Vital Question of Our Time

Often the leadership of Christian churches (including my own) appears not to give sufficient recognition to the importance of devotion to Jesus Christ. Strangely, some clergy seem troubled or annoyed by those for whom Christ is the most real person in their lives. Hostility to devotion takes many forms, including cold mechanical clericalism and an intellectualized form of belief that constantly attempts to express the faith in terms acceptable to the contemporary culture. Another source of opposition to devotion is a kind of religiosity that substitutes induced states of consciousness, like recollection and alpha rhythms, for mature prayer. New Age types of religiosity fall short because devotion is a personal relationship. Recollection and meditation can be helpful, but they are no substitute for a real relationship with Christ.

Strangely, there is no generally accepted definition of devotion. To some, the word signifies the most meaningful experience of daily life; to others, it suggests sentimentality, an embarrassment. Some of the very people who feel that the colorful devotion of simple souls is distressing may themselves be very devout and experience Christ's presence profoundly. They just fail to recognize the same reality in others who express it differently. A very devout young priest told me that as a result of prejudice from his seminary training, he felt an automatic chill when he heard the word "devotion".

When looking for a descriptive definition of Christian devotion, I turned to the account of the first recorded prayer to the ascended Christ—the words of St. Stephen at his martyrdom (Acts 7:55–60). First, the martyr sees the heavens open and the Son of Man standing at the right hand of God. As he is being stoned to death, he prays two distinct prayers: one asks that the Lord Jesus receive his spirit, and the other is a request that the Lord will forgive his enemies. These are clearly prayers to Jesus the Lord. Later we will explore the full significance of this type of invocation, especially in the Pauline writings.

After an analysis of many devotional prayers and some personal introspection, I think that a good descriptive definition of devotion to Christ will have the following elements.

1. A powerful psychological awareness of the personal presence of Christ, or a very strong desire for that presence.

2. An immediate appeal to Christ about personally significant things in one's life. This makes devotion a "real relationship" and not simply a meditation. The personally significant thing may be an imperative need ("Lord, receive my spirit") or a strong desire ("Lord, that I may see") or a fear ("Lord, save me lest I perish"). It may be a spiritual need ("Increase my faith"), or the need of someone dear to us ("Lord, have pity on my son"). It may be simply a desire to be silent in Christ's

presence ("Come aside and rest awhile"). We must relate to Christ not only with our minds but with our hearts.

3. We must be willing to do what He asks. This is interesting in Stephen's case. Not long before, Christ had given the command: "Love your enemies and pray for those who persecute you" (Mt 5:44). To people of that time such an injunction did not make sense. It had to be accepted on faith. With Stephen, we see a follower of Christ fulfilling this command for the first time in the most dramatic circumstances. Stephen does what Jesus asks, although he may not really have understood why he had to love his enemies. I am not sure that we understand it well even now.

4. Stephen did not fail, but we often do. Some of the psalms (Psalm 51, for example) are beautiful prayers of repentance, and we see repentance in the New Testament—that of St. Peter, for instance—following the failure to be loyal to Christ. Repentance is always part of Christian devotion.

5. Devotion must include trust in Christ. Christ often rebukes the disciples for their little faith, in the sense of trust in Him. He also praised the faith of those who did trust in Him. Faith in the Gospel is always immediate, personal, and includes the idea of trust. Trusting himself to Christ in the hour of death, Stephen makes a clear statement of his belief in life after death; "Lord Jesus, receive my spirit" (Acts 7:59).

Not only does Stephen trust, but he petitions: "Receive my spirit." In most cases devotion includes a prayer for God's merciful providence to grant some favor or grace. The centurion asking for the healing of his boy (servant or son) does so with a confidence that impresses even Jesus (Mt 8:5–11).

6. Finally, mature Christian devotion has a kind of simple eschatological element to it, in which the devout person is thinking not necessarily of the end of the ages, but of his own mortality. The devout are sustained by the hope that at the time of death, they will "see" the face of Christ in a new way, that He awaits them.

To summarize this definition, we can define Christian devotion as a powerful awareness of or longing for Christ's presence, accompanied by a trustful surrender to Him of our personal needs. To this is joined a willingness to do His will and a sense of repentance for any previous failure to do so. We must trust Him not only with our present need but also with the salvation of our souls and those we care about. Finally, in some way we must anticipate our meeting with Him at the hour of death.

With this definition of devotion in mind, we begin our journey through twenty centuries of Christian history. There will be divisions, scandals, failures, persecutions, and every other kind of trouble and tragedy that descends on men. The history of Christianity is not a trip to the land of Oz; it is an integral part of the struggle of human existence. Christians fail, sin, and do stupid things; they fight with and kill others. Crimes and atrocities will be committed in Christ's name. On a personal level, those who try to follow Him will go off the path. Some will give up altogether. Through it all, however, there will be a Presence, one so subtle that a fool may ignore it his whole life while claiming to be Christian. This Presence is so powerful that those who pursue and embrace it throughout life may, according to Christ's own promise, do greater works than He did. "Lo, I am with you always, to the close of the age" (Mt 28:20).

Our personal response to these words and to that Presence is Christian devotion. It was there when the first Christian martyr surrendered his spirit to Christ. That Presence and that devotion will also be there when the last Christian, at the point of death, prepares for the face-to-face encounter with the risen Lord.

Suggestions on How to Read This Book

I am hoping that many people who are not avid readers of long books will nonetheless find this book interesting and helpful to them. If you are familiar with substantial books these suggestions are not for you. But for those who are somewhat daunted by the length of *I Am with You Always*, I would like to make the following suggestion: that you read the first two chapters and then look through the table of contents, picking out chapters that are in line with your own interests. For instance, if you are a Protestant, you will find Chapters 10, 13, 15, 16, 20, 22, and 24 particularly interesting. Those who are Orthodox will find the chapters on the early Church along with Chapters 18 and 25 of special significance. If you are a Catholic who, for example, loves French spirituality, then Chapter 14 will be particularly to your liking. After you read the chapter in which you have the greatest interest, then you may want to look at the chapters around it or go back chronologically to see how it fits in. It is not expected that everyone who approaches this book will read every line. It might be very helpful, however, for all readers to examine the portions devoted to the twentieth century to find out where we seem to be going with devotion to Christ.

PART ONE

CHRIST FROM THE EARLY DISCIPLES TO THE AGE OF FAITH

I Finding the Lost Christ

Only someone who has been devoted to Jesus Christ and has learned to make some sense out of life because of Him can appreciate what it means to love Him. Yet how can we be devoted to or say that we love someone whom we have never seen, whose human voice we have never heard, whose hand we have never touched? Those with no faith in Christ find such personal devotion incomprehensible; those with little faith find it annoying because, sadly, they feel left out. Yet they may be moved or at least impressed by the vibrant relationship with Christ they find in someone else, especially if the devoted person is a simple soul. Skeptics may be touched by the faith of a poor old woman, but smirk at the sincere devotion of an educated person. Those with a weak, secularized faith, partially undermined by rationalism and materialism, will often criticize those who say, "I know him" (1 Jn 2:4). And it is they themselves who do not realize that they have little faith.

A Desperate Situation

If I have learned anything from five decades of work as a priest who is also a psychologist, it is that ultimately we are all desperate. Some cannot avoid a continual, sometimes acute sense of desperation. Others, who consider themselves quite healthy, fall imperceptibly into what Thoreau calls "lives of quiet desperation". Still others pass through times when they wonder if they can survive the day. The reason for this sense of desperation is not difficult to discover: the human situation is desperate in itself. Most of us seem to be on a journey from obscurity to oblivion. Those who have achieved some notice by the rest of the world often appear to be fools. They may not, in fact, be any more foolish than the rest of us, but their folly is celebrated or at least exposed. The few with real virtue who are well known often manifest a seriousness or ironic quality that suggests they know that the human situation seen apart from the promise of eternal life is desperate. I recall this message coming across clearly but subtly in a conversation with the novelist Walker Percy. He revealed both a strong Christian hope and a bleakly realistic view of the human situation. Only through a personal faith in Christ had he escaped Thoreau's "quiet desperation".

A Passing World

Our cherished relationships and all the things that we value are fragile; all we have will disappear in the inescapable event of death. Faced with this reality, thoughtful people search for an answer to the riddle of human existence. Different religious figures have given different answers, shown different ways, made different promises, and have led very different lives—the tranquility of the Buddha, the passionate battle of Muhammad, the awesome and truly God-given authority of Moses. All of these are inspiring responses to the sorrows and difficulties of life, to the desperate human situation. And then there is the response of Jesus, called the Christ.

Jesus of Nazareth

No great religious figure, no prophet is as inscrutable, as mysterious, or as enigmatic as Jesus of Nazareth. Obscurity, political insignificance, fatigue, betrayal, torture, and finally capital punishment hardly seem to provide answers that will attract those who desperately seek the meaning of life. His words are not like an epic poem. His short life, though sorrowful, does not read like a Greek tragedy. He is not a hero pitted fatefully against an evil world. His most famous followers—Paul of Tarsus, Francis of Assisi, Catherine of Siena, and Teresa of Avila—seem to have more of the overt characteristics of great religious figures than He does. There are many prophets, apostles, mystics, and martyrs of charity; but there is none like Him. Jesus of Nazareth stands alone because simply, directly, without any inner conflict He does the will of His Father, whom he calls His Abba. And He calls others to find the answer to life's desperate questions by doing the same. His words "Thy kingdom come, Thy will be done" (Mt 6:10) are His answer to the desperate human condition.

He is not consoling like the Buddha or charismatic like Muhammad, or mystically directed like Moses. This thoroughly devoted Person of simple purpose does many things that we moderns find difficult to accept. We would reject them as distasteful, outrageous, and even paranoid, should we discover them in the life of a contemporary. Indeed He is always a problem for those who study Christianity from the outside and even for those believers who study it from within. They are shocked by Him. He claims to have come down from the heavenly Father, to be one with God, to give His Flesh and Blood as a sacred Meal in memory of Himself; He condemns the hardhearted if they do not accept Him. Not only does He promise eternal life but He says He will return from the dead and take His followers to His Father's house. Innumerable people through the centuries have believed that He does exactly this. He continues to draw millions of souls to Himself in our day, and many more will follow Him in the future.

Who is Jesus of Nazareth? Who is He to me, to you, to the people of our postmodern age? This question has elicited many answers, the first from His closest associates on earth, and His very early disciples, including one who claimed to have met Jesus on the road to Damascus after He had died and risen to life. Answers have also come from those who were deeply influenced by His disciples in the first three centuries. In turn, these early leaders and bishops influenced an impressive collection of brilliant and dedicated men, the Fathers of the Church, beginning with the Council of Nicaea (A.D. 325). It was these bishops (or overseers) who codified the writings that make up the New Testament. Thus the final collection of those books was approved as public revelation almost four hundred years after Jesus' death. A powerful, consistent, intellectually impressive body of thought about Him became the living tradition of the Church. The writings of the early Church Fathers and the pronouncements of Church councils provided the foundation for future beliefs on the subject of Jesus Christ.

A Sign of Contradiction

In the course of the centuries, some questioned the teaching of the early bishops, as others had questioned the apostles before them. The resulting controversies have continued to give rise to clearer definitions, always with the goal of keeping the original experience of the apostles alive and whole. We will survey some of these controversies, especially the decisions of the early Church that were meant to preserve the mystery and meaning of the original message of Jesus Christ.

Jesus and the Scholars

In recent centuries scholars have tried to reconstruct from the Scriptures and other ancient writings a picture of the historical Jesus. Some such scholars were committed to Christianity; others were indifferent; and a number were actually hostile to it, although in a camouflaged manner. Unfortunately, in much historical reconstruction, theory replaced faith. Because so much of this research is done without the "obedience of faith" (Rom 16:26), and because the acceptance of particular theories is so dependent on the fashions of the moment, these endeavors have often done more harm than good to those seeking to know Jesus Christ.

As Pope Benedict XVI points out in his book *Jesus of Nazareth*, the search for the historical Jesus and the historical-critical school of biblical scholarship that this search engendered are flawed for a number of reasons. He states:

> As historical-critical scholarship advanced, it led to finer and finer distinctions between layers of tradition in the Gospels, beneath which the real object of faith—the figure . . . of Jesus—became increasingly obscured and blurred. At the same time, though, the reconstructions of this Jesus . . . became more and more incompatible with one another. . . . If you read a number of these reconstructions one after the other, you see at once that far from uncovering an icon that has become obscured over time, they are much more like photographs of their authors and the ideals they hold.[1]

[1] Pope Benedict XVI, *Jesus of Nazareth*, trans. Adrian J. Walker (New York: Doubleday, 2007; San Francisco: Ignatius Press, 2008), xii.

The Holy Father shows us that most of the attempts to conjure up a historical portrait of Jesus that is scientifically reliable "have produced a common result: the impression that we have very little certain knowledge of Jesus and that only at a later stage did faith in his divinity shape the image we have of him. This impression has by now penetrated deeply into the minds of the Christian people at large."[2] He goes on to point out that this is a bad situation for faith because "its point of reference is being placed in doubt: Intimate friendship with Jesus, on which everything depends, is in danger of clutching at thin air."

A different and more sensible approach is recommended by the Holy Father and has been detailed in a document of the Pontifical Biblical Commission.[3] The commission, under the director of then Cardinal Ratzinger, called for an approach to interpretation and understanding of Scripture that may be characterized as symphonic or holistic and by the combination of different approaches—textual, critical, narrative, traditional, doctrinal, and practical—in defining the pastoral and spiritual use of the Scriptures.

The Purpose of This Book

The purpose of this book is neither to offer a critique of contemporary biblical studies nor to point out the spiritually debilitating effects of some of these studies. My hope is to assist the committed disciple of Christ toward a better appreciation of the meaning of Christ and the Paschal mystery of His life, to open the eyes of those who seek meaning amid the desperate turmoil of earthly existence. Most committed disciples can probably see their own desperation described by Augustine in the *Confessions*: "I was sick at heart and in torment, accusing myself with a new intensity of bitterness, twisting and turning in my chain in the hope that it might be utterly broken.... 'And thou, O Lord, how long? How long, Lord? ... Remember not our former iniquities.' "[4] Those desperately seeking Christ will only be confused by the muddle of theories, ideas, and conjectures that they may hear when the Gospel is supposed to be preached. To them I hope to offer some clarity and help.

Jesus and the Individual

Soon after his election as Bishop of Rome, Pope John Paul II published an encyclical letter called *Redeemer of Man*, which became the cornerstone of his pontificate. He called Christians to center all thought and action on the mystery of Christ. The Pope, a very active participant in the Second Vatican Council, could see that it was necessary at this time for Catholics to focus their collective and individual attention on Christ:

---

[2] Ibid.

[3] "The Interpretation of the Bible in the Church". See *Origins*, CNS Documentary Service, 23, no. 29 (Jan. 6, 1994).

[4] Augustine, *The Confessions of Saint Augustine*, trans. Frank Sheed (New York: Sheed and Ward, 1965) bk. 8, chaps. 6, 7.

> Through the Church's consciousness, which the Council considerably developed, through all levels of this self-awareness, and through all the fields of activity in which the Church expresses, finds and confirms herself, we must constantly aim at Him "who is the head," "through whom are all things and through whom we exist," who is both "the way, and the truth" and "the resurrection and the life," seeing whom, we see the Father, and who had to go away from us—that is, by his death on the Cross and then by his Ascension into heaven—in order that the Counselor should come to us and should keep coming to us as the Spirit of truth. In him are "all the treasures of wisdom and knowledge," and the Church is His Body. "By her relationship with Christ, the Church is a kind of sacrament or sign and means of intimate union with God, and of the unity of all mankind," and the source of this is he, he himself, he the Redeemer.[5]

This impassioned plea may seem at first rather generalized, calling for a corporate commitment of the Church to Christ; however, the Pope quickly emphasizes that this first concern of the Church for union with Christ is also most particular and individual:

> The Council points out this very fact when, speaking of that likeness, it recalls that "man is the only creature on earth that God willed for itself." Man as "willed" by God, as "chosen" by him from eternity and called, destined for grace and glory—this is "each" man, "the most concrete" man, "the most real"; this is man in all the fullness of the mystery in which he has become a sharer in Jesus Christ, the mystery in which each one of the four thousand million human beings living on our planet has become a sharer from the moment he is conceived beneath the heart of his mother.[6]

John Paul II then extends his plea for a well-informed devotion to Christ, seeing this devotion as the foundation of all genuine ecumenical endeavors. He introduces an idea that he will develop later in his pastoral office, namely, that although Christian churches are divided, they are united in proclaiming Christ as Savior of the world:

> All of us who are Christ's followers must therefore meet and unite around him. This unity in the various fields of the life, tradition, structures and discipline of the individual Christian Churches and Ecclesial Communities cannot be brought about without effective work aimed at getting to know each other and removing the obstacles blocking the way to perfect unity. However, we can and must immediately reach and display to the world our unity in proclaiming the mystery

[5] Pope John Paul II, *Redemptor Hominis*, 7.3, in *The Encyclicals of John Paul II*, ed. J. Michael Miller, C.S.B. (Huntington, Ind.: Our Sunday Visitor, 1996), 54–55.

[6] Ibid., 13.3; 65–66.

> of Christ, in revealing the divine dimension and also the human dimension of the Redemption, and in struggling with unwearying perseverance for the dignity that each human being has reached and can continually reach in Christ, namely the dignity of both the grace of divine adoption and the inner truth of humanity, a truth which—if in the common awareness of the modern world it has been given such fundamental importance—for us is still clearer in the light of the reality that is Jesus Christ.[7]

Every year, millions of people end their earthly lives filled with hope in Christ, seeing in death a passage to a far better life. Hundreds of millions, in fact, almost two billion, call Him their Savior because they believe that He has saved them from a meaningless existence followed by a descent into endless oblivion. Throughout the centuries, billions have called Christ their Deliverer from futility, despair, and eternal nothingness, while millions have fought against Him. His teaching and His Church have been bitterly resented by those whose hope did not go beyond this world. The twentieth century saw the worst of Christ's enemies. The bizarre scene of Josef Stalin spending his last moments shaking his fist at the heavens is an incredibly ironic symbol of modern hostility to Christ.

Different ages have seen Christ as a Savior in different ways. One age has stressed that He is the Eternal Word of the Father, another has seen Him as King of Kings, and yet another has concentrated on His suffering humanity. In our time He has been viewed by some as the liberator of the oppressed, while to others He is the living expression of the Divine Mercy. Each of these titles is important; each reveals an aspect of the mystery of Christ, of God come among us. For many reasons it seems that the Christ of our time is the Divine Friend, not simply the Friend of all, but the Friend of each one, the Friend of those who are desperate in their loneliness. It is not surprising that at a time like ours, when individual fulfillment and the right to privacy are emphasized, that Christ will be seen by sensitive souls as the Divine Friend.

A Christless Christianity

Recently, an eminent European prelate and scholar, Cardinal Christoph Schönborn of Vienna, remarked that Jesus had become a distant and obscure figure to many in northern Europe. He is not denied, but has become unknown. This is not an accident. The rationalist biblical scholar Rudolf Bultmann, who was very much in vogue for several decades, observed that the more he studied Jesus of Nazareth, the more obscure He became. Perhaps the obscurity was due to the way He was studied. One cannot begin by studying God. One begins by worshipping God and then goes on to contemplate Him with awe and reverence.

[7] Ibid., 11.4; 61.

As a result of an excessively intellectualized approach to theological studies one often hears that the preaching of the Gospel is "out of touch" with the needs of people. Much preaching is academic, hamstrung by the limitations of rationalism. Another complaint is that preaching has become purely ethical and largely humanistic. Serious young people, born into the mainstream churches, including the Catholic Church, depart for Evangelical or Fundamentalist churches, because they "did not hear Christ preached" in their first church.

What's wrong? I think the problem is that many believe in Christ but do not truly know Him. Some even deny that there is a way to know Him, even through the dark glass of faith (see 1 Cor 13:12). This book is about knowing Christ as we must come to know Him in the context of our lives, through the teaching of the Christian faith, which has grown and developed continuously from the original revelation two thousand years ago.

They Did Not Worship Him[8]

As Christ becomes more and more obscure to us, reverence for His sacred person continues to be eroded. What follows is a blatant disrespect for life, the environment, one another, family, friends—God Himself. Often religious people, with an incredible lack of sensitivity, dispense with signs of reverence toward God. We see this on the part of both Catholics and Protestants. One is happy to say that this is much less obvious in the Eastern churches, whether Orthodox or Catholic. For example, despite St. Augustine's admonition that to approach the Holy Eucharist without a prostration or bow is a serious sin of irreverence,[9] one observes a distressing lack of reverence on the part of Catholics for this central mystery of the Church's worship. Things are not much better among Protestant Christians. A famous Protestant preacher and politician once addressed a national political convention with St. Paul's words to the Corinthians (Eye has not seen, etc, . . . [what we are going to do]) regarding the mystery of eternal salvation as a description of his party's platform. This was shocking, if not intended, irreverence.

As the word of God, Scripture must evoke profound reverence. Yet careless preachers often reduce these words to a handful of confetti. In the blandest of tones a well-meaning but thoughtless person may dispense ill-conceived ideas lacking in a grasp of the teachings of the Church Fathers, the decisions of ecumenical councils, or, on the part of Catholics, the authoritative teaching of the Pope. Such casual arrogance stems from a lack of awe and an inability to respond to the mystery of God; it leads to the trivialization of the Gospel, religious indifference, and ultimately to a loss of faith.

---

[8] See Rom 1:21.

[9] See *Enarratio in Ps. 98*, chap. 9, in *Patrologia Latina* (PL hereinafter), 37: 1264.

A Book for All Devout Christians

Despite many problems, there are still strong signs of religious faith in the Western world. These signs are most obvious in the United States, but they exist in most of the industrialized nations. Vital signs of faith are even seen where committed Christians comprise only a small percentage of the population. Regardless of their sectarian affiliation, these Christians believe that the resurrected Jesus of Nazareth, now reigning at the right hand of the Father, knows them immediately and individually, calls them to a greater discipleship, responds to their prayers, judges their sins, offers merciful forgiveness, and waits for them at the end of their lives with the salvation He bought by His life and death.

By an odd set of circumstances—and I hope by the workings of Divine Providence—I started to write books and preach the Gospel message in the media (usually EWTN) in the early 1980s. The ensuing publicity was unplanned, unexpected, and undesired because of the spiritual danger of vanity. Most of what I hope the Holy Spirit has led me to say and write has been addressed to my fellow Catholics and to Orthodox Christians. It has been a delightful surprise, however, to find that many Protestants and even members of other faiths respond to what I preach. I regularly receive encouraging letters from people who are not Catholics. Temptations to vanity are fended off by critical letters from some Catholics and others who think that I am too conservative. Although I try to accept criticism and learn from it, I never accept being called either "conservative" or "liberal": these are essentially political designations. "Conservative" means maintaining the status quo, and I think the status quo stinks.

When I try to sort out the critical reactions I receive and that others receive, I am often left with the feeling that we are criticized because we try to be devout. This does not mean that we are more faithful or virtuous or Christlike, but that we find devotion—a personal loving response to Jesus Christ—to be the most important element of our faith experience. Christian devotion is not limited to any denomination; it is obviously widespread and varies with intensity throughout the Christian world. So this important topic gave me the chance to write a book for all devout Christians—something I have always wanted to do.

I began this book on a pilgrimage in the Holy Land. There I found the concepts and chapters opening effortlessly before me. I was deeply moved to walk the streets of old Jerusalem and the Via Dolorosa, along the shores of the Sea of Galilee, and to go into the dungeon of the house of Caiaphas. This proved to be the perfect setting in which to write. It brought me to the realization that this book has been inside me for years. The sacraments are the most important spiritual encounters with Christ in my life, but these God-given signs focus our minds and hearts on the more general encounter with our Savior that all Christians share. The individual's inner icon or image of Christ is expressed in devotion. It represents the encounter with God's saving grace intelligently and devotionally formed by the shining picture of Christ given in the Scriptures, expressed especially in the Gospels and left to us by those who knew Him personally when He walked among us.

The image of Christ, provided essentially by revelation and early tradition, changes in perspective and emphasis from age to age, from culture to culture, from denomination to denomination. Christians in the industrialized nations will have an image of Christ very different from that of their co-religionists at the time of the Reformation. We need to look as objectively as possible at this devotional image as Christians move into the third millennium, not to discredit this image, but to sharpen it and make it more consistent with the New Testament and the ancient Church. This will help us embrace the image of Christ more devoutly. Though we all see through a glass darkly, we must try to see as accurately and devoutly as we can so that some day we may know him as we are known by Him (see 1 Cor 13:12).

2 You Have Known Him

Knowing Someone

Before considering devotion to Christ, we must ponder the psychological process of knowing another person, especially one we have neither seen nor touched. Some personal psychological introspection will be helpful here. In the following analysis of the process of knowing another person, I will avoid complex terminology but attempt to use insights from accepted theories drawn from the study of human cognition.

There are many ways to know a person. All are colored by the needs and experience of the one who does the knowing. For example, let's consider Marie, a mother of three. To her parents Marie will always be their child, even if she is caring for them in their old age. To her husband, she is a very different person. He knows her in an entirely different way, yet he loves her as much as her parents do, perhaps even more. She is known and loved as a spouse. To her oldest child—a fourteen-year-old boy—she is a source of conflict. He loves his parents, but resents them because they are in the way of his need for independence. He knows his mother both as the source of his own life and its greatest opposition. To her nine-year-old daughter, Marie is the greatest mom in the world, the giver of almost all blessings and the center of all authority. To her four-year-old boy, Marie and her husband stand at the center of the universe. They are, in fact, in the place of God.

Marie is seen differently by her siblings, her in-laws, her friends, the people in the church choir, and the garage mechanic, whom she does not trust. She is seen very differently by her brother's ex-wife, who thinks Marie interfered in their marriage. She is seen differently yet again by the crabby lady down street who called the police because Marie's dog chased her cat. Finally, there is the person Marie knows as herself.

The question of identity becomes more complicated when we consider someone who is absent. Marie has cousins in Ireland whom she has never seen. They write occasionally, exchange pictures, and speak on the phone at the holidays. She is the smiling face in a family snapshot, the friendly voice on the phone. Someday Marie, like all of us, will be simply a memory in this world. Voices filter through time and imagination: "That's your grandmother Marie, the one on the left in the wedding picture in the blue dress. She was a great girl, Marie. It's too bad she died so young. She was very brave and had a lot of faith, but the cancer finally got her. A great person." But someone pipes up, "She was bossy and too religious. She used to say that she prayed in tongues. My family thought it was all crazy." Others join in: "Listen, if it weren't for Marie, where would your family have been when the house burned down? Marie made room for everyone." "Yeah, but she was bossy." "Don't talk about my aunt that way. She's with God." Obviously there are many ways to know the same person. Even you.

Knowing Someone You Never Met

Before we come to the question, how do we know Christ? we must ponder the experience of knowing someone we have never met. First of all, we have intellectual notions of those we have not met, and in this way we can be said to know them. Millions of television viewers in the last decade of the twentieth century had the impression that they knew Pope John Paul II or Mother Teresa, an impression that came from information read or heard, and especially from television images. Many people meet me for the first time and say, "I know you from EWTN." Some actually act surprised that I don't know them as well. We also may feel that we know historical or religious figures: Abraham Lincoln, for example, or St. Thérèse of Lisieux or Anne Frank. Mental images of such people are so alive in the imaging faculty of the mind that we may feel we know a person from history better than we know the person next door.

It is obvious that we are able to know a person better if there is an emotional as well as intellectual component in our experience of knowing. I may also know someone who hates me but who does not really know me. I may resemble somebody whom my enemy is uncomfortable with or feels threatened by. Hatred, jealousy, and resentment may color a person's knowledge of another, so that it can be said that only an image, and not the person, is truly known. This image may profoundly influence the behavior of the person who thinks he knows another. One may spend much energy hating an image that doesn't represent reality. Images of people we have never actually known are particularly powerful; they color our lives, direct our actions, and even shape our path in this world. For example, Frenchmen differ greatly about the image of Napoleon, and Englishmen see Henry VIII in a variety of ways. If all this is so, then we must accept that our individual image of Christ will greatly shape our understanding of the Christian life.

Knowing a Saint in Heaven

Many Christians, myself included, try to know and even prayerfully communicate with those who have passed into the transcendent reality of eternal life. If you grew up in the old Catholic world you knew the saints and thought of them as your friends. You believed that they knew you and would pray for you. I continue to pray to saints and count many of them as my friends. How this communication is accomplished I leave to God.

St. Augustine is one of the few people in the ancient world who ever engaged this question. In the *Confessions*, speaking of his friend Nebridius, whom he considers so pure a soul that he is already with God, he writes:

> [H]e was a most zealous seeker of the truth. Not long after our conversion and regeneration by Your baptism, You took him from this life, by then a baptized Catholic and serving You in Africa in perfect chastity among his own people, for he had made his whole family Christian. And now he lives in Abraham's bosom. Whatever is meant by that bosom, there my Nebridius lives, my most beloved friend, Your son by adoption and no longer a freed-man only. There he lives. For what other place is there for such a soul? There he lives, in the place of which he asked me, an ignorant poor creature, so many questions. He no longer puts his bodily ear to my lips, but the lips of his spirit to Your fountain, drinking his fill of wisdom, all that his thirst requires, happy without end. Nor do I think he is so intoxicated with the draught of that wisdom as to forget me, since You, O Lord, of whom he drinks are mindful of us.[1]

Augustine obviously assumes that God Himself, His ubiquity, His omniscience, and His love for creation are the medium by which those in eternal life know and are known by the people on earth. In the early Church there are many examples of people knowing, honoring, and offering prayers to saints. Thus in the Vatican necropolis, where the bones of St. Peter were discovered (and in 1968 declared authentic by Pope Paul VI[2]), the following inscription from the first half of the fourth century was found, clearly asking the intercession of this apostle:

> PETER, PRAY CHRIST JESUS FOR THE HOLY CHRISTIAN MEN BURIED NEAR YOUR BODY.[3]

There are many ancient examples of Christians believing that a saint may know and care about the living on earth. More important is the fact that early in the Christian era people believed that they were friends of the saints. This was especially true of the Mother of Jesus, whom early Christians saw as the Gate of Salvation and Mother of the Church. Prayers to Mary date from as early as the third century.

As time went on, explicit prayers to other New Testament figures, such as John the Baptist, Peter, Paul, and John the Apostle, became common. By the fourth century, in both East and West, in public and

---

[1] Augustine, *The Confessions of Saint Augustine*, trans. Frank Sheed (New York: Sheed and Ward, 1965), bk. 9, chap. 3, pp. 186–87.

[2] See John Evangelist Walsh, *The Bones of St. Peter: The First Full Account of the Search for the Apostle's Body* (Garden City, N.Y.: Doubleday, 1982), 1–2, 128–29.

[3] Ibid., 85–86.

in private, people prayed to the saints.[4] They believed the saints knew them and interceded for them before God.

In devotion to the saints there is a consistent experience of being known by someone, a human being beyond this life, and also of knowing that person from Scripture or accounts of religious history. There is also the very strong experience of being helped by them.

Knowing the Angels

Apart from praying to saints, there is the profoundly mysterious devotion to the angels. This is a deeper mystery even than knowing a saint, who once lived in the world and shared our human experience. Almost all who are called saints left some historical record behind. Angels are unknown, except by some extraordinary revelation, usually in the Scriptures.

Beginning with the obvious fact that these mysterious beings are helpers sent by God—hence their name, which means "messenger"—believers in the God of Abraham have always had a healthy respect for angels. The evangelists speak of the appearance of angels at the Annunciation or the Incarnation of Jesus, at His birth, His temptation in the desert, His agony, and His Resurrection. It is not surprising that Christians were curious about angels and soon began to ask for their help.

All of this is of particular interest to us as we consider how you can know a person whom you have not met. How do you know an angel or even imagine one? We must rely on revelation or theological tradition for the little we can know about angels. Most of what theologians tell us is in the negative: how angels differ from us and yet remain persons, how they are ultimate sources of responsible action, that is, responsible individuals. Faith sees them as nonhuman persons. St. Thomas Aquinas tells us that each angel is unique, that they are not members of a species, as we are. They exist out of time. They had one choice for good or evil at the beginning of their existence, and that choice determined whether they would be angels of light or darkness.

People have some images of angels from the Bible. Among the most powerful of these for me is the angel of the agony, who comforted Christ in the Garden of Olives (see Lk 22:43). This deeply moving image has inspired many to pray to the angels to be with them in their suffering or peril, and especially at the hour of death.

It is an angel who brings the good news of salvation, the message that is also the occasion of the virginal conception of Jesus Christ. Great artists have often tried to capture that mysterious moment on which the fate of the world hangs. From the mystical communication between the Virgin and the angel painted by Blessed Fra Angelico to the extremely sensitive Annunciations of the Pre-Raphaelite English painters of the late nineteenth century, these invisible noncorporeal

[4] *New Catholic Encyclopedia* (New York: McGraw-Hill, 1967), 12:962, s.v. "Saints, Devotion to the".

beings have been celebrated in paintings. The premier African American artist, Henry Tanner, in his mystical painting of the Annunciation that hangs in the Philadelphia Museum of Art, depicts the angel as a mysterious shaft of light. Nevertheless, the expression of the humble Virgin clearly demonstrates that she is being addressed by a real but not human person.[5]

Can We Pray to Jesus Now?

Devotion to Jesus (experientially but not theologically) has much in common with devotion to angels and saints. It is relating to an unseen person. It has been part of Christian life since the Church's earliest days. Beginning with the prayer of St. Stephen, "Lord Jesus, receive my spirit" (Acts 7:59), there has been deep, spontaneous prayer to Christ. It has grown theologically and psychologically as people became more aware of their inner selves and needs. In East and West, personal devotion to our Savior has been the outstanding feature of Christian life.

It is particularly interesting to note that when Protestant Christians rejected the idea of devotion to the angels and saints, they did not reject devotion to Jesus Christ. While such devotion was not obvious in the Calvinist tradition in its beginnings, fervent prayer to Christ grew and flourished among Lutherans, Anglicans, Baptists, and others. In the great religious revival of the early nineteenth century, devotion to Christ was warm and fervent, especially under the influence of John Wesley's disciples and the many people influenced by their piety.

Is Devotion to Jesus Special?

We come to the question of whether there is anything specific about devotion to Christ. Most readers will probably agree that there is something unique about such devotion, but what is it? Does this difference pertain to how Christians at a particular time understand Christ as known from the Scriptures or the tradition of the ancient Church? Is the difference determined by secular history, education, or culture? Of greatest importance is the question: Do some of these differences arise independently of the individual who prays? Simply put, is a believer's experience different when praying to Christ from the experience of asking the intercession of a saint or an angel? It is important to emphasize that theologically, there is an essential difference between asking something in prayer of a saint, even the Blessed Virgin, or an angel, and asking the help of Christ, the Son of God. It is the difference between the creature and the Creator. Devotion to Christ is made further complex by the fact that you cannot pray to Him only in His

[5] When I began this book, I asked the gifted artist Fr. John Lynch to paint a depiction of the Annunciation for the cover. Fr. Lynch, who has done covers for many of my books, worked for several years on this beautiful painting, in which he seeks to communicate the dynamism of the Holy Spirit filling the Virgin as she speaks to the archangel. Although his paintings are done in a purely classical style, he strives to present a quality familiar to contemporary believers.

divinity or only in His humanity. He is one Divine Person with both human and divine natures.

In the Gospel account of the marriage feast of Cana (Jn 2:1–11), we observe the intercession of the Mother of Jesus, as well as her apparent disregard for His preference not to help the embarrassed host. Once importuned (so to speak, since there is no accurate word for this interaction of a human with the Divinity in these familiar terms), however, Christ acquiesces to His Mother and works an astonishing sign, fulfilling at one and the same time the role of Son of God and son of Mary, that is, Son of Man. The vocabulary developed by humans for their dealings with one another is inadequate to describe our interactions with God. It is all the more inadequate in describing God's initiatives or responses to us. Even the Scriptures limp because of this inadequacy of language. Some inspired writers struggle with this problem by using superlatives, metaphors, and similes. St. Paul occasionally coins new words. It is important to think about the fact that the words we use to describe our dealings with God and especially His dealings with us were not developed for this purpose. We must always approach the Divine Being through a cloud of profound mystery. Even the term "God" and others directed to Him—"divinity", "transcendent", "adoration", "infinite"—are not fully understood by those who use them. In fact, they are very imperfectly understood. Human language, like human understanding, though important, ultimately fails us in our search for God, as St. Paul reminds us when he asks, "For who has known the mind of the Lord, or who has been his counselor?" (Rom 11:34).

A Warning against Superficiality

Here a warning must be made. We need to grasp firmly the essential idea of the infinite mysteriousness of God. Scripture puts this warning very simply: "As the heavens are higher than the earth, so are my ways higher than your ways and my thoughts than your thoughts" (Is 55:9). This analogy, contrasting the opaque reality of rocks and soil with the quasi-infinite clarity of the sky, is even more meaningful to us who live in a time of great telescopes than it was to those before us. We should keep in mind the mystery of God as we ask: Does Jesus know and care about us individually? Do we believe that He knows and can help us? This leads to further speculation. Can He who once lived on earth and experienced the limitations of physical existence—hunger, fatigue, death—know all the people on earth and relate to each in a way totally beyond our comprehension? The way the ascended Lord knows us transcends the way a saint or angel can know us. Christ, who is God, knows us with the knowledge of God. Our analogy for dealing with this astounding mystery is our own very limited relationships with one another. Even the most intimate human relationships fall short of what faith tells us about Christ's relationship with each one of us. As the eternal Son of God, He has perfect knowledge of each person at any time and thus knows far more than we do about ourselves.

St. Paul observes that spiritual things can be understood only by spiritual minds (see 1 Cor 2:11–16). We must approach the great mystery of our relationship with Christ reverently and keep before us the immense mystery of divine knowledge and divine love. Our two most powerful analogues, one drawn from physical reality, the quasi-infinity of the heavens, and the other from psychological realities, the complexity and richness of a loving human relationship, invite us to the far greater experience of believing that the eternal Word of God, Jesus Christ, knows and loves us in a divine way.

The First Prayer to Jesus in Heaven

As we saw, the prayer of St. Stephen at his martyrdom is regarded as the first recorded prayer to the ascended Lord. Since that time the devout have gradually come to believe that they know Christ, that they are known by Him, and that in prayer they speak to Him. For many this is a deeply felt reality. Many of the earliest prayers to Christ are found in the accounts of martyrdom, such as the following from the acts of St. Theodotus of Ancyra, a tavern keeper who died around the year 302: "Lord Jesus Christ, who hast made heaven and earth, and who never forsakest those who hope in thee, I give thee thanks that thou hast granted me to conquer the dragon and to crush his head. Give rest to thy servants, grant that I may be the last victim of the violence of our enemies. Give peace to thy Church, snatch her from the tyranny of the devil. Amen."[6]

Prayer: Personal, But Not Liturgical

The prayer of Theodotus is personal. It assumes Christ hears and responds to the one who prays, and that the supplicant knows that Christ is forgiving and compassionate. It is, to put it simply, a devotional prayer. It is not liturgical, because it is not a prayer of the whole Church as the Mystical Body of Christ on earth. Liturgical prayer is efficacious because it is the prayer of Christ Himself. The prayer of an individual Christian is efficacious insofar as that person is open to Christ's grace and allows Christ to pray in him. The following prayer is even more obviously personal. It comes from the ecclesiastical writer Origen (184–254):

> Jesus, my feet are dirty. Come and slave for me; pour your water into your basin and come and wash my feet. I am overbold, I know, in asking this, but I dread what you threatened when you said: "If I do not wash your feet, it means you have no companionship with me." Wash my feet, then, because I do want to have companionship with you. And yet, why am I saying: "Wash my feet"? It was all very well for Peter to say that, for in his case all that needed washing was his feet: he was clean through and through. My position is quite different: you may wash me

[6] Rt. Rev. Fernand Cabrol, O.S.B., *Liturgical Prayer: Its History and Spirit* (repr., Westminster, Md.: Newman Press, 1950), 118.

now, but I shall still need that other washing you were thinking of, Lord, when you said: "There is a baptism I must needs be baptised with."[7]

Extraliturgical prayer, what we will call devotional prayer, does not compete with liturgical prayer but complements it. In private prayer the assumption need not even be made that the individual meets and knows Christ by reason of membership in the Mystical Body. A non-Christian may pray simply as a member of the great family of God. The assumption in private prayer is that the one praying is known and loved by God as an individual, either as a member of the Church or not. The person may know little or nothing about the nature of salvation and may not even be baptized; yet he calls out to Christ like the Syrophoenician woman in St. Matthew's Gospel (15:21–28) and is heard. It is a dangerous presumption on the part of a Christian to decide whom God will hear or not hear.

Devotion in the Old Testament

The assumption that personal prayers are heeded is based on Old Testament accounts in which God responds to the prayers of individuals, even those who are not members of the people of God. Among the most moving of these is the prayer of Hagar in the wilderness, a prayer that her son, Ishmael, who is clearly excluded from the inheritance of Abraham (Gen 21:8–21), might survive. This prayer is answered, and Ishmael goes on to be the progenitor of a great nation. Although completely sovereign, absolutely mysterious, and above heaven and earth, the God of Abraham, Isaac, and Jacob cared for and responded to the cries of Hagar and many of His children—Jews and Gentiles. It could even be said that Moses spoke to Him as a friend:

> But Moses besought the Lord his God, and said, "O Lord, why does thy wrath burn hot against thy people, whom thou hast brought forth out of the land of Egypt with great power and with a mighty hand? Why should the Egyptians say, 'With evil intent did he bring them forth, to slay them in the mountains, and to consume them from the face of the earth'? Turn from thy fierce wrath, and repent of this evil against thy people. Remember Abraham, Isaac, and Israel, thy servants." (Ex 32:11–13)

Jesus Christ Devotionally Invoked as Lord and God in the First Century

In attempting to examine devotion to Christ during the years shortly after Jesus' death and Resurrection we face a problem: a scarcity of records. The Jewish Christians of the time and their Gentile converts were a small and not well tolerated group that lacked the ability to produce and preserve many documents beyond those that were eventually included in the canon of the New Testament itself. The problem is further complicated by the fact that the academic search for the

[7] Origen, Homily 52 on Isaiah, in *Early Christian Prayers*, ed. Fr. A. Hamman, O.F.M. (Chicago: Henry Regnery, 1961), 43. Original Greek text in *Patrologia Græca* (PG hereinafter), 13:235d.

historical Jesus in the nineteenth and early twentieth centuries led instead to a diminished Jesus who was little more than an itinerant Palestinian preacher and very different from the Christ found in St. Paul, the writings attributed to St. John, and in the early Church Fathers. Things were further confused by Wilhelm Bousset, whose influential study, *Kyrios Christos*, published in 1913,[8] argued that the worship of Christ as divine goes back not to Christ's earliest followers but arose later among Hellenistic Gentile communities under the influence of pagan cults of divine heroes and cultic divinities. Bousset believed that Jesus was called (and considered) Lord (*Kyrios* in Greek) later and first by these semiconverted Gentiles. This idea, he supposed, quickly gained dominance, replacing an original Hebrew notion of a purely human Jesus with the Hellenized idea of a god-man. Obviously these ideas strike at the very heart of Christianity and produce a Jesus unworthy of true devotion. In the face of such difficulties, can we really evaluate devotion to Christ in this period?

I believe we can, and in doing so we will make use of a remarkable book: *Lord Jesus Christ: Devotion to Jesus in Earliest Christianity* by Larry W. Hurtado, professor of New Testament language, literature, and theology at the University of Edinburgh.[9] I strongly suggest reading this monumental work both to obtain an understanding of early devotion and as a means of comprehending the impact of historical-critical studies on Christian life and practice.

Hurtado, writing nearly a century after Bousset, produces substantial evidence and paints a very different picture from that of his predecessor. Like Bousset, Hurtado approaches the problem, in part, through language, finding clues to devotion in the use of words. He demonstrates that the use of the word "*Kyrios*" (Lord) by Greek-speaking Christians definitely postdated the same use by Greek-speaking Jews, who regularly substituted the word "*Kyrios*" for God's name. It is also clear that in Aramaic-speaking circles Jesus was, in fact, called Lord from a very early time. "The formulaic acclamation of Jesus as *Kyrios* reflected in several Pauline passages (Rom 10:9–10; 1 Cor 12:3; Phil 2:9–11) and taken there as unexceptionally characteristic of Christian practice has to be seen in light of these things."[10] The word "Lord" was used by Greek-speaking Jews in the place of the divine name, which was considered unutterable, and it became part of the religious vocabulary of Christian Jews.

Rejecting Bousset's claim that the worship of Christ was borrowed from pagan cults in which the concept of divine sonship was fairly common, Hurtado demonstrates that Paul's concept of Jesus' divine

[8] Wilhelm Bousset, *Kyrios Christos: A History of the Belief in Christ from the Beginnings of Christianity to Irenaeus* (1913; repr., Nashville: Abingdon, 1970).

[9] Larry W. Hurtado, *Lord Jesus Christ: Devotion to Jesus in Earliest Christianity* (Grand Rapids, Mich.: William B. Eerdmans, 2003), 14.

[10] Ibid., 21.

sonship is unique, involving God's direct intervention, Jesus' special status with God, and Jesus' consequent honor and dignity. Paul refers to Christ as Son of God only four times, but he constantly refers to Jesus of Nazareth as *Kyrios* in exactly the way that Greek-speaking Jews (of which he was one) referred to God Himself.

Hurtado demonstrates that

> a noteworthy devotion to Jesus emerges ... early in circles of his followers, and cannot be restricted to a secondary state of religious development or explained as the product of extraneous forces....
>
> Second, devotion to Jesus was exhibited in an unparalleled intensity and diversity of expression, for which we have no true analogy in the religious environment of the time....
>
> Third, this intense devotion to Jesus, which includes reverencing him as divine, was offered and articulated characteristically within a firm stance of exclusivist monotheism, particularly in the circles of early Christians that anticipated and helped to establish what became mainstream (and subsequently, familiar) Christianity.[11]

Some Examples of Early Devotion to Christ

Hurtado uses a simpler, less comprehensive definition of devotion than we have used. This is because he has a more focused purpose. Christ-devotion—the term he uses—means all "the beliefs and related religious actions that constituted the expressions of religious reverence of early Christians".[12] He maintains with justification that devotion to Jesus as Lord began so early that there is no trace of its development—it simply suddenly exists—or any evidence of opposition to it. Although Paul's letters are early documents, some dating from less than twenty years after Christ's death and Resurrection, he clearly took over already existing devotional practices. He makes no apologies or explanations for his Christ-devotion.

Although most of St. Paul's prayers are addressed to God the Father, like the introductions to most of the epistles, God is specifically identified as the "God and Father of our Lord Jesus Christ" (2 Cor 1:3). Paul gives thanks to God "through Jesus Christ" in Romans 1:8. In his salutation and benedictions Paul invokes Christ together with the Father (Rom 16:20 and 1 Cor 16:22).[13] These are commonly thought to be uses of early Christian liturgical formulas. Perhaps the most impressive of these early invocations of Jesus is the *maranatha*, which Hurtado indicates was an imperative appeal addressed to Christ: "Our Lord, come!"[14] Apparently, this Aramaic expression was so familiar

---

[11] Ibid., 2–3.

[12] Ibid., 3. See also by the same author: *One God, One Lord: Early Christian Devotion and Ancient Jewish Monotheism*, 2nd ed. (Edinburgh: T. and T. Clark, 1998), and *At the Origins of Christian Worship: The Context and Character of Earliest Christian Devotion* (Grand Rapids, Mich.: Eerdmans, 2000).

[13] Hurtado, *Lord Jesus Christ*, 139.

[14] Ibid., 141.

to Greek-speaking Christians of Corinth that no explanation of it was necessary. The phrase "Jesus is Lord" (Rom 10:9–13) is seen as a ritual action because of Paul's adaptation of Joel 2:32 that all who call on the name of the Lord will be saved. To call on Jesus, according to Hurtado, was "initially the specific ritual (collective) confession/ acknowledgment of His exaltation as 'Lord'.... In 1 Corinthians 1:2 Paul refers to Christians everywhere ... as 'all those who call upon the name of our Lord Jesus Christ'".[15]

Thus we find in the devotion of the earliest Christians something vibrantly new and different: a mysterious but powerful awareness that Jesus and the God He proclaimed are inextricably linked in ways that no other human can claim; this is coupled with a definitive rejection of the polytheism that such an idea might have implied in the ancient world. All this is expressed in the regular, indeed, constant, use of the same language to refer to Jesus and to God, a language that proclaims them to be Lord, *Kyrios*, *Adonai*—the God over all whose name can never be uttered—a language that proclaims them to be one. Hurtado tells us:

> The most important points to make here are these, by way of summary: The high place of Jesus in the beliefs and religious practice of Judean Christianity that comes across in this evidence confirms how astonishingly early and quickly an impressive devotion to Jesus appeared. This in turn helps explain why and how it all seems to have been so conventionalized and uncontroversial already by the time of the Pauline mission to the Gentiles in the 50s.... [A] veritable explosion of devotion to Jesus took place so early, and was so widespread by the time of his Gentile mission, that in the main Christological beliefs and devotional practices that he advocated, Paul was not an innovator but a transmitter of tradition.
>
> In short, the most influential and momentous developments in devotion to Jesus took place in early circles of Judean believers. To their convictions and the fundamental pattern of their piety all subsequent forms of Christianity are debtors.[16]

Devotion to Christ in the Early Church

The Prayer of the Early Martyrs

In order to illustrate how devotion to Christ developed after the beginning of the second century, we will briefly survey the prayers to Christ by the martyrs and show how He was seen by later generations of disciples during the period of persecutions. Christians, accepting the divinity of Christ, have no trouble invoking the risen Jesus, as the Jews invoked God the Lord in the Old Testament. To the Christian the Lord God is known as the Father of Jesus. St. Polycarp, Bishop of Smyrna (died ca. 155), offered the following prayer as he prepared to be burned at the stake in his eighty-third year:

[15] Ibid., 143.

[16] Ibid., 214–16.

> Lord God Almighty, Father of Jesus Christ, that dear Child of yours, through whom we have come to know you, God of the angels and powers, God of all creation, God of the race that lives in your presence, the race of the just.
>
> I bless you because you have thought me worthy ... to be numbered among the martyrs and to drink out of the cup your Anointed has drunk from.... For this and all your blessings I praise you and give you glory, through the eternal high priest, Jesus Christ the heavenly, your dear Child.
>
> He is with you and the Holy Spirit. Through him may glory be given you now and in the ages to come. Amen.[17]

The distinguished Jesuit scholar Herbert Musurillo in his important work *Acts of the Christian Martyrs* has carefully sought to include only texts of the highest authenticity. The following account of three third-century martyrs in Asia Minor rings with a directness and poignancy that makes their simple devotion to Christ shine through brightly. Their dialogue with the crowds shows them to be simple, ordinary people rather than advanced spiritual souls, who are nonetheless completely deserving of the martyr's crown:

> When the proconsul observed their extraordinary patience he ordered them to be burnt alive, and going down they both hastened to the amphitheatre that they might all the more quickly depart from the world. First of all, Papylus was nailed to a stake and lifted up and after the fire was brought near he prayed in peace and gave up his soul. After Carpus smiled as he was nailed down. And the bystanders were amazed and said to him: "What are you laughing at?"
>
> And the blessed one said: "I saw the glory of the Lord and I was happy. Besides I am now rid of you and have no share in your sins."
>
> A soldier piled up wood and lit it, and the saintly Carpus said to him as he was hanging: "We too were born of the same mother, Eve, and we have the same flesh. Let us endure all things, looking forward to the judgment seat of truth." After he had said this, as the fire came close he prayed aloud saying, "Blessed are you Lord Jesus Christ, Son of God, because you thought me, a sinner, worthy of having this share in you!" And with these words he gave up his spirit.
>
> There was a woman named Agathonice standing there who saw the glory of the Lord, as Carpus said he had seen it; realizing that this was a call from heaven, she raised her voice at once: "Here is a meal that has been prepared for me. I must partake and eat of this glorious repast!"
>
> The mob shouted out: "Have pity on your son!"
>
> And the blessed Agathonice said: "He has God who can take pity on him; for He has providence over all. Let me do what I've come

[17] "Prayer at the Stake', in Hamman, *Early Christian Prayers*, 51.

> for!" And taking off her cloak, she threw herself joyfully upon the stake.
>
> Those who witnessed this lamented it saying: "It is a terrible sentence; these are unjust decrees!"
>
> There she was raised up and as soon as she was touched by the fire she shouted aloud three times: "Lord, Lord, Lord, assist me! For you are my refuge." And thus she gave up her spirit and died together with the saints.[18]

That the martyrs believed Christ was present for them at their trial is brought out with startling emphasis in this sermon by St. Cyprian, Bishop of Carthage. He was to die a martyr in the year 258 and was looking forward to his almost certain death when he wrote these stirring words: "How happy Christ was to be there, how gladly he fought and conquered in such servants! He protects their faith and gives strength to believers in proportion to the trust that each man who receives that strength is willing to place in him. Christ was there to wage his own battle; he aroused the soldiers who fought for his name; he made them spirited and strong. And he who once for all has conquered death for us, now continually conquers in us."[19]

Some sophisticated readers may be inclined to dismiss the prayers of the martyrs because Acts of the Christian Martyrs has not been subject to the same extensive critical evaluation as the Scripture texts. However, no one can question the existing archaeological evidence from the original sources. A sample of the prayer inscriptions from Rome, where they have been better preserved than in other Christian cities, is enlightening. The following Greek inscription, found in the cemetery of Domitilla, is remarkable: "Demetrius and Leontia [ask]: Lord Jesus, remember our daughter till the eternal resurrection".[20]

The Early Writers

Perhaps of greater weight as evidence of the early Christians' devotion to Jesus are the accounts of ecclesiastical writers. These are not written remembrances of the martyrs' deaths, but rather well-developed pieces of literature with high critical value. Two important ecclesiastical writers, neither of them now considered saints, are very well represented in the library of classic Christian literature. The first is Clement of Alexandria, who wrote the *Paedagogus*, or *The Teacher*, sometime before the beginning of the third century. A teacher at the theological school of Alexandria in Egypt, he later

[18] In Herbert Musurillo, S.J., *Acts of the Christian Martyrs* (Oxford: Clarendon Press, 1972), 27.

[19] From Letter 10, quoted in *The Liturgy of the Hours*, trans. International Commission on English in the Liturgy (New York: Catholic Book Publishing, 1975), 4:1314.

[20] Orazio Marucchi, *Manual of Christian Archaeology* (Paterson, N.J.: St. Anthony Guild Press, 1949), 228.

went into exile and disappeared in the persecutions at the beginning of the third century. The following beautiful prayer comes from the *Paedagogus*:

> Be kind to your little children, Lord: that is what we ask of you as their Tutor, you the Father, Israel's Guide; Son, yes, but Father as well. Grant that by doing what you have told us to do, we may achieve a faithful likeness to the Image and, as far as is possible for us, may find in you a good God and a lenient Judge.
>
> May we all live in the peace that comes from you. May we journey towards your city, sailing through the waters of sin untouched by the waves, borne tranquilly along by the Holy Spirit, your Wisdom beyond all telling. Night and day until the last day of all, may our praises give you thanks, our thanksgiving praise you: you who alone are both Father and Son, Son and Father, the Son who is our Tutor and our Teacher, together with the Holy Spirit.
>
> All things belong to the One. He it is who makes them exist and exist as one; he makes eternity and gives us all a share in his own life. To him be glory for ever.
>
> All belongs to God, the good, the beautiful, the wise, the just. To him be glory, now and age after age. Amen.[21]

Another of Clement's great works is his hymn to Christ the Savior. This well-known hymn should be read in its entirety. We quote only part of it here. The words directed to Christ are long, but here is a selection:

> King of the saints,
> invisible Word of the Father most High,
> wisdom's Prince, Ground of exertion, eternal Joy;
> Jesus, Saviour of this mortal race,
> you the Shepherd, Cultivator,
> you the Helmsman and the Rider,
> you the Wing that lifts to heaven
> all the company of the saints;
> Fisher of men;
> them you came to deliver from the waters of sin;
> to fish untainted by the envious sea
> you cast the bait of sweet fresh life.
> Guide your flock of spiritual sheep;
> guide, holy King, guide your unsullied children.
> The prints of Christ's feet show the way to heaven.
> Word everlasting, Age without end, undying Light,
> Fountain of mercy, Doer of virtuous deeds,

[21] *Paedagogus* 3:12, in Hamman, *Early Christian Prayers*, 37–38. Original Greek text in PG 8:680.

exalted Life of them that sing God's praises....
Let us together sing simple praises,
true hymns to Christ the King ...[22]

It is important to note in this prayer that Christ is invoked not only in biblical terms but also as "Helmsman ... Rider ... the Wing that lifts to heaven all the company of the saints". These nonscriptural allusions are sandwiched between two very well-known New Testament references: "Shepherd" and "Fisher of men". By the end of the second century, many Christians were converts from paganism. Although Clement uses hundreds of quotations from the books that would be included in the New Testament canon two hundred years later, he does not hesitate to make literary allusions that would be more familiar to his Alexandrian audience of sophisticated Greeks. Much later he was seen to have made some errors innocently and unwittingly, but there is no question that Clement of Alexandria invokes Christ as God.

Perhaps the greatest representative of the school of Alexandria is Origen (d. 253), a center of controversy during his life who remains so to this day. His powerful writings are quoted by all serious Christian theologians. Fr. Hamman, in *Early Christian Prayers*, says about Origen: "He made a critical edition of the Bible and then commented on the text with a view to discovering its allegorical or spiritual meaning.... Prayer flowed out as he wrote his commentaries; it was generally addressed to Jesus, and its strongly individual note—the affection in it and the devotion to Christ that prompted it—was novel and anticipated Bernard of Clairvaux and Francis of Assisi".[23]

The following exhortation is not addressed directly to Christ but illustrates Origen's profound devotion.

> Let us keep the Scriptures in mind and meditate upon them day and night, persevering in prayer, always on the watch. Let us beg the Lord to give us real knowledge of what we read and to show us not only how to understand it but how to put it into practice, so that we may deserve to obtain spiritual grace, enlightened by the law of the Holy Spirit, through Jesus Christ our Lord, whose power and glory will endure throughout the ages. Amen.[24]

The Later Martyrs

The end of the third century and beginning of the fourth brought a tremendous harvest of martyrs as the emperor Diocletian tried vainly to stop the spread of Christianity throughout the Roman Empire. These events provided the great impetus for the coming proclamation of Christ's divinity at the Council of Nicaea (325) shortly after the persecutions came to an end.

---

[22] Ibid. 3:12; 38–39, PG 8:681.

[23] Hamman, *Early Christian Prayers*, 40.

[24] Origen, Homily 6 on Leviticus, in Hamman, *Early Greek Prayers*, 41. Original Greek text in PG 12:475.

Another prayer, although not as well authenticated literarily as the writings of Clement and Origen, dates from this period. It is attributed to St. Afra, a martyr of Augsburg, Germany, and clearly shows devotion to Jesus. Afra is among the few women martyrs to leave behind any statements or quotations from the time of her death. She is also a penitent, and this unusual circumstance caused people to pay much attention to her death. The following prayer is given in her acts of martyrdom:

> O Lord God Almighty, Jesus Christ, who didst come to call not the just but sinners to repentance, thus confirming the promise thou didst vouchsafe to make saying, "In the hour when the sinner shall repent of his sins, in that same hour I will no more remember them," accept at this hour my martyrdom as a penance, and by the material fire prepared for my body deliver me from the everlasting fire which burns both body and soul.
>
> I give thee thanks, Lord Jesus Christ, that thou hast vouchsafed to accept me as a victim for the glory of thy name, thou who wast offered as Victim on the cross for the salvation of the whole world, the Just for the unjust, the Good for the wicked, the Blessed One for the cursed, the Innocent for the guilty. I offer my sacrifice to thee, who with the Father and the Holy Ghost livest and reignest God for ever and ever. Amen.[25]

This is one of many prayers indicating that the Church was already being prepared for the great declaration of the Trinity at Nicaea to counter the heresy of Arius. This and many other literary works, including some that we have quoted, indicate that the Trinitarian belief was by no means invented at Nicaea, but rather was given final clear expression at that council. The doctrine, which had developed during the turbulent period of persecutions, could be traced directly from the Gospels and other writings that would later be codified as the New Testament.

Devotion—A Real Experience

To sum up our discussion of devotion so far: we can be said to know a person we have never met by a combination of information, our personal responses (including devotion, respect, or veneration), a medley of thoughts, feelings, convictions, and desires. When it comes to knowing the saints, we add a further dimension, namely, a belief that through the power of God, they are aware of our existence and attention to them. Reverence adds a sense of the holy to the simple respect I might have had for a secular historical figure—Lincoln or Pasteur. If I also think they have assisted me in the past and inspired me by their holy lives, like St. Francis and St. Thérèse, I have a devotion to them. Devotion, however, must be carefully distinguished from worship, which

[25] Cabrol, *Liturgical Prayer*, 117.

is due to God alone. A much greater devotion is possible when it includes the element of friendship, which many believe they experience in relation to the Virgin Mother of Christ, the saints, and the angels.

Finally, in a separate category, there is devotion to God as the sovereign Godhead, or to the individual Persons of the Trinity. This may be expressed toward any Person of the Trinity, but it is most engaging when it refers to Christ, who lived among us. He is the Divine Person who was born and experienced human life, who suffered and died. Devotion to Christ is thus more easily apprehensible to our imagination and emotions than devotion to the Father or Holy Spirit. Our Savior Himself invites devotion: "Come to me, all who labor and are heavy laden, and I will give you rest" (Mt 11:28).

Obviously we are joined to Him in the all-encompassing prayer of the Mystical Body. To quote St. Augustine, "He prays for us as our priest, he prays in us as our head, he is the object of our prayers as our God."[26] But we also are individually and personally known and cared for by Him. To focus exclusively on the relationship of Christ to the whole Church is to miss an essential aspect—perhaps half—of the Christian life. And when we study His life and are effectively guided by His words, when we open ourselves to the mystery of His grace and allow Him into our inmost being, then we know Him. Is there any more profound expression of the experience of Christian devotion than these words, "If a man loves me, he will keep my word, and my Father will love him, and we will come to him and make our home with him" (Jn 14:23)? A Christian who lives with little devotion, or disdains it altogether, leads a sad, anemic existence. Lack of devotion to Christ saps the vitality of the Church. And it leaves many sincere but misled people as very sorry disciples, simply with ideas and concepts but without any feeling of joy or zeal. Augustine said somewhere, "*Qui amat, zelat.*" He who loves is zealous.

---

[26] *Commentary on Psalm 85*, quoted in *Liturgy of the Hours*, 2:367. See also *Augustine: Major Writings* by Fr. Benedict J. Groeschel, C.F.R. (New York: Crossroad, 1995), 76.

3 The All-Powerful One

During the age of the martyrs, the most meaningful image of Christ for the devout arose from their belief that He was with them in their hour of need, even as they faced execution. The earliest images of Christ are those of the Good Shepherd who never deserts His flock—a very biblical and theological image, yet an extraordinarily personal one as well. Christ called to every suffering soul, rich and poor, free and slave. Christ called to the poor and suffering, "Come to me." As we have seen, we have only the final statements of some of the martyrs written down after the events; we have no direct access to their feelings or thoughts. Yet we know from the literature of martyrology that the martyrs left behind a striking belief that they had experienced Christ's presence at the time of their execution.

A New Image of Christ

After the Edict of Milan (313), which made Christianity legal in the empire, martyrdom became rare and a new image of the Savior emerged: Christ came to be seen as the All-Powerful One, the Pantocrator, the "King of kings". Some writers, like Professor Jaroslav Pelikan, author of the extremely well-researched consideration of Jesus in the life of the Church, *Jesus through the Centuries*, have linked this new image of Jesus to the experience of the Roman emperor Constantine the Great. According to an account by his tutor, Lactantius, Constantine ascribed his victory at the battle of the Milvian Bridge to a dream, in which he was told to put the Chi-Rho and the sign of the cross on the shields of his soldiers. He won the battle in October of 312.[1]

This image of Christ as the All-Powerful One might have emerged anyway, even without Constantine, as the idea of divine power emanating from the emperor was strong at the time. Why should people not relate this image of divine power to Him who said, "My kingship is not of this world" (Jn 18:36)? For those who have grown up in a democratic system it is difficult to imagine how much personal authority an emperor had. With the significant exception of the Jews, almost all ancient people tended to see emperors as having divine appointment, as people

[1] Jaroslav Pelikan, *Jesus through the Centuries* (New Haven: Yale University Press, 1985), 51–57.

again did from the sixteenth to the eighteenth centuries, when many believed in the divine right of kings.

The relationship of the power of Jesus Christ as King with the power of earthly kings produced different theories and systems in East and West. In the East, power was seen to devolve from God the Father to His Son, and thence to the emperor, as the divinely appointed earthly ruler. "The emperor was 'crowned by God ...', a belief reflected in the Byzantine ceremony of coronation."[2] As for the Patriarch of Constantinople, his authority could be said to derive from the emperor, who at the patriarch's consecration would declare: "By the grace of God and by our imperial power, which proceeds from the grace of God, this man is appointed Patriarch of Constantinople."[3]

In the West, Christ the King was seen to transmit power to St. Peter as head of the apostles, thence to his successor the Pope, and from him to earthly rulers. This chain of authority was epitomized in the year 800, when Pope Leo III crowned Charlemagne emperor. Thus, in both East and West, Christ came to be seen as King of Kings.

Throughout the empire, the victory of Constantine through the cross meant that Christ was King over all, the All-Powerful One. Every possible attempt was made to extol Christ as King.[4] Scripture quotations relating to the kingship of Christ were emphasized. Pilate's question, "Are you the King of the Jews?" (Jn 18:33), and Christ's answer, "My kingship is not of this world" (Jn 18:36), were often repeated. The rhapsodic words of St. Paul, "He is the image of the invisible God ... all things were created through him ..." (Col 1:15–16), and the vision of the King of Kings in the Book of Revelation (see Rev 19:11–16) served as powerful examples of the absolute sovereignty and benevolent kingship of the crucified carpenter who was God's chosen One. And in prayers such as the following, composed by St. Gregory of Nazianzus (329–390), the devout Christian invoked Christ as King of all creation:

> O Christ my King. You turned aside the dire might of Amelech, when your servant Moses raised his pure hands after the pattern of the cross in prayer upon the mountain. You fettered the savage jaws of lions and the sharp strength of their claws for Daniel's sake when he stretched out his hands. When Jonas opened wide his arms in prayer within the monster's entrails, he was delivered by your power from the whale.... Once, in order to deliver the storm-tossed disciples from the waters, you trod on foot the face of the turbulent deep stilling the waves' and the winds' might. For many a person you have rescued soul and body from disease. You who are God became man and mingled with mortals.

[2] Ibid., 54.

[3] Ibid.

[4] See ibid; the entire fourth chapter is an excellent review of this phase of Christian devotion.

> God from all time, you were manifested to us in the fulness of time.... Thus, when I call on you, come as blessed and propitious God. Come to me with helping hand, O my propitious God. Save me, overwhelmed as I am amid war, and wild beasts, and fire, and storm. I have nowhere to turn my gaze except to God alone. All this is brought upon me by evil men, the destroyers of life.... Their chief animosity is directed against people who love God....
>
> From these, O Christ, deliver me. Spread your sheltering wings about me always. O King, drive hateful cares far from your servant. Let not my mind be harassed by grave anxieties, such as this world and the prince of this world devise for hapless mortals.[5]

The Cross—Sign of Victory and Life

Gradually the pagan nobility joined the Church, adopting the emperor's new sign of the cross. Meanwhile the peasants and slaves realized that the cruelest sign of their noncitizenship, death by crucifixion, had become sacred to the emperor himself, who now prohibited the use of crucifixion as a form of capital punishment.[6] The descendants of crucified slaves or noncitizens responded enthusiastically to this amazing transformation of the cross from a barbaric punishment into a powerful religious symbol and royal ensign.

To our own day, the image of the all-powerful Christ in cathedral domes in the West and especially in the East tells us much about devotion to the crucified Messiah now glorified. Few have given a more compelling voice to this burgeoning devotion than St. Ephraem the Syrian (306–373), one of the Church's great poets and hymnists:

> I give you glory, O Christ, because you, the Only Begotten, the Lord of all things, who alone are without sin, gave yourself to die for me, a sinner, unworthy of such a blessing: you died the death of the cross to free my sinful soul from the bonds of sin.
>
> What shall I give you, Lord, in return for all this kindness?
> Glory to you for your love.
> Glory to you for your mercy.
> Glory to you for your patience.
> Glory to you for forgiving us all our sins.
> Glory to you for coming to save our souls.
> Glory to you for your incarnation in the virgin's womb.
> Glory to you for your bonds.
> Glory to you for receiving the cut of the lash.
> Glory to you for accepting mockery.
> Glory to you for your crucifixion.
> Glory to you for your burial.

[5] Poem 1, "Concerning His Own Affairs", opening prayer, in *Saint Gregory of Nazianzus: Three Poems*, trans. Denis Molaise Meehan, O.S.B., vol. 75 of The Fathers of the Church (Washington, D.C: Catholic University of America Press, 1987), 25–26.

[6] Pelikan, *Jesus through the Centuries*, 104.

Glory to you for your resurrection.
Glory to you that were preached to men.
Glory to you in whom they believed.
Glory to you that were taken up into heaven.[7]

Thus was the Friend and Companion of the Martyrs, the Crucified Shepherd, the Lamb Slain, replaced by the glorious King of Kings. His suffering and death were never forgotten. The paradox, in fact, was celebrated with the cross becoming the symbol of victory emerging from utter defeat.

The Word of God

As the Church rejoiced at the end of the persecutions, all were astonished by the toleration of Christianity as an official religion of the Empire, which occurred less than ten years later (A.D. 313). However, a mysterious refrain that had run through the history of Israel was about to be heard again, this time in the Church: the theme of difficulty and danger coming immediately after success. The signs of conflict within the Christian community are apparent in the Acts of the Apostles and the epistles. No sooner had the communities of the new converts been established in the open than conflict and schism appeared, ending the brief moment of success and peace with a powerful new heresy: Arianism. Arius was a brilliant and energetic priest of Alexandria, the center of Christian learning and intellectual life even during the persecutions. He brought into the Church an element of incipient paganism, a disguised polytheism; Arianism represented the last vestiges of the idea that there can be more than one god. From our perspective, it seems that Arius' great temptation was success. He actually could easily have been a Father of the Church. The throngs of the pagan world, mostly religious people who built temples and offered sacrifice to a veritable gallery of gods, suddenly found their religion collapsing. Arius had something for them: a demigod. His Christ looked like Jesus of Nazareth yet had something in common with Apollo. Not the Lord of heaven and earth, he was divine nonetheless. He came out of the other world, the world of the spirit. He was a savior indeed; but although divine, He was less than His Father. All this was implied in the statement that summed up Arius' teaching: "There was a time when the Word was not."

Arius' teaching would obviously be even less acceptable to Jews than that of one God in three equal Persons. However, a pagan drawn to the new faith might find the Arian doctrine natural. In pagan belief, after all, there were centaurs, who were half men and half horse, and mermaids, who were half women and half fish; in fact, all the gods had their too-human side. Why not a Son of God who was not quite

[7] "Prayer to the Suffering Christ" (excerpt), from "Sermon on the Passion", no. 9, excerpted in *Early Christian Prayers*, ed. Fr. A. Hamman, O.F.M. (Chicago: Henry Regnery, 1961), 180–81.

equal to the Father and therefore capable of taking on mortal flesh? It all seemed plausible, but it flew in the face of the Gospels, the New Testament writers, especially John and Paul, and the tradition that had developed during the early persecutions. Ultimately Arius' attack on this apostolic tradition had the effect of strengthening the unity and authority of the Church.

In 325, at Nicaea in Asia Minor, Constantine summoned a council made up mostly of Eastern Greek-speaking bishops, although the Bishop of Rome was represented by Hosius, Bishop of Córdoba. At the Council of Nicaea, Christ, who had been called the Word, or Logos (a term borrowed from Plato as early as the Gospel of John), was clearly proclaimed on the basis of Scripture and tradition to be "God from God, Light from Light, true God from true God, begotten not made, of one substance with the Father, through whom all things came to be". At the same time there was a condemnation, an anathema, against Arius and his followers. Christ is even called "Light from Light". This phrase was used to forestall anyone's thinking that being born or begotten of God suggests that there was an interval between the existence of the Father and the Son. Using an analogy, we can think of God the Father as fire, and the Son as light. "Once there is fire, there is light. So with the Father and the Son; their existence is simultaneous and eternal."[8]

It is vital to recall the opening of St. John's Gospel: "In the beginning was the Word, and the Word was with God, and the Word was God. He was in the beginning with God". It is no accident that the evangelist takes us immediately to the heart of the mystery of who Christ is. We find Him "in the bosom of the Father" (1:18). Not only do these words of St. John provide us with meditation for a lifetime, but the Church has considered them so important that for centuries in the West they were read at the end of Mass, a constant reminder of the identity of Christ as both Son of the eternal Father and the Incarnate Word.

The Council at Nicaea also proclaimed that God is three Divine Persons, who are simultaneously a single identical reality, one substance—in Greek, *homoousios*. The Father, the Son (the Word), and the Holy Spirit are entirely equal, all of the same nature. This is the dogma of the *Triunitas*, or Trinity. Christ's identity in the Church was now solidly built on Scripture and the writings of the Fathers.

The great Creed of Nicaea firmly founded the Church on the Trinity but left many questions open. Some of these are absolutely mysterious and will remain so forever; others are more capable of intellectual examination and rational illustration. Many questions would recur, because Arianism persisted for a long time and was occasionally even favored by Constantine's successors.

[8] Msgr. James T. O'Connor, *The Father's Son* (Boston: St. Paul Editions, 1984), 68.

As we shall see, there were attempts to explain the meaning of Nicaea itself, which would prove more theologically troublesome and yet ultimately more fruitful in enlightening the mystery of Christ. These attempts were judged by later councils, especially Ephesus and Chalcedon, to be inconsistent with the Scriptures and the proclamations of Nicaea.[9] We need to ask, did these new developments bring a new and more articulated devotion to Christ than what had existed in the days of the martyrs? The expression of Christ as the All-Powerful King and as the Logos was the beginning of the beautiful, incredibly long-lasting history of Christian art in liturgy, music, painting, and architecture. A new Christian world was beginning despite the threat of barbarian invasions. In fact, these same terrifying populations would themselves bring into Europe a human stock that would become the foundation of the medieval world. Personal devotion to Christ was now an integral part of the life of the Church. Christ as solace of the martyrs, King of Kings, and Eternal Word of God—He was known and celebrated as all these in prayer and personal devotion.

Christ Is Everywhere

As a result of the conflict with Arianism, Christians in the East and West grew in appreciation of Christ as true Son of God and equal to the Father. This understanding became the principal theme of devotion among members of the Catholic Christian Church during the centuries that Arianism raged. Thus Christ had to be everywhere, because the heavenly Father, as the foundation of all being, was ubiquitous—everywhere. This is an important step in the development of devotion. Not only was Christ there when we called to Him; He was with us always.

This idea is expressed very beautifully by St. Augustine. "I will speak, then, to our Lord Jesus Christ; I will speak, and let him hear me. I believe him present; I do not doubt it at all. For he himself has said, 'I am with you always, even unto the consummation of the world'" (Mt 28:20).[10]

Augustine then asks of God what it means when He says, "Unless you believe that *I am* ..." (Jn 8:24—emphasis added). The great Doctor comments that many things are—the heavens, the earth, angels, men. What does God mean when He says, "I AM WHO I AM" (Ex 3:14)? Are these other things not? Speaking of the people who heard Christ say these words, St. Augustine comments: "Though they were sinners, yet they were men. Then what do I make [of this]? What is this making things to be? Say it, Lord, to the heart, say it within, speak within. Let the inner man hear, let the mind understand this [truth] ... 'to be,' for Being always is in the same way".[11]

---

[9] See ibid., especially pp. 63–114.

[10] Commentary on the Gospel of St. John, tractate 38, nos. 9, 10.

[11] Ibid.

In this prayer and important commentary, Augustine equates the being of Christ with the universal, absolute being of the Godhead. Christ is everywhere. This is extremely important in understanding the unique devotion to Christ that existed then and exists now. We can call on a saint and trust that God will permit our prayers to be heard, but when we call on Christ, it is the same as calling on the Father. He is everywhere, and He is with us till the end of the world. This is the unique quality of Christian devotion.

Devotion and Love

We must interrupt our historical survey briefly to discuss some key ideas included in the term "devotion", which is, after all, simply a loving knowledge of God. What kind of love exactly is described by devotion? Here I borrow from one of the most perceptive modern Christians, C. S. Lewis. In his classic work *The Four Loves*,[12] Lewis distinguishes four definitions of love that are pertinent to our discussion of the form of love we call devotion. He uses Greek names for his four loves: *eros*, *agape*, *philia*, and *storge*. Lewis identifies *eros* simply as the love for what is fulfilling, a response to a need, especially a sexual need. Unfortunately, I think Lewis, for the sake of clarity, underemphasized the fact that in Greek (both ancient and modern) *eros* simply means "love of what fulfills a need" and may not relate to sexuality at all. Quite different from *eros* is *agape*, or charity, the selfless love that rejoices in giving itself. *Agape* is epitomized in Christ's love for us; we hope it is found in some of our responses to Him or those whom we love in His name. Then there is *philia*, the love of friends, a love that is mutual, encouraging, and reliable, but one that does not imply the selfless dedication of *agape*. It might be said that friendship is a step behind *agape*. Friendship can be taken for granted and is based on a shared need or fulfillment. The fourth type of love is *storge*, what Lewis calls "affection". This love is based on a need other than simply pleasure or fulfillment. It is founded very much on the need of an infant for its mother and the mother's need to love and care for the infant. *Storge* is a need to receive or a need to give. It has an important place in life. Lewis identifies *storge*, or affection, as the least expressive and the most common of loves. It is little spoken of, but it is found everywhere.

It seems to me that Lewis has missed another kind of love, namely, the love for one's own family, town, country, church, people, and, if you're global-minded, one's world. Things as different as patriotism and loyalty to a denomination are loving attitudes, although they may not be addressed to an individual. If I may presume upon Mr. Lewis' book, then I would consider affection for one's group much the same as affection for those on whom we are dependent, such as parents and close family members. Affection, or *storge*, in this specific sense constitutes a great deal of what is called the love of God in the Jewish Scriptures. If you loved God, you loved and served Israel and

[12] C. S. Lewis, *The Four Loves* (New York: Harcourt, Brace, 1960).

supported His people who were your people. *Storge*, seen here as generalized affection, does not imply intimacy, or even sharing of feelings, but it certainly implies the sharing of goals and values.

Worship as a Form of Love

Worship can mean different kinds of love for different people. This is obvious when we consider the variety of Christian worship found in a city like New York with its many nationalities, and denominations. Parishes or denominations with strong ethnic roots are often characterized by ritualistic customs and services that are repeated with little or no apparent feeling. Even the word "liturgy", which means "public act or service", has implications of *storge* that will baffle someone who has grown up in a very devotional church like that of the Pentecostals. Such enthusiastic religious experience is much more an expression of *philia*, a friendship with the "sweet Lord Jesus", or even a kind of affection expressed on the familial level, "dear Jesus". Some, whose religion is not expressive, think that very devotional experiences are sublimated forms of *eros*, but along with Lewis, I am suspicious of those who identify other people's affections only in this way. Even within a single religious group public worship can express different forms of love. Compare the Sunday Mass of the monks of Solesmes with a meeting of charismatic Catholics.

Impressive liturgical worship came to flower in Christianity when the simple liturgy of the persecuted Church began to include customs that contained elements of national or ethnic love, or *storge*. In the West, we see this especially in the work of St. Ambrose, Archbishop of Milan, a converted Roman official who developed liturgical forms, especially for the sacraments. A contemporary of Ambrose, St. John Chrysostom, Patriarch of Constantinople, had so great an impact on the public liturgy of the East that most Christians there still enjoy his liturgical expressions, which have remained quite stable over the centuries. In neither the Eastern nor the Western liturgical traditions were the expression of warm feeling prominent. The same, however, could not be said of other Oriental rites, especially those found in India and Ethiopia.

It is worth noting that we can participate in liturgy with attention and reverence, expressing faith and hope, and still not experience an intimate encounter with the person of Jesus. The awareness of inner feelings required for intimacy may not be available to some people at liturgical services. This has caused some of the more liturgically minded to disparage devotion, the religious experience of *philia*. In fact, the resistance and at times hostility to Eucharistic devotion observed recently in some segments of the Church seems to be specifically aimed at avoiding or even prohibiting personal devotion.[13] Whenever one thinks

---

[13] Fr. Benedict J. Groeschel, C.F.R., and James Monti, *In the Presence of Our Lord: The History, Theology, and Psychology of Eucharistic Devotion* (Huntington, Ind.: Our Sunday Visitor, 1997), 164–67.

about these developments, it is obvious that liturgical piety, insofar as it is a form of love, is actually a ritualized expression of *storge*, love that needs to receive or give something. This does not mean, however, that other kinds of love, especially *agape* and *philia*, need to be avoided if a person is engaged in primarily liturgical piety.

Love of a Friend

Vast numbers of Christians relate to Christ in a more or less intimate way. He is there for them as a Friend. They believe that He knows them personally, that He helps them with their struggles and receives their devotion in a personal way. This relationship to Christ, a form of personal devotion, exists among all types of people from great theologians, scholars, and mystics to scientists, farmers, and even prisoners.

Respectable Christians are often amazed that inmates in correctional institutions or those of doubtful virtue pray and ask Christ to help them. Most frequently this devotion expresses affection (*storge*). With others, however, devotion rises to a kind of friendship (*philia*), a feeling of mutuality and sharing, an ability to take God's love for granted in a reverential way. For the spiritually advanced, devotion grows gradually into *agape*, selfless love. But whether it is *storge, philia*, or *agape*, it is one of the marks of the authentic Christian. When all is said and done, devotion has always been a profoundly Christian experience.

As we return to our historical analysis, the question arises: How broad was popular devotion to Christ the Pantocrator in the first centuries after the persecutions? Could it appeal to people who were Christian simply out of a sense of loyalty to the tribe? The all-powerful King and Eternal Word, however beautifully portrayed in early icons, is a complex way of understanding Christ and hardly appeals to all. Was there another devotional image of Christ in the early Church, something more personal and intimate than Christ in eternal splendor? In our search for an answer we will examine a very natural type of devotion found in the early Church as it emerged from its catacombs.

A Very Early Christian Devotion—Christ the Healer

In virtually every culture religion deals with physical and emotional illness. Jesus was often surrounded by the sick. He healed their bodies, minds, and spirits by a prayer, a word, a gesture—by His presence. It is not surprising that in the second and third centuries, in the lulls between persecutions, we find Christian writers advising people to turn to Christ as healer and away from the pagan worship of the health-giver, the god Asclepius. Great crowds, desperate for healing, came to the shrines of this Greek god. Origen, who combated this cult, advised Christians to turn instead to the "Great Physician".[14] Arnobius the Elder of Sicca, who wrote of the shrines of Asclepius, described them

[14] Rudolph Arbesmann, O.S.A., "The Concept of '*Christus Medicus*' in St. Augustine", *Traditio* 10 (1954): 3.

as filled with the wretched and the ill. He, too, calls for the sick to turn instead to Christ. The image of Christ as Healer was a natural and obvious alternative to this pagan cult. The renowned ecclesiastical historian Eusebius of Caesarea called Asclepius a "downright destroyer of souls, drawing them away from the true Saviour". Similarly, Lactantius, Constantine's tutor, deemed Asclepius an "archdemon".[15] When Lactantius' student became emperor, he destroyed the shrine of this god at Aegae.[16] Christianity was quite capable of taking on a rival.

Although Origen is apparently the first Greek writer to invoke Christ as Physician, the devotion became most popular in Roman Africa with the Latin-speaking faithful. Citing Isaiah (50:50 and 53:4), Tertullian describes Christ's role on earth as preacher and healer (medicator).[17] St. Cyprian of Carthage tells us that Christ's mission on earth was to be the Divine Physician who heals the wounds caused by Adam's fall, neutralizing the poison of the serpent and giving prescriptions to Christians on how to avoid relapse.[18] Even the heretic Pelagius speaks of Christ's role as that of a doctor.[19] Although the idea of Christ the Physician was preached in order to draw the naïve and superstitious away from the cult of Asclepius and later from the Oriental cults of Isis, Mithras, and Serapis, the role of physician was acknowledged to fit the personal history of Jesus well. He certainly cured the physically ill during His earthly life, and redemption can be described aptly as a recovery from a fatal illness—an everlasting illness. In all presentations of Christ the Physician, He was seen as interested in and helpful to the individual.

After the popularity of pagan cults had subsided, St. Augustine, taking a cue from his teacher St. Ambrose, often called on people to turn to Christ the Physician. He explained with metaphors and similes how Christ would operate in their lives like a physician. There are more than forty references in Augustine's writings to *Christus Medicus*. For our purposes, it is important to demonstrate that for the African Christians of Augustine's time Christ was seen as interested in and responsive to each person's personal, prayerful requests.

Unfortunately, there are few archaeological remains of the Christian Roman community in North Africa. The stone of Timgad, a small monument with an inscription to Christ the Physician, is one of the few physical indications of the devotion to *Christus Medicus*. This stone was probably made by members of the short-lived sect called the Donatists, who in almost all external ways were similar to the Catholics in North Africa and who were recognized by Augustine as a dissident part of the Church possessing valid sacraments, including holy orders.

[15] Ibid., 4.
[16] Ibid.
[17] Ibid., 6.
[18] Ibid., 7.
[19] Ibid.

Year after year Augustine's sermons repeated the theme that Christ is the Physician of our salvation. Throughout the *Confessions* he implies that God knows us individually, listens to us, and responds to our requests. The *Confessions* is, among other things, a classic of devotional literature. An early reference in the saint's writings to Christ the Physician reads: "I am in deep trouble. See, I do not hide my wounds. You, O Lord, are the Physician; I am the sick man. You are merciful, and I need mercy." [20] Later on he went much further. He insisted that if we pray with real devotion, our prayer must bear some fruit; otherwise, it is simply a personal experience that goes nowhere. Consequently, St. Augustine uses the figure of *Christus Medicus* in the following practical ways: (1) to teach and illustrate humility; (2) to cure physical and mental illness; (3) to cure the vice of pride; (4) to teach forgiveness after the example of Christ; (5) to show how Christ uses suffering to cure the soul and restore it to health; (6) to show that patience in the spiritual struggle is necessary while the Divine Physician works; (7) to demonstrate that sick humanity is actually being cured by the disasters that are coming upon the empire; and (8) promotion of devotion to Christ, who alone can cure our souls.

In all these sermons Augustine calls the believer to trust the Divine Physician, to maintain hope in the face of pain and adversity, and to imitate the Divine Physician by compassion and care of the sick and unfortunate. The following selections will illustrate Augustine's prayerful use of this devotion.

1. *The Medicine of Christian Humility*

In a letter to Dioscurus, a young Greek scholar seeking to submit himself to Christ, Augustine writes that there is only one way to follow the Divine Master: "This way is first humility, second humility, third humility, and however often you should ask me I would say the same." This is Christianity's basic doctrine, humility. It is "the medicine of Christian humility by which alone the tumor [of pride] is cured." [21] Augustine continues: "Because man's spiritual disease had become such that it appeared to be incurable by the ordinary methods of divine dispensation, 'there came that humble Physician, found the patient prostrate, and shared in man's frail nature, calling him to be partaker in His own divine nature.... He provided a food for us to receive and become whole. Whence is this food, and whom does it nourish? Those who imitate the Lord's humility.' " [22]

2. *Curing the Physically and Mentally Ill*

Not content to show Christ as a healer of the physically ill, Augustine also speaks of Christ restoring health to the mentally ill:

---

[20] Augustine, *Confessions* bk. 10, chap. 28. Translation by the author.
[21] Arbesmann, "The Concept of *'Christus Medicus'* in St. Augustine", 10.
[22] Ibid., 11.

For a Physician He was, and to cure the insane patient He had come. Just as a human physician does not care whatever insulting remarks he may hear from an insane patient, but how the mad person may recover and become sane; nor even if he receive a blow from the insane patient does he care, but while the mad person inflicts new wounds upon him, he cures the patient's old fever: so also the Lord came to the sick man, came to the mad man to pay no heed to whatever He may hear, to whatever He might suffer, by this very example teaching us humility that, being taught by humility, we might be healed from pride.[23]

3. *Curing Pride*

The Way is Christ, the humble Christ; the Truth and Life are Christ, who also is God on high. If you walk in the lowly way, you will come to the height above. If you do not spurn the lowly way in your infirmity, you will remain full of strength when on high. For what is the cause of Christ's humility if not your infirmity? You were afflicted with a serious and incurable disease, and this your condition caused such a great Physician to come to you. For if your sickness were at least such that you were able to go to the Physician, it would seem to be bearable. But since you were not able to go to Him, He came to you. He came, teaching us humility, that, by this way, we may return to life.[24]

4. *Teaching True Forgiveness*

He was flogged, yet He went on healing. He bore with the insane patient, and did not abandon him: He was seized, bound, struck with fists and the reed, ridiculed and insulted; finally, brought into court, He was condemned, suspended on the cross, and treated from all sides with scoffs and jeers, yet He continued to be the Physician. Having lost their minds, they raged against Him and, in their delirium, shed His blood: yet from His very blood He prepared the remedies for the insane patient. When after the descent of the Holy Spirit they heard the unlearned apostles speak in different languages, they were amazed, they did penance, they were converted and healed.[25]

There was sent the Physician whom the patient did not know. "For if they had known [Him], they would never have crucified the Lord of glory" (1 Cor 2.8). But just the killing of the Physician became a powerful medicine for the patient: He came to call on the patient, He was killed to cure him.[26]

Desperately ill is he who, in his delirium, strikes the Physician. Of what nature then must be the madness of the patient who kills the

---

[23] Ibid., 12.

[24] Ibid., 14.

[25] Ibid., 17–18.

[26] Ibid., 18.

Physician? And how great, indeed, must be the goodness and power of the Physician who, from His blood, has prepared the medicine for His killer?[27]

5. *How Suffering Can Cure the Soul*

As the human physician sometimes cures by contraries, thus the Lord causes pain in order to give to man health everlasting. Human physicians do many things against the will, though not against the health, of their patients. Though, unlike the Divine Physician, who never makes a mistake, they are subject to error, often a patient puts his trust in such a physician, knowing perfectly well that it will mean not the application of a painless plaster but burning or cutting or even taking off a limb. Why then should we not allow the Divine Physician to proceed in the same manner in the interest of our spiritual health? The example of Christ Himself should encourage the Christian to submit patiently to trials ordained by God's providential method of healing: If He who had no festering wound was cut, if our very Medicine [Christ] did not reject the healing fire, should we bear impatiently with the Physician who burns and cuts, that is, who tests us by all kinds of tribulations and heals us from sin?... If you join the physician in fighting the fever, you will be two; if you join in with the fever, however, the physician will be defeated, yet to the detriment of the patient, not the physician.[28]

6. *Encouraging Patience in the Spiritual Struggle*

Even after remission of sins the soul itself is still affected by certain passions; still it is threatened by dangers of temptation; still it takes pleasure in certain suggestions: with some it is not pleased, but it consents to some with which it is pleased, and is taken a captive. This is infirmity; but He heals all your infirmities (cf. Deut. 7:15). All your infirmities shall be healed, fear not. They are great, you will say; but the Physician is greater. To the Almighty Physician no infirmity is incurable.... The human physician sometimes is deceived and promises health in the human body.[29]

We should, therefore, put ourselves wholly into the hands of the Physician. For He will not make the mistake of cutting off a healthy part instead of the festering: He knows what He examines; He knows what is wrong, because He Himself has made our nature; He discerns what He Himself has created, and what has been added by our own cupidity.[30]

---

[27] Ibid.

[28] Ibid., 22–23.

[29] Ibid., 20.

[30] Ibid.

7. Showing That the Human Race Suffers Because of Its Need to Be Cured by the Divine Physician

> The human race suffers not from bodily diseases, but from sins. The giant patient lies stretched out over the whole world from east to west. To cure the giant patient, the Almighty Physician descends from heaven, humbling Himself to mortal flesh, to the bed, as it were, of the patient. He gives wholesome prescriptions. He is spurned. But those who follow them, are cured. He is spurned when powerful friends say: "This Physician has no knowledge." But if He had no knowledge, His power would not fill the nations.[31]
>
> Seeing that men in their wretchedness are restless under the load of their cares, and taken up by the affairs of this world, which strangle their souls, God comes as a Physician. And they are so bold as to say: "Since Christ came, we have these horrible times; since there are Christians, the world is failing in every respect." O foolish patient! Not because the Physician came, your sickness became more serious: the good, kind, just, and merciful Physician foresaw that illness; He did not cause it. He came to comfort you that you may become really whole. For what does He take away from you if not things which are superfluous? You were fond of things which are harmful. You were held in bonds by them. These things you were fond of did not help to cure your fever. Is a physician unkind because he snatches poisonous fruit from the hand of his patient? What did the Divine Physician take away from you if not a harmful security which you were about to win? Cast off your ruinous affections: the things you bemoan and grumble at are part of His medicine.[32]

St. Augustine was not afraid to point out that from a spiritual point of view, the collapse of the Roman Empire was not necessarily an overwhelming disaster; rather, society was like a prostrate sick man awaiting medical assistance.

> Brethren, look with sober eyes at these amphitheaters whose walls are now crumbling. It was extravagance that built them. Or do you believe that righteousness erected them? It was the extravagance of godless men that raised them. Do you not wish that now at last the work of extravagance crumble away, and that the work of righteousness begin to rise?. . . Now they say: "The Christian times are evil . . ." There is a physician, brethren, and he knows to cut away a festering limb lest also the other parts grow putrid. One finger, he says, is cut away, because it is better that there is one finger less than that the whole body grows putrid. If a human physician does this because of his expert knowledge, and medical skill cuts away some part of the

[31] Ibid., 23–24.
[32] Ibid., 24.

limbs lest all grow putrid, why should God not cut away in men whatever He knows to be putrid so that they may attain to salvation?[33]

8. *Devotion to Christ, Our Only Hope*

> Relieve my deep wound after thy great mercy: the wound I have is deep, but in the Almighty I take refuge; I would despair of my own so deadly wound, unless I could find such a great Physician.[34]
>
> What was I, unless Thou didst heal? Where was I lying, unless Thou didst come to me? Indeed, with a huge wound I was endangered, but that wound of mine called for the Almighty Physician. To the Almighty Physician nothing is incurable.[35]

The image of Christ the Physician in many ways parallels modern devotions like the Sacred Heart or the Divine Mercy. The ascended Christ is seen as being aware of and involved in the struggles of the devout soul. He is also seen as seeking out those who reject Him, those who, like a demented person, attack the doctor. Christ is interested in the plight of the individual and of society. He is addressed by heartfelt petitions, in which the individual is revealed in the most personal way.

Fr. Arbesmann, to whom we owe much of what we know about Christ the Physician, makes it clear that this devotion was popular especially in the West over a long period of time. Several important early writers mention it, including Tertullian, Lactantius, and St. Augustine, as we have seen, and St. Ephraem the Syrian, St. Jerome, St. Cyprian of Carthage, and even Pelagius. Those who question whether devotion is appropriate or whether its expression should be limited to liturgical and scriptural prayers must recall that even in the age of the martyrs and extending into the post-Nicene Fathers, there is a popular devotion to Christ that can still have meaning for Christians sixteen hundred years later.

Devotions usually become known by works of art and popular paintings. The means for this kind of popularization were not available in St. Augustine's time. Devotions spread widely through art and books only as printing and the graphic arts became more developed in the fifteenth century. In the ancient Church, however, devotion was there, and great multitudes believed that Christ, who had ascended into heaven, knew them and continued to say to them individually, "Come to me, all who labor and are heavy laden, and I will give you rest. Take my yoke upon you, and learn from me; for I am gentle and lowly in heart, and you will find rest for your souls" (Mt 11:28–29).

---

[33] Ibid., 24–25.

[34] Ibid., 20.

[35] Ibid.

4 Son of God and Son of Mary

The Creed of Nicaea, which was augmented by the First Council of Constantinople, left many questions open. Nicea had defined that Jesus of Nazareth was both God and man. But how was this unique union to be understood? The theological difficulty of such inquiries is that they deal with mysteries so impenetrable that even in the Kingdom of God we will not comprehend their deepest aspects. The human mind, however, is curious, and so the Church was and is compelled to make decisions about theological theories.

The first great question about Christ after Nicaea was posed by Nestorius, Archbishop of Constantinople, around 425, and seemed at first a problem regarding the use of language. What words could be used to describe Jesus Christ and specifically His relationship to His Mother? It had long been the custom, especially in the East, to call Mary the *Theotokos*—the God-bearer, or the Mother of God. At the end of the apostolic age St. Ignatius of Antioch wrote that Jesus our Lord was really conceived of Mary.[1] St. Justin Martyr, the first great Christian apologist, who wrote about A.D. 150, was surprisingly explicit in his teaching about Mary in his Dialogue with Trypho, directed to an imaginary Jewish critic of Church teaching. In a few lines he shows the direction of accepted Christian teaching in the century immediately following Christ and the apostles. "Christ became man by the Virgin so that the disobedience which proceeded from the serpent might be destroyed in the same way as it originated. For Eve, being a virgin and undefiled, having conceived the word from the serpent, brought forth disobedience and death. The Virgin Mary, however, having received faith and joy, when the angel Gabriel announced to her the good tidings . . . answered: 'Be it done to me according to thy word.' "[2]

Thus Mary was seen as the new Eve very early on. The same parallels—death and sin through Eve, life and salvation through Mary—are expressed by St. Irenaeus, who was born in Asia Minor and became

[1] Ignatius of Antioch, Letter to the Ephesians, nos. 7, 18, in *The Fathers of the Church*, trans. Francis X. Glimm et al. (New York: Cima, 1947): 90, 94.

[2] *Dialogue with Trypho*, 100, 5, quoted in Hilda Graef, *Mary: A History of Doctrine and Devotion* (London: Sheed and Ward, 1963), 38.

Bishop of Lyons, France (died A.D. 202), and Tertullian, the first important Christian writer in Latin (died c. 220). Clement of Alexandria (died c. 215), who was one of the first professional Christian teachers, not only accepted Mary as the new Eve but taught that she remained a virgin during the birth of Christ as well as after it.[3] Origen (d. 253), the great pupil of Clement and one of the most powerful theological minds of the ancient Church, maintained that Mary was a virgin throughout her life. In his homilies on St. Luke, Origen does not hesitate to label as heretics those who claim that the "brothers" of Jesus were Mary's children. Origen maintained that they were Joseph's children by an earlier marriage.[4]

While all of this early Marian teaching may be a bit disconcerting to Protestants, one must also mention, to the discomfort of Catholics, that Origen, along with several other early Fathers of the Church, taught that Mary had faults. He maintained that her faith wavered at Calvary, as did that of the apostles, although there is no scriptural evidence for this. Nevertheless, Origen describes the Mother of Jesus as the new Eve and for the first time that can be verified refers to her as Theotokos—"she who gives birth to God".[5] This reference is before the middle of the third century.

Two centuries later St. Augustine, the recognized Doctor of grace and exponent of the universality of original sin, relying on St. Paul, taught against Pelagius that all human beings were subject to this mysterious wound of sin. However, he exempted Mary. In saying that all men had original sin, he adds, "except the holy Virgin Mary, about whom, for the honour of the Lord, I want there to be no question where sin is mentioned, for concerning her we know that more grace for conquering sin in every way was given to her who merited to conceive and give birth to him, who certainly had no sin whatsoever."[6]

This very brief review of the early Fathers makes it clear that soon after the end of the apostolic age, even during the early persecutions, the importance of Mary as the new Eve and Mother of God was recognized. It goes beyond the scope of this book to give a complete review of Marian teaching in the postapostolic period up to Ephesus, the Marian council in the fifth century. Several such reviews of this development have been done by competent authors, including *Mary: A History of Doctrine and Devotion* (2 vols.) by Hilda Graef. Of particular interest to Protestant readers is *Mary through the Centuries* by Jaroslav Pelikan.

Marian Devotion in the Church of the Martyrs

Most Christians are unaware of the very early Marian teachings in Christianity. Even in the second century there was what might be called devotion to the Mother of Jesus—books of devotion containing

[3] Graef, Mary, 43.
[4] Ibid., 45.
[5] Ibid., 46.
[6] Augustine, *De Natura et Gratia*, no. 42, quoted in Graef, *Mary*, 98–99.

legends and fables about Christ and His Mother. Although they have little or no historical value, these popular works are interesting. They show that a colorful devotional literature began long before the New Testament canon was codified at the end of the fourth century and that the ordinary Christian convert sought a personalized approach to the sober facts presented in the Gospels. These writings, which, for example, give us the names of Joachim and Anna, the parents of Mary, made a profound impact on popular piety despite the fact that the Church Fathers almost entirely ignored them. Some, especially St. Jerome, heaped scorn and derision on these unhistorical writings.

There are several of these apocryphal works, the most important of which is the *Protoevangel of James*,[7] which appears to have been written early in the Christian era, probably in Egypt toward the end of the second century. As obscure as its authorship is and despite its rejection by the Church Fathers, over thirty ancient copies of this work survive in Syriac and Coptic, as well as Greek and Latin, showing its wide popularity and that it must have significantly influenced the life of the Church.[8]

The *Protoevangel* illustrates how the ordinary Christian thought about the Mother of the Messiah. The legends of the *Protoevangel* emphasize the purity of Mary. She is said to have been raised in a chamber where her feet did not touch the ground until being presented in the Temple at the age of three. At that time she is said to have danced at the altar "and all the house of Israel loved her". The *Protoevangel* tells that she was nourished by angels until she was twelve, when she had to leave the Temple because she was then a young woman. So the priests assembled all the widowers of Israel, and Joseph was chosen as her husband. Old and reluctant because of his own sons, he accepted the task only when threatened with the wrath of God by the high priest.[9] The obvious message of this legend, or rather this parable, is that Mary was chosen by God to be Mother of the Messiah and she was preserved by God from all that might harm her unique purity. The story also conveys the idea that Joseph only reluctantly takes on the task, which is assigned to him by the high priests, thus linking the Old and the New Testaments, as is done in the Lukan narrative of the birth of John the Baptist.

Naturally there has been a rationalistic tendency to see the teaching of the early Church as a by-product of the *Protoevangel*. This assumption, however, goes both ways. Before the *Protoevangel* appeared, St. Irenaeus and Origen both saw Mary as the new Eve and stated that she remained a virgin even after the birth of Christ. Irenaeus, the great teacher of the second century, explicitly says that through her

[7] M. R. James, *The Apocryphal New Testament* (Oxford: Clarendon Press, 1924), 38–49, cited in Graef, *Mary*, 35.

[8] Graef, *Mary*, 35.

[9] Ibid., 36.

obedience Mary became the "cause of salvation" for the human race, just as Eve had been the cause of its loss. He sees Mary as interceding for all mankind, "the pure womb which regenerates men unto God".[10] Pelikan is of the opinion that Irenaeus was expressing a point of view already familiar to his readers, because this great bishop saw himself as carefully preserving the tradition of the apostles.[11] It is significant that Irenaeus was not favorable to new ideas.

It is important to note that certain early Fathers saw Mary as having faults. Despite their acceptance of her vital position in redemption and despite the lack of biblical evidence, Irenaeus believed that Christ repels Mary's importuning of Him at Cana (see Jn 2:1–11). He does this even though Christ works His first sign at Mary's request. Origen believed that Mary was scandalized along with the apostles at the Passion of Christ: "If she had not suffered scandal in the passion of the Lord, Jesus would not have died for her sins. But if 'all have sinned' . . . (Rom 3:23), then Mary, too, was scandalized at that time."[12] Origen saw evidence of her coming scandal in the prophecy of Simeon: "Your own soul a sword shall pierce" (Lk 2:35). But neither in St. Luke nor elsewhere in the Scriptures is there evidence of Mary being scandalized. Actually, Origen and Irenaeus were struggling with a question that would be repeated for centuries, namely, how Mary could be without sin and yet be redeemed. The answer would await the teaching on the simultaneous creation and redemption of Mary, proposed by Blessed John Duns Scotus and known to Catholics as the doctrine of the Immaculate Conception. This teaching maintains that Mary was simultaneously created and redeemed by Christ, thus remaining sinless.

What is most significant for us is that the early Fathers believed in Mary's essential role in redemption and in her perpetual virginity without any direct reference to the fables of the *Protoevangel of James* or other apocryphal books. It is much more plausible to hold that the poorly informed author of the *Protoevangel*, who is ignorant of most Jewish customs, derived the idea of Mary's perpetual virginity and purity from apostolic teaching and patristic tradition than it is to say that the Fathers derived their belief in Mary's perpetual virginity from the *Protoevangel* or other such documents. The author of the *Protoevangel* obviously borrowed uncritically from many sources, while the Fathers are very careful and avoid any reference to fabulous tales or things outside of the Scriptures.

An Early Marian Apparition

Reports of appearances of the Blessed Virgin Mary are disconcerting to many modern Christians, yet these apparitions have received a great deal of notoriety in the last two or three centuries. The first account

[10] Irenaeus, *Against the Heresies*, 4, 33, 11, cited in ibid, 40.

[11] Jaroslav Pelikan, *Mary through the Centuries* (New Haven: Yale University Press, 1996), 43.

[12] Origen, "Homily 17 on Luke", quoted in Graef, *Mary*, 45–46.

of an apparition of the Blessed Virgin, however, comes from before the year 270. St. Gregory of Nyssa wrote that St. Gregory the Wonder-Worker had a vision of the Blessed Virgin before his death. Hilda Graef points out that although Gregory of Nyssa wrote a century later, it is quite probable that the vision is authentic. Well-known scholars call the testimony of Gregory of Nyssa unimpeachable, since he is one of the most cautious of the ancient Fathers.[13] It is interesting that Mary appears in this vision with St. John the Apostle. A similar vision of these two great witnesses of the life of Christ was reported by simple country people in the 1870s at Knock, Ireland.

Why This Early Emphasis on Mary?

It was of the greatest importance for the early Church to fend off the idea that Christ was not truly human. Some at the time maintained that His body was merely an apparition or phantom. St. Augustine mentions this error as late as the end of the fourth century in describing his hope for his deceased friend Nebridius.[14] Irenaeus, while defending the virginity of Mary and proclaiming her as the Second Eve and the Mother of the Redeemed, rejected the assertions of the followers of the Gnostic teacher Valentinus that Jesus really had not been born of the Virgin Mary but had "passed through Mary as water runs through a tube" without any other participation on her part.[15]

Gnostic and Manichaean writers denied the mystery of the Incarnation of Christ with great determination. The former saw Him as being like the divine men of Greek and Roman mythology; the latter denied His physical reality and humanity entirely, since they despised all physical things, including the human body. The Mother of Jesus became very important in the battle against both heretical positions. The Council of Chalcedon (451) finally proclaimed that Jesus Christ was both God and man in a single Divine Person. Mary had to be the mother in this world of that Divine Person. She had to be a real mother, but she did not have to be a real wife in the sexual meaning of that term; hence they reiterated the dogmatic teaching of the Council of Ephesus on the Virgin Birth. This apparently fine point of theology on the divine personhood is really the cornerstone of the Christian concept of the Incarnation. So to speak, the two sides of the arch, divinity and humanity, would come together in a dynamic relationship in the single person of Jesus of Nazareth. He is both Son of God in His divinity and Child of Mary in His humanity. Mary is the Mother of this person. Obviously she could not give Him His divinity, but she did give Him His humanity, including the capability of suffering and dying.

---

[13] Graef, *Mary*, 47.

[14] *The Confessions of Saint Augustine*, trans. Frank Sheed (New York: Sheed and Ward, 1965) bk. 9, chap. 3.

[15] Pelikan, *Mary through the Centuries*, 47–48.

We see how important it was for the early Church to emphasize the role of the Virgin Mary in order to teach that Jesus Christ was human, as well as divine. At the same time she is also truly the Mother of God. This is very close to her title *Theotokos*. By her fiat at the Annunciation she participates so intimately in the divine plan that the Son of God receives His humanity through her, and she becomes the Mother of God.

The Council of Ephesus (431)

The Council of Ephesus proclaimed that Mary is the Mother of Jesus, who is both God and man. She truly and willingly gives her participation so that the Son of God may receive humanity from her, a humanity that, by the power of God, is united to His divinity in the single person of Jesus.

On this point let us recall the case of Nestorius, Patriarch of Constantinople (428–431), who held that in Christ a Divine Person and a human person were joined in perfect harmony, thus denying that Christ, as a single Divine Person, possessed both human and divine natures. It is extraordinarily important to note that when the Council of Ephesus condemned Nestorius and deposed him as patriarch for denying that Mary was the Mother of God, it also approved the use of many verbs and predicables to speak of the Messiah. These forms of speech pertained to the fact that He is truly God and truly man. Nestorius' problem was "with the 'communication of idioms,' whereby what is properly attributed to Christ's manhood can be predicated of God, e.g., that God is born of the Virgin Mary, etc." [16] With the doctrine of the communication of idioms (we would say the teaching on language), the Church Fathers permitted such expressions as that in Christ—God was born, walked, suffered, and died. This is true because the Son of God, when He came into this world, had a human mother. One can push this further and state accurately that God became a carpenter. It was not God the Father who did these things, or the Holy Spirit, but the Son. Decades before the Councils of Ephesus and Chalcedon, Augustine observes that the eternal Word, who created all time, "caused the day of His birth to take place in time". He continues:

> With the Father He precedes all the ages of the world, by the Mother He set Himself on this day in the course of the years. The Maker of Man was made man, that the Ruler of the stars might suck at the breast; that the Bread might be hungered; the Fountain, thirst; the Light, sleep; the Way, be wearied by the journey; the Truth, be accused by false witnesses; the Judge of the living and the dead, be judged by a mortal judge; the Chastener, be chastised with whips; the Vine, be

[16] Frederick Jelly, O.P., *Madonna: Mary in the Catholic Tradition* (Huntington, Ind.: Our Sunday Visitor, 1986), 93.

> crowned with thorns; the Foundation, be hung upon the tree; Strength, be made weak; Health, be wounded; Life, die.[17]

Because Mary had made all this possible by her consent, she became the spiritual agent of mankind and a cause of its salvation, just as Eve had been the cause of its damnation. For this reason devotion to Mary sprang from devotion to Christ. After the Council of Ephesus and the proclamation of the "Divine Maternity" (as it was called), there was a surge of interest in the Mother of Jesus. Pope Sixtus III built the basilica of St. Mary Major, at Rome. In the West, interest centered on the relationship of Mary and the Church, which had been the particular focus of St. Ambrose and St. Augustine. As the Mother of Christ, Mary is also the Mother of the Church and of the faithful. If she is the Mother of the faithful, is it not appropriate for her to be involved with us as an intercessor? Devotion to the Blessed Virgin Mary was seen as a complement to devotion to Christ, but she was always seen only as an intercessor.

In the Eastern Church, interest in the Mother of God became even more enthusiastic. A whole literature concerning the personal life of Mary and especially her death came into being. A collection of writings called the *Transitus Mariae* flourished in the ancient Church. The Fathers of the Church tried either to ignore this popular literature or to scorn it, as St. Jerome did. Yet we must reiterate that these writings, from the *Protoevangel of James* at the end of the second century to works in the fifth and sixth centuries, give us unique insight into the popular devotion of the ancient Church. One of the most beautiful passages of this writing concerns the Assumption of Mary. In the following Coptic account, written by Theodosius of Alexandria, Christ is pictured as standing over the dead body of His Mother, saying:

> Arise from thy sleep, O thou holy body, which was to Me a temple.... Arise. Why sleepest thou yet in the earth? Array thyself with thy soul, and come to the heavens with Me, unto My good Father and the Holy Spirit; for they long for thee. Arise, O thou holy body, from which I built Me My flesh in a manner incomprehensible; wear thy soul which was to Me a dwelling place.... Arise, O thou holy body; be joined to the blessed soul. Receive from Me thy resurrection before the whole creation.[18]

Our treatment of early Marian devotion is scarcely more than a sketch. For those interested in the history of devotion to Jesus Christ, further study will show that the strengths and weaknesses of popular

[17] Augustine, Sermon 191, in Fr. Erich Przywara, S.J., ed., *An Augustine Synthesis* (New York: Sheed and Ward, 1945), 180–81.

[18] Theodosius, *The Falling Asleep of Mary*, 8, 10ff., quoted in Alfred C. Rush, C.Ss.R., "Mary in the Apocrypha of the New Testament", in Juniper B. Carol, O.F.M., *Mariology* (Milwaukee: Bruce, 1954): 166.

devotion today are mirrored in the popular interests of Christians almost two thousand years ago.[19] For this reason the importance of early Marian devotion is difficult to overestimate.

Many Christians, even many Catholics, erroneously think that devotion to the Mother of Christ began in the Middle Ages or is the result of the reported apparitions in modern times. Nothing could be further from the truth. Fr. Walter Burghardt, S.J., mentions that such devotions as the Queenship of Mary find their roots in the Church Fathers. He also suggests that "the idea of Mary's universal mediation" is "rooted in her function as Second Eve and [is] suggested so vividly by Ambrose".[20]

Magnificent hymns like the Akathistos, a poem of twenty-four stanzas celebrating the Incarnation, are filled with the most beautiful praises of the Mother and Child and intercessions to both. In this hymn Mary is praised as "the raising up of the fallen Adam, a height inaccessible to human thoughts ... the bridge that leads from earth to heaven ... the field that yields a harvest of mercies", along with many other poetic metaphors. She is the object of so much praise not because of any power of her own but because she is the Mother of God. Graef also points out that these popular devotions should not be taken as the Mariological doctrine of the time, but as poetic expressions, given on occasion with a certain imprecise hyperbole.[21]

Jesus Christ and His Mother

The relationship between devotion to Our Savior and devotion to His Mother can be summed up in the following prayer, which is recorded on a papyrus in the John Rylands Library in Manchester, England. The text is found word for word in the Eastern liturgies and in the Ambrosian Rite in the West and is assigned to the third century: "We fly to thy patronage, O holy Mother of God; despise not our petitions in our necessities, but from all dangers deliver us, O glorious and ever blessed Virgin."

Catholics familiar with the Latin liturgy will recognize this prayer as a form of the *Sub tuum præsidium*, perhaps the oldest invocation to the Blessed Virgin. An even more popular prayer, the Ave Maria, is found in an ancient text discovered in a Coptic monastery. This document seems to be from the sixth or seventh century. The prayer appears to have been said after the reading of the Gospel for some Marian commemoration, perhaps the feast of the Presentation.

---

[19] Along with the comprehensive study of Hilda Graef, at least the following chapters of Juniper Carol's *Mariology* (vol. 1) are very informative: "Mary in Western Patristic Thought", by Walter J. Burghardt, S.J.; "Mary in the Apocrypha of the New Testament", by Alfred C. Rush, C.Ss.R.; "Mary in the Eastern Liturgies", by Very Rev. Cuthbert Gumbinger, O.F.M. Cap.; and "Mary in the Western Liturgy", by Simeon Daly, O.S.B.

[20] Burghardt, "Mary in Western Patristic Thought", in Carol, *Mariology*, 155.

[21] Hilda Graef, *The Devotion to Our Lady*, Twentieth Century Encyclopedia of Catholicism (New York: Hawthorn Books, 1963), 31–32.

Hail Mary, full of grace;
the Lord is with you, the Holy Spirit too.
Your priests shall be robed in justice,
they that honour you shall rejoice and exult.
For David's sake, your servant, Lord,
save, Lord, your people, bless your chosen portion.

Hail to the glorious virgin, Mary, full of grace.
The Lord is with you.
Blessed you are above all other women
and blessed is the fruit of your womb:
for he you conceived was Christ, the Son of God,
and he has redeemed our souls.[22]

Devotion to Jesus has always been helpful to Christians in integrating psychologically the physical and the spiritual components of human life. It has always brought together the intellectual and the emotional, the universal truth and the deeply personal needs of the individual. All devout Christians will recognize this by simply reflecting on their own individual relationship with our Lord Jesus Christ. The devotion to Mary is parallel and subsidiary to this devotion. Devotion to the Mother of Christ developed among Christians of the East and West because of their deeply felt need for motherly love. To this day Christians find in Marian devotion a personal love completely united with Christ. This is true for members of the Catholic and Orthodox churches, the Eastern churches in union with Rome, and the apostolic churches. It is also true for many Anglicans and even some Protestants.[23]

Well-developed and ancient theological insights provide a framework that supplies the theological foundation for the devotion to Mary. Marian devotion is comprehensible only when one realizes its single reason for existence: devotion to the Incarnate Son of God, the new Adam of Redemption.

---

[22] Translated in A. Hamman, O.F.M., ed., *Early Christian Prayers* (Chicago: Henry Regnery, 1961), 76.

[23] See, for example, David Van Biema, "Hail, Mary", *Time* 165 (March 21, 2005): 61–69.

5 The Holy Face: The Image Made without Human Hands

The human mind (except in the case of a person born blind) has a powerful ability to picture abstract ideas in symbols and images. We use this faculty—imagination—to recall persons, places, things, and events. We would have difficulty learning from the past or planning for the future if we could not imagine what has happened or what will happen. The accomplishments of the sightless are all the more astonishing when we realize that, for them, this imaginative faculty must operate in other ways. It is assumed that there is a primarily auditory, or subvocal, accommodation for the sightless, but how, then, can we adequately appreciate the accomplishments of heroic souls like Helen Keller who neither see nor hear?

For most, the processes of thought are intimately linked with the capacity to make mental images. For this reason man has always used symbols, sacred rituals, and images in seeking God. There is always the danger that any such image or symbol may assume an importance apart from what it symbolizes, thus opening the way to idolatry. The Hebrews made effective use of signs and symbols, but were deeply opposed to images because of the first commandment, which broadly condemned idolatry. Nevertheless, various images occur in Hebrew history, including the cherubim on the Ark of the Covenant and the bronze serpent used by Moses in the desert. The conviction that God could not be pictured along with the proscription of images contributed to a vital awareness of divine transcendence in Judaism, then in Islam, and later in some forms of Protestantism. It is interesting that most of these groups have come to live with photographic images, pictorial representations in art and history, and images on television and the Internet.

It should not surprise us that such scruples regarding images are also found in early Christian history.[1] Since the very heart of paganism was the veneration of idols, it is only natural that early Christians were deeply opposed to them. No Christian could make his living by producing idols for sale.[2] Nevertheless, images of Christ as the Good

[1] H.P. Gebhard, *The World of Icons* (New York: Harper and Row, 1957), 14 ff.

[2] Ibid., 17.

Shepherd existed from the second century onward. Early in the fourth century the ecclesiastical historian Eusebius (263–340), whom we met in Chapter 3 above, writes very negatively of the veneration of images of Christ and the apostles in the postapostolic period. The apocryphal Life of St. John the Evangelist, written in the middle of the second century, mentions the same thing.[3]

Usually these early Christian images were made by Gentiles who had converted. In these images Christ often resembles a Greek or Roman, short-haired and without a beard. However, early in the fourth century we find a painting in the Roman Cemetery of Domitilla, showing Christ with a full beard, long hair parted in the middle, and Semitic features.[4] These early images have a realism about them that is totally consistent with Græco-Roman art of the time.

The use of images of Christ was accepted only gradually: along with the Hebrew religious proscription and the fear that images would lead to idolatry, there were theological reasons for this. Clement of Alexandria agreed with many of his contemporaries that only God the Father ever created a true image: His own image in the form of the Logos, His Son. Since man can be said to resemble God because he has reason, in some sense man is an image of God. But, according to Clement, because God could not be imaged and because the Son could be imaged by none but the Father, Christians should not use images of Christ in worship.[5] Early in the fourth century, a provincial council held at Elvira, in Spain, forbade paintings in church. Yet a few decades later in the East several of the greatest Church Fathers defended the use of images, including SS. Basil the Great, Gregory of Nazianzus, Gregory of Nyssa, and John Chrysostom. St. Basil, perhaps the most ardent defender of images, even ordered that paintings of Christ be used to teach the faithful. A few centuries later, his monks would become staunch defenders of Christian iconography against the iconoclasts. These Greek Fathers defended images as educational tools and sources of edification. Sacred images speak without words. Disrespect to an image was seen as disrespect to the person it represented; therefore, images of Christ and the saints deserved respect and reverence.

The use of paintings became popular a little later in the West. St. Paulinus, Bishop of Nola (d. 431) and a friend of St. Augustine, arranged for many educational paintings in church. In fact, panel paintings were first called iconica by St. Gregory of Tours (d. 594).[6] Later, St. Gregory the Great (d. 604) encouraged the use of paintings of our Savior to recall the Son of God but warned against the

[3] *The New Catholic Encyclopedia* (New York: McGraw-Hill, 1967), 7:324. See the excellent article "Icons" by L. Ouspensky.

[4] See R. P. du Bourguet, S.J., *Art Paléochrétien* (Paris: Editions Cercle d'Art, 1970).

[5] Gebhard, *World of Icons*, 18.

[6] Ibid., 25.

worship of such paintings.[7] In both East and West in the fifth and sixth centuries, images were seen as representations of the Lord, His Mother, and the saints. Soon miracles were reported in response to prayer before a particular image.

The True Face of Christ

From the fifth century on, there was a vigorous effort to discover the true appearance of Christ, the Mother of God, and the apostles. St. John Chrysostom, annoyed by this, counseled people to concentrate on the presence of Christ in the Holy Eucharist: "How many there are who still say, 'You want to see his shape, his image . . . his clothing, his sandals.' Behold, you do see him, you touch him, you eat him!"[8]

This admonition of the great patriarch of the East fell on deaf ears. All were eager to know what Christ looked like. In the middle of the sixth century the so-called Abgar legend told of a picture of Christ not made by human hands. According to the legend, before Christ's Passion He sent His image, pressed on a piece of cloth, to King Abgar V of Edessa to cure him. This object, called the mandylion, was afterward kept in Edessa (modern Turkey). At the end of the sixth century a similar object was reported to be in Cappadocia (also modern Turkey).[9]

In a recent work on icons, Michel Quenot sees these stories as related to the legend of Veronica's veil, onto which Christ supposedly imprinted His face on the way to Calvary.[10] The name Veronica means "true icon" (*vera icon*). Although this event is not in Scripture, it is familiar to Catholics as the Sixth Station of the Cross. Images like Veronica's veil and the mandylion are called *acheiropoietoi*, meaning icons "made without human hands".[11] The intense interest in the Shroud of Turin gives evidence that believers still yearn for an image of Christ not made by hands. In fact, some think that the Shroud of Turin is really the mandylion of Edessa unfolded.

Of course most icons were not believed to be of miraculous origin, and schools were established to teach icon writing. Some of the greatest icon painters, like Andrei Rublev, were canonized by the Orthodox Church. But the style of icons was at least assumed to follow the original picture not made by human hands. Moreover, they were properly made only with long prayer, fasting, many blessings and anointings, and the following of rituals and classical models.

---

[7] Ibid.

[8] John Chrysostom, *In Matthaeum Homil.*, Patrologica Graeca (hereinafter PG) 57–58, 741–44, quoted in Msgr. James T. O'Connor, *The Hidden Manna: A Theology of the Eucharist* (San Francisco: Ignatius Press, 1988),47.

[9] Gebhard, *World of Icons*, 26.

[10] Michel Quenot, *The Icon: Window on the Kingdom* (Crestwood, N.Y.: St. Vladimir's Seminary Press, 1996), 23.

[11] Christoph Schönborn, O.P., *God's Human Face: The Christ-Icon* (San Francisco: Ignatius Press, 1994), 159.

Can You Picture Christ at All? Two Sides of a Great Controversy

I must now attempt the difficult task of describing the controversy over icons evenhandedly, and so I should begin by admitting my biases: I love icons and am among those Latin Rite Catholics who find much spiritual depth in this form of sacred art. According to our rule, the only images in the chapels of our Franciscan community are the icon crucifix of San Damiano, so beloved by St. Francis (before which he received his vocation), and the miraculous tilma, or blanket, of the Mexican peasant St. Juan Diego, which preserves an image of the Virgin Mary believed to be made without human hands.

Although I appreciate and use sacred art in my own devotional life, I must always remember that many defended the Church's earlier position during the persecutions that images were forbidden by divine law. Even St. Augustine, who wrote eloquently of the beauty of Christian hymns, was restrained in his enthusiasm for images.

The view of the iconoclasts of the eighth and ninth centuries that Christ cannot be pictured will resonate with some Protestant readers. Orthodox Christians, with considerable support from Catholics, tend to see the iconoclasts as all bad. We will see that they had their theological positions, which could be profound, although in fact they were often cruel and dictatorial. I would invite all readers to at least study the icon, the most spiritual genre of Christian art, with the understanding that even non-iconic Christian art that is deeply spiritual, like that of Blessed Fra Angelico (d. 1455), owes a debt to it. Here we present a brief sketch focused not on icons themselves but on what made them so beloved of some of Christ's followers and so detested by others.

Icons and Iconoclasts

A great Orthodox scholar of icons, L. Ouspensky describes this form of art as follows:

> The specific pictorial language of the icon was formed on Byzantine soil from elements of the arts of the different nations belonging to the Byzantine Empire or having cultural relations with it. The main characteristics of this language already marked the art of Roman catacombs: it is frontal, laconic, and lacking in shadows. This pictorial language of the icon developed in very close connection with the spiritual life of the Church, with the formation of its liturgy and its dogmatic definitions.[12]

Icons, which vary by culture and historical period, are the pride of Eastern Christianity; to speak of paintings in the Orthodox Church is to speak of icons. Despite this, the presence of icons has recently become noticeable in the West, even in Protestant circles. The Taizé Community, for example, has introduced this powerful form of religious art in Western Europe.

---

[12] Ouspensky, "Icons", 324.

Icons found their greatest defender in St. John of Damascus (675–749). Providentially, he was immune to the violence of the iconoclasts, which began with the Byzantine emperor Leo III (717–741) and continued under his successor, Constantine V (741–775). St. John of Damascus lived in the Monastery of St. Sabbas in the Holy Land, then ruled by Muslims. During the controversy, Leo forced the Patriarch of Constantinople, Germanus, to resign in 730 and imposed his own iconoclastic candidate, Anastasius (730–741). A decree ordering the destruction of icons, crosses, and even relics was issued but was unevenly applied because of the opposition of monks and many civil servants. Asia Minor seems to have provided the military recruits who went about their work of destruction with fanatical zeal. The Latin-speaking West sided with those who venerated icons; "Popes Gregory II (715–731) and Gregory III (731–741) wrote letters of protest, and the Roman Synod of 731 expressed its opposition."[13] None of this had an effect, as the Western Church was weakened politically and adjusting as best it could to the barbarian kingdoms.

St. John of Damascus, spokesman for the Patriarch of Jerusalem, wrote three treatises on icons that still make beautiful spiritual reading.[14] He showed that although the iconoclasts did not have a well-thought-out position, the Fathers of the Church constructed a powerful defense both from history and theology.

Leo III and his followers seem simply to have relied on the Old Testament objection to images and perhaps were even influenced by the Muslim caliph Yazīd II, who issued a decree against images. The original iconoclasts believed that an image was one in essence with what it portrayed. This way of thinking is foreign to modern people, but we may recall that early Christian martyrs died for refusing to step on a cross or symbol of Jesus. The tendency to see a picture as one with its subject gave iconoclasm a semblance of validity: any image that purported to be of the Son of God would automatically be an idol and contrary to the whole idea of Christ as the Son of God, because God could not be imaged.

In one of his treatises, St. John of Damascus discusses the prohibition against idol worship in Old Testament law and then makes an important distinction under the New Covenant between an image and the One who is worshipped.

> I heed the words of Him who cannot deceive: ... "You shall not make for yourself a graven image or any likeness of anything that is in heaven above, or that is in the earth beneath," and, "All worshippers of images are put to shame, who make their boast in

[13] *New Catholic Encyclopedia*, 7:327.

[14] John of Damascus, *On the Divine Images*, trans. David Anderson (Crestwood, N.Y.: St. Vladimir's Seminary Press, 1980).

> worthless idols." ... In this way and in a similar manner God spoke in times past to the fathers by the prophets, but last of all in these days He has spoken to us by His only-begotten Son, by whom He made the ages. He says: "This is eternal life, that they know Thee, the only true God, and Jesus Christ, whom Thou hast sent." I believe in one God, the source of all things, without beginning, uncreated, immortal and unassailable, eternal, everlasting, incomprehensible, bodiless, invisible, uncircumscribed, without form. I believe in one superessential Being, one Godhead greater than our conception of divinity, in three persons: Father, Son, and Holy Spirit, and I adore Him alone.... I do not adore the creation rather than the Creator, but I adore the one who became a creature, who was formed as I was, who clothed Himself in creation without weakening or departing from His divinity, that He might raise our nature in glory and make us partakers of His divine nature. Together with my King, my God and Father, I worship Him who clothed Himself in the royal purple of my flesh.... [J]ust as the Word made flesh remained the Word, so also flesh became the Word, yet remained flesh, being united to the person of the Word. Therefore I boldly draw an image of the invisible God, not as invisible, but as having become visible for our sakes by partaking of flesh and blood. I do not draw an image of the immortal Godhead, but I paint the image of God who became visible in the flesh, for if it is impossible to make a representation of a spirit, how much more impossible is it to depict the God who gives life to the spirit?[15]

In another passage the saint defends the use of sacred images because of the Incarnation.

> It is obvious that when you contemplate God becoming man, then you may depict Him clothed in human form. When the invisible One becomes visible to flesh, you may then draw His likeness. When He who is bodiless and without form, immeasurable in the boundlessness of His own nature, existing in the form of God, empties Himself and takes the form of a servant in substance and in stature and is found in a body of flesh, then you may draw His image and show it to anyone willing to gaze upon it. Depict His wonderful condescension, His birth from the Virgin, His baptism in the Jordan, His transfiguration on Tabor, His sufferings which have freed us from passion, His death, His miracles which are signs of His divine nature, since through divine power He worked them in the flesh.[16]

[15] "First Apology of Saint John of Damascus Against Those Who Attack the Divine Images", in ibid., 15–16.

[16] Ibid., 18.

An Important Theological Aspect of the Icon

In modern times, the position of the Byzantine iconoclasts has no defenders. Their cause was lost long ago. Every year many of the Orthodox churches celebrate the first Sunday of Lent as Orthodoxy Sunday to recall the restoration of icons.[17] Traditional Protestants, especially Baptists and some Calvinists, however, often became so iconoclastic that they would not even use a cross to mark their churches. They did not experience any need to study or defend the actions of Leo the Emperor and his son, although they sometimes ended up with the same Puritan conclusions—no images, sacred signs, or objects at all. Protestant objections were largely motivated by a literal, if selective, interpretation of the Old Testament, as well as hostility to things "Romish". Most Protestants have moved a bit on this point. One now sees crosses even on fundamentalist chapels, and I have seen a statue of Martin Luther in a Lutheran church and a life-size image of John Knox in the center of St. Giles Church in Edinburgh, the mother church of Scottish Presbyterianism. They were not there for the same reasons that one finds images in Orthodox or Catholic churches, but they were there.

A number of theologians have taken up the questions posed by the iconoclasts of old, and the issue is worth exploring as it brings out important considerations concerning devotion to Jesus Christ.

Can Christ Be Pictured?[18]

This question has been well explored in a profound theological examination by Christoph Cardinal Schönborn of Vienna, the principal editor of the *Catechism of the Catholic Church*. Schönborn points out that St. Athanasius countered the Arian position with the concept that Christ is the perfect image of the Father: "Only if the Son is the Father's perfect image, which in no way diminishes the brightness of its original, only then can he reveal the Father without alteration and loss. Only then is the Son the full revelation of the Father, only then is the Son the direct way to the Father. We touch here on the ultimate root of all theology of the icon: God has a perfect icon of himself".[19]

Arianism: Christ a Lesser God

As we have seen, Arius did not accept the clear position of Christ in the Gospel: "He who has seen me has seen the Father also" (Jn 14:9). Cardinal Schönborn cites Dom Odo Casel, who distinguishes between Arianism and the position of the Church enunciated at Nicaea (325):

> Arianism intended to incorporate the separation of God and world, typical of late antiquity, into the Christian dogma. When the Church,

[17] Timothy Ware, *The Orthodox Church* (London: Penguin Books, 1997), 31.

[18] Readers to whom the subject of Christological heresies and controversies is not appealing, or those who perhaps feel ill-equipped to grasp the more subtle points of Christology, may want to skip ahead to Chapter 6. Those who move ahead at this point may find that they will gain much insight if they return to this section later.

[19] Schönborn, *God's Human Face*, 13.

> in 325 A.D., determined the consubstantiality of Father and Son, in opposition to Arius, it safeguarded the Christian doctrine of salvation against the intrusion of later antiquity's paganism. . . . The Son not only resembles the Father, but is identical to him; and thus Christ, who remains Son even in his humanity, is the unmediated access to the Father. With this, Christian art finds its justification.[20]

St. Augustine taught that Jesus of Nazareth was truly Son of God and one with the Father, and the Fathers of the East were developing other and more subtle distinctions concerning Christ. This process continued even after the Council of Chalcedon, when the divine and human natures were defined as united in the single Person of the Logos, the eternal Son of God. The question of the definition of "person", thus, moved to the center of Christian theology. A person was no longer seen simply as a participant in a nature, so that being a person was almost a limitation. St. Gregory of Nyssa saw that the Divine Persons were different from one another in their missions, even though they had a single nature of divinity.[21] The Father is the ultimate source, the unoriginated origin: "The ascent to this origin is the path onto which revelation itself guides us: from the Spirit as the giver of God's gifts, through the Son as the Mediator of these gifts, to the Father as the ultimate origin".[22]

Following upon this, Schönborn adds: "The Church Fathers of the fourth century express this in their own language when they say: the gift of salvation, coming to us from Christ in the Holy Spirit, makes us godlike. Yet Son and Spirit can make us godlike only if they themselves are God".[23]

Schönborn cites references to SS. Athanasius and Gregory of Nazianzus to the effect that God became man that men might become gods, an almost universal understanding among the ancient Fathers. As Schönborn says, "the importance of this 'fundamental Christian experience' can hardly be overestimated."[24]

The person of the Son, even when He is united with a true human soul and a true human body in the womb of the Virgin (as Ephesus had proclaimed), remains divine. This simply must be; otherwise He could not say "that they may all be one; even as thou, Father, art in me, and I in thee, that they also may be in us" (Jn 17:21). This great truth is in constant danger of being minimized in the effort to make Jesus like us in all things except sin (see Heb 4:15), a text that is so often quoted out of context.

---

[20] Dom Odo Casel, "Glaube, Gnosis und Mysterium", in *Jahrbuch für Liturgiewissenschaft*, cited in ibid.

[21] Schönborn, *God's Human Face*, 25.

[22] Ibid.

[23] Ibid., 26.

[24] Ibid.

But how is Jesus God? He walks, talks, sleeps, and yet the Psalmist says that He "who keeps Israel will neither slumber nor sleep" (Ps 121:4).

Cardinal Schönborn refers to two Church Fathers who are not well known in the West, St. Cyril of Alexandria (d. 444) and St. Maximus the Confessor (d. 662). Cyril of Alexandria's great insight is that Christ is "God visible in the flesh". His powerful teaching, which agrees with Athanasius, is: "The very character of the Father's substance is by its nature transmitted to the Son, so that the Son reveals in himself the Father".[25] Is this not what St. Paul means when He says, "For what we preach is not ourselves, but Jesus Christ as Lord, with ourselves as your servants for Jesus' sake. For it is the God who said, 'Let light shine out of darkness,' who has shone in our hearts to give the light of the knowledge of the glory of God in the face of Christ" (2 Cor 4:5–6). Notice that he speaks of the face of Christ. Can there be a picture of Christ, if from the face of Christ shines the light that was there at the creation of the world? Schönborn sums up this profound truth in the following two paragraphs:

> Once the Incarnation is accepted as reality, it follows that "the flesh assumed by the Word does not remain foreign and accidental to this Word but becomes one with it" (PG 69:561B). The flesh is not "an extrinsic cover" but belongs to the very identity of the Logos. For this reason is "the Lord Jesus Christ one undivided identity" (PG 69:576BC), for the Word "did not dwell in a man—it became man" (PG 76:261C). "'The image of the invisible God' (Col 1:15), the reflection of the Father's substance and his imprint (Heb 1:3), has assumed the form of a slave (Phil 2:7), not by adding a man unto himself, as the Nestorians teach, but by making himself into such a form and yet at the same time preserving his likeness unto the Father" (PG 75:1329AB).
>
> To take the Incarnation seriously means: not to take the humanity of the Logos merely as an instrument, a garment, an extrinsic dwelling place, but rather as "the flesh of the everlasting God" (PG 75:1265A). Therefore, if the flesh is intrinsic to the Word, and if the Word remains consubstantial with the Father, then the Word, even in his Incarnation, "preserves his likeness to God the Father".[26]

St. Cyril's doctrine, summed up here, ought to be a subject of meditation for everyone these days when the divinity of Christ is often played down.

> "For God who said, 'Out of darkness light shall shine' (Gen 1:3), has shone in our hearts in order to irradiate the knowledge of God's glory that shines on the face of Christ" (2 Cor 4:6). Note that "on

---

[25] Cyril of Alexandria, quoted in ibid., 81.

[26] Schönborn, *God's Human Face*, 81–82.

> the face of Christ" there radiates the light of the divine and ineffable glory of God the Father. For the only-begotten Son reveals in himself the glory of the Father, even after having become man. Only in this and in no other manner is he recognized and named the Christ. If not, then let our adversaries tell us how an ordinary man could ever reveal to us or make known to us the light of God's glory. For, surely, we do not behold God in just any man, except he be the Word incarnate, having become one like us, which even in his Incarnation still preserved the true nature of the Son.[27]

I have been reading the Fathers of the Church for years, and I have not read anything that is a more powerful elucidation of the words of Jesus to Philip in John 14. When Philip requests that Jesus show the Father to them, the Savior answers, "Have I been with you so long, and yet you do not know me, Philip? He who has seen me has seen the Father; how can you say, 'Show us the Father'? Do you not believe that I am in the Father and the Father in me?" (Jn 14:8–10).

Monophysitism: The Inhuman Christ

The obvious danger in proclaiming the divinity of Christ is that of losing sight of His humanity. After the Council of Ephesus proclaimed that Jesus is God as well as man, the monk Eutyches and his followers did exactly that, initiating the heresy of Monophysitism, or the theory of the single nature. They taught that Christ's humanity had lost its identity by being absorbed by His divinity.

Monoenergism: The Jesus Who Does Not Act

Despite the condemnation of Eutyches at the Council of Chalcedon (451), the same error reappeared twenty years later, presenting itself this time as Monoenergism (meaning one source of action or energy). Some theologians taught that Jesus had only one source of energy: His divinity. But this position raises obvious questions: How did our Lord become tired? How did He experience the agony in the garden? Monoenergism was another attempt to solve the mystery of the Incarnation by an error similar to the heresy that Christ had only one will. The Second Council of Constantinople, in 553, condemned this as a theological trick; if Christ has only divine energy, then He is not man. The Council Fathers proclaimed Christ as "one of the Trinity who suffered for us".[28]

Monothelitism: The Jesus Who Does Not Will

Some continued to stumble at the idea of the divine and the human joined in a single person. Thus a theory evolved that at first seemed harmless, namely, that Jesus had only one will, which was divine. From our time it is difficult to see how this doctrine, known as Monothelitism, could have been proposed, given the obvious contrast between

[27] Cyril of Alexandria, quoted in ibid, 82–83.

[28] Schönborn, *God's Human Face*, 132.

Christ's human will and divine will during His agony in the garden. Cardinal Schönborn's comments on this controversy are enlightening:

> In Christ, therefore, human nature conforms always and in everything to the counsel of the divine will, without this divine will remaining merely extrinsic to the human will. For Christ's human will never had any stirring of opposition to the divine counsel. Even the spontaneous movement of the will against suffering and death, especially against undeserved suffering, a movement inherent in human nature and manifest as an indomitable drive for self-preservation, was in Christ replaced by the recasting and remolding of the will that characterized his human existence at its root.[29]

This last great Christological heresy was condemned at the Third Council of Constantinople in 681. The council, by recognizing the will as part of human nature, maintained that Christ must have two wills because He had two natures. The Gospel passage concerning the agony in the garden (see Lk 22:39–46), especially the words "not my will, but thine, be done", guided the decision of the council.

St. Maximus the Confessor Leads Us to the Heights

To find the answer to the question of Christ's will, which was left unresolved by the Council of Chalcedon, Cardinal Schönborn suggests that we consult St. Maximus the Confessor (580–662), author of what the cardinal calls "the most wonderful christological synthesis of the ancient Church . . . he is . . . one of the great mystics and spiritual guides of the Christian Orient".[30]

St. Maximus' synthesis of Christology is neither well known nor well understood because it brings us to the depths of the profound mystery of the life of the Trinity and of the life of the Incarnate Son of God. St. Maximus emphatically does not try to explain the mystery of God. He challenges our minds that we "may have power to comprehend with all the saints what is the breadth and length and height and depth, and to know the love of Christ which surpasses knowledge, that [we] may be filled with all the fulness of God" (Eph 3:18–19).

While I encourage the reader to attempt to scale the heights in Cardinal Schönborn's study, I will try to summarize the salient points so that with prayer and meditation we may look more realistically into the mystery of Christ. Schönborn, as we have seen, works toward a comprehensive intellectual analysis of the mystery of the Trinity, using St. Maximus the Confessor as the summit. Having gone to these heights, I suggest that we now fly to the top of the mountain and work our way back to where we were. It might be easier to climb down than up.

[29] Ibid., 127.
[30] Ibid., 102.

Millions have been awestruck by the photographs of the Hubble space telescope and their revelations of the heavens. These photographs show hundreds of galaxies that are millions of light-years across and billions of years old. Incredible photos of galaxies crashing together and making a new field of stars greet us in the morning newspaper. How wonderful it would be to pick up one of these magnificent photographic studies of astronomical events that took place before our solar system even existed and then read the following words of St. Maximus the Confessor:

> Yes, for the sake of Christ—rather, for the sake of the mystery that is Christ—all the eons, and all that the eons contain, have received the origin of their being from Christ and find the destiny of their being also in him. For the final purpose as designed in God's mind, and conceived in anticipation from the beginning, was the unification of all the eons: the union of what is specific with what is unspecific; of what is measured with what is unmeasured; of what is limited with what is unlimited; of the Creator with the created; of what is [unchangeable and] lasting with what is [changing and] in motion. And this union has been revealed at the end of time in Christ, who in himself brought God's foreknowledge to its fulfillment.[31]

This powerful expression of faith—a commentary on John 1:3, that "all things were made through him"—moves us toward that mysterious Person who was born so long after the creation of the universe. How could an itinerant rabbi who never traveled two hundred miles beyond the place of His birth be the One through whom all things are made? St. Maximus tells us:

> This is the great and hidden mystery. This is the blessed destiny for which the cosmos was brought into existence. This is the ultimate design which God had in mind before the beginning of anything created—the end foreknown, by reason of which all things exist, but which in turn does not exist by reason of any other thing. With this final destiny in mind, God created the substances of all things. This is the destination and the ultimate purpose toward which the Divine Providence and everything guided by Divine Providence is aimed and oriented, so that everything created by God would finally be in him recollected into the original unity. This is the great mystery that embraces all the eons, and that reveals the infinitely inexhaustible and immense design of God, a design eternally beyond all the eons. The "angel" of this design is the Word of God himself, who in his essence became man and (through this very act), we dare say, revealed the heart of hearts of the Father's loving-kindness, so that he might show

[31] PG 90:621BC; *Maximus der Bekenner*, 78, quoted in ibid., 124.

> to us, in his own person, the ultimate destiny toward which has been created everything that arose and came into being.[32]

Cardinal Schönborn, speaking of this quotation of St. Maximus, puts it in perspective.

> In this splendid conception of God's salvific economy, Maximus identifies the Incarnation as the heart of the divine design. . . . The Logos is not merely the cosmic instrument of God . . . God's own freedom is completely safeguarded, even—and especially—as it extends to the ultimate obedience of the Son, who himself comes forth from this freedom, so much so that he becomes the revelation of "the heart of hearts of the Father's loving-kindness". . . .
>
> The Incarnation reveals the meaning and the destiny of all creation. Maximus most assuredly was not the first to proclaim this teaching. . . . He launches the theology of the Incarnation in a new direction by conceiving the Incarnation entirely as flowing from the trinitarian "will" (cf. Eph 1:9) of God, whose "messenger" was Christ. Maximus is thus in a position to recognize in the union of Christ's two natures "the blessed purpose" of the work of creation. Creation, in this paradoxical union, finds its natural and its supernatural fulfillment: natural, because it has been created by God for this very union (already in God's image!); supernatural, because the type and manner of this union transcends not only man's fallen state, but the natural order itself. In this union, then, created nature is perfectly preserved and yet at the same time elevated to a mode of existence transcending this nature.[33]

As I read the words of St. Maximus and Cardinal Schönborn's commentary, I understood that I had realized something of this shining message many years ago while looking at the stars in the country sky. However, it was John and Paul, Augustine and Francis, rather than St. Maximus, who taught it to me: "We have beheld his glory, glory as of the only Son from the Father, full of grace and truth" (Jn 1:14); and, "He is the image of the invisible God, the first-born of all creation; for in him all things were created, in heaven and on earth, visible and invisible, whether thrones or dominions or principalities or authorities—all things were created through him and for him" (Col 1:15–16).

The Ways of Following Christ

The next selections summarize two approaches to a profound devotion to Jesus Christ, the Incarnate Word, God Made Man. Both call us to follow Christ in such a way that we are united with the Triune God: the first by enlightened humility, and the second by an abundance of deeply expressive love.

[32] Ibid., 90:621AC; 77–78, 122–23.

[33] Schönborn, *God's Human Face*, 123–24.

St. Augustine wrote the following to some Egyptian monks who were trying to contemplate the mystery of the Trinity.

> Who can contemplate with calm and pure mind this whole being ... and blessed by this contemplation press on to the sight of that which is beyond all known by our perception—to be clothed with everlasting life and obtain eternal salvation? Who can do this but someone who has admitted his sins, leveled his pride to the dust and knelt in meekness to receive God as his teacher?
>
> This can only happen by getting rid of pride by humility of spirit so that we can be lifted up. Such a humility was provided for us in a way that was filled with glory but most gentle, converting our haughty hearts by persuasion rather than by force. This was done by the Word by whom God the Father reveals Himself to angels, His Son who is his Power and Wisdom, hidden from human hearts blinded by worldly desires, humbling Himself to come in human form. This humble example of God makes us more afraid of being proud than of being humiliated like Him.[34]

St. Francis of Assisi, so different from St. Augustine, takes an approach that is poetic, ecstatic, and direct. In the twenty-third chapter of the earlier rule of his order he breaks into a song of praise to God the Father, which is sometimes called the canticle of the Redeemed, or a creed of praise. It represents direct devotion to the Son of God and to His heavenly Father. The prayer itself is addressed to the Father.

All-powerful, most holy,
Almighty and supreme God,
Holy and just Father,
Lord King of heaven and earth
we thank You for Yourself
for through Your holy will
and through Your only Son
with the Holy Spirit
You have created everything spiritual and corporal
and, after making us in Your own image and likeness,
You placed us in paradise.

Through our own fault we fell.

We thank You
For as through Your Son You created us,
So through Your holy love
With which You loved us

[34] Letter 232, quoted in *Augustine: Major Writings* by Fr. Benedict Groeschel, C.F.R. (New York: Crossroad, 1995), 163–64.

You brought about His birth
As true God and true man
By the glorious, ever-virgin, most blessed, holy Mary
and You willed to redeem us captives
through His cross and blood and death.

Because all of us, wretches and sinners,
Are not worthy to pronounce Your name,
We humbly ask
Our Lord Jesus Christ,
Your beloved Son,
in Whom You were well pleased,
together with the Holy Spirit,
the Paraclete,
to give You thanks,
for everything
as it pleases You and Him,
Who always satisfies You in everything,
through Whom You have done so much for us.
Alleluia![35]

How Possible Is It for Jesus to Be God and Man?

Now we come to the mystery of how this is possible. We have seen that in the person of Jesus of Nazareth the divine and human natures were united without being confused or mixed. St. Maximus is emphatic, as was St. Leo in his letter to the Council of Chalcedon, that natures by definition cannot be shared; otherwise one ends up with what the ancient Greeks believed a god to be: a divine man. From the early councils, however, we learn that the two natures remain distinct. Christ's human nature is a "compound"—a union of body and soul, as with all human beings. But the divine and human natures can be united only by something other than these natures. That something is the person, the thinking, acting individual person. This person is the Eternal Son of God. He did not begin to exist in the womb of the Virgin Mother. He took upon Himself a human nature, a true human body with a true human soul with its own will and energy. Christ's humanity is real, but so is His divinity.

What is the identity of this person? Obviously there are things that make each of us unique: the physical and psychological characteristics we receive from heredity and environment and the exercise of our knowledge and freedom. But what was Christ's inner uniqueness like? The answer is found in the great insight of St. Maximus, although it is also implicit in many of the Church Fathers, especially St. Augustine, and in mystics like St. Francis.

---

[35] *Francis of Assisi: Early Documents*, ed. Regis J. Armstrong, O.F.M. Cap., et al. (New York: New City Press, 1999), 1:81–83.

The mode of Christ's being as God becomes the mode of His being as man. This is why Jesus of Nazareth is not only the revelation of God the Son; He is the revelation of the Holy Trinity. The three Persons are distinct only by reason of what they do. They are otherwise identical. St. Maximus writes:

> God's Word himself teaches us that he is perfect in his nature and essence, according to which he is identical and consubstantial with the Father and the Holy Spirit; yet also, that he preserves the distinct difference in personhood, according to which he is in person and hypostasis separate from the Father and the Holy Spirit.
>
> Through the Holy Spirit, he has taken on flesh out of Mary, the Virgin and Mother of God, and has become completely man; which means, he has become a complete man through the assumption of flesh animated by a spiritual soul, and this flesh receives in him his nature and his hypostasis, that is, being and substance. From the instant of conception on, Word and flesh are one; for the Word himself is in a sense the seed of his own Incarnation. Thus in his hypostasis he has become a compound, even though in his own [divine] nature he is one and uncompounded.[36]

We may ask what this Triune God is like. What is it that the Son shows us? He shows us that God is love, and because He is divine love, He is free and His love knows no limits. The coming of the Logos to our fallen race was completely free, and that is why it is called love. To come at all was an act of ultimate generosity, of setting aside the mystery, majesty, the peace and joy of the Godhead, which are beyond human comprehension. The Church Fathers, following St. Paul and the other New Testament writers, say that this coming was for the purpose of enabling us to share in the divine life.

Christ did not come to receive glory and awe. He came to be a slave. The familiar words of St. Paul should be meditated on in this context. "Have this mind among yourselves, which is yours in Christ Jesus, who, though he was in the form of God, did not count equality with God a thing to be grasped, but emptied himself, taking the form of a servant, being born in the likeness of men. And being found in human form he humbled himself and became obedient unto death, even death on a cross" (Phil 2:5–8).

The Face of the Son

The face of Jesus of Nazareth was the human face of God. For this reason the attempt by artists to portray Him is justified. His physical face is an image of His personality. This was all the more true considering that in His face there was neither conscious deception nor unconscious distortion. He had no defense mechanisms, which are essentially unconscious lies we tell ourselves and others. This fact may

[36] PG 91:553C–556A, quoted in Schönborn, *God's Human Face*, 107.

explain the incredible influence He had over those He met. They either loved and followed Him or hated and rejected Him.

The face of Christ is the external symbol of His inner being. For this reason St. Maximus observes: "In his outward appearance he was like us; for in his boundless love he took it upon himself to become creature, yet without changing [His divinity], and thus he became the image [*typos*] and symbol of himself: he has revealed himself symbolically out of his inner being; through himself who is visible he has drawn the whole of creation to himself who is invisible and totally hidden".[37]

Of course, for Him to function in everyday life His divinity had to be veiled. He did not coerce anyone. Love does not and cannot do this. In the Transfiguration, however, His divinity shines through, revealed in the very humanity of Jesus. Cardinal Schönborn says that on Mount Tabor the divine glory breaks through for a moment, and yet St. Maximus points out that what has happened is that Christ "has revealed himself symbolically out of his inner being". It is His transfigured humanity that shows Himself, but his visible self is the same one who is invisible and hidden. Because of the union of the two natures in the single person of Christ the Son of God, we cannot divide that person between humanity and divinity; they are the same.

The Visible Face of Jesus

This brings us to the question of His visible face. The human likeness of Jesus is the image of the Son of God. In His words, "If I be lifted up I will draw all things to myself" (Jn 12:32), Jesus indicates that He brings all of creation to the Heavenly Father. He is the only way to the Father, and to find Him means we have also found the Father. Cardinal Schönborn says that there is "no other access to God's glory than the face of Christ".[38] St. Paul tells us: "For it is the God who said, 'Let light shine out of the darkness,' who has shone in our hearts to give the light of the knowledge of the glory of God in the face of Christ" (2 Cor 4:6). What is even more important in the spiritual life is that if we allow ourselves to be led by Him on the spiritual journey, which is the Passover, we will be changed "into his likeness from one degree of glory to another" (2 Cor 3:18).

Thus, we see the importance of the face of Christ in our spiritual lives. Those who distort this face into that of a person who did not know His destiny or who came only gradually to know who He was ignore the very essence of Christianity.

Cardinal Schönborn provides an excellent summary of the dogmas of the Christian faith. Speaking of the long Christological controversies and the definitions they gave rise to, he says that there was a consistent core of teaching from the time of the apostles. Although

---

[37] Ibid., 91:1165D–1168A, 130.

[38] Schönborn, *God's Human Face*, 131.

this teaching never directly pertained to the face of Christ until the iconoclastic disputes, it prepared for the position that the Church supported, and the use of icons flourished during that time. It will help the reader to have in mind this brief summary of the development of Christology given by Cardinal Schönborn:

> The christological controversies dragged on through centuries. During all this time, the Church never stopped to *profess* the mystery of Christ revealed and yet hidden in the holy face of Jesus. In Nicea (325 A.D.), she professed Christ as the consubstantial image of the Father; in Ephesus (431 A.D.) as the unchanged Word become flesh; in Chalcedon (451 A.D.) as true God and true man; in Constantinople (553 A.D.) as "one of the Trinity who suffered for us"; and again in Constantinople (681 A.D.) as the Word of God, whose human acting and willing was in perfect unison with God's counsel, even unto death. After these long centuries of turbulent, consequential struggles for the profession of the true Christ, our gaze comes to rest to contemplate a quiet image: *the icon of Christ.*[39]

The Image Made by Human Hands

If Christ's human face expressed His inner person and was the true icon of His inner being, then it is logical that to make an icon is not to go against God, but humbly to imitate Him. St. Germanus, Patriarch of Constantinople from 715 to 730, was deposed by Emperor Leo (III) the Iconoclast and condemned by the iconoclastic council in 754, along with St. John of Damascus. Germanus' well-thought-out defense should be noted because even though the conflict raged until 843, the basic defense of icons remained the same throughout that time.

> We allow icons to be fashioned and painted with wax and colors.... Of the invisible deity we make neither a likeness nor any other form. For even the supreme choirs of the holy angels do not fully know or fathom God. But then the only-begotten Son, who dwells in the bosom of the Father (cf. Jn 1:18), desiring to free his own creature from the sentence of death, mercifully deigned, according to the Father's and the Holy Spirit's counsel, to become man. He took on our own flesh and blood, one like us yet without sin, as the great Apostle says (Heb 4:15). For this reason we depict his human likeness in an image, the way he looked as man and in the flesh, and not as he is in his ineffable and invisible divinity.[40]

As the controversies went on, the most insightful and psychological of the defenders of icons was St. Theodore the Studite (759–826), who suspects the iconoclasts of holding on to old heresies and

---

[39] Ibid., 132.

[40] J. D. Mansi, *Sanctorum conciliorum nova et amplissima collectio* 13:101AC, quoted in ibid., 181.

denying the theology of the Incarnation, which had been well developed by that time.

> If Christ, paradoxically, has taken on flesh in his own person, but if then, as you assert, this flesh is not "characterized" or expressing someone in specific terms, rather "man" generically, how could his flesh [His humanity] ever possess a subsistence in him? . . . For Christ would not possess a human nature at all unless it dwells in him, in his particular person, in individual existence. If it were not so, the Incarnation would be a fictitious fantasy; Christ could not be touched nor portrayed with various colors: this would be nothing but the Manichaean viewpoint.[41]

St. Theodore displays a good sense of the psychology of devotion when he defends the icon on the basis of the need to image events in order to contemplate them. "The painted image is for us a sacred light, a salvific monument, as it holds up before us Christ in his birth, his baptism, his miracles, on the cross, in the tomb, in his Resurrection and Ascension. In all this we are not being deceived as though these events would not have happened. For what our eyes see supports our spiritual contemplation, so that through both experiences our faith in the mystery of salvation is strengthened".[42]

Theodore draws parallels between sight and hearing, thus showing his awareness of our need for images that appeal not just to sight but to the other senses as well: "Imprint Christ . . . onto your heart, where he [already] dwells; whether you read a book about him, or behold him in an image, may he inspire your thoughts, as you come to know him twofold through the twofold experience of your senses. Thus you will see with your eyes what you have learned through the words you have heard. He who in this way hears and sees will fill his entire being with the praise of God".[43]

Inadequate Pictures of Christ

There can be no completely adequate image of Christ, and many icons fall far short of the mark. No prayer uttered by the human voice, no human thought, can ever encompass God. It is part of the humility of the Incarnation that the Logos accepted a human nature at all—it was His *kenosis*, His self-emptying.

I have seen many beautiful paintings of Christ but never found one that was totally satisfying. This is not only because He is the Eternal Word of God but also because like everyone else, I am drawn to look for the perfect, the one, the true, and the beautiful. The restlessness of heart Augustine spoke of possesses us all until we come to the face of God in eternity.

[41] PG 99:396D–397A, quoted in Schönborn, *God's Human Face*, 222.

[42] Ibid., 99:456BC, 231.

[43] Ibid., 99:1213CD, 232. On the correlation between hearing and sight, see also PG 99:344C, 349A, 392A–D, 1217C.

There are, as we have mentioned, many Christians who still have profound problems—biblical, theological, cultural, or personal—with images of Christ, the angels, or the saints. From all that I have said about icons, I might seem to be totally unsympathetic to their position. I am not. I do disagree, but I understand their difficulty, for it is obvious that no one can adequately picture Christ. This is all the more clear if we consider the position of St. Maximus that Christ's face is the human face of God. For this reason it is almost unknown for any Christian church that promotes devotional depictions of Christ to use a photograph of a model as an object of devotion. Even a photograph used to illustrate a sacred scene has great limitations. I recall seeing photographs in a college chapel of a devout-looking young woman that were used to illustrate the words of Mary's prayer in St. Luke's Gospel: "My soul magnifies the Lord." I found the display somehow distasteful. There is something about a painting or statue that communicates, "This is just a symbol, just an attempt." A photograph, however, implicitly does more.

All Christians will agree that the Christ who is known by grace cannot be precisely pictured. We can know Him only "through a glass darkly" because of our human limitations and also because of the influence of culture, history, prejudice, or personal need. Remember, we know only a few of the words He spoke during His life. If we passed Him on a dusty road in Galilee, would we recognize Him? We hope we would. We do believe and hope that we will see Him when we finally close our eyes on this world.

We also know that He is with us now and to the end of the world. He has told us that we can see and serve Him in the hungry, the naked, the sick, and the imprisoned. The great question is: How do we serve and honor Him when He is actually seen in those He has said represent Him best? Are we ourselves conformed to the divine image, not by how we look or what we imagine, but by what we do? I conclude with this pointed quotation from Cardinal Schönborn:

> Christ, therefore, represents for us the mold, the original form of God's image; and man is his image by creation and call. Since the Son's mode of existence bestowed on the human freedom of Christ a new form, we all can from now on in our freedom participate, in grace, in his freedom. In this life already, we can participate in Christ's mode of existence, in his new humanity, if only our humanity is rooted in Christ's humanity. This is the divinization of man, so often discussed by the Fathers. It represents the "counterpart", the corresponding reality, to the humanization of God: God and man engage in a "wondrous exchange", which does not destroy the specific structure of human nature but rather, through supernatural means, leads it to its completion.[44]

[44] Schönborn, *God's Human Face*, 130.

6 Light Shining in the Darkness

A Starlit Night

Many historians consider the term "Dark Ages" to be unfair. Still, there is no denying that the barbarian invasions of the fifth century plunged the western part of the dying Roman Empire into chaos and cultural regression. St. Augustine in *The City of God* made it clear that the citizens of the empire had brought this calamity on themselves by centuries of immorality and by a disregard for the natural virtues their ancient philosophers had valued. It was a time of war, pillage, and destruction. Whole civilizations, like Roman Africa, vanished in the face of barbarian assault. Apart from a few periods of peace, like the ninth-century Carolingian Era, Western Europe was a scene of constant warfare.

Yet while the second half of the first millennium may be called a dark age, it was also a starlit night: constellations of sensitive, intelligent people brought out of these troubled times the immensely rich civilization of the later Middle Ages. The saints and scholars of the Dark Ages made innumerable contributions to Western civilization in almost impossible situations. Time has dimmed the memory of their achievements, but it is important to recall that almost all the great figures of the Dark Ages were deeply religious, and many shared a profoundly contemplative spirit. Despite the scorn heaped on this period by the Age of the Enlightenment, Christians, Jews, and Muslims from the fifth to the tenth centuries created beautiful works of art and devotion. Until recently it has been largely ignored that the Christian East flourished during this time, as we have seen in our discussion of icons. The flowering of Islamic culture and the remarkable accomplishments of the Jewish Diaspora have also been largely overlooked. It was the Christian West, however, that bore the brunt of the invasions, saw the establishment of barbaric kingdoms, and endured two periods of great destruction, the centuries immediately before Charlemagne (742–814) and those that succeeded the end of his powerful influence.

Those who lived through much of the twentieth century witnessed wars, holocausts, and brutal colonialism. We might, therefore, reflect compassionately on times when bitter struggles necessarily occurred as the world grew smaller and as ancient cultured people clashed with primitive tribes. The almost mythic scene of Pope St. Leo the Great persuading Attila the Hun in 452 to turn back from the gates of Rome can be taken as a logo of the Dark Ages. This event signifies the barbarian clash with the old inhabitants of Europe. While this was going on, monks, nuns, and, much later, canons regular quietly laid the foundations of a new civilization by educating the children of the barbarians. We must not forget that a majority of those who read these pages are descended from the very tribes who were thought to be bringing about the end of the world.

The Great Spiritual Lights of the Dark Ages

In 410 the unthinkable happened: Alaric, a barbarian chieftain, sacked Rome. As Augustine lay dying twenty years later, Vandal bands blocked the harbor of his city, Hippo. His priceless library survived almost miraculously and was transferred with his body to Sardinia. Later his remains were removed to Pavia by another barbarian king, Odoacer. By then a converted Christian, Odoacer (433–493) hoped this would confer dignity on his new capital in northern Italy. Augustine's body remains enshrined in the splendid Church of St. Peter in the Golden Sky, so-called because it once had a ceiling of gold.

St. Benedict and the Love of Christ

The knowledge and love of Christ did not perish in these invasions. A century after Augustine's death, monasticism began to flourish and St. Benedict of Nursia (c. 480–547) wrote his famous rule and instituted his new monastic tradition. The center of this rule was the simple formula, "[N]ot to value anything more highly than the love of Christ".[1] Borrowing from monastic traditions of the East, St. Benedict made prayer and work the heart of his rule, and centered all on Christ. Benedictines were to "renounce themselves in order to follow Christ ... advance in the ways [of Christ] with the Gospel as our guide ... share by patience in the passion of Christ" so as to come to His kingdom.[2] Christ was to be seen everywhere, but especially in guests and pilgrims, who were to be received as Christ. This charity to guests is still beautifully observed in Benedictine houses.

St. Gregory the Great (c. 540–604)

The influence of St. Benedict and his sister, St. Scholastica, was of great importance from the sixth century onward. However, the spiritual giant of the West who, along with Augustine, would be the guiding light of believers in these dark times was a Benedictine who became pope, St. Gregory the Great (c. 540–604). This remarkable man was literally left with the government of the empire as well as the Church when the emperor fled in panic. Among the last of the Church Fathers, he lived in the ruins of the empire and is responsible for the first signs of the new European civilization. Dom Jean Leclercq, the eminent

[1] Prologue of the *Rule of Saint Benedict*, as quoted in Jaroslav Pelikan, *Jesus through the Centuries* (New Haven: Yale University Press, 1985), 112.

[2] Ibid.

Benedictine historian, writes that Gregory's "teaching, developed in the atmosphere of that [patristic] tradition, became the chief source of medieval spirituality".[3] Gregory stands on the threshold of the new age, casting his luminous reflection over the five hundred years after his death.

The Bible's teaching is reflected in Gregory's whole life. As a layman, he had been prefect, or mayor, of Rome and had turned his home into a monastery. One of the regional deacons of Rome, he was responsible for the poor, and from 570 to 586 he represented the Western Church in Constantinople. In 590, at the age of fifty, he became Bishop of Rome and labored tirelessly until his death in 604. His letters on Job and on the Gospels are still included in the Liturgy of the Hours, his blunt criticisms of the clergy brightening up the Office readings with wry humor. His observation that there are many priests but few apostles is often quoted, as is his designation of bishops who are silent in the face of evil as "watchdogs that cannot bark".

Despite his responsibilities, Gregory maintained a deeply contemplative spirit. For him God is "boundless light . . . incomprehensible, ineffable . . . without limits. He is eternity . . . the one self-existent Being." He is "immutable and foreign to him is that change 'which is an imitation of death'. . . . He is simple, 'he is all that he has'. . . . He is eternal: not only unending, but ever wholly present to himself, altogether identical with himself, and with himself alone. He is unchangingly one and the same Being".[4] God is hidden but active in the depths of our hearts, a witness dwelling in the center of our souls, ever coming to our aid, arranging things for our welfare and giving us abundant grace. "We are one, we are close to each other in him who is everywhere", a fact that is the beginning of the knowledge of God and all charity.[5] In fact, Gregory's description fits well into the psychological description of devotion that is the theme of this book.

In Gregory we hear the echo of Augustine, his teacher. We learn that he saw man as weighed down by Adam's sin and even more burdened by personal sins, which lead away from God. Since sin begets sin, we have within ourselves every root of vice. Gregory's experience of a dying civilization no doubt brought him to his powerful experience of Christ as Mediator of salvation and Light of the soul. For him, Christ shines like the figure of glowing brass seen by Ezekiel, and the amberlike alloy of silver and gold (electrum). We must meditate on the Passion of Christ because there we see the Lord most clearly as Mediator and Redeemer.[6] The grounds of our personal hope

---

[3] Dom Jean Leclercq et al., *The Spirituality of the Middle Ages*, vol. 2, *A History of Christian Spirituality* (New York: Seabury Press, 1982), 3.

[4] Gregory the Great, *Morals on Job*, quoted in ibid, 12–13.

[5] Gregory the Great, *Epistles*, V, quoted in Leclercq, *Spirituality of the Middle Ages*, 14.

[6] Leclercq, *Spirituality of the Middle Ages*, 16.

are the Resurrection and Ascension of Christ.[7] Gregory, immersed in the troubles of his time, saw Christ suffering in the Church. He stressed that we must pray to Christ even though the saints are interceding for us. The Psalms speak to him of Christ, and he often ended his sermons with doxologies to Christ.

The following selection from St. Gregory illustrates his beliefs with a clarity desperately needed in his chaotic times. Those who followed him would rely on his writings for half a millennium of stormy history.

> There comes to my mind what the bystanders said derisively of the crucified Son of God: "If he is the king of Israel, let him come down from the cross, and we will believe him." If he had yielded to their derision, and come down then from the cross, he would not have demonstrated to us the virtue of patience. Instead, he waited for a while; he endured their taunts, he bore with their mockery, he preserved his patience, he deferred their esteem, and he who did not will to come down from the cross rose from the sepulcher.
>
> Rising from the tomb was a greater thing than coming down from the cross. Destroying death by rising from the dead was a greater thing than preserving life by descending from the cross. When the bystanders saw that he was not coming down from the cross at their derisive remarks, when they saw him dying, they believed they had prevailed. They rejoiced as if they had consigned his name to oblivion. But see how his name has increased throughout the world, how the multitude which rejoiced over his slaying now grieves over his death! They perceive that it is through his suffering that Christ has arrived at glory.[8]

Devotion to Christ in the Barbarian Kingdoms—East and West

While the growth of Christianity had been gradual during the first five centuries, the first great wave of conversions in the West began with the work of Gregory and his contemporaries and went on into the seventh and eighth centuries. A similar surge of conversions in the East was sparked by SS. Cyril and Methodius, brothers who converted the Slavs and laid the foundation of the Slavic civilization. Many large cities of what was then the new world had been only outposts of the empire or simply forest land when Christ walked the earth. Today these places are dotted with churches named after the monks and missionaries who converted the hordes pouring out of the North and East into the ruins of the empire.

Although many of the first missionaries were martyred, as Leclercq observes, "[E]verywhere young nations with no traditional culture accepted the Gospel with fervour and simplicity".[9] In Spain, especially,

[7] Ibid.

[8] Quoted in John Leinenweber, *Be Friends of God: Spiritual Reading from Gregory the Great* (Cambridge, Mass.: Cowley Publications, 1990), 137–38.

[9] Leclercq, *Spirituality of the Middle Ages*, 46.

Christianity had been purified of Arian influences, which the barbarians first encountered when they received the Gospel. Saints like Leander and, later, Isidore of Seville, Braulion of Saragossa, and Ildephonsus of Toledo used the Christology of the great councils to imprint the knowledge of the God-Man on Iberian life and culture.

The Centrality of the Eucharist and the Word of God

Long before the sixth century, the celebration of the Eucharistic liturgy was the center of life for Catholic Christians (a name which distinguished them from Arian Christians and other dissident groups). Apart from the Mass, the spiritual expressions of the people of that time would be familiar to Evangelical Protestants today. Early medieval prayers and devotions were drawn almost entirely from the Bible. Along with devotion to the Mother of Jesus and the saints, Christian piety was strongly biblical. Most saints after the time of the apostles were martyrs, although a number of confessors emerged during this period—those who had lived for but had not been called to die for Christ. Most popular among the postpersecution saints were Augustine; his mother, Monica; Jerome; Pope Leo; and, of course, Gregory the Great. In the East, John Chrysostom and the three Cappadocians, (Gregory of Nyssa, Gregory of Nazianzus, and Basil) had the first places.

The Christians of these dark times, however, cherished the Bible, particularly the Psalms and the Gospels. In East and West, the Church gave the Psalms to the ordinary people, most of whom could not read and learned them by rote, by means of the Divine Office. The whole Psalter was read in a week, according to the pattern legislated by the Rule of St. Benedict. Each psalm was preceded by a brief commentary, or antiphon, a verse usually drawn from the Bible and usually relating to Christ.[10] "[E]very psalm was held to have been said by Christ, written in foreknowledge of his redemptive work, or meant to be recited in reference to the mysteries of his life."[11] The commentaries remained in widespread use until the thirteenth century. They came from the Greek and Latin Fathers and especially from Origen.[12] In Eastern parishes using the rite of St. John Chrysostom, people to this day sing psalms and Scripture verses rather than popular hymns.

The Light from the Cross

The Fathers, especially John Chrysostom and Augustine, had dwelt on the Passion of Christ and the power of the Cross to bring redemption. Christ is seen as Redeemer not only by His glorious Resurrection but also by His death on the Cross. St. Augustine put it this way:

> Therefore, the Christ who is preached throughout the world is not wearing an earthly crown, nor a rich Christ, but Christ crucified. At

[10] Ibid., 63.
[11] Ibid.
[12] Ibid.

> first this Christ was ridiculed by many, and the ridicule goes on. A few believed at first but now whole nations. Because when Christ, despite the ridicule of men, was first preached the lame walked, the dumb spoke, the deaf heard and even the dead came back to life. This finally convinced some of the proud that even among the visible forces of the physical world there is nothing more powerful than the Humility of God. All this took place that we might struggle to be humble, shielded from the contemptible assaults of human pride by the example of a humble God.[13]

After Emperor Constantine's legendary dream (see Chapter 3 above), the Cross became fixed as the sign of Christ's suffering love for mankind and of His victory over death. The second half of the first Christian millennium saw devotion to the Cross become increasingly widespread. Christians in East and West made use of crosses and, later, crucifixes with the image of the body of Christ, as well as the gesture known as the Sign of the Cross. Professor Pelikan gives a fascinating account of this gesture of devotion. He cites Tertullian, who early in the third century wrote about the Sign of the Cross, originally made with a thumb on the forehead: "[A]t every forward step and movement, at every going in and out ... in all the ordinary actions of daily life, we mark upon our foreheads the sign."[14] Pelikan states that this "became the prime evidence for the existence of an unwritten tradition that everyone observed even though it was not commanded in the Bible".[15] He also recalls that the emperor Julian the Apostate (c. 331–363), who renounced Christianity and relapsed into paganism, complained of Christians: "You adore the wood of the cross and draw its likeness on your foreheads and engrave it on your housefronts."[16] Despite the tragic schism between East and West, the Sign of the Cross continues to unite Orthodox and Catholic Christians.

When Protestants removed crosses from churches and ended the custom of making the Sign of the Cross, it did not imply a rejection of devotion to Christ's Passion but an opposition to visible symbols much like that of the iconoclasts. In the eastern United States, where Protestantism was first established in colonial times, one did not see crosses on Protestant churches at all. A simple cross mounted on a steeple was the sign of a Latin-Rite Catholic Church and the triple cross the sign of an Orthodox or Eastern-Rite Catholic Church. We see today crosses on many Protestant and Evangelical churches, marking a significant change in attitude.

---

[13] Letter 232, translated in *Augustine: Major Writings*, ed. Fr. Benedict J. Groeschel, C.F.R. (New York: Crossroad, 1995), 164.

[14] Tertullian, *The Chaplet* 3, quoted in Pelikan, *Jesus through the Centuries*, 96.

[15] Pelikan, *Jesus through the Centuries*, 96.

[16] Julian, *Against the Galileans*, quoted in ibid.

Three Powerful Influences

Possibly the most important aspect of the veneration of the Crucified King was that it brought together three powerful historical influences, which gave early Christianity its sociocultural location. The Cross symbolized not only what Christians believed but how they thought and experienced that belief. The first of these forces is the Hebrew religion, with all its developments up to the time of Christ, including the books written in the Diaspora by Greek-speaking Jews. The second is Greek philosophy, especially the insights of Plato on the four transcendent attributes of being—the one, true, good, and beautiful—as well as his mysterious idea of the *logos*, the word. The final influence came through the customs of Græco-Roman pagan religion.

Admittedly, Christians of the first seven centuries had conflicts with the representatives of these very different influences, and followers of Christ often defined themselves by contradicting these influences. The Catholic Christian bishops, as they were called even in the second century, criticized the Jews while accepting their Bible as revelation. They argued with Platonists even while using their philosophical concepts. They denounced paganism while exorcising and consecrating its temples for Christian worship. The very language they used to speak of the Trinity and the God-Man was drawn from all these sources because they wanted to use only the most accurate words to describe the truths revealed by God.

Christians still express and experience their faith in ways deeply influenced by these three forces—Judaism, Greek philosophy, and Roman pagan religious expression. Simply say the words of the prologue of St. John's Gospel and you have touched on all of these influences in the New Testament itself. Why is this? Not only because of the laws of culture, sociology, and anthropology, although they are obviously operative, but also because the Word of God, who would become Jesus Christ, was present in the world in which the Jews, Greeks, and Romans lived. As the liturgy of Holy Saturday says: "Jesus Christ yesterday, today, and forever". Once the Resurrection occurred, His followers knew that whether Jew or Greek, slave or free, all were united in His presence (see Gal 3:28).

I Am with You: The Universality of Christ

The risen Jesus was present to individuals in their real-life situations and when they came together as communities of worship. He was present to Paul and Lydia when she became the first Christian convert in Europe (Acts 16:14–15). She was able to speak of God only in the language of the Græco-Roman religion on that portentous day when she met the Jewish preacher by the brook by the Ignatian Way. And Paul had to put into comprehensible Greek the teachings of the Hebrews and the astonishing revelation of God's Son. He called on the Holy Spirit to do this in inspired ways. Clement of Alexandria and his fellow philosopher-converts brought with them powerful intellectual insights that affect the thinking of every devout Christian today—a system of thought that would evolve concepts like the Trinity to describe the Christian God.

The question arises immediately: Could Christianity adopt influences from outside the Græco-Roman and Jewish worlds? It already had in India, where the tradition of the Apostle Thomas still exists. The same can be said of Ethiopia. Both areas had received some Greek influences, yet both remained very isolated from the rest of Christianity until modern times. Although the barbarians had been converted, they left their cultural mark wherever they invaded and, therefore, influenced the life of the Church. This was true especially in Visigothic Spain and among the Slavs. Still, in matters of religion, they largely, almost passively, accepted the new faith with its complex cultural influences, becoming Greek or Latin Christians in a single universal Church.

The Celts

There soon came into prominence a culture with a greater sense of itself than had other barbarians, one that did not arrive with a horde of nomadic warriors in the fourth and fifth centuries of the Christian era but had been in Europe for more than half a millennium, spreading from Asia Minor and Eastern Europe to the British Isles. In the far western areas of Britain and Ireland it was dominant, a culture in which the Græco-Roman religion played no part. The religion of the Celts was one of darkness and light, of wind and sea, of fear, death, and intense feasting and revelry. Celtic gods inspired as much fear as awe, yet there was a strong mysticism about these people that allowed them to be deeply affected by a relatively small group of Christian monks that came from Egypt early in the fourth century. The Celtic religion was one of high kings and druids, of earthly heavens and hells, and from our perspective it almost seems that these people were waiting for the Gospel of the loving, forgiving High Priest and High King to arrive.

St. Patrick's Mission

Among the most successful apostles of Christianity was Patricius, or Patrick (390–461), a Latin-speaking Gallic monk (a Romanized Celt himself), who converted an entire people. The only other example of a whole nation converted by a single person is that of Armenia, the first Christian nation, converted by St. Gregory the Illuminator at the beginning of the fourth century, a decade before the Edict of Toleration.

Patrick was a pragmatic missionary: if it worked and was not immoral, he used it. He ordained the second or third son of chieftains as priests, even if they were married, despite the requirement of celibacy mandated by the regional, or plenary, Council of Elvira (371). He identified the Church so much with the tribes that to this day Irish diocesan borders are a crazy quilt, with one diocese having churches within another, because they follow tribal lines sixteen hundred years old. Patrick was a monk who trusted monks. Thus the Irish Church became strongly monastic, its bishops being celibate monks of a strict rule. He set up schools to teach Roman culture, which in time became the best schools in Europe. Nevertheless, he let the people use many Celtic religious customs to express the new faith, and thus a fourth powerful cultural influence entered the expression of Western Christianity.

It is beyond our purposes to examine the history of Celtic Christianity or to trace the missionary efforts that brought it to the far north of Scandinavia and as far south as the Italian Alps. The faith of the Celts even mingled with the Greek-derived Slavic Christianity in Eastern Europe. We should note, however, that the Celtic influence is still powerful and even today it is the focus of much study not only in Ireland but also in Scotland, Wales, and even England, where the Roman influence tended to dilute but not entirely absorb it.

Our goal, instead, is to look for the personal presence of and devotion to Jesus Christ in this culture, and we do not have far to look. Among the Celts Christ was seen as the High King, an effective image for a society that was "tribal, rural, hierarchical and familiar".[17] The kings of Ireland were not rulers of a great empire, distant from the people and considered divine. They ruled over relatively small tribes and needed to exert their personality in order to gain loyalty, even to death. They needed to be dynamic and just, and it helped if they were admired for virtues like courage. No one, however, suggested that they were divine. Christ, on the other hand, was the divine High King, who was also a real man.[18]

An ancient Irish poem goes:

> O King of Kings,
> O sheltering wings, O guardian tree!
> All, all of me,
> Thou Virgin's nurseling, rests in thee.[19]

Since Irish monasticism was influential at home and throughout much of Europe, we must mention the Celtic monks' relationship with Christ. The following prayer shows a depth of intelligence as well as the power of devotion among the monks. It was written by one of the *Celi De*, or Servants of God, a reform movement of Celtic monasticism that flowered in the eighth and ninth centuries.[20] The prayer is attributed to Oengus.

> The time is right and I repent
> every trespass, O my Lord.

[17] Máire de Paor and Liam de Paor, *Early Christian Ireland* (New York: Frederick A. Praeger, 1958), 31.

[18] Ibid.

[19] Quoted in Uinseann O Maidin, O.C.R., *The Celtic Monk: Rules and Writings of Early Irish Monks*, trans. Robin Flower (Kalamazoo, Mich.: Cistercian Publications, 1996), 189.

[20] O Maidin, *Celtic Monk*, 2.

Pardon me my every crime,
Christ, as Thou art merciful.

By Thy incarnation sweet,
by Thy birth, my sacred King,
by Thy lasting baptism here,
pardon me my every wrong.

By Thy hanging, filled with love,
by Thy rising from the dead,
all my passions pardon me,
Lord who art truly merciful.

By Thy ascension—glorious hour—
to holy Heaven, to the Father
(promised ere thou didst depart)
pardon me my every wrong.

By Thy coming holy word
to judge the hosts of Adam's seed,
by heaven's orders nine revealed
be my offence forgiven me.

By the ranks of profit true,
by the martyr's worthy throng,
by the train of noble Fathers,
pardon the crimes that mastered me.

By the band of the pure apostles,
by the chaste disciples' host,
by each saint of royal favor,
pardon me my evil deeds.

Lord, O Lord, hear me,
Fill my soul, Lord, with Thy love's ray,
Fill my soul, Lord, with Thy love's ray,
Lord, O Lord, hear me.[21]

In this poem, we get the sense of a reform that laid "great stress on the seeking of perfection in the monastic state, on meditation, and on the study and perfection of the Liturgy".[22]

The best known Celtic prayer is the "Deer's Cry", or "St. Patrick's Breastplate". Its Latin name refers to the *lorica*, or battle armor, that protected the heart of the soldier. The conflict here is with the spiritual enemy. There is no doubt that part of this prayer goes back to the old Celtic religion. According to legend, St. Patrick and his companions said this prayer when they confronted the high king at Tara

[21] Ibid., 199–200.

[22] De Paor and de Paor, *Early Christian Ireland*, 72.

by lighting a beacon in honor of Christ. This legendary event is said to have taken place on Holy Saturday in the year 433. The prayer, according to John Taylor, who wrote about Christianity in Africa, "sums up and contains all the spiritual awareness of the primal vision and lifts it into the fullness of Christ". He adds, "Would that it were translated and sung in every tongue of Africa!"[23]

> I arise today
> Through a mighty strength,
> the invocation of the Trinity,
> Through belief in the threeness,
> Through confession of the oneness
> Of the Creator of Creation.
>
> I arise today
> Through the strength of Christ's birth
> with His baptism,
> Through the strength of His crucifixion
> with His burial,
> Through the strength of His resurrection
> with His ascension,
> Through the strength of His coming down for Judgement.
>
> Christ to shield me this day,
> So that there come to me abundance of reward.
> Christ with me, Christ before me, Christ behind me,
> Christ in me, Christ beneath me, Christ above me,
> Christ when I lie down, Christ when I sit,
> Christ when I arise,
> Christ in the heart of every man who thinks of me,
> Christ in the mouth of everyone who speaks of me,
>
> Christ in every eye that sees me,
> Christ in every ear that hears me.[24]

Although we have used Irish selections, there is also Christian Celtic poetry from Scotland, Wales, and England, where St. David (d. 589) and his monks had a profound influence, which in turn sent the English monk St. Boniface (d. 754) to Germany. We must remember that throughout the Celtic world Christ as High King, Center of the Universe, and Crucified One is the central theme of this remarkable and at that time new face of Christianity.

The Second Darkness

The ninth century was ushered in by the coronation of Charlemagne as Holy Roman Emperor by Pope St. Leo III on Christmas Day in

[23] Quoted in Esther de Waal, *Every Earthly Blessing: Celebrating a Spirituality of Creation* (Ann Arbor, Mich.: Servant Publications, 1991), 15.

[24] Excerpted from translation in ibid., 15, 17.

800, a rather auspicious beginning for a century. Charlemagne brought order, peace, and culture to a dark continent. Unfortunately, his descendants were unable to maintain either the emperor's vision or the peace and religious development he had brought to Europe. Gradually, anarchy returned. The Church fell under the control of the secular powers. Rulers were often brutal and malicious. Bishops and abbots had to learn to lead armies, as law and government gradually disappeared. Even the fervent Church in Ireland went into decline. The lowest point in the history of the papacy occurred in the middle of the eleventh century, with the shameful career of Pope Benedict IX (1032–1045). Yet for many this was also a time of religious fervor. There were constant attempts at Church reform. These did not succeed but prepared the way for the reforms that were to come and sustained the hopes of the faithful.

Northern Italy and France were seedbeds of reform whose strength came from monastic life. Eastern Europe was half a millennium beyond the collapse of the Roman Empire in the West. And the East was recovering from the turmoil of the iconoclast controversy and learning to live with the Muslims who ruled beyond the Bosporus and in the Holy Land. The beautiful ancient city of Ravenna in northern Italy, famous for its spectacular Christian mosaics and churches, gave the world two of its great religious reformers, whose lives were similar but whose personalities were quite distinct: John of Fécamp (990–1078) and St. Peter Damian (1007–1072). We shall come to Peter Damian in the next chapter, but we pause here to see how the grace of God could produce a gentle, devoted, and cultured disciple of Christ at the end of five hundred years of chaos and confusion.

Poor John of Fécamp

The monk and spiritual writer who called himself Poor John—and who was known by the nickname Jeannelin, or Johnny—had an immense influence on medieval piety (according to Fr. Leclercq, who played a significant role in the rediscovery of his fellow Benedictine in our century).[25] It is claimed that John of Fécamp was one of the most widely read spiritual writers until Thomas à Kempis in the fifteenth century. His name is not so well known, because many of his writings were popularly attributed to St. Ambrose, St. Augustine, Cassian, St. Anselm, and St. Bernard. Priests for centuries offered John's prayer "To the High Priest" before Mass, thinking it was the work of St. Ambrose. It could be found at the back of every altar missal.

Lord Jesus Christ,
I approach your banquet table
in fear and trembling,
for I am a sinner,

[25] Leclercq, *Spirituality of the Middle Ages*, 122.

and dare not rely on my own worth
but only on your goodness and mercy. . . .
Praise to you, saving sacrifice,
offered on the wood of the cross for me and for all mankind.
Praise to the noble and precious blood,
flowing from the wounds of my crucified Lord Jesus Christ
and washing away the sins of the whole world.
Remember, Lord, your creature,
whom you have redeemed with your blood.[26]

Although drawn into the struggle for Church reform by his uncle, St. William of St. Volpiano, John of Fécamp sought to live as a hermit. He became a monk and then the abbot of the Abbey of the Holy Trinity at Fécamp, in France. The desire to be a hermit never left him in his very engaged life, and, consequently, we find in his writings the contemplative, the scholarly, and the apostolic. Leclercq says of him: "He is a perfect representative of the medieval spirituality which preceded him, for in him blossom forth the traditions of the Fathers, of early monasticism, of St. Gregory and the writers and reformers of the Carolingian and later centuries".[27]

John of Fécamp takes inspiration from St. Augustine. His writings are confessions and praises of God. He waits for divine inspiration. "He tells of his gratitude for the mysteries of our redemption, of his poverty and need of God's grace. He finds the words he needs in Holy Scripture, in St. Gregory, in the Carolingian *Libelli Precum*, in the liturgy." [28]

Jeannelin brings together two powerful spiritual insights: the absolute transcendence of God and the mediation of Jesus, who makes God accessible to us in prayer and the sacraments, especially the Eucharist. He is powerfully drawn to Christ, who shows His love for us in the Passion. He is very personal in his devotion. "*Te Christe . . . te volo*", he writes. (You, Christ, you do I desire.) John of Fécamp did not attempt to teach a way to the experiential knowledge of God that comes with contemplation. Instead, he maintained that it was simply the practice of deep prayer itself that led to the contemplative experience. For this reason he composed prayers as guides and inspirations for others. The following prayer from the end of Jeannelin's major work, *Confessio theologica*, is a beautiful way to sum up half a millennium of Christian prayer struggle, in which the Gospel overcame the darkness of the world and gave birth to the age of faith:

[26] *The Roman Missal: The Sacramentary*, trans. International Commission on English in the Liturgy (New York: Catholic Book Publishing, 1974), 1006–7.

[27] Leclercq, *Spirituality of the Middle Ages*, 123.

[28] Ibid., 124.

> There are various kinds of contemplation, by whose aid the soul which has devoted itself to thee, O Christ, finds joy and advancement. Yet my spirit rejoices in none of them as in that wherein, putting aside all else, she raises the eyes of her heart purely and simply towards thy Godhead only. What peace and joy, what rest does the soul which tends to thee enjoy! When my soul longs for the divine vision, and as far as it is able sings of its glory, behold the burden of the flesh is less wearisome, the tumult of thought grows quiet, the weight of our mortality and our sorrows no longer deadens our faculties as they are wont to do; all is peace and quiet. The heart is aflame with love, the soul joyful, the memory strong, the understanding full of light: and my whole spirit, burning with the desire of beholding thy beauty, is borne away by the love of the unseen realities.[29]

This profound prayer, which could have been written a thousand years later as an expression of the spiritual struggles of our own time, illustrates how devotion to Christ was the center of life for one of the most cultured men of a very dark time. The same Jesus Christ who appeared to Stephen, who was invoked by the martyrs, the same Divine Physician and King of Kings, was also the only door by which the soul could come into the brightness of divine life.

---

[29] Quoted in ibid., 125. Latin text in J. Leclercq and J.-P. Bonnes, *Un maître de la vie spirituelle au XIe siècle: Jean de Fécamp* (Paris, 1946), 182.

7 The Darkest Night and the Early Dawn

An analogy from nature fits the tenth and eleventh centuries in Western Europe: the darkest, coldest part of the night comes before the first signs of dawn. The collapse of the Carolingian empire left Western Europe, especially central and southern Europe, in a state of lawless strife. By the tenth century the Church had fallen under the power of petty nobles and warring princes who had little interest beyond wealth and power. Leclercq sums it up well: "Great abuses were the result: schisms and scandals in the Papacy, churches and monasteries seized by seculars, and among the clergy simony and incontinence." [1] But even then there was an opposing tendency, a powerful movement toward reform, which took on many interesting aspects, all of which were motivated by and expressed in a personal devotion to Jesus Christ.

The Reform of Cluny

Reform began in the abbeys, especially in the Benedictine abbey of Cluny in eastern France. The first abbot, St. Berno, removed the abbey from the control of secular rulers, uniting it with the Pope. St. Odo, abbot from 924 to 942, began a reform of liturgical life so comprehensive that it brought spiritual order to a world familiar only with chaos. The monks of Cluny celebrated the liturgical year in a manner that recalled that divine worship was the "service of the King of kings". The monks were called to an authentic spiritual life with "sustained effort and perpetual self-abnegation".[2]

The focus of this effort was the celebration of the mysteries of Christ, beginning with the first Sunday of Advent and culminating in the Sacred Triduum of Holy Week. Pentecost was seen as the beginning of "Ordinary Time" because life was to be lived as a continuation of the coming of the Holy Spirit at Pentecost. The principal duty of the monk, according to St. Benedict, was the *opus Dei*, or work of God. The center of life was the celebration of the Eucharist. Christ in His mysteries was celebrated at all times, and outside the hours of divine

[1] Dom Jean Leclercq et al., *The Spirituality of the Middle Ages*, vol. 2, *A History of Christian Spirituality* (New York: Seabury Press, 1982), 95.

[2] Ibid., 107.

worship, the monks occupied themselves with works of charity. The Cluniac reform and the many abbeys that followed its lead provided the model for the restoration of Benedictine life in the nineteenth and twentieth centuries.

So powerful did the Benedictine ideal become at the end of the Dark Ages that it set the tone for the reform preached at the end of this age by such eleventh-century Christians as Pope St. Gregory VII (Hildebrand—d. 1085), St. Anselm of Canterbury (d. 1109), and St. Peter Damian (d. 1072). All these were either monks, like Anselm, or students formed at Benedictine abbeys, like Pope Gregory and Peter. They all learned from the monks the centrality of the love of Christ and were devoted to Him and the reform of His Church.

St. Anselm and the Love of Jesus Crucified

The most important religious figure at the transition from the Dark Ages to the high Middle Ages is St. Anselm, Archbishop of Canterbury (1033–1109). Born in Aosta in northern Italy, he became abbot of Bec in Normandy and subsequently succeeded Lanfranc, his predecessor at Bec, by becoming England's second Norman archbishop. He guided the developing English Church, blending the Saxon and the Norman into a coherent whole. Anselm was a bridge between epochs and civilizations. Yet he was persecuted and exiled. A gentle man and spiritual director whose philosophy and theology would remain vital for a thousand years, Anselm deeply influenced modern philosophers through his ontological argument for the existence of God. Pelikan states that Anselm "shaped the outlook not only of Roman Catholics, but of most Protestants, many of whom have paid him the ultimate compliment of not even recognizing that their version of the wisdom of the cross comes from him, but attributing it to the Bible itself".[3]

In his monumental work *Cur Deus Homo* (*Why God Became Man*), Anselm sought to explain how the suffering and death of Christ was necessary and how it accomplished our salvation. He realized that several strains of thought regarding this run through the New Testament and the Fathers but that no clear answer to this question was obvious, because ultimately the answer is locked in the unsearchable mystery of God. Anselm relied on the Epistle to the Hebrews and the concept of redemption, or the ransoming, of the human race. Pelikan gives a fine summary of this teaching. Beginning with the sin of Adam, Anselm taught that the "rightness" of moral order required that it be restored properly. But no one could redeem a divine offense except God Himself. Pelikan writes:

> Such was the divine dilemma to which the wisdom of the cross provided a resolution, according to Anselm's reasoning. For the justice

[3] Jaroslav Pelikan, *Jesus through the Centuries* (New Haven: Yale University Press, 1985), 106–7.

> of God, having pronounced that violation of the moral will was worthy of death, clashed with the mercy of God, which desired life rather than death. The one who was guilty of the sin, man, could not pay the penalty except by being lost forever; the one who wanted to forgive, God, could not do so except by undercutting the moral order of the universe. Only a being able to pay the penalty (by being human) but capable of making a payment that was of infinite worth (by being divine) could simultaneously carry out the imperatives of divine mercy and satisfy the demands of divine justice. The payment, moreover, had to be voluntary, and could not be made by someone who owed it on his own behalf, for that would not avail for others. Therefore God had to become a man, and moreover had to die on the cross, so as to achieve the ends of divine mercy and yet to render satisfaction to divine justice and thus uphold "rightness." His death on the cross made it, one may say, morally possible for God to forgive.[4]

Whatever the theological adequacy of Anselm's teaching, it brought the mystery of Jesus Crucified into focus in the lives of the devout. Sometimes this approach was overdone by certain preachers, who give the impression of an angry God demanding the blood of Christ before opening the gates of eternity. But medieval piety was untroubled by such concerns. Anselm prepared the way for the immense piety of the high Middle Ages and opened the door to the devotion called *compositio loci*, which characterized the prayer of St. Francis and the multitudes he influenced. Through this devotion the Gospel scenes would come to life as the devout imagined themselves at the side of the Crib or beneath the Cross. In the same way they recalled the presence of Christ with them during their own life struggles.

The Reform of the Apostolate

Along with the Benedictine reforms there was a fascinating collection of growing spiritual movements in Europe. Besides the monastic ideal were at least two distinct currents of reform: the reform of the clergy and the growth of the mission to pagans. The reform of the apostolic life sought especially the reform of diocesan clergy. Little is known about its inception, but starting with the Council of Aix in 817, there was a strong movement for priests to live and pray together in what were called collegiate churches. Binding themselves to the common recitation of the Divine Office, these priests were called canons. Today's custom of Catholic priests living together in a rectory finds its roots in this movement.

St. Peter Damian (1007–1072), among the most determined reformers of his century, began his adult life as a hermit and ended it as a cardinal and close adviser to the Pope. Seeing himself simply as a faithful worker for Christ, he labored tirelessly for the reform of the clergy, confronting every type of scandal and disorder. Writing about another

[4] Ibid., 107.

such reformer, St. Romuald (d. 1027), Peter recalls that this founder of the Camaldolese hermits would be reduced to tears of divine love and cry, "Beloved Jesus, beloved Jesus, thou art sweet to me as honey, thou art my ineffable desire".[5] Devotion to Jesus clearly had survived the darkness of the times, burning brightly in the souls of many during a difficult period of transition.

A significant aspect of the reform of apostolic life was the decision to spread the Gospel to those who had not heard it. The remarkable missionary efforts of the Irish monks from the sixth to the ninth centuries and the endeavors of the Studite monks in the East did much to revive the enthusiasm of Christians at the time. St. Adalbert (d. 997), a missionary bishop and martyr in Poland, had left his homeland "to go into exile ... so as to become old in poverty under a foreign sun; all hard and bitter things seemed sweet to him because of Jesus, his well-beloved".[6] Adalbert indeed suffered and was twice exiled as Bishop of Prague. Like the other saints of the time, he was deeply influenced by the Benedictine ideal, lived for a time as a monk, and was a close friend of the abbot of Cluny.[7]

Our consideration of diocesan and nonmonastic clergy of the time must take into account the fact that there were as yet no seminaries; thus, the preparation of clergy was haphazard. Some were well trained in abbey schools and some at collections of monasteries, which eventually evolved into universities, like Oxford and Paris. Others were trained by capable parish priests appointed by the bishop. In many places, however, students were simply prepared by parish priests and monks of local abbeys with very uneven results. Meanwhile, simony, the selling of sacred offices or services, led to grave abuses. Pope St. Gregory VII brought the wrath of kings and many others down on his head by fighting against simony and lay investiture, or the control of ecclesiastical offices by the nobility. In such an atmosphere the requirement of celibacy was often ignored. Many priests lived publicly as fathers of families. This was uncanonical in the West, although marriage had always been permitted to candidates for the priesthood in the East. It was not so much that these married priests in the West led scandalous lives; often they were good family men. Yet their very situation put them outside the laws of the Church, and they were called irregular priests.[8]

---

[5] Peter Damian, *Life of St. Romuald*, cited in Leclercq, *Spirituality of the Middle Ages*, 112.

[6] *Passion of Saint Adalbert*, chap. 13, quoted in Leclercq, *Spirituality of the Middle Ages*, 117.

[7] *Butler's Lives of the Saints*, ed. Fr. Herbert Thurston, S.J., and Donald Attwater (New York: P.J. Kenedy, 1963), 2:152.

[8] Such situations existed as late as 1572. In that year, by a quirk of ecclesiastical history, the irregular priest Andrew Wouters freely accepted imprisonment and martyrdom at Gorkum, in Holland. His martyrdom was seen as sufficient penance, and he was canonized in 1867, along with eighteen other martyred priests and religious. He is commemorated on July 9 as one of the companions of St. Nicholas Pieck (Thurston and Attwater, *Butler's Lives of the Saints*, 3:56).

Priests Together: The Canons Regular

To combat these difficulties and to encourage prayer and devotion the reformers of the ninth to eleventh centuries urged diocesan priests to live together and celebrate the Office of the Church in common. Up to this point, the scarcity and cost of hand-lettered Psalters exempted those who did not join in the public recitation of the Liturgy of the Hours (made up primarily of psalms) from private recitation. Now, however, private recitation of the Office and the private celebration of Mass began to be seen as a desirable form of piety, especially because of the Cluniac reforms.[9]

It is not surprising that some groups of priests and clerics living together drew up rules and adopted aspects of religious life. Called pastoral canons, they eventually became vowed religious whose work was the care of souls. Such men lived a pastoral life rather than the isolated, contemplative life of the monks, and their form of life harkened back to the *Servi Dei*, St. Augustine's community of clergy and laity, who lived together, vowed to poverty, chastity, and obedience. The eleventh-century development of pastoral canons would eventually give rise to vast armies of friars (Dominicans, Franciscans, Augustinians, Carmelites, and Servites) and clerks regular (Jesuits, Redemptorists, and Passionists), who would play a significant part in Church reform movements of the next thousand years.

The most illustrious of the pastoral canons was St. Norbert, Archbishop of Magdeburg who founded his first house of canons at Prémontré, in France, around 1120. A man of great austerity and apostolic zeal, he had been a diocesan canon and went through a conversion in 1115.[10] His devotion to the Church and the presence of Christ in the Eucharist was typical of the reform movements of the time. His community, the Norbertines, to this day sees its apostolate as a combination of liturgical prayer, education, and the care of souls.

In many respects the life of the canons regular resembled the life of monks. Founders like St. Norbert emphasized personal poverty and simplicity. He even went barefoot as an example of poverty, a custom later adopted by the mendicant friars. Leclercq says the coming of the pastoral canons "encouraged the appearance in the Church of more and differing states of life.... [T]here were various ways of fulfilling the ideal of the Gospel".[11] In a book called "The Diverse Orders of the Church", Raimbaud of Liège distinguished various kinds of monks and canons, some dwelling "far from men" and some "near to men", and along with these there were hermits, all of whom were seen as lawful and admirable.[12]

It would seem that the acceptance of diversity in following Christ is historically part of the development of European civilization as it left

[9] Leclercq, *Spirituality of the Middle Ages*, 109.
[10] Ibid., 145.
[11] Ibid., 150.
[12] Ibid.

the Dark Ages and entered the high Middle Ages. It shows clearly that Christ can be sought and followed in many different ways.

An amazing variety of communities of canons regular was established throughout central Europe and then in the rest of the Western Church. It should be noted, however, that the institution of pastoral canons has never been as prestigious as that of monks. This may have been due to the fact that the life led by the canons was generally not as austere as that of the monks. Moreover, some of the most illustrious canons, like St. Dominic, made yet other reforms, which led to the first mendicant friars. We will come to these shortly.

The Reform of Cîteaux

As Western Europe recovered from the dark centuries, a new approach to the Benedictine ideal appeared. The leader (though not the founder) of this reform, called the Cistercian Order (from their early abbey at Cîteaux), was both a genius and a saint. St. Bernard of Clairvaux (1090–1153) was a complex man of great talent, whose life was filled with startling successes and terrible defeats. Sometimes called the last of the Church Fathers, he also might be considered the first modern man. He was criticized for habitually taking the "middle way" between opposing positions,[13] and yet he had strong views himself—a well-developed identity, we might say in the language of psychology. The following insights of Leclercq sum up St. Bernard very well. Speaking of the saint's inner conflicts, he says:

> He had to be the master of an exceptionally many-sided nature, to reconcile different talents, and with many gifts to remain single-minded. This resulted in his being able to take up various attitudes and different activities. His was the nervousness of a sick man, the ardour of the man of action, and an exaggerated sensibility coupled with the acuteness of a brilliant intelligence. Above all, in the midst of these contrasts, and thanks to the conflict they imposed, he lived intensely the mystery of Jesus Christ. . . . The power of Christ shone forth in Bernard, giving him a supernatural prestige and an influence which can only be explained in terms of a testimony to the resurrection of him in whose Passion he shared profoundly.[14]

Although the Cistercian reform was founded by others (St. Robert of Molesmes, St. Alberic, and St. Stephen Harding) as a reaction to the growing wealth of Cluny, St. Bernard put this reform on the map. It was an effort to return to a very literal observance of the Rule of St. Benedict, seeking solitude, poverty, and the following of the humble Christ. The Cistercians introduced innovations such as the establishment of lay brothers who were not choir monks or clerics, the intentional selection of the poorest geographic sites for monasteries,

---

[13] Ibid., 192.

[14] Ibid.

and a simplicity of life similar to the ideals of the early canons regular and the hermits. Bernard was also willing to borrow from the experiences of St. Bruno, who had founded his austere order of hermits, the Carthusians, in 1084. Bruno's ideal of "God alone" fit well with Bernard's sense of the absolute, yet despite his absolutism and uncompromising goals, Bernard worked more than anyone else for the Crusade against the Turks to free the Holy Land. At the same time he not only condemned a pogrom against the Jews, but actually left his monastic solitude to go to Germany to stop the fanatical persecutor in his tracks. The following quotation from Joshua Ben-Meir, a Jewish writer and contemporary of St. Bernard, illuminates a side of Bernard's character that receives little attention:

> The Lord God was moved by the groans of His people. He remembered His covenant with them and renewed His great mercies. Against this son of Belial [Rodolph, the instigator of the pogrom] He raised up a wise man, named Bernard of Clairvaux, a town in France. This religious (according to their manner of speaking) calmed the people and said: March towards Sion, defend the sepulchre of Christ, but touch not the Hebrews. Speak to them with kindness, for they are of the flesh and bone of the Messiah: to harm them is to wound the Saviour in the apple of His eye.... Thus spoke this wise man, and his voice prevailed, because he was loved and revered by all. The multitude listened to his counsels and the fire of their anger cooled. The priest Bernard, however, received neither gold nor ransom from the Jews. It was his heart that led him to love them and prompted him to speak good words for Israel.[15]

St. Bernard's own sermon to the people included the following remarks. Speaking to Rodolph rhetorically, he says:

> Your doctrine is not your own, but derived from your father, the devil, who sent you. For he was a murderer from the beginning; he is a liar and the father of lies (John viii, 44). And it is enough for you that you lie like your master (Matt. x, 25). O most abominable doctrine! infernal wisdom! opposed to the teaching of all the prophets and apostles, destructive of charity and grace. O foulest of heresies, full of blasphemy and sacrilegious impiety, which, inspired by the spirit of lies, hath conceived sorrow and brought forth iniquity (Ps. vii. 15)![16]

Part of Bernard's motivation in stopping the attack on the Jews was his recognition that they were Christ's own people. He called for the Crusade against the Turks, on the other hand, because they had made

[15] Quoted in Ailbe J. Luddy, O.Cist., *Life and Teaching of St. Bernard* (Dublin: M.H. Gill and Son, 1927), 532. Corroborated by Rabbi David Blumenthal.

[16] Quoted in Luddy, *St. Bernard*, 531.

themselves enemies of Christ by virtually destroying the Church in the Holy Land. They also threatened the very existence of Christian Europe by their "holy war" and forced conversions.

Christ was the heart of Bernard's life and spirituality. This is brought out in his *Five Books on Consideration* (*De Consideratione*), a work of advice he wrote to Pope Eugene III, a former Cistercian abbot and disciple of Bernard who was elected pope in 1145. Professor Pelikan describes Bernard's letter to the new pope and its effect.

> Drawing upon the monastic distinction between the contemplative life and the active life, Bernard admonished his former pupil not to allow the administrative details of the papacy to deflect him from what was primary in the church: the person of Jesus Christ. The pope should not, he urged, become the successor of Constantine, but of Peter. For the monastic ideals of contemplation and study were not irrelevant to the governance of the church, but central to it.[17]

A New Step in Devotion to the Divine and Human Christ

Bernard's devotion to Christ gives us the opportunity to examine some important distinctions in how Christ was perceived by those who followed Him. On one hand, there was the mystical vision of Christ as the Word of God, the Logos, emphasized by Origen and the early Fathers. On the other hand, there was the human life of Christ emphasized by St. Augustine: Christ the Suffering Servant of God who was born in a stable and died on the Cross. In St. Bernard's writings these two approaches do not contradict each other in their practical expression of devotion. The late Professor Ewert Cousins selected the following quotations from Bernard to illustrate his "carnal", or human love, of the person of Jesus of Nazareth. "Notice that the love of the heart is, in a certain sense carnal, because our hearts are attracted most toward the humanity of Christ and the things he did or commanded while in the flesh. . . . The soul at prayer should have before it a sacred image of the God-man, in his birth or infancy or as he was teaching, or dying, or rising, or ascending".[18]

Bernard gives as the principal reason why God became man that "he wanted to recapture the affections of carnal men who were unable to love in any other way, by first drawing them to the salutary love of his own humanity, and then gradually to raise them to a spiritual love." [19]

St. Bernard sees these affections, this love of the heart, not as an end but as a means to inspire the soul to a contemplative love beyond knowledge and human affections. This goal became the essence of Cistercian spirituality. In his sermons and writings on the Song of Songs (which he and other mystics see as an allegory of contemplation), he expresses

---

[17] Pelikan, *Jesus through the Centuries*, 119.

[18] Ewert Cousins, "The Humanity and the Passion of Christ", in *Christian Spirituality: High Middle Ages and Reformation*, ed. Jill Raitt (New York: Crossroad Publishing, 1988), 378.

[19] Bernard, *Sermons on the Song of Songs*, 20:6, quoted in ibid., 378, 380.

Christian contemplative love in terms of the Bridegroom of this canticle, who is Christ. The experience of Christian love for the Savior is about to take another great step—that of the Bride. The following citation from St. Bernard assumes that the reader is aware of his profound gratitude to Christ for salvation through His birth, life, death, and Resurrection. Bernard awaited the coming of Christ in the encounter of death and the Second Coming.

First Leclercq gives us an insight that will guide us in understanding St. Bernard's pivotal teaching on divine love. Speaking of the object of contemplative activity according to St. Bernard, Leclercq writes:

> This object is the person and work of Jesus Christ, by whom the Blessed Trinity is revealed to us, and we receive the divine life.... Bernard's devotion to Jesus must, however, be seen in its true light: it rests neither in a sensible love for his humanity, nor in mystic contemplation of the Word.
>
> It would be truer to say that Saint Bernard points out above all the divine condescension by which the Word ... is offered us in the flesh, thus once more becoming accessible to us. By Christ in the flesh the treasures of the loving-kindness hidden in the bosom of the Father are made manifest, to excite us to confidence, to give us a greater knowledge of the goodness and mercy of God and to draw us to imitate him and love him.[20]

With this clarification in mind, we can ponder the following passage about divine love, based on the Song of Songs. It will help us to understand Bernard, as well as Francis, John of the Cross, and Teresa of Avila, all of whom follow Bernard in this mystical tradition. Although the Orthodox and Protestant mystics often had little knowledge of St. Bernard, we will see that the experience of the love of Jesus is similar in their writings and perhaps, at least in the Protestant tradition, less likely to be understood by their contemporaries.

> Love is sufficient of itself, it gives pleasure by itself and because of itself. It is its own merit, its own reward. Love looks for no cause outside itself, no effect beyond itself. Its profit lies in its practice. I love because I love, I love that I may love. Love is a great thing so long as it continually returns to its fountainhead, flows back to its source, always drawing from there the water which constantly replenishes it. Of all the movements, sensations and feelings of the soul, love is the only one in which the creature can respond to the Creator and make some sort of similar return however unequal though it be. For when God loves, all he desires is to be loved in return; the sole purpose of his love is to be loved, in the knowledge that those who love him are made happy by their love of him.

[20] Leclercq, *Spirituality of the Middle Ages*, 198–99.

> The Bridegroom's love [that is, Christ's love], or rather the love which is the Bridegroom, asks in return nothing but faithful love. Let the beloved, then, love in return. Should not a bride love, and above all, Love's bride? Could it be that Love not be loved? ...
>
> And when she has poured out her whole being in love, what is that in comparison with the unceasing torrent of that original source? Clearly, lover and Love, soul and Word, bride and Bridegroom, creature and Creator do not flow with the same volume; one might as well equate a thirsty man with the fountain....
>
> It is true that the creature loves less because she is less. But if she loves with her whole being, nothing is lacking where everything is given.[21]

Those who disparage medieval Christianity should study St. Bernard. As we move on, we will see that in the Eastern Church after the division and in the very best of the Protestant tradition, the love of Christ can reach great heights. But it is Bernard who first articulated this experience with power and clarity, directing it to Jesus Christ in His humanity as well as His divinity.

The Centuries of Devotion

Historians have noted that the twelfth and thirteenth centuries saw a remarkable development of Christian devotion in Western Europe. This devotional life continued to flourish in the dark fourteenth century despite wars and the Black Death. Eamon Duffy of Cambridge University has contradicted accepted theories by showing that devotions were a healthy, powerful aspect of English life immediately before the split between Henry VIII and the Church.[22] The early life of Luther illustrates that in countries that later became Protestant, especially Germany, devotion would remain strong until the eve of the break with the Catholic Church. We shall also see that devotion to Christ would grow from its old Catholic roots and flower in many segments of the Protestant world. A similar revival of devotion took place in the East in the fourteenth century. We will consider this in a later chapter.

The flowering of devotion in the West during this period extends from the heyday of St. Bernard's influence to the decline of that of St. Francis long after his death.[23] It is vital to recall the distinctions between liturgical piety, individual contemplative-style prayer, and devotion. The two great saints, Bernard and Francis, one at the beginning of the period and the other at its apex, included in their personal spiritual expressions all three aspects of religious experience. Perhaps

---

[21] Bernard, *Sermons on the Song of Songs* 83:4–6, as quoted in *The Liturgy of the Hours* (New York: Catholic Book Publishing, 1976), 4:1333–34.

[22] Eamon Duffy, *The Stripping of the Altars: Traditional Religion in England c. 1400–c. 1580* (New Haven: Yale University Press, 1992). The book's theme is the effects of that split on the Church in England.

[23] Leclercq, *Spirituality of the Middle Ages*, 243.

we see St. Francis as more personally devotional because of his simplicity of spirit and emotional temperament. However, he had a strong liturgical intuition as well as a deeply contemplative spirit.

Before we come to St. Francis, we must set the stage. Writing of major developments in late medieval devotions, Richard Kieckhefer, a historian of religion, says:

> In the last centuries of the Middle Ages, devotions of all kinds flourished in unprecedented profusion: pilgrimages, veneration of relics, Marian devotions, meditations on the passion of Christ, penitential exercises, and more.... Devotional literature proliferated even before the invention of printing, and all the more afterward.... Devotional art too enjoyed a heyday.... Themes with major significance in European devotional art, such as the pietà, emerged during this period; others, like the man of sorrows, attained new-found popularity. This explosion of devotional forms unmistakably changed the tenor of Christian life.[24]

Anyone visiting a museum's medieval gallery will find a profusion of devotional art with biblical themes. Such themes as the Annunciation and the Crucifixion were often repeated because each parish church, monastery, or chapel used these objects not only to encourage devotion but to instruct. The care, artistic quality, and indeed, in some cases, the genius in this art are unmistakable. The same can be said of accomplishments in music, the flowering of Gregorian chant, and sacred hymnology. Side by side with this devotion grew a rich and often hotly debated theology. Along with this, a thirst for contemplative prayer waxed strong and is reflected in the immense library of mystical literature from the time of St. Bernard to the writing of *The Imitation of Christ* three hundred years later.

A phenomenon so widespread, long-lived, and integrated into everyday life as medieval devotion must always be a mixed blessing, replete with abuses and exaggerations. Bizarre mixtures of piety and magic emerged along with occasional regressions to more animistic forms of religiosity. These were abetted by naïve readings of biblical texts: accounts such as that of the witch of Endor (1 Sam 28:7–25) or Jephthah's tragic sacrifice of his daughter (Judg 11:30–40) or the bronze serpent in the desert (Num 21:4–9) could appear to give biblical approval to theologically unacceptable religious practices. Statues meant to teach could be used as talismans, and prayers could be thought of as spells by the simple and uneducated.[25]

[24] Richard Kieckhefer, "Major Currents in Late Medieval Devotion", quoted in Raitt, *Christian Spirituality*, 75.

[25] A thorough and sympathetic treatment of this mix of piety and magic is given by Duffy, *Stripping of the Altars*, chap. 8.

Before we judge these primitive forms of religiosity too severely, however, we must realize that our own times are also prone to such ways of thinking regarding physical illness and medicine. Today we regularly view medical practice as miraculous ("miracle drugs", for instance). We are as willing to use nonconventional forms of the medical arts as some medieval people were to use holy water and blessed oil. The follies of mankind do not change; we simply express our superstitions differently.

Most, however, did not lapse into superstition but maintained a devotion, whose object was the increase of virtue, especially the three theological virtues of faith, hope, and charity. Serious voices were raised to keep devotion on the straight and narrow. Peter of Blois (d. 1200), a lay writer of psychological insight and faithfulness to the spirit of the Church Fathers, made the following observation about religious emotions and the experience of contrition, or sorrow for sin:

> There is no merit in any feeling of devotion unless it proceeds from the love of Christ. Many of the characters in tragedies and other poems and songs are wise and illustrious and powerful, and excite our love: they have every gift. The actors put before us the trials they endured, the injustices they suffered ... and the audience is moved to tears. Thou art touched by these fables. When thou dost hear our Lord spoken of devoutly and art so moved, hast thou truly the love of God? Thou hast compassion for God ... thy tears are in vain if thou dost not love God, and thy tears of devotion and penitence flow not from the sources of our Saviour, that is from hope, faith and love.[26]

Christ: The Center of Medieval Devotion

The center of medieval devotion was the humanity of Christ.[27] The primary focus of piety in the first thousand years was on the divinity of Christ as Logos, but believers never lost sight of His humanity, especially His sufferings. However, in the Middle Ages, perhaps because people had become more aware of their own humanity and psychology, the human life of the Son of God became the focus of attention. Rarely was the acceptance of His divinity compromised, and this was mostly by the coming of Unitarianism in the mid-Renaissance. Every aspect of the life of Jesus of Nazareth was expressed and celebrated. New feast days were added in Ordinary Time (from Pentecost until Advent). Corpus Christi, the Transfiguration, and the Exaltation of the Cross were widely celebrated; the Office of the Passion of Christ, the Rosary, with its fifteen evangelical themes, all focused on the Son of God in His humanity.

---

[26] Peter of Blois, *Treatise on Sacramental Confession*, quoted in Leclercq, *Spirituality of the Middle Ages*, 244.

[27] Cousins, "Humanity and Passion of Christ", in Raitt, *Christian Spirituality*, 375.

The devotion to Christ in the Holy Eucharist with solemn adoration of His divinity was possible only because of the theological realism of Christ's words at the Last Supper: "[T]his is my body" (Mt 26:26). Even the Marian devotions were ultimately Christocentric. Mary was celebrated as the holy Mother of God and also as one of us—*Notre Dame*, "Our Lady". Later some of these devotions would move in wrong directions, causing Catholic and, later, Protestant writers to become critical. The distinguished contemporary Mariologist René Laurentin writes of fourteenth-century piety: "Repelled by a desiccated intellectualism, men [sought] life on the imaginative and sentimental plane. Throughout this period of decadence popular enthusiasm for the Blessed Virgin never faltered, but the adulterated fodder it was nourished on consisted of trumpery miracles, ambiguous slogans, and inconsistent maundering." [28] Despite all of this, devotion to the Mother of Jesus gave rise to magnificent hymns and sermons, cathedrals, shrines, and endless acts of charity done under her patronage.

Jesu, Dulcis Memoria

Devotion to Christ was often expressed with great loveliness during these centuries. Nineteenth-century writers like Tennyson and Scott in England, Whittier and Longfellow in America—all of them Protestants—were entranced by the beauty of medieval piety. The following hymn, or at least excerpts from its sixty stanzas, illustrates well the devotion to Christ, the Son of God and Son of Mary, in the eleventh and twelfth centuries. Although it is often attributed to St. Bernard, it was written at the end of the twelfth century, apparently by an English Cistercian. The long work, called *Jubilus Christi*, or the celebration of Christ, is a masterpiece of Medieval Latin poetry. For this reason the Latin is given, along with the translation by the prolific and masterful nineteenth-century English hymn translator Fr. Edward Caswall of the Birmingham Oratory. Here we cite only the first two stanzas to bring to a suitable ending this chapter on the love of Christ during the early Middle Ages.

Jesu, dulcis memoria,	Jesus, the very thought of Thee
Dans vera cordis gaudia:	With sweetness fills the breast;
Sed super mel et omnia	But sweeter far Thy face to see,
Ejus dulcis praesentia.	And in Thy presence rest.
Nil canitur suavius,	Nor voice can sing, nor heart can frame,
Nil auditur jucundius,	Nor can the memory find
Nil cogitatur dulcius,	A sweeter sound than Thy blest Name,
Quam Jesus Dei Filius.	O Savior of mankind!

[28] René Laurentin, *Queen of Heaven: A Short Treatise on Marian Theology* (London: Burns, Oates and Washbourne, 1956), 60.

8 The Thirteenth Century: The Age of the Love of Christ

Some have called it the greatest of centuries. Perhaps. Undoubtedly, it is the century when in theology and poetry, in music and art, in acts of religious devotion and charity to the poor and sick, an impressive number of people in Western Europe lifted their hearts and minds to Jesus Christ. Like any age, it had its scandals and knaves, and there were dark sides: the misdeeds of the Crusaders, especially to Eastern Christians and Muslims, and the ill-treatment of the Jews. Even these, however, were somewhat offset by the positive accomplishments of the Crusades and the flowering of Jewish culture in medieval Europe.

The century began with one of history's greatest popes, Innocent III, and his council of reform, Lateran IV, held at Rome in 1215. The Church had been challenged to reform by the spirit of the times, which involved a desire for evangelical simplicity and a fervent piety among the laity. Innocent III, with characteristic vitality and insight, had taken up the challenge. He was well aware of the need for reform: twenty years before the council he wrote a book on "The Misery of the Human Condition", which reflected the severe difficulties of his time.[1]

Six years before the great council there appeared before Innocent III an odd itinerant band of penitents, led by a rich man who had become a beggar. Their first meeting annoyed the Pope. He assumed them to be yet another lay group trying to take reform into their own hands, preempting Church authority by their own assumed divine inspirations. Innocent would have dismissed them altogether except for a troubling dream in which he saw the penitent beggar supporting the crumbling walls of the Lateran Basilica. The next day the Pope again received the little brothers, as they called themselves. He approved their way of life and received their pledge of loyalty and obedience. Thus began the Franciscan Order.

The little penitent, forever to be known by a nickname his father had given him, Francesco (the little Frenchman; his baptismal name

[1] Dom Jean Leclercq et al., *The Spirituality of the Middle Ages*, vol. 2, *A History of Christian Spirituality* (New York: Seabury Press, 1982), 259.

was John), captured the imagination of his own time and of all subsequent centuries. His personal sanctity, the purity of his life and message, and the charity of his heart made him one of the few popular saints who encountered no real enemies in his own lifetime.

St. Francis, the Lover of Christ

From the day of his conversion Francis of Assisi burned with a personal love for Jesus Christ. He is, in fact, a paradigm of Christian devotion according to the descriptive definition we have used in this book. From the hauntingly beautiful days of Francis' initial conversion, Christ was real and present to him. He saw Christ everywhere: in nature; in birds and animals; in lepers and all the sick; in friends and enemies; in laity, religious, and clergy; in the bishop and the Pope. He writes in his *Testament* that early in his life "it seemed too bitter for me to see lepers. And the Lord Himself led me among them and ... what had seemed bitter to me was turned into sweetness of soul and body."[2] Shortly after his conversion, which climaxed in his mystical experience before the Crucifix of San Damiano, Francis would go through the streets of Assisi banging on doors and saying tearfully, "Love is not loved."

St. Francis did not intend to establish a religious order, and he brought to this task none of the organizational genius of St. Benedict or of his own contemporary, St. Dominic. Things got out of hand very early, because he lacked the perspicacity and critical judgment necessary to oversee a large group. He made the tragic mistake of assuming that everyone who followed him had the same ideals and experience of divine love that he had.

As a result of his lack of organization and limited appreciation of human weakness, Francis' order started to come apart even before his death. The huge number of friars (five thousand) elected his nemesis, Brother Elias, in his place. During the intervening centuries his order has split into three or four huge trunks, innumerable branches, and twigs (I belong to a twig). Considering the diversity of the Franciscan family, it is unsurprising that there always have been administrative difficulties. There are friars, nuns (called Poor Clares after their foundress, St. Clare of Assisi), active sisters, and lay members (now oddly called Secular Franciscans—an oxymoron). Francis really started a movement rather than a religious community. Franciscanism is really something larger than a religious community, although it contains many of them.

Francis was devoted to the Mass, profoundly moved by the presence of Christ in the sacrament of the Eucharist, and it was he who popularized devotion to the Blessed Sacrament outside the liturgy. Although there is compelling evidence that Eucharistic devotion had

[2] The *Testament* of St. Francis, quoted in *Francis of Assisi: Early Documents*, ed. Regis J. Armstrong, O.F.M. Cap., et al. (New York: New City Press, 1999), 124.

already arisen, at least in northwestern Spain by the end of the seventh century,[3] it was St. Francis who sought to make it universal. In so doing, he was following the express wishes of Innocent III at the Lateran Council and of his successor, Pope Honorius III, Francis' personal supporter. The following quotation is one of many of the saint's concerning the reservation of the Holy Eucharist.

> Let all of us, clergymen, consider the great sin and the ignorance some have toward the most holy Body and Blood of our Lord Jesus Christ and His most holy names and written words that consecrate His Body. We know It cannot be His Body without first being consecrated by word. For we have and see nothing corporally of the Most High in this world except [His] Body and Blood, [His] names and written words through which we have been made and redeemed from death to life (1 John 3:14)....
>
> Are we not moved by piety at these things when the good Lord offers Himself into our hands and we handle Him and receive Him daily with our mouth? Do we refuse to recognize that we must come into His hands? Let us, therefore, amend our ways quickly and firmly in these and all other matters. Wherever the most holy Body and Blood of our Lord Jesus Christ has been unlawfully placed and left, let It be moved from there, placed in a precious place and locked up.[4]

Francis wrote in the same vein to the superiors of the growing number of friars in 1217.

> I beg you with all that is in me and more that, when it is fitting and you judge it expedient, you humbly beg the clergy to revere the most holy Body and Blood of our Lord Jesus Christ and His holy name and written words that sanctify His Body above all else. They should hold the chalices, corporals, appointments of the altar, and everything that pertains to the sacrifice as precious. If the most holy Body of the Lord is very poorly reserved in any place, let It be placed and locked up in a precious place according to the command of the Church. Let It be carried about with great reverence and administered to others with discernment.[5]

St. Francis also wrote to rulers and heads of government, from mayors to kings, asking them all to show the greatest respect to Christ.[6]

---

[3] For the evidence of an early extraliturgical Eucharistic devotion in Lugo, Spain, see Fr. Benedict Groeschel, C.F.R., and James Monti, *In the Presence of Our Lord: The History, Theology, and Psychology of Eucharistic Devotion* (Huntington, Ind.: Our Sunday Visitor, 1997), 193–98.

[4] In *St. Francis of Assisi: Writings for a Gospel Life*, ed. Regis J. Armstrong, O.F.M. Cap., et al. (New York: Crossroad, 1994), 45–46.

[5] Ibid., 47–48.

[6] Ibid., 49.

This great love and reverence for Christ led him to spread devotion not only to the Eucharistic presence but also to the Lord's birth and death. The prayer form known as *compositio loci* had no greater practitioner than Francis of Assisi, and it was he who popularized two very obvious examples of it: the Christmas crib, or crèche, and the commemoration of the Passion, a devotion that would lead in the fifteenth century to the Stations of the Cross.

Borrowing from the peasant custom of going from the church to a stable on Christmas Eve, Francis spread the devotion of the crèche, something that continues to this day, reminding us dramatically of the meaning of the word "Emmanuel": Christ is here among us.

The Middle Ages had a number of devotional practices recalling the Passion of Christ. Prayers or dramas invited the faithful to contemplate the sufferings of our Savior from His condemnation to His death and entombment. Francis composed an "Office of the Passion", and his enthusiasm for devotion to Christ Crucified led to the popular but incorrect belief that he had instituted the Way of the Cross. All of these devotions—the Crib, the Cross, and the reservation of the Blessed Sacrament—focus attention on the suffering or the humility of Christ.

The Living Crucifix

Two years before St. Francis' death at the age of 45, the mysterious, awe-inspiring phenomenon of the stigmatization occurred in the remote solitude of Monte Alverno. Much has been written about this event from points of view ranging from deep devotion to radical skepticism. Having had some firsthand experience dealing with people undergoing this phenomenon, I readily admit to a purely psychological explanation in some cases. Stigmata that can be explained psychologically usually occur to a devout, emotionally vibrant individual, but by no means necessarily to someone who is emotionally disturbed. That these marks are related at least to some subjective influence can be seen by the fact that in recent years the location of the marks has moved from the palm of the hand to the wrist. In the past thirty-five years, scientific investigation has strongly suggested that Christ was crucified through His wrists. In response to this information the stigmata have tended, then, to move to the wrists.

In the case of St. Francis there was no precedent for such a powerful psychological response to devotion to Christ. He is the first known stigmatic. In a great number of cases of stigmatic wounds that have been studied, the marks are superficial and transitory. In the case of St. Francis, however, the wounds were very deep and appeared to have structures within them similar to nails, but apparently formed of congealed blood.

The stigmata in the life of St. Francis are, after all, an awesome and mysterious sign of the love of Christ that went beyond what most of the saint's followers ever hoped to achieve. If we believe in Divine

Providence, these marks of love and gratitude to the suffering Messiah are most appropriate. Padre Pio, who also bore the stigmata and is one of St. Francis' great modern disciples, stated that these marks were both painful and humbling. Anyone with a reasonable estimation of his own spiritual limitations and myopia would be wise to pause in prayerful reflection before such a life of divine love as St. Francis lived, and to accept with awesome silence and respect these signs of the suffering Son of God.

St. Francis left a series of admonitions that are not well known, because they are disconcerting to our mediocrity. In the following one we can see both his devotion to Christ and his willingness to participate in Christ's sufferings, no matter what the cost.

> Let all of us, brothers, consider the Good Shepherd Who bore the suffering of the cross to save His sheep.
>
> The Lord's sheep followed Him in tribulation and persecution, shame and hunger, in weakness and temptation, and in other ways; and for these things they received eternal life from the Lord.
>
> Therefore, it is a great shame for us, the servants of God, that the saints have accomplished great things and we want only to receive glory and honor by recounting them.[7]

The Gospel Life

For reasons that are complex and not entirely clear, the thirteenth century brought about a strong and widespread desire to lead a more literal Gospel life. Groups of itinerant penitents and evangelizers became a common scene along the roads of Europe during this time. They were often made up entirely of laymen; in the case of St. Francis, there were a few priests and clerics of lower rank. There is a long-standing tradition that St. Francis himself was a deacon or subdeacon. If this assumption of a clerical role is true, it was certainly downplayed during his life.

If the itinerants had made public vows of poverty, chastity, and obedience to the Pope or to the diocesan bishop, or if there were priest members, then the group was officially religious and recognized by the Church. The Servite Order began with a group of Florentine businessmen who formed a penitential community. At this time also, different bands of penitents began to coalesce into such groups as the Franciscan Third Order Regular of Penance and also into the early Carmelite and Augustinian friars.

Many other bands were not formally recognized, and some, as we have mentioned, found themselves at odds with Church authority for teachings contrary to the Catholic faith. All of these groups, either those at peace with the Church, like the friars, or those at odds with the Church, like the followers of Peter Waldo (Pierre Valdès; d. 1218),

[7] Armstrong, *Writings for a Gospel Life*, 156.

sought explicitly to follow the life of Christ as indicated by the Gospel as literally as possible.

Many of these groups became mere footnotes in history. One such community was the Poor Men of Christ, founded by St. Stephen of Muret (d. 1124), which later flourished as the Order of Grandmont and then disappeared. On the other side were the Lombards, or Arnoldists, inspired by Arnold of Brescia, who, after asking the blessing of the Pope, bitterly denounced the clergy. He went so far as to teach that it was impossible for clerics who possessed property to be saved. Eventually condemned as a heretic, he was burned alive by imperial order in 1155. Hugo Speroni, who took up Arnold's point of view, went even further and maintained that "the rites of the Church are inventions of the priests and idolatrous materializations of the true religion", which Christ intended to be purely spiritual. For Speroni, what counted was "interior baptism, spiritual communion with the Word, and inner compunction".[8]

It is interesting that the revered Russian monk St. Nil Sorsky (1433–1508) and his followers presented a case against all monastic ownership in the Russian Church Synod of 1503. Although Nil was always faithful to the Orthodox teaching, there were heretical movements in the East that echoed the same demand for the complete lack of ownership.[9]

Another reformist movement of the twelfth century involved the Humiliati, or Poor Men of Lyons, and Peter Waldo, a devout merchant of that city who died in 1218. Peter embraced a life of penance and poverty around 1170 and preached a love of poverty and the example of Christ. After fourteen years Pope Lucius III forbade the Poor Men to preach for a number of reasons. They came to deny the whole sacramental doctrine of the Church while retaining the signs, and they taught that the validity of the sacraments depended on the sanctity of the minister: a return to the Donatist position St. Augustine had defeated in the fourth century. Waldo himself, although not ordained, conferred baptism, confirmation, absolution of sins, and Communion. It is not surprising that three hundred years later the sixteenth-century reformers would see the Waldensians as their forerunners.

Another person seeking to lead a Gospel life, Amalric de Bène (d. 1207), taught in Paris, but his teaching became suspect. He went to Rome, appealing to Pope Innocent III for protection but was refused. His followers added a hint of pantheism to their evangelical aspirations and eventually sided with the apocalypticism of Joachim of Fiore (1130–1202).[10]

---

[8] Ibid., 263.

[9] Sergei Hackel, "Late Medieval Russia: The Possessors and the Non-Possessors", in *Christian Spirituality: High Middle Ages and Reformation*, ed. Jill Raitt (New York: Crossroad, 1988), 223.

[10] See Delno C. West and Sandra Zimdars-Swartz, *Joachim of Fiore: A Study in Spiritual Perception and History* (Bloomington, Ind.: Indiana University Press, 1983).

Joachim is of less interest to us because he was not directly part of the movement to lead a Gospel life. His thinking and popularity influenced many, however, including the Franciscan reform movement, the "Spirituals", who sought to return to the simplicity of St. Francis' early experience. Joachim, Cistercian abbot in Calabria, taught that a new and third age was about to dawn (the Old Testament was the first and the New Testament and the Church were the second). He maintained that the third age would see the Scriptures renewed spiritually, as if Christ had been born again and as though He were raising the dead and breathing into His disciples the gift of the Holy Spirit. The belief in a new age of the Holy Spirit, or a golden millennium, has often arisen in Christianity since the time of Joachim. We see it in some Pentecostal groups today.

Later, almost a century after the death of St. Francis, the Spirituals would put emphasis on "absolute poverty" and have a head-on collision with Popes Boniface VIII (1294–1303) and John XXII (1316–1334). The Spiritual Franciscans were always better at poverty than at obedience or charity. One of them, Ubertino of Casale (died c. 1330), was the first to call a pope the Beast of the Apocalypse and the Roman Curia the Whore of Babylon. Although Ubertino was always a friar and a Catholic, he used these slanderous titles which survive to this day among many prejudiced people, who nevertheless see themselves as devout followers of the humble Christ.

Among all these souls attempting to follow the Gospel life there were very few with any intellectual interests. Obviously there were bright people, capable of inspiring others, but whether Catholics or the first forerunners of Protestantism, they appear not to have been informed about the teachings of the Church Fathers. Their understanding of early Christianity was based on their own reading and interpretation of the New Testament rather than on the writings of Ignatius of Antioch, Irenaeus, or Cyprian. They tended to create an image of the early Church from their own conclusions about the early Christians and even about their sacraments and clergy.

The Teachers of the Gospel Life

St. Anthony of Padua

While all this discord was going on, much of it occasioned by real abuses among the clergy and religious, a large number of intellectually gifted men entered the Order of St. Francis. The best representative of this group is probably St. Anthony of Padua, a popular preacher whose sermons show a warm and devotional Christianity centered directly on Christ. In a sermon written for the feast of St. John the Evangelist, the Lisbon-born preacher discusses the following of Christ, taking as his text: "When Jesus had finished speaking, he said to him, 'Follow me'" (Jn 21:19).

> "Follow me!" Jesus said to Peter, and today He repeats these same words to every Christian.... In the third chapter of Jeremiah, we

read, "You will call me 'My Father' and never cease to follow me" (3:19). Follow me, then, by casting aside anything that weighs you down, for if you are thus burdened, you will not be able to keep up with me since I am running in haste.

In the words of the psalmist: Christ says, "I ran in thirst" (61:5; DRV), thirst for the salvation of all. Where did he run? To the Cross! You too should run after Him, carrying your cross after Him who so eagerly carried His Cross for you....

"Follow me" for I know where to take you. The Book of Proverbs says, "On the way of wisdom I direct you, I lead you on straightforward paths" (4:11).... The way of wisdom is the way of humility: every other way is that of ignorance and pride. Jesus showed us the way of wisdom when he said, "Learn from me" (Mt 11:29). When we follow Christ, who guides us by His example, we walk a very narrow path, a path of poverty and obedience.

Although obedience and poverty seem to confine and restrict our freedom, nevertheless, poverty makes us rich, and obedience makes us free. Whoever follows Jesus along the straight and narrow path will not be hampered by attachment to riches and to his own will.[11]

St. Dominic and the Preaching Friars

When St. Francis was spreading his Gospel message, a number of others who were faithful to the Church were also attempting to lead the Gospel life. Preeminent among these was Dominic Guzman (1173–1221), a Castilian canon regular with much in common with the Norbertines. St. Dominic preached against heretical movements, especially the Albigensians, or Cathari. This group had revived many of the ideas of the Manicheans, whom Augustine had defeated almost a millennium before. Unfortunately, the writings and sermons of St. Dominic were lost, and few of his own words remain. It is known that he was deeply dedicated to Gospel poverty and prayer. It was noted that he had no cell or room of his own in any of the houses of his growing order, but slept wherever he found a place.

It has always been believed that Dominic and Francis were friends, although obviously they had very different personalities, with different approaches to the Gospel life. To this day the members of each order refer to the founder of the other order with an affectionate honorific: the Franciscans refer to the great preacher as Holy Father St. Dominic and vice versa. On their respective feast days fraternal visits are exchanged: Dominicans preach on St. Francis' day and Franciscans on the feast of St. Dominic.

The two founders sought to follow the Gospel life through preaching, poverty, and devotion. Early on, each order gave rise to men of great intellectual acumen who would become Doctors of the Church.

[11] *Saint Anthony: Herald of the Good News*, ed. and trans. Claude M. Jarmak, O.F.M. Conv. (Ellicott City, Md.: Conventual Franciscan Friars, 1995), 176–77.

During the first century of existence there were two Doctors in each order: Sts. Thomas Aquinas and Albert the Great among the Dominicans, and SS. Anthony of Padua and Bonaventure among the Franciscans.

St. Albert the Great and St. Thomas Aquinas

The names of these two Dominican geniuses are usually associated with intellectual accomplishments rather than devotion. They brought Aristotelian thought into the philosophical tradition of the Church. Albert (1206–1280) was one of the first Europeans to make a systematic study of the natural sciences. He wrote commentaries on Aristotle, whose philosophy was just coming to be known in the Christian world through contact with Muslim philosophers. He also wrote spiritual works, particularly a book called *Clinging to God*, a mystical work on union with Christ through the renunciation of all things. He explicitly writes on the redeeming blood coming from the Heart of Christ. This Heart of the Son of God gives life to the whole Mystical Body of Christ, thus linking devotion with the foundations of Christian theology. Albert's devotion to Christ is well illustrated by the following prayer at the conclusion of his sermon for the Fourth Sunday of Advent, one of many such prayers he addressed to his Savior.

> Lord Jesus Christ, listen to the voice of our distress in the desert of penitents crying out to you; that we may not be deceived by the falsehood of discussions in nobility of birth, from superstition of religion, from curiosity of knowledge tempting us; grant us to prepare the way to you through the desert driven away of sin, by the purpose of repenting, by the remission of wrongs, by contempt of temporal [things], and by the observing of the commandments. May your paths be made straight in us by the renunciation of our own will, feeling, self-confidence, by the spending over and above of counsels/deliberations; that in the house of Bethany of obedience baptized with the water of true contrition, with the Holy Spirit and with fire across the Jordan, and after the river of the last judgment we may perfectly know you, the Mediator of virtue and knowledge, the Mediator of God and men.[12]

Although St. Albert served for a short time as Bishop of Ratisbon, he subsequently resigned and returned to study, teaching, and spiritual direction and attended the second Council of Lyons in 1274. In the twentieth century St. Albert was declared a saint and Doctor of the Church. Perhaps the reason for this long delay is that he was so greatly surpassed by his remarkable student, Thomas Aquinas (1225–1274). It far exceeds the scope of this book to examine the mystical theology of St. Thomas and its effects on so many others, especially St. John of the Cross. His teachings have been summarized and adapted to our

[12] Translated from the text in P. G. Meersseman, O.P., *Introductio in Opera Omnia B. Alberti Magni OP* (Bruges: Charles Beyaert, 1931), 123.

time, especially by the eminent Dominican mystical theologian Fr. Reginald Garrigou-Lagrange.[13] For our purposes we need to take note of St. Thomas' description of contemplation as essentially an act of the intellect, a divine light and supernatural mode of knowledge. But contemplation is impregnated by love. He stressed the need for the gifts of the Holy Spirit, especially wisdom and a response of perfect docility to God. His contemplative devotion to Christ is centered on the Holy Eucharist and is enshrined in the Mass and liturgy for the feast of Corpus Christi. Although some dispute his authorship, less than thirty years after Thomas' death the Dominican General Chapter referred to him as the composer of this Mass. The hymn "*O Salutaris Hostia*", familiar to Catholics for centuries as a hymn sung at Benediction of the Blessed Sacrament, is really the end of a much longer hymn composed by St. Thomas. It is, however, more than enough to illustrate his profound devotion to Christ.

O salutaris hostia, *Quae caeli pandis ostium,* *Bella premunt hostilia.* *Da robur fer auxilium.*	O Sacrifice for our salvation, Who Gate of Heaven opens wide, Our enemies press hard around us. Assist us strongly, be our guide.
Uni trinoque Domino *Sit sempiterna gloria,* *Qui vitam sine termino* *Nobis donet in patria.*	To the One and Triune God, Be glory and eternal praise. May He grant us life forever And to our home our souls upraise.[14]

St. Bonaventure (1221–1274)

With great loyalty to St. Francis, of whose order he became the sixth general minister, Bonaventure made Scripture the foundation of all his works. His body of work is less original than that of his contemporary St. Thomas because he remained firmly in the Augustinian-Platonic tradition and is clearly not Aristotelian. His goal as a spiritual writer is to help Christians make progress on the spiritual journey to contemplation by loving God. Following St. Francis, he sees contemplative prayer as affective, directed toward the life of Christ and its different events, especially Christ's death. Christ alone lifts fallen man "broken and bowed" to salvation and holiness. One becomes a new creation in Christ, following the threefold way. At the end of his work called *The Threefold Way* he sums up the classic steps of the journey of the soul to God in strictly Christocentric ways. The spiritual journey is a journey to Christ.

---

[13] Among the works of Fr. Garrigou-Lagrange currently in print are *Life Everlasting and the Immensity of the Soul*; *Christian Perfection and Contemplation*; *The Mother of the Saviour and Our Interior Life*; *The Three Conversions in the Spiritual Life*; and *Our Saviour and His Love for Us* (TAN Books).

[14] *Verbum Supernum Prodiens* (part of St. Thomas' Office for Corpus Christi), quoted in *Devoutly I Adore Thee: The Prayers and Hymns of St. Thomas Aquinas*, trans. and ed. Robert Anderson and Johann Moser (Manchester, N.H.: Sophia Institute Press, 1993), 97–99.

Thus do thou distinguish the steps that lead to the way of union:
let vigilance make thee attentive, for the Bridegroom passeth swiftly;
let confidence make thee strong, for he cometh without fail;
let desire enkindle thee, for he is sweet;
let fervour raise thee up, for he is sublime;
let delight in him give thee repose, for he is beautiful;
let joy inebriate thee, for he is the fullness of love;
let attachment unite thee to him, for his love is full of power.
And mayest thou ever, O devout soul, say to the Lord with all thy heart:
I seek thee, I hope for thee, I desire thee, I raise myself up toward thee,
I lay hold on thee, I exult in thee, at last I cleave to thee.[15]

An even greater emphasis on the need for devotion and affection is found in the following citation, in which Bonaventure insists on the priority of affective love over intellectual contemplation.

> But if you wish to know how these things come about,
> ask grace not instruction,
> desire not understanding,
> the groaning of prayer not diligent reading,
> the Spouse not the teacher,
> God not man,
> darkness not clarity,
> not light but the fire
> that totally inflames and carries us into God
> by ecstatic unctions and burning affections.
> This fire is God,
> and his furnace is in Jerusalem
> [Is 31:9]; and Christ enkindles it
> in the heat of his burning passion,
> which only he truly perceives who says:
> My soul chooses hanging and my bones death
> [Job 7:15]. Whoever loves this death
> can see God
> because it is true beyond doubt that
> man will not see me and live
> [Ex 33:20]. Let us, then, die
> and enter into the darkness;
> let us impose silence
> upon our cares, our desires and our imaginings.[16]

[15] Bonaventure, *De triplici via*, pt. 2, chap. 3, no. 5, quoted in Leclercq, *Spirituality of the Middle Ages*, 310.

[16] *The Soul's Journey Into God*, quoted in *Bonaventure: The Soul's Journey Into God; The Tree of Life; The Life of St. Francis*, ed. and trans. Ewert Cousins (New York: Paulist Press, 1978), 115–6.

The ecstatic language of St. Bonaventure may go beyond the experience of people in our own time. To us his prayers can appear overly sentimental. I suspect that Bonaventure's way of relating to Christ is so individual, so intense, and at times so ecstatic that the alienated people of today may find him incomprehensible. However don't count Bonaventure out. I have reason to expect a return to his style based on direct expressiveness of experience as the twenty-first century progresses. It is worth noting that Pope Benedict XVI was influenced in his formation by Bonaventure.

The two great Christian minds, Thomas and Bonaventure, whose lives and work almost exactly overlapped, were very different. Thomas was clear-sighted, lucid, and intellectually comprehensible, except for the last four months of his life when he maintained a mysterious silence, which has been seen as the result of a profound contemplative experience.[17] Bonaventure, on the other hand, although intellectually brilliant, is primarily affective and even ecstatic. This spirituality of experience would link St. Augustine and St. Bernard to the high Middle Ages, which Bonaventure so clearly represents.

Dominican spirituality gave rise to its own mystical tradition in Germany, especially among cloistered nuns, and in Italy with so great a soul as the ecstatic laywoman St. Catherine of Siena; however, the Franciscan tradition would prove to be more popular. Books like *The Meditations on the Life of Christ* (attributed to St. Bonaventure, but written by a friar after his death) would focus on the birth, childhood, Passion, and death of Christ.[18] The following counsel from the *Meditations* communicates this affective spirituality, which so clearly has its origin in the experience of St. Francis: "Take delight and rejoice. Compassionate with his [Christ's] sufferings. By familiar friendship, confidence, and love, imitate Jesus with all thy heart and with all thy strength."[19]

This spirituality of the love of Christ and meditation on His life in every conceivable aspect is what links the devotion of St. Bernard to that of the fourteenth century, when the so-called *devotio moderna* was about to begin. The meditation of St. Bernard and St. Francis was still anchored to the objective contemplation of Christ's mysteries. However, devotion began to drift more and more toward the subjective and personal, toward the individual's own mind and imagination. This trend would become increasingly pronounced as time passed and would prove to be immensely popular as the Reformation dawned. Unfortunately, devotion's very subjectivism would effectively remove it at times from the authentic experience of Christian spirituality based solely on the New Testament.

---

[17] Josef Pieper, *The Silence of St. Thomas*, trans. Daniel O'Connor (London: Faber and Faber, 1957), 45–47.

[18] Leclercq, *Spirituality of the Middle Ages*, 314.

[19] Ibid.

9 The Women of Christ

Perhaps in an analogy to Christ and His Mother, Christianity had often linked a man and woman together in some great spiritual movement or accomplishment. Augustine and his mother, Monica; Benedict and his sister, Scholastica; Francis and his most loyal disciple, Clare, are shining examples. There were, however, other women who made it on their own, so to speak, but these were often Christian royalty. Saints like Helen, Margaret of Scotland, or Elizabeth of Hungary, as well as abbesses of great monasteries, like St. Hilda of Whitby and St. Odilia of Alsace, combined both ecclesiastical and civil authority.

With the end of the Middle Ages and the beginning of the Renaissance, however, we find two women mystics who deeply inspired history on their own—St. Catherine of Siena, who literally saved the papacy, and St. Joan of Arc, the ecstatic maiden who changed the course of European history. From then on there would be a train of great Christian women. Before we proceed in our history to the age when women were able to take their equal place, we must survey the devotion of great women to Christ up to the end of the medieval period.

We must recall that until recent times women rarely participated in public life as did men. Thus, humanity has been deprived of half of its great writers, composers, and civil leaders. It did not, however, sustain such losses in the sphere of spirituality and devotion. In fact, the first great women writers in Western civilization were mystics of the Church.

Beginning in the second century, there were celebrated women martyrs in East and West, but unlike the Church Fathers, they left few writings. Recently a Protestant theologian, Christopher Hall, working on a New Testament commentary based on the writings of the Church Fathers, has asked the question: Where are the Mothers of the Church? He has come up with some interesting candidates: Marcella, a Roman widow and ascetic praised by St. Jerome; Paula, friend of the same Church Father who was struck by her intellect as well as her "willingness to endure separation from her children for the sake of the Gospel"; Melania the Elder, the learned student of all the ancient commentators, including three million lines of Origen;

Olympias, deaconess of the Church at Constantinople; and Macrina, sister of Gregory of Nyssa.[1]

The first major feminine contribution to devotion to Christ was made by St. Helen, mother of Constantine, who opened the Holy Land to pilgrims and brought the relics of the Cross to Byzantium, whence they spread throughout Europe. Helen, however, left no writings. Even the great abbesses of the Dark Ages and early Middle Ages have left little to tell us about their devotion.

The most remarkable exception to this feminine silence is that intrepid pilgrim of the late fourth century, Egeria (also called Aetheria), who traveled from northern Spain to the Holy Land. Her diary is among the most interesting travelogues in all literature. The following piece shows how her writing reflects, rather than fully illustrates, her warm devotion to Christ.

> On the following day, after crossing the sea, I arrived in Constantinople, giving thanks to Christ our God who deigned to bestow such favor on me, an unworthy and undeserving person. Not only did He deign to fulfill my desire to go there, but He granted also the means of visiting what I desired to see, and of returning again to Constantinople.
>
> After arriving there, I did not cease giving thanks to Jesus our God, who had deigned to bestow His grace upon me, in the various churches, that of the apostles and the numerous shrines that are here.[2]

Another woman who has left a record of her devotion is the ninth-century poet Casia (also Kasia), reputedly a Byzantine nun and founder of a convent in Constantinople. Various liturgical hymns have been attributed to her, though her authorship of some is doubtful. Her hymns became part of the Byzantine liturgy. The "Ode for the Wednesday of Holy Week" is one of her best and reflects a deep, personal love for Christ.

Lord, the woman fallen in many sins, seeing Thy Divinity,
Taking the part of myrrh-bearer, wailing bringeth to Thee myrrh against Thy burial;
"Alas!" she crieth, "for that night is to me the wildness of sin, dusky and moonless, even the love of transgression;
Accept the springs of my fears, who with clouds partest the waters of the sea;
Bend to the groanings of my heart, who has brought down Heaven by Thine ineffable humiliation:
I will kiss again Thy stainless feet,
I will wipe them with the hair of my head;

[1] Christopher A. Hall, *Reading Scripture with the Church Fathers* (Downers Grove, Ill.: InterVarsity Press, 1998), 43ff.

[2] *Egeria: Diary of a Pilgrimage*, ed. George Gingras (New York: Newman Press, 1970), 88.

Thy feet, whereof when Eve in Paradise heard the sound, she hid herself for fear;
The multitude of my sins, and the depths of Thy judgment, who shall explore, Saviour of souls, my Redeemer?
Forget not me, Thy servant, Thou, whose mercy is infinite!"[3]

In the absence of much writing by women, we know that monks and bishops often wrote to them, as the Fathers of the Church had frequently written to devout laywomen. St. Augustine's letters to Proba, for example, clearly indicate her spiritual depth and natural talents.[4] I have often regretted that we do not have her contribution to this correspondence. SS. Jerome and John Chrysostom and John of Fécamp are among those who included nuns, abbesses, and queens among their correspondents. They have given us a view of Christian women that causes us to regret even more that the interesting people they wrote to left little writing behind them.

The twelfth century produced two Benedictine nuns who became well-known spiritual writers, both of them mystics and visionaries. The most important was St. Hildegard of Bingen (1098–1179), a woman who struggled all her life with serious illness and yet traveled all over Germany giving counsel and settling disputes. She attributed her vast synthesis of natural and spiritual knowledge to divine enlightenment, yet she was a practical, capable administrator of her abbey. She saw world history as a great conflict between good and evil with Christ as the final victor.

Jesus Christ, the love that gives love,
You are higher than the highest star;
You are deeper than the deepest sea;
You cherish us as your own family;
You embrace us as your own spouse;
You rule over us as your own subjects;
You welcome us as your dearest friend.
Let all the world worship you.[5]

St. Hildegarde's good friend, St. Elizabeth of Schönau (1129–1164), was a visionary who claimed in her visions to have encountered various friends of Christ from the Gospels. Although the very extent of her revelations and their lack of historical accuracy have much reduced the importance of this nun, she had great influence in her own time. Elizabeth's emphasis on liturgical piety and on the daily reception of

[3] Quoted in H.J.W. Tillyard, *Byzantine Music and Hymnography* (London: Faith Press, 1923), 30.

[4] See *Augustine: Major Writings*, ed. Benedict J. Groeschel, C.F.R. (New York: Crossroad, 1995), 154–55.

[5] *HarperCollins Book of Prayers* (Edison, N.J., Castle Books, 1993), 196.

the Eucharist made her an important influence in keeping Christians focused on the Gospel and the life of Christ.

St. Clare of Assisi

As literacy spread during the high Middle Ages, women writers emerged who were spiritual persons of great insight. The writings of St. Clare of Assisi reflect not only a deep personal spirituality but also an extraordinarily pure soul dedicated to the Gospel life. Her writings, mostly in the form of letters of counsel to her sisters, are characterized by a profound, yet simple, contemplative spirit. Clare's love of Christ was very influenced by the spirituality of St. Francis, and she was his most loyal disciple. However, those who know St. Clare well recognize the unique quality of her individual contribution. She brought her own sense of presence, common sense, and profound dedication to her writings. Perhaps of all the earlier women writers, Clare is most able to speak to our time in ways we can understand.

In the following selection St. Clare is writing to Agnes, a princess and daughter of the king of Bohemia, who had received papal permission to open a convent of Clare's new order, the Poor Ladies. It was an event of great notoriety and edification because among the first sisters were several noblewomen along with the princess. Clare is really congratulating Agnes on her growth in the knowledge and love of Christ.

> Happy, indeed, is she to whom it is given to share in this sacred banquet so that she might cling with all her heart to Him / Whose beauty all the blessed hosts of heaven unceasingly admire / Whose affection excites / Whose contemplation refreshes, / Whose kindness fulfills, / Whose delight replenishes, / Whose remembrance delightfully shines, / By Whose fragrance the dead are revived, Whose glorious vision will bless all the citizens of the heavenly Jerusalem: which, since it is the splendor of eternal glory, is the brilliance of eternal light and the mirror without blemish.
>
> Gaze upon that mirror each day, O Queen and Spouse of Jesus Christ . . .
>
> Look at the border of this mirror, that is, the poverty of Him Who was placed in a manger and wrapped in swaddling clothes.
>
> O marvelous humility! O astonishing poverty! The King of angels, the Lord of heaven and earth, is laid in a manger!
>
> Then, at the surface of the mirror, consider the holy humility, the blessed

poverty, the untold labors and burdens that He endured for the redemption of the whole human race. Then, in the depth of this same mirror, contemplate the ineffable charity that led Him to suffer on the wood of the Cross and to die there the most shameful kind of death.

Therefore, that Mirror, suspended on the wood of the Cross, urged those who passed by to consider, saying: "All you who pass by the way, look and see if there is any suffering like my suffering!"

Let us respond with one voice, with one spirit.[6]

The Brides of Christ

The Rhineland and the Low Countries would give rise to a school of mystical devotees of Christ, a movement owing much to the bridal mysticism of St. Bernard and his commentaries on the Song of Songs. Lacking the Puritanism of later European culture, the expressions of love on the part of these mystics, both men and women, can be difficult for the modern mind to deal with. Medieval writers had none of the Victorian reticence about human love that has become part of our thinking. Consequently, they accepted the analogues of human love as it relates to divine and spiritual devotion without embarrassment or repressed meaning. The modern mind tends to be either repressive and puritanical or given to pansexualism. In either case, it cannot deal appropriately with analogues used by spiritual writers inspired by the Song of Songs.

The Nuns of Helfta

Four nuns of Helfta, a Saxon convent, were noted spiritual writers who focused on the Heart of Jesus as a symbol of His love for mankind and an emblem of divine mercy.[7] These remarkable women—Mechtild von Magdeburg, St. Mechtildis von Hackeborn, Gertrude von Hackeborn, and St. Gertrude the Great—united a personal devotion to Christ with a strong liturgical piety and became the great lights of northern Europe in the thirteenth century. Mechtild von Magdeburg (1207–1298) wrote a powerful work, *The Flowing Light of the Godhead*, in the form of a dialogue between the soul and its betrothed, Christ. The Lord invites the soul into an eternal embrace of divine mercy. The soul that divests itself of all things will embrace the Lord and experience what the angels cannot receive.[8] While Mechtild may be accused of hyperbole and of being on the edge of theological accuracy, her writing is one of the first examples of what may be called

[6] Fourth letter to Blessed Agnes of Prague in *Clare of Assisi: Early Documents*, ed. and trans. Regis J. Armstrong, O.F.M. Cap. (New York: Paulist Press, 1988), 48–49.

[7] Dom Jean Leclercq et al., *The Spirituality of the Middles Ages*, vol. 2, *A History of Christian Spirituality* (New York: Seabury Press, 1982), chaps. 6, 7.

[8] Ibid., 376.

Wesenmystik, or mysticism of the essence. This approach to spirituality implies that the soul is made in the image of God. The image, however, has become obscured, and the spiritual journey is, in fact, the soul's return to its lost likeness to Him. The means of this transformation are threefold: the grace of Christ, who calls the soul to a total self-stripping; an intuition that becomes clear vision; and a love that eventually becomes undivided possession.[9]

Mysticism of the essence is in some contrast to the more traditional spirituality, or *Brautmystik*, which employed the more obvious Gospel values of commitment to Christ, meditation on the events of His life, and the humble acceptance of His gifts. It is not always easy to distinguish these two emphases, since many great saints and mystics combine both. The mysticism of the essence, or the return to God, has its roots in the Platonism of the early Church Fathers, especially St. Augustine and St. Gregory of Nyssa. The latter Father pictures the soul as stamped with the seal of God's image, which becomes obscured by the remains of sin and imperfection and needs to be cleansed. It seems to me that this is the initial insight of the mysticism of the essence.[10]

It is interesting that *Wesenmystik* has always been characteristic of northern Europe. Some of those who wrote in this vein, like Meister Eckhart, the Dominican whose works were censured after his death, lacked caution. Others, like St. Gertrude, stayed within the tradition of the Church, probably safeguarded by their reliance on the liturgy to guide them in their spiritual experiences.

St. Gertrude the Great

We do not have the luxury of reviewing all of these mystics, but we must look at the devotion of St. Gertrude the Great (ca. 1255–1302), another of the extraordinary quartet of Helfta nuns. Like Mechtild, Gertrude was guided by the liturgy and Scripture to the love of Christ's humanity, embodied in the Heart of Christ. Gertrude wrote her book *The Legate of Divine Love* in hopes that it would lead souls to the love of Christ. Speaking to Christ of these devout souls, she ended the book with this prayer: "May so sweet a fragrance arise to thee from the golden censers of their hearts full of charity, as to make amends abundantly for all the defects of my ingratitude and negligence."[11]

This prayer is characteristic not only of St. Gertrude but of the devotees of the Sacred Heart of Jesus centered around St. Margaret Mary Alacoque in the seventeenth century. The idea that the individual can offer prayers and acts of penance to the Son of God in gratitude and reparation will later become a powerful source of Christian devotion. As one might suspect from this, St. Gertrude was profoundly aware of the Mystical Body of Christ and its real identity

[9] Ibid., 362.

[10] See *From Glory to Glory: Texts from Gregory of Nyssa's Mystical Writings*, trans. and ed. Herbert Musurillo, S.J. (New York: Charles Scribner's Sons, 1961).

[11] Leclercq, *Spirituality of the Middle Ages*, 454.

with the Incarnate Word. She saw Christ suffering and coming to the spiritual rescue of His members who were wounded by sin and weakened by mediocrity.

Hadewijch and the Beguines

Toward the end of the twelfth century, especially in northern Europe, collections of pious women and separate groups of pious men began to live near each other, close to a particular church or chapel, in order to practice the evangelical life. The women were called Beguines, probably because of the color of their robes, which was similar to beige; their clothing was actually made of undyed wool. They did not have vows, but were expected to live in chaste celibacy and to pray together. They accepted the authority of an appointed superior, a coordinator of activities rather than an abbess or prioress. The men—the Beghards—earned their living by manual work, and the women by arts like sewing and caring for the sick.

So undefined were the borders of this movement that it is often difficult to tell who actually belonged. Some identify Blessed Juliana of Mont-Cornillon (d. 1258) as a Beguine. This mystic, apparently an exiled abbess, is most responsible for the establishment of the feast of Corpus Christi in Liège, Belgium, from which it spread to the universal Church.

Since they were not canonical religious, they were often the object of suspicion. In fact, some of the Beguines and Beghards were condemned in 1311 at the Council of Vienne. The year before, Marguerite Porete, a Beguine who was perhaps the author of *The Mirror of Simple Souls*, was burned at the stake in Paris for heresy.[12] Perhaps because of its inherent lack of stability and authority, the movement was variously accused of pantheism, Catharism, quietism, and immorality. Nonetheless, several papal documents spoke favorably of them. In 1321, Pope John XXII claimed that there were two hundred thousand Beguines who remained faithful.

On the positive side, the well-behaved Beguines and Beghards not only followed an evangelical life but were deeply devoted to Christ, to the mystery of the Incarnation, to His childhood, and to the Passion. They carried on widespread work for the poor, ran hospitals and shelters for the infirm, and supported the Crusades.

The Beguines were often dedicated to personal poverty in imitation of the poor Christ. One of the founders of the movement, Marie d'Oignies, wished to live on the roads in rags as a beggar in order to follow Christ. The best known of the Beguines is Hadewijch of Antwerp. Her actual dates are unknown, but she lived in the mid-thirteenth century, not long after Jacques de Vitry had obtained papal approval for the Beguines and Beghards from Pope Honorius III in 1216.[13] Like later mystics of northern Europe, Hadewijch believed

[12] Ibid., 357–78.

[13] Ibid., 354.

that one can come into contact with God only by a love that goes out of itself. Leclercq points out that in Hadewijch's writings theological content is less important than affectivity and religious emotion, which became almost ends in themselves. In the following selection Hadewijch presents Christ as the model we must strive to imitate.

> This is the way on which the Son of God took the lead, and of which he himself gave us knowledge and understanding when he lived as Man. For from the beginning to the end of the time he spent on earth, he did and perfectly accomplished, amid multiplicity, the will of the Father in all things and at all times, with all that he was, and with all the service he could perform (Matt. 20:28), in words and works, in joy and pain, in grandeur and abasement, in miracles, and in the distress of bitter death. With his whole heart and his whole soul, and with all his strength (Deut. 6:5), in each and every circumstance, he was ready to perfect what was wanting on our part. And thus he uplifted us and drew us up by his divine power and his human justice to our first dignity, and to our liberty (Gal. 4:31), in which we were created and loved, and to which we are now called (Gal. 5:13) and chosen in his predestination (Eph. 1:4–5), in which he had foreseen us from all eternity.
>
> That cross which we must bear with the Son of the living God (Matt. 12:38) is the sweet exile that we bear for the sake of veritable Love. . . .
>
> And thus we must always persevere with renewed ardor: with hands ever ready for all works in which virtue is practiced, our will ready for all virtues in which Love is honored, without other intention than to render Love her proper place in man, and in all creatures according to their due. This is to be crucified with Christ (Gal. 2:19), to die with him, and to rise again with him (Col. 3:1). To this end he must always help us; I pray him for this, calling upon his supreme goodness.[14]

An anonymous writer, known as the second Hadewijch, pushed the original dedication to poverty even further. The latter's absolute poverty of spirit and almost Oriental fascination with emptiness are both interesting and dangerous. In seeking the poverty and simplicity of Christ, the author follows a train of thought that risks losing a theological understanding of faith almost entirely. The following poem (XXVI) shows the extremes to which a soul can go to become poor in imitation of Christ.

> Naked love which spares nothing
> In its wild death
> When every accident is left aside
> Finds itself again pure essence.

[14] Letter 6, in *Hadewijch: The Complete Works*, trans. and ed. Mother Columba Hart, O.S.B. (New York: Paulist Press, 1980), 62–63.

In love's pure abandon
No created good can subsist:
For love strips of all form
Those whom it receives in its simplicity.

Freed from every modality,
Alien to every image
Is the life here below
Of the poor in spirit.

All is not found in poverty,
Exile, and all such ways:
The poor in spirit must dwell
Without notions in a vast simplicity,

A simplicity without end, and having no beginning
Neither form, modality, reason, nor object,
Without opinion, or thought, or intention, or learning:
One that is boundless and without any limit.

Here in this wild desert
Dwell in unity the poor in spirit.
Nothing is there for them save freedom in a silence
Ever answering to Eternity.[15]

This strange world of ethereal simplicity contrasts to the personal devotion of St. Clare, St. Gertrude, and the nuns of Helfta, who are all guided by the liturgy, Scripture, and tradition. The humanity and even the Heart of Christ become not only an object of devotion but also the means of rising to spiritual heights by a complete detachment based on love of Christ. With some of the Beguines and Meister Eckhart, devotion to Christ is not rejected but catapulted into a stratosphere where nothing exists in the pure vacuum of eternity. Although such a mystical tradition may be fascinating, sincere, and demanding, it appears to move further and further from the Gospel and the Church. The question posed by the medieval women mystics is, can there be a synthesis of these two themes: a consuming personal love and devotion to Christ on the one hand and the attraction of the depths of eternity on the other? The answer may be found in one of the most remarkable women who ever lived—Catherine of Siena.

St. Catherine of Siena

In a very short life of thirty-three years Catherine of Siena (1347–1380), a laywoman whose single ecclesiastical distinction was that she was a Dominican tertiary or lay affiliate, changed her world and, arguably, ours too. She was such a powerful individual that it is difficult to trace the specific historical influences that shaped her. Although the

[15] Leclercq, *Spirituality of the Middle Ages*, 362–63.

Dominican Order can claim her with legitimate pride, her spirituality was not in the tradition of the mystics of that order in Germany, where there was a flowering of speculative mysticism among nuns directed by the Friars Preachers. And although the friars generously and energetically supported her, Catherine seems to represent the original impulse of St. Dominic to lead the Gospel life totally dedicated to the person of Jesus.

Because of her highly intuitive personality, her passionate devotion to Christ, and her apostolic zeal for the reform of the Church and the conversion of sinners, many writers compare Catherine to St. Francis rather than to the great intellects of the Dominicans.[16] In fact, one of St. Francis' most respected biographers, Johannes Jørgensen, is equally celebrated for his life of St. Catherine.[17] Those unfamiliar with St. Catherine's life should read Jørgensen, as well as one of the excellent studies that have come out more recently as a result of Catherine's being declared, along with St. Teresa of Avila, a Doctor of the Church in 1970.

The Church was at a low ebb during Catherine's life, which coincided with what is called the "Babylonian Captivity" of the papacy. Under the domination of the French kings, seven popes had resided at Avignon in southern France. So great was Catherine's reputation as a mystic and reformer that Pope Gregory XI returned to Rome on January 17, 1377, at her direction. It can be said with some truth that she saved the papacy on the eve of the Great Schism when there were no fewer than three men who simultaneously claimed to be pope.

We know of Catherine's spirituality mostly from her *Dialogue*, written between December 1377 and October 1378. Her letters, which are spontaneous and revealing, are also essential if we are to understand this great woman. Uninterested in abstract theological questions or speculative mysticism, she was concerned with responding to the love that the Holy Trinity showed to the individual soul. She believed she was guided by an interior Master, the Holy Spirit, to whom she gave herself totally and who in mutual love gave Himself back to her. The words of St. Francis to the friars, "Give yourselves totally to Him so that He may give Himself totally back to you", could have been said just as well by Catherine. She saw herself as nothing and heard these words addressed to her mysteriously by Christ: "Know, daughter, that I am he who is, and thou art that which is not."[18] This sounds like the Rhineland mystics, but again it is more like the sentiments of St. Francis.

St. Catherine experienced her Lord very much as a living human being who is a Divine Person: the Incarnate Word who is Jesus of

[16] Ibid., 409.

[17] Johannes Jørgensen, *Saint Catherine of Siena* (New York: Longmans, Green, 1938).

[18] Quoted in Leclercq, *Spirituality in the Middle Ages*, 412.

Nazareth. He visits and speaks to her. Catherine does not generally stress the spousal theme characteristic of St. Bernard. Instead she sees Christ as a personal friend.

For this reason, unlike many other mystics, Catherine is intensely concerned about the spiritual welfare of her neighbor, of the whole Church, and indeed of the whole world. Christ demonstrates His mercy for the world in the Incarnation and His mercy for the Church in the specific call for reform, especially in the hierarchy. While many reformers of this time condemned the papacy and the hierarchy, Catherine of Siena was calling them to personal conversion and reform. In her letters she directly addressed the rather worldly pope as "Dear Christ on Earth", a salutation that must have been disconcerting, to say the least. Catherine believed that she could best serve Christ by bringing sinners back to the state of grace through prayer and holiness of life, and she frequently prayed, "O eternal Father, accept the sacrifice of my life for the mystical body of Holy Church."[19] She called others to prayer, penance, and works of love.

Such a spirit of reform and concern for others could have masked fanaticism, especially in such an intense person, who, according to one of her sympathetic biographers, was capable of being "touchy and unsociable, stubborn and imperious".[20] The important psychological antidote to this possible fanatical streak was Catherine's conviction of the necessity of self-knowledge. She wants to know all she can about God and the things of God, but she also wants to know herself. The clear desire for knowledge and orthodoxy links her with her Dominican roots, and yet her ecstatic quality and reliance on the interior Master, the Holy Spirit, make her resemble St. Francis. She was a truly original personality.

This great woman was a true lover of Christ. Seldom do we find someone who could have fitted so easily into the Gospels and the life of Christ. The following prayer, which expresses St. Catherine's devotion to Christ, leaves no doubt that if she had lived in Jerusalem fourteen centuries earlier, she would have been one of that very small group of women who stood beneath the Cross.

> O eternal Truth
> what is your teaching
> and what is the way
> by which you want us to go to the Father,
> the way by which we must go?
> I know of no other road
> but the one you paved
> with the true and solid virtues

[19] Letter 371 (Feb. 15–16, 1380), quoted in ibid., 414.

[20] R. Fawtier and L. Canet, *La double expérience de Catherine Benincasa* (Paris, 1948), quoted in Leclercq, *Spirituality in the Middle Ages*, 411.

of your charity's fire.
You, eternal Word,
cemented it with your blood,
so this must be the road.

Our sin lies in nothing else
but in loving what you hate
and hating what you love.
I confess, eternal God,
that I have constantly loved what you hate
and hated what you love.
But today I cry out in the presence of your mercy:
grant that I may follow your truth
with a simple heart;
give me the deep well and fire of charity;
give me a continual hunger
to endure pains and torments for you.
Eternal Father,
give my eyes a fountain of tears
with which to draw your mercy down
over all the world,
and especially over your bride.

O boundless, gentlest charity!
This is your garden,
implanted in your blood
and watered with the blood of your martyrs,
who ran bravely after the fragrance of your blood.
You, then, be the one to watch over it.
For who could prevail
over the city you were guarding?
Set our hearts ablaze
and plunge them into this blood
so that we may more surely conceive a hunger
for your honor
and the salvation of souls.

I have sinned against the Lord.
I have sinned!
Have mercy on me![21]

The Other Catherine—St. Catherine of Genoa

The writings, career, and impact of Catherine of Siena have somewhat eclipsed her namesake, who resembled her in a number of ways—St. Catherine of Genoa (1447–1510), who was born exactly a century after the great Sienese mystic, in an even more troubled time of Church history,

[21] *The Prayers of Catherine of Siena*, ed. and trans. Suzanne Noffke (San Jose and New York: Authors Choice Press, 2001), 70–71.

namely, the scandalous pontificate of Alexander VI on the eve of the Reformation.[22] Catherine Fieschi Adorna was very much a mystic in her own right. Although there are many parallels between her teaching and that of St. Catherine of Siena, especially the complete dedication of their lives to Christ and their message of Church reform, there are differences. While both were drawn intuitively to the love of the Holy Trinity and to a personal, burning love of Christ, and while both relied on the Holy Spirit, it was Catherine of Genoa who would have a substantial influence on the Catholic and Protestant reformations.

Except for St. Francis, no Catholic saint ever had more influence with Protestants than Catherine of Genoa because of her profound experience of the guidance of the Holy Spirit, the interior Master. She even speaks of the baptism of the Holy Spirit. She began the first prayer groups, which invited laity and clergy to pray and study the Scriptures together. This movement, still alive today, is called the Oratory of Divine Love. These prayer groups—*oratorios* in Italian—gave rise to the powerful musical form of this name, which employs scriptural themes and was made immortal by Palestrina and Handel.

Catherine was a married woman who converted her wealthy rake of a husband into a devout Franciscan tertiary who tended the sick poor. She became the director of the Pammatone Hospital for the poor, which in her time was the largest such institution in the world. She influenced Catholic reformers, especially Cardinal Giles of Viterbo, who preached and inspired reform among his Augustinian confreres in Germany, including Martin Luther. In his monumental study of Catherine's life and spirituality Baron Friedrich von Hügel traces her influence in such diverse people as St. John of the Cross, St. Francis de Sales, and Luther.[23]

Catherine's great work is *The Purgatory*, a powerful description of the purgation of the soul by divine love both in this world and the next. This remarkable work shows the need for cooperation with divine love in the process of coming to God. When we consider the book's subject matter, it seems astonishing that three hundred years after her death American Protestants of the holiness movement in the nineteenth century would publish six editions of the life of this Catholic mystic, whom they referred to as Madame Adorna. They were deeply impressed by the spiritual heights attained by a laywoman who was an apostle, an angel of mercy to the poor, and the charismatic founder of the first prayer groups.

Catherine of Genoa's personal devotion to Jesus was almost entirely focused on the reception of the Holy Eucharist. She somehow had

---

[22] See *Catherine of Genoa: Purgation and Purgatory, The Spiritual Dialogue*, trans. Serge Hughes, introduction by Benedict J. Groeschel (New York: Paulist Press, 1979). Much of the material on Catherine of Genoa is drawn from this book.

[23] See von Hügel's two-volume work, *The Mystical Element of Religion* (London: James Clarke, 1961).

received permission to receive the Eucharist every day, which was decidedly unusual in her time. There are many quotations concerning her devotion to Christ in the Eucharist in an early *Life* of the saint.[24] Baron von Hügel's work, published in 1908, is a psychological study of Catherine, in which he gives the following description of her devotion, citing passages from the *Life*.

> [T]here is a most characteristic eagerness for interiorization, for turning the Holy Eucharist, perceived without, into the heart's food within; and a corresponding intensity of consciousness and tenderness at the moment of reception. "When she saw the Sacrament on the altar in the hands of the priests, she would say within herself: 'Now swiftly, swiftly convey it to the heart, since it is the heart's true food.' " And "one night she dreamt that she would be unable to communicate during the coming day, and waking up, she found that tears were dropping from her eyes, at which she wondered, since hers was a nature very slow to weep." And "when at Mass, she was often so occupied with her Lord interiorly, as not to hear one word of it; but when the time for Communion arrived, at that instant she would become conscious of exterior things." And she would say: "O Lord, it seems to me, that if I were dead, I should return to life to receive Thee; and that if an unconsecrated host were given to me, I should recognize it to be such by the mere taste alone, as one discerns water from wine."[25]

The Girl Who Called to Jesus

The most popular saint of the troubled period between the Middle Ages and early modern times is clearly the Maid of Orléans, who loved and followed Christ to the loss of her own life. Although she never wrote a word and probably was illiterate, the history of Europe was changed forever after a single year of public life of the girl who believed she had been called by God—Joan of Arc.

Her life is so well known that there is no need to review it here. What is important is that, when she was canonized a saint five hundred years after her death in 1431, the Church recognized neither her mission to save her homeland nor the remarkable spiritual quality of her voices and the victory they procured. Joan was canonized for her unfailing obedience to God and her unshakable trust in His providence when, forsaken by those she had saved, she faced torture and death alone.

It can be said that Joan's canonization hung entirely on the last moments of her life as the smoke rose around the stake in the marketplace of Rouen. Her last prayer enshrined the simple faith of

[24] The earliest biographical document, or *Life*, of St. Catherine is the *Vita e Dottrina*, first published in 1551. It is the work of Cattaneo Marabotto, her confessor, and Ettore Vernazza, one of her spiritual disciples. See von Hügel, *Mystical Element of Religion*, 1:90ff.

[25] Von Hügel, *Mystical Element of Religion*, 1:115.

millions of European peasants over the centuries. Her final words were a repetition of the name of Jesus six times until the flames silenced her earthly voice. Joan had said that her voices called her "Daughter of God". The best that the Church could do after its authority had been so abused at her trial was to proclaim most solemnly that the title of saint was justified in her case beyond all human validation.

The Woman of the New Age: St. Teresa of Avila

Although it is impossible to date precisely the end of the medieval period and the beginning of the Renaissance, there is little argument that St. Teresa of Avila (1515–1582) was among the first great saints of that new age. Her autobiography is the greatest personal spiritual testament in that genre since *The Confessions of St. Augustine*, written more than a thousand years before. Although cloistered, St. Teresa profoundly affected her own time, influenced both secular and religious history, and opened up new horizons for women in the Church. Her writings as well as her life are accepted as a significant part of the treasury of Spanish literature and life. The order she founded, despite its roots in the very ancient tradition of Carmel, was substantially changed by her own experience of God and man. In many ways she stands with Augustine, Basil, Benedict, Dominic, Francis, and Ignatius as the founder of a great tradition of religious life.

Teresa was a reformer and suffered much for her efforts. Despite her holy life, she saw herself as a penitent and a poor sinner entirely dependent on the mercy and love of Christ for salvation. It has been said that hers was the most authentic type of reform because it began with a true reform of herself. Her incredibly precise description of the developmental stages of the spiritual journey and her personal account of the states of advanced contemplation are the aspects of her life that attract the attention of scholars and biographers. Here, however, we focus on her personal devotion to Christ. It is simply extraordinary. For Teresa, Christ is the Lord and King—"His Majesty". He is the Lord of her soul, her glory, Spouse, Bridegroom, and Brother. St. Teresa's prayers reflect her profound conviction that Christ is consubstantial with the Father. For example, in the following prayer she often refers to Christ simply as God, but from the context it is clear that the prayer is to Christ.

> O God of my soul, how we hasten to offend You and how You hasten even more to pardon us! What reason is there, Lord, for such deranged boldness? Could it be that we have already understood Your great mercy and have forgotten that Your justice is just?
>
> *The sorrows of death surround me.* Oh, oh, oh, what a serious thing sin is, for it was enough to kill God with so many sorrows! And how surrounded You are by them, my God! Where can You go that they do not torment You? Everywhere mortals wound You.

> O Christians, it's time to defend your King and to accompany Him in such great solitude. Few are the vassals remaining with Him, and great the multitude accompanying Lucifer. And what's worse is that these latter appear as His friends in public and sell Him in secret. He finds almost no one in whom to trust. O true Friend, how badly they pay You back who betray You! O true Christians, help your God weep, for those compassionate tears are not only for Lazarus but for those who were not going to want to rise, even though His Majesty call them. O my God, how You bear in mind the faults I have committed against You! May they now come to an end, Lord, may they come to an end, and those of everyone. Raise up these dead; may Your cries be so powerful that even though they do not beg life of You, You give it to them so that afterward, my God, they might come forth from the depth of their own delights.[26]

St. Teresa did not intend to begin a work of Church reform, nor did she dream of a work that would spread throughout the world. Her work and prayer for years had been to restore the primitive observance of the rule of her order in imitation of the hermit fathers on Mount Carmel. Her immediate vision was focused on the one monastery of reformed Carmelites she knew she had been called to establish. The spread of her reform came later.

> At about this time[27] there came to my notice the harm and havoc that were being wrought in France by these Lutherans and the way in which their unhappy sect was increasing. This troubled me very much, and as though I could do anything, or be of any help in the matter, I wept before the Lord and entreated Him to remedy this great evil. I felt that I would have laid down a thousand lives to save a single one of all the souls that were being lost there. And . . . as my whole yearning was, and still is, that as He has so many enemies and so few friends, these last should be trusty ones, I determined to do the little that was in me—namely, to follow the evangelical counsels as perfectly as I could and to see that these few nuns who are here should do the same, confiding in the great goodness of God, who never fails to help those who resolve to forsake everything for His sake.[28]

She urged her fellow religious to offer their prayers also for "those who are defenders of the Church", for the "preachers and learned

---

[26] Soliloquy no. 10, in *The Collected Works of St. Teresa of Avila*, vol. 1, 2nd ed., trans. and ed. Kieran Kavanaugh, O.C.D., and Otilio Rodriguez, O.C.D. (Washington, D.C.: ICS Publications, 1987), 452.

[27] At the time of the foundation of the first reformed convent, St. Joseph's in Avila, in 1562.

[28] Teresa of Avila, *Way of Perfection*, trans. E. Allison Peers (New York: Image Books, 1991), 36–37.

men who defend her". Her call was a battle cry of reform: "Oh, my sisters in Christ! Help me to entreat this of the Lord, who has brought you together here for that very purpose. This is your vocation; this must your business; these must be your desires; these your tears; these your petitions.... The world is on fire. Men try to condemn Christ once again, as it were, for they bring a thousand false witnesses against Him. They would raze His Church to the ground."[29]

It is well known that St. Teresa stressed the need to contemplate the humanity of Christ, especially in His passion, and this was born of her own personal experience. For a time, as she was trying to find her way in the life of prayer, she made mistakes and took false turns. When she began to experience the prayer of quiet, she tells us, she turned aside "from everything corporeal ... and no one could have made me return to the humanity of Christ". She later recalled this period with sorrow and felt herself a "dreadful traitor—although in ignorance". Characteristically, St. Teresa, who is so great of heart, always admits her mistakes, as much to humble herself as to warn others not to repeat her errors. She soon recovered a more balanced view in prayer and says: "I had been so devoted all my life to Christ ... and thus I always returned to my custom of rejoicing in this Lord, especially when I received Communion. I wanted to keep ever before my eyes a painting or image of Him since I was unable to keep Him as engraved in my soul as I desired."[30]

In a celebrated passage from her *Life*, the first draft of which was completed in 1562 just before the founding of St. Joseph's, St. Teresa describes Christ, the great Friend:

> Whoever lives in the presence of so good a friend and excellent a leader, who went ahead of us to be the first to suffer, can endure all things. The Lord helps us, strengthens us, and never fails; He is a true friend. And I see clearly, and I saw afterward, that God desires that if we are going to please Him and receive His great favors, we must do so through the most sacred humanity of Christ, in whom He takes His delight. Many, many times I have perceived this truth through experience. The Lord has told it to me. I have definitely seen that we must enter by this gate if we desire His sovereign Majesty to show us great secrets....
>
> This Lord of ours is the one through whom all blessings come to us. He will teach us these things. In beholding His life, we find that He is the best example. What more do we desire than to have such a good friend at our side, who will not abandon us in our labors and tribulations, as friends in the world do? Blessed are they who truly love Him and always keep Him at their side![31]

[29] Ibid., 38.

[30] *The Book of Her Life*, chap. 22, in *Collected Works of St. Teresa of Avila*, 1:192.

[31] Ibid., 194

There are often similarities in the writings of St. Teresa and St. John of the Cross, the first friar of the reform. Here we can detect an echo of her fellow reformer's well-known phrase: "Love is repaid by love alone."

> As often as we think of Christ we should recall the love with which He bestowed on us so many favors and what great love God showed us in giving us a pledge like this of His love, for love begets love. Even if we are at the very beginning and are very wretched, let us strive to keep this divine love always before our eyes and to waken ourselves to love. If at some time the Lord should favor us by impressing this love on our hearts, all will become easy for us, and we shall carry out our tasks quickly and without much effort.[32]

The impact of this most remarkable woman has been recently recognized in a single year's time by the bestowal of the title Doctor of the Church on St. Thérèse of Lisieux, and the canonization of the contemporary martyr of the Holocaust, St. Teresa Benedicta of the Cross (Edith Stein)—both daughters of the Discalced reform.[33] Anyone familiar with the very personal writings of St. Teresa of Avila begins to feel a personal relationship with her. It is easy, therefore, to imagine Teresa rejoicing at the honors bestowed on her spiritual daughters and at the same time telling the Lord that in no way were these triumphs anything that she, poor sinner, had to do with.

---

[32] Ibid., 198.

[33] In 1970, St. Teresa of Avila and St. Catherine of Siena were the first women to receive the title "Doctor of the Church".

PART TWO

CHRIST FROM THE RENAISSANCE TO MODERN TIMES

Introduction

The Christ of the New World

The phrase "the New World" is often used to describe the Western Hemisphere, almost unknown to Europeans until the time of Columbus. Here I am using it with a larger meaning. For our purposes, the phrase refers to a world reborn at the end of the medieval period in Europe. In any real understanding of the processes of history we can see the beginnings of a new age in the climax of the preceding one. St. Francis may have been the most authentic representative of medieval Christianity; yet anyone familiar with Renaissance history realizes that he, the first few generations of Franciscans and Dominicans, and their contemporaries were laying the foundations of the new world that would emerge in Western Europe at the end of the fifteenth century.

Professor Jaroslav Pelikan has explained the ways in which the Renaissance was not initially a revolt against Christ, but rather a fresh way of seeing Him as the divine and human model for mankind in a new world.[1] So creative is Pelikan's analysis and so contradictory to the accepted theory, which considered the Renaissance a revolt against faith and Christianity, that as I read his words, I kept arguing with him in my mind. Standard histories have assumed that the Renaissance was a rejection of and revolt against the faith of the Middle Ages and ultimately a rejection of the Gospel. Pelikan uses Konrad Burdach's well-thought-out contradiction of this accepted wisdom in a very powerful summary: "The Renaissance, which establishes a new concept of humanity, of art, and of literary and scholarly life", arises "not in opposition to the Christian religion but out of the full vitality of a religious revival."[2]

It dawned on me that so much of the art of this period was focused on Christ—from the pre-Renaissance paintings of Giotto in Assisi to the great masters of Rome and Florence, like Michelangelo and Leonardo. It is true, as Pelikan points out, that there was a development of ideas that challenged the relative simplicity of medieval thought, including the way that all Christians perceived Jesus Christ as the true

[1] See *Jesus through the Centuries*, chapter 12, "The Universal Man" (New Haven: Yale University Press, 1985).

[2] Konrad Burdach, quoted in ibid., 146.

God and perfect man. Of course, elements of the Renaissance led to a loss of faith for many; its pride and narcissism are all too obvious. But whether it was Fra Angelico, Raphael, Ignatius Loyola, Thomas More, Erasmus, Luther, Zwingli, or Calvin—all in their own way Renaissance men—they looked to Jesus Christ as the Universal Man and Mirror of the Eternal, to use Pelikan's phrases. A new adventure in faith begins with the rebirth, or Renaissance, of Europe. Our task—and our adventure—is to see how people were devoted to Christ in this age, which has so profoundly affected our own.

A Note to the Reader

As we leave the medieval period, our focus, devotion to Christ, will become more difficult to narrate for several reasons. One is that European history becomes much more complex; more knowledge of the events of this history are known. Also, the number of devotional works grows exponentially with the invention of printing and the spread of literacy. The need to be selective is painfully necessary, especially as we survey the Protestant Reformation and its many different and often conflicting expressions, from the relatively Catholic observances of the Scholastic Luther to the pious anarchy of the early Baptists. Catholicism itself became much more complex as the Jesuits and other new communities came into existence without the customs of the monks and friars. The Catholic Reformation—which actually began with St. Catherine of Genoa and the Oratory of Divine Love three decades before Luther's challenge to the papacy—ironically added an important spiritual dimension to the Protestant Reformation—so did *The Imitation of Christ*, written by a Catholic religious shortly before that time. While all this was going on, the Eastern churches, now separated from the West, continued their growth and development in the face of incredible challenges from the Tartars in the north and from the rest of the Muslim world in the south. After we consider the Reformation and its aftermath, we must pause and catch up on all that was going on in the eastern half of the Christian world.

At several stages I have had to pass over significant developments and interpretations of history, ecclesiology, and faith and simply illustrate how devotion to Jesus flourished. I will be grateful if my readers bear in mind that this is an overview, a flight over the Alps. I hope to point out the great mountain passes and look into the deepest valleys; perhaps some readers will be inclined to explore parts of this great panorama in a more scholarly way. If you feel that I have given short shrift to something important, then for heaven's sake study, read, and perhaps write about that area of the immense drama of Christian devotion. What a magnificent ecumenical project it could be to learn how all our forefathers responded to Jesus' invitation, "Follow me".

I would ask the reader also to bear in mind that I am resolved not to make this a polemical book—a covert attempt to prove the Catholic position and put down Orthodox or Protestant piety and devotion.

As a teenager, I became friends with a Presbyterian minister, Linn Creighton, and his wife, Lois (later also a minister), and since that time I have been deeply impressed by the fact that spread throughout the Christian denominations are many who strive to love Christ as best they can and as they have learned to do. I am aware that many of my biases are unconscious. I confess this freely, since I love the spiritual home God gave me, the Catholic Christian Church.

In seven decades of daily association with my Church, I know very well the problems, shortcomings, and contradictions that occur in any age-old association of human beings. I long for reform in the Catholic Church and have tried to dedicate my efforts to this end. This love for and conviction about the Church, however, does not keep me from appreciating the dedicated love and devotion of other Christians. The last four popes have done precisely this. If you read this book as an Orthodox, Protestant, Lutheran, or Anglican Christian and you feel that you have been misrepresented or slighted, please accept my apology, write a critique, and even ask for a retraction. But do know I have tried to open the discussion of what we all agree on and what we should all daily grow in: our own love of our Savior, Jesus Christ.

The Thrust of Renaissance Devotion

According to many authors, the Renaissance was most deeply affected by the religious experience of St. Francis, although much of its later humanism would have left the seraphic saint very uncomfortable. The Renaissance-style Basilica of St. Mary of the Angels, below Assisi, built over the tiny fieldstone chapel of the Portiuncula, is a powerful symbol of this anomaly. Those familiar with the life of St. Francis can easily imagine him attacking this noble humanist edifice with a sledgehammer.

The devotion of the early Renaissance was focused on the humanity of Christ, who is nonetheless divine. St. Francis' devotion and his idea of the love of Christ in His humanity characterized much of the popular piety of the time. With his unusual insight contradicting the traditional view of the Renaissance, as opposed to the mystical and even the religious, Pelikan sees in the popularity of the devotion of St. Francis a rebirth of Christian humanism, which would color the religious movements of Western Europe for centuries to come.

> The Christ of Francis was not one in whom the presence and power of the divine had anesthetized his human nature so that the pain of the cross left him unaffected. Rather, as the New Testament had said, "we have not a high priest who is unable to sympathize with our weaknesses, but one who in every respect has been tempted as we are, yet without sinning" (Heb 4:15). The experience of Francis as the second Christ, and specifically of his conformity to the cross, served to endow painting and poetry with a new realism, as they struggled to give form to the fundamental conviction that in the suffering and death of Jesus

> on the cross both the mystery of divine life and the mystery of human life had become manifest.[3]

St. Francis' popularity with many Protestants is not simply an admiration of his gentle and prayerful ways or of his love for nature. The devotion of St. Francis and his contemporaries to the human, yet divine, Christ, their compassion for His suffering, and their gratitude for His presence and grace of conversion characterized all Catholic and Protestant devotion in the Reformation. It may annoy Catholics who regularly point to St. Francis' explicit loyalty to the Church and to the Pope to be reminded that he has deeply influenced the prayer life of Protestants, but this cannot be denied. When I started to preach in Protestant churches back in the 1960s, I became aware not only that we prayed to the same Savior but that we often prayed to Him in much the same way.

Setting the Stage for the Devotion of the Reformation

Although the expression of devotion to Christ in the late sixteenth century was more or less distinct on the part of Catholics on the one hand and the various Protestant movements on the other, there were at the beginning of the Reformation obviously common roots. These roots were to be found not only in the biblical piety of the high Middle Ages expressed by the Franciscan vision, but also in two other influences shared by almost all Christians of the time: a return to ancient sources and the *devotio moderna*, or the new way of devotion. To understand the piety of the Protestant and Catholic reformations, it is important to grasp these two influences.

Ad Fontes

The Latin phrase *ad fontes*, meaning "to the sources", was the intellectual battle cry of the Renaissance with its partial rejection of the medieval world. The medieval mind took for granted that its speculations on Scripture, tradition, and what had been preserved of classical antiquity by the monks of the Dark Ages were simply the next step in human development—in other words, progress. Later the Scholastic theologians like St. Thomas Aquinas assumed that they were making progress in a straight line, basing their writings on Scripture, tradition, and the ancient philosophers, some of whose works had recently been discovered. In the thirteenth century it was thought that there had been very little human development or change between the collapse of the Western empire during the patristic age and the beginning of Scholasticism in the eleventh and twelfth centuries. The Scholastics tried to patch together the broken fabric of civilization where they found it. Later the Church, the repository and guardian of all learning, implicitly assumed that all the initial medieval assumptions about early Christian times and pagan antiquity were simply true.

[3] Pelikan, *Jesus through the Ages*, 140.

There are countless examples of these assumptions, which were made because no one had any reason to question them at the time. A little vignette may be helpful. The Cathedral of Pavia, a city established by the barbarian king Odoacer in the fifth century (see Chapter 6), contains an altar obviously from a much later period celebrating the fact that the first Christian bishop of this city was St. Cyrus. This legend, enshrined in Renaissance-style marble reliefs, shows Cyrus as a child giving the loaves and fishes to Christ at the miraculous multiplication in the Gospel. Cyrus is also shown later being ordained bishop by St. Peter, wearing a tiara and full pontifical regalia. It would not have occurred to people at that time to question the validity of this legend. They even missed the fact that five centuries had elapsed between Christ's multiplying the loaves and fish of the little boy and the ordination of Bishop Cyrus.

The men of the Renaissance confronted with such a myth would shout, "Back to the sources—*ad fontes.*" The study of Scripture and the Fathers, as well as classical writers, became the highest priority. Especially in the case of Scripture, this study was essential to the spirit of the Protestant Reformation. However, the Catholics were not to be left out. For a thousand years people had understood the Scriptures in Latin in the excellent fifth-century edition of St. Jerome. Now vernacular translations were demanded, based on the original Hebrew and Greek. The demand was felt not only by Protestants but also by Catholics. It will surprise many that the Catholic English Bible, the Douay-Rheims edition, preceded by a number of years the King James translation. Nonetheless, Martin Luther's translation was not only a great literary accomplishment but also the very symbol of the desire to return to the original sources.

Devotio Moderna

The *devotio moderna*—the new or modern devotion—was a move away from the highly liturgical and scriptural piety of the first twelve hundred years of the Church. Whereas in the past people had prayed together, they now sought to pray alone, in meditation or spiritual exercises. Personal needs, concerns, and affections were increasingly expressed in one's own words. In many respects this trend merely continued the ongoing personalism of the high Middle Ages. The roots of *devotio moderna* can be found in St. Bernard's tender affection and in St. Francis' deep love for Jesus Crucified. Later we shall see how this devotion is related directly to Christ the God-Man, who knows the individual and seeks Him with tender love. Scripture and tradition are not abandoned, but they are no longer the sole expression of piety.

An illustration of how the *devotio moderna* changed things can be found by considering the Office of the Passion written by St. Francis. Based almost entirely on psalms and antiphons, this Office rather startlingly does not express his tender devotion. In the thirteenth century, however, the best way to express this devotion was in the liturgical form of an Office, that is, psalms with antiphons. Later *The Imitation of Christ*, the epitome of the *devotio moderna*, would use phrases one can imagine St. Francis saying but which, in fact, he never uttered.

As their principal book indicates, the goal of the followers of the "new devotion" (sometimes called the New Devout) was the imitation of Christ. Although not apparently written by a member of the New Devout, *The Imitation* was the guidebook of a movement that became the Brothers and Sisters of the Common Life. In the enlightening introduction to his translation of *Devotio Moderna: Basic Writings*, John Van Engen makes the following observation pertaining specifically to devotion.

> The person of Jesus Christ stood central to this New Devotion. Here the brothers and sisters inherited a tradition derived ultimately from the Cistercians and Franciscans, which by the Late Middle Ages had spread across nearly all orders and levels of Western Christendom.... "Imitation" is probably a misleading term for their outlook. Their emphasis fell neither on imitation in a strict sense, as in works of mercy, nor on "mystic union," as in the teachings of many late medieval authors, but rather on an individual and affective identification with particular moments in Christ's life, chiefly his passion, the result or purpose of which was ideally fourfold: to "relive" with Christ his virtuous life and saving passion, to have him ever present before one's eyes, to manifest his presence to others, and to orchestrate, as it were, all of one's mental and emotional faculties around devotion to him. This emphasis was entirely positive: to have the New Devout live in Christ and Christ in them. There was no proto-Protestant repudiation of Mary or the saints, whose model and intercession were taken entirely for granted and also mentioned. Yet this focus on the person of Jesus Christ was so total, as the works translated here should make abundantly clear, that there was in effect, if not necessarily in conscious intention, something of a shift toward a more exclusively Christocentric form of piety.
>
> To focus on the life and passion of Christ was to read the Gospel and the writings that explained and ordered it. The contemplative reading of holy writings, especially Holy Scripture, was prescribed for all brothers and sisters, who were expected additionally to make up a kind of "notebook" (*rapiaria*) of those passages they found most compelling. Here too the New Devout stood heirs to a long monastic tradition, best exemplified in early medieval *florilegia*, now effectively extended to those outside the orders. Scripture plainly received special emphasis: Brothers and sisters were expected to read it daily in their own rooms, while the formal theology of the schools went almost entirely unread. Consistent with this emphasis was a concern to make

> Scripture available in the vernacular as well, a right stoutly defended on behalf of sisters and lay brothers.[4]

It is important to point out that the New Devotion preceded the Reformation by a century. The notion that focusing on the vernacular Scriptures was a new idea of Luther's is historically inaccurate. The following passage from a manual of devotion for the Sisters and Brothers of the Common Life makes this very clear. The instructions given here were written in the early 1400s, as was *The Imitation of Christ*.[5] *The Imitation* was popular in translation as far away as Italy by the first half of the fifteenth century, and at least the third book was most likely written by Thomas à Kempis (1379–1471), a Canon Regular of St. Augustine.

The instruction on "knowing Christ", or meditations, reveals a Christocentric piety of great intensity. This was the devotion that moved people so powerfully in the dark century before the Reformation. The writing is an instruction by Gerard Zerbolt of the Brothers of the Common Life.

> When you read that Christ suffered some punishment or mockery, do not think of it as just any man bearing it but as something unspeakably beyond every other man. And you ought diligently to gather its causes into your heart, for they are great stimulants to compassion. Knowing how much someone can be tortured and afflicted by a certain punishment, you must consider how much more he felt it as something unfitting. Moreover, the more lively the sensibility of a man, the more he will suffer from a punishment and in turn be tortured by his sensitivity. But Christ's was the most lively and nobly dignified of all natures, and therefore suffered those punishments more than any other. See if there is any sorrow like unto his sorrow. Think therefore how intolerable for you or some other tender person would be some punishment such as having the head punctured with spines, the whole body brutally whipped, and so on, and how much more awful that punishment was for Jesus Christ, man and god, with his noble and delicate nature.
>
> Second, Christ suffered as much as he willed. For according to the evangelist Jesus undid himself, not the passion. He was likewise offered up because he so willed. He undertook his passion for the satisfaction of original sin, which had despoiled the whole human race of its original righteousness, infecting human nature and spoiling its eternal bliss. He also took on the passion and death so that he would be the sufficient sacrifice for all men, and because the works of God are perfect it seems that Christ assumed the most bitter of all deaths. . . .

[4] *Devotio Moderna: Basic Writings*, trans. John Van Engen (New York: Paulist Press, 1988), 25–26.

[5] Ibid., 8–9.

> Indeed the doctors say that his death was the most bitter and aggravated, exceeding the grief of all men ever to have suffered death since the beginning of the world.
>
> Third, it increased Christ's grief no little that he suffered this passion at the hands of people upon whom he had conferred so many benefits, to whom he could rightly say: "You are my people because I am your God; what could I have done for you that I have not done?" But how could you have repaid me worse than to have inflicted such a death? . . .
>
> [A]pply Christ's passion usefully and fruitfully to yourself, in imitation of his virtues and in flight from the vices. To this end you must direct your whole intellect and affections toward sensing how Christ conducted himself inwardly and outwardly in all his deeds, words, and responses as recorded in the text of the Gospel, that is, how he acted inwardly and outwardly in different places and times, as well as the Jews, Pilate and Herod, his mother Mary and Mary Magdalene, and so on. This way you will find in his passion a plenitude of every virtue and the best medicine against every vice. . . .
>
> [F]uel your mind from the bitter passion of the Lord's passion with a rich devotion and so enkindle your affections to love. Think that you, dear man, were the cause of so much grief, so much bitterness. Seize then upon this benefit: Think of Christ as dying for you alone. Thence will arise gratitude, for he suffered to effect your illumination, redemption, justification, and glorification.[6]

Modern people may be unprepared to examine closely the depth of feeling that accompanied the *devotio moderna*. The following passage from *The Imitation of Christ* reveals the love, the loyalty, and the trust that these people had in Christ and felt they could express to others.

> Gladden, then, this day the soul of Your servant because I have raised my heart to You, O Lord Jesus. I long to receive You now, devoutly and reverently. I desire to bring You into my house that, with Zacheus, I may merit Your blessing and be numbered among the children of Abraham.
>
> My soul longs for Your Body; my heart desires to be united with You. Give me Yourself—it is enough; for without You there is no consolation. Without You I cannot exist, without Your visitation I cannot live. I must often come to You, therefore, and receive the strength of my salvation lest, deprived of this heavenly food, I grow weak on the way. Once, most merciful Jesus, while preaching to the people and healing their many ills, You said: "I will not send them away fasting, lest they faint in the way." Deal with me likewise, You Who have left Yourself in this Sacrament for the consolation of the

[6] Gerard Zerbolt, *The Spiritual Ascents*, in *Devotio Moderna*, 282–84.

faithful. You are sweet refreshment to the soul, and he who eats You worthily will be a sharer in, and an heir to, eternal glory.[7]

The First Protestants

The linking of church and state, a model as old and universal as civilization itself, began to come under great pressure as townspeople who were not part of the religiously mandated nobility began to gain power and influence. Modern people cannot be expected fully to realize that secular rulers in ancient times were regarded as having a sacred trust from God; their installations often included many sacramental signs. Monarchs were anointed with sacred chrism, and bishops blessed newly ascended dukes and princes. We retain a remnant of this in the United States: the swearing-in of public officials is often done with a Bible.

The alliance of religion and civil government in the West had often been under great tension because of the theological and practical independence of the papacy. The Church alone could call a king or emperor to task and even impose severe spiritual sanctions if he was a tyrant or if he betrayed the Church. Sometimes the nobles and the Church made common cause, as when Stephen Cardinal Langton wrote the Magna Carta and the English barons forced King John to sign it. Still, many times there were abuses, and the common people rebelled, as in the Peasants' Revolt of 1381 in England. Their rising was against not the lords secular alone but also against the lords religious—the bishops and abbots of large monasteries, which had huge landholdings and many employees.

The thirteenth-century movement toward leading a Gospel life, which was exemplified by St. Francis and a number of religious, also, as we have seen, included many like Peter Waldo (see pp. 104–5 above), who were at odds with the Church. Inevitably, in the great turmoil of the fourteenth century, these movements would find many devout adherents who had lost faith in the bishops and in the clergy.

Later on, when the Anabaptists emerged in Germany, Austria, and the Low Countries, one of the most important contentions was that civil society and the Church were corrupt. When one recalls all that had happened in the thirteenth and fourteenth centuries, there is much to be said for this judgment. The close affiliation of Luther with the German princes and the largely successful attempts of Zwingli and Calvin to create a Christian republic were despised by the Anabaptists. The latter were simply against the government; although, paradoxically, they became involved in a disastrous attempt to set up a theocratic state at Münster themselves under a wild, charismatic figure named Thomas Müntzer. No doubt some of the brutality of the persecution of these simple folk was motivated by the idea that they were traitors

[7] Thomas à Kempis, *The Imitation of Christ*, bk. 4, chap. 3 (Milwaukee: Bruce, 1940), 221. (Many editions and translations have been published.)

to the state. The same explains the brutality of the treatment of both Catholics and then the first members of the Church of England under successive Tudor monarchs.

The first Protestants saw the Church as made up only of the very seriously committed. In his preface to *Early Anabaptist Spirituality*, Hans J. Hillerbrand says:

> Anabaptism emerged as a conscious and explicit challenge to the understanding of Christianity, and therefore of reform, on the part of the reformers, notably Martin Luther and Huldrych Zwingli. The charge was that these reformers had not fully returned the church to its apostolic origins and faith; too much popery had remained, and it was only among the Anabaptists that the true apostolic faith was restored. The Anabaptists charged that the mainstream reformers were thieves and murderers, shepherds who led their sheep astray, wolves who attacked the flock. . . .
>
> The bill of particulars against Zwingli and Luther (no less than against the Catholic Church) was the important point of departure for Anabaptist spirituality: the Christian faith was utterly serious business. Thus the first (and perhaps foremost) characteristic of the Anabaptist understanding of the Christian faith lies in the categorical opposition to the notion that the civic community and the Christian church were identical and that all people were in fact "Christians". . . .
>
> To the reformers' rejoinder that they, too, saw the Christian faith as serious, the Anabaptists responded that there was no visible evidence among them to substantiate their contention.[8]

Despite their rejection of the government of the Church and their even more strenuous rejection of civil authority, the Anabaptists preserved some Catholic forms of devotion to Jesus. The following poem from Michael Sattler, an early Anabaptist, could have been written by a Franciscan, Dominican, or Augustinian friar.

As Jesus with his true teaching
Gathered to himself a small flock
He told them that each with patience
Should daily carry his cross

And he said, You my beloved disciples
You should always be glad
On earth love nothing else
Than me and following my teaching

The world will persecute you
And mock and scorn you

[8] *Early Anabaptist Spirituality: Selected Writings* (New York: Paulist Press, 1994), xix.

Hunt you and publicly say
You have Satan in you . . .

Look to me, I am God's son
And have always done well
I am the best of all
But was killed anyway . . .

O Christ, help your people
Who follow you truly
So that through your bitter death
They will be saved from all need[9]

In *A Distant Mirror*,[10] her historical review of the fourteenth century, Barbara Tuchman has reminded us that this time, which brought on the problems of the Reformation, was one of chaos and cruelty. The Black Death had the effect of an atomic war, carrying off one-third of the population and, in percentages, much larger numbers of clergy and religious. However, Tuchman fails to give credit where it is due and does not mention that the clergy and religious died in such great numbers because they cared for the dying. The Franciscan province of Paris, founded by St. Bonaventure, is said to have been wiped out to the last man. The Church, especially the papacy, fell under the domination of kings, and even such prophetic figures as St. Catherine of Siena, St. Vincent Ferrer, St. Bernardine of Siena, and Savonarola could not stem the tide and make a lasting reform.

Many others also worked and prayed for reform, including the sophisticated Erasmus and Thomas More, the ecstatic laywoman St. Catherine of Genoa, and Cardinal Giles of Viterbo, a former general of the Augustinians. Despite voices raised here and there—many of them impressive—there was no serious movement toward reform on the part of the papacy or the bishops. The storm that threatened the unity of Christendom continued to gather momentum.

[9] Michael Sattler, Song no.7, cited in *Early Anabaptist Spirituality*, 54–55.
[10] New York: Knopf, 1978.

10 The Devotion of the First Protestants

The Anabaptists

Throughout Europe, especially in German-speaking areas, devout souls believed they were led to make the most radical break possible with the Church. The Anabaptists, so-called because they insisted that their new members be rebaptized, sought to return to the early Church as they imagined it—without liturgy, sacraments, clergy, or places of worship. Anabaptists paid scant attention to the early Fathers or even to the Church as it is seen in the pastoral epistles. Instead, they sought an ideal church made up solely of those sanctified by the grace of Christ. The following poetic passage was written by Peter Rideman, a member of an Anabaptist community called the Hutterites, in 1540.

> The Church of Christ is the basis and ground of truth, a lantern of righteousness, in which the light of grace is borne and held before the whole world, that its darkness, unbelief and blindness be thereby seen and made light, and that men may also learn to see and know the way of life. Therefore is the Church of Christ in the first place completely filled with the light of Christ as a lantern is illuminated and made bright by the light: that his light might shine through her to others.
>
> And as the lantern of Christ hath been made light, bright and clear, enlightened by the light of the knowledge of God, its brightness and light shineth out into the distance to give light to others still walking in darkness ... Which thing, however, cannot be other than through the strength and working of the Spirit of Christ within us.[1]

Totally unliturgical, the worship of the Anabaptists was a gathering of the devout, who were served by brothers who ministered to them, instructed, and encouraged them in the word of God. Interestingly, in addition to baptism, a kind of communion was held weekly; it involved, however, few recognizable ceremonies and did not acknowledge the Eucharist's sacramental nature.[2]

---

[1] From Peter Rideman, *Confession of Faith: Account of Our Religion, Doctrine and Faith* (Rifton, N.Y.: Plough Publishing House, 1970), 39–40.

[2] *Mennonite Encyclopedia* (unpublished ms.), s.v. "Worship, Public Anabaptist".

The following prayer of Hans Schlaffer, an Anabaptist executed in 1528, could have been written by a Catholic under Henry VIII. It is important to notice that the ideas of total dedication, complete trust in God, the damage caused by original sin, and the power of grace to strengthen us are fully consistent with the very medieval piety that the early Anabaptists thought they had rejected.

> Almighty God! I want to accept the cup of salvation and call upon your Name. Yes, I want to give you a voluntary sacrifice and confess your Name. I will pay my debt to you before all people, and those who fear you will see that I have hoped in your Word.
>
> Therefore, Almighty God, reveal your strength and great power in my weak earthly vessel, in which you have laid and hidden the noble treasure that you showed me. Let the price of everything you have given me be my weak body and miserable life, for I have nothing more. O my God! What need and blows I am suffering here! In this I begin to recognize the fall of Adam and how it has damaged me. In this the fight between flesh and spirit begins, which nobody can discover unless he experiences it. O my God, how will it continue?
>
> But now, Lord, I lay all my anxiety, need, and fear on you. I have felt your help powerfully until now. You will never take it from me to the end but in my great need and weakness you will show your greatest help and strength to me, in my shame and disgrace you will proclaim your glory, and in my temporal death you will reveal eternal life to all who in Christ's faith surrender to you and endure to the end in your will. Come, O beloved Father, Come![3]

Perhaps the most interesting element of the early prayers of the Anabaptists and the Hutterites, (who lived in communal villages sharing work, prayer, and meals) is the concept of spousal love between the individual and Christ. You will recall that this trend in Christian piety owes its development to St. Bernard of Clairvaux. This kind of spousal piety was common in the Middle Ages; it is not, however, associated with early Protestantism, nor is it generally part of Protestant thinking today. The following prayer of Hans Denck (c. 1500–1527) reminds us very much of St. Bernard.

> Love is a spiritual power by which one is united or longs to be united with another. Where love is perfect, the lover does not hold apart from the beloved, but forgets himself as if he no longer existed, and takes no heed of pain, which he suffers for the sake of the one he loves. Yes, the lover is not satisfied with what he has done until he has proved to the utmost, and in every danger, the love he bears to his beloved, and where it is possible (as it is possible) that this would be for the good of the one he loves, he would freely and joyfully

[3] From a handwritten Hutterian codex.

> surrender himself in death for his beloved. . . . The less the loved one recognizes the love that the lover bears him, the more pain is felt by the lover, and yet he cannot desert love, but must prove it to the utmost, even though no one were ever to recognize it.[4]

The early Anabaptists suffered cruelly at the hands of both Catholics and Protestants, and their devotion was colored by this constant persecution. The following selection is from a German Hutterite prayer, "Dialogue between Jesus and the Soul", preserved originally in handwritten form and then in translation. In this cherished part of the Hutterites' spiritual literature, the anonymous writer shares his sentiments with Christ in His Passion.

> Soul: Whither wilt thou go, dearest Lord Jesu? My mind is made up to stand constantly by thee. Therefore will I follow thee gladly withersoever thou goest, and never forsake thee.
>
> Jesus: Oh, dear soul, this time thou canst not follow me. For a while we must part. Yet thou wilt follow me from afar and, weeping, behold what cometh upon me.
>
> Soul: I am ready to suffer imprisonment with thee, to die with thee or to fight with thee, therefore with courage and joy I shall go with thee. Though I fare as thou, I can do naught else.
>
> Jesus: Unto death is my soul troubled. O sinners, sinners, what have ye done! The cruel wrath of God threateneth and terrifieth me. The jaws of hell are opened to swallow me.
>
> Soul: Now I have known for the first time what cometh from sinning against God. My Jesus, now that I have seen thy suffering, I shall all the more jealously shun evil.[5]

In their attitudes toward the nature of the Church and liturgy and their relationships to the civil government, the early Anabaptists and the Catholics (and indeed the Lutherans and Calvinists) could not have been further apart. Anabaptists represented the most radical departure from the Catholic Church possible. Yet Anabaptist piety owed much to the devotion of the medieval Church. This devotional continuity between deeply divided groups arose, not only because they had common sources in ancient and medieval spirituality but because the Anabaptists had learned to pray and be devoted to Jesus Christ from their Catholic parents and grandparents.

The Common Bond

It is essential to keep in mind the common roots of Christian devotion and its common history of fifteen hundred years. It is also vital to remember that the Christ to whom all the increasingly diverse and

[4] Unpublished translation of "*Von der wahren Liebe*", trans. Eberhard Arnold (Hutterite Community).

[5] From a copy of a handwritten English text of the prayer.

divided Christian groups prayed is a real person dwelling in eternal glory at the right hand of God (Acts 2) and that He responds in a real but intangible way to all who call on Him. Not only were all these Christians devoted to the same Jesus Christ, but He was devoted to them. Although His love for individual souls is often overlooked, it is the most important fact in all of Christian history. He loves us all even when we all go astray.

Luther and His Beloved Savior

Martin Luther inspires a strong reaction. Although not the founder of the Reformation—several men before him could claim that title—he is certainly its father. He strongly objected to anyone's use of his name as a designation, and yet today tens of millions of people call themselves Lutherans.[6] Contrary to popular belief, he did not walk directly out of the Catholic Church or the Augustinian Order on that fateful day in 1517 when, following a traditional custom for academic disputations, he posted his Ninety-Five Theses. The next year he freely explained his position to the papal legate, Cardinal Cajetan, in Augsburg and continued a dialogue with the Catholic authorities for two more years until his excommunication in 1520. As late as 1531, ten years after the civil recognition of the Protestant Confession (Diet of Augsburg), a compromise agreement on terminology was worked out between Luther's followers and Catholic authorities. It was, however, rejected by Rome because the Pope saw it as an agreement of words rather than belief. Unlike the beginnings of the Anabaptists, Luther's break was neither a sudden nor absolute rejection of the old faith. He maintained much of Catholic liturgy, including commemorations of the Blessed Virgin and the saints. Compared to his contemporaries Andreas Carlstadt, Huldrych Zwingli, and John Calvin, Luther is very Catholic, and many Lutherans to this day prefer not to be called Protestants.

Catholics are often aware of only the extreme abuses and scandals Luther denounced, while Protestants fail to recognize that Luther himself was only one of a number of Catholic priests and religious working for the reform of the Church at that time. A shining example is that of Fr. Johann Staupitz, Luther's own Augustinian superior and spiritual guide. Luther and Staupitz belonged to an order within an order—the Reformist Augustinians, of which Staupitz was vicar general, or representative of the general of the Augustinian Order.

It is important for Catholics to realize that Luther was a man of enormous talent and indefatigable zeal for the Gospel message as he understood it. The definitive edition of his works (books, articles, and sermons), *Weimarer Ausgabe*, contains one hundred large volumes.[7] Beyond that he wrote more than twenty-five hundred existing letters

---

[6] Marc Lienhard, "Luther and the Beginnings of the Reformation", in *Christian Spirituality: High Middle Ages and Reformation*, ed. Jill Raitt (New York: Crossroad, 1988), 272.

[7] James Atkinson, ed., *The Darkness of Faith: Daily Readings with Martin Luther* (London: Darton, Longman and Todd, 1987), 63.

of spiritual counsel, along with thirty-six hymns, some of which are sung today in Catholic churches. His translation of the New Testament was completed a few months after he left the Augustinian Order, and his translation of the Old Testament was published some years later. They are considered masterpieces and among the foundations of the modern German language.

Martin Luther was deeply devoted to Christ as His Savior and Redeemer. His devotion grew out of a conviction that corrupt human nature absolutely needs to be saved. This was by no means a new concept or emphasis in Christianity. The idea is at least as old as St. Paul, and in the West it had been powerfully clarified by St. Augustine and his allies in the fifth-century conflict with Pelagius. But as the contemporary Lutheran theologian Marc Lienhard points out, Luther went far beyond St. Augustine—in fact further than any recognized Christian theologian before him. Lienhard writes:

> The bishop of Hippo found nothing in himself after his conversion but a remnant of the weakness of the flesh. Luther, on the contrary, situated sin as a permanent reality in the will itself, in the tendency of human beings to affirm themselves over against God. But it was in Augustine that Luther discovered a hymn to the omnipotence of grace. Salvation was conceived entirely as the work of the grace of God. The virtue of pagans was denied as well as the ability of sinners to prepare themselves for grace and to acquire any merit whatsoever. But there again, a difference appears: for Augustine, grace was a gift of God, a reality infused in persons which conferred on them qualities and new strengths; for Luther, grace was an attitude of God and not an objective quality susceptible of being detached from God.[8]

While I disagree with Lienhard's analysis of St. Augustine's view of the permanent effects of original sin, I agree with his view that Luther saw the effects of original sin in a totally different way. Actually Augustine saw the lasting effects of original sin as the darkening of the intelligence, the weakening of the will, and the casting of the emotions into disorder, which leads to the disruption of the social order. Augustine would not have limited the effects merely to a weakness of the flesh.

The earlier Catholic Scholastic theologians whom Luther rejected—Aquinas, Bonaventure, and Albert—along with the later ones, like William of Ockham and Gabriel Biel, in no way disagreed with Luther on the reality of original sin. Their position on the nature of grace, however, which followed St. Augustine and the Church Fathers, was very different from Luther's. In Catholic belief grace is not simply a redemption imputed to the fallen creature by God's mercy, but rather

[8] Lienhard, "Luther and the Beginnings", 271.

a transforming change taking place in the person's being, worked by the divine mercy through the salvation won by Jesus Christ.

The debate over grace, which in recent years has become a fruitful dialogue, gives us a way of appreciating Luther's unique devotion to Christ arising from his theology of grace. As with St. Augustine and St. Bonaventure, Luther's theology was rooted in personal experience. While still an Augustinian and a Catholic professor, he wrote, "Learn to know Christ and Christ crucified; learn to sing his praise, to despair of yourself and to say: You, Lord Jesus, you are my justice, but I, I am your sins; you have assumed that which is mine, and you have given me that which is yours.... In effect, Christ lives only with sinners.... Think of this great love and you will see there the sweetest consolations. In effect, if it is possible to come to a quiet conscience by our efforts and our trials, why, then, did Christ die?"[9]

As we have seen, there was a powerful movement at this time for the direct use of the Bible. Anyone informed about medieval piety and theology from Bernard and Francis to Thomas Aquinas and Duns Scotus will realize that the Scriptures were the fountain of all they did and taught. But as the various modern languages developed and the popular knowledge of Latin declined, the Scriptures became more and more mediated to the people—passed on by sermons, art work, religious plays, and so on. The movement we have already spoken about, *ad fontes*, was already strong when Luther was a friar, and it was in his new role as a reformer that it became even more pronounced. The following passage beautifully illustrates Luther's devotion to Christ and his love of the Bible.

> The whole of Scripture deals with Christ, from beginning to end. Every word of the Bible peals "CHRIST". Its whole concern is Christ.
>
> Because Christ was born a man for our sake, and was sent by God to redeem us from sin and death, he must needs step into our place and become a sacrifice for us. He himself had to bear, and render satisfaction for, the wrath and the curse into which we had fallen and under which we lay.
>
> You may ask, "What then does it mean to know Christ?" Or, "What benefits does he bring us?" The answer is that you begin to learn to know Christ when you begin to understand the words of St. Paul in 1 Corinthians 1:30: thanks to God you have your existence in Christ Jesus. God is the source of your life in Christ Jesus, whom God made your wisdom, righteousness and sanctification and redemption.[10]

We have already seen that finding Christ present in one's own life was part of the vision of St. Francis: the medieval Christmas crib, the

[9] Ibid., 270–71.

[10] Atkinson, *Darkness of Faith*, 9.

wayside Crucifix, the devotion to Christ present in the Eucharist all shout, "Emmanuel, Christ is with us."

The disciples of Luther clearly saw this and left us with a splendid artistic legacy. Albrecht Dürer's hauntingly beautiful etchings and drawings and the powerful Cranach paintings bring together the medieval vision of Christ's humanity as seen a century before by Blessed Angelico. They also present Luther's vision of Christ saving a totally corrupt world.

Professor Pelikan, himself a Lutheran pastor at the time of his writing *Jesus through the Centuries*, insightfully stresses that Christ as the Mirror of the Eternal was the key metaphor of Reformation thought.[11] The glass mirror had become an important symbol and was often depicted in paintings of the time. The concept of Christ as the image of the Father goes back to the New Testament and the earliest Fathers of the Church. Speaking of the Reformation, Pelikan says:

> [T]he Reformers ... would all have agreed in principle with what we have seen to be the universal Christian consensus that Jesus, as Mirror of the Eternal, was the revelation of the True, the Beautiful and the Good.... Yet it was only on his significance as Mirror of the True that they would have found substantial agreement: Christ was the true revelation of what Luther called "the hidden God [Deus absconditus]," and the source of divine Truth as this had been set down in the Scriptures. Calvin was no less persuaded than Luther that for the true knowledge of God it was necessary to look to the revelation that had come in Jesus, the Mirror of the True.[12]

It is interesting to note that Catholics had also used the image of Christ as the Mirror of God. The constitutions of the Capuchin reform of the Franciscan Order in 1536 invoke Christ as "God and Man, the True Light, the Brightness of Glory and of Eternal Light, the Spotless Mirror and Image of God".[13]

Luther lived when rationalism, the naïve belief that the human mind can comprehend all things, was taking hold. Although he was no rationalist, relying on revelation to lead him to the truth, which was to be found in Christ, he unwittingly joined the rationalists by denying the importance of mystery. This denial would later give rise in Protestantism to two opposing camps—rationalism and fundamentalism, both of which tend to deny or disengage the concept of mystery. In defense of Luther it must be said that the Scholastic philosophy of his time tended toward a kind of rationalism. Although Luther denounced William of

[11] Jaroslav Pelikan, *Jesus through the Centuries* (New Haven: Yale University Press, 1985), 158.

[12] Ibid., 158–59.

[13] *The Capuchin Constitutions of 1536*, chap. 12, no. 152, quoted in John C. Olin, *The Catholic Reformation: Savonarola to Ignatius Loyola* (New York: Fordham University Press, 1992), 181.

Ockham, the popular Scholastic nominalist of the late Middle Ages, he "remained in some way a debtor to Ockhamism", as Lienhard says.[14]

The following quotation from a sermon well illustrates Luther's impatience with philosophy and his conviction that the appeal of faith is the only way to be a true Christian.

> God is invisible, inscrutable, incomprehensible, and so on.... Give up all such speculating, which is utterly unrelated to the word of God anyhow. God is saying to you, From the unrevealed God I shall become your own revealed God: I shall incarnate my own beloved Son.... "This is my beloved Son. Hear you him." Behold his death, his cross, his passion. See him hanging on his mother's breast, and hanging on the cross. What Christ says and does, you may be sure of. "No man cometh to the Father but by me." "He that hath seen me hath seen the Father." What God is saying to you is this: "Here in Christ you have me, here in Christ you will see me."
>
> If you want to escape from despair and hatred of God, let speculation go. Begin with God *from the bottom upwards, not from the top downwards*. In other words, begin with Christ incarnate, and with your own terrible original sin. There is no other way. Otherwise, you will remain a doubter for the rest of your life.
>
> At all costs cling to the revealed God. Allow no one to take the child Jesus from you. Hold fast to Christ, and you will never be lost.[15]

It is puzzling that Luther, who so loved Augustine, would have taken this stand against mystery and the philosophical preludes to faith. Any reading of the latter books of Augustine's *Confessions* will demonstrate that Luther's rejection of mystery and his definition of original sin and grace far exceed Augustine's positions.

Luther, so often preoccupied by an awareness of human misery, may appear very grim. We, therefore, must remind ourselves how much he rejoices in Christ. The following Christmas sermon gives the light along with the darkness of Luther's thought.

> To the Kingdom of Christ belong only poor, suffering men. It was for their sake that this King came down from heaven to earth. Therefore is his Kingdom a kingdom for hearts which are fearful, sorrowful and miserable. To such I now preach, just as the angel preached to the poor, frightened shepherds: "Behold, I bring you good tidings of great joy!"
>
> True enough, this great joy is offered to all people, yet it can be received only by those who have a troubled conscience and a grieving heart. The angel is saying, "To those I have come, for such people is my message, to them my good tidings."

[14] Lienhard, "Luther and the Beginnings", 271.

[15] Atkinson, *Darkness of Faith*, 47.

> Is it not a great miracle, that where the anxiety of conscience is greatest shall this joy be nearest; that where you are disheartened by fear and anxiety there shall come such sweet and abundant joy, that the human heart is too narrow to comprehend it? . . .
>
> Listen to the angel's song, all you who have a troubled heart. "I bring you good tidings of great joy!" Never let the thought cross your mind that Christ is angry with you! He did not come to condemn you. If you want to define Christ rightly, then pay heed to how the angel defines him, namely, "A great joy!"[16]

Luther was no mystic; his impatience with the mysterious, as well as his lifelong polemical use of his own psychological anxiety, precluded any mystical possibilities. In this sense Louis Bouyer, trained as a Calvinist pastor, questions the possibility of spirituality in the contemplative sense in the early days of the Reformation. There is surely a difference between the Anabaptists, who obviously had mystical tendencies, and the Lutherans and Calvinists, who were uncomfortable with mystery and the mystical.

Luther's minimalization of the mystical element in religion, however, did not rule out a real personal devotion to Christ. He had a loving devotion to Christ, which is illustrated in the following prayer.

> O heavenly Father, God of all comfort, I thank thee that thou hast revealed to me thy beloved Son, Jesus Christ, in whom I have believed, whom I have preached and confessed, whom I have loved and praised. . . .
>
> I pray thee, dear Lord Christ, let me commend my soul to thee.
>
> O heavenly Father, if I leave this body and depart this life, I am certain that I will be with thee for ever and ever, and that I can never, never tear myself out of thy hands.
>
> So God loved the world that he gave his only-begotten Son, Jesus Christ, that whosoever believeth in him should not perish, but have eternal life.
>
> Father, into thy hands I commend my spirit. Thou hast redeemed me, thou true God. Amen.[17]

Luther's Spiritual Legacy

After the dust of the Reformation had settled, Lutheranism would produce one of the greatest cultural accomplishments of Western Christianity—the music of Johann Sebastian Bach and his contemporaries. The great Masses of Bach were written around the frame of the Latin Mass, which Luther retained. Bach has been called the fifth evangelist because he interpreted the Christian message so forcefully. His great *Passions* include some of the most powerful Christian poetry. While

[16] Quoted in ibid., 54.

[17] Quoted in ibid., 26.

purists may deny that these prayers have a truly mystical component, the music that accompanies them soars and lifts the spirit.

We will look at some prayers drawn from the *Saint Matthew Passion* that were composed by Lutheran writers of the seventeenth and eighteenth centuries and incorporated into the text. It is interesting to note that the *Passions* are oratorios, arrangements of Scripture with hymns and meditations meant for nonliturgical worship and meditation.[18]

For those unfamiliar with Lutheran writings, a sample drawn from the *Saint Matthew Passion* might give an insight into the spirituality and devotion that arose, at least partly, from Luther's experience. Each of the following verses is identified with its author. Among the most beautiful prayers that Bach used were those written by Paul Gerhardt, one of Lutheranism's greatest poets.

Receive me, my Redeemer,
My Shepherd, make me Thine;
Of every good the fountain,
Thou art the spring of mine.
How oft Thy words have fed me
With milk and sweetened fare,
How oft Thy grace hath led me
With gentle, heavenly care.[19]

Here would I beside Thee stand;
Lord, bid me not depart!
I would be ever at Thy hand.
Though breaks Thy loving heart.
When bitter pain shall hold Thee
In agony opprest,
Then, then will I enfold Thee
Within my loving breast.[20]

Throughout the *Passion*, Bach inserted hymns that summoned the members of the audience to participate personally in the Passion narrative, to respond to Christ. The following chorale (no. 35), written by Sebald Heyden, brings us very much into the personal life of Christ.

O man, thy heavy sin lament,
For which the Son of God was sent
To die upon the Cross.

[18] See Chapter 9 above for a discussion of St. Catherine of Genoa and her new *oratorios* (prayer groups), which gave their name to the musical form, as well as her influence on Church reform through Giles of Viterbo and reform-minded Augustinians.

[19] *Erkenne mich, mein Huter* (Chorale), translated in libretto, Roswita Cervone, ed., in *Matthaus-Passion*, Karl Richter, Munchener-Bach Orchester/Munchener-Bach Chor (Hamburg, Germany: Polydor International GmbH, Deutsche Grammophon/Archic Produktion, no. 413613-2, 1980), pt. 1, no. 21, p. 45.

[20] *Ich will hier bei dir stehen* (chorale), in Cervone, *Matthaus-Passion*, pt. 1, no. 23, p. 47.

He left His Father's throne above
To save thy soul, o wondrous love!
From everlasting loss.

He healed the sick, He raised the dead
And hungry multitudes He fed
Until the time drew nigh,
When He should be betrayed and slain
That we God's pardon might obtain.
O praise the Lamb, the Lamb for aye![21]

When one reviews the hymns used in the *Saint Matthew Passion*, there is little doubt that Paul Gerhardt's are the most beautiful and powerful. He was obviously a student of ancient music, choosing one of the great medieval hymns attributed to St. Bernard of Clairvaux, *Salve Caput Cruentatum*, for the *Saint Matthew Passion*. Eventually this hymn, "O Sacred Head, Surrounded", became one of the most popular in the English language. The following chorale (no. 53) is again by Gerhardt and clearly invites the audience to share in the Passion.

Commit thy way to Jesus,
Thy burdens and thy cares;
He from them all releases,
He all thy sorrows shares.
He gives the winds their courses,
And bounds the ocean's shore,
He suffers not temptation
To rise beyond thy power.[22]

One can only wonder what a dialogue might be like today between Luther and his associates on one hand, and Cardinals Giles of Viterbo and Cajetan and the reform-minded Pope Adrian VI on the other. Adrian VI and those cardinals were as convinced as Luther that the Church needed reform. Adrian, who succeeded Pope Leo X, reviewed Luther's works again before he reiterated the condemnation of his predecessor. It is tragic that despite their theological disputes, they could not at least find common ground in their devotion to Christ, our only Savior and Lord.

Key Issues

It has often been said that if Luther had not begun the Protestant Reformation, someone else would have. This observation does not diminish Luther's importance; it indicates that reform was in the air among those who would remain with the old Church as well as those

[21] *O Mensch, bewein dein Sunde grof* (chorale), in Cervone, *Matthaus-Passion*, pt. 1, no. 35, pp. 57, 59.

[22] *Befiehl du deine Wege* (chorale), in Cervone, *Matthaus-Passion*, pt. 2, no. 53, p. 73.

who would leave. As we have seen, the two Catherines were both powerful reformers, and Catherine of Genoa directly influenced Luther through the Augustinian Order. Later we will examine Catholic reformers such as St. Thomas More and Pope Adrian VI (d. 1523). It is interesting to note that in the various movements that would come to be called Protestant and in the devout Catholic experience, those who believed in reform were drawn to devotion to Jesus Christ. Both Protestants and Catholics strove to return to a purer, more authentic expression of Christ's teachings.

Two key issues, which are often not discussed in historical analyses of Reformation times, will be the focus of our attention as we examine devotion to Christ. First, the nature of Christian spirituality, or how one grows as a disciple of Jesus, and second, the significance and meaning of the Eucharist. How do the words "This is my body ... This is my blood ... Do this in memory of me" apply to the life of a Christian?

As Bouyer points out, this question—often ignored by contemporary Protestants—is a persistent one in Protestant history. It troubled Luther, causing him to revise his original ideas on the nature of the Eucharist as being merely symbolic. It was a key issue in Anglican history and in modern times has somewhat reshaped that church. It was a most important subject with John Wesley and the first Methodists, and it has emerged among modern European Protestants with such movements as Taizé. Surprisingly, the Eucharist was also an important issue in Calvinist theology. Both these issues pertain to the present study: How do we see Christ present in our lives? Of course, there are many other issues surrounding the Reformation, and these will touch on our discussion in so many ways that we must be almost painfully restrictive, always staying with our central question. But we must move on to expressions of the Reformation that differed significantly from the Anabaptists and the Lutherans.

The Reform Piety of Zurich: Zwingli and Bullinger

Situated in the beautiful foothills of the Alps, Zurich was the center of activity of Huldrych Zwingli (1484–1531) for twelve years, a period that makes his reform efforts almost exactly contemporaneous with the early Luther. As a Catholic, Zwingli held the title of canon at the "Great Church" in Zurich, a post he retained until his death in the battle of Kappel, Switzerland, in October of 1531. Zwingli had none of the popular piety of Luther or Calvin. He had been the object of a scandal as a priest. His argument against celibacy was that it did not work. The occasion for his departure from the Church had not been a disagreement over theology, but a dispute over eating sausages in Lent. Zwingli was a rather joyous, robust person, friendly and outgoing. Although enjoying the rank equivalent to a monsignor today (he had papal honors), he participated in the battle of Kappel as a military officer against the Catholic "foresters". Because

Zwingli was dressed as an army officer, the Catholics who found his body did not realize that this was the man who had fought and defeated them in the past.

Zwingli's work was continued by Heinrich Bullinger (1504–1575), who ably led the Reform movement for over forty years. Except for the radical Anabaptists, the reform of Zurich moved furthest from Catholicism. The contrast is important for an understanding of Protestant piety.

We must look at another important distinction, one between Luther and the Zurich reformers. Luther gradually came to believe that he was beginning a kind of Lutheran Catholicism in which the Church would be purified by his ideas. For this reason he retained Catholic usages and a strong dependence on the Church Fathers, especially St. Augustine. The Eucharist as an encounter with Jesus Christ occupied his attention and caused considerable anxiety and reappraisal. While Luther's ideas on grace, justification, and the evil of human nature left no room for what Catholics saw as spiritual growth and development, he retained many practices of piety that exist to this day in strongly traditional expressions of Lutheranism.

Zwingli had no such inclination. Like the Anabaptists (whom he otherwise feared because "they overturn everything"),[23] he tried to return to the life of the early Church. Also, like the Anabaptists, he seemed unaware of the risk of fantasizing what the early Church was like and almost entirely ignored the Fathers and other writers who immediately succeeded the apostles. There was an important distinction, however, between Reform Protestants (as we shall now refer to them) and Anabaptists. The latter were often self-educated laymen or priests with minimal education, although a few, like Carlstadt, were well trained. They found themselves attacked on all sides by the authorities—civil and religious, Catholic, Lutheran, Reform, and, later on, Anglican. The Zurich reformers were former priests, pastors of parishes concerned for their flocks and for their society in general, and so they attempted to form a *respublica christiana*. The Reform leaders avoided setting up a purely secular Christianity only by constant reference to the inspiration of the Holy Spirit; in fact, Luther called them spiritualists.[24] This insistent appeal to the Holy Spirit required the Reform theologians not to ignore the old Church, which all knew was the work of the Holy Spirit, but rather to claim that they were returning to its earliest form.[25]

In an important statement of purpose the Swiss reformers claim to be a "simple clarification of the orthodox faith and of the general

[23] Quoted in Timothy George, "The Spirituality of the Radical Reformation", in Raitt, *Christian Spirituality*, 341.

[24] Fritz Büsser, "The Spirituality of Zwingli and Bullinger in the Reformation of Zurich", in Raitt, *Christian Spirituality*, 301.

[25] Ibid., 301–2.

teaching of the pure Christian religion by the servants of the Church of Christ in the Swiss Confederation"—that they are "in unity with the old true church, that they spread no new and false teachings and therefore have nothing in common with various sects or false doctrines".[26] This appears to be a clear reference to the Anabaptists.

The Spirituality of Zurich

Zwingli and Bullinger did not share the profound pessimism about human nature of Luther and Calvin, nor are the Zurich reformers deeply concerned about predestination. In fact, the anxiety about salvation that pervaded Europe at the end of the Middle Ages does not seem to be of great importance for them. Zwingli does not appear to have been as deeply influenced as the other reformers by the notion of an arbitrary Divine Will flowing from the philosophy of Ockham and the other nominalists. Although aware that we are all sinners in need of the salvation that Christ gives, Zwingli sees the Lord as the Head and Captain of the Church. The Church guided by the Holy Spirit and by Scripture alone finds Christ not primarily in the celebration of the Eucharist but in the preaching of the word. Zwingli and Bullinger probably preached every day. The spirituality that developed in Zurich was "an ever deepening and maturing personal relationship with God in Christ".[27]

Zwingli's approach to the Eucharist appears a bit contradictory. He wrote: "I preserve entire in the supper the things that ought to have been preserved in the Mass, namely, prayers, praise, confession of faith, communion of the Church or the believers, and the spiritual and sacramental eating of the body of Christ, while, on the other hand we omit all those things which are not of Christ's institution."[28] Here his omissions included praying for the living and the dead, praying for the remission of sins, and so on.

The real difference in terms of the Eucharist was that Zwingli and the Zurich reformers "replaced transubstantiation by asserting that the community of believers was transformed into the body of Christ through the work of the Holy Spirit" and the reception of communion was the symbol and necessary sign of this transformation. Indeed, this transformation of the community is one of the aspects of the Eucharistic theology of the Church Fathers, but it is only one aspect of the Catholic (and Orthodox) belief about Christ's presence in the Eucharist. It is clear that the Zurich reformers' views on the celebration of the Lord's Supper were very different from those of other Christians (including Luther and Calvin) when we realize that Zwingli and Bullinger celebrated the Lord's Supper only on Christmas, Easter, Pentecost, and the anniversary of the dedication of a church.

---

[26] From the title of the *Second Helvetic Confession*, quoted in ibid., 302.

[27] From *Brockhaus Encyclopedia*, quoted in Büsser, "Zwingli and Bullinger", 301.

[28] *Christianae fidei*, quoted in Büsser, "Zwingli and Bullinger", 308.

The Presence of Christ in Early Reform Protestantism

The two ideals in the Reform Protestant expression were the *respublica christiana* and the presence of Christ exclusively in the congregation. These gave rise to a religious ambiance far removed from traditional Catholicism or Orthodoxy, one in which there was a complete absence of the mystical or transcendent. Writing of Reform spirituality, Büsser notes that even today, while spirituality certainly exists, there are no adequate descriptions of it in German theological dictionaries or lexicons.[29] This made his task in writing about Reform spirituality more challenging. Bouyer is more critical in his appraisal. With his own powerful sense of spirituality and liturgical piety, Bouyer sees Zwingli's teaching as a rejection of the supernatural.

> Indeed we could say that Zwingli achieved the realization of a perfect natural religion or morality—where the Gospel is reduced to an interiorization of the Old Testament precepts, and the beatitudes and the announcement of the Kingdom of God are no more than a picturesque way of describing the advent of a wholly inner religion and a religious moralism instead of ceremonial religion. The folly of the cross, the ecstasy of the soul, have no place in this bourgeois and rational piety, where the parables are seen as no more than a poetic and popular expression of a religion of commonsense.[30]

While admitting that Zwingli resembled Calvin with his strong social sense, Bouyer reminds us that this responsibility for the welfare of others was an important part of medieval piety too. With Zwingli, however, more than anyone else it must be said that Christ was found in the community and in the world around him.

Reform piety deeply influenced the English Puritans through their relationship with the Dutch reformers; in fact the Pilgrim Fathers stayed in Holland before they arrived at Plymouth. Their intent was to set up a *respublica christiana* in America. It is interesting, however, that their efforts ultimately led rather to the establishment of the first secular state in modern times, in which there is a very strong separation not only of church and state but also of religion and public life. This, of course, is the United States of America.

Later we shall see that Reform Protestantism did eventually produce individuals with a strong spiritual or mystical sense. Nevertheless, to this day the principles of Zwingli and Bullinger are active not only in Reform Protestantism but also in many forms of mainstream Protestantism in the United States.

The emphasis on a piety of this world and a kind of subtle ignoring of the world to come is striking to anyone who belongs to a religion

---

[29] Büsser, "Zwingli and Bullinger", 300–1.

[30] Louis Bouyer, *Orthodox Spirituality and Protestant and Anglican Spirituality*, vol. 3, *A History of Christian Spirituality* (New York: Seabury Press, 1982), 81 (hereinafter cited as *Spirituality*).

with a stronger element of the supernatural. I am quite prepared to understand the Protestants' reluctance to pray to the Blessed Virgin Mary or the saints. I was astonished, however, by an objection that a devout Protestant of the Reform tradition used in response to this devotion. Speaking of praying to the Virgin Mary, she said, "I don't speak to dead people." This woman had no sense of the communion of saints or of the existence of Christ's friends and disciples who have passed from this world to the next. Surely a Reform theologian would have corrected her, but it was interesting that she did not have a sense of the saints' being alive in the world to come. Nonetheless, she was a very active member of a church in the Reform tradition.

Calvin—Glory to God Alone

Because the Reformed churches adopted the model of church government advocated by Calvin—government by elected councils of elders or presbyteries—Calvinism and the Reform tradition have long been confused. However, vast differences existed between Zwingli and Bullinger on the one hand and Calvin on the other. For example, Calvin, like Luther, refused to see the Eucharist as a symbol. Calvin's profound anticlericalism contrasted with Zwingli's attitudes; the latter, having been a monsignor, always retained the clerical style. And finally, Calvin's uncompromising sense of the transcendence of God and the supernatural made him quite different from the more earthy Reform tradition.

Luther rejected the Catholic Church but kept close to its traditions. Calvin neither understood nor appreciated the Catholic tradition, but he shared one thing with Catholicism: his mystical sense of the transcendence of God.[31] Early Calvinists would be astonished to hear the word "mystical" applied to this strict logician and humanist with his own vast theological system (unique among reformers), but Bouyer, a well-trained scholar in both Calvinism and Catholic spirituality, has this to say when he declares Calvin a mystic: "If this assertion sounds like a paradox to a number of Catholics as well as Protestants, this is due entirely to a series of prejudices and misunderstandings. And if Catholics and Calvinists seem to agree in regarding Calvin as essentially anti-mystical, it is because, as a rule, Calvinists are incredibly ill-informed about Catholic mysticism, viewing it wholly on the surface, while Catholics know only the externals of Calvinism."[32]

To understand the piety of Calvinism, especially as it later grew into English Puritanism and Dutch and French Calvinism, it is necessary to grasp Calvin's guiding insight, *Soli Deo gloria* (Glory to God alone). Herein is an essential difference between Calvin and Luther. The goal of Luther's theology of justification was the salvation of the individual; thus, he reflected much of the late medieval preoccupation with salvation. In the

[31] See Louis Bouyer, *The Spirit and Forms of Protestantism* (Westminster, Md.: Newman Press, 1961), chaps. 3, 4.

[32] Ibid., 64–65.

turbulent, plague-ridden fifteenth century, people dreaded God's judgment, and Luther's thought is consistent with this.

Although certainly concerned with salvation, Calvin moved the center of his attention from man to God. He did not see justification as the be-all and end-all of the drama of the Christian life but rather the sanctification of the individual for the glory of God. We are called not simply to be saved but to be saints for God's glory. Most Catholics and, in fact, most Protestants do not realize that in returning to the traditional idea of personal sanctification by grace alone through faith, Calvin was going back to the theology of ancient Catholicism and Orthodoxy. Calvinism at its deepest level is a religion in which God is all—the means as well as the end. The human being exists to give glory to God and will do so either in heaven or in hell. Starting from this point of view, Calvin rejected much of the Catholicism of his time as idolatry. People prayed to God and the saints for help in earning their daily bread, for health and safety, and even to get rich. Against this humanism of late medieval piety Calvin stressed the figure of the Old Testament God. Salvation is God's pure gift in Christ our Redeemer. Calvin taught a double predestination: God is totally responsible for the salvation of the just and also for the damnation of the lost. This is a chilly doctrine. Few of Calvin's followers today stress this aspect of his teaching, but even here Calvin tried to see this somber theory in a positive way.

> See, then, how much we ought to be so much the more strengthened in our expectation of salvation, since God concerns himself with it, and makes it his own cause. This is a point we ought to observe well. For, however much God adjures us, time and again, to be solicitous for our salvation, since we are distrustful by nature, we remain ever in doubt of achieving it. But, when it is put before us that God will maintain his right, that he will not suffer his majesty to be trampled under foot by man, here we have a doctrine that should set us in a resolute assurance. And then it is certain that God gives us this favour of associating his glory with our salvation, binding them inseparably one to the other. There is here no infallible certainty that our Lord Jesus will come and give us respite and repose; particularly as God is bound to uphold the rights of his majesty against the pride and revolt of man. Observe, then, that Jesus Christ can only maintain the glory of his Father in the measure he declares himself to be our Redeemer. The two things are inseparable. See in that the infinite love of God towards those faithful to him, uniting himself to them so closely that, as he cannot overlook the claims of his glory, he makes it our salvation.[33]

[33] From a sermon of Calvin's on the Second Coming, quoted in Bouyer, *Spirit and Forms of Protestantism*, 66–67.

Something needs to be said about that aspect of Calvinist piety which captures the attention of most Catholics, namely, the predestination to hell of the lost. To Catholics and most Protestants this is appalling. How could God possibly send someone arbitrarily to hell? Since some people appear actually to be lost according to the New Testament and the words of Christ Himself, how could this happen unless it was the will of God? This question had been considered by Catholic and Orthodox theologians, and it preoccupied a good deal of the attention of St. Augustine and St. Thomas Aquinas. How did Calvin get to such a radical view (and, in fact, Luther was not far behind him)?

Seeds of the Reformation

The person to blame for Calvin's extreme views on predestination is probably an English Franciscan friar who died under excommunication, William of Ockham (c. 1285–c. 1349). We have mentioned him earlier, but here we must speak of his influence on the Reformation, an influence so strong that he is sometimes called the "first Protestant". Ockham belonged to a school of philosophy called nominalism, a decline of medieval Scholasticism that was really a form of skepticism, which is still alive today in modern philosophy. The most important aspect of nominalism was called voluntarism. This did not mean that the nominalists simply believed in free will like many other Scholastics. But with Ockham in the lead, nominalists maintained that all distinction between right and wrong and between good and evil belonged to God and had to be determined by His will. This ultimately implied a complete denial of the whole Scholastic tradition going back to its roots in the philosophy of Plato and Aristotle.

Scholastic philosophy saw good and evil as coming from the nature of things and held that evil was essentially a lack of a good that ought to be there. St. Augustine had said in the *Soliloquies* that God revealed to those who clung to Him that evil ultimately was nothing at all (Nimis non est). Goodness is part of the very essence of God, and He does not need to choose something to be good or evil. Ockham's God, however, was arbitrary; theoretically, He could choose that theft was an act of virtue and that honesty was an act of evil. Ockham did say at least that God's intelligence would always cause Him to choose the good.

Therefore, it was a very small step to say that God could send the apparently good person to hell and the apparently bad one to eternal life. Calvin and Luther both subscribed to much of Ockham's thinking, although they disagreed with his regressive kind of Scholasticism. It is unfortunate that both of them knew Scholasticism only through the prism of nominalism.

This kind of so-called voluntarism opened the door to Calvin's idea that God could damn an apparently good man to hell. First of all, Calvin denied there was such a thing as a truly good man, and, secondly, one's eternal fate was unrelated to whether one was virtuous or vicious. Calvin clearly saw the problem here, and that is why his doctrine of sanctification is so important. As one reads some of his statements on sanctification, one wonders whether he modifies his teaching about the absolute autonomy of God's judgments concerning the saved and the lost. Calvin makes it very clear that God's grace cannot operate in a soul that rejects it. Ultimately he maintains in spite of himself the salvation of the good. It is not enough to be predestined to heaven; to get there one must also lead a devout Christian life.

It goes beyond the scope of this book to examine Calvinist theology in depth. However, we must note the problems raised by Calvin's doctrine of predestination if we are going to understand his devotion to Christ. While it would be unfair to say that Luther's or Calvin's doctrine of justification by faith alone led to a denial of morality, it is true that the idea of personal sanctification was foreign to Luther and acceptable to Calvin. Luther rejected the possibility of sanctification as an error of medieval piety, although the idea of growth in holiness goes back to the very ancient Church and is found in the writings of St. Gregory of Nyssa and St. Augustine.

According to Calvin, "faith was authentic and saving only if it showed itself in a sanctification of the whole being".[34] His monumental work, the *Institutes of the Christian Religion*, grew and was augmented in the course of his life (especially his teaching on the Church). In the *Institutes*, Calvin gives his view of spiritual development.

> For at first the devout mind does not dream up any kind of God, but contemplates him who is the one true God. Nor does it imagine him according to its own opinion, but is satisfied to accept him according to his own revelation; it takes the greatest possible care not to be led away by any rash folly to wander about outside the bounds of what he has declared. Having thus come to know God, and that he governs all, it confides in his protection, and places itself entirely in his care. Because it knows him as the author of all good, as soon as it feels affliction or need, it turns to him, confident in his succour. Persuaded of his goodness and mercy, it rests on him in sure confidence, and does not doubt that for all adversities his compassion has prepared a remedy. Looking on him as Lord and Father, it judges it right to acknowledge his dominion, honour his majesty, advance his glory, obey his commands. Since it recognises in him a just judge, armed to punish sin with severity, it has his tribunal always present, whose fear restrains it from provoking his wrath. However, it is not so terrified at the thought of

[34] Bouyer, *Spirituality*, 86.

> judgment as to wish to hide away from him, even if escape were possible; rather, it accepts him as judge of sinners as readily as rewarder of the good, for it realises that his glory is concerned equally with the chastisement of the evil and the admission of the just to eternal life. Furthermore, it does not refrain from sin solely through fear of punishment, but because it loves and reverences God as a father, it serves and worships him as Lord and Master; even were there no hell, it would have a horror of offending him. This is true, genuine religion, namely, faith united with a lively fear of God. It conjoins fear with a willing reverence, and entails the worship and service prescribed by the law of God.[35]

It is clear, then, that the "saved" person is one who by God's help is living the life that Christ preached. It is interesting to note that both Calvin and Luther appealed to two Catholic saints, Augustine and Bernard, to justify their assurance of salvation apart from any worth of the individual.[36] Both Augustine and Bernard, as well as countless others, would agree that our salvation is purely a grace and that even our ability to accept this grace is a gift of God. The Catholic saints do not continue with this logic, which in Calvin's theology removes all freedom from the individual who is lost. In Catholic thinking, a person does something good simply by not rejecting grace and, when grace is given freely, by uniting his will with this action of God.

It must not be thought that Calvin ultimately agreed completely with the saints of the old faith in his doctrine of sanctification. According to Calvin, God's grace does not change a person inwardly but rather, as Luther said, imputes a justification that is external. However, Calvin's positive contribution to the Protestant vision was to see that the individual must lead a developing Christian life (especially the death of self). Otherwise, faith is unreal and useless.[37]

Calvin and the Eucharist

Calvin's doctrine on the Eucharist reveals a radical sense of transcendence, which Zwingli did not possess. Calvin held that the sacraments were not merely symbolic gestures; he retained the Catholic thinking that sacraments were pledges or promises of God's grace. The meaning of the Latin word *sacramentum* is precisely that—a pledge. The Lord's Supper, according to Calvin, entailed the presence of the body and blood of Christ, but not in either a Catholic or a Lutheran sense. Christ's body in heaven does not come down to the bread and wine. Bouyer tells us that for Calvin "the Word of God, by offering us Christ's body and blood by means of the species, raised us up to the heaven

[35] Calvin, *Institutes of the Christian Religion*, bk. 1, chap. 23, quoted in Bouyer, *Spirit and Forms of Protestantism*, 70–71.

[36] Ibid., 95.

[37] Bouyer, *Spirituality*, 86.

where he dwelt, so that we were truly nourished by his flesh and blood, though spiritually".[38] Although this teaching is very different from the Catholic belief, the explanation is not totally lacking in mystery or transcendence. Bouyer sums up Calvin's teaching this way:

> There can be no doubt that Calvin wanted this to be understood in just as real a sense as the Catholic or Lutheran sense of presence. It was the corner-stone of his mystical doctrine of the union of the Christian with Christ and of his incorporation with his risen being, and formed the basis of his doctrine of the Church. All this is very Pauline and seems to bring us very near to Catholic doctrine. Moreover, Calvin drew the logical conclusion and insisted on frequent communion—without very much success, be it said, even in Geneva. He would have liked to restore the Eucharistic Supper to its normal place after the service of readings and prayers, at least every Sunday.[39]

In fact, Calvin's Geneva is the first place in the world where a layperson could receive the Eucharist daily if he so desired. Apparently, however, few people were moved to become Calvinist daily communicants.

As the years went on, Calvin paid increasing attention to the doctrine of the Church. He rejected Luther's notion, expressed in the Augsburg Confession, that the Church was simply the word faithfully preached and the sacraments performed in community. He also rejected both the organic growth of the Church from apostolic times and the sacrament of holy orders (unlike Luther and Zwingli, he had never been ordained a Catholic priest). In his view, the sacraments did not in themselves contain or do anything;[40] they expressed only the commission of the contemporary community to perform a function in its name. There was a very real denial of the idea of a continuous and organic growth begun by Christ with the apostles and proceeding through the regular succession of bishops. Calvin's idea of the sacraments was that they summoned up the heavenly Church, which was made one with the body of the risen Christ. This did not bring the mysterious presence of Christ to our midst but rather raised our thoughts to heaven by reason of the word and the signs that accompanied the Word of God.[41] For this reason, Calvin felt that he could make up the words of the liturgy. He felt no obligation, as Luther did, to retain the Catholic liturgy or to adapt it to fit his own theology. The following prayer from Calvin's service of the Lord's Supper will illustrate his simultaneous dependence on and rejection of the old liturgical formulas.

---

[38] Ibid., 90.

[39] Ibid.

[40] Bouyer, *Spirituality*, 89–92.

[41] Ibid., 92.

And as our Lord Jesus
Not only offered for us
Once on the cross
His body and His blood
For the remission of our sins,
But also willed to share them with us
As nourishment in life eternal,
Give us such grace that,
With true sincerity of heart
And a burning zeal,
We may receive from Him
Such a great benefit and gift
That in sure faith we may receive
His body and His blood.
Likewise it is entirely His
As He, being true God and true man,
Is verily the holy, heavenly bread
To quicken us,
So that we may no longer
Live in ourselves and according to our own nature,
Which is entirely corrupt and vicious,
But that He may live in us
To lead us to the holy life,
Blessed and everlasting.[42]

The Glory of God

"Glory to God alone", as it was understood by Calvin, was the central principle of his religious movement. Unfortunately, although widely used, this phrase was never entirely accepted, especially as Calvinists and Reform churches were blended together in different countries and in different ways. These expressions of Reform Calvinism, that is, the linking of Zwingli's and Calvin's thought, range from the French Huguenots and the English Protestants to the Congregationalists in America.

At its best, Calvinism represented a severe morality, detailed rules of conduct (almost monastic in their thoroughness), a heavy-handed civil government, and a piety that often impressed people as long-winded and boring. It is unfortunate that the lackluster quality of services that came from the combined Reform Calvinist tradition has obscured some of its strong morality and spirituality. When the Baptist movement spread throughout the Calvinist world, it was perhaps the popularity and spontaneity of this more emotional approach to Protestant Christianity that caused people to leave the Calvinist tradition for the Baptist or Pentecostal faith. For all his rejection of monasticism and the old Catholicism, Calvin was quite an ascetic himself. Catholics and

[42] Quoted in *The Piety of John Calvin*, ed. and trans. Ford Lewis Battles and Stanley Tagg (Grand Rapids, Mich.: Baker Book House, 1978), 123.

Orthodox Christians often don't recognize this fact, because they misunderstand his application of the theory of double predestination. Calvin often stated his strict morality as part of the means of being saved: "For, as Christ our Redeemer once appeared, so in his final coming he will show the fruit of salvation brought forth by him. In this way he scatters all the allurements that becloud us and prevent us from aspiring as we ought to heavenly glory. Nay, he teaches us to travel as pilgrims in this world that our celestial heritage may not perish or pass away".[43]

Behind Calvin's thought was a spirituality of giving all to God—what he called the consecration. The twentieth-century theologian Karl Barth tried to restore the Reform and nominally Calvinist world from a sell-out to the Enlightenment. He emphasized the total sovereignty of God reflected in Calvinism at its best—everything we admire in the faith of the Pilgrim Fathers. It is a fascinating fact of Christian history that at the very time Calvinism was spreading its message of the sanctity of God alone, St. John of the Cross, the Carmelite mystic (1542–1591), was teaching his doctrine of *todo y nada*, or seeking and serving God alone. Both men drew from identical biblical sources and came to the same absolutist conclusion—one *todo*, and the other *solus* (*Soli Deo gloria*). It is important to recognize that both of these ideas echo the *Deus meus et omnia* (My God and my All) of St. Francis of Assisi.

Bouyer tells of a personal interview with an outstanding member of the French Calvinist Church, Auguste Lecerf, a person "most learned in Calvinism, as well as embodying in himself the highest type of strictly Calvinist spirituality".

> [W]e read to him [Lecerf], without comment, some of the salient passages of the *Ascent of Mount Carmel*, of St. John of the Cross. After listening with the closest attention, he answered in perfect sincerity and without hesitation: "If that is the real Catholic mysticism, it is precisely the religion for which Calvin fought all his life."[44]

[43] Calvin, *Institutes* 3, 7.3, in *Exploring the Heritage of John Calvin*, ed. David E. Holwerda (Grand Rapids, Mich.: Baker Book House, 1976), 117.

[44] Bouyer, *Spirit and Forms of Protestantism*, 65.

11 The Devotion of the Catholic Reformers

I have considered first the devotion to Christ among the early Protestants for several reasons. The most compelling was a desire to be fair. Second, because the Protestant Reformation was an event of such historic importance, it defined this age as much for the Catholic Church as for those who left its fold. As we have seen, many movements toward reform flourished especially in the areas of Europe that remained Catholic. We have already considered the call to Church reform at the time of the two Catherines, of Siena and Genoa. The profound love for Christ of these two laywomen is rivaled only by that of the great contemplative nun who wrote her great works on the spiritual life while the religious storm was raging, St. Teresa of Avila.

Just as Catholics often know little about early Protestant devotion to Christ and have seen the Reformation largely in theological or even political terms, Protestants are often unaware of the movements for reform among Catholics before and after the breakup of the Church in the first half of the sixteenth century.

It is perfectly obvious that many of the Church's problems came from its close ties to civil rulers influenced by the somewhat mad notion of the divine right of kings. At times the independent religious role of the papacy was a challenge to autocratic civil rulers. At other times the papacy itself was co-opted by those who wished to use it for their own ends. This was the case in the early fifteenth century, when popes were controlled by the kings of France. Meantime the failure of the Crusades to stem the Muslim threat, the Hundred Years' War that tore Europe apart, and the Black Death combined to leave the Church prostrate. The beginning of what was to become Renaissance skepticism, the decline of medieval society, and the constant attempts of royalty to control the appointment of bishops and even the election of popes cumulatively took a terrible toll on the Church.

That the desire for reform was a powerful current in the later Middle Ages is made evident by the publication of many influential books about spirituality and devotion as well as reform—from the devout criticism found in the works of Dante, Chaucer, and William

Langland, to the uplifting call to perfection in *The Imitation of Christ.* These books were aimed at the reform of the individual and of the Church. That these books were written by loyal Catholics is obvious. These and other works demonstrated the power of the movement toward reform. St. Bernardine of Siena (1380–1444), the Franciscan apostle of devotion to Christ and His Holy Name, and the Dominican friar Girolamo Savonarola (1452–1498), are both examples of the reform spirit in the century before the Reformation. It is important to point out that the desire for Church reform goes back to St. Bernard and St. Francis, who saw their struggle as a response to their own personal love for God and to the contemplation of Jesus Christ as His beloved Son, who they believed was still with them.

Whereas the early Protestant reformers focused on salvation and one's grateful response to Christ and complete trust in Him for this gift, Catholics focused on His whole life from the Annunciation to Pentecost. Catholic devotion in the sixteenth century centered strongly on the Eucharist, where both the historical events of Christ's life and His final return came into sharp focus in the Mass. Even after the eleventh-century break between Eastern and Western churches, both Catholics and Orthodox continued to see the celebration of the Eucharist as a mysterious and mystical representation of the whole Paschal mystery and Christ's work of salvation. Especially as a result of the piety of St. Francis and a succeeding group of remarkable canonized preachers from several orders, the Catholic West was intensely responsive to the sacramental presence of Christ in the Eucharist. As a result, every parish church was seen as a house of God and gate of heaven. Even without the devotion to the Eucharistic presence outside the liturgy, this same vision of the local church building as a house of God was equally strong—perhaps even stronger—among Eastern Christians, who do not reserve the Blessed Sacrament for worship, as is done in the West. The Orthodox response to sacred icons kept in their churches at least partially explains this vision.

Protestant church buildings became edifying structures for preaching, hymn singing and public prayers, but in no sense were they seen as the house of God. It must be mentioned that Luther was very much in the middle of this. Although he denied the traditional theology of the Eucharistic sacrifice, he returned to, or recaptured, the deeply moving belief that the blessed bread and wine really contain the Body and Blood of Christ, to use a more Lutheran formula. (It is significant that the verb "contain" was used by the Council of Trent as well; however, in the conciliar document the subject of the verb is simply the appearances of bread and wine, not the substance.) The unadorned Protestant places of worship from Geneva to Amsterdam and later in New England make clear that a church building was a simple structure where one could raise one's mind and heart to the God who dwelt in heaven. Calvin's idea that communion was an invitation to the soul to rise to heaven to be communicated to Christ Himself seems to be brought out by the very design of the Pilgrims' meetinghouse.[1]

The Catholic Reformers

The list of Catholic voices raised for reform (excluding England, which we will discuss in the next chapter) is led by Pope Adrian VI of Holland. Born in Utrecht, he was the last non-Italian pope until John Paul II. He was elected by what was either a historical fluke or Divine Providence—or perhaps both—and took the place of the worldly Leo X (1513–1521), who had issued the condemnation of Luther. Adrian was a brilliant man of humble and ascetical ways and a disciple of the Brothers of the Common Life, who popularized *The Imitation of Christ.* This devout man of integrity and perhaps saintliness was opposed by worldly members of the Curia in Rome and put his trust in Christ. Adrian VI is often overlooked because of his premature death (after only twenty months as pope), brought on by exhaustion and opposition on all sides. Nonetheless, he is important not only as a reformer but also as the first pope to be obviously inspired by the *devotio moderna.*

In many respects the followers of the *devotio moderna,* Catholic and later Protestant, could look back to SS. Francis and Bernard and even Augustine to justify their more subjective approach to the Christian life and the experience of personal prayer. The *devotio moderna* reflected the intense subjectivity of this historical moment, when the first writers with psychological acumen similar to that of St. Augustine were beginning to appear after about a thousand years. People became increasingly aware of the subtleties and demands of inner experience. In fact, this reflective interest would come to full flower in the mid-twentieth century. But whereas some went off into subjective mysticism, most clung to the traditional theology of the Fathers and Scholastics. This is equally true of those who were influenced by the *devotio moderna,* although they professed to be far less interested in the study of philosophy or theology.

St. Ignatius and the Jesuits

A perfect example is St. Ignatius Loyola, a converted Spanish soldier whose devotion to Christ is enshrined in his *Spiritual Exercises.* Ignatius called his new order the Society of Jesus, and through the centuries his many influential followers, a number of them saints, have pursued an incredible variety of tasks, living a life of poverty, chastity, and obedience without the customs of monasticism.

The following brief citation from the *Spiritual Exercises,* or thirty-day retreat, of St. Ignatius underscores the Christ-centered devotion of this remarkable religious figure. His fervent devotion is combined

[1] See Rev. Joseph N. Tylenda, "Calvin and Christ's Presence in the Supper—True or Real", in *Scottish Journal of Theology* 27 (Feb. 1974): 65–75.

with a powerful intellect and ability to inspire—qualities not so different from those possessed by the leaders of the Protestant Reformation.

> Those who wish to show the greatest affection and to distinguish themselves in every service of their Eternal King and Universal Lord, will not only offer themselves entirely for the work, but by working against their own sensuality and carnal and worldly love, will make offerings of greater value and importance saying: Eternal Lord of all things, I make this offering with Thy grace and help, in the presence of Thy infinite goodness and in the presence of Thy glorious Mother and of all the Saints of Thy heavenly court, that it is my wish and desire, and my deliberate choice, provided only that it be for Thy greater service and praise, to imitate Thee in bearing all injuries, all evils, and all poverty both physical and spiritual, if Thy most Sacred Majesty should will to choose me for such a life and state.
>
> Take, O Lord, and receive all my liberty, my memory, my understanding, and my entire will, all that I have and possess. Thou hast given all to me, to Thee O Lord, I return it. All is Thine; dispose of it according to Thy will. Give me Thy love and Thy grace, for this is enough for me.[2]

St. John of the Cross and the Carmelites

A very different experience of reform—that of the retiring mystic who nonetheless made a profound impact on religious history—can be seen in the life of the friar whom St. Teresa conscripted to help in her reform of the Carmelite nuns, which she later extended to the friars. The writings of St. John of the Cross (1542–1591) demonstrate a thorough knowledge of Scripture, as well as a solid grounding in Scholastic theology and philosophy acquired in his studies at the University of Salamanca. His major prose works are the development, or commentary, on his poetry, composed in the form of love ballads, and among the most powerful mystical poetry ever written. The Church regards him as its Mystical Doctor, and most critics consider him the finest poet in the Spanish language.

Although St. John of the Cross is not an apparently devotional writer, his poetry and mystical theology focus ultimately on reaching that state of union with God through Christ at the summit of the mountain. In his decisive, lapidary style he advises us in his great work *The Ascent of Mount Carmel* to focus on Christ, the summit of our life, whom we must strive always to imitate.

> Have a habitual desire to imitate Christ in all your deeds by bringing your life into conformity with His. You must then study His life in order to know how to imitate Him and behave in all events as He would. . . .

[2] *The Spiritual Exercises of St. Ignatius*, trans. Anthony Mottola (Garden City, N.Y.: Image Books / Doubleday, 1963), 68, 104.

> In order to be successful in this imitation, renounce and remain empty of any sensory satisfaction that is not purely for the honor and glory of God. Do this out of love for Jesus Christ. In His life He had no other gratification, nor desired any other, than the fulfillment of His Father's will, which He called His meat and food. (Jn 4:34)[3]
>
> * * *
>
> A man makes progress only through imitation of Christ Who is the Way, the Truth, and the Life. No one goes to the Father but through Him, as He states Himself in St. John. (Jn 14:6) Elsewhere He says: *I am the door, if any man enter by Me he shall be saved.* (Jn 10:9) Accordingly, I should not consider any spirituality worthwhile that would walk in sweetness and ease and run from the imitation of Christ.[4]

The love of Christ calls for the total transcendence of all personal goods, the renunciation of all things, the seeking of nothing but Christ, and these are the themes found in all of the Carmelite's writings. The sternest, most unworldly of Anabaptists could feel at home with the all-consuming fire of John's love of Christ. In the following passage St. John expounds on the unfathomable riches and mysteries of Christ that await the soul determined to seek Him above all things.

> There is much to fathom in Christ, for He is like an abundant mine with many recesses of treasures, so that however deep men go they never reach the end or bottom, but rather in every recess find new veins with new riches everywhere. On this account St. Paul said of Christ: *In Christ dwell hidden all treasures and wisdom.* (Col. 2:3) The soul cannot enter these caverns or reach these treasures if, as we said, she does not first pass over to the divine wisdom through the straits of exterior and interior suffering. For one cannot reach in this life what is attainable of these mysteries of Christ without having suffered much, and without having received numerous intellectual and sensible favors from God, and without having undergone much spiritual activity; for all these favors are inferior to the wisdom of the mysteries of Christ in that they serve as preparations for coming to this wisdom. When Moses asked God to reveal His glory, God told Moses that he would be unable to receive such a revelation in this life, but that he would be shown all good, that is, all the good revealable in this life. So God put Moses in the cavern of the rock, which is Christ, as we said, and showed His back to him, which was to impart knowledge of the mysteries of the humanity of Christ.

---

[3] *The Ascent of Mount Carmel,* bk. 1, chap. 13, nos. 3–4, in *The Collected Works of St. John of the Cross,* ed. and trans. Kieran Kavanaugh, O.C.D., and Otilio Rodriguez, O.C.D. (Washington, D.C.: Institute of Carmelite Studies, 1973), 102.

[4] Ibid., bk. 2, chap. 7, no. 8, 124.

> The soul, then, longs earnestly to enter these caverns of Christ in order to be absorbed, transformed, and wholly inebriated in the love of the wisdom of these mysteries, and hide herself in the bosom of the Beloved.[5]

Todo y nada (all and nothing) is a phrase used to describe the saint's uncompromising pursuit of union with God, for which all earthly things must be forsaken. In a remarkable sketch he made of Mount Carmel, symbolizing the mount of perfection, he gives a list of maxims to guide those who would scale the mountain. They are repeated in the treatise itself. The contrast is always between the "all" and the "nothing".

> To reach satisfaction in all
> desire its possession in nothing.
> To come to possess all
> desire the possession of nothing.
> To arrive at being all
> desire to be nothing.
> To come to the knowledge of all
> desire the knowledge of nothing.
> To come to the pleasure you have not
> you must go by a way in which you possess not. . . .
> When you turn toward something
> you cease to cast yourself upon the All.
> For to go from all to the All
> you must deny yourself of all in all. . . .
> In this nakedness the spirit finds
> its quietude and rest.
> For in coveting nothing,
> nothing raises it up
> and nothing weighs it down,
> because it is in the center of its humility.[6]

The Capuchins— The New Franciscan Reform

Along with many individual reformers, the older orders began to awaken from the lethargy of the fifteenth century. The largest of these reform movements was the Capuchins, a group of Franciscans from the century-old reform of St. Bernardine of Siena, who sought to lead a prayerful religious life serving the poor and doing evangelical preaching. Like all movements of that time, their beginnings were stormy. Their simple message of a Gospel life in literal imitation of Christ's own apostles won the admiration of Catholics, especially on the border areas of the new Protestant states. In northern Italy, France, Switzerland, southern Germany, and Tyrol, they gave an example of religious life that

[5] St. John of the Cross, *The Spiritual Canticle*, st. 37, lines 4–5, in *Collected Works*, 551.
[6] *Ascent of Mount Carmel*, bk. 1, chap. 13, no. 11, in *Collected Works*, 103–4.

challenged the charges of clerical luxury and indulgence, which Protestant preachers could so easily point to. The early Capuchins included peasant farmers like St. Felix of Cantalice; aristocrats like Ange de Joyeuse, hereditary marshal of France; and great scholars like St. Lawrence of Brindisi. When we look at these devout reformed Franciscans, we encounter deep personal devotion to Christ. The following quotation from the earliest constitutions of the Capuchin reform is an eloquent example of Catholic Reformation piety. To appreciate it, we must recall that the men who wrote these lines struck a note of awesome contradiction to the worldly Renaissance style. They dressed in heavy, worn robes, shaved their heads, wore long beards, lived in the humblest dwellings, and conducted shelters (called hospitals at that time) for the poor and sick in the slums of cities like Rome and Genoa.

> In Christ then, Who is God and Man, the True Light, the Brightness of Glory and of Eternal Light, the Spotless Mirror and Image of God; in Christ, appointed by the Eternal Father to be the Judge, Lawgiver and Savior of men; in Christ, to Whom the Holy Ghost has given testimony; and from Whom are all our merit, example, help, grace, and reward; in Whom be all our meditation and imitation; in Whom all things are sweet, learned, holy, and perfect; in Christ, Who is the light and expectation of the Gentiles, the end of the law, the salvation of God, the Father of the world to come, our final hope, Who of God is fashioned the Wisdom and Justice, Sanctification and unto us Redemption, Who with the Father and the Holy Ghost, co-eternal, consubstantial, and co-equal liveth and reigneth one God, be everlasting praise, honor, majesty, and glory, world without end. Amen.[7]

Catholic Devotion to Christ

A variety of specifically Catholic devotions with roots in medieval piety now came to full flower. The Christmas crèche, the Stations of the Cross, Passion plays, citywide missions and revivals, the celebration of Corpus Christi, pilgrimages and visits to shrines—all were specifically Catholic ways of taking the message of the New Testament to large, mostly illiterate, populations.

As the spirit of reform caught on, preachers went everywhere preaching the Gospel and encouraging veneration of Christ. There is no denying that the generation of Protestant divines who succeeded the original reformers concentrated on the use and knowledge of the Bible with an enthusiasm and comprehensive intellectual acumen unique since patristic times. It is also true that the Catholic preachers and faithful were equally enthusiastic in their devotion to Christ in more traditional ways, ranging from recitation of the Rosary with its meditations on the mysteries of the lives of Jesus and Mary to the solemn celebration of the liturgical seasons.

---

[7] *The Capuchin Constitutions of 1536*, chap. 12, quoted in John C. Olin, *The Catholic Reformation: Savonarola to Ignatius Loyola* (New York: Fordham University Press, 1992), 181.

The Similarity of Devotion

As the wars of religion subsided and the bloody persecutions came to an end, a remarkable but often overlooked similarity in devotion emerged. The Catholic Church and the Protestant churches, which were now growing in number, had drawn as far away from each other as possible and continued to denounce each other. Yet both sides began to embrace forms of piety and devotion that became increasingly similar.[8] From the seventeenth century onward, devotion to Christ would develop in the various divided groups along strikingly similar lines. Bitter acrimony gradually gave way to silence, and the different trends in the Protestant world shaped themselves into new identities, often in conflict, as between Anglicans and Puritans in England or between Baptists and Lutherans in Germany. Despite division, persecutions, and animosity, a remarkable but largely unrecognized common ground appeared—a renewed devotion to Christ in His divinity and humanity. Is it possible that this historically inexplicable similarity between warring churches had its roots in a reality beyond them all and yet present within those who sincerely sought to be disciples of the same Christ? Is it possible that Christ's grace was calling all who sincerely invoked His name, that the same dynamism of grace shaped the spiritual lives of those who sought Him and drew close to Him in the different churches? Is it possible that this great dynamism and mystery of Christianity with all its wounds and scars is the universal presence of the Holy Spirit? And does this Spirit not invite to a mysterious center all who believe and trust in Him with all their desire? This emerging common devotion to Christ is what we shall now examine.

[8] See Louis Bouyer, *Orthodox Spirituality and Protestant and Anglican Spirituality* (New York: Seabury Press, 1982), 99–168. Bouyer tends to see this gradual confluence as a return to Catholic tradition. It may also be seen as the effect of devotion to Christ, which all shared in common, and as the effect of the grace of the Holy Spirit in members of the different churches.

12 Christ in England

Each age, culture, and people will generate its own image of and devotions to Christ. We have neither the time nor space to study these varied and rich interpretations, but I believe there is a need to examine Christ as He is known to English-speaking peoples. Although my own country has been described as a melting pot of many cultures, the foundational and, up to this time, dominant one is that of the British Isles. Although this country was born of revolution against the British Crown, much of American literature, art, and even religious sense came from England or the lands it occupied. Those whose native language is English cannot know themselves well if they are unaware of the many images of Christ in the English-speaking world.

Legend relates that Christianity came to Britain with someone who actually knew Christ—Joseph of Arimathea, the disciple who removed Jesus' body from the Cross. That Joseph of Arimathea ever went to England is obviously legend, but it gave English Christians a sense that they belonged to Christendom as much as did the Greeks or Romans, who actually knew the apostles. It was especially important for them to make this claim because the French, by an even more incredible legend, claimed St. Anne, the grandmother of Jesus, as one of their own.

For nearly a thousand years, the Christianity of these misty isles was shaped first by monks, the earliest ones of Egyptian origin and culture, later by Irish missionaries, and finally by their own Anglo-Saxon Benedictines. This fascinating Church history begins with the Glastonbury thorn, a bush said to have been planted by Joseph of Arimathea from a shoot from the crown of thorns. Again, this is only legend, but the story links the people of Britain with the events of redemption. A piety similar to what we found in the Celtic church in Ireland (see Chapter 6) developed in the Saxon church. In England, Christ was a high king, although His presence in more humble forms could be found in the great forests and at the family hearth. The knowledge of Christ's life was entwined with the liturgy of the Mass. The following prayer of the Celtic Church reminds us of this piety. "O holy Jesus; O gentle friend; O Morning Star; O midday Sun adorned.... For the sake of thy kindliness (affection, love, mercy), hear the entreaty of this man and wretched poorling and weakling for the acceptance of this sacrifice on behalf of all Christian churches, and on mine own behalf."[1]

Although Irish missionaries had made inroads in the north of Britain, the conversion of England to Christianity is generally reckoned from the end of the sixth century, when St. Augustine of Canterbury, at the request of Pope Gregory the Great, arrived at Dover. The new faith rapidly took hold in the seventh and eighth centuries. Monastic establishments multiplied, as did schools; and a religious literature in the vernacular developed, providing beautiful Christian piety—simple, direct, and biblical.

From the age of *Beowulf* there survive a number of religious poems, the greatest of which is *The Dream of the Rood*, dating probably from the eighth century. Its authorship has been long debated and will probably always remain unknown. It is certain, however, that the author was literate, familiar with Sacred Scripture, and devoted to the redemptive love of Christ. In *The Dream of the Rood*, we see the flowering of piety in the Anglo-Saxon Church. The Cross itself in this work becomes a figure in the drama of salvation, speaking to us and inciting in us a loving response to the crucified Savior. Here we give only a few excerpts from the work, which the interested reader could profitably meditate on in its entirety.

> Long ago was it that I was cut down at the edge of the forest, moved from my trunk. Men bore me on their shoulders, they set me on a hill. I saw then the Lord of mankind hasten with great zeal that He might be raised upon me.
>
> Then the young Hero—He was God almighty—firm and unflinching, stripped Himself; He mounted on the high cross, brave in the sight of many, when He was minded to redeem mankind. Then I trembled when the Hero clasped me; yet I durst not bow to the earth, fall to the level of the ground, but I must needs stand firm.
>
> As a rood was I raised up; I bore aloft the mighty King, the Lord of heaven. They pierced me with dark nails; the wounds are still plain to view in me, gaping gashes of malice. I was all bedewed with blood, shed from the Man's side, after He had sent forth His Spirit. I saw the God of hosts violently stretched out. All creation wept, lamented the King's death; Christ was on the cross.
>
> Now the time has come when far and wide over the earth and all this splendid creation, men do me honor; they worship this sign. On me the Son of God suffered for a space; wherefore now I rise glorious beneath the heavens, and I can heal all who fear me."[2]

[1] Conrad Pepler, O.P., *The English Religious Heritage* (London: Blackfriars Publications, 1958), 19.

[2] Quoted in *Anglo-Saxon Poetry*, trans. R.K. Gordon (London: J.M. Dent and Sons, 1957), 235–37.

Toward the end of the poem, the poet drops the device of the personified Cross and speaks for himself: "Then glad at heart, I worshipped the cross with great zeal. Now I have joy of life that I can seek the triumphant cross, do it full honor. Great is the desire for that in my heart, and to the cross I turn for help. May the Lord, who here on earth suffered aforetime on the cross for the sins of men, be a friend unto me; He has redeemed us and has given us life, a heavenly home." [3]

The shining light of the Anglo-Saxon Church was Venerable Bede, saint and Doctor of the Church (672–735). His method of dating historical events from the birth of Christ spread throughout the West, becoming a lasting legacy. Bede tells us at the end of his great history of the English Church that he had been raised since the age of seven by Benedictine monks at Wearmouth and Jarrow abbeys and had become a monk and then was ordained a priest by St. John of Beverley. At the end of his monumental book he writes these revealing lines about death: "And I pray Thee, loving Jesus, that as Thou hast graciously given me to drink in with delight the words of Thy knowledge, so Thou wouldst mercifully grant me to attain one day to Thee, the fountain of all wisdom and to appear forever before Thy face." [4]

Although the Norman invasion of 1066 ended the age of the Saxon Church, it did not end devotion to Christ. In fact, the hymn composed for the coronation of William the Conqueror, the new Norman king, was "*Christus vincit* (Christ Conquers)". Nor did the Normans really try to obliterate the Saxon Church. At first William permitted and then encouraged devotion to the penultimate Saxon king, St. Edward the Confessor, whose son he had defeated at Hastings. In fact, before the Conquest, the English Church had suffered from all the usual symptoms of the Dark Ages, including simony, lax observance, ignorance, and worldliness. After William the English Church was known for its zeal, hard work, and learning.[5]

Devotion to Christ during the high Middle Ages in England was a rich and all-encompassing experience of faith in the Son of God. Among its most important figures was one who continues to engage the attention of modern people, the converted sinner Thomas Becket (1117–1170). Archbishop of Canterbury, he was murdered by the henchmen of the tyrannical king Henry II. The following quotation from his writing is a small but telling example of medieval devotion to Christ.

> If we who are called bishops desire to understand the meaning of our calling and to be worthy of it, we must strive to keep our eyes on him whom God appointed high priest for ever, and to follow in his footsteps. For our sake he offered himself to the Father upon the altar

[3] Ibid., 237–38.

[4] *The Catholic Encyclopedia* (New York: Appleton), 2:384.

[5] Ibid., 15:643.

> of the cross. He now looks down from heaven on our actions and secret thoughts, and one day he will give each of us the reward his deeds deserve. . . .
>
> Remember . . . how our fathers worked out their salvation; remember the sufferings through which the Church has grown, and the storms the ship of Peter has weathered because it has Christ on board. Remember how the crown was attained by those whose sufferings gave new radiance to their faith. The whole company of saints bears witness to the unfailing truth that without real effort no one wins the crown.[6]

The Ancrene Riwle

Among the most interesting documents in the history of English medieval spirituality is the rule for anchoresses written in the early thirteenth century by an unknown spiritual guide. Intended for three gentlewomen who were attempting to lead a life of prayer, withdrawn from society, this way of life became so popular that the rule was edited, expanded, and translated, going far beyond the west of England. Although the *Ancrene Riwle* lacks the profound spirituality of St. Bernard and the early English mystics, it is practical, devout, and provides a window into the thought of devout thirteenth-century European Christians. It also illustrates a devotion to Christ as the great saving Knight of the Holy Trinity.

There is much in the rule about devotion to Christ, to "our Ladye Sainte Marye", and to the saints. However, we need only to ponder the following excerpt to see how Christ the Savior appeared to the people of this age of chivalry.

The Parable of the Knight and His Shield

The parable begins with a lady "completely surrounded by her enemies. Her land all laid waste, and she herself destitute in an earthen castle".[7] The king comes to her rescue with food, jewels, and an army. He is beautiful and his speech is of such delight as to raise the dead. Yet she disdains him. He offers to make her queen of all he possesses, and she still disdains him. The king finally offers to save her by going into battle, although he knows he will die. The king did all this and was "outrageously tortured and finally slain. But by a miracle he rose from death to life. Would not this lady be of an evil nature had she not loved him thereafter beyond everything else?"[8]

The following selection from the next passage is a beautiful medieval appreciation of Christ the King.

> This king is Jesus, the Son of God, who in just this way sought our soul's love when it was besieged by devils. And He, like a noble lover,

[6] Letter, quoted in *The Liturgy of the Hours* (New York: Catholic Book Publishing, 1975), 1:1279ff.

[7] *Ancrene Riwle*, trans. M. B. Salu (Exeter, U.K.: University of Exeter Press, 1990), 172.

[8] Ibid., 173.

> after having sent many messengers and many good gifts, came to give proof of His love, and showed by knightly deeds that He was worthy of love, as knights at one time were accustomed to do. He entered the tournament, and like a brave knight had His shield pierced through and through for love of His lady. His shield, concealing His Godhead, was His dear body, which was extended upon the cross, broad as a shield above, where His arms were stretched out, and narrow below, where, as many think, one foot was set upon the other.[9]

After the use of several Old Testament quotations about love and about shields, the legend continues.

> "But why, master?" you will say. "Could He not have delivered us with less pain?" Yes indeed, quite easily, but He did not want to. Why? So that we might not have any excuse for not giving Him our love, when He had bought it so dearly. A thing little loved is cheaply bought. He bought us with His heart's blood—never was price more dear—in order to win from us our love for Him, which cost Him so much. In a shield there are three things, the wood, the leather, and the painting. So too is this shield: the wood of the cross, the leather, which was God's body, and the painting, the red blood which colored it so fair. . . .
>
> After the death of a brave knight, his shield is hung high in the church in his memory. And so is this shield, the crucifix, set in the church, where it may be most easily seen, that it may remind us of Jesus Christ's deed of knighthood on the cross. Let His beloved see by that how He bought her love, allowing His shield to be pierced, His side opened, to show her His heart, to show her how completely He loved her, and to win her own heart.[10]

No one reading the *Ancrene Riwle* could disdain medieval devotion to Christ. As we study English spirituality, the example of devout people living as anchorites, as monks and nuns, or as friars working with the people should make us well aware that there were a great many sensitive, devoted souls who sought to please Christ out of personal love and devotion.

The English Mystics

The history of devotion to Christ in England is comprised of many strands and currents of thought that influenced social and religious history and human activity on every level. While much of the Christian world was preoccupied with a fear of hell and while the notion of divine sovereignty was growing in ways that contradicted the teachings of the Fathers and the commentaries of the medieval Scholastics, a group of mystics budded forth in England who became known for

[9] Ibid.

[10] Ibid., 173–74.

their perfect trust in God and their personal friendship with Christ. Their writings stand out against a background of popular piety marked by attempts to influence God. They are also in sharp contrast with the later Protestant preoccupation with double predestination. The English mystics are not opposed to all of this; they are simply above it.

In a book of singular beauty, *The Mediæval Mystics of England*, Eric Colledge traces the English mystical tradition to St. Paul and St. Augustine. The link is obvious when we think of the influence of St. Anselm, an Italian who was an abbot, and then primate and guide for the developing Norman church. The following quotation from this remarkable man gives a taste of the devotion to Christ that inspired the man who linked the emerging Norman-English church with Rome and ultimately with the Church of the apostles.

Who will snatch me from the hands of God?
Who shall be my help, my salvation?
Who is the one called "the angel of great counsel,"
the one called savior, that I may call upon his name?
It is Jesus, yes, Jesus himself.
He is the judge between whose hands I tremble.
But breathe now a sigh of relief, O sinner,
yes, breathe a sigh of relief, and do not despair.
Hope in him whom you fear.
Flee to him from whom you fled.
Insistently invoke the one whom your pride provoked.
Jesus, Jesus, because of that name treat me according to that name.
Jesus, Jesus, ignore the proud man who provokes you,
see only the wretched one who invokes you.
Sweet name! Name full of delights!
Name that comforts sinners and brings them blessed hope.
For what is Jesus if not savior?
Therefore, Jesus, because of who you are, be Jesus for me.[11]
You who fashioned me, let me not perish.
You who redeemed me, let me not be condemned. . . .
If you let me into the wide embrace of your mercy,
it will not be narrowed because of me, O Lord,
Admit me therefore, O dearest Jesus,
admit me among the number of your elect,
so that with them I may praise you, enjoy you, and glory in you.[12]

St. Aelred of Rievaulx

Anselm was not alone; several others of the English school of mystics who spanned the period from the twelfth to the fifteenth centuries

[11] This phrase would be echoed centuries later at Tyburn by many of the English martyrs, whose last words were: "*Jesu, Jesu, esto mihi Jesus.*"

[12] From Meditation 1 of St. Anselm, quoted in William H. Shannon, *Anselm: The Joy of Faith* (New York: Crossroad, 1999), 73–74.

are of importance. Among these is St. Aelred, abbot of Rievaulx who was born in 1109, the year Anselm died. His greatest work, *The Mirror of Love*, began as instructions for novices and was published at the insistence of St. Bernard. Aelred illustrates many of the characteristics of the English mystical tradition.

> Who will give me wings, as of a dove, that I may fly, and find rest? Till then let my soul be fledged, Lord Jesus, let it grow wings, I pray You, in the nest of your chastening: let it rest in the cleft of the rock, in the cavern of Your wounds. Let it embrace You, the crucified one: let it take from You the draught of Your precious blood. While I wait, let this sweet meditation fill my memory, lest forgetfulness darken it for me: while I wait, let me look upon myself as knowing nothing, except my Lord, and Him crucified, lest empty error seduce my knowledge from the firm foundation of the Faith, let the delight of all my love be in You, lest I be taken up by any worldly desire.[13]

In this passage we see a deep relationship with Jesus Christ profoundly rooted in the historical facts of Christ's life. In a few lines Aelred invokes Christ's salvific death and by implication His glorious Resurrection. He acknowledges his total dependence on Christ to save him from error and worldliness and to bring him to salvation.

Richard Rolle

As the *devotio moderna* took hold in England, many were more interested in their own love of Christ than in the interpretations of Scripture provided by philologists like Erasmus or the theological debates of the later Scholastics like Ockham and Biel. One of the earliest representatives of this tendency (it was never an organized movement) was Richard Rolle de Hampole (ca. 1300–1349). Although he studied at Oxford, Rolle left the university with his education incomplete to live in a forest as a hermit. His *Fire of Love* describes the purgative and illuminative ways and the arrival at contemplation. Eventually he moved his cell near a monastery of Cistercian nuns who preserved and published his writings.

After Rolle's death his tomb became a place of pilgrimage and reported miracles, and his writings became increasingly popular, especially when printed books appeared. Rolle translated large sections of the Bible into English, a fact that annoyed the disciples of the reformist priest John Wycliffe, who claimed their leader as the earliest translator. Many have held that Rolle, along with the other English mystics, would have been canonized if the Reformation had not almost obliterated English Catholicism. The beautiful devotion to Jesus of this humble, learned hermit provides one of the bright sides of late medieval English piety. In fostering our devotion to Christ, we could scarcely

[13] Aelred of Rievaulx, *The Mirror of Love*, chap. 5, quoted in Eric Colledge, O.S.A., *The Mediæval Mystics of England* (New York: Charles Scribner's Sons, 1961), 109–10.

do better than to read Rolle's work *I Sleep and My Heart Wakes* (see Song of Songs 5:2), in which we find the following lines of meditation on the Passion of Christ.

> It was my King who shed those bitter tears, who bled
> Waiting in mortal dread till His betrayers led
> Him to be tormented.
> Pitilessly did they strike Him and at the pillar smite Him,
> Spitting in His fair face so foully to despite Him.
>
> My King's crown is of thorns, that cruelly pierce His brow.
> Alas, my joy, my love is dragged to judgment now.
> Nails pierced His feet and pierced those hands so dear,
> And His unblemished body was wounded with a spear.
>
> Naked is His white breast, red is His bleeding side,
> Livid His lovely face, and His wounds deep and wide:
> From those five wounds, as though a crimson tide,
> The blood runs down: His pains no man can hide....
>
> Bring me to Thy love: O Jesu, take my heart,
> Cleanse it from every sin, and let us never part.
> Thou art my whole desire: I long to be with Thee:
> Kindle within me fire, that I, of earth's dross free,
> May climb where I aspire, at last Thy face to see.[14]

This very personal devotion can be seen as a development of St. Aelred's piety and illustrates the tendency of later medieval people to be more aware of their own feelings. We have seen this illustrated beautifully in the life of St. Francis.

The Cloud of Unknowing

Although *The Cloud of Unknowing* is not usually considered a devotional work, this treatise on the contemplative life is the great spiritual classic of the fourteenth-century mystical movement in England. We could scarcely look at this period without acknowledging so significant a work. The nameless author is thought to have been a priest with a wide experience of souls, possibly a member of a religious order and a mystic. Beyond that, little can be said of him, so successfully has he preserved his anonymity, though much speculation concerning his identity continues to be made.[15] The author, it seems, preferred that attention be focused on his teaching, not on himself.

The Cloud of Unknowing teaches us important things about devotion to Christ. In the early stages of the spiritual life discursive meditation is indispensable, focusing on the life of Christ, on His humanity, using

[14] Quoted in Colledge, *Medieval Mystics of England*, 150–51.

[15] In addition to the works cited in this section, see Phyllis Hodgson's edition of *The Cloud* (New York: Early English Text Society, 1944); and David Knowles, *The English Mystical Tradition* (New York: Harper and Brothers, 1961).

scenes from the Gospel. Later, if the soul continues to advance, it will attain what St. Teresa calls the "prayer of quiet" and, perhaps in the higher stages of contemplation, the prayer of union. Devotion and our understanding of Christ must not dwell solely on Christ's humanity but lead us into the mysterious person of Christ, who is the Eternal Word of the Father made flesh. In turn, Christ, the Son, leads us to His Father.

The author tells us: "The higher part of the active life, and the lower part of the contemplative life, consists in good spiritual meditations and earnest consideration of a man's own wretched state with sorrow and contrition, of the passion of Christ and of his servants with pity and compassion, and of the wonderful gifts, kindness, and works of God in all his creatures, corporeal and spiritual, with thanksgiving and praise."[16]

In *The Epistle of Privy Counsel*, in many ways a companion piece to *The Cloud*, the same author treats certain points made in *The Cloud*. He "stresses that Christ is the only way to contemplation of the divinity: there is no other path",[17] as indeed our Lord Himself has told us: "I am the way, and the truth, and the life" (Jn 14:6). In addition, as the way to God, "our Lord is not only porter himself, but also the door: the porter by his Godhead, and the door by his Manhood."[18] Christ is both the gate and the gatekeeper: "I am the door of the sheep.... [I]f anyone enters by me, he will be saved" (Jn 10:7–9). "[H]e who does not enter the sheepfold by the door but climbs in by another way, that man is a thief and a robber" (Jn 10:1).

Fr. Johnston summarizes: "The author's teaching is based on a sound theology which states that in Christ there is one Person who is both man and God. As man, Christ is the door; as God, He is the porter. Through the door (and there is only one door) the contemplative enters to meet the porter who is the Second Person of the Blessed Trinity."[19]

Although it derives from the venerable apophatic tradition of mystical writers from the sixth-century Pseudo-Dionysius, the teaching of *The Cloud* can be difficult for modern people, for whom the acquisition of knowledge and the operation of reason, even in spiritual matters, are of overriding importance. Nor are human intellectual gifts placed at the service of God to the extent that they were in the past. In the contemplation of God human knowledge will not help us. The soul is enveloped in a "cloud of unknowing" and goes to God by

[16] *The Cloud of Unknowing*, chap. 8, ed. James Walsh, S.J. Classics of Western Spirituality (New York: Paulist Press, 1981), 137.

[17] William Johnston, *The Mysticism of* The Cloud of Unknowing (St. Meinrad Ind.: Abbey Press, 1975), 73.

[18] *The Epistle of Privy Counsel*, chap. 9, ed. Abbot Justin McCann (London: Burns and Oates, 1964), 128.

[19] Johnston, *Mysticism of* The Cloud, 78.

love. Ultimately every Christian must learn that of all the gifts God has given to us, it is love He wants most in return. The intellect is of limited use, but love will bring us to the heart of God. "No man can think of God himself. . . . [H]e can certainly be loved, but not thought. He can be taken and held by love but not by thought."[20]

The Blessed Lady of St. Julian

Another English mystic popular with Christian readers is the anonymous anchoress of the church of St. Julian in Norwich, East Anglia. Even during her lifetime she appears to have been called Lady (Dame) Julian. The ecstatic laywoman Margery Kempe, who visited her, refers to her in this way.[21] She was probably born in 1343, and thirty years later on a single day in May she experienced several "shewings", or revelations. They appear to have been what St. John of the Cross would later describe as intellectual visions: revelations that are given to the soul by grace and are so vivid that they seem to be seen although they are not apparitions of figures in the external world. The action of God's grace is assumed because the visions, though interior, are completely spontaneous and differ dramatically from the expected thoughts and assumptions of the individual. Such experiences are not really that unusual in the lives of very devout persons.[22]

What makes Julian's visions so remarkable is the commentary she wrote about them thirty years later and which are now called "the long text". David Knowles has said that the revelations "treat of many of the deepest topics of nature and grace, of good and evil, of the hypostatic union of the divine and human natures in Christ, and of the identification with Christ, the inclusion in Christ, and all those predestined to eternal salvation".[23]

So profound are the observations of this woman who calls herself "a simple unlettered creature" that scholars see the influence not only of Rolle and the earlier English mystics but also of the later writers, like the author of *The Cloud of Unknowing* and the twelfth-century Cistercian writer William of St. Thierry (1085–1148). Julian was obviously well-read and makes good use of the Latin Vulgate Bible. That such writings were available to her before the advent of printing (1477) is not a surprise, since her anchorhold was across the street from an Augustinian priory, and the church to which she was attached was associated with Carrow Priory.

Julian seems to have remained in the anchorhold at the little church until her death sometime after 1417. It was not unusual for a church to have a solitary attached to it, and these folk were often recognized

[20] *Cloud of Unknowing*, 130.

[21] Colledge, *Medieval Mystics of England*, 285.

[22] See Fr. Benedict J Groeschel, *A Still, Small Voice* (San Francisco: Ignatius Press, 1993), and A. Poulain, S.J., *The Graces of Interior Prayer*, trans. Leonora L. Yorke-Smith (London: Routledge and Kegan Paul, 1957).

[23] *English Mystical Tradition*, 130.

by the bishop as recluses. They earned their keep by tending to the church, keeping the candles burning, and seeing to it that thieves were kept out. Julian's popularity in our own time is partly due to her remarkable theological and psychological sensitivity, and partly to her recognition, along with other great writers like Augustine, Anselm, Mechtild, Bridget of Sweden, and Catherine of Siena, of a motherly aspect of God. Her strong affirmation of the need to trust in the loving providence of God and the merciful love of Christ are messages deeply appreciated by our own neurotic age.

Julian's great work, *The Revelations of Divine Love*, is familiar to many. The first part relates the revelations of Christ in His Passion, which she received in 1373. The following selections illustrate her tender response to the suffering Christ, which she describes with homely imagery and her longing to be united with Him in His suffering.

> This revelation of Christ's pains filled me full of pains, for I know well that he suffered only once, but it was his will now to show it to me and fill me with mind of it, as I had asked before. And in all this time that Christ was present to me, I felt no pain except for Christ's pains; and then it came to me that I had little known what pain it was that I had asked, and like a wretch I regretted it, thinking that if I had known what it had been, I should have been reluctant to ask for it. For it seemed to me that my pains exceeded any mortal death. I thought: Is there any pain in hell like this pain? And in my reason I was answered: Hell is a different pain, for in it there is despair. But of all the pains that lead to salvation, this is the greatest, to see the lover suffer. How could any pain be greater than to see him who is all my life, all my bliss and all my joy suffer? Here I felt unshakably that I loved Christ so much more than myself that there was no pain which could be suffered like the sorrow which I felt to see him in pain.[24]

Throughout the *Revelations*, Julian is eager to communicate the loving relationship between God and the soul. Toward the end she tells us that "love is our Lord's meaning.... And in this love he hath done all his works." And in His love He is ever merciful and ready to forgive our sins.

> And this is a supreme friendship of our courteous Lord, that he protects us so tenderly whilst we are in our sins; and furthermore he touches us most secretly, and shows us our sins by the sweet light of mercy and grace. But when we see ourselves so foul, then we believe that God may be angry with us because of our sins. Then we are moved by the Holy Spirit through contrition to prayer, and we desire

[24] *Julian of Norwich: Showings*, trans. and ed. Edmund Colledge, O.S.A., and James Walsh, S.J. (New York: Paulist Press, 1978), 209, 212.

> with all our might an amendment of ourselves to appease God's anger, until the time that we find rest of soul and ease of conscience. And then we hope that God has forgiven us our sin; and this is true. And then our courteous Lord shows himself to the soul, happily and with the gladdest countenance, welcoming it as a friend, as if it had been in pain and in prison, saying: My dear darling, I am glad that you have come to me in all your woe. I have always been with you, and now you see me loving, and we are made one in bliss.
>
> So sins are forgiven by grace and mercy, and our soul is honourably received in joy, as it will be when it comes into heaven, as often as it comes by the operation of grace of the Holy Spirit and the power of Christ's Passion.[25]

Walter Hilton

The prior of the Augustinian Canons of Thurgarton, in Nottingham, wrote beautiful mystical works meant to serve as guidebooks for those on the spiritual journey. A century after his death, in 1395, Hilton's *Ladder* (or Scale) *of Perfection* was among the first mystical books to be printed in England (1494), only seventeen years after the introduction of printing. Hilton was much involved with the Carthusians, and he was seen as a solid spiritual guide, although he humbly disclaims having any of the friendly familiarity with Christ that he describes in his books. He taught that the soul is first restored to the image and likeness of God by faith and then by faith and feeling. Assisted by humility, the soul passes through the dark night, which is a withdrawal from earthly things by great desire and yearning to love. Then it will see and feel Jesus fully, united with Him in the "softness of love".

Rolle, Julian, and now Hilton all blended orthodox religious faith with warm personal experience—something St. Bernard, St. Francis, and their followers had done a few centuries before, and that Augustine had experienced a millennium earlier. All these English mystics, as well as the author of *The Cloud of Unknowing*, emphasized a gentle trust in God and a peaceful mystical spirit focused on personal love and devotion to Christ. Later we will see this same spirit echoed in the seventeenth century in the writings of Fr. Augustine Baker, O.S.B., author of *Holy Wisdom*, and the Capuchin exile Benet of Canfield. We will also discover among some English Puritans strong mystical elements reflecting the same emphasis as the earlier experience of the English mystics. The following passages from Hilton illustrate this mystical piety well.

> If then you want to know what this desire is, truly it is Jesus, for He creates this desire in you, and He gives it to you, and it is He in you Who desires, and it is He Who desires: He is everything, and He does everything, if you could only see Him. You do nothing but allow Him to work in your soul, assenting with great joy of your

[25] Ibid., 246.

> heart that He vouches safe to do this in you. You, with all your reason, are nothing but an instrument with which He works; and therefore when you feel your thoughts, touched by His grace, taken up by desire towards Jesus, with a powerful and devout will to please Him and love Him, think then that you have Jesus, for it is He Whom you desire. Look at Him well, for He goes before you, not in His bodily appearance, but invisibly, through the secret presence of His power. See Him therefore in the spirit, if you can, or else believe in Him and follow Him wherever He goes, for He will lead you on the right way to Jerusalem, which is the vision of peace in contemplation.[26]

Hilton sees Jesus as the interior master or spiritual guide of the soul. He is present and active; in fact, all that is of value is His. Writing of trials and darkness, Hilton continues:

> Since then they are so good and so restful, though they may only be short, this darkness and this night which consist of nothing but desire and longing for the love of Jesus and of a blind thinking about Him, how good and how blessed it is to feel His love and to be illumined by His blessed and invisible light so that we may see the truth. A soul receives this light when the night ends and the day dawns. I believe that it was this night which the prophet meant when he said "My soul has longed for You in the night." It is much better to be hidden in this dark night from the contemplation of the world, even though the night be an affliction, than to walk in the false pleasures of this world, which seem so shining and so full of comfort to those who are blind to the light of spiritual knowledge. For when you are in this darkness, you are much closer to Jerusalem than when you are in the glare of that false light. Therefore let all your heart be moved by grace, and practise living in this darkness, and often try to accustom yourself to it; and soon it will bring rest to you, and the true light of spiritual knowledge will shine on you, not all at once but in secret, little by little.[27]

This remarkable passage reminds us of the writings of St. John of the Cross almost two centuries later. The essential elements of devotion we described in the death of St. Stephen are here. Jesus is actually present in the darkness. He asks for our trust in Him during trials; He hears our cry, and finally, He requires that we do His will and follow His teaching.

The Later Medieval Period

The most powerful expression of faith in England was the Mass. In the popular mind the Mass and its mystery, along with the profound theology of the Holy Eucharist, were enshrined in the Arthurian legend of

[26] Walter Hilton, *The Scale of Perfection*, chap. 24, quoted in Colledge, *Mediæval Mystics of England*, 256–57.

[27] Ibid., chap. 25, pp. 262–63.

the Holy Grail. England also prided itself with the title "Our Lady's Dowry", because there were so many churches named for the Virgin Mother. Christ was envisioned in many ways: the eternal King, the Suffering Servant, the crucified and risen Lord. The Church became wealthy, prosperous, and frequently embroiled in disputes with the king and the nobility, who looked upon its possessions with undisguised greed.

As time went on faith became entwined with legend and superstition. A general preoccupation with personal salvation spread over Europe, accentuated in the fourteenth century by the Black Death and the Peasants' Revolt. Piety became increasingly a matter of making bargains with God, seen as similar to the covenants of the Old Testament. The injunction of Moses, "Do this and you shall live", came to be interpreted as salvation through good works. People did this or that, went here or there, or made sacrificial gifts in order to strike bargains with God. They were familiar enough with the Old Testament to recognize the same impulse in Abraham, Moses, and David. Such thinking, especially about the assurance of salvation and the sufferings of Purgatory, led to what would be denounced as superstition by the Protestant reformers, beginning with the English priest John Wycliffe (ca.1330–1384). They repudiated the idea of a salvation based on works and not on faith, seeing in the popular piety of the time what Christ and St. Paul had denounced in the Pharisees. Though, as Louis Bouyer has pointed out, the dogmatic teaching of the Church against Pelagius going back to St. Augustine and the Second Council of Orange (529) and its confirming decrees (531) by Pope Boniface II was clear that salvation depends on Christ alone.[28]

[28] Louis Bouyer, *The Spirit and Forms of Protestantism* (Westminster, Md.: Newman Press, 1961), 43ff. The decrees of this council were against Pelagius, and their confirmation by the Bull of Boniface II, *Per Filium nostrum*, of Jan. 25, 531, makes them binding *de fide*—or obligatory articles of faith—for Catholics. The fifth conciliar Canon states: "If anyone says that the increase, or even the beginning, of faith, or the inclination to believe, which leads us to faith in him who justifies the ungodly, and to regeneration by Baptism, are innate in us, and are not the effect of grace, that is, of the Holy Ghost who, by his inspirations, turns our wills from unbelief to faith, from ungodliness to piety; such a one must be held to oppose the doctrines of the Apostles." Again, in Canon 18 we read: "Whatever good works we do are deserving of reward, not through any merit anterior to grace; their performance, rather, is due to a prior gift of grace to which we have no claim." Lastly, in Canon 6 the Council proclaimed: "If anyone says that God has mercy on us when, without his grace, we believe, will, desire, strive, work, watch, study, ask, seek, knock, and does not confess that we believe, will, and are enabled to do all this in the way we ought, by the infusion and inspiration of the Holy Spirit within us; or makes the help of grace depend on the humility or obedience of man, rather than ascribing such humility and obedience to the free gift of grace; he goes counter to the Apostle, who says, 'What hast thou that thou hast not received?' and 'By the grace of God I am what I am' (1 Cor. 4:7 and 15:10)."

It must be obvious that when people of the fourteenth and fifteenth centuries, even led by ill-informed clergy, sought to win grace by actions such as gaining indulgences, they went absolutely against the *de fide* teachings of the Catholic Church. These teachings were then reaffirmed by the Council of Trent, which says of justification: "Its single formal cause is the justice of God, not that by which he himself is just, but that by which he

Despite these teachings, the actual piety of this time involved many superstitious elements, culminating in the ultimate outrage of the selling of indulgences.

It would, however, be a great mistake to see the Church in medieval England as simply a circus of superstitions. There are two distinct and sharply contrasting views of the late medieval English church. One reflects the Protestant position that the English church was diseased nearly to the point of death and that Henry VIII simply finished it off. The other, more recent view maintains that a still-vibrant English church was destroyed by political intrigue and government suppression. Anyone interested in Reformation history should read A. G. Dickens' *The English Reformation*[29] for the older view, and Eamon Duffy's *The Stripping of the Altars*,[30] which makes the case for a revision in the estimate of the English church. Duffy's work is a strong critique of Dickens', although both are competent historians and each attempts to present a balanced point of view. Neither condemns nor accepts entirely the Catholic or Protestant side of the argument. Let it be said that true to the English tradition of devotion to Christ, Catholics and early Protestants considered themselves loyal disciples of Jesus Christ. Thus, the English Reformation is one of the saddest chapters in Christian history, with devout souls being martyred on all sides by those who thought of themselves as followers of the Gospel.

Almost all those who went to death in this struggle devoutly and confidently invoked Christ in their final moments. Most of these could have saved their lives by denying what they believed about Christ and His teaching, but they would not. Although some vacillated, many calmly went to torture and execution for their beliefs. The vast majority on all sides went to death with the same composure and trust as King Charles I, a High Church Anglican who a century later told his Protestant executioners that he traded a perishable crown for a heavenly one. The profound convictions of Catholic, Protestant, and, later, Anglican martyrs, so similar despite their profound religious differences, suggest that the roots of devotion to Jesus Christ once grew very deeply in the soil of Britain.

---

makes us just, a gift by which we are renewed in the spirit of our mind, and are not only accounted, but are truly called, and are, just."

[29] Schocken Books, 1964.

[30] Yale University Press, 1992.

13 England and the Reformation

As already mentioned, an interesting debate in academia involves how and why England passed in a single century from a vibrant, loyal Catholic country to the most antipapal of all Protestant nations. This controversy ranges far beyond our consideration, yet we must acknowledge it. Consequently, our considerations at times may appear contradictory, especially to those who approach this history from a polemical point of view, pitting one set of martyrs against another or heaping evidence of abuse on one side and canonizing the other. Our goal is simply to present the best efforts of each side in terms of devotion to Jesus Christ. Loyalty and fervent devotion to Christ will be seen on all sides and may serve to remind us that in any controversy there may be those who for identical reasons embrace positions that are diametrically opposed. The inescapable fact will emerge that by the end of the sixteenth century, after the violence of the reform period ended, there is ample evidence of a distinct Anglican spirituality, a Protestant Puritan spirituality, a nonconformist Anabaptist spirituality, and finally, a hidden, recusant Catholic spirituality that relied on the Catholic Reformation piety of continental Europe for its expression.

The emergence of these four distinctly English spiritualities and their own expressions of devotion to our Savior are of greater interest to us than the mixture of royal absolutism, political intrigue, and religious persecution, which boiled over in England throughout the sixteenth century. We will be best served by emphasizing a few representative individuals rather than whole movements. In this way we will find our way through a complex time, about which many misconceptions linger.

John Wycliffe and the Lollards

John Wycliffe (1324–1384), a parish priest and doctor of theology, began as a leader in the movement to remove all property from religious orders and from the Church itself, an idea which claimed some inspiration from the radical poverty espoused by St. Francis. Since dioceses and religious orders, especially monastic orders, had great land holdings, the dispossessed peasants found this teaching very attractive. The Peasants' Revolt of 1381 gave a loud and at times violent voice to this idea. Although Wycliffe himself cannot be held responsible for the bloodshed caused by this revolt, his radical teaching against ecclesiastical ownership was part of the mix of historical events that led to it. He was often charged with heresy related either to ecclesiastical property or to the sacraments, particularly the Holy Eucharist. Powerful friends, however, usually enabled him to avoid answering these charges. Finally in 1380, four years before his death, he attacked the doctrine of transubstantiation. Consequently, he was forbidden to preach and was summoned to Rome to explain himself. He was, however, too infirm to respond.[1] Wycliffe had sent out what were called "poor priests"—apparently, mostly laymen—to preach his opposition to the authority of both church and state. While it is difficult to find a direct link between Wycliffe and the first English Protestants at the time of Henry VIII 150 years later, his insistence on the Bible as the only rule of faith, his rejection of Catholic teaching on the Eucharist, and his opposition to ecclesiastical authority have caused him to be seen by friend and foe as the first Protestant.[2]

Wycliffe's followers came to be called Lollards, a name that was not a compliment. It is thought to derive from a medieval word meaning "idler" or "mumbler".[3] That the Lollards were unsure of their position at times is shown by the fate of different Lollard theologians at Oxford who were called to trial for heresy in opposition to the university. Two of these men made abjurations or denials of their positions. One, Philip Repington, went on to become Bishop of Lincoln and a cardinal; a second, John Aston, returned to his original position as leader of the Lollards. A third, Nicholas Hereford, appealed to the Pope then returned to England, where he continued to preach Wycliffe's theology. He subsequently changed his mind and died a hermit at Coventry Charterhouse.

During the fifteenth century the word "Lollard" was used for almost any movement against church authority. Sometimes, especially as learned men stepped away from this movement, ideas that were foreign to Wycliffe flourished. These included forbidding the eating of pork and the observance of Saturday rather than Sunday as the Sabbath. This was the result of uneducated men simply reading the Bible on their own. This experience led to a way of thinking similar to the German-speaking Anabaptists, whom we described in Chapter 10. Their ideas persisted to the time of Henry VIII and eventually became the English Baptist tradition, which is historically and even theologically quite different from the English reform tradition of the Puritans. The latter could trace themselves to John Calvin and especially to Huldrych Zwingli.

Historians have generally been unsympathetic to the Lollards. They were often an unattractive, disorganized group, bound together by

---

[1] See *The Catholic Encyclopedia* (New York: Robert Appleton, 1912), 15:722ff.

[2] Ibid.

[3] *The New Catholic Encyclopedia* (New York: McGraw-Hill, 1967), 8:973ff.

antiestablishment and antisacramental convictions. The central idea of the Reformation, usually referred to as justification by faith (although Bouyer has pointed out that this phrase has an interpretation that is acceptable to Catholics), is not found in Wycliffe or other early Lollards. Having rejected ecclesiastical authority in whole or in part, especially when exercised by those who seemed unworthy, Wycliffe and his disciples had to accept Scripture alone as the rule of faith. At first they did not reject the ancient tradition of the Church, but were forced to do so eventually because it was inconsistent with their accepted position.

The literature on Wycliffe and the Lollards reveals few prayers, and most of these are polemical. This probably reflects the fact that they were often in a very defensive position. The following lines are said to have been written from Newgate Prison by Robert Smith, a Lollard who was burned at Uxbridge in August 1555 during the reign of Queen Mary.

> Content thyself with patience
>   With Christ to bear the cross of pain,
> Which can and will thee recompense
>   A thousandfold with lyke again.
> Let nothing cause thy heart to quail;
>   Launch out thy boote, haule up thy sail,
> Put from the shore;
>   And at the length thou shalt attain
> Unto the port that shall remain
>   For evermore.[4]

The Reformation Comes to England

Although the Lollards remained a presence in England, the later disciples of Wycliffe did not start the Reformation there. The ideas circulating in Europe between 1500 and 1530 inevitably found a growing acceptance in England, although they were initially undetected because the very people who accepted the new ideas were men of influence in the old Church. Catholics who blame the greed and cupidity of Henry VIII for the attack on Catholicism miss the significance of the English Reformation. Protestants who see the reform only as a response to a Church that had become corrupt do the same.

Here and there in England, young men, often diocesan priests or friars, electrified by the new humanism epitomized by Erasmus, a priest and the Renaissance figure par excellence, met in quiet groups. Intrigued by the call to return to the sources (*ad fontes*), and disgusted at the superstition of popular piety, these men also became disenchanted with the papacy, which had fallen prey to many worldly Renaissance values. These values were reflected in art, music, and clothing, rather

[4] Quoted in W.H. Summers, *The Lollards of the Chiltern Hills* (London: Francis Griffiths, 1906), 181.

than in serious theological debate, like that being conducted beyond the Alps. Compared to Popes Alexander VI and Leo X, Luther, Calvin, and even Zwingli (despite his somewhat tarnished reputation) looked, in the sixteenth century, like sincere Christians. The voices raised for reform south of the Alps, like those of Cardinal Giles of Viterbo and St. Catherine of Genoa, St. Bernardine of Siena and Savonarola, were often drowned out by the din of the largely corrupt papal court.

The young priests and friars found support for their views among the nobility and even the bishops who resented the influence of those who, like Cardinal Wolsey, represented the union of church and state. They also resented the widespread abuse of appointing nonresidential bishops to English sees. Many English dioceses at this time had not seen a residential bishop in decades. Their bishops were Italians living in Italy on the income of the diocese.

The Catholics who would remain loyal to the old Church when the storm broke, like John Fisher, Bishop of Rochester, and Thomas More, Lord Chancellor, were as critical of this state of affairs as anyone else. Nonetheless, the genuine Catholic piety of the time, with its stately liturgy and popular devotions intended to bring the Gospel alive, unfortunately kept many people from seeing the need for reform. Those who did see such a need were the priests and friars who met in quiet corners. The idea, largely accepted without question, that these reformers founded an Anglican, or English, church identical in most things with the old Catholic Church except for the papacy is a historical myth. It is a paradox of history that the one person who clearly intended to keep the old Church and its teachings and customs, but free from the papacy and the influence of religious orders, was Henry VIII.[5]

The Protestant Church of England was founded not by Henry, but by bishops and clergy who were influenced by Zwingli, less by Calvin, and still less by Luther. Although they preserved some of the ritual and structure of the Catholic Church, they were fully convinced of the general body of ideas that is called Protestantism. There was, however, always a reaction to these Protestant trends in the newly established Church of England, and so there would frequently reappear forms of liturgy and piety that expressed more Catholic sentiments and customs, as we shall see.

It is interesting that the more Catholic side of Anglicanism came to the fore half a century later with Bishop Lancelot Andrewes, who was not widely accepted. In the seventeenth century a Catholic trend emerged again with Archbishop Laud, who was executed by the Protestant Oliver Cromwell. Again in the eighteenth century we see the Catholic trend in the writings of John Wesley. Finally, Catholic trends flowered in the nineteenth century with the Oxford movement.

[5] See Philip Hughes, *A Popular History of the Reformation* (New York: Image / Doubleday, 1960), and J.J. Scarisbrick, *Henry VIII*, 2nd ed. (New Haven: Yale University Press, 1997).

Thomas Cranmer While Anglo-Catholics may not like to admit it, the theological and liturgical founder of the Church of England was Thomas Cranmer, who was appointed Archbishop of Canterbury by Henry VIII and approved by Pope Clement VII in 1533 while the controversy over Henry's divorce from Catherine of Aragon was raging. Although Cranmer was burned at the stake during the reign of the Catholic Queen Mary, he is not generally seen by Anglicans as a martyr, because he vacillated at the time of his death. Catholics generally see him as an evil genius who used and was used by Henry in his scandalous and homicidal affairs. This view, however, fails to give Cranmer his due. The fact is that Thomas Cranmer gradually became a Protestant in his own convictions. He was, however, in the dangerous and eventually fatal position of being a Catholic archbishop at the time.[6]

Bouyer, who writes as a Catholic critic of Cranmer, states that his first Prayer Book (1549) is "without doubt his masterpiece from the point of view of the composition of services and the style of the formularies—a style at least as admirable as that of Luther's Bible".[7] The second Prayer Book, (1552) written without the restraints of Henry VIII, who desired to preserve the entire Catholic tradition, truly reflected Cranmer's Protestant thought.[8] Here the Eucharist is presented as simply a commitment on the part of the recipient to the Christian life, the position of the reformed Protestants who followed Zwingli. Although Cranmer was not a pious man or a devout soul, he translated and composed many liturgical prayers. They are of interest because they fall between the old Catholic liturgical prayers and the ideas of the new Protestant piety. The following prayer illustrates Cranmer's ability to write Reformation thinking into traditional Catholic forms. "O God, the king of glory, which hast exalted thine only son Jesus Christ, with great triumph unto thy kingdom in heaven; we beseech thee, leave us not comfortless; but send us thine holy ghost to comfort us, and exalt us unto the same place whither our savior Christ is gone before; who liveth and reigneth &c."[9]

The Episcopal churches of Scotland and of the United States used Cranmer's first Prayer Book, thus remaining closer in thought to Catholicism, especially regarding the Eucharist. Bouyer points out a great irony of religious history—one that reveals the general misunderstanding of

---

[6] See Scarisbrick, *Henry VIII*, especially chapter 2.

[7] Louis Bouyer, *Orthodox Spirituality and Protestant and Anglican Spirituality*, vol. 3, *A History of Christian Spirituality* (New York: Seabury Press, 1982), 105 (herein after cited as *Spirituality*).

[8] Ibid., 106.

[9] Collect for the Sunday after Ascension, in *The Collects of Thomas Cranmer*, compiled and presented for devotional use by C. Frederick Barbee and Paul F. M. Zahl (Grand Rapids, Mich.: William B. Eerdmans, 1999), 64. The Collects presented in this edition are for the most part Cranmer's translations of pre-Reformation Collects from the fifth- and sixth-century Sacramentaries of Leo I, Gelasius, and Gregory the Great. In other words, they are not original compositions. There are few exceptions, as, for example, the Second Sunday of Advent, the First Sunday of Lent, and the one cited here.

Calvin—namely, that Cranmer's second Prayer Book was rejected in Scotland because it reflected Zwingli's denial of the real presence in the Eucharist.[10] The Scottish Calvinists were too loyal to Calvin's teaching to accept Cranmer's symbolic interpretation of the Eucharist. Anglicanism has always maintained an ambiguity regarding the Eucharist as sacrifice, sacrament, and presence, which is illustrated by the contrast between Cranmer's first and second Prayer Books. Cranmer, moreover, intended ambiguity, using prayer formulas that allowed others to read into his work ideas that represented traditional Catholicism, Calvinism, Lutheranism, or the radical denials of Zwingli.

This ambiguity began with the very personality of Thomas Cranmer. He managed to be a married man while a Catholic archbishop. He served a monarch who, despite his rejection of the papacy, demanded the continuation of medieval Catholic customs. Although Cranmer has a bad reputation among Catholics, he apparently tried to save both Thomas More and Bishop John Fisher by keeping them out of harm's way in the Tower of London.[11] When Cranmer went to the stake, he was still ambiguous, or perhaps conflicted. He missed becoming the great Anglican martyr by recanting his Protestant positions and then by recanting his recantation. For this reason neither Cranmer nor, still less, Henry VIII can be seen as the founder of what would become a unique element in the European and American religious scene, a genuine Anglican piety and spirituality.

Since devotion was so linked in people's minds with Catholicism, Cranmer worked out an expression of devotion that was specifically English, yet was rooted in Catholic liturgy and which avoided conflicts about the Eucharist. Cranmer's great contribution to the history of the Reformation was a popular and eloquent reform of the Divine Office—the liturgical prayer outside the celebration of the Mass. The Divine Office, with its various hours spread throughout the day, had always been intended as a continuation of the Eucharistic liturgy and was seen as an integral part of the celebration of the Paschal mystery. Cranmer, however, separated it from and substituted it for the Mass. Nonetheless, he took over this ancient monastic prayer form, using a reform of it that had been recently made by the Franciscan Cardinal Quiñones. Yet another of Cranmer's complexities can be seen here. Quiñones' Office was a revision of the Divine Office as originally used in the papal household and elsewhere in Rome, which the Franciscan Order had adopted and spread throughout the Church. Ironically, Cranmer popularized the papal form of the Office in Protestantism! He reduced the hours to Morning Prayer and Evensong, inserting into them elements of Matins, Lauds, Prime, Vespers, and Compline.

---

[10] Ibid. See also W. Jardine Grisbrooke, *Anglican Liturgies of the Seventeenth and Eighteenth Centuries* (London: SPCK, 1958).

[11] Scarisbrick, *Henry VIII*, 331ff.

Bouyer sums up Cranmer's work with this great appreciation. "The splendid language of religious majesty and the melodious style in which these formulas were expressed made them a means of education by worship, of which no Church, Catholic or Protestant, has the equivalent today".[12]

Cranmer's Office, which expressed the reformist humanism of Erasmus, appealed greatly to the university-educated clergy of the Church of England. It preserved much of the Catholic heritage of England while avoiding the profound questions of the Eucharistic mystery. In the United States and other English-speaking countries more influenced by reformed Protestantism, Cranmer's Morning Prayer often supplanted the celebration of the Eucharist on Sunday.

It took almost half a century for a truly Anglican spirituality to grow. Calm and a sense of identity are necessary to the development of new responses to the Gospel call and to the challenge of Christ. If this array of responses is basically coherent, expressed in an integrated way, and reflecting the grace of the Holy Spirit in the lives of truly sincere people attempting to be fervent followers of Christ, a distinct spirituality will be born.

> Anglican spirituality takes its character from the Book of Common Prayer. It is not essentially mystical, though it may . . . be for some of its practitioners metaphysical, which I adopt to mean simply "poetic". . . . The Book contains the seeds of that moralism which is so vital a part of classic Anglicanism, which for a while in the eighteenth century took over and is inseparable from the Caroline and Tractarian longing for holiness. The aim of the Prayer Book is "a godly, righteous and sober life." It does not encourage flights into the spiritual empyrean. . . . For some it may be the starting point of "a devotion of rapture," but not for most; it does not encourage enthusiasm nor the perfectionism which was so much part of the Christianity of the radicals of 1640–1660 and of John Wesley.[13]

John Fisher, Bishop of Rochester

Although Thomas More is seen as the icon of Catholic opposition to Henry VIII, the facts reveal that the implacable foe of the king from the beginning of his divorce attempts was John Fisher, the brilliant, fearless Bishop of Rochester.[14] He was so highly respected that

---

[12] Bouyer, *Spirituality*, 107, and footnote. See also *The First and Second Prayer Books of Edward VI*, ed. E. C. Ratcliff (New York: Everyman's Library, 1949), 448.

[13] Gordon S. Wakefield, "Anglican Spirituality", in *Christian Spirituality: Post-Reformation and Modern*, ed. Louis Dupré and Don E. Saliers (New York: Crossroad, 1996), 263.

Although it is only fair to point out that Gordon Wakefield argues that Anglican spirituality begins with Thomas Cranmer and his two Prayer Books, there is no doubt that the Prayer Book of 1552 did much to define what would become Anglicanism. However, I think that Wakefield might more accurately have said that Cranmer began the Anglican theological position rather than its spirituality.

[14] See Rev. John Lewis, *The Life of Dr. John Fisher*, vol. 1 (London: Joseph Lilly, 1855); E. E. Reynolds, *Saint John Fisher*, rev. ed. (Wheathampstead: Anthony Clarke Books, 1972).

he had preached the funeral sermon of Henry VII, emphasizing the king's great sorrow for his sins, a clever way not only of distancing himself from the king's bad reputation but also warning those present to prepare for their own final judgment. The fact that the king had often favored Fisher did not keep the bishop from being realistic about the king's need for repentance. Fisher was a deeply spiritual man, one so ascetical that his portraits have a skeletal look; indeed, he kept a model of a human skull on his dinner table.[15] Along with being deeply penitent, he was so dedicated to the Scriptures that he carried his New Testament with him to Tower Hill, his place of execution. He was everything that the Lollards and the early Protestants could want in a Christian leader, except that he was totally dedicated to the old faith and very willing to confront the homicidal wrath of the king. In his literary evaluation of Fisher, C. S. Lewis sees him as "almost a purely medieval writer, although scraps of humanistic learning appear in his writings". Eamon Duffy in his enlightening summary of John Fisher's piety sees him differently, as representing the coming together of the new and the old, while admitting that he was imbued with the rich tradition of English spirituality.[16]

Fisher is indebted to Rolle, Hilton, the anonymous author of *The Cloud of Unknowing*, as well as to Augustine, Bernard, and the Victorines. He insists on the need for prevenient grace and the gratuitousness of salvation.[17] He did not, however, reject the images and devotionalism of late medieval piety, or its rich emotional quality. He wanted that piety deepened and purified of superstitious features. He was greatly devoted to his patron, St. John the Baptist, and is frequently identified with the Precursor: his emaciated figure, the hair shirt worn under his bishop's robes, his fearless opposition to the king, his defense of marriage and family, and his eventual beheading by an adulterous monarch.[18]

Fisher, imbued with devotion to Christ Crucified, was a deeply devout Christian trying to make his way in a hurricane of historical confusion. Fearlessly loyal to the Gospel, he dedicated himself to the moral and spiritual reform of his Church.

He appealed for reform in many ways. In 1518, when Cardinal Thomas Wolsey was made papal legate to England, a council was held in order to examine the situation of the Church in England. The following excerpt from Fisher's sermon to the bishops at that council shows the dedication of this man to the reform of the Church.

[15] Lewis, *Dr. John Fisher*, 215.

[16] See *Humanism, Reform and the Reformation: The Career of Bishop John Fisher*, ed. Brendan Bradshaw and Eamon Duffy (Cambridge: Cambridge University Press, 1989), 205ff.

[17] Ibid., 215ff.

[18] For more on Fisher's asceticism, see Rev. T. E. Bridgett, *Life of Blessed John Fisher*, 4th ed., (London: Burns, Oates and Washbourne, 1922), 65ff.

> For what should we exhort our flocks to eschew and shun worldly ambition, when we ourselves that are bishops do wholly set our minds to the same things that we forbid in them?
>
> What example of Christ our Saviour do we imitate, who first executed doing and after fell to teaching? If we teach according to our doing, how absurd may our doctrine be accounted! If we teach one thing and do another, our labour in teaching shall never benefit our flocks half so much as our examples in doing shall hurt them who can willingly suffer and hear with us, in whom (preaching humility, sobriety, and contempt of the world) they may evidently perceive haughtiness in mind, pride in gesture, sumptuousness in apparel, and damnable excess in all worldly delicacies?[19]

We have seen that it is a tragedy of history that fervent disciples of Christ could misunderstand one another so badly. It is also a tragedy that during the Reformation there were so many people on different sides who agreed about the causes of the Reformation and were profoundly dedicated to reform. Unfortunately these men were divided by profound religious beliefs and were sadly unable to recognize the sincerity of others.

Thomas More (1478–1535)

Thomas More is one of the most admired men in Western civilization. Some years ago, the Anglican vicar of the Church of St. Peter in Chains at the Tower of London told me that Thomas More was the greatest man whose bones rest in the ossuary under the church. More's inspiring statue, adjacent to Chelsea Old Church, his personal parish, calls him statesman, writer, and saint, and indeed he was canonized a martyr of the Catholic Church, along with John Fisher, on May 19, 1935.

Because he stood up to the charges made against him, more likely to expose the injustice of the system than to win his freedom, and because he never compromised himself, his case is well known. He brings together the disparate roles of philosopher, statesman, administrator, Renaissance thinker, devout Catholic, as well as defender of his conscience against a murderous tyrant. For this reason even his greatest admirers seem to overlook his deep personal devotion to Jesus Christ.

As one might expect, More's devotion was well thought out and very focused on the New Testament and especially the Gospels. His final work, *De Tristitia Christi* (*On the Sorrow of Christ*), is among the most remarkable books in the history of devotion. Its understanding of the Passion is based on commonsense questions asked about the Passion narrative that invite the reader to share in Christ's sufferings. Published only in 1976, *De Tristitia Christi* was written when More was imprisoned in the Tower and being gradually deprived of all comforts, even those a condemned

[19] Quoted in Fr. Vincent McNabb, O.P., *Saint John Fisher* (London: Sheed and Ward, 1935), 41.

man might expect in a civilized nation. As he wrote, the book was taken in sections from the Tower by his daughter Margaret (later Roper), who was allowed to visit for a time and bring him supplies.

More than his other writings, *De Tristitia Christi* reveals Thomas More's love for Jesus Christ. He gave much thought to Christ's sufferings in the text of the Gospels, and he put himself in them. We must recall that as More wrote this last meditation, he was cruelly deprived of all books. At any time he could have gone free by the simple denial of the Pope's authority and acceptance of the king as head of the Church. Such a statement would not only have won him his freedom but gained him an exalted position with Henry VIII. Fisher had probably gone too far to take anything back effectively, but More was still the "King's good servant". For reasons of morality and personal spiritual conviction and most of all because of his loyalty to Christ, More went instead to the block. A few lines from *De Tristitia Christi* will illustrate his deep love for Christ. Considering that he was facing a traitor's death of being hanged, drawn, and quartered, this meditation is all the more moving.

> O saving Christ, only a little while ago, you were so fearful that you lay face down in a most pitiable attitude and sweat blood as you begged your father to take away the chalice of your passion. How is it that now, by a sudden reversal, you leap up and spring forth like a giant running his race and come forward eagerly to meet those who seek to inflict that passion upon you? How is it that you freely identify yourself to those who openly admit they are seeking you but who do not know that you are the one they are seeking? Hither, hither let all hasten who are faint of heart. Here let them take firm hold of an unwavering hope when they feel themselves struck by a horror of death. For just as they share Christ's agony, His fear, grief, anxiety, sadness, and sweat (provided that they pray, and persist in prayer, and submit themselves wholeheartedly to the will of God), they will also share this consolation, undoubtedly they will feel themselves helped by such consolation as Christ felt; and they will be so refreshed by the spirit of Christ that they will feel their hearts renewed as the old face of the earth is renewed by the dew from heaven, and by means of the wood of Christ's cross let down into the water of their sorrow, the thought of death, once so bitter, will grow sweet, eagerness will take the place of grief, mental strength and courage will replace dread, and finally they will long for the death they had viewed with horror, considering life a sad thing and death a gain, desiring to be dissolved and to be with Christ.[20]

[20] Thomas More, *De Tristitia Christi*, in *The Complete Works of St. Thomas More*, ed. and trans. Clarence H. Miller (New Haven: Yale University Press, 1976), 14:413–21; see also *The Sadness of Christ*, ed. Gerard Wegemer, trans. Clarence Miller (Princeton, N.J.: Scepter Press, 1993), 75.

The last pages of the unfinished manuscript are almost entirely New Testament quotations centered on trust in Christ and our willingness to participate in His suffering. Obviously More chose these to help prepare him for torture and execution. It is unfortunate that literary and dramatic presentations of his life usually neglect this book and the powerful spiritual message it contains.

English Spirituality: From Conflict to Spirituality

The Beginnings of Anglican Spirituality and Devotion

The turbulent climate of theological controversy mixed with political ambition and so many currents from outside did not prevent the development of a spirituality reflecting the new English church independent of the papacy and the old Catholicism. Duffy has made it clear that there was a vibrant devotional life everywhere in England before the time of Henry VIII. This was focused on Christ, His life, presence, and spiritual teachings, as well as on the Virgin, the angels, and the saints.[21] Initially the English Reformers cut away anything reflecting mystery or a contemplative spirit, but they rarely replaced these with devotion, emphasizing instead the intellectual study of the Bible.

During the tumultuous succession of monarchs after Henry VII—Edward, the boy Protestant; Lady Jane Grey, the Nine Day Queen; Mary, the isolated Catholic; and finally Elizabeth, a heroine to Protestants—devout believers of all persuasions shifted for themselves. Catholics became more and more influenced by continental Catholicism, since their underground priests studied in such places as Douai, Lisbon, and Rome. The Lollards and first Baptists came out of hiding and found a common cause with the European Baptists. The Calvinists were beginning a movement of English Puritanism, not realizing they were following Zwingli rather than Calvin. But throughout the realm the clergy of the new Church of England went about preaching, teaching, baptizing, and blessing marriages. They were able to express a wide range of ideas so long as they did not appear too Catholic. Anglicanism began to exist on its own and produce some outstanding Christians, who were neither Catholic nor Protestant in a strict sense. They were the first real Anglicans.

Richard Hooker (1554–1600)

The most impressive of the first Anglicans was Richard Hooker, a country parson of great erudition, whom Bouyer considers the real founder of Anglicanism. He describes Hooker as having "a mind capable of vast critical learning combined with wide and, above all, deep human and spiritual experience, together with an imperturbably serene judgment ... one of the greatest [minds] in religious history".[22] Bouyer does not hesitate to compare Hooker's *Laws of Ecclesiastical Polity* to the *Summa Theologica* of St. Thomas. In terms of Reformation theology, Hooker was

---

[21] See Eamon Duffy, *The Stripping of the Altars: Traditional Religion in England c.1400–c.1580* (New Haven: Yale University Press, 1992).

[22] Bouyer, *Spirituality*, 109.

the first to reject the idea that God had absolute power to determine good or evil, salvation or damnation, an idea essential to the harsh approach to predestination favored by Luther and Calvin. Hooker returned to the Scholastic idea of divine law and good coming from the very being of God, an idea consistent with St. Thomas. Human beings, however much wounded by original sin, still aspired to follow the love and redemption of Christ. Most important for our consideration is that Hooker, while accepting the idea of justification by faith alone, also mentioned that "secret grace" should transform our lives into the life of Christ within us.[23] This comes close to the teaching of St. Thomas on sanctifying and actual grace, but Hooker wisely avoided mentioning the source of his theology, thus avoiding disputes with the English Protestants.

Hooker rejected the two basic Protestant conceptions of the Church: a free association of believers (Zwingli's notion) or an entity to be constructed from ideas selected from New Testament exegesis (the Baptist goal). He believed instead that the Church was a historical reality growing originally from the ancient body established by Christ. It was the Church of the apostles and the Fathers, struggling along with its current members who are wounded by original and actual sin but nonetheless being transformed into Christ by His grace. Hooker even used the ancient patristic ideas of virtue, grace, purification, illumination, and union with God to describe the devout Christian walking on the spiritual road and being a member of the Mystical Body of Christ.

> For your better understanding, what this severing and separating of themselves doth meane, we must know, that the multitude of them which truly believe ... is all one body, whereof the head is Christ, one building, whereof he is the cornerstone, in whom they as the members of the body being knit, and as the stones of the building, being couple, grow up to a man of perfect stature, and rise to an holy temple in the Lord. That which linketh Christ to us is his mere mercy and love towards us. That which tieth us to him is our faith in the promised salvation revealed in the word of truth. That which uniteth and joyneth us amongst ourselves, in such sort that we are now as if we had but one heart and one soul, is our love. Who be inwardly in heart the lively members of this body, and the polished stones of this building, coupled and joined to Christ, as flesh of his flesh and bones of his bones by the mutual bond of his unspeakable love towards them, and their unfained faith in him, thus linked and fastened each to other by a spiritual, sincere, and hearty affection of love without any manner of simulation, who be Jews within, and what their names be, none can tell, save he whose eyes do behold the secret disposition of all men's hearts.[24]

[23] Ibid., 111.

[24] Richard Hooker, "The First Sermon upon Part of Saint Jude", *Tractates and Sermons* (Cambridge, Mass.: Harvard University Press, 1990), 25–26.

The Anglican Church is often described as a bridge between the Catholic and Protestant traditions. Hooker deserves recognition as one who genuinely tried to bridge the gap between Catholic theology (often indistinguishable from Eastern Orthodox theology) and the Lutheran and Calvinist positions. Thus, Catholics may be struck by the Catholic flavor of Hooker's devotion and that of other Anglicans. Yet Protestants may find enough similarity between their own theology and that of the Episcopal Church in the United States to accept Episcopalians as fellow Protestants.

The Anglican religious experience is an echo of the piety and erudition of Richard Hooker, who after a difficult stay at Oxford as Master of the Temple returned to a country parish to pray, meditate, and write his monumental theological works.

Lancelot Andrewes (1555–1626)

Born only a year after Richard Hooker, Lancelot Andrewes, who served as bishop in three Anglican dioceses, is one of the shining lights in the history of Christian devotion. His prayers and meditations display extraordinary erudition yet can be spiritually satisfying to a reasonably informed but simple believer. They are so imbued with insights of Christ that they do indeed bridge gaps in all directions. Cardinal Newman always kept Andrewes' prayers at his prie-dieu for use during his thanksgiving after Mass, and Newman has provided us with a splendid translation of these prayers.[25] It is some measure of Andrewes' erudition that he composed these meditations in Hebrew, Greek, and Latin, depending on the sources he was using.

Andrewes was one of the principal authors of the King James Bible. Many a Gospel Protestant would be shocked to find that the only translation acceptable to him was made by so Catholic a man as Bishop Andrewes. In fact, Andrewes would have been one of the Lords Spiritual of the Church of England who were held in great contempt by the English Puritans.[26] He was also a bishop at the court of Queen Elizabeth when the Catholic martyrs suffered most. This same man who left profoundly beautiful devotional writings and moving contemplative prayers of repentance and contrition was also a totally dedicated pastor of souls and a bishop.

Bouyer calls Andrewes "the most perfect embodiment of the accomplished scholar that the Anglican Church has ever produced. Stupefyingly erudite ... he was none the less a pastor unreservedly dedicated to his flock, and ... practised a spirituality of inner contemplation that approached mysticism".[27]

---

[25] See *The Devotions of Bishop Andrewes*, in John Henry Newman, *Prayers, Verses, and Devotions* (San Francisco: Ignatius Press, 1989). The bulk of this volume is given to Newman's own *Meditations and Devotions*, as well as his *Verses on Various Occasions*.

[26] Bouyer, *Spirituality*, 117.

[27] Ibid.

Andrewes' *Private Prayers* in Latin are very revealing of his spirituality. These prayers proved popular in translation, providing the Anglican Church with its first great expressions of personal piety. In every respect the devotion of Bishop Andrewes was scriptural and patristic and yet reflective of late medieval piety. Personal devotion to Jesus Christ is seen on every page. The following selection shows how this man could be a guide to Newman, the Catholic convert and cardinal, 250 years later.

A PREPARATION FOR HOLY COMMUNION

O Lord, I am not worthy, I am not fit,
that Thou shouldest come under the roof of my soul;
for it is all desolate and ruined;
nor hast Thou in me fitting place to lay Thy head.
But, as Thou didst vouchsafe
to lie in the cavern and manger of brute cattle,
as Thou didst not disdain
to be entertained in the house of Simon the leper,
as Thou didst not disdain
that harlot, like me, who was a sinner,
coming to Thee and touching Thee;
as Thou abhorredst not
her polluted and loathsome mouth;
nor the thief upon the cross
confessing Thee:
So me too the ruined, wretched,
and excessive sinner,
deign to receive to the touch and partaking
of the immaculate, supernatural, life-giving,
and saving mysteries
of Thy all-holy Body
and Thy precious Blood.
Listen, O Lord, our God,
from Thy holy habitation,
and from the glorious throne of Thy kingdom,
and come to sanctify us.
O Thou who sittest on high with the Father,
and art present with us here invisibly;
come Thou to sanctify the gifts which lie before Thee,
and those in whose behalf, and by whom,
and the things for which,
they are brought near Thee.
And grant to us communion,
unto faith without shame,
love without dissimulation,

fulfillment of Thy commandments,
alacrity for every spiritual fruit;
hindrance of all adversity,
healing of soul and body;
that we too, with all Saints,
who have been well-pleasing to Thee from the beginning,
may become partakers
of Thy incorrupt and everlasting goods,
which Thou hast prepared, O Lord, for them that love Thee;
in whom Thou art glorified for ever and ever.
Lamb of God,
that takest away the sin of the world,
take away the sin of me, the utter sinner.[28]

Andrewes and Hooker begin an impressive list of religious scholars, writers, and theologians who literally made the Anglican Church. The poet John Donne, the parson-poet George Herbert, and his devout parishioner Henry Vaughan, and such sadly overlooked lay writers as Izaak Walton, Sir Thomas Browne, and the mystical eccentric Richard Crashaw all belong to this period in the history of devotion. (It is worth noting that a number of these Anglican poets are found in the poetry selection at the end of the Catholic *Liturgy of the Hours* in English.) These writers gave the Anglican Church both a literary and spiritual identity, as well as a respectability, after its stormy and embarrassing beginnings. They prepared for the next generation of Anglicans, who cemented this tradition.

Jeremy Taylor (1613–1667)

Among the most representative of the second generation of Anglicans was Bishop Jeremy Taylor. Only thirteen when Bishop Andrewes died, Taylor inherited much of the old Catholicism that Andrewes, Hooker, and others had preserved. Although part of the first generation to be raised on the King James Bible, Taylor was basically Catholic in his understanding of grace and the sacraments. When Laud and the king were defeated in the Civil War with the Protestants, Taylor was imprisoned for a time but spent most of Cromwell's Protectorate in a comfortable exile called Golden Grove, in Wales. There he wrote a good deal, but sorrow and trouble followed him, as he was virtually an underground priest of the Church of England during the Protectorate. Finally Taylor went to Ireland. After Cromwell's death he became Bishop of Down and Conor, which lacked both cathedral and bishop's house and had virtually no Anglican clergy. He spent the rest of his life in conflict with the Scottish Presbyterians in Ireland. Bishop Taylor's last years were marked by sorrow. He buried each of his seven sons and was rejected by the

[28] Quoted in Newman, *Prayers, Verses, and Devotions*, 94–96.

very church he had suffered to defend. Finally in 1667 he succumbed to a fever he caught when ministering to the sick.

One must admire the beauty and spirituality of the writings of a man who endured so many difficulties. The following selection from a recent edition of Taylor's works provides an example of the Anglican spirituality that grew to maturity under the persecution of the English Protestants.

> Holy Jesus, make me to acknowledge Thee to be my Lord and Master, and myself a servant and disciple of Thy holy discipline and institution; let me love to sit at Thy feet, and suck in with my ears and heart the sweetness of Thy holy sermons. Let my soul be shod with the preparation of the gospel of peace, with a peaceable and docile disposition. Give me great boldness in the public confession of Thy name and the truth of Thy gospel, in despite of all hostilities and temptations. And grant I may always remember that Thy name is called upon me, and I may so behave myself, that I neither give scandal to others, nor cause disreputation to the honour of religion; but that Thou mayest be glorified in me, and I by Thy mercies, after a strict observance of all the holy laws of Christianity. Amen.[29]

Many have the impression that Cranmer's theology of the Eucharist, very much like that of Zwingli, obliterated in Anglicanism the traditional understanding of the Eucharist and the priesthood, which is so closely bound to it. Recall that the reformers stressed that the Eucharist was a commemoration and not a sacrifice. The Catholic position, simply put, united the celebration of the Mass with the eternal Paschal mystery in heaven and the sacrifice of Christ on the Cross. The following passage is from Bishop Taylor's work *The Worthy Communicant*. It is especially informative for Catholic and Orthodox readers, since it reveals that his position was closer to Catholic and Orthodox Eucharistic belief than to Cranmer's understanding.

> It is the greatest solemnity of prayer, the most powerful liturgy and means of impetration in this world. For when Christ was consecrated on the cross and became our high-priest, having reconciled us to God by the death of the cross, He became infinitely gracious in the eyes of God, and was admitted to the celestial and eternal priesthood in heaven; where in the virtue of the cross He intercedes for us, and represents an eternal sacrifice in the heavens on our behalf.
>
> Now what Christ does in heaven, He hath commanded us to do on earth, that is, to represent His death, to commemorate this sacrifice, by humble prayer and thankful record; and by faithful manifestation and joyful eucharist to lay it before the eyes of our heavenly

[29] Discourse 7 of Faith, quoted in *Jeremy Taylor: Selected Works*, ed. Thomas K. Carroll, Classics of Western Spirituality (New York: Paulist Press, 1990), 277.

> Father, so ministering in His priesthood, and doing according to His commandment and His example.... As Christ in virtue of His sacrifice on the cross intercedes for us with His Father, so does the minister of Christ's priesthood here, that the virtue of the eternal sacrifice may be salutary and effectual to all the needs of the church both for things temporal and eternal.... Our blessed Lord was pleased to command [that] the representation of His death and sacrifice on the cross should be made by breaking bread and effusion of wine; to signify to us the nature and sacredness of the liturgy we are about ... we are ministers in that unchangeable priesthood, imitating in the external ministry the prototype Melchisedec ... and in the internal, imitating the antitype or the substance, Christ Himself; who offered up His body and blood for atonement for us, and by the sacraments of bread and wine.[30]

We come now to another interesting aspect of Anglican spirituality: the lay spiritual writer, a tradition very much alive in the writings of people like C. S. Lewis and T. S. Eliot. The presence of lay mystical writers and poets is more noticeable in Anglicanism than in any other Christian denomination, and it started at this time with a remarkable group of poets.

John Donne (ca. 1572–1631)

The poet and preacher John Donne is the best known of the early Anglicans; his poems remain classics of English literature. Donne left the Catholic Church after a solid Jesuit education and late in life became a fervent member of the Anglican clergy, yet he remained deeply identified with his Counter-Reformation training. Any selection of his *Divine Poems* will demonstrate the method of meditation taught by St. Ignatius Loyola.[31]

Catholics have often called Donne's religious sincerity into question, since he earned a handsome income as the Anglican dean of St. Paul's at a time when, as a Jesuit, he would have been a hunted outlaw and possibly a martyr. Bouyer, however, rejects the charge of insincerity, claiming that Donne would have seen the Roman Curia as bogged down in temporal concerns and politics and the Anglican Church as a more cultured and humanistic expression of Christianity. Donne's poems reveal a sincerity of repentance and a willingness to acknowledge sin. Despite his suspicion of Catholics, Donne is paradoxically perhaps the most Catholic of Anglicans, since his religious education was entirely Catholic. Even a reading of the following brief selections will illustrate both the devotion and Catholic emphasis of his poetry. Those familiar with the Spiritual Exercises of St. Ignatius Loyola will notice this immediately. Jesus is very much the Incarnate

[30] *The Worthy Communicant*, chap. 1, section 4, in Caroll, *Taylor: Selected Works*, 209–10.

[31] Bouyer, *Spirituality*, 113–14. See also chapter on Donne in Louis Martz, *The Poetry of Meditation* (New Haven: Yale University Press, 1954).

Word coming into our fallen world out of divine love for souls and for the individual crying out for salvation.

Annunciation

Salvation to all that will is nigh,
That All, which always is All every where,
Which cannot sinne, and yet all sinnes must beare,
Which cannot die, yet cannot chuse but die,
Loe, faithfull Virgin, yields himselfe to lye
In prison, in thy wombe; and though he there
Can take no sinne, nor thou give, yet he'will weare
Taken from thence, flesh, which deaths force may trie.
Ere by the spheares time was created, thou
Wast in his minde, who is thy Sonne, and Brother,
Whom thou conceiv'st, conceiv'd; yet thou art now
Thy Makers maker, and thy Fathers mother,
Thou'hast light in darke; and shutst in little roome,
Immensity cloysterd in thy deare wombe.

Nativitie

Immensitie cloysterd in thy deare wombe,
Now leaves his welbelov'd imprisonment,
There he hath made himselfe to his intent
Weake enough, now into our world to come;
But Oh, for thee, for him, hath th' Inne no roome?
Yet lay him in this stall, and from the Orient,
Starres, and wisemen will travel to prevent
Th'effect of Herods jealous generall doome;
Seest thou, my Soule, with thy faiths eyes, how he
Which fils all place, yet none holds him, doth lye?
Was not his pity towards thee wondrous high,
That would have need to be pittied by thee?
Kisse him, and with him into Egypte goe,
With his kinde mother, who partakes thy woe.[32]

Henry Vaughan (1622–1695)

Vaughan was a young man in the parish of Bemerton, near Salisbury, when George Herbert (1593–1633), a mystical poet, served there as rector. A physician and attorney, Vaughan combined devotion with a love of nature that characterizes many later English poets.[33] His poem *Silex Scintillans* is filled with this and even a touch of alchemy. Catholic readers of the poetry in the *Liturgy of the Hours* will recall "The World", with its startling first lines

[32] John Donne, *The Complete English Poems* (London: Everyman's Library, 1991), 430–31.

[33] For a profound and thorough analysis of Vaughan and his devotion to Christ, see E. I. Watkin's *Poets and Mystics* (London: Sheed and Ward, 1953).

I saw Eternity the other night
Like a great Ring of pure and endless light.

Vaughan's devotion to Christ was deep but a bit different from what we have become accustomed to. Christ is Lord of life and death and the one who saves the soul. One thinks of the Pantocrator of ancient times in this Ascension hymn:

Dust and clay, man's ancient wear,
Here you must stay, but I elsewhere!
Souls sojourn here, but may not rest;
Who will ascend must be undressed.

And yet some, that know to die
Before death come, walk to the sky
Even in this life; but all such can
Leave behind them the old Man.

But since he that brightness soil'd,
His garments be all dark and spoil'd,
And here are left as nothing worth,
Till the Refiner's fire breaks forth.

Then comes he! Whose mighty light
Made his clothes be like Heav'n all bright;
The Fuller, whose pure blood did flow,
To make stain'd man more white than snow.

He alone and none else can
Bring bone to bone and rebuild man;
And by his all-subduing might
Make clay ascend more quick than light.[34]

The English Puritans

While the Anglican Church struggled to find its identity and to survive under Cromwell (1599–1658), the English Puritans had the upper hand. They had driven Anglicans from parishes, especially after the abolition of the episcopate in 1645. Often these Puritans are considered cruel fanatics, like the fiery general Oliver Cromwell, especially because of their brutal treatment of the Irish. However, there were among them people of genuine spirituality who even tried to soften the blows against Catholics. Surprisingly, there is also a mystical devotion to Christ. There is a particular importance in looking at the relationship between the English Puritans and the Anglican Church because, in fact, this conflict rages in Northern Ireland to this day. It would be wise for us to know something of the authentic religious devotion

[34] From "Ascension-Hymn", quoted in *Sacred Poems of Henry Vaughan* (London: Pickering, 1847), 117; spelling slightly modernized.

that inspired these Puritans as they attempted to take control of England and to create a state based on their own understanding of the Bible.

The Puritan Mystics of England

Americans think they know something of the New England Puritans, and therefore of the English Puritans. Actually, most people know little about the Puritans, and what few ideas they possess are often badly distorted. For this reason many will likely be surprised by the phrase "Puritan mystic". The popular view of the stoic Pilgrim father, next to his pale, almost androgynous wife and perfectly behaved children, gives us the adjective "puritanical". Whatever this word means to the average reader, it has nothing to do with warm or ecstatic mysticism. This brief study of the Puritan mystics will be a great surprise—a pleasant one to Catholics and perhaps a disconcerting one to Protestants, because this tradition of Puritan mysticism appears largely to have been lost.

We do not have the space to record the complex events that mark the history of the British Isles from the death of Elizabeth (1603) to the restoration of the monarchy (1660). The Catholic faith had been so persecuted by this time that it survived only in small pockets among what were called recusants.[35] The Catholic Church was still very much alive but persecuted in Ireland and in remote sections of Scotland. Contrary to popular belief, the Protestant Scots, although noisily antipapal, were not given to violence against their fellow Scots who were Catholic. For this reason Scotland at this time provided only one canonized Catholic martyr, St. John Ogilvie, whereas hundreds of English and Irish martyrs from this period were later beatified and canonized.

The Scots had been deeply influenced by John Knox (ca. 1514–1572), who made his country a vibrant center of Calvinism undiluted by the reform Protestantism of Zwingli. These Scottish Calvinists were Presbyterians—an adjective that ironically means "priestly" but in this case refers to a strong central church government. They were quite different from the English Puritans and eventually did battle with them at Winchester in 1651.

From the time of Henry VIII there had been a genuine Calvinist movement in England. At the death of Queen Mary (1558), Calvinist exiles returned from Europe, increasing their ranks, especially among the new middle class and the growing body of educated people. Calvinists gradually gained political control of England between 1603 and 1640 and in the latter year abolished the episcopacy. This eventually led to the execution of William Laud, Archbishop of Canterbury, and finally in 1649 of the king himself. Their political leader, Oliver Cromwell, was, oddly enough, not affiliated with any Puritan congregation, but his chaplains

[35] A recusant was a person who refused (*recusare*) to attend services at the Protestant church, an offense punishable by a fine of £20 *per annum* (later greatly increased) following passage of the Act of 1583.

and supporters were members of the Calvinist, or Puritan, church in England. These chaplains were very influential during the period when Cromwell ruled as Lord Protector until his death in 1658. Two years later, the monarchy was reestablished with Charles II, whose wife, Henrietta Maria, was Catholic. The king attempted to gain some freedom for Catholics but was unsuccessful, because he had to negotiate with Anglicans, Puritans, and other influential anti-Catholic forces. This difficulty worsened following the fictitious Popish Plot concocted toward 1678–1679 by a bitter ex–Jesuit seminarian, Titus Oates.

Throughout this turmoil a Puritan mystical tradition of deep personal piety was developing. It borrowed from late medieval piety, as well as from the *devotio moderna*, although direct allusions to these sources were rare because of anti-Catholic feeling. It is astonishing to note that Cromwell's chaplains, especially Peter Sterry, of whom we will hear more below, tried to relieve the pressure on Catholics. More astonishing still, considering his severe treatment of the Irish, is the fact that Cromwell himself tried to take pressure off Catholic recusant nobility by allowing many of them to buy back lands that had been confiscated by the Crown or at least to oversee them as government agents.[36] He admitted to Cardinal Mazarin that persecution of Catholics was tyranny over conscience and called the confiscation of Catholic property an "arbitrariness of power".[37]

With Cromwell and the two kings—Charles I and Charles II, one coming before and one after Cromwell—having some sympathy for English Catholics, is it surprising to find echoes of Catholic devotion among Puritan preachers? Bouyer states that a number of Cromwellian chaplains were characterized by a "vehement mystical feeling for Christ" and were closer to the devotion presented by the Jesuits and the Visitation nuns (disciples of St. Francis de Sales) than were traditional Anglicans of the time.[38]

In her book *English Devotional Literature (Prose) 1600–1640*, Helen C. White, an erudite Catholic scholar and professor of English literature at the University of Wisconsin, sought to establish a strong connection between the Protestant and Anglican devotional literature of the first half of the seventeenth century and its Catholic sources. Richard C. Lovelace, professor of Church history at Gordon-Conwell Theological Seminary in Massachusetts, is selectively critical of White's judgments, acknowledging the value of her contribution but pointing out instances where Protestant writing directly attacks or at least rejects earlier Catholic spiritual writers as a "rotten generation of mongrel divines".[39] It is worth noting that Lovelace does not take into consideration any of the

[36] *New Catholic Encyclopedia*, 4:470.

[37] Ibid.

[38] Bouyer, *Spirituality*, 134.

[39] Richard C. Lovelace, "Puritan Spirituality: The Search for a Rightly Reformed Church", in Dupré and Saliers, *Christian Spirituality*, 296.

important writers we are discussing here. He concludes his summary, as White does, with those writers up to 1640. Had he gone as far as 1660, after Cromwell's time, he would perhaps have seen the more obvious Catholic influences on people as different as Francis Rous and Thomas Goodwin, whom we will consider next.

Francis Rous (1579–1669)

Francis Rous, a layman and educator, was Speaker of the House of Commons under Cromwell. He wrote a commentary on the Song of Songs called *The Mystical Marriage, or Experimental Discourses of the Heavenly Marriage between a Soul and her Saviour.*[40] When one puts the following key citations from Rous in the context of Calvin's view that human nature is "totally depraved", it seems obvious that there has been a change of emphasis, to say the least.

> For the Deity, and that humanity being united, make our Saviour, Head and Husband of souls; and thou being married to him who is God, in him art also one with God. He one by a personal union, thou one by a mystical. And being thus united and married to him, his spirit flows into thy spirit, and the sap of the Deity feeds itself into thy soul. . . . The Son of God so loved the souls of men, that he would make them a wife, and marry them. And that he might make this wife to be brought into his Father's house, he left his Father to come to his wife, that he might cleanse her from spots and blemishes, and present her pure and glorious to his father.[41]

This is a clear theological statement, one remarkably similar to the decree of the Council of Ephesus (431) describing Christ's salvific mission and His divine and human natures in one person. Rous is also in agreement with the spousal mysticism of St. Bernard and especially of St. John of the Cross, whose works were well known by the time Rous wrote. The following prayer uses the spousal imagery in an even more daring way than St. John of the Cross did in his own commentary on the Song of Songs.

> Let thy spirit then look and long, and lust for this Lord who is the spirit, the chiefest spirit; let it cleave to him, let it hang about him, and never leave him till he be brought into the chambers of thy soul. Yea, tell him resolutely thou wilt not leave him, till thou hear a voice in thy soul, saying, "My beloved is mine, and I am my well-beloved's." To this end be still gazing on him and still calling on him: "Kiss me with the kisses of thy mouth." Yea, kiss my soul with such a kiss of thy spirit, that they may be no longer two, but one spirit.

[40] Bouyer, *Spirituality*, 136. Rous' work was first published in 1635. An edition printed at the Kings-head, London, in 1656, is in the possession of the Stanford (Calif.) University Library. See also Gordon S. Wakefield, *Puritan Devotion* (London: Epworth, 1957).

[41] Francis Rous, *The Mystical Marriage* (London: Kings-head, 1656), chap. 1, 686–87, spelling modernized.

> Say to him, Whom have I in heaven but thee, and whom have I desired on earth besides thee. My soul thirsteth, and panteth for thee, the living God. Tell him that thou art sick of [with] love. Vex him with importunity, and put him out of hope of ease (as the widow did the Judge) but only by satisfying thy desires.[42]

These citations are characteristic of the entire work. As E. I. Watkin has pointed out, the similarity of Rous' writings to those of the great Carmelite Doctor cannot be mere coincidence.[43]

The conclusion of Francis Rous is almost identical with the experience of union in the medieval mystics, especially St. John of the Cross. The following quotations, the first from Rous and the next from St. John of the Cross, are similar in their mystical descriptions and theology.

> For when Christ visiteth the soul, as he doth clarifie her with light, and ravish her with joy, so he doth beautifie her with holiness. . . . In these actions of Christ there are heights of union and the increases of union bring with them increases of uniformity. The Spirit of union is fire, and fire turn that into itself to which it is united. And the fuller and closer this union is, the more is this turning. So Christ Jesus, the more he comes into a soul by his Spirit, the more spiritual doth he make her; yea, the more doth he melt a soul into himself; the more doth he turn her will into his will, and the more doth he increase his own image in her.[44]

In the following passage the Carmelite Doctor comments on the verse "Let us rejoice, Beloved, and go to see ourselves in Your Beauty" from his *Spiritual Canticle*. Although no research is available on this question, one may justifiably suggest that John of the Cross had at least some indirect influence on Rous.

> That I be so transformed in Your beauty that we may be alike in beauty, and both behold ourselves in Your beauty . . . that each looking at the other may see in the other his own beauty, since both are Your beauty alone, I being absorbed in Your beauty; hence, I shall see You in Your beauty, and You shall see me in Your beauty, and I shall see myself in You in Your beauty, and You will see Yourself in me in Your beauty; that I may resemble You in Your beauty, and You resemble me in Your beauty, and my beauty be Your beauty and Your beauty my beauty; wherefore I shall be You in Your beauty, and You will be me in Your beauty, because Your very beauty will

[42] Ibid., 687.
[43] See Watkin, *Poets and Mystics*, 153ff.
[44] Rous, *Mystical Marriage*, 724; spelling and punctuation slightly modernized.

be my beauty; and therefore we shall behold each other in Your beauty.[45]

The rest of Rous' remarkable work is in the same mystical vein as that of St. John of the Cross. Watkin makes the point that between Puritan piety and devotion and Catholic Counter-Reformation devotion of the mystical type there was at least a profound similarity, if not a conscious borrowing.

Thomas Goodwin and the Heart of Jesus

If it seems strange that we can suspect the influence of a Catholic mystic on a Puritan writer, it may appear even more astonishing to see the possible influence of a Puritan on the most popular Catholic devotion, namely, the Sacred Heart of Jesus. The facts are simple. One of the most respected and popular of the Puritan divines, Thomas Goodwin (1600–1680) was chaplain to Cromwell. Unlike other chaplains, who seemed sympathetic to the plight of Catholics, Goodwin was strongly opposed to any influence of popery in the Puritan church. His preaching was founded on his own religious experience of conversion and complete discipleship. Like all Puritans, he sought a total involvement of his life with the cause of Christ, echoing a theme of the Anabaptists, a theme that was also the foundation of the spirituality of monks and friars, as well as of new orders like the Society of Jesus.[46]

For a Calvinist, his description of his total conversion seems quite voluntarist: "And what I did was from deliberate choice.... The weeds that entangled me in those waters, I swam and broke through with as much ease as Samson ... for I was made a vassal and a captive to another binding."[47]

These remarks sound so un-Calvinist that John Brown, Goodwin's sympathetic biographer, finds it necessary to explain them: "Possibly to some people this may sound like old-world talk which has grown obsolete in these latter days.... There is more in it of living reality and firm grasp of spiritual fact than some may be prepared to admit. And one thing is certain: no man will ever understand how Puritan preaching laid hold of men as it did, made such heroic, courageous, commanding souls as it did, till he has accurately gauged a profound religious experience like that which Thomas Goodwin has laid bare for us in himself."[48]

In fact, Thomas Goodwin's conversion was profoundly serious and, according to his own words, went on all his life. His sermons, Brown

[45] St. John of the Cross, *The Spiritual Canticle*, st. 36, in *The Collected Works of St. John of the Cross*, trans. Kieran Kavanaugh, O.C.D., and Otilio Rodriguez, O.C.D. (Washington, D.C.: Institute of Carmelite Studies, 1973), 547.

[46] See John Brown, *Puritan Preaching in England* (London: Hodder and Stoughton, 1900).

[47] Quoted in ibid., 103.

[48] Brown, *Puritan Preaching*, 103–4.

asserts, demonstrate a deep love for Christ and a personal desire to respond to Him.

Before we examine Goodwin's remarkable sermon on the Heart of Jesus, we should recall that devotion to the Heart of Christ can be found as early as the thirteenth century, among the German mystical nuns, and in the writings of St. Bonaventure, the sixth general of the Franciscans. It is our contention that this devotional picture of Christ caring for sinners has its roots in the first devotion to Christ the Physician. Goodwin's understanding of the Heart of Christ, filled with concern for the welfare of sinners, appears similar to St. Augustine's picture of *Christus Medicus* (see Chapter 3 above). Later, when we consider the writings of St. John Eudes, St. Margaret Mary, and St. Claude de la Colombière, we will see the similarity of ideas and the struggle with the mystery of how Christ, now in eternal glory, still is concerned about souls and can be said to suffer for those who have gone astray.

> I shall now annex this discourse that follows, which lays open THE HEART of Christ, as now he is in heaven, sitting at God's right hand and interceding for us; how it is affected and graciously disposed towards sinners on earth that do come to him; how willing to receive them; how ready to entertain them; how tender to pity them in all their infirmities, both sins and miseries. The scope and use whereof will be this, to hearten and encourage believers to come more boldly unto the throne of grace, unto such a Saviour and High Priest, when they shall know how sweetly and tenderly his heart, though he is now in his glory, is inclined towards them; and so to remove that great stone of stumbling which we meet with (and yet lieth unseen) in the thoughts of men in the way to faith, that Christ being now absent, and withal exalted to so high and infinite a distance of glory, as to "sit at God's right hand," etc., they therefore cannot tell how to come to treat with him about their salvation so freely, and with that hopefulness to obtain, as those poor sinners did, who were here on earth with him.[49]

Although Goodwin reiterates the Calvinist notion that Christ is far away in heaven, he nevertheless sees Christ as compassionate and at least present by His knowledge and concern for suffering sinners.

> The drift of this discourse is therefore to ascertain poor souls, that his heart, in respect of pity and compassion, remains the same [as] it was on earth; that he intercedes there with the same heart he did here below; and that he is as meek, as gentle, as easy to be entreated, as tender in his bowels; so that they may deal with him as fairly about the great

[49] *The Heart of Christ in Heaven towards Sinners on Earth*, Vol. 4, *The Works of Thomas Goodwin* (Edinburgh: James Nichol, 1862), 95.

> matter of their salvation, and as hopefully, and upon as easy terms to obtain it of him, as they might if they had been on earth with him.[50]

It is very clear, then, that Christ is at least aware and present in that sense—compassionate, understanding, and forgiving—as He was to the poor sinners we meet in the Gospel. The purpose of this is to give hope to the devout Puritans who listened to Goodwin when he was president of Magdalen College, Oxford, and when he was a popular preacher in London. Goodwin then takes up Christ's action of washing the apostles' feet at the Last Supper. He says: "This preface was prefixed by the evangelist, on purpose to set open a window into Christ's heart, to shew what it was then at his departure, and so withal to give a light into, and put a gloss and interpretation upon all that follows."[51]

Goodwin summarizes the exalted and beautiful words of Christ in the Gospel of John, words that speak of His relationship with the Father and His concern about the apostles.

> What was Christ's heart most upon, in the midst of all these elevated meditations? Not upon his own glory so much, though it is told us that he considered that, thereby the more to set out his love unto us, but upon these thoughts his heart ran out in love towards, and was set upon, "his own": "having loved his own", says the 1st verse.... The elect are Christ's own, a piece of himself ... "he came unto his own, and his own received him not".
>
> One would think that when he was meditating upon his going out of this world, his heart should be all upon Abraham, his Isaacs, and his Jacobs, whom he was going to; no, he takes more care for his own, who were to remain here in this world, a world wherein there is much evil.[52]

Goodwin then makes the point that Christ was so much concerned about the apostles and that He tenderly cared for them. "He lets them see what his heart would be unto them, and how mindful of them when in heaven, by that business which he professeth he went thither to perform for them; concerning which, observe first, that he lovingly acquaints them with it aforehand what it is, which argued care and tenderness.... Yea, he carrieth their names written in his heart."[53]

Presuming, of course, that it was the Apostle John who received the revelation in the Book of Revelation, he mentions that sixty years after His Ascension, when Christ was reigning in heaven, He was concerned about the hearts of men.

[50] Ibid., 95–96.
[51] Ibid., 96.
[52] Ibid., 97.
[53] Ibid., 99.

> Christ cries out as loud from heaven, "Come," in answer to this desire in them; so that heaven and earth ring again of it. "Let him that is athirst come to me; and let him that will come, come, and take of the waters of life freely." This is Christ speech unto men on earth. They call him to come unto earth, to judgment; and he calls sinners to come up to heaven unto him for mercy. They cannot desire his coming to them, so much as he desires their coming to him. Now what is the meaning of this, that upon their calling upon him to come, he should thus call upon them to come? It is in effect as if he had plainly uttered himself thus: I have a heart to come to you, but I must have all you my elect that are to be on earth, come to me first. You would have me come down to you, but I must stay here till all that the Father hath given me be come to me; and then you shall be sure quickly to have me with you. Hereby expressing how much his heart now longs after them.[54]

In the second part of his presentation, Goodwin calls the reader to "take our hands and lay them on Christ's breast, and let us feel how his heart beats and bowels yearn toward us, even now he is in glory—the very scope of these words being manifestly to encourage believers against all that may discourage them, from the consideration of Christ's heart towards them now in heaven".[55]

Any person seriously interested in comparisons of spirituality should read Goodwin's sermon and also study the Catholic doctrine of the Sacred Heart of Jesus and its more modern version, the devotion to the Divine Mercy. Obviously there are Calvinist elements in Goodwin's presentation, especially his emphasis on Christ's being in heaven. Catholic mystics would stress very much Christ also being here, both in the Eucharist and by divine grace in the soul. Apart from that, however, the tender devotion, the recognition of Christ's warm human and divine love for souls, His compassion and mercy are so close to being identical that it would be a quibble to separate them.

Incredible Similarities

The end of the sixteenth century and the entire seventeenth century were times of great religious and spiritual activity. England was beginning to spread its language and religious traditions to the colonies and what would become the new nations. For this reason we must soon bring to an end our consideration of the specifically English devotion to Christ. Anglicans, Puritans, Baptists, and underground Catholics, still strong in Ireland and with a remnant in England, would all seek to export their beliefs and devotions to Christ. Because of the bitter polemics of the time, and especially because of the religious-political entanglements of these various groups, they failed to recognize that

[54] Ibid., 109.
[55] Ibid., 111.

they resembled each other remarkably. There are deeper reasons for their unrecognized similarity, however: mysterious influences of grace, which we should assume were operating in all who sought to be disciples of Christ and who attempted to build their lives on the Gospel. Rarely did they see the grace of Christ operating in the lives of their religious antagonists. From the distance of half a millennium, however, we can easily do so.

A New Face of God

Protestants of the seventeenth century lived in a world far different from that of Luther and Calvin. The Black Death was a distant memory and Renaissance ideas had been incorporated into the thinking of the various churches. The Council of Trent had produced a reformed Catholicism. The reformation churches, from Anglican to Baptist, were able to study the Bible with a bit more peace, and the polemics had finally died down.

Pierre de la Ramee

In *The New England Mind*, the distinguished historian of American Puritanism Perry Miller has established the importance of what is called Ramist logic. Pierre de la Ramée (1515–1572) was an outstanding logician and a lector at the Collège de France. He died in the criminal massacre of St. Bartholomew's Day at the hands of the henchmen of his lifelong foe, Jacques Charpentier.

Ramée (or Petrus Ramus, as he is also known) stressed in his vigorously anti-Aristotelian philosophy that divine will is not an arbitrary authority requiring blind submission. He emphasized the unity of reality, of thought, and of experience expressed in the proper use of language and demanding the art of logic. Ramée left the Catholic Church in 1561 and found that his almost fanatical approach to logic made him a popular hero, not only to French and German Protestants but also to English Puritans. Although a royal decree in 1554 proscribing Ramée's works and lecturing was later lifted through the intervention of the Cardinal of Lorraine,[56] Ramée apparently found the Catholic system of thought too narrow. Although the philosophy of St. Thomas Aquinas was not as popular in Catholicism at the time as Augustinian thought, Ramée's opposition to Aristotle and indirectly to St. Thomas no doubt made him feel more at home outside the Catholic Church. On the other hand, Protestants who were uncomfortable with an arbitrary God were desperately seeking a way to maintain their belief in Sacred Scripture and yet not be slaves to an arbitrary understanding of the divinity. Ramée's rules for logic (a compact fifty pages), the *Dialecticae* (1556), were extremely popular. He himself had translated them into the vernacular and saw to translations into other languages.[57]

[56] Perry Miller, *The New England Mind: The Seventeenth Century* (New York: Macmillan, 1939), 116.

[57] For an excellent summary of these issues, see ibid., especially chap. 5.

In the midst of all the enthusiasm by Protestants and Catholics alike, a revolution was occurring in Protestant thought. Bouyer says that Ramée put an end to the whole system of Ockham and his notion of *potentia absoluta*, which had permeated Luther's thought and which Calvin "had carried to its logical conclusion with his theology of law and predestination and, finally, his understanding of the Word of God".[58] If all this is a bit abstract, you might consider the small number of Fundamentalist Protestants (usually from the Anabaptist tradition) who still maintain that the earth is only six thousand years old. How did they get themselves into this position? Their spiritual ancestors obviously did not accept Ramée. Anglicans from Hooker to Laud rejected Ramist logic for other reasons, probably because they suspected the minimizing of tradition and the Church Fathers, which it implied. This is possibly the explanation why a number of early American universities—Harvard, Yale, Columbia, Princeton—began in the Puritan tradition, rather then as Anglican establishments. Miller points out the need to appreciate Ramée and his contribution of a totally logical method congruent with faith in order to understand mainstream American Protestantism. We are of course interested in understanding the response of the Puritans to Ramée and its effect on their devotion to Christ, which now began to flow from their logical study of the Bible.

The Covenant Theology—A Puritan Way Out

William Perkins (1558–1602), a Puritan theologian strongly attached to the Calvinist doctrine of the divine will, fell back into a position similar to Ockham's: what God wills becomes reasonable because of that very fact. Like Ockham, Perkins tried to package the concept of an arbitrary divine will by softening it because of God's goodness. Obviously, this put him into a closed circle that was illogical. His disciple William Ames (1576–1633), looking for a spiritual expression of Ramée's logic, created a theology of the covenant. Simply put, God had created Adam to be perfect, but the Fall destroyed this perfection. However, the Fall brought a new covenant, which began with Abraham and arrived at perfection in Christ. This covenant does not do away with the immutable law of nature; but by firm faith in the grace of Christ the Mediator, human nature regains the power to accomplish what it had originally lost. It may not seem obvious, but this view contains strong elements of Platonic thought. According to Bouyer, "In this way all arbitrariness in the divine will disappeared. Faith was no longer in opposition to reason, and grace no longer condemned nature. Rather, faith restored perverted reason just as grace healed vitiated nature."[59]

Anyone familiar with Platonism will realize the danger here, namely, that of equating grace and nature, of confusing faith with reason, and of the identification of the two.

---

[58] Bouyer, *Spirituality*, 144.

[59] Ibid., 145.

Despite all the anti-Catholic rhetoric of the time, there is no doubt that the theological trends of the period fostered a spirituality and devotion that approached the Catholic spirituality of the past. Not only was classical Catholic spirituality, although unrecognized as such, returning to the Protestant world, but all parties, from Catholics to Baptists, were producing a devotional literature with strong similarities. Except for Bouyer, very few people have pointed this out, but it is one of the most important elements in any ecumenical encounters of believing Christians.

One can hardly speak of devotion, as we have defined it, and at the same time speak of an angry and arbitrary God. The early Lutherans and Calvinists found some relief from this image in the figure of the suffering and risen Christ. But the angry image of God continued to present problems for the later Calvinists (and, as we shall see, the Lutherans). They needed, as Ames had recognized, a beautiful face of God. Responding to this need was a remarkable group of Puritan Platonists led by Peter Sterry.

Peter Sterry (1613–1672)

Sterry was a chaplain to Oliver Cromwell and attended him at the hour of death. A man of remarkable complexity in a time of war and religious discord, he considered himself a perfect Calvinist. Yet he opposed the Scottish Presbyterians, considering them worse than Catholics. His attitude toward Catholics was complex. Following the style of the times, he saw Catholics as the "Ghost of Judaisme", but as his principal biographer, Vivian De Sola Pinto, says, Sterry praised Romanists because "they take, and give a large scope to the understanding and affections in generous contemplations, in mystical divinity".[60] De Sola Pinto goes on to say that if Sterry's upbringing had been Catholic, he might have been happy in the Church of St. Teresa and Richard Crashaw, the mystic and poet.[61]

Sterry was a man of his own convictions. It was primarily he who induced Cromwell to take pressure off the Catholic recusants. Despite his devout Calvinism he preached a friendly picture of Christ quite different from Calvin's. In a sermon on forgiveness, Sterry reveals a loving devotion to Christ and a remarkably positive attitude toward the whole human race.

> Forgiving one another freely for Christ's sake, is the language of St. Paul. Look upon every person through this two-fold Glass, the Blood, and the Beauties of Christ. Christ hath died for all. The natural Being of every person hath his Root in the Grave of Christ, and is watered with his blood. Christ lives in all. His Resurrection is the life of the whole Creation. He is the Wisdom, the Power, the Righteousness of

[60] Quoted in Vivian de Sola Pinto, *Peter Sterry: Platonist and Puritan* (Cambridge: Cambridge University Press, 1934), 24.

[61] *Peter Sterry*, 24.

> God in every work of Nature, as well as of Grace. He is the Root, out of which every natural, as well as every spiritual, plant springs, which brings forth himself through every natural existence, and brings forth himself out of it, as the flower, the brightness of the Glory of God. He is the Root and Truth of all things. All things are by him, and for him, to the praise and glory of God in him. His name is excellent through all the Earth. Read then this Name of Excellency, of Glory, the Name of Christ in every part and point of the Earth, the darkest, the lowest, the least; forgive the spots upon this Name in every person, for the Names-sake engraven upon it.
>
> Receive one another into the Glory of God, is the Rule of St. Paul. Divines distinguish between the person, together with the nature of the Devil, and the evil. The person, the nature, springs forth from God, and so is good, hath a Divinity and Glory in it; a Divine Root, a Divine Image. It stands in the Glory of God, as a Flower in the Garden, a Beam in the Sun, it is maintained by a continual emanation from the bosom of the supream [sic] Glory. Thus thou art to receive every person, clouded with the greatest evils, as he is the work of Nature, and of God into the Glory of God. Thus every other person is to be thy Neighbour, thy Brother in the Glory of God; and the Object of a Divine Love.[62]

John Smith and the Cambridge Platonists

The ancient Greek philosophers were creators of new ways of thinking. Of the three greatest—Socrates, Plato, and Aristotle—Plato by far had the most profound impact on Christianity and how it would present the revelation of Jesus to the world. Not only did Plato supply the philosophical foundations for the teaching of the early Church, giving it concepts and names used in things as sublime as the Trinity, but he also produced terms used of Christ by the evangelist John. The term "Word" in the prologue of the Johanine Gospel is directly from Plato.

The Church Fathers from East and West used Platonic concepts without apology or explanation, even though they knew the difference between philosophy and revelation. Peter Sterry was accused of losing the distinction between nature and grace—a false accusation, it seems to me. This charge would be made by other Puritans—the right wing, if you will—against the group of Puritan Platonists at Emmanuel College, which the Puritans themselves founded at Cambridge.[63] Benjamin Whichcote (1609–1685) was the leading originator of the group and taught that right reason could only be found where there was right faith. God was perfect reason and goodness, and reason and goodness were natural to man despite the Fall. Since the Fall, man's reason, like his natural religious nature, needed to be reinforced and restored by revelation, that is, by Christ as our life and

[62] Quoted in ibid., 127.

[63] Bouyer, *Spirituality*, 148–49.

our Savior. If one is not careful, thinking like this could become a natural supernaturalism, which could obliterate the distinction between nature and grace. As Bouyer points out, this has always been a temptation among Christian Platonists. However, the Cambridge Platonists were cautious on this point.

Bouyer believes that Whichcote's ideas can be given an interpretation like that given by the Greek Fathers, especially Gregory of Nyssa, who said that the image of the Trinity was printed on the soul but needed to be cleansed of sin.[64] St. Bonaventure taught a similar doctrine, that human beings cannot think or reason at all without direct divine illumination.

It is difficult to distinguish Whichcote's picture of mankind from that of traditional Catholic theology. In the words of St. Bonaventure, "Man is good but broken and bowed because of original sin and unable to free himself." Catholic and Orthodox theology never denied the essential goodness or divine root of human nature or the reality of the Fall.

The Platonists turn our thoughts to how mysterious a human being is. The Cambridge Platonists, all fervent Calvinists but products of their own time, seem to have come a long way from Calvin. Despite his short life, John Smith (1618–1652) is the most interesting of them. In a study for the tercentenary of Smith's death, Watkin praised him in this way: "[H]is positive testimony remains to an intellectualism which is genuine, consistent and truly rational because it is not rationalist but spiritual, and to a vital knowledge of God which is His own illumination of the soul, a communication to her of His light and life."[65]

Smith was described as "a living library and a walking museum".[66] Not only did he have a thorough knowledge of Hebrew but also of rabbinical and Cabalistic Judaism. Unfortunately, little survives of his writings. Smith is a Christian mystic, and his teaching reflects what one finds in the writings of Catholic mystics. He sees Jesus as a model of gentleness and sweetness, "a knowing of the truth that is in that sweet, mild, humble and loving spirit of Jesus". Smith's basic doctrine can be seen from the following quotation: "God hath stamped a copy of His own archetypal loveliness upon the soul, that man by reflecting into himself might behold there the glory of God.... Reason in man being *lumen de lumine*, a light flowing from the fountain and father of lights ... was to enable man to work out of himself all those notions of God which are the true groundwork of love and obedience to God and conformity to Him."[67]

[64] See *From Glory to Glory: Texts from Gregory of Nyssa's Mystical Writings*, trans. and ed. Herbert Musurillo, S.J. (New York: Charles Scribner's Sons, 1961), 112–17.

[65] Watkin, *Poets and Mystics*, 255.

[66] Bouyer, *Spirituality*, 150.

[67] John Smith, *The Excellency and Nobleness of True Religion*, quoted in *Poets and Mystics*, Watkin, 243.

He speaks of us, saying, "Moses-like conversing with God in the mount and there beholding His glory shining out upon us in the face of Christ, we should be deriving a copy of that eternal beauty upon our own souls, and our thirsty and hungry spirits would be perpetually sucking in a true participation and image of His glory".[68]

Perhaps the clearest expression of Christian devotion in Smith is the awareness of something that mystics often speak of: Christ being formed in the human soul by the Holy Spirit.

> The more this sensual, brutish and self-central life thrives and prospers, the more Divine Faith languisheth; and the more that decays and all self feeling, self love and self sufficiency pine away, the more is true faith fed and nourished, it grows more vigorous; and as carnal life wastes and consumes the more does faith suck in a true, divine and spiritual life from the true life who hath life in Himself and freely bestows it to all those that heartily seek for it.... We are told of Christ being formed in us and the Spirit of Christ dwelling in us; of our being made conformable to Him, of having fellowship with Him, of being as He was in this world, of living in Him and His living in us, of dying and rising again and ascending with Him into heaven: because the same Spirit that dwelt in Him derives itself in its mighty virtue and energy through all believing souls, shaping them more and more into a just resemblance and conformity to Him as the first copy and pattern.[69]

Summarizing Smith's beliefs, Watkin characterizes him as distinctly mystical. "The principles which for him determine the genuine religious life—a progressive influx of the Divine life, unity, interior solitude, complete reliance on God, profound distrust and progressive abnegation of self—are the principles which determine the way of Divine Union."[70] The parallels with the teachings of SS. John of the Cross and Teresa of Avila and other Catholic mystics are obvious. In Peter Sterry and John Smith we find what we found with Francis Rous: a true Christian mystical experience in the Calvinist tradition.

The Last Two Catholics

This title does not imply that the Catholic faith ended in England during the sixteenth century, but the Catholic Church, as a functioning entity, did. In "The Present Position of Catholics in England", Newman describes the Church's situation at the beginning of the nineteenth century as resembling bits and pieces of flotsam distributed on a beach. Most Catholic activity on the part of English-speaking people necessarily took place on the Continent or in the colonies.

---

[68] From *Legal Righteousness and of the Righteousness of Faith*, quoted in *Poets and Mystics*, Watkin, 243–44.

[69] Ibid., 252.

[70] Watkin, *Poets and Mystics*, 253.

English Catholics were served at this time by what were called seminary priests, who had studied in Europe and were often martyred. A collection of religious priests, often operating from the embassies of Catholic countries, also shaped the devotional life of this remnant. These included the Benedictines, the old founding order of England; the Jesuits, whose beginnings were almost contemporary with the persecution; and the French Capuchins, who, like the Jesuits, were a significant part of Counter-Reformation devotion and piety.[71]

Benet of Canfield (1562–1611)

William Fitch, who in religious life took the name Benet along with the name of his place of birth, according to the old custom of the Franciscan and Capuchin friars, was born in Essex in the early part of the reign of Queen Elizabeth.[72] Benet's family was Protestant,[73] inclined to Puritanism, and little is known of his early life. In 1580 he was admitted to the Middle Temple in London to study law.[74] Benet's own account suggests some youthful idleness and dissipation until he read *The First Book of Christian Exercise Appertaining to Resolution* (albeit in a form adapted for Protestant use) by Fr. Robert Persons, S.J.[75] This seems to have brought on a spiritual crisis that turned him to a life of reform. Determined to seek the truth between the Catholic and the Protestant positions, he felt suddenly illumined as to the truth of the Catholic religion.[76] He was received into the Catholic Church by a Carthusian priest, a prisoner at Newgate, on August 1, 1585. Six months later, he left for France, making Douai his first stop.

In his autobiography Benet recorded his impressions on first reaching French soil.

> We arrived at the desired haven, namely, a Catholic country, where for the first time I saw the majesty, beauty, and magnificence of Thy Church, and with what joy and satisfaction I remarked . . . the order reigning in this Church militant and celestial hierarchy, from the Pope at the head . . . down to the secular clergy. . . .

[71] See Fr. Cyprien de Gamache, *Memoirs of the Mission in England of the Capuchin Friars of the Province of Paris from the Year 1630 to 1669*. This is volume 2 of *The Court and Times of Charles the First* (London: Henry Colburn, 1848). Volume 1 is a collection of letters public and private. The annotations in Fr. Cyprien's volume are frequently marked by a strong anti-Catholic bias.

[72] For a study of Benet of Canfield see the work of his earliest biographer, Jacques Brousse, *The Lives of Ange de Joyeuse and Benet Canfield*, trans. Robert Rookwood, ed. T.A. Birrell (London: Sheed and Ward, 1959), especially the excellent introduction. See also Henri Brémond's *A Literary History of Religious Thought in France*, vol. 2 (London: SPCK, 1930). Depending on the source, Benet's family name is given variously as Filch, Finch, and Fitch. We follow the spelling according to Brousse and the *Dictionary of National Biography*.

[73] However, an aunt, Jane Wiseman, was a staunch Catholic who suffered some years' imprisonment under the penal laws of the time.

[74] Brousse, *Ange de Joyeuse and Benet Canfield*, xxii.

[75] Ibid.

[76] Ibid., 113ff.

> When I beheld the lofty and magnificent buildings of Thy temples, the great and spacious monasteries, beautiful within and without with sculpture, paintings, exquisite carvings, I could think of nothing but the gravity and majesty of Thy holy Church. . . .
>
> The glorious services of Thy Church to my mind embellish and magnify the whole. For, beholding the great solemnity of the Mass, celebrated by priests, deacons, sub-deacons, acolytes, each with the ornaments of his rank and each performing his own office; beholding the dressed altar glittering with candles and encircled by the choir; beholding the devotion and piety with which they censed it with goodly fragrance, and the great and solemn processions of thronging worshippers with torches, candles and numberless tapers . . .[77]

We might see here the enthusiasm and loss of objectivity of a new convert. Yet while we read much about the troubles and failures of the Church at this time, it is worth noting that there were spiritually sensitive people who experienced something other than chaos and corruption.

Benet continued to Paris, where he entered the Capuchins at the convent of Saint-Honoré in 1587. It was not long, however, before he became a cause for concern among his new confreres, as he would fall into ecstasy for extended periods of time. In the summer of 1599 he attempted to return to England, where a number of French Capuchins were working underground through the French embassy and some of the Catholic recusant nobility. Almost immediately after landing near Dover, he was imprisoned. The French king, Henry IV, insisted on his being sent back to France, and he was deported early in 1603.

Although Benet was learned, "the book which he held continually in his hands and turned often every day . . . was the cross and passion of Our Saviour".[78] He worked for many years as a spiritual director and always preached the doctrine of the Cross. "The sublimity of his doctrine has been known and searched after in the cloisters . . . and God only knows the number of religious men and women who, having been comforted by his exhortations and aided by his doctrine, both by word of mouth and writing, have been exalted to the high state of perfection".[79]

France was on the threshold of a great religious renaissance, and according to Brémond, the renowned scholar of the time, it was Benet who gave this renewal its authentic Christian mysticism. His *Rule of Perfection (Règle de perfection)* is described by Brémond, who can be very caustic and critical, as a "beautiful book glowing and luminous".[80] Although the book was put on the Index in 1689 at the time

---

[77] Quoted in Brémond, *Religious Thought in France*, 113–14.

[78] Brousse, *Ange de Joyeuse and Benet Canfield*, 144.

[79] Ibid.

[80] Brémond, *Religious Thought in France*, 116.

of the Quietist controversy where it remained until modern times, it was rediscovered in the twentieth century, largely by people like Brémond, Huxley, and Watkin.

The core of Benet's teaching was the "active and heroic surrender" of one's life to the divine will.[81] This is Canfield's "golden key" to holiness: to do all "from the sole motive of pleasing God, all one is aware that God desires, commands, counsels, and inspires".[82] Later we shall see this teaching, which ran through much of the spirituality of the time, come to its most popular expression in the eighteenth-century classic *Abandonment to Divine Providence* by the French Jesuit Jean-Pierre de Caussade.

It is important to consider how Benet of Canfield teaches people that they may come to the unitive way, the closest possible association with God in this world. Perhaps the most important chapter in the third part of his *Rule of Perfection* is devoted to the need to imitate and contemplate our Lord's Passion. Using the analogy from the story of Rahab (see Josh 2:18), he says:

> The scarlet rope that Rahab put at the window of her house shows that God wishes us to put his red and bloody Passion at the window of our inner house, which is our understanding, so that we might be able always to meditate upon and contemplate it there. But if one should consider the immensity of this sovereign majesty, and what it is that such sublimity and omnipotence should suffer so cruelly, as it did, wholly in order to give us an example, he would concede easily that this mystery truly deserves to be contemplated our whole lives.[83]

Benet teaches that once we have come to contemplate the divinity in our being, the soul must cling to Gospel scenes of the Passion, "even", according to Brémond, "when a soul has attained those heights which dominate from afar created images, even the holiest": "Then God Himself seems to summon the soul to contemplate only divinity, but the soul clings to the Gospel scenes of the passion. *Dimitte me*, Christ says to her, *aurora est*—cease to touch my human nature, for thou seest true day dawning, my divinity. But the soul responds: . . . I will not leave Thee. And that, I mean, to cling close to the God-man, is essential, because not only Christianity, but the highest contemplation itself is won thus".[84]

Benet also makes clear that he does not wish to lose the images of the life of Christ and especially of His Passion. Those familiar with the writings of St. John of the Cross will recall his counsel not to dwell on visual images. Nonetheless, even he experienced a vision of

[81] Ibid., 118.

[82] Ibid.

[83] Kent Emery, Jr. *Renaissance Dialectic and Renaissance Piety: Benet of Canfield's Rule of Perfection* (Binghamton, N.Y.: Medieval and Renaissance Texts and Studies, 1987), 230.

[84] Brémond, *Religious Thought in France*, 124.

Christ Crucified, which he tried to record with a sketch that is still in existence.

The last of the Catholic writers before the Church entered the dark tunnel of complete persecution in England, Benet of Canfield brings to the history of Christian mysticism a profound love of Jesus, especially of Him crucified. Even in the midst of the highest mystical experiences he returns to Christ's Passion, anchoring his devotion to biblical scenes and historical events of Christ's life.

Augustine Baker (1575–1641)

If the life of Benet of Canfield was exciting and came at the beginning of the revival of spirituality that was to sweep through France in the seventeenth century, the life of Dom Augustine Baker, one of the first of the refounded English Benedictines, is remarkable because of its quiet in the midst of turmoil. Although he is not among the great mystics, *Holy Wisdom*, an anthology of his writings, has been of immense help to those who were called to contemplation, but not to the greatest heights. E. I. Watkin states that while Baker's teaching is in conformity with the most sublime doctrine, he tempers the application of the most challenging teachers to the weakness of the majority, especially of contemplatives.[85] Watkin concludes that Baker's writings can be put safely and profitably into the hands of anyone interested in contemplation.

Baker was born in Abergavenny, in Wales, and was baptized in the Church of England. Following his education at Oxford, he became a lawyer. As a young man, he lost his faith, but in 1600 had a remarkable conversion. His horse brought him to a footbridge so narrow that he could go neither forward nor back, and he resolved: "If ever I escape this danger I will believe there is a God who hath more care of my life and safety than I have had of His love and worship." [86] He was converted to a serious pursuit of the Gospel and began to study the controversies of the Reformation. This led him to the Catholic Church, and at his first confession, he recalled, "There sprang up a desire of spiritual perfection to be purchased with the loss of all sensual pleasures and abandoning all secular designs".[87]

In London, Baker met some undercover Benedictine monks (of the Italian Cassinese Congregation) and decided to enter religious life, which he did at Padua in 1605. He fell ill and was sent home, arriving just in time to receive his father into the Catholic Church. It is an incredible fact that the English Benedictine Congregation had just been reestablished, or rather continued, when two Italian monks became affiliated with Dom Sigebert Buckley, the last survivor of Westminster Abbey. In the 1630s Baker spent several years at St. Gregory's Abbey,

[85] Watkin, *Poets and Mystics*, 188.

[86] Ibid., 190.

[87] Ibid.

Douai, in Flanders (now Downside Abbey), although officially he was a member of the community at Dieulouard, in Lorraine (present-day Ampleforth). Dom Augustine (his religious name) also spent nine years as chaplain to the newly founded (1623) convent of English Benedictine nuns at Cambrai (later Stanbrook Abbey), and thus he was associated with the roots of Benedictine life in England today. While at Cambrai, he wrote the majority of his treatises; he was also director to Dame Gertrude More the great-great granddaughter of Thomas More and a spiritual writer in her own right.

Like St. Teresa of Avila, he records a second conversion in his book the *Secretum*, referring to his return to the practice of mental prayer in 1608. He had a profound experience of "passive contemplation", an ecstasy he described as "a speaking of God to the soul". The experience was brief, but the result was that it made his prayer "far purer, far easier, less painful to nature and more abstract from sense.... It wrought a stability or perfect settledness of prayer".[88]

Baker's ecstasy left him with an interior illumination, which, according to Watkin, gave him "a personal assurance of the truth of Catholic doctrine".

> I would tell you of the wonderful proof and satisfaction that a soul hath of the verities of Christian religion by one of the said passive contemplations.... The soul most clearly seeth that all is most assuredly true that in such work is manifested or told unto her, as are the verities and mysteries of Christianity. O happy evidence of our belief. No thanks to them that believe after such a sight. A man may say that God is not beholden to them for believing that which they have so clearly, evidently and manifestly, as it were, seen with their eyes and handled with their hands. Such sights of the soul are far more clear than are the sights or feelings of our outward senses.[89]

After his conversion, Baker went through years of spiritual darkness and desolation. Apparently, he gradually left off the life of interior prayer, but in the darkness he did not give up the practice of faith, hope, and charity. In 1613 he was ordained a priest in the Benedictine Order. His identity as a Catholic priest (a treasonable offense in England at that time) did not prevent him from working as a lawyer, mostly on charity cases, for "widows, orphans and distressed persons".

In 1620, he returned to the practice of mental prayer and achieved a high degree of active contemplation, that is, interior prayer directed by his own will and acts of love for Christ and the heavenly Father. He was guided by the English classic of the fourteenth century *The*

---

[88] Watkin, *Poets and Mystics*, 191.

[89] From the *Confession of Venerable Father Baker*, excerpted from Augustine Baker, *Secretum*, ed. Abbot Justin McCann (London: Burns, Oates and Washbourne, 1922), quoted in Watkin, *Poets and Mystics*, 191–92.

Cloud of Unknowing, as well as by Walter Hilton's *Scale of Perfection*. In this way, Baker's work is part of the profound tradition of the English mystics. Toward the end of his life, he ceased writing and lived as a fugitive just before the time of Cromwell. From a private letter we learn that his prayer had become totally passive, that is, directed by the Holy Spirit rather than by himself. A fugitive and separated by a misunderstanding from the Benedictines, Baker seemed a pitiful old man, yet he wrote that his sufferings were "the greatest tastes of heaven that this life is capable of".[90]

Baker died in London on August 9, 1641, and in 1657 his contemporary and fellow Benedictine Dom Serenus Cressy, published an anthology of his writings under the title of *Sancta Sophia*, or *Holy Wisdom*.

As we focus on his devotion to Jesus Christ we must ask if a mystic drawn into the Godhead by active and passive contemplation can still be a person of devotion to Christ. Unfortunately, many later editions of *Holy Wisdom* omit the long recitation of Baker's personal prayers to Christ. The following selection from these prayers will make clear that this profound mystic could have a devotion to Jesus Christ as fervent and well articulated as anyone in any of the traditions of the time—Anglican, Protestant, or Catholic:

> Hail, sweet Jesus, who with an unspeakable charity hast instituted the Sacrament of the Eucharist, and with a wonderful liberality hast in it given Thyself to us; stir up in me a desire and enkindle in the interior of my soul a vehement thirst of this most venerable Sacrament.
>
> Hail, sweet Jesus; praise, honour, and glory be to Thee, O Christ, who didst hang (Thy hands and feet being pierced) three hours upon the shameful wood of the cross ... shedding in great abundance Thy Precious Blood.... O that Thou wouldst purge and thoroughly heal me, being washed with this Thy Precious Blood!
>
> Hail, sweet Jesus, who wouldst that Thy side should be opened with a soldier's lance ... that Thy mellifluous Heart should be wounded for me; O that it might please Thee to make a most deep wound in my heart with the lance of Thy love, and unite it to Thy most Sacred Heart, in such manner that I may have no power to will anything but that which Thou wilt! Bring in, O my Lord, bring in my soul, through the wound of Thy side, into the bosom of Thy charity and treasure-house of Thy Divinity, that I may joyfully glorify Thee, my God.[91]

The Primers

No one can grasp devotional life at this time without some appreciation of primers. These were prayer books of devotion that spread like

[90] Watkin, *Poets and Mystics*, 198.

[91] Augustine Baker, *Sancta Sophia*, ed. Dom Norbert Sweeney, O.S.B. (London: Burns and Oates, 1876), 567–86. Punctuation slightly modified.

wildfire with the introduction of printing into England at the end of the fifteenth century. Apart from Bibles, the most common books printed were primers, a name that derived from the fact that they included prayers from the first hour of the Divine Office, or Prime. Helen C. White made a fascinating study of these popular prayer books in *The Tudor Books of Private Devotion.*

Early Catholic Primers

As printing became widespread in the very decade of the Reformation, primers spread throughout England and the Continent. Whether they should be written in Latin, especially the Scriptures, or include the vernacular, was a subject of controversy. The most popular of the original primers in English was published at Rouen in 1538 and shipped to England. Gradually, the Catholic primer came to include the Little Office of Our Lady, but inserted before it were a calendar of major feast days and a series of familiar prayers, the Commandments, the seven penitential psalms, litanies, prayers for the dead, the psalms of the Passion, and the Passion narrative according to St. John. Though different primers contained different prayers, they all centered on Christ, emphasizing His Passion and death.

Perhaps most representative of these Catholic devotional prayer books are the prayers called the "Oes", of St. Bridget of Sweden. According to a legend, Bridget, a widowed aristocrat and mystic, recited these prayers every day before a crucifix in St. Paul's Church in Rome. The following selection of these prayers, included in Catholic and, later, Anglican primers, demonstrates the warm devotion to Jesus Christ that people loved at that time:

> O Jesu, endless sweetness of loving souls! O Jesu, ghostly joy passing and exceeding all gladness and desires! O Jesu, health and tender lover of all repentant sinners, who loves to dwell, as Thou said Thyself, with the children of men! For that was the cause why Thou were incarnate, and made man in the end of the world.
>
> O blessed Jesu, lovable king and friend in all things. Remember Thy sorrows when Thou hungest naked and despised on the cross. And all Thy friends and acquaintances stood against Thee, in whom Thou foundest no comfort, but only in Thy blessed mother.[92]

Protestant Primers

Primers were important enough that after the break with Rome it was necessary to reissue them. As White has pointed out, they were powerful tools that shaped the ideas of the people. Bishop John Hilsey, who succeeded John Fisher at Rochester, was given the task of producing a primer suitable to the Church of England. Interestingly, he

[92] Quoted in Helen C. White, *The Tudor Book of Private Devotion* (University of Wisconsin Press, 1951), 218.

included the Oes of St. Bridget in the work, which was published in 1539.[93]

As the English became more Protestant, the primers changed into what were called books of devotion. *The Imitation of Christ*, already over a century old, provided an unusually popular model. Series of prayers, based largely on biblical quotations, became even more popular in the reign of Queen Elizabeth.[94] The emphasis changed to explanation of facts drawn from the Gospels, and less attention was paid to the feelings and responses of the reader. The following selection is from John Bradford's *Godly Meditations on the Lord's Prayer, Belief, and Ten Commandments, with other Exercises*, published in 1562. His handling of the sufferings of Christ is different in tone and historically more precise than the earlier Catholic meditations.

> Thy body was racked to be nailed to the tree, thy hands were bored through, and thy feet also; nails were put through them to fasten thee thereon: thou wast hanged between heaven and earth, as one spewed out of heaven, and vomited out of the earth, unworthy of any place: the high priest laughed thee to scorn, the elders blasphemed thee and said, "God hath no care for thee:" the common people laughed and cry out upon thee: thirst oppressed thee, but vinegar only and gall was given to thee to drink: heaven shined not on thee, the sun gave thee no light, the earth was afraid to bear thee, Satan did sore tempt and assault thee, and thine own senses caused thee to cry out, "My God, my God, why hast thou forsaken me?"[95]

The Common Ground of the Various Primers

Histories of the Reformation usually stress the theological controversies and political aspects of this most important conflict in Western Christianity. Religious faith, however, is far more grounded in the experience of great multitudes of believers, who hardly grasp the complexity of theological debates and have no control over political forces. The devout are far more interested in spiritual goals—in pleasing God, in following Christ's example, in their own struggles against human weakness. However enthusiastically enmeshed in their theological controversies, they were Christians because they sought to "know Christ Jesus" and to spread the knowledge of His saving grace to others. The most important aspect of their lives was their personal devotion to Christ, expressed in prayer, song, worship, and in good deeds done in His name. The primers provide a source of insight into the lives of the divided Christians of these times.

Although the Catholic, Anglican, Protestant, and Anabaptist primers have their own characteristics, each preserves the intent of the early books, which were fashioned by the desire and experience of

[93] White, *Tudor Book of Private Devotion*, 216–17.

[94] Ibid., 134ff.

[95] Quoted in ibid., 147.

vast numbers of people—clerical, religious, and lay. These simple books present a picture of a devout society in which people sought the presence of Christ through prayer and meditation. The primers show that these multitudes of Christ's followers who were in profound conflict with one another were nonetheless united in devotion of Jesus Christ.

14 The Spiritual Renewal in France

The later part of the sixteenth century and the hundred years that followed saw an intense spiritual renewal in continental Europe among both Catholics and Protestants. The movements of these two groups have been assumed by historians to be distinct, as the followers of the old Church and those of the new churches rarely communicated. Perhaps there was little dialogue, but apparently they did read each other's works, for we find a surprising similarity in their experiences and especially in their devotion to the one figure beloved by them all—Jesus Christ.

A Century of Spiritual Dynamism

As we have seen, Benet of Canfield and Augustine Baker encountered a devout Catholicism in Europe a generation or two after the Reformation. This fervent piety, co-existing with confusion and scandal, gave rise unexpectedly to a rich and vibrant seventeenth-century French Catholic spirituality, a phenomenon astonishing for several reasons. This spiritual renaissance was initially sparked and sustained by converts like Benet and by laypersons, some of them raised among Protestants. It was guided and inspired by members of the new orders—Jesuits, Capuchins, and Discalced Carmelites.[1] The renewal gave rise to an army of preachers and spiritual directors, among them the Vincentians (the Congregation of the Mission), founded by Europe's great apostle of charity, St. Vincent de Paul (ca. 1580–1660). Side by side with them were the Oratorians, founded by Pierre (later Cardinal) de Bérulle (1575–1629). Jean-Jacques Olier and the Sulpicians worked along with these, especially for the reform and education of priests. The Jesuits provided legions of dedicated men beginning with Pierre Coton, adviser to Henry IV, and going on to Père Louis Lallemant (1587–1635), who almost by accident was a powerful spiritual writer and whose notes were published after his death; and Père de Condren. The immense Jesuit contribution to the unparalleled age of spirituality comes to its climax only in the next century

[1] Henri Brémond, *A Literary History of Religious Thought in France*, vol. 2 (London: SPCK, 1930). See also Michael J. Buckley, S.J., "Seventeenth-Century French Spirituality: Three Figures", in *Christian Spirituality: Post-Reformation and Modern*, ed. Louis Dupré and Don E. Saliers (New York: Crossroad, 1996), 29.

with Jean-Pierre de Caussade, whose *Abandonment to Divine Providence* is among the greatest books of Catholic spirituality.[2] Bringing this time to a beautiful and integrated conclusion were St. John Eudes and St. Louis de Montfort, as well as St. Margaret Mary Alacoque and her spiritual director, St. Claude de la Colombière.

A list of priests and religious, however, can be deceptive. Among the most remarkable figures of the period were laywomen like Marie de Valence and Madame Acarie. To prepare for this little-known time, coming on the heels of the Reformation, we cite the historian Henri Daniel-Rops: "Has it been sufficiently appreciated that the first sixty years of the seventeenth century stand out as a period of strength within the Church, an epoch of rare beauty and fruitfulness, certainly as rich as the greatest moments of medieval Christianity? Has it been really appreciated that this was an era of youthful bloom and dazzling revival?" [3]

This spiritual springtime extending from the mid-sixteenth century to about 1670 has been described by Abbé Brémond in his classic *Literary History of Religious Thought in France.* It is important to recognize that in terms of devotion to Jesus Christ, this age began not with intellectual convictions but a mysticism directed toward the simple awareness of the presence of God. It came to flower with perhaps the most beautiful Christocentric spirituality since the time of St. Francis. We shall see that this remarkable time can be viewed as an integrated whole that reached the most beautiful expression of personal relationship with the living Christ. The devotion that flourished in seventeenth-century France began, continued, and was perfected in the hearts of those who sought the love of Christ. While all this was going on, there were powerful discordant elements, particularly Jansenism and Quietism. These movements would eventually move into such excess as to require the corrections of the Church.[4] No one can deny that however divisive and erroneous these movements may have become, they were, however, part of a remarkable moment in the history of devotion to Jesus Christ.

Humble Beginnings

Brémond recognizes as the first significant person in this age the peasant woman Marie Teyssonnier, born around 1575 at Valence, in the Dauphiné, and who died a Beguine in 1648.[5] Marie led a quasi-religious life as a widow and was called Soeur Marie. After the manner of many saints, the name of her hometown is added as well, so that she is known as Marie de Valence. It is interesting that although her parents were Catholics when she was born, they became Huguenots and she was baptized in their temple (as Protestant churches are

---

[2] See Buckley, "Seventeenth-Century French Spirituality", 54ff.

[3] Henri Daniel-Rops, *The Church in the Seventeenth Century*, trans. J.J. Buckingham (New York: Doubleday, 1964), 1:75.

[4] See Louis Dupré, "Jansenism and Quietism", in Dupré and Saliers, *Christian Spirituality.*

[5] Brémond, *Religious Thought in France*, 33.

called in France). She was betrothed to a Calvinist notary at the age of thirteen. By this time the family had returned to the Catholic Church. Nonetheless at the age of fifteen she was sent to Beaume, a Huguenot village, where she scandalized everyone at church by following Catholic customs, like kneeling down. Her husband was a heavy drinker who joined the army when Marie was in her early twenties. He died, leaving her a little cottage in Valence, which she made into a chapel. There, occasional Masses were offered in this Huguenot area. Around 1599, guided by mystical experience, which she neither expected nor understood, she found a spiritual guide in the remarkable Jesuit Père Pierre Coton, spiritual adviser to King Henry IV and his devout successor, Louis XIII.

Only Providence could have linked this humble peasant woman with this remarkable Jesuit, who Brémond says did more than anyone to found the "Renaissance of Mysticism".[6] But Coton was not the only well-known person Marie was to influence. There was a monk of the order known as the Minims, Louis de la Rivière, an accomplished spiritual writer, who knew Marie for thirty years and became her biographer. Jean-Jacques Olier, who founded the Sulpicians, a group of reforming diocesan priests, and who was a gifted spiritual writer, cherished a spiritual friendship with Marie and saw their friendship as a providential gift that strengthened him in the crises of his life. Even Cardinal Richelieu, the secretary of state and a man of great power, came to Marie's little cottage. He questioned her for an hour. Despite the fact that she treated him with great reserve and did not speak of her extraordinary communications with God, the cardinal departed totally satisfied with her answers.[7] It was Richelieu who advised her to accept the invitation to meet with the Queen Mother, which she did reluctantly.

How did it happen that this humble soul welcomed such distinguished visitors to her cottage chapel? Monsieur Olier recounts how he visited her with another priest, M. de Bretonvilliers, who related the extraordinary impression that she made on him. "Methought I saw an angel in Heaven rather than a creature still living on earth; so filled with the Spirit of God did she appear, and such an impression did the charming modesty of her countenance, which had something supernatural about it, make on me, that even today, although many years have passed since we met, I am as much moved when I recall it as if I were still hearing her voice".[8]

Marie seems to have made no effort to initiate or direct her spiritual experiences. She simply experienced the presence of Jesus spontaneously as a blessed intrusion into her life.[9] Although she could not read, she insisted on having a New Testament near her, as if she derived

[6] Ibid., 54.
[7] Ibid., 34.
[8] Ibid., 40.
[9] Ibid., 42.

spiritual nourishment by its presence. When we read her biography by Rivière and comments from perceptive people, like Olier, Bérulle, Francis de Sales, and Vincent de Paul, we realize that this illiterate mystic had to be experienced in order to be fully appreciated. She makes no plans, teaches no doctrine, and yet is deeply concerned about the salvation of souls through the grace of Christ. In return, she seems to experience the world around her and life itself as they might have been if man had never fallen. The following observations of Rivière about the last years of Marie's life are intriguing.

> She enjoyed for the last two years of her life especially, a particular presence of God, pure and simple. We have often had long conversations, she and I, on this mode of Presence. The terms she used to explain her meaning were these: to see God, to see God in God, to see the creatures in God and oneself in God. She used these phrases simply and freely. But when I represented to her that it was not probable that she had seen the Divine Essence, humble and simple as she was she acquiesced and was content to believe that she had seen only a pure light, which to her figured the Divine Essence.[10]

This experience of God might remind us of lines we saw in Chapter 13 by the contemplative country physician and Anglican mystic Henry Vaughan:

> I saw Eternity the other night
> Like a great Ring of pure and endless light,
> All calm, as it was bright . . .

One may ask, where is the explicit devotion to Jesus to be found? We do not see it in the experience of John Smith, the Puritan Platonist, or even of Benet of Canfield or Marie de Valence. We should view the experience of the mystics of this time as a whole, with individuals taking only a part in a particular phase. Such souls drawn to the simple experience of divine light can thus be seen as laying the foundations for the mystical love of Jesus Christ, which is to be experienced after them. This is exactly what happened as the seeds planted by the simple peasant woman of Valence grew into an amazing spiritual renaissance that produced the richest devotion to Christ in Church history.

The World's First Ecumenist

Marie de Valence not only attracted the attention of Père Pierre Coton (1564–1626); she affected him deeply. She predicted that he would become a friend and adviser to the king, and so it happened. Recall that she had lived devoutly as a Catholic married to a Protestant in a completely Protestant area. In the beginning of his priesthood, Coton had been involved in dialogues with Protestant clergy. He was known

[10] R. P. L. de la Rivière, *Histoire de la vie et mœurs de Marie Tessonier* (Lyon, 1650), 437, quoted in ibid., 45.

for his "human touch" in these debates. Anyone familiar with the elegant French writers of the time, known for finesse and precision, will realize that these debates were held at an extremely high level. Coton was so understanding of the position of his Calvinist adversaries that they spread the word that the Jesuit was becoming a Huguenot. Coton was required to defend himself publicly from the charge of treason, brought against him by some Catholics who did not understand a man who could say to Huguenots, "We are brothers, not on the mother's side, for we have not the same Church as mother, but on the side of God, our Father and Saviour." [11]

On the cover of a book, Coton wrote the words of Proverbs 15:1: *"Responsio mollis frangit iram"* (A soft answer turns away wrath). History was to prove how important this maxim would be for Coton. The Jesuits had been suppressed in France by royal decree, but through Coton's effort the ban was lifted by Henry IV, who, after all, was a convert to the Church and somewhat unfamiliar with these things. The king required conditions that seemed restrictive and humiliating to the general of the Jesuits. Coton, caught in the middle, was blamed by the general for the king's decree. Coton advised the humble surrender of some rights common to religious orders for the sake of working in France for the glory of God and the salvation of souls. Coton tried to placate the general and be a loyal Jesuit, Catholic, and Frenchman all at once. This was the same man who relied so much on the counsel and prayers of the peasant woman of Valence.

In the midst of diplomatic missions Père Coton maintained a profound spiritual life. He directed not only Marie de Valence but also Madame Acarie, a sophisticated aristocrat who brought the first nuns of the Teresian Carmelite reform to France and who will be the subject of our next consideration. Coton wrote on the spiritual life for the educated people of his time while he was busy counseling peasant women. His little book on the interior prayer of the devout soul makes the following suggestion—one that might seem surprising for an adviser to the king. Coton suggests "when contemplating a garden or flowerbed, you exclaim: If this passing world is so beautiful, what will be that of immortality? Seeing a flowery meadow: The fragrance of the Son of God and the Child of Mary is as that of a field on which Heaven has shed its benediction." Coton goes on to say that when smelling a bouquet of flowers one might say: "Such is the scent of my Jesus, my Beloved." [12]

Does this sound like a man who could also endure the wrath of kings and the displeasure of the authorities of his order? Does it sound

[11] Jean-Marie Prat, *Recherches historiques et critiques sur la Compagnie de Jésus en France du temps du Père Coton* (Lyon, 1876), 1:411, 417, quoted in Brémond, *Religious Thought in France*, 59.

[12] Pierre Coton, S.J., *L'intérieure occupation d'une âme dévote*, quoted in Brémond, *Religious Thought in France*, 76.

like someone who with elegant diplomacy could deal with court intrigues and jealous enemies? How did he do it? The answer is to be found in the following paragraph from his sermons.

> The spiritual man, although speaking, acting, working in public, fixes his gaze on none save the King of heaven and earth there truly present, in comparison with Whom all monarchs and potentates of this world are but flimsy rags. Should he endeavour to please anyone, it is God; should he fear to displease, it is God also; he will take no heed of men, save only because God wills that he should try to make himself agreeable to them for their good. And doing this, he attains so high that he can tread under foot the things of this world.[13]

Since the *Spiritual Exercises* of St. Ignatius, the foundation of the whole life and attitude of any true Jesuit, are founded on loyalty to and grateful love for Jesus Christ, it should be no surprise that Père Coton was far more explicit in his devotion to Christ than the peasant woman who saw God in everything.

Immense crowds, greater than any that had ever been seen in Paris (by some estimates, two-thirds of the city), came to the Jesuit chapel on March 19, 1626, to pray over the body of this remarkable priest. He was buried by the Archbishop of Paris that evening at the foot of the altar. Coton, always dedicated to his guardian angel, had long before believed that while celebrating Mass for Marie de Valence, his angel and hers had appeared to him. Perhaps the accomplishments of his life, more incredible than fiction, can be understood from the following quotation from Louis de la Rivière, Marie's biographer: "I am not surprised that living the angelic life down here as he did . . . the angels should sometimes have complimented him with their presence. One thing is certain, that on his return from Rome he declared to Soeur Marie that, while celebrating in the holy chapel of Our Lady of Loretto, his good angel appeared to him, in company with those of the said Soeur Marie and the Demoiselle Marguerite Chambaud".[14]

Madame Acarie

We now consider Barbe Avrillot, 1566–1618, better known as Madame Acarie, or as Blessed Marie of the Incarnation, a lay sister of Carmel, where she spent the last four years of her life.[15] Like Marie de Valence, Madame Acarie wrote nothing. Yet, she, more than anyone, was the catalyst of that spiritual age which began in the last thirty years of her

[13] *Sermons sur les principales et plus difficiles matières de la foi*, preached by R.P. Pierre Coton and edited by him in the form of Meditations (Paris, 1617), 447, quoted in Brémond, *Religious Thought in France*, 93.

[14] Rivière, *Histoire* 99, quoted in Brémond, *Religious Thought in France*, 84–85.

[15] Marie of the Incarnation's beatification in 1791 went virtually unnoticed. No public recognition was possible as revolution raged in France. Today, unfortunately, this courageous woman who contributed so much to the spiritual renaissance in France is largely a forgotten figure.

life. She brought to France the Discalced Carmelite nuns, founded a few decades earlier by St. Teresa. At her death they numbered seventeen convents. She helped develop the Ursuline nuns and sparked a reform among Benedictine abbeys. Brémond states, "She knew, grouped, stimulated and directed well-nigh all the leading religious spirits of her day", although she was an invalid and lived only fifty-two years.[16]

Madame Acarie's father was a middle-rank nobleman who was financial counselor to the Queen of Navarre. He was ruined, however, as a result of the political upheaval caused by the Holy League, led by devout Catholics who did not trust the convert king, Henry IV. As a girl, Barbe wanted to be a nun, but her mother was determined to marry off her only child. At sixteen she wed another victim of the same political scene, Pierre Acarie. One day Pierre noticed his young wife reading a romantic novel. Although not devout himself, after consulting with his confessor he presented his wife with a pile of pious books, admonishing her not to waste her time on romances. Little did Pierre know that he had opened a Pandora's box of mysticism, visions, and incredible undertakings for the cause of Christ. Nor did he realize he would have to adjust his own life, as his home would become the center of spirituality in Paris for decades.

Madame Acarie read the books avidly. One day Pierre's confessor quoted her a line: *"Trop est avare à qui Dieu ne suffit"* (Avaricious indeed is the one for whom God does not suffice), and this caused a complete turnabout in the life of the twenty-two-year-old, upper-class Parisian wife and mother. Almost immediately she experienced a series of profound ecstasies, a sense of the presence of God so overwhelming that she appeared often to be unconscious. For example, one day she did not return home after Mass. Alarmed, her family and friends searched for her and in the evening found her in the chapel, still "in an ecstasy, like one dead".[17] When she came to, she asked if the Mass was finished. These ecstasies, which she tried to prevent because of embarrassment, were beyond her control. They were associated with keen suffering, to which was added the intense pain of the stigmata in her hands and feet. She disguised these marks sufficiently so that only Père Coton, her spiritual director, knew of them. By that time, however, Madame Acarie was permanently on crutches because of several broken bones.

Religious ecstasy—literally standing or being outside of oneself—is a temporary unconsciousness (or dissociation, to use a modern psychological term), which in true mystical experience is brought on by the fact that the psyche cannot deal with so great a grace given at that time. Ecstasy is not in itself a sign of virtue; indeed, a similar state can be brought on by totally natural causes. It is observable that the ecstasies of deeply

[16] Brémond, *Religious Thought in France*, 145.

[17] Ibid., 154.

religious people seem to come under control as they mature. What appears to happen is that the psyche (the complexity of psychological functions and the organic structure they depend on, especially the central nervous system) adapts to the strength of the individual's mystical experience. This apparently is what happened to Madame Acarie. Yet even when, as a psychologically and spiritually mature woman nearing fifty, she was clothed as a Carmelite at Amiens, the ceremony (at that time public) was held in early morning in case she went into ecstasy and caused shock and puzzlement to the local laity.[18]

About five years after her "conversion" from romantic novels to devout reading, Benet of Canfied, who was considered a great spiritual authority, was consulted about her ecstasies. His verdict was that all the phenomena came from God and that Madame Acarie must allow God to fulfill His designs in and through her.[19] Wanting more assurance, Pierre Acarie went to a Jesuit. He also complained to his parish priest that his ecstatic wife was neglecting her duties, and Madame Acarie had to listen to herself being denounced from the altar. She was even once refused Holy Communion, an indignity she accepted without complaint.

Madame Acarie's life was by no means simply a series of ecstasies. When she was twenty-eight, her husband, as a result of his role in the Holy League, was exiled, leaving her and their six children on the verge of destitution. Madame Acarie had to go to court to save what little remained. She left the judges and lawyers astounded by her defense, which was clear and complete.

From then on, the mystic displayed a genuine practical genius, which enabled her to obtain help from the best spiritual minds of the time, including Canfield, Bérulle, Père Coton, St. Francis de Sales, and her cousin François du Tremblay, later Père Joseph, the Capuchin diplomat and Richelieu's *eminence grise*. "She assembled within this group all the energies vital to the rebirth of French spirituality."[20]

Her practical and spiritual gifts enabled her to coordinate many facets of a project and overcome obstacles. This was especially true of the plan to bring the Carmelite reform of St. Teresa to France. The Spanish were reluctant to come and had to be persuaded; permission had to be secured from the Pope and the French king; property had to be acquired and a monastery erected in Paris. Through delegates she brought it all to a successful conclusion by 1604. She had handpicked young women to be the first French Carmelite novices and selected those who traveled to Spain to escort the "Spanish mothers" to Paris.[21]

[18] Ibid.

[19] A. R. Salmon-Malebranche, *Madame Acarie*, trans. Jeanne Dumais, O.C.D.S., and Sr. Miriam, O.C.D. (Eugene, Ore.: Four Corners Press, 1981), 11.

[20] Buckley, "Seventeenth-Century French Spirituality", 30.

[21] Among the six Spanish foundresses, some of whom had known and lived with St. Teresa, were Blessed Anne of St. Bartholomew, who had been the saint's nurse, and the

Madame Acarie also forged a link between mysticism and social responsibility, something characteristic of French piety to our own day. She worked for the poor and inspired others to do the same. René Gauthier, councillor of state, stated in his sworn testimony for the cause of her beatification that ten thousand conversions were traceable to her.[22] Undoubtedly we can learn much from studying her life. But our question is, what is her devotion to Christ and how did it express itself?

To answer this question we must raise another. What was it about this invalid mystic that moved so many people, including some of the most revered spiritual thinkers of French history? Her biographer, André Duval, professor of theology at the Sorbonne, writes that she had "in a sublime degree" the gift of discernment of spirits.[23] This means that by a special gift she could penetrate the interior of a person's soul and recognize the spring of all the spiritual movements therein. Brémond sees this kind of discernment in an inexperienced and untrained person as both a grace and a "sort of spiritual instinct". In the case of Madame Acarie he adds another ingredient: "personal experience of sublimest mysteries, a sharpened sense ... of Divine Presence and Influence".[24] The Jesuit provincial Père Binet wrote: "What she told me was known to God alone; she showed me all the consequences which the business might entail, and nothing could have been truer."[25]

We are of course reminded of Marie de Valence. How can an untrained and, in Marie's case, an unlettered layperson offer the most reliable degree of spiritual advice to prelates, royalty, clergy, and laity, some of whom were outstanding spiritual guides themselves? The only answer is the mysterious gifts of the Holy Spirit, especially wisdom, knowledge, and counsel.

The exploration of Madame Acarie's devotion is problematic because she wrote nothing except for letters and retained, as far as we know, absolute discretion about what she experienced in her long ecstasies; consequently, there is little to go by in the way of written evidence.

Her well-authenticated stigmata certainly indicated a profound identity with Christ and His sufferings. Dr. Duval affirms her stigmata, as does Père Coton, but they were very circumspect on the subject because Pope Sixtus IV had forbidden, under pain of excommunication, the attribution of the stigmata to anyone but St. Francis.[26]

Venerable Anne of Jesus, leader of the group and prioress of the Paris Carmel. She went on to found other monasteries, including several in the Spanish Netherlands. She died at Brussels in 1621 with a reputation for great holiness. It was Anne of Jesus who, as prioress of Granada, had requested St. John of the Cross to write his commentary on the *Spiritual Canticle*.

[22] Brémond, *Religious Thought in France*, 168.

[23] Ibid., 179.

[24] Ibid., 181.

[25] Quoted in ibid.

[26] Brémond, *Religious Thought in France*, 154.

Despite her extreme reticence, we get glimpses of her inner life. Once, in the process of opening a Carmel in Rouen, Duval recalls that Madame Acarie, seeing the city from a height, began to recite our Lord's words over Jerusalem: "O Jerusalem, Jerusalem . . . if thou hadst known."[27] Thus we see that the life of our Savior was in her meditation as she went about her daily events.

More revealing is a letter she wrote to Cardinal de Bérulle, which gives an indication of one of her ecstasies while she was gazing at a crucifix. It is important to note in this letter that she refers to her soul with the third-person feminine pronoun.

> The soul was so suddenly and sharply touched that I could no longer even look upon it outwardly, but beheld it interiorly. I was amazed to see the Second Person of the Most Holy Trinity served in this wise for my sins and those of mankind. It would be quite impossible for me to describe what passed within, particularly the excellence and dignity of this Second Person. . . . I remember well that the soul admired His Wisdom, His Goodness, and particularly the excess of His love towards mankind. . . . What did she not say to the Lord so surely present with her? What needs did she forget? What desires, aspirations, thanksgivings! Oh, how she entreated the efficacy of what He had done for our salvation![28]

What emerges from this letter is a deep devotion to and identification with the Second Person of the Blessed Trinity. By the use of the phrase "the soul admired His Wisdom", a new dimension is introduced into the vocabulary of spirituality. Bérulle, as we shall see, takes up this idea of admiration and makes a method of prayer of it. Obviously, the idea of rejoicing in the beauty and glory of God and of the Divine Word is not a new one in Christian spirituality. We have seen this in the experience of Francis Rous and St. John of the Cross. There is, however, a unique quality to the word "admire". The simple act of focusing on the admirable qualities of God with powerful devotion of heart and soul comes from the experience of Madame Acarie.

As spirituality developed through the seventeenth century, the concept of admiration grew. It was foundational to the Catholic piety of the first half of the twentieth century and is reflected in the writings of Marmion, Goodier, and Guardini. As we pass from Madame Acarie and Marie de Valence we are reminded of what Ted Campbell, the Methodist theologian, has recognized: these simple people, assisted by others of profound intelligence and piety, brought into European history a spirit of mysticism, a religion of the heart that would make this

[27] Ibid., 166.

[28] Quoted in ibid., 172.

age as important in Christian history as any other, including the high Middle Ages.[29]

St. Francis de Sales (1567–1622)

No study of Christian devotion could be complete without a recognition of the immense contribution of Francis de Sales. He is the writer par excellence on the nature of devotion and its psychological components. Fr. Michael Buckley accurately fits de Sales into the century we are studying: "If Benoît de Canfield nurtured the nascent mysticism of the dawning century and Madame Acarie gave it methods of interchange which allowed different traditions to be in communication with one another to their mutual enrichment, Francis de Sales led the entire century into the world of devotion and the love of God." [30]

Like Canfield, Marie de Valence, and even Père Coton, Francis de Sales had many contacts with the Protestant world. He was raised in a largely Protestant area of Savoy and became Bishop of Geneva, a city he could never enter because of its stern Calvinism. He labored in the Catholic areas of his Alpine diocese and in the border areas, where he won the respect of Protestants. With St. Jane Frances de Chantal (1572–1641) he founded the Visitation Order in 1610. We have already met Francis de Sales as one of the spiritual figures who influenced and was influenced by Madame Acarie. Although a retiring man, happy to work in his poor divided diocese, his recognized spiritual genius drew him into almost every important current of French spirituality—from devout humanism, which he especially represents, to Jansenism, which was far from his thought.[31]

It is important to take note of two aspects of this remarkable life. We focus on his theological emphasis on the universal salvific will of God in the face of the grim emphasis on predestination at the time and his analysis of religious devotion, which he usually calls charity, that is, "devotion bursting into flames".[32] The two great works of Francis de Sales are the *Introduction to the Devout Life*, a best seller in his own time, and the *Treatise on the Love of God*.[33] Although not an academic theologian, he was declared a Doctor of the Church in 1877, a title recognizing his profound contribution to the Church's teaching and thought. Actually, Francis was one of the great psychologists of Christian spirituality, and his contribution is both psychological and pastoral. Like Augustine, he analyzes the positive and unproductive

[29] Ted A. Campbell, *The Religion of the Heart: A Study of European Religious Life in the Seventeenth and Eighteenth Centuries* (Columbia: University of South Carolina Press, 1991).

[30] Buckley, "Seventeenth-Century French Spirituality", 32.

[31] For an excellent appreciation of Francis de Sales see Michael de la Bedoyere, *Saint Maker* (Manchester, N.H.: Sophia Institute Press, 1998).

[32] See *Introduction to the Devout Life*, trans. Michael Day, C.O. (Westminster, Md.: Newman Press, 1956). See also *Introduction to the Devout Life* and *Treatise on the Love of God*, ed. Wendy M. Wright (New York: Crossroad, 1993).

[33] See *On the Love of God*, trans. John K. Ryan (Rockford, Ill.: Tan Books, 1975).

forms of Christian devotion and relates these experiences to the principal doctrines of Christianity, especially those concerning God the Father and the Incarnate Word, Jesus Christ.

We recall that the post-Reformation era put much emphasis on predestination, especially Calvin and Luther's idea that some could be consigned to hell before they even existed. The Catholic responses to this teaching, made largely by Dominicans and Jesuits but also by some Scotists (Franciscans), were colored by the theology of Augustine and Thomas. To Catholics of our own time even these would appear somber. In his erudite and enlightening study, Fr. Buckley focuses on Francis de Sales' unique contribution to theology, one that begins not with predestination, but with God's universal salvific will. This traditional teaching of the Fathers East and West emphasizes that "God does not will the death of the wicked" (Ezek 18:23) and that in some sense He wills all to be saved and mysteriously offers this grace to all.[34] Since the time of Francis of Assisi, no one had emphasized the love of God and love of Christ for the individual like Francis de Sales. Buckley sees de Sales' contribution as having a lasting effect on theologians as different as Alphonsus Liguori, Matthias Scheeben, and Karl Rahner. (We could also add Hans Urs von Balthasar, Dietrich von Hildebrand, and Pope John Paul II.)

De Sales' theology, which is never distinct from his spirituality, began with an experience of near despair. On the testimony of St. Jane Frances de Chantal, given during the process of Francis' beatification, we have a compelling account of his deliverance from hopelessness. Protestant readers will recall a similar experience in the life of Luther. De Sales studied at the Jesuit College of Clermont, at Paris. His piety reflected the austerity and grim thinking of the times, and he took upon himself some of the austere practices of the Capuchins—fasting, wearing a hair shirt, etc.—since he was much influenced by Benet of Canfield and Ange de Joyeuse. After six weeks of terrible torment during which he could not shake the conviction that he was eternally lost, he entered the Lady Chapel of the Church of Saint-Étienne-du-Grès. He prayed to God the Father and to Jesus with this prayer recorded by St. Jane Frances.

> Whatever happens, O Lord, You hold everything in Your hands, and all Your ways are just and true. Although You have veiled my eyes before the eternal secret of predestination and reprobation—You whose judgments are unsearchable, You who are just judge and a merciful Father—I shall love You, Lord, at least in this life, even if I am not allowed to love You in eternity. At least I shall love You here below, O my God, and I shall always hope in Your mercy. Always I shall continue to praise You, whatever the angel of Satan may do to prevent me. O Lord Jesus, You

[34] Buckley, "Seventeenth-Century French Spirituality", 32–41.

> shall always be my hope and my salvation in the land of the living. And if it is inevitable that I must be damned among the damned who will never see Your gentle face, let me at least be spared from the company of those who will curse Your Holy Name.[35]

As he finished the prayer, he found a card with the Memorare to the Blessed Virgin by St. Bernard. Praying this prayer, he felt like a leper seeing his sores disappear. "A delirious sense of spiritual and bodily peace came over him." Years later what he had experienced that day would be recalled in a letter to a nun. "My daughter, I beg you to see to it that those meditations of man's four last ends finish up with hope and trust in God, not with fear and fright. When they finish in fear, they are dangerous. . . . God is not so terrible for those who love Him. . . . He asks little of us because He knows how little we have".[36]

In the *Introduction to the Devout Life*, de Sales describes devotion as a "spiritual alertness which makes us respond heartily and promptly to what love asks of us". Philothea (the person to whom the introduction is ostensibly written) is told to make a clearly willed desire to do God's will and then to confirm this by a decision to belong to God alone. She is taught to meditate on the life of Christ, to pray and respond to the life of grace and the sacraments. De Sales is the apostle of leading a devout Christian life in whatever circumstances one finds oneself. In the *Treatise on the Love of God*, he describes the origin of the spiritual life in the soul, the union with God that makes the soul tend toward God, and the phenomenon of standing outside oneself (*ex-histanai*) or losing oneself in the love of Christ.[37] Christ is to be found in one's neighbor; Jesus is both the object of our love and the model for the lover. Friendship in its diverse elements is included: God for the individual, the believer for God and neighbor, the freedom and the friendship of Christ. St. Jane Frances wrote in a letter a year following his death: "God had flooded his entire soul with such brilliant light that he had the power to survey the truths of faith at a single glance and to explain them."[38]

St. Francis defines contemplation as a loving, pure, permanent attention to God and the things of God. This contrasts with meditation, which is a discursive set of ideas about God or the life of Christ. Buckley also helpfully defines another concept: *indifference*. We have come upon this idea in the English mystics, especially in Benet of Canfield. The idea became more defined in Francis de Sales. It is a "habitual union and conformity with God's will that goes beyond the

[35] Quoted in Bedoyere, *Saint Maker*, 22–23.

[36] Quoted in ibid., 24.

[37] For a good summary of his spirituality, see Elisabeth Stopp, "François de Sales", in *The Study of Spirituality*, ed. Cheslyn Jones, Geoffrey Wainwright, and Edward Yarnold, S.J. (London: SPCK, 1986), 382–85.

[38] Ibid., 384.

acquiescence of resignation and loves all things only as they are caught up and exist within the divine will".[39]

This teaching is eloquently brought out in a letter from St. Jane Frances to her brother, André Frémyot (1573–1641), who was Archbishop of Bourges. We can see from the letter that de Sales taught an indifference that was quite the opposite of Quietism.

> Since God, in His eternal goodness, has moved you to consecrate all your love, your actions, your works, and your whole self to Him utterly without any self-interest but only for His greater glory and His satisfaction, remain firm in this resolve. With the confidence of a son, rest in the care and love which divine Providence has for you in all your needs. Look upon Providence as a child does its mother who loves him tenderly. You can be sure that God loves you incomparably more. We can't imagine how great is the love which God, in His goodness, has for souls who thus abandon themselves to His mercy, and who have no other wish than to do what they think pleases Him, leaving everything that concerns them to His care in time and in eternity.[40]

The spirit of abandonment to God, or trust in Him, which St. Francis de Sales taught so well to his closest disciples, was deeply identified with the Passion of Christ and the sufferings of His Mother. A beautiful letter to St. Jane Frances, who was at that time suffering greatly, brings to light how the Bishop of Geneva identified himself, and called on his disciples to identify themselves, as partners in Christ's Passion.

> Therefore, my dearest daughter, remain thus in the darkness of the Passion. I say "in the darkness" for I leave you to ponder this: when our Lady and St. John stood at the foot of the Cross in the strange and frightening darkness that surrounded them, they no longer heard nor saw our Lord and felt only bitterness and distress; and although they had faith, this too was in darkness, for it was necessary that they should share in our Savior's sense of abandonment. How fortunate we are to be the slaves of this great God who became a slave for our sake![41]

In the *Treatise on the Love of God* de Sales shows what he means by charity, the subject of his book, and *complacence*. In chapter 5 of book 5, which is on this precise subject, he gives these insights into meditating on Christ's Passion. He makes a number of biblical allusions, like the thorn bush of sorrow and the statement from the Song of Songs: "I am black but beautiful."

---

[39] Buckley, "Seventeenth-Century French Spirituality", 65.

[40] Quoted in *Francis de Sales, Jane de Chantal: Letters of Spiritual Direction*, trans. Péronne Marie Thibert, V.H.M. (New York: Paulist Press, 1988), 201.

[41] Quoted in ibid., 154–55.

> When I see my Savior on the Mount of Olives with his "soul sorrowful even unto death" [Mt 26:38], I say, "Ah, Lord Jesus, what has brought those sorrows of death into the soul of life except love which arouses commiseration and by it draws our miseries into your sovereign heart?" How can a devout soul seeing this abyss of weariness and distress in the divine lover be without a sorrow both holy and loving? On the other hand, reflecting that none of the beloved's afflictions come from imperfection or lack of strength but from the greatness of his most dear dilection, the soul cries out, "I am black," with sorrow brought on by compassion, "but I am beautiful" with love caused by complacence.... I who am ever exposed to the sorrows that I receive by condolence from the incomparable torments of my divine Savior, I am completely covered over with distress and rent by sorrow. But because the dolors of him I love come from his love, to the extent that they afflict me through compassion they bring me delight through complacence. How could a faithful lover fail to have the greatest content at seeing herself so greatly loved by her heavenly spouse?
>
> For this reason love's beauty lies in the deformity of sorrow. If I wear mourning for the passion and death of my king and am all burned and blackened with grief, I do not cease to have consolation incomparably sweet at seeing his surpassing love amid all his travails and sorrows....
>
> Love makes lovers equal. Ah, I see him, this dear lover, a fire of love burning in the thorn bush of sorrow [see Ex 3:2]. I am the same: I am wholly on fire with love within the thickets of my grief.... Do not look only at the horrors of my piercing sorrows, but see the beauty of the love that comforts me. Alas! that beloved divine lover suffers from unbearable sorrow.... He loves his torments and dies with joy at dying in torment for me. Wherefore, even as I sorrow over his sorrows, so also am I ravished through and through with joy in his love. Not only do I grieve with him, but I am glorified in him [see Rom 8:17].[42]

The devotion of Francis de Sales represents the highest form of devotion to Christ and received the attention and support of many Protestants during those most unecumenical of times. In spite of the bitterness connected with the persecution of Catholics (Mary Queen of Scots was beheaded while St. Francis was a student at Clermont College, where he was taught by exiled English Jesuits), Francis had a great love for England and wished to work for its return to the Church. Even more surprising is the popularity of his two great works, especially the *Introduction to the Devout Life*, among English Protestants.

---

[42] St. Francis de Sales, *On the Love of God*, trans. John K. Ryan (Garden City, N.Y.: Image Books, 1963), bk. 5, chap. 5, 246–47.

Marie de Médicis, widow of Henry IV, sent a richly bound copy of the *Introduction* to King James I of England, which he carried with him and studied for several weeks. When Francis heard about this, he is reported to have said, "I would give my life a thousand times over to bring England back to the fold, but of course our Holy Father, the pope, would have to be pleased to send me on this mission."[43]

French Protestants also read de Sales. St. Jane Frances notes that "even Huguenots think very highly of this book for what it teaches them about right behavior and the practice of virtues".[44] When we recall the dark controversy over predestination, it is astonishing that this gentle pastor of souls could win people on all sides to an admiring love of God.

Pierre de Bérulle (1575–1629)

Another graduate of the Jesuit College of Clermont who became a powerful figure in the spiritual renewal of France was Pierre de Bérulle. Apart from his mystical teaching and work as a spiritual director and guide to many reform-minded religious, his clerical career was fascinating and stormy. He started early on the spiritual road, having made an Ignatian retreat in 1602, three years after his ordination at the age of twenty-four. The retreat may have made him aware that the mystical experiences of his contemporaries were too abstract and needed an explicitly Christological focus.[45]

At the age of twenty-eight Bérulle was named by the Holy See as one of the three superiors of the first French community of Carmelites of the Teresian reform.[46] As a result of his involvement with the new Carmel in Paris, Bérulle came under the influence of Mother Anne of Jesus. Formed in Carmel by St. Teresa, Anne of Jesus stressed the need to focus on Christ's humanity in prayer. Tolerating no attempt to bypass this essential element in the spiritual life, she was critical of any abstract form of mysticism. She influenced Bérulle and many others, and Bérulle "grew decisively Christocentric about this time (1605–1610) as evidenced in his writings".[47] An explicitly Christocentric mysticism and devotion continued to flourish in France for the next seventy-five years and came to its final flowering with St. John Eudes and St. Margaret Mary Alacoque's devotion to the Sacred Heart of Jesus.

In 1611 Bérulle founded the French Oratory following the model begun by St. Philip Neri. Bérulle's deep devotion to Christ drew him

---

[43] See Elisabeth Stopp's excellent article "Healing Differences: St. Francis de Sales in Seventeenth-Century England", *The Month* 38 (1967): 53.

[44] Ibid., 54.

[45] *Bérulle and the French School: Selected Writings*, ed. William M. Thompson, trans. Lowell M. Glendon, S.S. Classics of Western Spirituality (New York: Paulist Press, 1989), 13.

[46] Bérulle's association with the Carmelites is the subject of another book, but we will only point out here that his failure to understand and respect the ideals and vision of St. Teresa led to many difficulties. He also successfully barred the Discalced Carmelite friars from France for several years, thus consolidating his own influence in the French Carmels.

[47] Thompson and Glendon, *Bérulle and the French School*, 13.

to make a dramatic consecration in the form of a vow of servitude to Jesus and Mary. Had Bérulle confined this vow of servitude to the Oratory, all might have been well, but his attempt to have it gain acceptance among the Carmelites proved unfortunate. Although in the best light the vow could be viewed as a logical and intense prolongation of baptismal vows, Bérulle brought on controversy which continued for years. Madame Acarie, by then a Carmelite, was very opposed to Bérulle's idea, and the ensuing differences clouded their long friendship during her last years. Even though some Carmelites embraced the idea of the vow, it was alien to the spirit of St. Teresa. After a defective copy of the vow was found in 1620, Bérulle was accused of heretical leanings and censured by two theological faculties.

Bérulle's thought at this time was influenced by another remarkable but hidden woman, the daughter of a devout aristocrat, who was only twenty-two when he met her. Along with St. Francis de Sales and St. Jane Frances de Chantal (still a layperson), Bérulle met the talented and spiritual Mademoiselle de Fontaines at Tours. She became Mother Madeleine of St. Joseph, and Brémond calls her, along with Madame Acarie, "the glory of the French Carmelites".[48] Twenty years later Mother Madeleine published the life of another Carmelite, Catherine of Jesus, with a preface by Bérulle. It was a powerful statement of the highest Christocentric spirituality. In the preface he extolled the idea of humility and spiritual childhood, a concept closely connected to the idea of humility and abandonment. The concept of the humility of God, who abased Himself for us at the Incarnation, and the idea of spiritual childhood, the soul's complete dependence on God, as well as devotion to Jesus especially as a child, were strong currents in the French Carmels for more than two centuries. They are perhaps best exemplified in the spirituality of St. Thérèse of Lisieux in the nineteenth century.

Bérulle writes in his preface:

> Great and sweet is it to behold Jesus, in Whom is the fullness of Divinity and Eternal Wisdom, united to a little child and it to Him; happy child to be so close to the Heart where dwells and triumphs the Trinity itself. But if this thought is sweet and great, though the meaning to which it leads us is strong and severe, its result is mighty and its end seems strange. For Jesus, by act and word, not only abases the great of this earth—that would be a small thing—but also the great of His Divine and Celestial dwelling-place, by the formidable negation, the searching pronouncement: "Unless you become as little children, you shall not enter the kingdom of heaven." This oracle should arrest us, this spectacle draw tears from our eyes, should melt pride by the sweetness of Jesus and cast down for ever the highest

[48] Brémond, *Religious Thought in France*, 239.

cedars of Lebanon at the Feet of Jesus and those of the little ones of Jesus upon earth.[49]

In a dramatic turn of history, Pope Urban VIII came to Bérulle's defense and even made the embattled priest a cardinal in 1627, calling him the "apostle of the Incarnate Word".[50] Unfortunately, the Pope, while very pro-French, was also very interested in politics, and Bérulle was caught between great forces. He was criticized for his strong stand against the Huguenots, and when Richelieu achieved complete power, Bérulle was forced out of public life in 1629. His enemies, however, continued to attack him, accusing him of heresies ranging from Monophysitism to Nestorianism—almost contradictory positions. Shortly after his public "disgrace" this man of great piety, who had led such a controversial life, died while offering Mass.

Bérulle's experience is the high-water mark of a personal and thoroughly informed devotion to Christ. The Catholic Church would wait almost three hundred years until the time of Blessed Columba Marmion to again see a personal devotion so highly articulated in rich theological language. In Bérulle's case some of his language was so new that it aroused charges of heresy. Since there is renewed interest today in what is called the French School, of which Bérulle is the founder, a brief review of his particular approach may be helpful.

Bérulle speaks of the states (*états*) of Christ. He writes of "Jesus living in three different and wonderful states, that is, in the heart of the Father, in our humanity, and in his Eucharist".[51] Like St. Francis de Sales, he sees the Incarnation putting the human race in a much more positive light than do Calvin, Luther, or even Augustine and most of the Scholastics. The fact that we are a race adopted by God through the grace of Christ is a very specific and Christian insight into the universal salvific will of God. "The same Word, who is necessarily begotten within eternity, wanted to be begotten a second time in the fulness of time; and by this second birth he wanted to imprint on this humanity the adorable character of his divine and eternal filiation, which it receives and bears for eternity. For he possesses this humanity not just as God, but as Son of God, and in this quality he imprints on it his proper and personal subsistence."[52]

Bérulle puts many of the intuitions of medieval piety into theological language. In Christ, God has become human and will remain so forever in His risen glory. Even the various stages, or *états*, of Jesus' life, from infancy to suffering and death—"all the moments of that life"—live on in Him so that He enters into and makes His own all-human experience (except sin) "from the weakness and dependence

[49] Quoted in ibid., 245. Scripture quotation is in Latin in the original.

[50] Thompson and Glendon, *Bérulle and the French School*, 16.

[51] John Saward, "Bérulle and the 'French School'", in *Study of Spirituality*, 386ff.

[52] From Bérulle's *Grandeurs de Jésus*, 6, 11, quoted in ibid., 390.

of life in the womb to the ultimate poverty of death. Not only did he appropriate all our human states, he also sanctified and deified them."[53]

Saward explains Bérulle's devotion clearly:

> Bérulle's great insight is that, while the exterior circumstances of these various states and mysteries of Christ's life are past, the interior state or living disposition within Christ's human soul remains, and it is this disposition which can have an effect, as *vertu* or *mérite*, on us. The "interior states" of the mysteries of our Lord's life produce correlative "states" in chosen souls. "They are past with regard to execution, but they are present with regard to their efficacy (*vertu*)".[54]

Bérulle, according to Saward, explains this with the example to our Lord's wounds. "[I]f Jesus could take the scars on his body into glory, "why will he not be able to preserve something in his soul, in the definitive state of his glory? . . . What remains in him of these mysteries forms on earth a kind of grace, which pertains to those souls chosen to receive it". All the mysteries of Christ's life, because of the interior dispositions and sentiments in his soul corresponding to them, affect and vivify us."[55]

What does a devout Christian do with this insight? How do we participate in the states of Christ's life? To answer this Bérulle appeals to two essential insights of St. Thomas Aquinas. Thomas teaches that Christ is the head of the Church of which we are the members, echoing one of the most important and mysterious teachings of St. Paul: "It is no longer I who live, but Christ who lives in me" (Gal 2:20). The humanity of Jesus is the instrument of the Incarnate Word as head of the Church on earth. Saward rightly quotes Bérulle saying, "It pleases him [Christ] to imprint on souls his states and effects, his mysteries and his sufferings, and one day it will please him to imprint on us his grandeurs and his glory."[56]

Bérulle's insight into the states of Christ and our participation in them illuminates several aspects of Christian devotion that are puzzling to Protestants and even to some Catholics. Because of his prestige as a mystic and poet-saint, people are comfortable enough with Francis of Assisi praying to the Divine Child at Gubbio or to the crucified Savior. Yet when such devotion is presented today, it is dismissed as medieval. It was Bérulle's genius to see that our link with the Infant Christ and the crucified Savior is our own lives and the various states we move through as members of the Mystical Body and as human beings. Which of us does not at times feel the weakness and dependency of a child? Who does not feel rejection or emotionally

[53] Saward, "Bérulle", 390.

[54] Ibid.

[55] Ibid., 391.

[56] Bérulle, *Opuscules de Piété*, 78, quoted in ibid.

crucified at times? How can we realistically relate in a spiritual way to the state of the suffering and death that marked the end of our Savior's earthly life?

Saward reminds us of the Gospel counsel to accept the Kingdom of God as children. The childhood of the Incarnate Word provides an example for us. We also receive from the Incarnate Word the grace to follow Him in the humility and humiliation of His suffering and death. The reality of following Christ's example and relying on His grace is all the more obvious when we suffer and take up our cross with Him.

We do not think often enough of the *imitatio Christi*—the need to model ourselves on Christ in all things. This is not just a theory; it is an obligation, and it is made possible through grace and the mysterious reality of the Mystical Body of Christ. We do good and endure suffering and death with Him as members of His body, a theme integral to the theology of St. Paul. We also see and serve Christ in the poor, the needy, and the suffering. He is in us and around us.

Bérulle, quoting almost literally the words of St. Augustine about the chain of love—*vinculum caritatis*—saw this union with Christ especially in the Eucharist. In his great work *Discourse on the State and the Grandeurs of Jesus*, he writes the following, which sums up a devotion to Christ in the Mystical Body, which is familiar to people of our time.

> There is a divine and inviolable chain of unity and charity, of the charity of the Father and of the Son towards men, and of the unity of the Father with the Son in the Trinity, of the unity of the Son with human nature in the Incarnation, and of the unity of the body of Jesus Christ with us. . . .[57]
>
> But of course the chain is not simply an external connection. It is through the "substantial and corporeal residence of the living and glorious body of the Son of God" in our mortal bodies through Holy Communion that we share in his holy and divine life, the life He shares with the Father.[58]

Bérulle's theology inspired a group of writers known as the French School, of which the principal representatives are Jean-Jacques Olier, founder of the Sulpicians; St. John Eudes, founder of a community of priests and women religious; the Venerable Madeleine de Saint-Joseph, who founded several French Carmels; and St. John Baptist de la Salle, founder of the Brothers of the Christian Schools. The themes of the French School continued in the writings of St. Louis de Montfort, who founded a congregation of missionaries and sisters. Related to all of these are the revelations of the Sacred Heart of Jesus to St. Margaret Mary Alacoque and the writings of her spiritual director, St. Claude de la Colombière.

---

[57] Bérulle, *Grandeurs de Jésus*, 6, 4, 248, quoted in Saward, "Bérulle", 393.

[58] Ibid.

All of these writers stress the two steps of admiration and loving response. The ideas of consecration of one's whole life to Christ in a complete service of love (sometimes called "servitude") and total acceptance of God's will become clearer and clearer in the writings of the French School.

Jean-Jacques Olier (1608–1657)

The rich piety of Jean-Jacques Olier is similar to that of Bérulle but founded on the centrality of our response to Jesus. Olier's comprehensive approach to devotion arises from the life of Christ as the foundation of the life of every Christian. This new emphasis of total dedication will also be the central theme of the devotion to the Sacred Heart proposed by St. John Eudes (1606–1680).

Those familiar with Olier emphasize that his devotion was very quiet. In our noisy world this has caused him almost to disappear. I was able to find only a few of his works, almost all of them in French, in a century-old seminary library conducted by the Society of St. Sulpice, which he founded.

Despite the popular image of a quiet, retiring Olier, his writings reveal a life of warm personal devotion. His list of qualities of the self-centered person and the person who practices self-denial (only briefly cited here) is a commentary on the prayer of St. Francis of Assisi, based in turn on his admonitions.

The self-centered person is full of himself	The Christian is empty of himself.
The self-centered person is always preoccupied with himself.	The Christian always forgets himself.
The self-centered person loves praise and seeks it.	The Christian is confused by praise and flees it.[59]

Olier's personal love for Jesus Christ showed itself, as it did in the life of St. Francis, in a love of material poverty.

> Thus a soul, withdrawn into God and clothed with the dispositions of Jesus Christ, discovering in him such great wealth, cannot desire earthly goods. If it did have the slightest appreciation of them, it would be like a king who, not being satisfied with his glory and majesty, would go looking for wealth and splendor in the sackcloth of a peasant.
>
> We are called to poverty and detachment from all the world's goods because of the immense and infinite riches that we find in God. . . .
>
> Our Lord enjoyed and possessed God in this world. He was saturated and satiated in his soul by what God is in himself. And since he

[59] Jean-Jacques Olier, *Introduction to the Christian Life and Virtues*, quoted in Thompson and Glendon, *Bérulle and the French School*, 263–64.

> enjoyed in himself true wealth, he could have no desire for what was only its shell and surface.[60]

Olier resembled St. Francis in his dedication to love of neighbor out of love for Christ. In his words on charity we see his warm emotional and spiritual devotion. "True and perfect love can be recognized by the great love we have for everyone. This love would like to set everything ablaze, even to seeing itself filled with a fire, a passion and a zeal to make God known and loved everywhere."[61]

The great theme of the French School, that Christian lives are the life of Christ, becomes even more apparent in St. John Eudes, Olier's contemporary, who outlived him by many years.

St. John Eudes and the Two Hearts

St. John Eudes (1601–1680) represents the final development of the French School, and he expressed a phase of development that would succeed the piety of the French School: devotion to the Sacred Heart of Jesus and the Immaculate Heart of Mary. We have seen that the idea of praying to the Heart of Jesus had a long Catholic tradition and that focusing attention on the Heart of the Savior was even in keeping with the Puritan devotion of Thomas Goodwin. The best and most theologically developed expression of this was that of John Eudes, who founded the Congregation of Jesus and Mary (1644). In his enlightening study, Ted Campbell has summarized Eudes' teaching well and recognized its theological importance. In the popular Catholic mind devotion to the Heart of Jesus comes from the private revelations to St. Margaret Mary Alacoque. St. John Eudes' writings on the Sacred Heart, however, antedated publication of St. Margaret Mary's visions by a number of years. The first apparition to St. Margaret Mary was on December 27, 1673, but this was not made known until 1682, and then only in the Visitation Monastery where she lived. By then John Eudes had died, and so it is safe to say that Margaret Mary did not influence him. It is interesting to speculate on whether his writings influenced her.

Campbell sums up the contribution of Eudes to the religion of the heart.

> Eudes advocated devotion to the sacred heart of Jesus and to the immaculate heart of the Virgin Mary. He had studied previous spiritual writers on the subject, and endeavored to interpret this devotion against the background of traditional Catholic teachings about the Trinity and human salvation. Eudes insisted that as Jesus is human and divine, and united to the Trinity, devotion to any specific aspect of Jesus (i.e., to the sacred heart) becomes worship of Christ and of the whole godhead. He further clarified that the love revealed in

[60] Ibid., 254–55.
[61] Ibid., 270.

devotion to the sacred heart is the love for God lost because of human sin, and restored through the grace of Christ expressed in the sacraments. He also cited specific Catholic saints who had expressed similar forms of devotion. In this way Eudes provided an explanation for the practice of devotion to the sacred heart in which it could be understood as broadly harmonious with traditional Catholic theology.

Within this orthodox framework, however, Eudes explicated a Catholicism focusing on the encounter with God through the affections. The heart of Jesus becomes the heart of the believer.[62]

Eudes' expression of the total gift of self through consecration to Christ and Mary continues the thought of Bérulle and his vow of servitude. There have been many expressions of total self-giving to God in the course of Christian history. In the French School, and especially in St. John Eudes, it reaches a high level. The following excerpt from the vow that John Eudes made on March 25, 1637, epitomizes his teaching. Not only do consecration and self-sacrifice become explicit but the identity with Christ in His sufferings and in union with His Mother is central.

> O good Jesus, receive and accept this vow of mine and this sacrifice which I make to Thee of my life and my being in homage to and by the merits of the most divine sacrifice Thou didst make of Thyself to Thy Father on the Cross. Look upon me henceforth as an offering and victim dedicated to be wholly immolated to the glory of Thy holy name. Grant, through Thy great mercy, that my whole life may be a perpetual sacrifice of love and praise for Thee. Grant that I may live a life that may perpetually imitate and honor Thine own holy life and that of Thy Blessed Mother and holy martyrs; that I may never pass a day without suffering something for love of Thee; and that I may die a death conformable to Thy holy death.[63]

St. Vincent de Paul (1580–1660) and St. Louise de Marillac (1591–1660)

We have left the devotion of the two great French apostles of charity to the end for an important reason. Although they lived during a time of incredible spiritual activity and mystical movements, they did not lead these events. Quite the opposite. Biographers of St. Vincent de Paul make it clear that his life and work represent the result rather than the cause of this great time of spiritual renewal in France. While never a great sinner, he was gradually converted over a period of two decades from being a worldly cleric to becoming the apostle of charity. Canfield and Madame Acarie, Bérulle and St. Francis de Sales, all

[62] Campbell, *Religion of the Heart*, 37–39. The citation of St. John Eudes is from his work *Le Coeur admirable de très sacrée Mère de Dieu*. The English translation is by Dom Richard Flower, *The Sacred Heart of Jesus* (New York: P.J. Kenedy and Sons, 1946), 96–97. See also Flower, 25–35, 40–45, 60–65, 72–76.

[63] Quoted in Peter Herambourg, C.J.M., *Saint John Eudes, a Spiritual Portrait*, trans. Ruth Hauser, ed. Wilfrid E. Myatt, C.J.M. (Westminster, Md.: Newman Press, 1960), 309.

envisioned a France converted to Christian values and filled with charity. The best results of these efforts by God's grace are Vincent de Paul, his mission, and the Vincentian family. The latter was to be composed of devout women, many of whom became vowed religious, following his spiritual daughter, Louise de Marillac, and many laypeople. Although the leader of the reform of Catholic life, clerical and lay, in France, he was not one of the founders. The reformers themselves were the instruments of grace to convert this complacent ecclesiastic. Once converted, he led by his zeal and example the continuation of the reform that had changed his own life.[64]

The principles that grounded this apostle of charity are simple and are so familiar that they appear commonplace: to be led by Divine Providence, to work to fulfill the needs at hand (no grand schemes), and to give oneself completely to God out of love for Christ. Vincent's emphasis was the care of the immense number of desperately poor people he encountered, most of them refugees from the wars of Europe and the civil war in France.

Together with the Ladies of Charity, one of the first organized volunteer movements in history, and the Daughters of Charity, one of the first active, noncloistered communities of women, the Lazarists (as the Vincentian priests and brothers were first called) worked tirelessly. In addition, Vincent de Paul wrote an astonishing twenty-eight hundred letters, most of them concerned with spiritual direction or exhortation.

Behind all of this was a series of conversions, of steps that were guided by devotion to Jesus Christ. Influenced as he was by Bérulle and de Sales, Vincent did not publish the rule, or constitutions, of the Congregation of the Mission until three decades after it began. This rule was unusual in that it was not written in a legal style. Instead Vincent de Paul presented a series of meditations on the life of Christ, into which he wove a pattern for his followers in the Congregation of the Mission to imitate Christ.

> I have tried to base all the rules, where possible, on the spirit and actions of Jesus Christ. My idea was that men who are called to continue Christ's mission, which is mainly preaching the good news to the poor, should see things from his point of view and want what he wanted. They should have the same spirit that he had, and follow in his footsteps.[65]

St. Louise de Marillac follows the model of the French spiritual reformers more than her spiritual father. Her road to holiness began

[64] *Vincent de Paul and Louise de Marillac: Rules, Conferences, and Writings*, ed. Frances Ryan, D.C., and John E. Rybolt, C.M., Classics of Western Spirituality, (New York: Paulist Press, 1995). The reader is referred especially to the excellent chapters on St. Vincent by Hugh F. O'Donnell, C.M., and the one on St. Louise by Louise Sullivan, D.C.

[65] Ryan and Rybolt, *Vincent de Paul and Louise de Marillac*, 86–91.

with a profound mystical experience.[66] Devout, guided by a spiritual director, and influenced by the growing tide of spirituality in France, she requested to enter the newly established Daughters of the Passion in Paris. The Capuchin provincial, who apparently had responsibility for admission to this new community, rejected her and prophetically told her that God had other designs for her.[67]

She was then married into the highest sphere of influence in France. Her husband, Antoine Le Gras, was personal secretary to the Queen Regent, Marie de Médicis. Le Gras, who was chronically ill, died after fifteen years of marriage, leaving her with a son, who was a constant source of concern. Two years before her husband's death Louise had had a powerful illumination, which she called a light, on Pentecost 1623.[68] During a novena from Ascension Day to Pentecost she was deeply disturbed by the thought that she should leave her husband, live a religious life, and serve the poor, according to a promise she had made. Louise also experienced great doubts about the immortality of the soul. She describes this experience.

> God gave me the grace to make a vow of widowhood should he call my husband to himself. On the following feast of the Ascension, I was very disturbed because of the doubt I had as to whether I should leave my husband, as I greatly wanted to do, in order to make good my first vow, and to have greater liberty to serve God and my neighbor.
>
> I also suffered greatly because of the doubt I experienced concerning the immortality of the soul. All these things caused me incredible anguish which lasted from Ascension to Pentecost.
>
> On the feast of Pentecost, during holy Mass or while I was praying in the church, my mind was instantly freed of all doubt. I was advised that I should remain with my husband and that a time would come when I would be in a position to make vows of poverty, chastity, and obedience and that I would be in a small community where others would do the same. I then understood that I would be in a place where I could help my neighbor but I did not understand how this would be possible.[69]

Within the next three years, Louise met Vincent de Paul, her husband died, and the Archbishop of Paris approved the establishment of the new Congregation of the Mission. A letter of Vincent's to Louise written seven years before his establishment of the Daughters of Charity with her, reflects the gentle wisdom for which this humble priest is known. Vincent had had to leave Paris unexpectedly and had not informed her. He writes: "Our Lord will use this little mortification

[66] Ibid., 227.
[67] Ibid., 41.
[68] Ibid.
[69] Ibid., 226–27.

to advantage if he wishes, and he himself will act as your director. Yes, he will surely do so, and in such a way that he will lead you to see that it is he himself. Be then his dear daughter—quite humble, submissive, and full of confidence—and always wait patiently for the manifestation of his holy and adorable Will." [70]

During the next few years, Louise helped establish the Confraternity of Charity, known now as the Society of St. Vincent de Paul. The young aristocrat grew spiritually during these years. She also grew in the development of managerial skills, which would be necessary when she began what would become the first worldwide order of active religious women. Like her spiritual father she was not given to making plans or setting long-term goals. The following passage, written six years before her death, illustrates St. Louise's devotion to Christ and explains the great dedication and humility of someone who could have lived amid the comforts of the French aristocracy. Her words also indicate how she and her director were consistently content to be led by Divine Providence.

> On the Feast of Saint Genevieve, in 1660, as I was receiving Holy Communion, I felt, upon seeing the Sacred Host, an extraordinary thirst which had its origin in the belief that Jesus wanted to give himself to me in the simplicity of his divine infancy. When I was receiving him and for a long time afterward, my mind was filled by an interior communication which led me to understand that Jesus was bringing not only himself to me but also all the merits of his mysteries. This communication lasted all day. It was not a forced, interior preoccupation. It was rather a presence or a recurrent recollection, as sometimes happens when something is troubling me.
>
> I felt that I was being warned that, since Jesus had given himself entirely to me, laden with the merits of all these mysteries, I must make use of this occasion to participate in his submission to humiliations.
>
> One means to attain this end is to be found in the fact that, without any cause in me, I appear to others as having received some graces from God. This both humbles me and gives me courage.
>
> No desires, no resolutions. The grace of my God will accomplish in me whatever he wills.[71]

The works of Vincent, Louise, and the Vincentian family are legion, and their impact profound. To this day, visitors to the motherhouse of the Daughters of Charity, in Paris, are filled with a spirit of peace.[72] Throughout the world the Daughters of Charity have spread the word

[70] Letter, Oct. 30, quoted in ibid., 152.

[71] Ibid., 230–31.

[72] Many pilgrims each year visit the chapel of the Daughters of Charity, where in 1830 the Blessed Virgin appeared to St. Catherine Labouré to reveal to her the message of the Miraculous Medal.

of God and the charity of Christ, especially in times of war, when they have been seen on the battlefield caring for the wounded on both sides.

The Jansenists and the Quietists

A review of seventeenth-century French Catholic devotion would be incomplete without mention of two important spiritual movements, which for different reasons ended up at the outer edges of the Church. Professor Campbell refers to the "religion of the heart": Jansenism and Quietism were precisely this. Campbell describes religion of the heart as a movement that emphasizes four elements: (1) the conviction that "human beings in their 'natural' state are separated from God", (2) that this separation is overcome by "heartfelt experience", (3) that this experience focuses on "repentance (sorrow over sin) and faith (personal trust in God)", and (4) sometimes it includes "vivid experiences of personal illumination".[73]

It must be obvious from this definition, that religion of the heart would involve devotion. However, both Jansenists and Quietists in their own ways minimized devotion. Jansenists, devotional themselves, scoffed at the devotion of others. Contradictions such as this were intrinsic to both movements, and neither ever embraced a settled position, like Thomism and Calvinism. They grew in fascinating ways, turned back on themselves, went in two directions at once, and often denied what they appeared to have said. In both cases, when the Church issued critical evaluations and censured their teachings, they declared that they never held the ideas that were condemned. As someone with partial French ancestry, I hope I will be forgiven for saying that most other countries and languages would not have given rise to such subtle and intellectually precise controversies.

We need not review the complex histories and ideas of these movements in order to consider their devotion to Christ. A few general observations will suffice. In terms of our discussion, Dr. Campbell's work is highly recommended.

Jansenism

France was enjoying the first decades of the remarkable century of spirituality when Jacqueline-Marie Arnauld (1591–1661), still a child of ten, was appointed abbess of the ancient monastery of Cistercian nuns at Port-Royal des Champs, near Paris. Mère Angélique, as she was known in religion, underwent a powerful religious conversion in 1608 as a result of the preaching of an itinerant Capuchin friar and commenced a much-needed reform of her monastery along the best traditional lines. All this is similar to the work of St. Teresa. By 1625 the nuns had moved to Paris, their Cistercian identity replaced by that of their own new community, the Order of the Blessed Sacrament. These two events reflect the great success of the reform, and it seemed

[73] Campbell, *Religion of the Heart*, 2–3.

that Mère Angélique was headed for her own niche in the history of reforming mother foundresses.

In 1633, Père Jean Duvergier de Hauranne (1581–1643), called the Abbé de Saint-Cyran because he was a titular, or honorary, abbot, became spiritual director of the new convent Port-Royal de Paris. At the old abandoned monastery of Port-Royal des Champs, Saint-Cyran founded a community of men and women hermits, known as the Solitaries of Port-Royal. Saint-Cyran vigorously opposed the Jesuits, whom he considered semi-Pelagian because of their practices of penance and their idea that one could be absolved from sin in confession even if one's motive were only fear of God (attrition) rather than love for God (contrition). All this proved to be too much for Cardinal Richelieu, and Saint-Cyran was imprisoned. He died shortly after his release in 1643.

Saint-Cyran was a friend of Cornelius Jansen, Bishop of Ypres (Belgium), then in the Spanish Netherlands. This committed reformer, also an enemy of the Jesuits, died in 1638 while Saint-Cyran was in prison. Two years after Jansen's death, his monumental work, *Augustinus*,[74] was published. In it he attacked semi-Pelagians in general and the Jesuits in particular. Seen from our perspective, nearly four hundred years later, this seems puzzling because the Jesuits were dedicated to spiritual reform. The Jansenists have often been seen as spiritual elitists, despising the conversion of simple souls whose first impetus to reform is fear of standing before the judgment seat of God. From this perspective, the extreme Augustinianism of Jansenism seems like Calvinism in Catholic attire. They apparently thought of themselves as the elect, as did the Calvinists, and believed they had but to stay on a straight and narrow path in order to avoid losing divine election. The best side of Jansenist spirituality was their gratitude that God in His mercy had drawn them from the abysmal state of fallen human nature. In their opinion, however, this grace did not extend to all. In fact, a distinctly heretical tenet of the *Augustinus* is that Christ died only for the elect.

Obviously, their idea of election was in opposition to the thinking of other Catholic reformers, like St. Francis de Sales, who emphasized the universal salvific will of God, and St. Vincent de Paul, whose passionate devotion was to serve Christ in the poor. Eventually, the Jansenists attacked devotion to the Sacred Heart as "cardiolatry" and became increasingly puritanical about the sacraments, which they valued so highly that they believed few were worthy to receive them. Anyone approaching the sacraments had to have a deep love for and commitment to Christ deriving from admiration and gratitude rather than from mere sorrow for sin and its effects. This approach was taken

[74] The *Augustinus* was condemned for the first time in 1642 by Pope Urban VIII in the papal bull *In eminenti*.

by Mère Angélique's younger brother, Antoine Arnauld, an apologist for Jansenism, in his work *On Frequent Communion* (1643), in which he stressed the need for severe penance and extended preparation for Communion. For this and other works, he was formally censured and his doctorate withdrawn by the Sorbonne.

Jansenism might have been a footnote in the history of religion except for the entrance on the scene of Blaise Pascal (1623–1662), one of the great minds of the century and perhaps of the millennium. Our world of computers, electronic calculators, and statistical inference is built on the monumental discoveries of this "father of statistics". His *Provincial Letters*, written at the request of the Solitaries of Port-Royal, are a series of fictitious letters to a friend intended to further the Jansenist cause and ridicule Jesuit positions on a number of issues. Clever, witty, and polemical, they are a marked contrast to his *Pensées*, which were published posthumously (1670) and based on his private notebooks of meditation and observation. Both works are classics of French literature.

The Jesuits, meanwhile, were not idle. Through their influence, a series of five propositions distilled from the *Augustinus* were condemned by a group of theologians at Louvain. They were similarly condemned by Pope Innocent X (*Cum Occasione*) in 1653, and several papal interventions followed over the next sixty years. The popularity of Jansenist ideas endured, however, especially among the French clergy. This alarmed Louis XIV, who was anxious to quell all discord and religious controversy during his long reign. The ideas, already influential in the Spanish Netherlands, were spreading, through priests trained in France, to Ireland and other countries. The historical phenomenon of Jansenism came to an end in the Catholic Church in 1711, when the king ordered the monastery of Port-Royal destroyed. Two years later the last significant condemnation of the movement was issued by Pope Clement XI in the bull *Unigenitus Dei Filius*.

Despite this, Jansenism, like most heresies, did not completely disappear. In the eighteenth century, odd groups trying to be Jansenist danced in the spirit, celebrated the Eucharist with laymen and women acting as priests, and requested physical punishment, even crucifixion. At the end of the nineteenth century St. John Bosco could complain of the Jansenist atmosphere in the seminary he attended in northern Italy. Even in the middle of the twentieth century, anyone seeking a fervent observance of religious life or even of Catholic lay life might be branded a Jansenist by people who did not have the slightest idea what the word meant.

Jansenist devotion (and many Jansenists would have rejected the term as an oxymoron) is perhaps best seen in the famous mystical document called Pascal's "Memorial". This paper, which he wore sewn inside his clothing, is a deeply moving and insightful description of a mystical experience of God and still ranks as one of the most revealing documents of an intense encounter with God.

Memorial

In the year of grace 1654
Monday, 23 November, the day of St. Clement,
Pope and Martyr, and others in the Roman Martyrology,
the eve of St. Chrysogonus, Martyr, and others, etc. . . .
From about half past ten in the evening
Till about half an hour after midnight

FIRE

God of Abraham, God of Isaac, God of Jacob
not of the philosophers and the learned.
Certitude joy certitude emotion sight joy
God of Jesus Christ
Deum meum et Deum vestrum.
Thy God shall be my God.
Forgetfulness of the world and of everything other than God
He can be found only in the ways taught
in the Gospel. Greatness of the human soul.
Good Father, the world has not known
Thee, but I have known Thee.
Joy Joy Joy and tears of joy
I have separated myself from Thee
Dereliquerunt me fontem
my God wilt Thou leave me
let me not be eternally separated from Thee
They have life eternal, they that know Thee
Sole true God and He Whom Thou hast sent
Jesus Christ
Jesus Christ
I have separated myself from Him I have fled renounced
crucified Him.[75]

In this document, the sophistication and literary skill of the great mathematician are nowhere in evidence. Gone, as well, are distinctions and controversies, although Pascal's values still reveal themselves in his experience. His "Memorial" represents the highest expression of spiritual emotion and is in complete accord with our descriptive definition of devotion.

From our moment in history, it is easy to attack Jansenism because of its excesses as well as the pessimism and the crabbiness of those who are regarded today as Jansenists. In a well-balanced assessment, however, Louis Dupré, while acknowledging the movement's elitism,

[75] As quoted in *The Soul Afire: Revelations of the Mystics*, ed. H. A. Reinhold (Garden City, N.Y.: Image Books, 1973), 356–57.

pride, and subordination, makes this positive observation, backing it up with quotes from the *Pensées*.

> Yet in the later Pascal, as in so many now forgotten members of the Port-Royal movement, it was carried by the humble awareness of an unmerited union with God. Port-Royal was originally, and always remained for its finest members, a center of piety more than of controversy. Its devotion book, the *Exercises*, reveals its spirit far more than Arnauld's noisy polemics. In the *Pensées* we find that piety reflected in the passages on the knowledge of the heart.[76]

> "Those to whom God has given religious faith by moving their hearts are very fortunate, and feel quite legitimately convinced, but to those who do not have it we can only give such faith through reason, until God gives it by moving their heart, without which faith is only human and useless for salvation."[77]

The conclusion of those who have studied Jansenism seriously is that it was not merely an elitist, self-righteous movement, hostile to the other movements of its time and especially to the reforms led by the Jesuits. Its genuine anti-Pelagianism led to a real honesty about the limitations of human nature and its total dependence on God. The writings of some modern Catholic authors like François Mauriac and Georges Bernanos reflect some of Pascal's thinking. In fact, in the mindless optimism of contemporary psychospirituality, a dose of Pascal would be a welcome and sobering relief.

Quietism

If the Jansenists represented a distortion of St. Augustine's teaching on grace, their contemporaries, the Quietists, can be seen as an exaggeration of the Carmelite spirituality of St. Teresa and St. John of the Cross. There are many differences between the two movements, although there is some evidence that the most celebrated Quietists, Madame Guyon (1648–1717) and Archbishop Fénelon (1651–1715), had been distantly related to the Arnaulds of Port-Royal.[78] Like the Jansenists, the Quietists were condemned by the hierarchy and then by Pope Innocent XII. However, their attitude toward their critics and the controversies swirling around them was entirely different. As one might expect from their name, Quietists maintained a holy indifference, an attitude of detachment. As a rule, they even accepted and signed the corrections that were made to their writings. Some powerful and gifted ecclesiastics like Jacques-Bénigné Bossuet, the great court orator and Bishop of Meaux, as well as the king judged the Quietists harshly, considering them a danger to the unity of France. Others, including

[76] Louis Dupré, "Jansenism and Quietism", in Dupré and Saliers, *Christian Spirituality*, 127.

[77] *Pensées*, no. 110, quoted in ibid., 127–28.

[78] Ronald A. Knox, *Enthusiasm* (New York: Oxford University Press, 1950), 319.

the Jesuits, supported them in their trials; in fact, the same pope who condemned Fénelon expressed his admiration for this devout and brilliant man.

A careful study of Quietism demonstrates how orthodox spiritual writers can become carried away with their own ideas and slip into hyperbole and error. The history of Quietism also shows how mystical writers were vulnerable to the attacks and misunderstanding of loyal churchmen like Bossuet, who seems to have had no real understanding of mysticism. When Innocent XII was pressed into condemning some of Fénelon's writings, the Pope questioned whether in doing so he was not actually condemning St. Teresa.[79]

One aspect of the history of Quietism especially draws our attention. Beginning with Miguel de Molinos (1640–1697), a Spanish writer who taught that the soul abandoned to God must be completely passive in the highest state of contemplative prayer, the Quietists tended to lack balance and perspective. Like Molinos, other Quietists made statements so extreme as to sound unorthodox. When they were corrected, however, they often retracted and repudiated their problematic statements. This was true of the most famous of those who exaggerated—Molinos and Madame Guyon. For the most part they denied what they were accused of saying or at least denied the meaning attributed to their words. Molinos was tried for heresy and retracted. With characteristic detachment he spent the rest of his life prayerfully in a papal prison following his condemnation in 1687.

Madame Guyon, one of the more colorful figures in the history of spirituality, was no theologian at all. Guided by her heart and intuition, she often found herself in trouble with those in authority and even went to the Bastille for a time. That Archbishop Fénelon, a cautious man of real spiritual depth, ever got involved with the histrionic Madame Guyon is a surprise, but we have seen that some of the spiritual leaders of the time were influenced by untrained religious women, like Marie de Valence and Madame Acarie. Fénelon discovered in the determined Madame Guyon and her spiritual director, Fr. Lacombe, living examples of total dedication to God at a time when a kind of pedantic intellectualism was prevalent in the Church and at the royal court of Versailles.

When Madame Guyon was accused of the same errors as Molinos, and when Bossuet warned his friend Fénelon against her teaching, she asked that her writings be formally examined and judged. Putting her head into the lion's mouth, she sent all her writings to Bossuet. At the same time Fénelon further angered Bossuet by supporting her with extracts from the works of orthodox mystics. Despite

[79] Elfrieda Dubois, "Fénelon and Quietism", in Cheslyn Jones, Geoffrey Wainwright, and Edward Yarnold, S.J., *The Study of Spirituality* (New York: Oxford University Press, 1986), 411.

Fénelon's vote of confidence, there was good reason to suppose the verdict would go against Madame Guyon: Louis XIV was already opposed to her because of his wife,[80] and Bossuet was very much the king's man. Nevertheless, because of Fénelon's arguments, a compromise was reached, but it proved to be unsatisfactory to all. After Fénelon continued his defense Bossuet became enraged, and the Bishop of Meaux used his very considerable literary talents to attack his old friend savagely.

In the meantime Fénelon was named Archbishop of Cambrai. He published his citations of the mystical writers in defense of Madame Guyon as the *Maxims of the Saints on the Interior Life*. Urged by his wife and Bossuet, the king petitioned the Holy See to pass judgment on this entire work. After two years of study Innocent XII was coerced by royal pressure to condemn twenty-three of the work's propositions. Despite this he wrote a letter of personal sympathy and appreciation to Fénelon. The Archbishop of Cambrai emerged from this fray with his reputation intact, and he was close to being made a cardinal by Innocent's successor, Clement XI, when he died in January 1715.[81]

Like Madame Guyon, Fénelon retained a dignified silence, indicating his profound holy indifference and acceptance of God's will. Except for his extensive correspondence, he remained silent and isolated in exile at Cambrai during the last years of his life. As Thomas Merton has pointed out, Fénelon's correspondence shows that he was free of the errors of Molinos or Madame Guyon.[82]

Many have defended Fénelon's deep sense of the acceptance of God's will as the antidote to self-love and self-centered ambition.[83] Quietists were accused of deemphasizing the Incarnation and the sacraments. This charge appears to be valid in the case of Molinos and in a negative reading of Madame Guyon. Such a charge, however, can be unjustly leveled against a number of canonized mystics if their writings are taken out of context.

The following quotation, taken from an Advent letter of Fénelon to the Comtesse de Gramont, to whom he was spiritual director, clearly reveals his profound devotion to Christ.

---

[80] Madame de Maintenon (1635–1719), whom the king had secretly married in 1684, some six months after the death of his queen, Maria Theresa. A very religious woman, Mme. de Maintenon contributed much to the king's spiritual improvement and succeeded in raising the moral tone at court. She had long been opposed to Mme. Guyon and her views (as well as to Jansenism). At first friendly to Fénelon, Mme. de Maintenon had used her considerable influence at court to have him appointed tutor to the Duke of Burgundy, Louis' grandson and heir, but during the Quietist controversy she sided with Bossuet against him. Her influence may well have contributed to Fénelon's banishment from royal circles.

[81] Dubois, "Fénelon and Quietism", 411.

[82] Thomas Merton, "Reflections on the Character and Genius of Fénelon", in *Fénelon: Letters of Love and Counsel*, trans. and ed. John McEwen (New York: Harcourt, Brace and World, 1964), 11–30.

[83] Ibid., 29.

> The season of Advent should inspire us with a longing to surrender ourselves to God, to make ready in our hearts for the fulness of His grace and to prepare to be reborn with Jesus Christ: in other words to profit from His birth by achieving that union with Him that only a real love of God can bring about. We must realize that the words used by John the Baptist in calling the Jews to repentance—"Prepare ye the way of the Lord, make straight His paths"—are addressed likewise to each one of us in order that our hearts may be in a fit state to receive and spread abroad His blessing. This preparation consists of an ardent longing to possess Him. That is why Holy Church reminds us at this season of the desire of the Patriarchs to see the coming of the Messiah who for that very reason is referred to in Holy Writ as the Desired, or Desire, of all peoples. We encourage such desires when we pour out our hearts to God in prayer and implore Him to come and take possession of them. Jesus Christ has Himself taught us this kind of prayer when He told us to ask the Father that His Kingdom come, that is, that He should reign peacefully within us while we lovingly obey His laws and His Gospel.[84]

The experience of Fénelon, the abuse of royal power to attack him, his willingness to stand up to Louis XIV on the subject of unjust wars, and his humble acceptance of mistreatment and exile all show him to be a man of his convictions. The observation of Innocent XII, who signed the condemnatory decree against him, clinches the argument between Bossuet and Fénelon: "Cambrai [Fénelon] loved God too much; Meaux [Bossuet] loved man too little."[85]

Without minimizing the salvation wrought by Christ or the gratuity of grace, Fénelon sums up the mystic's way of being open as much as possible to God's grace and providence: "The surest and quickest way is to renounce oneself, forget oneself, abandon oneself, and to take no further thought of oneself except when this is required out of fidelity to God. The whole of religion consists simply in leaving oneself and one's self-love in order to tend to God."[86]

Later Luminaries of the Spiritual Age

Louis Marie Grignion de Montfort (1673–1716)

Along with Francis de Sales, Bérulle, and Fénelon, the spiritual age in Catholic France gave rise to many lesser-known people of great devotion to Christ. Some of these prepared the way for the Church to survive the coming storm of the French Revolution; others planted seeds that would produce a harvest of religious communities after the Revolution.

One of the most representative disciples of Christ at the end of this age was a startling evangelical figure, who unfortunately is often

---

[84] Quoted in ibid., 201–2.

[85] *Erravit Cameracensis excessu amoris Dei; peccavit Maldensis defectu amoris proximi*, quoted in Dubois, 415.

[86] Merton, "Character and Genius of Fénelon", 22–23.

misunderstood as a run-of-the-mill devotional cleric: Louis de Montfort, the "vagabond priest", is part St. Francis, part St. Vincent de Paul, part St. John the Baptist. Known for his devotion to the Virgin Mary, Louis has many unrecognized similarities with his Protestant contemporaries, the evangelical preachers of England and Wales, and especially with John Wesley, whom we will soon meet.

Unlike so many priests of previous ages, Louis Grignion (Montfort was the name of his village) was well educated by the Jesuits at Rennes and by the Sulpician followers of Fr. Olier in Paris.[87] He had the equivalent of sixteen years of education beyond elementary school, and he read the Church Fathers and medieval authors such as Bernard of Clairvaux and Thomas Aquinas. He was also steeped in the writings of his fellow Breton, Blessed Alain de la Roche, the little-known fifteenth-century Dominican promoter of the Rosary, and had been formed by the works of his near contemporaries—Francis de Sales, John Eudes, and Vincent de Paul. He was very loyal to the Church but "stayed carefully out of the system". In 1706, he was appointed apostolic missionary to France by Pope Clement XI, who had never heard of this poor young priest until he came to Rome for the papal blessing. It is typical of Louis de Montfort that at the age of nineteen, when, bearing gifts from friends and supporters, he left his home in Brittany to study in Paris, he gave away to the first beggars he met all his money and baggage and even exchanged his clothes with one of them.[88] He begged his way to Paris, arriving in rags. In the brief sixteen years he spent as an itinerant priest and servant of the poor, he laid the foundations for three religious communities: the Montfort Missionaries, the Daughters of Wisdom, and the Brothers of St. Gabriel.

The Jansenists were not amused by Louis' enthusiastic and joyful piety or by his encouraging people to receive the Eucharist daily. The clergy and laity of importance during the reign of Louis XIV saw him as a strange misfit.[89] His love for the Bible, his complete dependence on Divine Providence, and his enthusiastic devotion made him suspect by civil and religious authorities.

Two things have kept Louis de Montfort from receiving the recognition he deserves. (It is worth noting that his writings are not included in the standard works or anthologies that we have used for this study.) The first reason is that his theological, Christocentric spirituality is linked very strongly with devotion to the Virgin Mary. Misinterpretations of his writings have arisen despite his warning: "If devotion to Our Lady distracted us from Our Lord, we would have to reject it as an illusion of the devil."[90] Some have seen his emphasis on going to

---

[87] *God Alone: The Collected Writings of St. Louis Marie de Montfort* (Bay Shore, N.Y.: Montfort Publications, 1997). See introduction by J. Patrick Gaffney, S.S.M., vii–xvii.

[88] Ibid., x.

[89] Ibid., xii.

[90] *True Devotion to the Blessed Virgin*, chap. 2, no. 62, in *God Alone*, 308.

Jesus through Mary as theologically unbalanced, yet he explicitly teaches that the sole purpose of devotion to Mary is to provide "a smooth but certain way of reaching Jesus Christ". This true devotion, including complete trust, is "a way of reaching Jesus perfectly, loving him tenderly, and serving him faithfully".[91]

The second thing that has kept Montfort from taking his rightful place in the history of spirituality is that his teachings are clearly derived from writers who immediately preceded him. The influence of Francis de Sales, Bérulle, and Olier is manifest. Montfort emphasized that baptism is the foundation of the Christian life. Following Bérulle, he saw all dedication and consecration as an articulation of the baptismal promises, even the vows taken by religious.

There is nothing wrong with teachings that are derived from solid roots. Some mystics are very original, like St. Catherine of Siena and St. Catherine of Genoa. Some build on the insights of others. We will see this when we study Wesley and his debt to the evangelists who directly preceded him. Christ's disciples should be unconcerned as to whether they are bringing out an original point of view or simply bringing another's understanding of the Gospel to a faithful conclusion. They all see themselves as disciples, whether they are original or not, because there is only one master, Christ (see Mt 23:10).

Montfort's writings reveal a man of deep faith and love, of prayerful ideas gathered while walking the roads to preach the Gospel. He is a poet of the poor and humble. This selection from a poem on Holy Communion is representative of his deep, pure devotion.

> My Jesus, I long ardently
> For you to come to me this day;
> Without you life is misery.
> Come to me soon, I pray.
>
> Good Shepherd, bear your lost sheep home
> Within your arms, whene'er I stray;
> From ravening wolves that round me roam
> Oh, keep me safe, I pray.
>
> O bread of Life, for you I sigh,
> Give me yourself without delay;
> For otherwise my soul must die.
> Give me to eat, I pray.
>
> O fount of living waters clear,
> How long and weary is the way;
> Refresh my soul which thirsts for you.
> Give me to drink, I pray.[92]

---

[91] Ibid.

[92] *"Mille fois mon coeur vous désire"*, in *God Alone*, 539–40.

The First Modern Visionary: St. Margaret Mary Alocoque

Much of the spiritual life of devout Catholics has been shaped by mystical visionaries, especially since the seventeenth century. Visionaries—those who claim to have experienced the sights and sounds of eternity—have been part of the Judeo-Christian tradition since Moses and the prophets. These experiences, including those of universally admired saints like Francis of Assisi and Catherine of Siena, are difficult to assess. Encounters with the divine presence are often expressed in language and concepts that do not acknowledge the distinction between the natural and the supernatural worlds. Visionaries are often so difficult to evaluate that we simply leave their accounts dangling somewhere between reality and myth. If we try to judge them at all, we turn to more tangible indicators, like their deeds or their effect on history.

By the time of the great Carmelite mystics, especially St. John of the Cross, a more reflective, analytical, and critical approach toward mystical visions was entering Western European thought. The great Carmelite himself could be very critical of reported apparitions and even remained pointedly objective about the spiritual experiences of his mentor, St. Teresa of Avila. He may in fact suggest that some of her reports constitute intellectual visions,[93] very powerful religious experiences rather than apparitions, which are intrusions into this world from the world beyond by Christ, the Blessed Virgin Mary, or the saints.[94] Far from the naïveté of medieval times, St. John of the Cross advises those dealing with apparitions to begin with the assumption that they are diabolical in origin or the production of an overwrought imagination.[95]

While those studying mystical apparitions and experiences became more critical, those who actually received these graces were also becoming more perceptive concerning their own psychological states. Accounts

[93] See, for example, *The Living Flame of Love*, stanza 2 (9), in which he speaks in a general way of the transpiercing of the heart. He may have had in mind St. Teresa's own experience.

[94] See A. Poulain, S.J., *The Graces of Interior Prayer*, trans. Leonora L. Yorke-Smith (London: Routledge and Kegan Paul, 1957), especially chaps. 22–23; *Revelations and Mystics*, trans. L. Yorke-Smith (New York: Alba House, 1998), which consists of excerpts from *The Graces of Interior Prayer*. Anyone particularly interested in this area would do well to review Fr. Poulain's exhaustive study. See also Fr. Benedict J. Groeschel, C.F.R., *A Still, Small Voice* (San Francisco: Ignatius Press, 1993), 156ff.

[95] See *The Ascent of Mount Carmel*, bks. 2 and 3, for St. John's thorough treatment of private revelations, locutions, etc. He expresses strong disapproval of those who would seek such favors from God and discusses the harm that can thereby be done to souls. For those, however, whom God chooses to guide by what we would term today extraordinary religious experiences, the Mystical Doctor nevertheless insists that anything "received by the soul through supernatural means" ought to be "clearly and plainly, fully and simply" related immediately to a spiritual director and that this be done "for the sake of the humility, submission, and mortification of the soul". The director, in turn, should be open to receiving such confidences and should display no displeasure or antipathy at hearing them. The director is also cautioned to urge the penitent to live by faith, reminding him that just one work of charity is worth more in God's sight than "all the visions and communications" received from heaven.

from the small number of visionaries approved by the Church became better articulated and tended to include descriptions of the individual's feelings and personal responses. Visions became more like dialogues than the vast panoramas of the Apocalypse or the ecstatic encounters of St. Francis. The actual experience may not have changed, but their description became more discerning and more psychological.

One of the first of the newer, more personal, reports, and the one that has affected popular Catholic piety more than any other, involves the apparitions of St. Margaret Mary Alacoque (1647–1690). She was part of the new middle class emerging in Europe. As a result of her father's premature death, she grew up in an extraordinarily difficult home dominated by cruel relatives who abused her mother and her young siblings. This part of her life reads like a gothic novel. In 1671, at the age of twenty-four, she entered the relatively new Visitation Order, founded by SS. Francis de Sales and Jane Frances de Chantal. She was able to do this only because her oldest brother, having reached his majority, had taken control of things at home, restoring economic stability and freeing his family of the tyranny of servitude.

The drama of Margaret Mary's life is lost on most Catholics, who are familiar only with pictures of the saint kneeling in the mystical light of the apparition of Christ with His Heart exposed and surrounded by rays of glory. In the familiar picture of these events in the Visitation monastery and especially in the incredibly mystical contemporary painting in the dome of that very chapel, Margaret is pictured as someone who lived in another world, surrounded by a light never known on earth.

The fact is that she struggled with a gentle sort of worldliness. French provincial social life came to have a certain appeal for her once she was no longer under the domination of relatives.[96] But Margaret was a woman of deep prayer, who opened her house to the poor so that she could educate their minds and feed their bodies.[97] In a memoir, she describes her own rich inner life, especially centered on the reception of the Eucharist, even before she entered the convent. "On the eve of my Communions, I felt my soul so abyssed in recollection that I could speak but with the greatest effort; I was wholly taken up with the sublimity of the action I was about to perform. After my Communions, I desired neither to eat nor drink, to see anyone, nor to speak, so great were the peace and consolation I felt."[98]

It is not surprising that in the atmosphere of the very observant convent of the Visitation, she blossomed. Her superior, Mother Hieronyme Hersant, had known the foundress, St. Jane de Chantal, and for twenty years had St. Vincent de Paul as her spiritual director. Mother

[96] Emile Bougaud, *The Life of Saint Margaret Mary Alacoque*, trans. by a Visitandine of Maryland (Rockford, Ill.: Tan Books, 1990), 54ff.

[97] Ibid., 60–61.

[98] Quoted in ibid., 66.

Hersant was followed by other superiors who were quite demanding of the young religious, perhaps because many of them belonged to wealthy and privileged families.[99] The initial advice Margaret Mary received from the mistress of novices was: "Place yourself before God like canvas before a painter."[100] This became the guiding principle of this deeply spiritual soul. She was to learn quickly to rely on such advice because of a great disappointment. She was not permitted to take her vows at the customary time. Many in the community, recognizing Margaret Mary's intense prayer life, had a high opinion of her, but, as one sister said, "She was so extraordinary that perhaps she was not intended to live out her life at the Visitation."[101] Her fervor was well known, "though all did not approve her extraordinary ways". As another sister put it, Margaret Mary "was astonishingly fervent during her novitiate. But her extraordinary ways made us fear."[102] For all the wariness of the superior and community, however, Margaret Mary's profession was delayed only about four months. Perhaps because of her extraordinary piety and the concern of the sisters she was given the humble task of caring for the convent's domestic animals.

Margaret Mary's new superior, Mother de Saumaise, realized she had an unusual person in her care. There are many testimonies from the sisters given under oath during the process of Margaret's beatification. The following testimonies present a startling picture of this remarkable young woman. Sr. Marguerite d'Athose reported: "I attest to having seen the venerable deceased pass almost the entire day, particularly Sundays and feasts, before the Blessed Sacrament, on her knees, immovable, in recollection so profound that the whole community was surprised that she could remain so long in the same position, though her constitution was not the strongest." Sr. Elizabeth de la Garde, who later became superior, stated: "I certify that the venerable Sister was always most faithful to pass all her free time before the Blessed Sacrament, her hands joined in profound adoration. No movement on her part ever betrayed a wandering of mind. . . . On Holy Thursday, for several consecutive years, she passed from seven in the evening until the next morning kneeling in the same place, neither coughing nor moving."[103]

With personal intuition of apparently mystical nature, Margaret Mary realized that she would be under the spiritual direction of a fervent

---

[99] Bougaud, *Margaret Mary Alacoque*, 78.

[100] Ibid., 92.

[101] It must be remembered that one of the goals of the Visitation was to make religious life accessible to ordinary people, with a rather simplified structure for those who could not endure the long fasts and austere penances of monastic orders. The Visitation stressed ordinariness and a simple approach to God; singularity and extraordinary states were frowned on. In that atmosphere it is hardly surprising that the community scarcely knew what to make of Margaret Mary.

[102] Bougaud, *Margaret Mary Alacoque*, 103.

[103] Ibid., 120–21.

young Jesuit, Claude de la Colombière (1641–1682), an outstanding preacher who came to her monastery at Paray in October 1674. The destinies of this young nun (twenty-six at the time of the first revelation in December 1673) with extraordinary mystical ways and the brilliant and deeply devoted priest were to be forever entwined. Colombière's writings reveal a man of extraordinary virtue who had made a vow to observe perfectly all the requirements of his Jesuit life. He soon perceived in Margaret Mary "an extraordinary soul". Having been ordered by Mother de Saumaise to be completely open to this spiritual director, Margaret Mary disclosed to him the astonishing revelations of Christ's love for human beings. These revelations are the foundation of the modern Catholic devotion to the Sacred Heart of Jesus.

Before we read from these remarkable statements, it is important to recall that in a mystical experience of this type we are not dealing with the conversation of two people as it ordinarily takes place in the world around us. It is obvious from the description of St. Margaret Mary's ecstasies and profound prayer that she was in touch with another world and that she was withdrawn from this one. When it is assumed that God interacts with and manifests things to someone in this world, we must be aware that this is not ordinary direct speech. The individual's subjective elements can move in very easily. It is difficult for mystics experiencing visions to differentiate their own thoughts and observations from the content of the revelation that they experience as the voice of another person. This is not to assume that their presentations are inaccurate, only that they are very different from normal human speech.

St. Margaret Mary's experiences of the figure of the Sacred Heart of Jesus took place on three occasions over a period of two and a half years. The saint described the first revelation in testimony given with great reluctance. In fact, she prayed to be able to overcome her repugnance at recording what had happened. She is reported to have been dumbfounded and confused while writing an account of her visions.

The first revelation took place December 27, 1673. Saint Margaret Mary writes:

> Once, being before the Blessed Sacrament and having a little more leisure than usual, I felt wholly filled with this Divine Presence, and so powerfully moved by it that I forgot myself and the place in which I was. I abandoned myself to this Divine Spirit, and yielded my heart to the power of His love. He made me rest for a long time on His divine breast, where He discovered to me the wonders of His love and the inexplicable secrets of His Sacred Heart, which He had hitherto kept hidden from me. Now He opened it to me for the first time, but in a way so real, so sensible, that it left me no room to doubt, though I am always in dread of deceiving myself. . . .

> The Lord said to me, "My Divine Heart is so passionately in love with men that it can no longer contain within itself the flames of its ardent charity. It must pour them out by thy means, and manifest itself to them to enrich them with its precious treasures, which contain all the graces of which they have need to be saved from perdition." He added: "I have chosen thee as an abyss of unworthiness and ignorance to accomplish so great a design, so that all may be done by Me." [104]

The second revelation occurred sometime during the year 1674. No precise date is given.[105] This revelation is particularly interesting in that bright light and flame are constantly alluded to. Also, Christ's complaint here makes clear that there is little or no return made by men to His divine love. This revelation also introduces into the devotion to the Sacred Heart the idea that Christ still suffers, which presents some theological difficulties.

With the second revelation comes the element of reparation, which we can make by virtuous acts and the patient endurance of suffering. The idea of vicarious suffering with Christ is as old as St. Paul. The following is taken from St. Margaret Mary's account.

> Once when the Blessed Sacrament was exposed, my soul being absorbed in extraordinary recollection, Jesus Christ, my sweet Master, presented Himself to me. He was brilliant with glory; His five wounds shone like five suns. Flames darted forth from all parts of His sacred humanity, but especially from His adorable breast, which resembled a furnace, and which, opening, displayed to me His loving and amiable Heart, the living source of these flames. . . .
>
> He unfolded to me the inexplicable wonders of His pure love and to what an excess He had carried it for the love of men, from whom He had received only ingratitude. "This is much more painful to me than all I suffered in my Passion. If men rendered me some return of love, I should esteem little all I have done for them, and should wish, if such could be, to suffer it over again, but they meet my eager love with coldness and rebuffs. Do you, at least, console and rejoice me by supplying as much as you can for their ingratitude." [106]

Our Lord went on to make two requests: that Margaret Mary receive Holy Communion on the first Friday of each month as an act of reparation for man's rejection of divine love, and that she keep watch each Thursday night from eleven o'clock until midnight as an act of

[104] Quoted in ibid., 163–64.

[105] Although the exact date is unknown, it may have been around the feast of Corpus Christi, since the saint specifies that the Blessed Sacrament was exposed. It was certainly before the arrival of Fr. de la Colombière in the autumn.

[106] Bougaud, *Margaret Mary Alacoque*, 168–169.

reparation for sin and to console Him for all who have abandoned His loving Heart.

As Christ revealed Himself to St. Margaret Mary, it is clear that He can be said to suffer from the ingratitude of men. However, Christ is in eternal glory and presumably beyond suffering. These theological difficulties have not gone unrecognized, and theologians and even popes have attempted to clarify some of them.

In defense of Margaret Mary, it must be recalled that the visionary has no control over the vision. One cannot argue with a revelation as one can argue with oneself in an internal self-critical monologue.

As might be expected, such an overwhelming interior event was observable in its effects on the saint's behavior. She describes the reactions of others.

> "During all this time," says Margaret Mary, "I was unconscious, I knew not where I was. Some of the Sisters came to take me away, and, seeing that I could neither reply nor support myself on my feet, they led me to our Mother, who found me quite out of myself, trembling and as if on fire." When Margaret Mary told her what had just taken place, whether she believed or not, or whether she feigned not to believe it, Mother de Saumaise humbled her as deeply as she could— "which gave me extreme pleasure, caused me inconceivable joy," says Margaret Mary; "for I felt myself such a criminal, I was filled with such confusion that however rigorous might be the treatment bestowed upon me, it would still have seemed to me too lenient." [107]

Apparently, about the same time, Margaret Mary was attended by a physician, Dr. Billiet, who tried to moderate some sixty fevers that afflicted her. In an interesting turn of events, Mother de Saumaise ordered Margaret Mary under obedience to request a cure from God. Immediately the fever left her, and she rose from the bed, much to the physician's amazement. Somehow, despite all the superior's concern about the possibility of Margaret Mary's being deluded or deceived, she was given permission to receive Holy Communion on the first Friday and to spend the prior evening in a prayerful vigil.

It was about this time as she was receiving severe criticism from her community for her extraordinary behavior that Fr. de la Colombière came to the rescue. He cautiously, but unquestionably, came to believe in the validity of her experiences. While she was under the Jesuit's spiritual direction, the third and greatest of the revelations occurred on June 16, 1675.

> "Behold," said He to her, "this Heart which has so loved men that it has spared nothing, even to exhausting and consuming itself, in order to testify its love. In return, I receive from the greater part

[107] Ibid., 170.

> only ingratitude, by their irreverence and sacrilege, and by the coldness and contempt they have for Me in this sacrament of love. And what is most painful to Me," added the Savior, in a tone that went to the Sister's heart, "is that they are hearts consecrated to Me." Then He commanded her to have established in the Church a particular feast to honor His Sacred Heart. "It is for this reason I ask thee that the first Friday after the octave of the Blessed Sacrament[108] be appropriated to a special feast, to honor My Heart by communicating on that day, and making reparation for the indignity that it has received. And I promise that My Heart shall dilate to pour out abundantly the influences of its love on all that will render it this honor or procure its being rendered."[109]

One may be surprised that a supernatural vision would give directions so precise and related to a particular time. That God would be concerned with dates seems odd. However, the Jewish Scriptures offer many examples of precise divine instruction, especially in the Book of Leviticus. We have already seen how in the Middle Ages the feast of Corpus Christi had been established in honor of the Blessed Sacrament because of the visions of Blessed Juliana of Mont-Cornillon (see Chapter 9 above). By this time Corpus Christi had become a significant public event. During the octave following the feast, public demonstrations in honor of Christ were held everywhere. Apparently, the secular celebrations that surrounded these religious services became something of a carnival in various places and may have become almost sacrilegious. Placing the feast of the Sacred Heart immediately after the eight days of celebration in honor of the Eucharist as an act of reparation would, thus, have made sense to a person of the times.

It is beyond our scope to discuss the theological difficulties related to the problem of an apparently suffering Christ in eternal glory. Perhaps the key to understanding this is to remember that the realities of eternal life exist outside of time. We can say accurately that it is a mystery how Christ in eternal glory can be said to suffer. That He suffers in His Mystical Body most Christians would easily admit. That He suffers personally, that He is offended, even insulted by His creatures and that He grieves over these insults, is far more difficult to understand. It might be well to recall that the staunch Puritan divine Thomas Goodwin, whom we met in Chapter 13, saw the holy Heart of the Savior in eternal life responding with feelings of compassion to the needs of men.

Devotion to the Sacred Heart made it possible for large numbers of people to offer up their personal sufferings, and even excruciating pains to God as partial reparation for the sins of the world. Devotion to the

[108] That is, the feast of Corpus Christi.
[109] Bougaud, *Margaret Mary Alacoque*, 176.

Sacred Heart of Jesus gave a very healthy purpose to many suffering people. Older Catholics will certainly remember being told to "offer it up." This idea of vicarious suffering in union with Christ was not a new one, but it did take tremendous hold in the Catholic Church, particularly during the nineteenth century and later during the world wars. Even those who do not put much credence in the experiences of this devout nun must admit that the notion of suffering in union with Christ gave consolation and purpose to large numbers of the faithful for a long time. It is well known in England that Queen Mary sent a beautifully embroidered Sacred Heart badge to every Catholic serviceman in the British armed services during the First World War.

St. Paul in his Second Epistle to the Corinthians writes: "For as we share abundantly in Christ's sufferings so through Christ we shall share abundantly in comfort too" (2 Cor 1:5). In Philippians 3:10, he prays "that I may know him and the power of his resurrection and may share his sufferings, becoming like him in his death". An even more powerful text is this: "Now I rejoice in my sufferings for your sake, and in my flesh I complete what is lacking in Christ's afflictions for the sake of his body, that is, the Church" (Col 1:24).

The theological complexity and intense mystical fervor of Margaret Mary's experiences were a problem. She could not deny—nor did she wish to deny—that these things had happened, but she was highly aware that she was a very small vessel into which very large things had been poured.

She gave her superior, Mother de Saumaise, an account of her visions and revelations, and these, in turn, were entrusted to Fr. de la Colombière.

> That which finally convinced her of the truth of God's gifts to this soul [St. Margaret Mary] was the opinion of Father de la Colombière, S.J., whose virtue, as everyone knows, equalled his learning and who has since died in the odour of sanctity. This great religious examined the question thoroughly, and was so penetrated with esteem and veneration for her, that from that time he always looked upon her as a Saint, and wished for a special place in her prayers.[110]

This quiet cloistered nun was faced with the challenge of how to make known the vision she had received and the request that Christ had made to her to spread the devotion to His Sacred Heart. Here is where Colombière was so important. Margaret Mary writes: "I felt myself tormented and urged to make known this Divine Heart, without being able to find the means to do this, until Father de la Colombière was sent to me, and I could resist no longer. I was obliged in spite of myself to tell him all I had concealed with so much care,

[110] Quoted in Sister Mary Philip, *A Jesuit at the English Court* (London: Burns, Oates and Washbourne, 1922), 73.

because he had been chosen to carry out this great design of God, but I confess I was unable to express all that was revealed to me, for it was an abyss of God's mercy."[111]

Fr. de la Colombière was not simply a messenger of St. Margaret Mary but a deeply spiritual man. A study of his writings reveals his utter submissiveness to the divine will and his complete confidence in God, characteristics common to many of the mystics we have read of. We get a glimpse of Colombière's own ideas on the spiritual life in the following brief passage from his fifth meditation of the Passion.

> Would you see what occasions we have of imitating Jesus Christ, Who submitted Himself without reserve to the will of His Father? We shall find them in the changes of the season, in public calamities, in illness, in the worries of business, in all that concerns our relations, our children, our friends.... We shall find them in the faults of others, of children, of servants. What a vast field we have before us for the exercise of virtue! And if we look at ourselves the horizon is wider still: what occasions occur for self-abnegation in our own weakness and imprudence! We fall, we are wounded, we speak when we should have kept silence, or we say that which we should never have said: on the one hand, what weakness! but on the other, what a source of spiritual riches! If only we profited by the occasions, we should become holy in a very short time.[112]

In a letter he writes: "A soul who loves God desires only to suffer for Him, and loves all those who give her an occasion of suffering for her Beloved."[113] Fr. de la Colombière worked to popularize devotion to the Sacred Heart but had to be extremely discreet so as not to reveal the identity of the visionary. However, he did make it known that extraordinary mystical graces had been given in the name of the Sacred Heart of Jesus. St. Margaret Mary was not to enjoy his spiritual direction for very long. In 1676, the year after her third great vision, St. Claude de la Colombière was assigned to be chaplain to the Duchess of York, wife of the future James II, at the Chapel Royal of St. James' Palace, London, where he remained for two years. At that time the Catholic Church was still being persecuted in England, and Claude saw priests being led out of prison to be hanged, drawn, and quartered.

In the summer of 1678, Titus Oates, a man with a very checkered career, gave false evidence in court against a number of Catholics and revealed what he called a plot for the Catholics to take over England. As a result, many people were arrested, including Fr. de la Colombière. Because of his position and connection with the royal family and owing to the protection of the French king, he was released after

[111] Quoted in ibid.

[112] Quoted in ibid., 97–98.

[113] Letter 101, quoted in ibid., 100.

three weeks. He was given ten days in which to finish up his affairs; then, under guard, he made for the seacoast and returned to France in January 1679.

Colombière had been ill, apparently with tuberculosis, even from the days he knew St. Margaret Mary. His stay in a miserable English dungeon only made his condition worse. He was sent initially to Lyon and later to Paray, where he renewed his acquaintance with Margaret Mary at the Visitation. His health continued to deteriorate, and on the evening of February 15, 1682, having seen St. Margaret Mary only a few times since his return from England, Claude de la Colombière died at the Jesuit house in Paray. He was buried there, where his body can be venerated today at a beautiful shrine just a short walk from the Visitation chapel, the scene of God's singular favors that this apostle of the Sacred Heart helped so successfully to propagate. He was canonized in 1992.

After the death of her spiritual director and powerful supporter one might have expected that Margaret Mary's life would have become even more difficult. She was certainly still a cause of concern and apparently, at times, of consternation in the convent, simply because of her remarkable periods of recollection and prayer. As of yet only her superior and one or two others bound by confidence knew of the visions she had received. With the exception of Fr. de la Colombière himself, all seemed to have refrained from any judgment on their authenticity.

Despite this and with a good deal of unexpected support, Margaret Mary was appointed novice mistress of seven rather engaging women whose personalities are well sketched by her biographer, Bishop Bougaud.[114] A new superior, Mother Melin, entrusted the novices to the mysterious mystical sister but apparently kept a very careful eye on things.

The revelations continued, which the saint reported in her confidential writings. It is impossible now to discern whether these were new private revelations of the type we reported already or whether they were intellectual or imaginative visions. Often in the case of revelations accepted by the Church, one hears of numerous reported visions and experiences following upon the original powerful episode.[115] Fr. Poulain, the great authority in this area, states that the fact that the reports are numerous does not cause a doubt a priori about the authenticity of the experience. However, the possibility of mixing up one's own ideas and experiences becomes obvious, so that there is a very real danger of imminent deception, particularly if one publishes these experiences.

---

[114] Bougaud, *Margaret Mary Alacoque*, 221ff.

[115] See Poulain, *Graces of Interior Prayer*, 364, also pp. 299–396. Those interested will find this section very helpful.

Margaret Mary reported that she had such experiences every first Friday. "Every first Friday of the month the Sacred Heart of Jesus was represented to me as a brilliant light, whose rays fell on my heart and inflamed it with a fire so ardent that it seemed as if about to be reduced to ashes."[116]

A remarkable event occurred at this time that completely changed Margaret Mary's position in her convent. About two years after the death of Fr. de la Colombière the Jesuits in Lyon published some of his notes under the title *Spiritual Retreat*. One of the first copies was sent to the Visitation nuns. Without first reading the book herself, Mother Melin had it read aloud in the refectory. One day the reader, who happened to be one of Margaret Mary's novices, read the following lines while the saint was seated among the sisters at the table.

> I have recognized that God wishes me to serve Him by furthering the accomplishment of His desires concerning a devotion He has suggested to a person to whom He has communicated Himself very intimately, and to serve whom He has graciously pleased to make use of my weakness. . . . God, then, having revealed Himself to a person who, from the great graces that He has given her, we have reason to believe, according to His Heart, she explained them to me, and I obliged her to put in writing all that she told me.[117]

After some introduction Colombière then directly quotes St. Margaret Mary.

> "Being before the Blessed Sacrament during one of its octaves," said that holy soul, "I received from my God some most sublime graces of His love. I was filled with the desire of making Him some return, and of rendering Him love for love; but He said to me: 'Thou canst never do anything greater for Me than what I have already so many times asked thee.' And exposing to me His Divine Heart, 'See this Heart,' said He, 'which has loved men so much that it has spared nothing, even to exhausting and consuming itself, in order to testify to them its love. . . . It is for this reason that I ask thee that the first Friday after the octave of Corpus Christi be set apart as a special feast to honor my Heart, by making an act of reparation, and by communicating on that day to repair the indignities it sustained during the time of exposition on the altars.' "[118]

The novice reading this passage recalled years later that when she looked up at Margaret Mary, the saint "was sitting with her eyes lowered and looking profoundly annihilated". Later the reader approached Margaret Mary and asked, "My dear Sister, haven't you heard your

[116] Quoted in Bougaud, *Margaret Mary Alacoque*, 230.
[117] Ibid., 236.
[118] Ibid., 236–37.

manifestation in the reading today to your heart's content?" The saint lowered her head and "replied that she had great cause to love her abjection".[119]

The enthusiasm of the novices, who loved their mistress, took over, while the saint herself was deeply humiliated. Under a stairway they prepared an oratory with an altar and decorated the walls, ceiling, and rafters with flowers, stars, and fiery hearts. In the center of the altar they placed a picture of the Sacred Heart. Surprised and delighted when she saw this gift, Margaret Mary gave up some of her reticence and spoke to them in the most glowing ways about the devotion to the Sacred Heart.

The question remained: Would anyone celebrate devotion to the Sacred Heart of Jesus, which did not have official recognition? There was no question that during Margaret Mary's revelations our Lord had requested that a feast in His honor be established, but as yet there was no Church sanction for it. It was in every way still a private devotion. The community demurred from any kind of celebration, but the novices had permission to celebrate their own private feast.

From 1686 until St. Margaret Mary's death four years later, devotion to the Sacred Heart spread quietly in France, particularly among the religious of the Visitation and their friends. Rumors began to spread about Margaret Mary's sanctity, and visitors to Paray tried to catch a glimpse of her through the grille of the convent chapel. Many referred to her as a saint for her demeanor, humility, prayerfulness, and profound recollection.

As the year 1690 progressed, Margaret Mary frequently spoke about her death. Although she was not in very good physical health, her doctors assured her and her superiors that there was no danger. Even on the day before her death, when she requested Viaticum and the anointing of the sick, which were then given only to those very close to death, they were refused, the doctor insisting that she was not in danger. She had already told two of the sisters (her former novices) that they would be with her at the moment of her death, and it happened as she predicted. The community were astonished when they were called to her bedside to bid her farewell. By the age of forty-three this remarkable woman had made a change in the devotional life of Catholics, which would affect their perception of Jesus Christ for at least three centuries. The image of the loving Christ with His arms extended in an invitation of affection, His gentle face looking at them from statues and pictures, His Heart burning with love, and His assurances of salvation and forgiveness for sinners have profoundly affected the piety and attitudes of Catholics well into the present time.

As a result of another humble nun, St. Faustina Kowalska, a new image of Christ as a lover of mankind has emerged: the Divine Mercy.

[119] Ibid., 237.

We will consider this devotion at the end of this book. However, it is important to note that Sr. Faustina herself identified her mystical vision of Divine Mercy with the Sacred Heart of Jesus. She did not see this as a different devotion or a different revelation.[120]

The Last of a Great Age

The remarkable hundred years of French spirituality came to a very quiet end with an obscure writer whose work came to be known only in the late nineteenth century. Jean-Pierre de Caussade (1675–1751) was a Jesuit spiritual director. The eminent Benedictine historian Dom David Knowles, who studied de Caussade carefully, ranks him among the ten greatest Catholic spiritual guides since St. Bernard.[121]

We cannot fail to see de Caussade's story as an expression of the divine irony that is so often observable in matters spiritual: an age that began with an English Protestant convert, Benet of Canfield, and an illiterate peasant woman, Marie de Valence, should come to an end with a writer whose impressive work was unknown and unpublished for 110 years. In fact, de Caussade died thinking that he had written only one book. It appeared anonymously in 1741—a rather dry instruction on prayer "according to the teaching of Bossuet"—and for a time was attributed to his better-known contemporary, Père Antoine.[122]

De Caussade, ordained in 1704, received his doctorate in theology the next year. He appears to have spent some years preaching missions, and in 1729 he was appointed spiritual director to the Visitation nuns at Nancy. In 1731 he was withdrawn from this post and lived for two years in semi-disgrace in a seminary for "indiscreet words".[123] The nuns welcomed him back enthusiastically when this period of silence was over (1733), and he remained with them for six more years. He was then made superior successively of two Jesuit communities and ended his days as spiritual director to seminarians at the Society's seminary in Toulouse.

The important book for which de Caussade is known today, *Self-Abandonment* (or *Abandonment*) *to Divine Providence*, wasn't written for publication but is a series of conferences given at the Visitation (which the nuns copied down and preserved) and a collection of his letters, most of them written to the same nuns. The writings were put into logical order and published in book form in 1861 by Fr. Ramière, S.J.[124]

---

[120] See Robert A. Stackpole, *Jesus, Mercy Incarnate* (Stockbridge, Mass.: Marians of the Immaculate Conception, 2000), 101–13.

[121] Fr. J. P. de Caussade, S.J., *Self-Abandonment to Divine Providence*, trans. Algar Thorold (Rockford, Ill.: Tan Books and Publishers, 1987), see Fr. Knowles' excellent introduction, p. v. The Doubleday / Image edition of this work (translation by John Beevers) was published in 1975 but, unfortunately, without Père de Caussade's letters.

[122] Fr. John Joyce, S.J., in ibid., xx.

[123] Mark Gibbard, "Jean-Pierre de Caussade", in *The Study of Spirituality*, ed. Cheslyn Jones, Geoffrey Wainwright, and Edward Yarnold, S.J. (London: SPCK, 1986), 416.

[124] Joyce, foreword to de Caussade, *Self-Abandonment*, xx.

It is not surprising that *Abandonment* is not well known among American Jesuits or among those they direct. De Caussade's spirituality is definitely derived from two sources, neither of which is part of the Ignatian tradition: St. John of the Cross and St. Francis de Sales.[125] Although de Caussade cites Bossuet and, surprisingly, Fénelon, who was still under a cloud, and even though he draws on the Fathers and the mystics, he never mentions St. Ignatius. The Jesuit to whom he seems to owe the most is Louis Lallemant. Fr. Knowles sees a strong similarity between Caussade's self-abandonment and the "little way" of St. Thérèse of Lisieux.[126]

I find de Caussade's doctrine of abandonment to be a synthesis of the effective and practical means of the spiritual life offered by the great majority of Christian mystics. Knowles sees similarities between de Caussade and Carmelite and Dominican spirituality and with St. Benedict's "seeking for God".[127]

In my own struggles with spirituality I have found de Caussade's abandonment to mirror St. Francis of Assisi's poverty and devotion to Christ as Savior, as well as St. Bonaventure's devotion. In fact, de Caussade enthusiastically mentions his relationship with a convent of Poor Clares in Albi, who relied on Divine Providence for everything from day to day. He states that he has a great attachment to them because they practice abandonment "in admirable perfection".[128] It is worth noting that this eighteenth-century French Jesuit's writings are widely appreciated by spiritual writers of other faiths.

Fr. Knowles examines the theology behind de Caussade's thought. This is important, since his significant work is not an organized theological presentation. A few salient points will help us appreciate how this teaching on abandonment—almost Oriental-sounding to the uninformed—is centered on Jesus Christ alone. Following St. Francis de Sales, de Caussade sees all people potentially called to perfection. "Let us not distress or refuse anyone, or drive any away from eminent perfection. Jesus calls all to perfection.... If we knew how to leave God's divine hand free to act, we should attain the most eminent perfection. All would attain, for it is offered to all."[129]

The second point of emphasis is the divine indwelling, an idea dear to many mystics: "The presence of God which sanctifies our souls is that indwelling of the Holy Trinity which is established in the depths of our hearts when they submit to the divine will."[130] What is the goal of embracing the divine presence? Following St. Paul and the great medieval mystics, de Caussade says it is "to form Jesus Christ in

[125] Knowles, introduction to de Caussade's *Self-Abandonment*, vi.

[126] Ibid., xv.

[127] Ibid., xiv and v.

[128] De Caussade, *Self-Abandonment*, 118.

[129] Knowles, introduction in ibid., x.

[130] Ibid.

the depth of our hearts". This is a parallel to St. Paul's "It is no longer I who live but Christ who lives in me" (Gal 2:20).

The practical question, then, is what to do to advance in the spiritual life. Here de Caussade preaches Christ as his own interior guide who asks only for our total confidence.

> Imagine we are in a strange district at night and are crossing fields unmarked by any path, but we have a guide. He asks no advice nor tells us of his plans. So what can we do except trust him? It is no use trying to see where we are, look at maps, or question passers-by. That would not be tolerated by a guide who wants us to rely on him. He will get satisfaction from overcoming our fears and doubts, and will insist that we have complete trust in him.
>
> God's activity can never be anything but good, and does not need to be reformed or controlled.... [I]t does one thing today, another tomorrow, yet it is the same activity which every moment produces constantly fresh results, and it will continue throughout eternity. It produced Abel, Noah and Abraham—all different types.... Jesus Christ is the first-born, and the Apostles are moved more by the guidance of his spirit than by imitating his works. Jesus Christ did not restrict himself, for he did not follow all his own precepts literally. His most holy soul was always inspired by the Holy Spirit and always responsive to its slightest breath.... It is this same Jesus Christ, always alive and active, who continues to live and work fresh wonders in the souls of those who love him.
>
> If we wish to live according to the Gospel, we must abandon ourselves simply and completely to the action of God. Jesus Christ is its source.[131]

What is necessary here, of course, is faith—not simply theological faith in the truth of the Gospel but loving faith and confident hope. With these we can put ourselves completely into the hands of God.

> Here, in a few words, is what you ought to do in order to attain promptly to pure love and perfect self-abandonment. You must, first of all, ardently desire and energetically will it whatever the price you may have to pay. Secondly, you must firmly believe and say repeatedly to God, that it is absolutely impossible for you to acquire by your own strength such perfect dispositions, but, also, that grace makes everything easy, that you hope to receive this grace from his mercy, and you must beg it of him in and through Jesus Christ; thirdly, you must gently and quietly humble yourself, whenever you have withdrawn yourself from the holy bondage of his will, without discouragement, but on the contrary protesting to God that you will await

[131] *Abandonment to Divine Providence*, trans. John Beevers (New York: Doubleday / Image, 1975), 83–84.

> with confidence the moment at which it will please him to give you that decisive grace that will make you wholly die to yourself and live in him by a new life wholly hidden with Jesus Christ our Lord.[132]

De Caussade was not an enthusiast of explicit devotions. He saw a lot of devotions as a distraction and thought the same about many ascetical practices popular at the time. Rather, he offered the fiat of Mary at the Annunciation as the perfect example of a soul surrendered to God. Nevertheless he encouraged devotion to the Sacred Heart of Jesus, which was popular at the time. In a letter to a nun at the Visitation he writes:

> Your devotion to the Sacred Heart of Jesus Christ and the practices you have adopted in regard to it are true spiritual treasure which suffices to enrich both you and your dear daughters. The more you draw upon this treasure, the more there remains for you to draw, inexhaustible as it is. . . .[133]

And so this incomparable age of spirituality, filled with devoted souls of every rank and kind, draws to a close. This period of a century and a half was replete with unworldly cardinals and mystical housewives and had its full share of controversies. At the same time there were many unexpected parallels with Protestants, who were otherwise separated from the Catholic world by deep theological divisions and animosity. The last great figure who comes at the end of the age of the French School is a quiet, unassuming man who spent his life teaching a simple secret of holiness to members of his community and to cloistered nuns. His doctrine is not original. It is as old as the Gospel: "I have come down from heaven, not to do my will but the will of him who sent me" (Jn 6:38); "not my will but yours be done" (Lk 22:42); "Father, into your hands I commend my spirit" (Lk 23:46). And yet this humble soul, who was almost unknown in his lifetime, is compared by scholars with Bernard, Teresa, John of the Cross, and Francis de Sales. What is God saying to us? From a humble, humiliated, and holy man we learn the lesson of opening our hearts to the Lord: "Thy will be done". And Christ is more and more born into our souls.

[132] De Caussade, *Self-Abandonment*, 134–35. (See n. 121 above for edition information).
[133] Letter to Mother Marie-Anne-Sophie de Rottembourg (1739), in ibid., 430.

15 Pietism—The Second Protestant Reformation

It is a mistake for Catholics to think that while the golden age of Spanish mysticism was going on in the sixteenth century and France was experiencing its profoundly spiritual seventeenth century, nothing important was happening among Protestants. We have already seen that spreading through seventeenth-century England was a revival in English Puritanism; it was led by William Perkins, William Ames, Richard Baxter, and John Bunyan. Their writings on the Gospel and calls to conversion and total commitment of life are very similar to the meditations of St. Ignatius Loyola and even writings like those of Cardinal de Bérulle. None of these writers would have been pleased to learn of similarities between themselves and those on the other side of the religious battle lines, yet they all sought to be dedicated to the same Christ and they all invoked the same Holy Spirit.

We have also seen that the French spiritual revival was sparked, in part, by two Anglican converts to the Catholic Church: Benet of Canfield and Augustine Baker. Remarkably, one of the most influential figures in the movement to correct the spiritual decline caused by the Thirty Years' War that led to Protestant reform on the Continent was an ex-Jesuit, Jean de Labadie (1610–1674). Born of Huguenot converts to Catholicism,[1] he became in fairly rapid succession a Jesuit priest, an Oratorian, and then a Jansenist. After reading Calvin's *Institutes*, he became a Calvinist but eventually left to join a smaller group of French Reformed Protestants. Becoming a minister, he preached in France, the United Provinces (the Netherlands), and Switzerland. He was even invited by the great Protestant poet John Milton to take over an independent congregation in London, but he declined. Despite his tendency to move about, he was a leader of Reform Protestantism in Europe and in Britain.[2]

Labadie was markedly impatient with what he considered the need for "general reform" in Christianity and "particular evidence of a

[1] Ted A. Campbell, *The Religion of the Heart: A Study of European Religious Life in the Seventeenth and Eighteenth Centuries* (Columbia: University of South Carolina Press, 1991), 75ff.

[2] Ibid., 76.

general corruption among Christians". He especially called pastors to be agents of reform, lamenting the absence of zeal for Christ and the lack of signs of a sanctified life. One thinks of efforts at the same time in France on the part of St. John Eudes, St. Vincent de Paul, Monsieur Olier, and others to reform the clergy and, through them, the Church. Labadie called for a religion based on a divine anointing and an interior calling. He wanted a universal preaching of repentance, the establishment of separate seminaries to train pastors in a given catechesis so that the faith could be preached effectively and that congregations could be called to conversion. What St. Catherine of Genoa had called *oratorios*, or prayer groups, focused on Scripture and personal conversion, were now established for Protestants and called conventicles.[3]

Ever restless, Labadie, dismissed by the Reform congregation, founded his own separatist denomination. Losing interest in religious acts (sacraments), he focused instead on inner experience. It is thus not surprising that he opened discussions with the Quakers, but that ended in a personal struggle with William Penn.[4] Before his death he was attracted to Antoinette Bourignon (1616–1680), an ex–Carmelite nun in Amsterdam and who, as Campbell says, is hard to classify but who is "a somewhat eccentric example of the distortion of mystical theology".[5] Labadie established his own communal house, printing press, and a following. He was driven from Amsterdam (a rare event in that liberal city) and fled to northern Germany, where he died in 1674. He ended by focusing his spirituality on the end of the world and even commended some of the Jews of Amsterdam, who were propagating a false messiah named Shabbetai Tsevi.[6]

Despite his aberrations Labadie was for some time the most powerful voice in French Reform Protestantism and was highly regarded by Dutch Protestants. His great accomplishment was to make Continental Protestantism aware of the possibility of a personal relationship with Christ that encompassed all aspects of life. He also showed that such devotion could exist in a number competing and mutually exclusive religious persuasions from the Jesuits to the Quakers.

Pietism

Labadie was not the only voice raised for affective devotion in the Netherlands. Anyone familiar with Rembrandt's hauntingly beautiful paintings of Christ (he belonged to a small separatist denomination at the time of their painting) will know that devotion to Christ was very much in the air. A powerful religious current was spreading through German-speaking lands and England, especially with leaders like John Wesley. It then came to Colonial America. This current deeply influenced the

[3] Ibid., 77.
[4] Ibid., 78.
[5] Ibid., 31.
[6] Ibid., 78.

religious experience of Americans of all nationalities, especially African Americans. Unfortunately, this same current, important even today, is often belittled as being emotional and subjective. The leaders of major denominations tend to view Pietism as anti-intellectual, and out of touch with the work of contemporary theologians struggling to live with the continuing effects of the Enlightenment. For most, the word "pietistic" is pejorative, describing a Christianity that is sentimental, ill-informed, and psychologically embarrassing. This causes some to ignore the impact of Pietism, which is experiencing a comeback, often in the form of a vital and popular type of Evangelical Protestantism.[7]

Since Pietism represents a large and long-standing current in religious history, it is impossible to give more than a descriptive definition of it. As we have seen, it was a response to the "religious and moral lassitude" of Christians in several central European countries as a result of the Thirty Years' War (1618–1648), a seemingly interminable political conflict posing under the banner of religious conviction.[8] Much could be said to defend the hypothesis that at least in some respects this spiritual vacuum was caused by the end of monastic life and the suppression of the friars, who were popular preachers of personal Christianity.

The first generation of Pietists, despite their anti-intellectual protestations, were theological and polemic enough. Sometimes in the case of Lutheran and Reform Christians—and in their own way the Anabaptists—they were distracted from their express goal of leading a pure Christian life by the conflicts around them and ended up killing one another in the name of the gentle Christ. When they were not fighting each other, they were fighting the Catholics, who could be equally cruel in the name of the same gentle Christ. But as Bouyer has reminded us, times had changed from the early days of the Reformation.[9] It was the moment to get on with the goal of following Christ and loving Him and, through Him, the Trinity, and of loving one's neighbor because of Him.

Pietism was a reaction against a dry, verbose Lutheran or Puritan orthodoxy, as well as against an intolerance and even hatred aimed at various Protestant groups, especially those with little political clout, like the Anabaptists and the separatist denominations. Gradually some Pietists even opened dialogue with Catholics.

Nevertheless, Pietism was more than a reaction. Basing itself on the "new birth" of adult conversion and the decision to follow Christ

---

[7] *Pietists: Selected Writings*, ed. Peter C. Erb. Classics of Western Spirituality (New York: Paulist Press, 1983). See especially Erb's introduction, which is a comprehensive history of German Pietism.

[8] David W. Lotz, "Continental Pietism", in *The Study of Spirituality*, ed. Cheslyn Jones, Geoffrey Wainwright, and Edward Yarnold, S.J. (London: SPCK, 1986), 448.

[9] Louis Bouyer, *Orthodox Spirituality and Protestant and Anglican Spirituality*, vol. 3, *A History of Christian Spirituality* (New York: Seabury Press, 1982), 169.

entirely by accepting the call of grace and dedicating every action to living the Christian life, Pietism's adult conversion was very similar to the religious profession of medieval monks, friars, and nuns. It even more obviously paralleled the understanding of vows and promises made by members of the new reformed Catholic religious orders, like the total commitment of the Jesuits, the Discalced Carmelites (of St. Teresa), and the Capuchins. The "new man" was to take on the work of love, to do charitable deeds. Admittedly this new emphasis had to be explained and some compromise found between it and Luther's stern denial of good works as an essential part of the Christian life. Other aspects of the early Reformation, like arbitrary predestination, were softened, and the focus was placed on the assurance of salvation that comes from faith in Christ.

Personal piety in its Protestant forms—Bible reading, prayer, and meditation on the Holy Word—took the place for a largely literate population of the medieval acts of devotion: the reception of the sacraments, processions, pilgrimages, and the religious pageantry that had instructed the largely nonreading public in the past. Many belonged to the prayer groups, or conventicles, described in Labadie's work.

English Puritanism beginning with William Ames was a kind of Calvinist Pietism. All these movements proclaimed absolute loyalty to one or another of the reformers, but each mitigated the dark theology of the turbulent sixteenth century, as St. Francis de Sales and his contemporaries softened the edge of the Catholicism that had produced hymns like the *Dies Irae*. Pietists were even open to the medieval mystics, although they would have claimed that it was through Luther that they came to them. The writings or at least the ideas of St. Bernard, Thomas à Kempis, the Dominican John Tauler, and St. Francis de Sales were quietly used.[10] By the nineteenth century St. Francis of Assisi, that most medieval of Christians, was taken by many Protestants as the example of an almost perfect Christian.

After their recovery from Cromwell's Protectorate, the Anglicans were gradually influenced by Pietism, and an evangelical Anglicanism appeared, blending some of the remaining medieval devotion and liturgy with love of the Bible and personal prayer. It is not too much to say that eighteenth-century Anglicanism produced Wesley and Methodism as well as the Oxford movement, which was strongly influenced by Pietism. For instance, John Henry Newman, a founder of the Oxford movement, was deeply influenced by his mother's evangelical Anglicanism.

To understand Pietism, two great figures must be appreciated—Johann Arndt (1555–1621), who laid its foundations, and Philipp Jacob Spener (1635–1705), who can be said to be its founder. Many other interesting writers are important in the history of Pietism: August Hermann

[10] Lotz, "Continental Pietism", 450.

Francke (1663–1727), Gottfried Arnold (1666–1714), Johann Bengel (1687–1752), and the most fascinating, Count Nikolas Ludwig von Zinzendorf (1700–1760), the refounder of Moravianism. Nor should we forget that Calvin's idea of personal sanctification—a return to the spirituality of medieval Catholicism—opened the door to a Christianity of personal spiritual growth, always, of course, understood, as it must be, as a response to grace. The early Pietists may also have been influenced by the devout struggles for perfection of the Anabaptists, Mennonites, and similar groups who at this time were attempting to lead a literal Gospel life as they understood it.[11]

Johann Arndt and Philipp Jakob Spener

Johann Arndt, an orthodox Lutheran, became critical of the dry debates and abstract reasoning of the Protestant scholars who were then modeling their own form of Scholasticism on the Spanish Jesuits.[12] Arndt's great work, *True Christianity*, focused on personal renewal, individual growth in holiness, and religious experience.[13] Arndt's influence was strong, spreading even to Russia and contributing to the influential writings of St. Tikhon of Zadonsk (1727–1783).

Campbell cites the following passage from *True Christianity*, which sums up Arndt's hopes for a renewal among Lutherans and other Protestants. "True Christianity consists ... in the exhibition of a true, living faith, active in genuine godliness and the fruits of righteousness.... [It also shows] how true repentance must proceed from the innermost source of the heart; how the heart, mind, and affections must be changed, so that we might be conformed to Christ and his holy Gospel; and how we must be renewed by the work of God to become new creatures."[14]

Realistic and well read, Arndt was conversant with Christian mysticism, East and West, and took a down-to-earth approach to mystical spirituality reminiscent of St. Teresa of Avila and St. John of the Cross. "Perfection is not, as some think, a high, great, spiritual, heavenly joy and meditation, but it is a denial of one's own will, love, honor, a knowledge of one's nothingness, a continual completion of the will of God, a burning love for neighbor, a heart-held compassion, and, in a word, a love that desires, thinks, and seeks nothing other than God alone insofar as this is possible in the weakness of this life."[15]

Obviously, Arndt was deeply devoted to Jesus Christ. The following passage, in which he speaks of repentance and the following of Christ, gives us some sense of this fervent Christian's love for his Master.

---

[11] Erb, *Pietists: Selected Writings*, 4.

[12] Ibid., 3.

[13] Ibid., 4.

[14] Campbell, *Religion of the Heart*, 79.

[15] From the foreword to book 3 of *True Christianity*, in *Johann Arndt: True Christianity*, trans. Peter Erb. Classics of Western Spirituality (New York: Paulist Press, 1979), 224.

> God's Son did not become man for his own sake but for ours, so that he might unite us once again with God through himself, and make us participants of the highest good, and purify and make us holy once again. That which is to be made holy must be made holy through God and with God. As God is personally in Christ, so God must be united with us through faith and man must live in God and God in him; man must live in Christ and Christ in him.... Christ Jesus must be the medicine for our corrupted nature. The more Christ lives in man, the more is human nature made better....
>
> Christ's life is the new life in man, and the new man is the man in whom Christ lives in the spirit. Christ's meekness must be the meekness of the new man; Christ's humility, the humility of the new man; Christ's patience is the patience of the new man.... This is a new creature and the noble life of Christ in us as Saint Paul says: "It is no longer I who live, but Christ who lives in me" (Gal. 2:20).[16]

Philipp Spener is credited with founding Lutheran Pietism. He combined the insights of Arndt and the preexisting Reformed Pietism that he had encountered in Labadie. Born in Alsace, he studied at Strasbourg between 1651 and 1653. Later he read Labadie's writings in German translation, but he became acquainted with the author who had just been ordained a Reform minister and was already becoming famous. Spener was appointed a senior pastor in Frankfurt, preaching reform with considerable success. He founded conventicles so large that a whole church had to be assigned for their meetings. Spener published what would become the most influential work in early Pietism—the *Pia Desideria*—in 1675, the year after Labadie's death. Spener stressed the priesthood of all the faithful and that the laity should exercise this office in their study and teaching of the Bible. He stressed the need for works of kindness and generosity.

Spener's immediate success was partly due to an already growing sense of devotion in German Lutheranism. In Chapter 10 above, we met Lutheran hymn writers like Paul Gerhardt (1607–1676) who "plundered the riches of medieval devotion to produce intensely personal hymns"[17] that Bach incorporated into his magnificent oratorios. These works, like "Jesu, Joy of Man's Desiring", are profound expressions of Christian devotion.

It is no surprise that Spener ran into opposition. His critics called him and his disciples "Pietists", a term of derision, for the first time in the 1680s. Spener, however, was undeterred, and it is an indication of his insight into the need for reform and for a more devotional practice of the Christian faith that he was made preacher of a famous church in Berlin.

---

[16] Erb, *True Christianity*, bk. 1, chap. 11, pp. 65–66.

[17] Campbell, *Religion of the Heart*, 82.

That Spener was totally dedicated to Jesus hardly needs to be proved. While much of his preaching was instructive, it was also devotional. Spener wrote on prayer, "Whenever we pray with our mouths God looks at the same time not only upon our tongues but also on the base of our hearts out of which the tongue speaks."[18] He was particularly explicit about meditation on the suffering of Christ. "Our dear Savior purchased us with his suffering as his own possession. This act binds us to him since we are no longer ourselves but are truly his; we may then no longer live according to our own will but must live completely for his pleasure. As a result, as often as we consider the suffering of Christ, we must remember his act which impels us to earnest godliness."[19]

Like all truly devotional writers, Spener calls for a change of life, for action rather than words, and especially for personal acts of gratitude to Jesus Christ. "Let us not continue to talk but let us enter into the practice itself. We know that our blessedness rests in repentance, faith, and following Christ, and to this meditation on the suffering of Christ gives great aid; therefore, we ought to turn faithfully to our Savior to honor him for the good of our souls. Let us then not leave one another until we agree together to truly turn the present time to such a godly goal and work to heartily call to God for His grace."[20]

It will be instructive not only for Protestants but for Catholics and Orthodox to realize that Spener and the Lutheran and Anglican Pietists focused devotion not only on the reading of the Bible but also on the reception of the Eucharist. In a sermon on the method of prayer, which is in itself enlightening, Spener speaks of meditation on the Eucharist: "Likewise does meditation on the Holy Communion, which feeds us in a spiritual way so that our whole inner man is strengthened through the life-giving flesh and blood of Jesus Christ which has the Holy Spirit with it."[21]

Spener has no hesitation in saying that Christ really comes to the individual in Holy Communion. Writing about Holy Communion and Christian joy, he says: "Since Christ comes to us in [Holy Communion] he is often a special sweetness and joy which worthy communicants are allowed to sense. The body and blood which now are in eternal joy we taste and they bring with themselves something of that sweetness. As a result they are the most precious goods, namely the whole service of Christ in the Holy Communion, and therefore it does not remain without joy."[22]

---

[18] Spener, "God-Pleasing Prayer", in Erb, *Pietists: Selected Writings*, 90.

[19] Spener, "Meditation on the Suffering of Christ", quoted in Erb, *Pietists: Selected Writings*, 80.

[20] Ibid., 81–82.

[21] Spener, "God-Pleasing Prayer", in Erb, *Pietists: Selected Writings*, 91.

[22] Spener, "Christian Joy", quoted in *Pietists: Selected Writings*, 95.

The Halle Experience

Despite all the opposition, it is an observable historical phenomenon that when devotion has been lacking for a while in the life of a Christian people and the faith is going to survive, those who bring devotion to Christ back into focus are likely to meet with success beyond all expectations. This is especially true if the devotional movement coincides with historical and political factors that can be allied with it. This is what happened to German Pietism. The state of Brandenburg-Prussia was gaining power, and its leaders were anxious to avoid theological divisions in the state Lutheran Church. They could have been opposed to the return of Pietism, but the Pietists were open to other Protestants and saw the possibility of salvation for all who loved Christ. They were also unconcerned with theological debate. Such factors encouraged the Prussian government to smile on their efforts. As a result, a preexisting university at Halle became the center for Protestant German culture in the eighteenth century, as well as the spring of much German Pietism. This first modern university deeply affected German Lutheranism, as distinct from Scandinavian Lutheranism, creating a softer, more devotional public image.

August Hermann Francke, the genius behind Halle and its devout humanistic approach, had been converted on a Sunday evening with an experience not unlike that of Pascal. Campbell explains that after a long period of spiritual searching Francke was asked to preach on the text: "[T]hese are written that you may believe that Jesus is the Christ, the Son of God, and that believing you may have life in his name" (Jn 20:31). Feeling he lacked sufficient faith, Francke fell on his knees and was filled with the joy of conversion.

> Then the Lord heard me, the living God from his holy throne, as I was still on my knees. So great was his fatherly love that he would not take away such doubt and restlessness of heart little by little, with which I could have been quite content, but rather he suddenly heard me so that I would be all the more convinced and would bridle my strayed reason, to use nothing against his power and faithfulness; thus he suddenly heard me. Then, as one turns his hand, so all my doubts were gone. I was sure in my heart of the grace of God in Jesus Christ; I knew God not only as God, but rather as one called my Father. All sadness and unrest in my heart was taken away in a moment.[23]

It should not be surprising that Francke would draw on the bridal mysticism we have already observed in St. John of the Cross and the English Puritan Francis Rous. The Pietists were at home with poetry and hymns, perhaps a secondary sign of devotion. Among the beautiful hymns Erb has selected are these verses from Francke.

---

[23] Quoted in Campbell, *Religion of the Heart*, 87.

"Come" is the voice of your bride.
"Come" calls your pious beloved.
She calls and shouts loudly.
Come quickly, Jesus, come.
So come then, my bridegroom;
You know me, O lamb of God,
That I am betrothed to you.

But the proper time and hour
Are totally left to you.
I know that it is pleasing to you
That I with heart and tongue
Promise to come to you, and, therefore,
From now on direct my way
Toward you. . . .

O Jesus, my soul has
Has already flown up to you.
You have, because you are totally love,
Completely exhausted me.
Leave off, what are times and hours,
I am already in eternity
Because I live in Jesus.[24]

Francke visited Spener, joined forces, and was identified as a Pietist. As a result, he was forced to leave his first university post. He went to Halle, becoming both a professor and pastor of the local parish. Then followed thirty years of outstanding pastoral success, and German Pietism had its great day. Services ranged from the education of poor children through seminary training. A chemical laboratory with an apothecary were side by side with beautiful new Baroque churches. Everyone was called to a joyful repentance and a spiritual life. Biblical scholarship with practical exegesis had of course a respected position. How did all this fit in with Luther's gloomy approach to salvation and reprobation, to arbitrary predestination? Well, honestly it did not fit very well.

But Lutheran Pietism was alive. It could adjust, as Christianity had often adjusted in the past. The early Christians adjusted when their expectations of an imminent end of the world proved wrong. Scholars say that we can see that adjustment in the epistles of St. Paul, who in the First and Second Letters to the Thessalonians was very apocalyptic and then in the pastoral epistles looked forward to the Church being around for some time. In the past two centuries Christianity has adjusted better than anyone thought it could both to the separation of church and state and to complex scientific theories about the origin of life.

[24] From "Hymns from the Spiritual Songbook", Erb, *Pietists: Selected Writings*, 173–75.

So the Lutherans at Halle agreed that eternal life was based on God's foreknowledge rather than on predestination of those whom God would accept or reject arbitrarily. Based on the theology of Arndt, they focused on the present possibility of repentance and faith for all. At that moment, the Lutherans, of all people, saw the possibility of salvation in the broadest framework. One can picture Thomas Aquinas and Francis de Sales at an ecumenical dialogue with Arndt and Francke, something that would have been unlikely with Luther and Calvin.

From the Halle experience one learns that Lutheranism is capable of a true Christian humanism. Devout humanism had been part of Catholic history for a long time and part of the Anglican experience as well. The atmosphere in which the encounter of faith and human accomplishment interact peacefully and productively will be one of religious devotion. Without devotion to Christ, Christians are too easily drawn into a humanism that merely wears Christian belief as a cape. There is little or no real integration, and ultimately the Christian identity will be lost. With devotion, Christians will be able to adjust; a deep personal involvement with Christ will also keep them from falling down the slippery slope of unbelieving humanism.[25]

Anyone seriously interested in Christian devotion would be amply rewarded by reading the Pietists. Lovers of music would be particularly rewarded to discover that the oratorios and hymns of Bach and his contemporaries fit into a fascinating theological context. This is an example of Lutherans rediscovering the rich devotional experience of the late Middle Ages. The hymns of St. Bernard and the Franciscan Jacopone da Todi, author of the *Stabat Mater*, were streams that fed the composers of the age of Pietism.

A beautiful example of Christian devotional music comes from Halle and its many publications and endeavors. Johann Anatasius Freylinghausen (1670–1739) was one of the principle hymn writers for the Halle Spiritual Songbook. It seems obvious that he knew *Jesu Dulcis Memoria*, the early medieval hymn we have already seen.

> Jesus is the most beautiful image
> Which wisdom has illuminated
> Which so pure, calm, and mild
> Has been spun out by eternal love,
> Which the highest power of heaven
> Has ever brought forth.
>
> It is full art and decor,
> Enrapturing sense and heart.
> It is the masterwork of divinity

[25] For those interested in reading further on this subject, we suggest *The End of the Modern World* (New York: Sheed and Ward, 1956) by Romano Guardini, who was a professor at Berlin University during the 1930s.

In which it impresses itself immediately.
If you wish to see the form of God
Look to Jesus; you will see it immediately,

The grace and light of all angels,
The splendor and glory of all saints,
Is met a thousandfold
Alone in this image.
Whatever one can think
Is all met in Jesus.

Indeed, God himself, the eternal light,
Has never seen anything more beautiful,
And can never turn
His presence from him;
Say what you always will,
Jesus is the most beautiful image.[26]

For those who have the time to study the devout humanism of the Lutherans at Halle, of Anglicans at Oxford and Cambridge, and of Calvinists in Holland and later in the United States (for example, at Harvard, Yale, Columbia), much can be learned about the importance of devotion for those who tried to join a very real faith with secular learning and the appreciation of the arts and sciences. Though some of the people mentioned would not admit it, they were following the examples of the universities founded by monks and friars five hundred years before. It is not surprising, then, that we often find these very institutions using the architectural styles of the medieval universities. It was more than architecture; it was a sense of devotion that contributed to the effort to bring Gospel and secular values together harmoniously.

Arnold and the Radicals

Any movement that seeks to lead people to a more perfect observance of a spiritual ideal is going to give rise to more radical expressions of its own principles. This is not a theological observation, but one drawn from history and social psychology. Those drawn to doing the most—the *omnia*—can be sure that someone else will try to surpass them. This was observable in the early days of the Franciscan Order and the rise of the so-called spiritual brethren who radically did their own thing to the point of arrogance and self-will, but not without genuine sincerity, which at times even had beautiful expressions.

The German Pietists had the same experience with the radicals. Following the road that left Labadie on his own with his own church after having been ordained in several others, some Lutheran Pietists

[26] From "Hymns from the Spiritual Songbook", quoted in *Pietists: Selected Writings*, 177–78.

became separatists, convinced that they could obtain their goals only outside the structure of the German Lutheran Church. Some, like Gottfried Arnold (1666–1714), never quite left the Lutheran Church, but he inspired others who did leave, becoming radical separatists. Ernst Hochmann (1670–1721), for instance, was the founder of the Church of the Brethren, which opened a Protestant monastic community, the Ephrata Cloister, near Lancaster, Pennsylvania. This eighteenth-century community flourished for about seventy years.[27] The denomination's survivors today are called Dunkers.

All these movements were mystical in the sense that the spiritual experience of the presence of Jesus was of supreme importance. Among popular guides to this direct experience were the writings of Jakob Böhme and even the books of the Catholic Quietists.[28]

Arnold, who was never actually separated and accepted the post of a Lutheran pastor, is both the originator and easiest of the radicals to study. We will, thus, examine his approach to devotion to Christ to gain an appreciation of this movement. Before we begin, however, it is important to realize that he had been influenced at Halle by Christian Thomasius, who taught that piety was a matter of pure intuition, independent of theology. This form of subjectivism outraged both Calvinists and Lutherans. One Calvinist, Auguste Lecerf, called it a theory of the infallibility of heretics.[29] It is not surprising that the esoteric mystic Jakob Böhme, whom Spener had admired, was proclaimed by Arnold and the radicals as "a new Luther".[30] Arnold also saw Madame Guyon as the last incarnation of Sophia, no less. Piety was seen as an essentially feminine reality, and women were its best experts. Arnold attacked the authorities of all churches and theologians as false Christians. Erb sums up this position: "The true witnesses experienced the working of the divine, by the guidance of the Spirit in them were able to interpret the Scriptures properly and make correct theological judgements, and, established as the true Church, witnessed against institutional heresy about them."[31]

A large book would be needed to review the spiritual history of these radical movements, which are now represented by rather traditional conservative Christian communities in the United States, especially in the Midwest. A sense of this radical mystical feeling is expressed in the following verses. While one may not be at home with the radical subjectivism expressed here, the verses strongly suggest a kind of devotion based on the picture of Jesus as the Divine Word. We are familiar with this kind of expression from the popular old German hymn "Fairest Lord Jesus", which resembles this poem of Arnold.

[27] Erb, introduction to *Pietists: Selected Writings*, 15.

[28] Ibid.

[29] Bouyer, *Spirituality*, 175.

[30] Ibid.

[31] Erb, *Pietists: Selected Writings*, 14.

Walk with Jesus

It is true; outside it is pleasant
Where everything can bedeck itself with flowers.
I, however, go into my house
To walk in all stillness with my lamb.
There the sun shines and the nightingale sings;
There it is green, blossoms come forth, fresh springs rush out.
There I see nothing but Jesus.
His angelic choir fills all places.
He is the sun, love, song.
As a result hope is renewed and pure waters leap.
Is that not enough for my beautiful walk?
He is also to bring me to paradise.[32]

The following poem, like many of Arnold's writings on mysticism, including his teaching on the *Sophia*, calls to mind the radical poetry and art of William Blake, of a century later. Blake was influenced by German and Scandinavian spiritual ideas, many of which were heterodox. The following poem, called "Double Light", reads almost like a description of Blake's paintings and parallels his poetry.

Double Light

O beam of glory, you our sun,
You the source and fountain of light,
Send us your fire from the joy of your kingdom
Until our spirit is perfected in One.
At the same time ignite us more in your power;
Keep us in your love life.
What your thought creates for our love and peace
Is only given for common use.
Your gospel is for all of us
And must reach out to others
So that they may be truly one in you
Until your knowledge covers the earth.[33]

Although the language is not at all theologically precise and some phrases, if pushed to their conclusions, would lead far beyond orthodox Christianity, the tender and mystical love for Jesus, the Eternal Son and Light of the World, can find parallels in some Catholic and Anglican mystics. One thinks particularly of the poem "In the Beginning Was the Word" by St. John of the Cross. The wife referred to in this passage is fallen human man. The speaker is God the Father.

[32] Translated from Gottfried Arnold, *Gottliche Liebes-Funcken*, no. 87, in ibid., 238.

[33] Translated from Gottfried Arnold, *Neue Gottliche Liebes-Funcken*, no. 1, quoted in *Pietists: Selected Writings*, 240.

I would like to give you,
Son, a loving wife,
who by your worth deserved
to keep our company,
to eat bread at our table—
the same bread of which I eat—
to know the glories
that I've had in such a Son,
and to please me by rejoicing
in your grace and beauty.
"Father, I thank you dearly,"
the Son said in reply:
"On whatever wife you give me
I will shed my brilliance
and by it she will see
that my Father's worth is great,
that whatever being
I have, I received from him.
I will rest her on my arm
and she will burn in your love
and with eternal delight
make your goodness her own."[34]

Bouyer's evaluation of Arnold and his disciples is negative. He claims they tended to play up "themes of virginity and nuptial mysticism, but in a context of ... dubious sentimentalism and naïve eroticism". This, coupled with their attraction to monastic piety in the ancient Church, compromised them "for good and all in the eyes of healthy-minded Protestants".[35] Perhaps this explains why Professor Pelikan does not even deal with German Lutheran Pietism in his great summary of Christ, *Jesus through the Centuries*.

The Moravians and Count Zinzendorf

A traveler in east central Pennsylvania will recognize the Amish by their distinctive dress and customs and be a bit less aware of the Mennonites, who tend to blend in with the American scene in externals. Few, however, are aware of the Moravians, except for the name of their college and their beautiful Christmas observances around the city of Bethlehem.

Although these groups all began in Eastern Europe in the fifteenth and sixteenth centuries, each has its own history and identity, and they vary in terms of their devotional life. We will limit ourselves here to the Moravians who have had a great impact on Protestant devotional

[34] John of the Cross, "In the Beginning Was the Word", in *The Poems of St. John of the Cross*, trans. Ken Krabbenhoft (New York: Harcourt Brace, 1999), 65, 67.

[35] Bouyer, *Spirituality*, 175.

history. This is largely due to their contact with the early Methodists whom they met by a providential accident when the Wesleys were their fellow passengers on a voyage to Georgia in 1736. The story of the Moravians and their encounter with the devout Lutheran Count Nikolas von Zinzendorf (1700–1760) is one of the most remarkable elements in Protestant history because of the count himself, whom Bouyer describes as "one of the most astonishing figures of the eighteenth century".[36]

The early Moravians, like the Lollards and the first Anabaptists, came into existence in the mid-fifteenth century long before Luther and Calvin. They were originally part of the movement around the Czech Jan Hus (ca. 1370–1415), who insisted on the laity receiving Holy Communion under both species. After his disgraceful treatment and execution at the Council of Constance (he had appeared voluntarily and had been promised safe passage), one group of his followers founded a religious movement called *Unitas Fratrum* (or the Bohemian Brethren). They were subsequently driven from Bohemia to Moravia.[37] This group preserved a number of Catholic traditions, like the belief in apostolic succession of their own bishops and the hearing of confessions.[38]

A small remnant in Holland gathered by Bishop Jan Amos Komenský and another led by Bishop Christian David were given refuge by Count von Zinzendorf, a devout Lutheran Pietist who had established a community, the Herrnhut, in 1722 in Saxony.[39] Although Zinzendorf had been approved as a candidate for the pastorate in the Lutheran Church in 1737, he was in fact ordained by a Moravian bishop.[40] By this time, this group and the count himself were seen as a blending of Lutheran Pietism, Moravian customs, and their own religious services, which were an attempt to return to ancient Christian ways, like the love feast (separate from the Eucharist) and the Mandatum, or the washing of feet. All was very enthusiastic and devotional, in some measure due to the count's own emotional personality.

The theology of this group was anti-intellectual.[41] After all, they had blended two churches into one, with the emphasis on devotion and inward religion. They went beyond Spener and Francke and all at Halle, where they had been educated and to whom they were related.

The count himself was genuinely ecumenical and in many ways ahead of his time. He had been involved in the bicentenary of the Reformation, and through his contacts at Halle and with other Pietists he tried to work out an understanding between the Pietists and the orthodox Lutherans.[42] On the Catholic side he had corresponded with

[36] Ibid., 177.
[37] In contemporary terms, from the western to the eastern part of the Czech Republic.
[38] Campbell, *Religion of the Heart*, 92–94.
[39] See Erb, introduction to *Pietists: Selected Writings*, 19–24.
[40] Campbell, *Religion of the Heart*, 94.
[41] Ibid., 95–96.
[42] Erb, introduction to *Pietists: Selected Writings*, 22.

the Cardinal Archbishop of Paris, Louis de Noailles (1651–1729), until the latter's death.[43]

Zinzendorf published a number of studies that included a serious attempt to understand the psychology of religious development.[44] The count, of course, received much opposition and was banished from Saxony shortly before his ordination as a pastor. He was a friend of the King of Denmark and through this connection sent Moravian missioners to Greenland and the Virgin Islands.

It may surprise Protestants to learn that the count-pastor became very involved in a devotional preoccupation with the wounds and sufferings of Christ. Some of those associated with this movement went beyond the bounds of ancient Christian theology and taught that the Father had suffered and died on the Cross, reviving an old heresy called patripassionism, or modalism. Of special interest to us is Zinzendorf's love of Christ Crucified and his devotion to the Passion and death of Jesus. The following selection from his "Litany of the Life, Sufferings, and Death of Jesus Christ" may seem strange to Protestant readers, but older Catholics will find it familiar in many ways. The whole litany can be read with profit.

Leader:	From the sin of not believing in you, From all sins of the flesh and the spirit, From all self-righteousness, From all lukewarmness and drunkenness, From all indifference to your wounds and death.
Congregation:	Defend us, dear Lord God. There is nothing in us but poverty. By your blood, death, and suffering give us a warm, completely submissive heart. . . .
Leader:	By your holy simplicity
Congregation:	Make our hearts and minds simple!
Leader:	By your obedience and servanthood
Congregation:	Help us to be obedient in heart Make me like in mind to you, as an obedient child, meek and still. Jesus, now, help me that I might be obedient as you. . . .
Leader:	By your watching and praying
Congregation:	Teach us to be wakeful in prayer! . . .
Leader:	By your tears and cry of dread
Congregation:	Console us in dread and pain! You shed so many tears for us, So many drops of blood flowed out from you, So many are the voices which pray for us and plead for us.

[43] Campbell, *Religion of the Heart*, 92.

[44] Ibid., 95–96.

Leader: By your head crowned with thorns
Congregation: Teach us the nature of the kingdom of the Cross!
Leader: By your outstretched hands on the Cross
Congregation: Be open to us at all times!
Leader: By your nail-pierced hands
Congregation: Show us where our names stand written!
Leader: By your wounded feet
Congregation: Make our path certain!
Leader: By your pale beautiful lips
Congregation: Speak to us consolation and peace!
Leader: By the last look of your breaking eyes
Congregation: Lead us into the Father's hands!
Holy Lord God,
Holy strong God,
Holy merciful Savior,
You eternal God.[45]

Although Zinzendorf condemned the excesses of the Moravian devotees of the Passion of Christ, his community was compromised, and August Spangenberg became the accepted leader of the Moravians.[46] Both men came to Pennsylvania and founded a town called Nazareth. The Moravian influence in the Bethlehem area of that state, as we noted earlier, continues to this day.

Zinzendorf understood faith as an inward experience to the point of saying that dogmatic teaching was a burden to faith. He even got to the point of addressing the Trinity as Father, Son, and Mother. Despite all these "astonishing" details, Zinzendorf was a truly devoted man who led many of his more orthodox German contemporaries to a new ecumenical piety. Campbell sees Zinzendorf's experience as the origin of the nondenominational churches.

By the time of Zinzendorf's death others had taken over the leadership of the Moravians, and it was Spangenberg who would link this central European religion of enthusiasm with Wesley and the evangelical revival, which during the eighteenth and nineteenth centuries so powerfully affected Christianity in the English-speaking world. Although Zinzendorf's name is not well known, his thinking and experience are still very much a vital force in Christian churches, especially in the rural United States.

[45] Nicolas Ludwig, Count von Zinzendorf, "The Litany of the Life, Suffering and Death of Jesus Christ", trans. from Hans Urner, *Der Pietismus*, in Erb, *Pietists: Selected Writings*, 297–99.

[46] Campbell, *Religion of the Heart*, 95.

16 The Protestant Renewal in England and America

It is an unfortunate fact that for many Protestants as well as Catholics, contemporary Protestantism seems a tangled skein of customs, institutions, ideas, and names, with innumerable but unimportant differences. This can leave the very large reality that we call the Protestant world vulnerable to the winds of change and to the latest ideas popularized by the media. Historically, there is much more substance to the differences among Protestants than most people know. Although we are restricting ourselves to the question of devotion to Jesus Christ, we must take into account the many strands of belief and thought, as well as the varied expressions of Protestant devotion to Jesus, which emerged in these different traditions. I hope that Protestants will become more aware of the history of their own particular tradition, of why their forebears differed both from one another as well as from the Catholic and Orthodox. As we have seen, some will be very surprised by what Christians experienced in common about Christ.

The eighteenth and nineteenth centuries are close enough to us that the effects of the different Christian experiences and beliefs are still quite significant. Different Protestant denominations are visible everywhere. The history we are about to summarize briefly explains why in the United States especially there can be a church on every street corner.

William Law (1686–1761)—The Way of Reform

As Arndt began a profound reform movement in German Protestantism, so William Law, an ordained but deposed professor, or Fellow, at Emmanuel College, Cambridge, became the most powerful voice for reform in England. He is designated a nonjuror: an Anglican clergyman who refused to take the oath of loyalty to William and Mary following the revolution of 1688 because of a previous oath to the deposed king, James II. Expelled from the Church of England, the nonjurors functioned as an underground church with their own bishops, chapels, and clergy. They were High Churchmen and relied heavily on the early Church Fathers for their theology. They also used the rather Catholic forms of worship associated with Archbishop Laud, who had been executed in 1645 by Cromwell. The nonjurors were really the forerunners of the Oxford Movement.

When Law was deposed, he retired to Putney, a village near London. There he tutored the father of Edward Gibbon, the renowned historian, and he wrote his most influential work, *A Serious Call to a Devout and Holy Life*, in 1728. This powerful and devotional book, in many respects similar to St. Francis de Sales' *Introduction to the Devout Life*, was enormously popular and remains a classic.[1] Like de Sales, Law demonstrates "how to live the noblest ethical and ascetic ideals in terms of ordinary Christian experience".[2]

Law writes of recovering our lost integrity by being refashioned after the image of Christ. Reform requires leaving behind the things of the flesh, the world, and the devil by devotion and discipline. He was influenced by the Greek mystical writer St. Gregory of Nyssa and the writer known as St. Marcarius of Egypt,[3] as well as by the Catholic mystics Ruysbroeck, Tauler, and Thomas à Kempis. He also admired Fénelon, Francis de Sales, and the perennial favorite of Protestant spiritual writers, Jacob Böhme.[4]

The impact of *A Serious Call* can be measured by another great man of the times, Samuel Johnson, preeminent stylist and author of the first authoritative dictionary. When Johnson arrived at Oxford, he picked up *A Serious Call*, "expecting to find it a dull book (such books generally are) and perhaps to laugh at it. But I found Law quite an overmatch for me".[5] From the time he read *A Serious Call*, religion, according to his biographer James Boswell, became "the dominant object of his thoughts". Johnson called Law's work "the finest piece of hortatory theology in any language".[6] John Wesley published an abridged version of *A Serious Call* and Law's other classic, *Christian Perfection*, in his fifty-volume *Christian Library*.[7]

The center of Law's teaching is that complete moral conversion and the seeking of perfection at all times is the authentic living of the Christian life. This is what Law means by devotion, rather than simply a prayerful approach to Christ, and it is the central message of *A Serious Call*. An exile in his own country, Law moved from Putney to London and then, at the age of fifty-four, back to the place of his birth, King's Cliffe in Northamptonshire, to live out his days in a semimonastic community with two devout women under his spiritual direction.[8] He became

[1] Paul G. Stanwood, ed. *William Law*, Classics of Western Spirituality (New York: Paulist Press, 1978). This volume contains the text of *A Serious Call to a Devout and Holy Life* and *The Spirit of Love*.

[2] Ibid., 7.

[3] Ibid., 1–2.

[4] Ibid., 14–15.

[5] Ibid.

[6] Ibid.

[7] Ibid.

[8] Ibid., 22.

increasingly engrossed in the mystical but unorthodox writings of Jakob Böhme, who was strongly biased against formal religion and structure; this fitted in well with Law's position as a deposed cleric of the nonjuror movement. Law apparently did not function as an Anglican nonjuror priest, which he could have done at his little "monastery"; instead he regularly attended the parish church.[9]

During this time, relying increasingly on Böhme's writings, Law stressed that the whole purpose of the Christian life is for Christ to be born again in us. The atonement or redemption is not some exterior justification but rather a whole rebirth and renewal of life.

> "As in Adam all die, so in Christ shall all be made alive." This is the whole work, the whole nature, and the sole end of Christ's sacrifice of Himself; and there is not a syllable in scripture that gives you any other account of it. It all consists from the beginning to the end, in carrying on the one work of regeneration; and therefore the Apostle saith, the first Adam was made a living soul, but the last or second Adam was made a quickening spirit because sent into the world by God to quicken and revive that life from above which we lost in Adam. And He is called our Ransom, our Atonement. . . .
>
> The whole truth therefore of the matter is plainly this. Christ given for us is neither more nor less than Christ given into us. And He is in no other sense our full, perfect, and sufficient Atonement than as His nature and spirit is born and formed in us, which so purgeth us from our sins that we are thereby in Him, and by Him dwelling in us become new creatures having our conversation in Heaven.[10]

This much no Anglican or Catholic can ever argue with—or any Methodist, for that matter. Law was realistic about suffering and its place in the Christian life, which is not surprising since he is serious about the Christian life, as the very title of his book suggests. In *The Spirit of Love* he writes the following about Christians and the meaning of the Cross in their lives.

> Wonder not then that all the true followers of Christ, the Saints of every age, have so gloried in the cross of Christ, have imputed such great things to it, have desired nothing so much as to be partakers of it, to live in constant union with it. It is because His sufferings, His death and cross were the fullness of his victory over all the works of the Devil. Not an evil in flesh and blood, not a misery of life, not a chain of death, not a power of Hell and darkness, but were all baffled, broken, and overcome by the process of a suffering and dying Christ. Well therefore may the cross of Christ be the Glory of Christians.[11]

[9] Ibid., 15.

[10] *The Spirit of Love*, pt. 2, the Second Dialogue, in Stanwood, *William Law*, 434–35.

[11] Ibid., 451.

The question arises, did Law lose anything by his rather lopsided interest in the writings of Böhme? The following quotation from the Third Dialogue of *The Spirit of Love*, which appeared in 1754, after he had lived fourteen years at King's Cliffe and seven years before his death, shows the influence of Böhme's cosmology and strange theology.

> All evil, earthly beasts are but short-lived images or creaturely eruptions of that hellish disorder that is broke out from the fallen spiritual world; and by their manifold variety, they show us that multiplicity of evil that lies in the womb of that abyss of dark rage which (N.B.) has no maker but the three first properties of nature fallen from God and working in their darkness.
>
> So that all evil, mischievous, ravenous, venomous beasts, though they have no life but what begins in and from this material world and totally ends at the death of their bodies, yet have they no malignity in their earthly, temporary nature but from those same wrathful properties of fallen nature which live and work in our eternal fallen souls. And therefore, though they are as different from us as time and eternity, yet wherever we see them we see so many infallible proofs of the fall of nature and the reality of Hell. For was there no Hell broke out in spiritual nature, not only no evil beast but no bestial life could ever have come into existence.[12]

It is this kind of theology that must have repelled John Wesley, who turned away from Law, whom he had admired greatly because of *A Serious Call*. Subsequently Wesley had no use for Böhme and many years later called him an "ingenious madman" who "contradicts Christian experience, reason, Scripture, and himself".[13] Writing about Law's later works, especially *The Spirit of Love*, Bouyer recognized that there are passages of "high spirituality" but adds that "there is something definitely extravagant about them. Böhme's bizarre genius here turns into a very British kind of mild dottiness.... This, anyway, seems to have been the impression that Wesley came away with after his last pilgrimage to King's Cliffe."[14]

Austin Warren, who is legitimately impressed by Law (as indeed we all may be), sees him, however, as "obscurantist" and "rigorist", caught by a denial of Christian humanism.[15] Perhaps if history had allowed Law to lead a more normal life, rather than that of a monk with neither the spiritual direction nor the checks and balances of monastic life, he might be seen as a better-balanced genius. Despite the eccentricities of his later years, there is no doubt that Law was deeply devoted to Jesus Christ. The following words from the Third Dialogue touchingly demonstrate his

[12] *The Spirit of Love*, pt. 2, the Third Dialogue, in Stanwood, *William Law*, 484.

[13] From an entry in Wesley's *Journal* (July 12, 1773), quoted in Louis Bouyer, *Orthodox Spirituality and Protestant and Anglican Spirituality* (New York: Seabury Press, 1982), 188.

[14] Bouyer, *Spirituality*, 187.

[15] Austin Warren, foreword to Stanwood, *William Law*, 20.

lifelong devotion to His Savior. "For to seek to be saved by patience, meekness, humility of heart, and resignation to God is truly coming to God through Christ; and when these tempers live and abide in you as the spirit and aim of your life, then Christ is in you of a truth and the life that you then lead is not yours but Christ that liveth in you. For this is following Christ with all your power." [16]

Change and Revival in Eighteenth-Century Britain

Anyone who has visited an art museum is likely to be puzzled by the remarkable contrast between the genteel paintings of Thomas Gainsborough (1727–1788) and the etchings of William Hogarth (1697–1764), who showed England as a depraved world of drunken women and abandoned babies. Did they really live in the same country at the same time?

The fact is that English life, which was once concentrated on a quaint bucolic countryside, had changed too quickly with the invention of the water frame for weaving, the smelter, and the humble pump, which provided the opportunity for deep mining in the earth. Factories dominated the cities, and mines scarred the mountainsides. Campbell rightly states that the importance of these developments as factors in the growth of the evangelical revival cannot be overestimated. It was usually in the newly industrialized cities and suburbs and often among the army of immigrants to them that the earliest evangelical societies developed.[17]

I might add that less than two hundred years had passed since the monasteries, with their schools, farms, and infirmaries, had been suppressed. The violent political and religious conflicts occasioned by the Reformation had ended only in 1688. Life was a burden to many neglected people, whose alienation would become permanent when, forced by economic necessity, they left village and farm to work in factories and mines.

To the everlasting credit of Johann Arndt and the other Pietists, they reminded German Protestants of their responsibility to their neighbor and to the world in which they lived. The tradition of Christian social responsibility had always been part of life in Italy (witness St. Catherine of Genoa) and in France (witness St. Vincent de Paul). It was the Pietists and their descendants, the Moravians, who reminded Protestants that they were "their brothers' keeper". The Moravians brought this awareness to England when it was not a strong ideal among the Puritans, although there were still echoes of social responsibility among the Anglicans because of the remains of the monastic tradition in their life.

The influence of the new Evangelical Anglicans like Thomas Bray, who founded in 1698 the Society for Promoting Christian Knowledge (to this

[16] *Spirit of Love*, pt. 2, the Third Dialogue, in Stanwood, *William Law*, 489.

[17] Ted A. Campbell, *The Religion of the Heart: A Study of European Religious Life in the Seventeenth and Eighteenth Centuries* (Columbia: University of South Carolina Press, 1991), 99.

day, SPCK is a label in many fine books) and the Society for the Propagation of the Gospel in Foreign Parts (SPG), began to spread works of charity similar to what we have seen coming from Halle.[18]

The Welsh Revival

No place needed the Gospel message of faith and charity as much as Wales, a quiet bucolic corner of Britain, which was suddenly transformed into an immense, ugly coal-mining camp. The evangelization began with a country parson, Griffith Jones (1684–1761), who sought both to evangelize and to bring education and a knowledge of the Welsh language to the ordinary people. It is astonishing that in this little land in about forty years Jones established three thousand schools, circulated thirty thousand copies of the Welsh Bible, and, incredibly, taught 150,000 people to read.[19]

The revival took a huge step away from the Anglicanism of Jones with a young schoolmaster, Howell Harris (1714–1773), who had studied briefly at Oxford for holy orders but left because of the immorality he found there. Against Jones' own Anglican principles, Harris and others like him began a life of evangelical preaching as lay preachers, calling for repentance and acceptance of the salvation given by Jesus Christ. Recall that Jones, as an Anglican, would have believed that all preaching should be done in church by clergy. Campbell gives Harris' description of a celebration of the Lord's Supper in Wales.

> I was last Sunday at the Ordinance with Brother Rowlands where I saw, felt, and heard such things as I can't send on Paper any Idea of.... Such Crying out and Heart Breaking Groans, Silent Weeping and Holy Joy, and shouts of Rejoicing I never saw. Their Amens and Cryings Glory in the Highest &c would inflame your soul was you there. Tis very common when he preaches for Scores to fall down by the Power of the Word, pierced and wounded or overcom'd by the Love of God and Sights of the Beauty and Excellency of Jesus, and lie on the Ground.[20]

These meetings began to be called revivals and often focused on the wounds and suffering of Christ, a devotion borrowed from the Moravians,[21] but with its roots in the medieval piety of SS. Bernard and Francis. The presence of Jesus was very much the psychological center of these meetings. The belief that Christ was there can be seen from the fact that He was invoked as present. The focus was on the desire to follow Christ's teachings to the last detail. It is unfortunate that little is available about the Welsh revival apart from Campbell's detailed

---

[18] Ibid., 101.

[19] Ibid., 102.

[20] From Derec Llwyd Morgan, *The Great Awakening in Wales*, trans. Dyfnallt Morgan (London: Epworth Press, 1988), 23, quoted in Campbell, *Religion of the Heart*, 105.

[21] Campbell, *Religion of the Heart*, 106.

overview. Yet this revival was the most powerful element in Welsh life for about 250 years.

The English Revival

The English revival was the parent of the American revival of the mid-nineteenth century. Like many important movements, it began with personal conversions, this time of two people who could not have been less alike: George Whitefield (1714–1770), the son of a tavern keeper, and Selina Hastings, Countess of Huntingdon (1709–1791). What they had in common was a joyous moment of conversion that removed their burdens and guilt. Countess Selina was very ill when her sister-in-law told her of her own conversion and healing. Following is an account of the countess' experience lying on her sickbed.

> [F]rom her bed she lifted up her heart to God for pardon and mercy through the blood of his Son. With streaming eyes she cast herself on her Saviour: "Lord, I believe; help thou mine unbelief." Immediately the scales fell from her eyes; doubt and distress vanished; joy and peace filled her bosom. With appropriating faith, she exclaimed, "My Lord, and my God!" From that moment her disease took a favorable turn; she was restored to health, and what was better, to "newness of life."[22]

Whitefield met the countess in 1738, three years after his conversion and one year before his ordination as an Anglican priest. He was beginning to preach repentance and salvation to coal miners and to organize societies for prayer, Scripture study, and good works. He preached in America for two years and set up an orphanage there. By this time evangelical preaching had become unwelcome in Anglican parishes, so Whitefield built a large preaching house, The Tabernacle, in Moorfields. As early as 1720 the devout societies of Christians at Oxford had been meeting to study the Greek New Testament. These young men were so methodical in their religious observances that they were called the Holy Club or, with a certain irony, the Methodists.[23] John Wesley had been a member of such a club during his short stay at Oxford as a tutor.

These Methodists held their first conference in Wales in 1743, and Whitefield was made moderator for life, which made him a kind of bishop, as these are also appointed for life. Shortly after, Whitefield and his family went to work in North America, to return in 1748.

While Whitefield was evangelizing and organizing on two continents, Lady Huntingdon was responding to her own conversion in a

[22] From Helen C. Knight, *Lady Huntingdon and Her Friends: Or, the Revival of the Work of God in the Days of Wesley, Whitefield, Romaine, Venn, and Others in the Last Century* (New York: American Trust Society, 1853), 14–15, quoted in ibid., 108.

[23] A. Raymond George, "John Wesley and the Methodist Movement", in *The Study of Spirituality*, ed. Cheslyn Jones, Geoffrey Wainwright, and Edward Yarnold, S.J. (London: SPCK, 1986), 456.

less dramatic but no less determined way. She joined a joint Moravian-Anglican religious society, and after the death of her husband she worked full-time at evangelizing the British aristocracy. In general, they were as receptive as Voltaire was to the Jesuits. The countess was a true evangelizer and built beautiful chapels for preaching in spas like Bath, in hopes of drawing in those who might be looking for something to do between rounds of taking the waters.

When Howell Harris brought Whitefield to visit the countess after his return from America, she added him to the swelling ranks of her personal chaplains. This whole group, which worked very effectively and with great devotion, was given the very British and deceptively innocuous title "The Countess of Huntingdon's Connexion". After Whitefield's death the countess opened a Methodist seminary. Essentially she and her followers moved quietly out of the Anglican Church and into the chapels that were recognized now as independent Protestant churches.

The countess and her preachers, unequivocal Calvinists, held to the doctrine of predestination. This conflicted with their emphasis on the necessity of conversion for salvation and also with the very broad scope of their evangelization, which extended to the poor and the outcast. Traditional Calvinists often saw the poor and wretched as those predestined to hell. Any thoughtful Calvinist must have uncomfortably pondered the question, how do I know I am saved? The countess and her preachers focused on the experience of conversion, the conviction of one's own sins (a kind of confession), and the assurance of pardon as the "signs of grace received". Nonetheless, their belief in predestination notwithstanding, they energetically pursued the conversion of everyone they met. This seemed to bring them into the camp of the despised Jacobus Arminius (1560–1609), a Dutch Calvinist theologian who "claimed that God had decreed to save all who believed in Christ and condemned only those who would refuse an offer of saving grace".[24] The strict Calvinists thought that this was Pelagianism and would probably have compared it to the conversion required by Catholic saints, especially St. Ignatius Loyola in his *Spiritual Exercises*. The individual's free choice of Christ was most important. It is significant that Wesley, who expressed repugnance at Calvin's predestination, identified Ignatius as among the greatest men of Christian history.[25] Actually, no orthodox Catholic would ever deny that the choice for Christ requires both grace and the grace to accept grace (prevenient grace).

It is important to remember above all that the Evangelicals, including Whitefield and the countess, had experienced a grace of conversion, which they knew they had to accept. A rigid Calvinism could

[24] Eric Lund, "Second Age of the Reformation: Lutheran and Reformed Spirituality, 1550–1700", in *Christian Spirituality: Post-Reformation and Modern*, ed. Louis Dupré and Don E. Saliers (New York: Crossroad, 1996), 224.

[25] Bouyer, *Spirituality*, 189–90.

be in conflict with such an expression of conversion, and it was precisely this conflict around predestination that would eventually break up this group of English evangelists.

This controversy, called the "extent of the atonement", would eventually divide the Evangelicals, with the countess, Howell, and the strict Calvinists on one side, and the Wesleys on the other. Whitefield sided with the countess, and when he died, there was a difficult moment because John Wesley insisted on preaching his funeral sermon. Sometime earlier Whitefield had put a request to this effect in his will.[26]

One of the lasting effects of this controversy is the existence of the Welsh Calvinistic Methodist Church. To most people who know anything about John Wesley and make the common mistake of identifying him as the founder of Methodism, this name seems a contradiction in terms. How does one put Calvin and Wesley together since they differ so profoundly on election and predestination?

The English Evangelicals, even apart from the Wesleys and despite the controversies, did much good. Their unique blend of severe Calvinist theology and warm devotion of the heart, their belief in a limited atonement, which seemed to contradict their genuine concern for the poor and the downtrodden, is a complex piece of Christian spiritual theology. Largely due to Whitefield's early preaching and the astonishing success of Wesley's Methodist Church in the United States, this unusual blend of strict moralism and devotion has been the Christian expression of millions—especially among the working class.

The Wesleyan Movement

John and Charles Wesley—Brothers with Trembling Hearts

Just as Francis de Sales turned Catholic theology away from an emphasis on damnation to the hope of salvation, so the Wesley brothers, especially the more influential John, brought some sunshine into the Protestant world. Although demanding in their ethical teachings, the Wesleys saw God as a loving Father and Christ as a gentle Savior suffering for all. This brought light and warmth into Protestant Christianity.

We will focus on John Wesley (1703–1791), rightly recognized as the founder of the Methodist Episcopal Church in the United States. Because he was essentially a spiritual writer and teacher and not an academic theologian, writers of historical theology have given this remarkable man who was deeply attuned to the call of Christ less recognition than he deserves. An Anglican priest who was far more broad-minded than most of his contemporaries, he expressed a fraternal concern for Catholics. In fact, he was often accused of being a Catholic. Although these accusations were unfounded, in his own personal preaching and spiritual life he had much in common with the preaching friars of the Middle Ages. In this review we cannot adequately encompass even the most important facts of Wesley's life, but

[26] Campbell, *Religion of the Heart*, 127.

we can encourage the reader to get to know him better. All his life he sought only to be an authentic disciple of Jesus Christ.[27]

Wesley brought together his father's High Church Anglicanism and his mother's Evangelical nonconformity (independence of the established church). Ordained in 1728, he became a tutor of Greek at Lincoln College, Oxford, where he was very disedified by worldliness. Through his brother Charles (1707–1788), John became involved in the holy clubs at Oxford. One newspaper reported that these young men were taking on austerities, like fasting twice a week, "after the pattern of the ancient Alexandrian mystic, Origen".[28] Indeed they were interested in restoring the primitive Church of the Fathers whom they enthusiastically studied.[29] They were also influenced by the nonjurors, who brought the flavor of the medieval Church with them.

A list of writers and movements that affected the young John Wesley shows that he was open to many influences and able to tolerate their mutually exclusive elements in order to bring them into his own life and experience. He was especially drawn to embrace the most authentic and comprehensive Christian belief he could find. In his very synthesis of other people's ideas Wesley finds his creativeness.

Although staunchly Protestant and capable of writing books sharply critical of the Catholic Church (*Popery Calmly Considered*), he included seven Catholic authors in his *Christian Library*, including Pascal, Molinos, Fénelon, and Jean-Baptiste de Renty, a close friend of St. John Eudes. He admired *The Imitation of Christ* and the writings of Teresa of Avila, Ignatius Loyola, and Francis de Sales.[30] Interestingly, the library included neither Luther nor Calvin.

One thing always remained an absolute center in Wesley's immense preaching and writing. One goal determined all his attention and brought his wide-ranging religious interests together: to lead as perfect a Christian life as possible by accepting and using every grace and by following Christ's teachings in the Gospel as closely as possible. Faith and the life focused on Christ were the center of Wesley's thought and action. From the powerful moment of his conversion, he trusted in Christ alone. In his *Journal*, Wesley describes the event that took place at a meeting in Aldersgate Street on the Wednesday following Pentecost, May 24, 1738.

[27] Easily available to most readers is the volume *John and Charles Wesley: Selected Writings and Hymns*, ed. Frank Whaling, Classics of Western Spirituality (New York: Paulist Press, 1981).

[28] Campbell, *Religion of the Heart*, 117.

[29] Unfortunately, the interest of Wesley and his immediate followers in the Fathers of the Church was all but lost in America. The excellent *Ancient Christian Commentary on Scripture* in twenty-eight volumes, initiated by the eminent Methodist scholar Thomas Oden, signals a welcome return to patristics by some of Wesley's followers.

[30] Bouyer, *Spirituality*, 193.

> In the evening, I went very unwillingly to a society in Aldersgate Street, where one was reading Luther's Preface to the Epistle to the Romans. About a quarter to nine, while he was describing the change which God works in the heart through faith in Christ, I felt my heart strangely warmed. I felt I did trust in Christ, Christ alone for salvation; and an assurance was given me that he had taken away *my* sins, even *mine*, and saved me from the law of sin and death.
>
> I began to pray with all my might for those who had in a more especial manner despitefully used me and persecuted me. I then testified openly to all there what I now first felt in my heart. But it was not long before the enemy suggested, "This cannot be faith, for where is your joy?" Then was I taught that "peace and victory over sin are essential to faith in the Captain of our salvation but that, as to the transports of joy—that usually attend the beginning of it especially in those who have mourned deeply—God sometimes giveth, sometimes withholdest them, according to the counsels of his own will."
>
> After my return home, I was much buffeted with temptations, but cried out and they fled away. They returned again and again. I as often lifted up my eyes and he *sent me help from his holy place*. And herein I found [in what] the difference between this and my former state chiefly consisted. I was striving, yea, fighting with all my might under the law, as well as under grace. But then I was sometimes, if not often, conquered; now, I was always conqueror.[31]

Wesley's experience of the "heart strangely warmed" is a clear expression of devotion. A sensitive man, Wesley suffered much through the parting of friends like Whitefield, and his awkward attempts at marriage. He also suffered through his struggles in the American colonies and his concern for his own ability as a simple priest to ordain bishops for his new church in America. Through all this John Wesley trusted in Christ.

Like St. Louis de Montfort a generation before, the Wesleys resorted to poetry and hymns, which are perhaps the best windows into their inner experience. Providence had given John a brother whose musical and poetical abilities would earn him a unique place in the history of Christian hymnology. Ordained an Anglican priest in 1735, Charles Wesley had gone to Georgia to work for the conversion of the indentured servants and the poor of that area. He is the author of an astonishing 4,430 hymns. In fact, two of the most familiar hymns of the church year, both of them splendid in music and content, are his works "Hark! the Herald Angels Sing" and "Christ the Lord Is Risen Today". Many hymns are also attributed to John, who probably provided much

[31] From the *Journal* of John Wesley, quoted in Whaling, *Wesley: Selected Writings*, 107. See also Campbell on this event, 118–19.

of the phrasing and theological inspiration. Yet, Charles was no uncritical follower. In fact, he came to a very serious separation from his brother following a dispute over whether John could ordain bishops for the new church in America. The issue was whether a priest could ordain a bishop, and John Wesley argued that the priesthood of bishops and presbyters were one and the same. This was never the Christian tradition, and John Wesley's stand might make us suspect him of being a theological relativist. I'm not sure that is fair. He had a profound sense of his own call, one so strong that it appears to have caused him to be inconsistent with his own theological principles. His High Church Anglicanism had to be very severely bent in order for him to attempt to ordain a bishop. The seriousness of his decision may not be obvious to Protestant readers, but to High Church Anglicans, as well as to Catholics and the Orthodox, it was a momentous step. In the long run it made the Methodist Episcopal Church in the United States much more Protestant than Anglo-Catholic.

Wesley and Christian Spirituality

Wesley's great contribution to the history of Christianity, distinct from his work as an evangelist, is often overlooked. He made a significant contribution to the psychology of religious experience. As Campbell notes, John Wesley's diaries and journals are similar to many of the introspective psychological works of the times and particularly of the coming century.[32] Like Augustine some thirteen hundred years earlier, he learned about the experience of faith, hope, and charity from analyzing his own development and from studying the experience of others, as is evident in the collection he made in publishing the *Christian Library*. In this he also follows in the footsteps of St. Teresa of Avila and St. John of the Cross, who carefully studied their own responses to grace. Because Methodist spirituality and its emphasis on conversion was so widespread in the United States, it is not surprising that the first doctoral dissertation done in psychology studied the phenomenon of religious conversion.[33] The founding geniuses of the study of psychology of religious experience, William James and Friedrich von Hügel, were at least indirectly influenced by Wesley.

The most effective way to sample the devotion to Christ of John Wesley and his brother is to examine John's writings and their parallels in Charles' hymns. It must be kept in mind that it is often difficult to tell how much John had to do with particular hymns, but the assumption is that he provided some, if not most, of the theology in the choice of words. At least he led the two in terms of theological convictions.

In keeping with our descriptive definition of devotion, the following selections from John's prose and Charles' hymns will provide some

---

[32] Campbell, *Religion of the Heart*, 121.

[33] Edwin Diller Starbuck, *The Psychology of Religion: An Empirical Study of the Growth of Religious Consciousness* (New York: Scribners, 1911).

insights. A thorough study of the Wesleys' devotion to Christ would require a very large volume.

Christ Is Present to the Individual

An essential aspect of John Wesley's teaching was the recognition that one needed a deep sense of one's own sin and misery—in fact, "utter despair" of self and "of all else besides Christ". The antidote to this was complete trust in Christ, a very personal recognition that Christ knows, cares about, loves, and saves us. This is quite different from the general theological principle of the salvation of the whole world. The following quotation from Wesley's "Directions for Renewing Our Covenant with God" (1780) reminds us of the meditations in the *Spiritual Exercises* of St. Ignatius and particularly of the meditation called the "Two Standards".

> Choose Christ and his ways and you are blessed forever; refuse, and you are undone forever. And then, turn either to the right-hand or to the left; lay both parts before you, with every link of each; Christ with his yoke, his cross and his crown; or the Devil with his wealth, his pleasure and curse: and then put yourselves to it thus; Soul, you see what is before you, what will you do? Which will you, with the crown or the curse? If you choose the crown, remember that the day you take this, you must be content to submit to the cross and yoke, the service and the sufferings of Christ, which are linked to it. What say you? Had you rather take the gains and pleasures of sin, and venture on the curse? Or will you yield yourself a servant of Christ, and so make sure the crown?[34]

After a forceful exploration of the choices at hand and their results, Wesley concludes with a powerful prayer reminiscent of Ignatius. Its allusion to bridal mysticism is also interesting, since we know that Wesley was familiar with the Spanish mystical writers.

> O blessed Jesus, I come to you hungry, wretched, miserable, blind, and naked; a most loathsome, polluted wretch, a guilty, condemned malefactor, unworthy to wash the feet of the Servants of my Lord, much more to be solemnly married to the King of Glory; but since such is your unparalleled love, I do here with all my power accept you, and take you for my Head and Husband, for better, for worse, for richer, for poorer, for all times and conditions, to love, honor, obey you before all others, and this to the death. I embrace you in all your offices: I renounce my own worthiness, and do here avow you for the Lord my Righteousness: I renounce my own wisdom, and do here take you for my only guide; I renounce my own will, and take your will for my law.

[34] From *Directions for Renewing Our Covenant with God*, in Whaling, *Wesleys: Selected Writings*, 134.

> And because you have been pleased to give me your holy Laws as the Rule of my life, and the way in which I should walk to your kingdom, I do here willingly put my neck under your yoke, and set my shoulder to your burden, and subscribing to all your laws as holy, just, and good, I solemnly take them as the Rule of my words, thoughts, and actions; promising that though my flesh contradict and rebel, I will endeavor to order and govern my whole life according to your direction, and will not allow myself in the neglect of any thing that I know to be my duty.[35]

We must recall the idea of total consecration growing from baptism that was popularized by de Bérulle and others of the French School about a hundred years before Wesley began preaching. Also we think of the spiritual consecration of St. Louis de Montfort. Wesley obviously expresses similar sentiments.

The following hymn by Charles Wesley is one of many that reveal the pilgrim's sense of Jesus' presence and our reliance on His grace.

> Savior from sin, I wait to prove
> That Jesus is thy healing name,
> To lose, when perfected in love,
> Whate'er I have, or can, or am;
> I stay me on thy faithful word,
> The servant shall be as his Lord.
>
> Answer that gracious end in me
> For which thy precious life was given:
> Redeem from all iniquity,
> Restore, and make me meet for heaven.
> Unless thou purge my every stain,
> Thy suffering and my faith are vain. . . .
>
> Didst thou not die that I might live
> No longer to myself, but thee?
> Might body, soul, and spirit give
> To him who gave himself for me?
> Come then, my Master, and my God!
> Take the dear purchase of thy blood.[36]

An important part of the teaching of the Wesleys, like that of Law, is that we should try to be perfect Christians. The following quotation from John Wesley's *Christian Perfection* puts this succinctly.

> But whom then do you mean by *one that is perfect*? We mean one in whom *is the mind which was in Christ*, and who so *walks as Christ also*

[35] Ibid., 144.

[36] From the 1780 *Hymnbook of Charles Wesley*, no. 364, in Whaling, *Wesley: Selected Writings*, 225–26.

> *walked*; a man *that has clean hands and a pure heart*, or that is *cleansed from all filthiness of flesh and spirit*; one in whom is *no occasion of stumbling*, and who accordingly *does not commit sin*. To declare this a little more particularly: We understand by that scriptural expression, *a perfect man*, one in whom God has fulfilled his faithful word, *from all your filthiness and from all your idols will I cleanse you. I will also save you from all your uncleannesses*. We understand hereby one whom God has *sanctified throughout, in body, soul, and spirit*; one who *walks in the light as he is in the light, in whom is no darkness at all: the blood of Jesus Christ his son having cleansed him from all sin*.[37]

We Must Place All Our Trust in God

The conviction that the believer must be totally resigned to God's will and seek to have total trust that God will bring him to salvation and sanctification is a foundational principle of the spiritual life for the Wesleys. Indeed, it is a foundational principle of the spiritual life in general. John often used the expression "total resignation to the will of God".[38] Such an adage reminds us of French piety, both of the Quietists and of the orthodox Catholics.

The following advice comes from Wesley's Covenant Service.

> And this giving yourselves to him must be such as supposes that you be heartily contented.
>
> First, see what it is that Christ expects, and then yield yourselves to his whole will: do not think of compounding, or making your own terms with Christ, that will never be allowed you.
>
> Go to Christ, and tell him, Lord Jesus, if you will receive me into your house, if you will but own me as your Servant, I will not stand upon terms; impose upon me what conditions you please, write down your own articles, command me what you will, put me to any thing you see as good; let me come under your roof, let me be your Servant, and spare not to command me; I will be no longer my own, but give up myself to your will in all things.
>
> That he shall appoint you your station and condition; whether it be higher or lower, a prosperous or afflicted state: be content that Christ should both choose your work, and choose your condition; that he should have the command of you, and the disposal of you: make me what you will, Lord, and set me where you will: let me be a vessel of silver or gold, or a vessel of wood or stone, so I be a vessel of honor: of whatsoever form or metal, whether higher or lower, finer or coarser, I am content; if I be not the head, or the eye, or the ear, one of the nobler and more honorable instruments you will employ, let me be the hand, or the foot, one of the most laborious, and lowest, and most contemptible of all the Servants of my Lord, let my dwelling be upon the dunghill, my portion in the wilderness, my

[37] From *A Plain Account of Christian Perfection*, in Whaling, *Wesley: Selected Writings*, 315–16.
[38] Ibid., 355.

> name and lot among the hewers of wood, or drawers of water, among the doorkeepers of your house; anywhere, where I may be serviceable; I put myself wholly into your hands: put me to what you will, rank me with whom you will; put me to doing, put me to suffering, let me be employed for you, or laid aside for you, exalted for you, or trodden under foot for you; let me be full, let me be empty, let me have all things, let me have nothing, I freely and heartily resign all to your pleasure and disposal.[39]

These words, written in 1780, remind us of de Caussade. It is not possible that Wesley read de Caussade, because his book, although written approximately a decade before, was not published for another hundred years. However, the idea of total dependence on God and abandonment to His will had already been strongly suggested by devotion to the Sacred Heart of Jesus and by many in the French School. While Wesley's thoughts are parallel and nearly identical, we do not imply that he borrowed them from French Catholic spirituality. In fact, all these people were responding to the call of grace in a very particular time. Again we see the fascinating parallel between Protestants and Catholics experiencing similar challenges and coming up with similar responses.

Charles Wesley expressed the ideal of total renunciation of self-will and trust in God in his hymns. The following lines from "For Believers Praying" is typical of this teaching of complete confidence in God's will and in Christ as present.

> Jesu, my strength, my hope,
> On thee I cast my care,
> With humble confidence look up,
> And know thou hear'st my prayer.
> Give me on thee to wait,
> Till I can all things do,
> On thee almighty to create,
> Almighty to renew.
>
> I want a sober mind,
> A self-renouncing will
> That tramples down and casts behind
> The baits of pleasing ill:
> A soul inured to pain,
> To hardship, grief, and loss,
> Bold to take up, firm to sustain
> The consecrated cross.[40]

[39] From *Directions for Renewing Our Covenant with God*, quoted in Whaling, *Wesley: Selected Writings*, 139–40.

[40] From the 1789 *Hymnbook of Charles Wesley*, no. 381, in Whaling, *Wesley: Selected Writings*, 231.

How Christ Calls Us to a Higher Life

The concept that a true and right knowledge of Christ calls for greater and greater obedience to His teaching, to ever more perfect and complete discipleship, is one that is sadly lost on many Christians today. Even Christian meditation, as practiced in many "programs", is encouraging but not challenging. This is a kind of revival of Quietism. The Wesley brothers, truly devoted Christians, would have nothing to do with any of this. If you want to love Christ, you must do His will and put obedience to Him before everything else in life. Here the Wesleys became indistinguishable from Catholic and Orthodox mystics and even from spousal mysticism.

There are innumerable examples of the teaching of total self-giving in John Wesley. They remind us of St. Catherine of Genoa. The following letter written to a friend beautifully illustrates how Wesley sought to bring the ideal of pure love and total discipleship into the life of an ordinary layperson.

> "Walk in love," as Christ also loved us and gave Himself for us. All is contained in humble, gentle, patient love. Is not this, so to speak, a divine contrivance to assist the narrowness of our minds, the scantiness of our understanding? Every right temper, and then all right words and actions, naturally branch out of love. In effect, therefore, you want nothing but this—to be filled with the faith that worketh by love.[41]

The same conviction about total dedication to the Christian life is clearly expressed by the following hymn of Charles Wesley.

> Holy, and true, and righteous Lord,
> I wait to prove thy perfect will;
> Be mindful of thy gracious word,
> And stamp me with thy spirit's seal.
>
> Open my faith's interior eye:
> Display thy glory from above;
> And all I am shall sink and die,
> Lost in astonishment and love!
>
> Confound, o'erpower me by thy grace;
> I would be by myself abhorred:
> All might, all majesty, all praise,
> All glory be to Christ my Lord!
>
> Now let me gain perfections' height;
> Now let me into nothing fall;
> Be less than nothing in thy sight,
> And feel that Christ is all in all![42]

[41] Letter to Philothea Briggs, Jan. 5, 1772, in Whaling, *Wesley: Selected Writings*, 163.

[42] From the 1780 *Hymnbook of Charles Wesley*, no. 381, quoted in Whaling, *Wesley: Selected Writings*, 231.

Eucharistic Teachings and Hymns

Frequently we have surprised our readers with devout teachings about the Eucharist of different Reformation denominations. Beginning with Luther and Calvin, both of whom denied the Eucharistic realism of the Catholic Church and in particular the explanatory doctrine (not dogma) of transubstantiation, the reformers retained the ancient teaching that those who receive Holy Communion truly receive the Body and Blood of Christ. Although contemporary Protestants, even Methodists, seem unaware of how important Eucharistic theology and devotion was to John Wesley, it was in fact central to his evangelization and personal spirituality. In the fifth volume of his *Journal*, written in the last decade of his life, we read:

> LONDON—The number of communicants was so great that I was obliged to consecrate thrice; I preached and with Dr. Coke's assistance I administered the Sacrament to 11 or [12,000] communicants ...
>
> MANCHESTER—Easter Day, I think we had about [16,000] communicants.[43]

The first rule of the Methodist revival was to "be at church and the Lord's Table every week".[44]

Wesley's Eucharistic theology was explicitly not Catholic. Like all Protestants he rejected the concept of transubstantiation; yet, he held to such beliefs as the Real Presence of Christ in the Eucharist, and he understood the Eucharist as a memorial of the suffering and death of Christ, a sign and means of grace, and a pledge of eternal life. He also taught that the Eucharist is a sacrifice in which we offer ourselves in union with Christ our Priest.[45] These concepts, which seem to be startlingly Catholic, were based on the writings of Dr. Daniel Brevint, one of the Anglican clergy deposed at the time of King Charles I's execution and restored by his son Charles II, as dean of Lincoln. The Methodist theologian Dr. Rattenbury makes it clear that Brevint's influence on Wesley was hostile, or at least negative, in regard to Catholicism. However, Rattenbury's work was published before the ecumenical movement of the second half of the twentieth century. However, he cites Dom Gregory Dix, an Anglican Benedictine, as being in agreement with the sacrificial aspect of understanding Brevint, whereas most Catholics have seen Dix as closer to traditional Catholic theology.

Rattenbury sees the Wesleys as anti-Roman but Catholics of the ante-Nicene Church. He embraces the writings of the Anglo-Catholic Gregory Dix and says that it is "difficult to think of any work to which Free Church people can appeal with more confidence

[43] Quoted in J. Ernest Rattenbury, *The Eucharistic Hymns of John and Charles Wesley* (Akron, Ohio: OSL Publications, 1996), 3. This is a recent edition of a much earlier work.

[44] Ibid.

[45] Ibid., 11ff.

for the confirmation of their views on this subject than Dix's *The Shape of the Liturgy*".[46]

It seems to me that Wesley's teachings on the Eucharist if compared with those of Pope Pius XII and the Catholic liturgical writers after his encyclicals on the liturgy would be largely in agreement, showing much more similarity than Dr. Rattenbury found earlier on.

All this notwithstanding, few readers are aware of the Eucharistic devotion of the Wesleys. John Wesley insisted that hundreds of thousands of people receive Holy Communion every Sunday at a time when many Anglican churches celebrated the Eucharist only three times a year. It is no wonder that he was often accused of being a Catholic. The phrase used against him was that he was dragging "the rags of Popery" into the church.

There is no doubt that John Wesley saw the Eucharist as a source of grace. In his General Rules for the Methodist societies, in his commentary on the Lord's Prayer, he writes about the words "Give us this day our daily bread": "It was the judgment of many of the ancient Fathers that we are here to understand the sacramental bread also; daily received in the beginning by the whole Church of Christ, and highly esteemed, till the love of many waxed cold, as the grand channel whereby the grace of his spirit was conveyed to the souls of all the children of God."[47]

It is important to note that both John and Charles Wesley believed in the priesthood passed on by apostolic succession. In 1745 John defined his views on the priesthood in a letter to his brother-in-law, Westley Hall. He is careful to state the Anglican position on the bishops.

> We believe it would not be right for us to administer either Baptism or the Lord's Supper unless we had a commission so to do from those Bishops whom we apprehend to be in a succession from the Apostles. And yet we allow these Bishops are the successors of those who were dependent on the Bishop of Rome.
>
> We believe there is, and always was, in every Christian Church (whether dependent on the Bishop of Rome or not), an outward priesthood, ordained by Jesus Christ, and an outward sacrifice offered therein by (those) authorized to act as Ambassadors of Christ and Stewards of the Mysteries of God.
>
> We believe that the three-fold order of ministers ... is not only authorized by its Apostolic institution, but also by the written word.[48]

A thorough understanding of the Wesleys' teachings on the Eucharist would necessitate a real study of Brevint's theology, which is very

---

[46] Ibid., 125.

[47] "A Meditation on the Lord's Prayer. An Extract from Wesley's Sermon on the Mount VI", in Whaling, *Wesley: Selected Writings*, 116.

[48] Letter, Dec. 30, 1745, quoted in Rattenbury, *Eucharistic Hymns*, 68.

well developed. This, in fact, has been done by Rattenbury. Anyone interested in the subject would find a great deal there. The following passage from Brevint explains why Charles Wesley was able to write hymns, almost any of which a Catholic could sing at Mass today. Brevint writes:

> The main intention of Christ herein was not the bare remembrance of His Passion; but over and above, to invite us to His Sacrifice, not as done and gone many years since, but as to grace and mercy, still lasting, still new, still the same as when it was first offered for us.[49]
>
> This Victim having been offered up in the fulness of times, and in the midst of the world, which is Christ's great temple, and having been thence carried up to heaven, which is his sanctuary; from then spreads Salvation all around, as the burnt-offering did its smoke. And thus Christ's Body and Blood have everywhere, but especially at this Sacrament, a true and real Presence. When Christ made a self-offering upon earth ... [he] had made a way into heaven. Christ is gone up and sends down to earth the graces that spring continually both from this everlasting Sacrifice and from the continual intercession that attends it.[50]

The study of the Wesleys' Eucharistic teaching is too vast and complicated for us to examine. It is important, however, for Protestant readers to recall that Eucharistic devotion was an important part of the spirituality of the past. Dr. Rattenbury quotes 160 hymns on the Eucharist written by Charles Wesley, in which we can see the influence of Dr. Brevint. The following are splendid examples of Eucharistic devotion.

O Thou eternal Victim slain
A sacrifice for guilty man,
By the eternal Spirit made
An offering in the sinner's stead,
Our everlasting Priest art Thou,
And plead'st Thy death for sinners now.

Thy offering still continues new,
Thy vesture keeps its bloody hue,
Thou stand'st the ever-slaughter'd Lamb,
Thy priesthood still remains the same,
Thy years, O God, can never fail,
Thy goodness is unchangeable.

O that our faith may never move,
But stand unshaken as Thy love!

[49] Dr. Daniel Brevint, *The Christian Sacrament and Sacrifice*, sec. 2, quoted in Rattenbury, *Eucharistic Hymns*, 131, 135–36.

[50] Ibid. sec. 4, quoted in Rattenbury, *Eucharistic Hymns*, 136–37.

Sure evidence of things unseen,
Now let it pass the years between,
And view Thee bleeding on the tree,
My God, who dies for me, for me![51]

The Wesleys did not back away from the Catholic teaching that Christ's sacrifice was renewed mystically and sacramentally in the Eucharist, making their thought very different from that of Calvin and Luther. The following verses of a hymn of Charles Wesley illustrate this.

Jesu, at whose supreme command
We thus approach to God,
Before us in Thy vesture stand,
Thy vesture dipp'd in blood.

Obedient to Thy gracious word,
We break the hallow'd bread,
Commemorate Thee, our dying Lord,
And trust on Thee to feed.

Now, Saviour, now Thyself reveal,
And make Thy nature known;
Affix the sacramental seal,
And stamp us for Thine own.

The tokens of Thy dying love
O let us all receive
And feel the quickening Spirit move,
And *sensibly* believe.

The cup of blessing, blest by Thee,
Let it Thy blood impart;
The bread Thy mystic body be,
And cheer each languid heart.

The grace which sure salvation brings
Let us herewith receive;
Satiate the hungry with good things,
The hidden manna give.

The living Bread sent down from heaven
In us vouchsafe to be
Thy flesh for all the world is given,
And all may live by Thee.

[51] From *Hymns on the Lord's Supper*, no. 5, quoted in Rattenbury, *Eucharistic Hymns*, 162.

Now, Lord, on us Thy flesh bestow,
And let us drink Thy blood,
Till all our souls are fill'd below
With all the life of God.[52]

Summary of the Wesleyan Experience

Both in the United States and in England Wesley's followers, now called Methodists, were moving toward separation from Anglicanism. In America they were very obviously distinct from the Episcopal Church and had their own clergy, who had received ordination from John Wesley. Dr. Campbell points out that to his death, John denied that he had separated from the Church of England; yet he had approved moves that would make his society a denomination by the end of 1780. In 1784, he ordained two lay preachers as elders in North America and consecrated Dr. Thomas Coke, an Anglican priest, to serve as General Superintendent among the North American Methodists. To anyone who knows Greek, the title superintendent indicates a bishop, or overseer. By the end of the decade Wesley had ordained elders for Scotland, Wales, and England. In 1795, four years after his death, the Wesleyan Conference in Great Britain adopted a denominational structure.[53]

Despite all this history and controversy and the conflicting interpretations even of what the Wesleys believed, there is no doubt that they were totally dedicated to Jesus Christ. They believed, and caused their followers to believe, that Christ lived and operated within their lives, that He was available to them, that they had confidence in Him, and that above all they had to follow His teachings down to the smallest detail. The Wesleys are outstanding in the history of Christianity as devout disciples of Christ. Their spirituality, so similar to the Counter-Reformation spirituality of the Catholic saints on the Continent, should be recognized as a bridge between Catholics and Protestants and in fact even as a unifying example for all Christians who seek to say with St. Paul, "I live, no longer I, but it is Christ who lives in me" (Gal 2:20).

[52] Ibid., no. 30, quoted in Rattenbury, 168–69.
[53] Campbell, *Religion of the Heart*, 128.

17 Devotion to Christ in the East

Pope John Paul II began the new millennium by visiting centers of Eastern Christianity, especially Orthodox churches in Greece and Ukraine. This puzzled many, as did his expressed hope of visiting Russia. Sometimes he went as an unwelcome guest, making many Catholics wince and many Orthodox Christians annoyed. Even his apostolic letter *Orientale Lumen* of 1995, designed to make Western Christians aware of the rich heritage of the Christian East, seemed to have little impact on a relationship that has been stormy for a thousand years. Pope John Paul's apology for the injustices on the part of Catholics in the past, especially the sack of Constantinople in 1204, startled everyone and made it clear to all but the most prejudiced that his unilateral action came from a heartfelt desire for a reunion of Christianity. He especially sought a relationship between the five traditional patriarchates: Rome, Alexandria, Antioch, Constantinople, and Jerusalem, as well as Athens and Moscow, and the other Eastern Orthodox and apostolic churches.

Many Western Christians do not realize that a millennium-long controversy and history of misunderstanding, hostility, and mutual excommunication lay behind the reluctance of some Eastern Orthodox to welcome the Bishop of Rome.

Pope Benedict XVI also made a historic visit to Turkey in 2006, during which he met with Ecumenical Patriarch Bartholomew. Such visits are not meant to resolve theological differences but to establish an atmosphere of mutual respect and understanding, in which the Holy Spirit can operate and influence human freedom.

Even those Western Christians who admire the Eastern liturgy and icons and have devotion to Orthodox saints often have little appreciation of how historical forces in the East and West led to the development of different theologies of the Church, along with many subtle distinctions. For whole centuries these two worlds were barely aware of each other. When they did interact, it was often under pressure of political, economic, or military need, as happened during the Turkish and Mongol invasions.

But as Fr. Alexander Schmemann, an eminent Orthodox scholar, has noted, "[T]he twentieth century may be called the century of the discovery of the Christian East by the Christian West."[1] His outline of the historical causes of the Great Schism of 1054 and the reunion and new breaks after that is written from an Orthodox perspective but with real objectivity. He points out that as early as the Councils of Ephesus and Chalcedon in the fifth century, the Greek bishops remained silent when, through delegates, the bishops of Rome declared that they had unique authority to judge the actions of other bishops. He quotes an unidentified Russian historian as saying, "The Easterners not only did not object in time to the growing mystique of papal dogmas, they not only silently signed the papal formulations, but they themselves, by their appeals to Rome, heedless of the juridical implications, supported the sincere illusions of the Romans that the Greeks, too, shared the Western concept of the papacy."[2]

Fr. Schmemann gives accounts of situations where principal Eastern patriarchs even of Constantinople accepted the claims of the papacy. Bishop Kallistos (Timothy) Ware in his book *The Orthodox Church* summarizes the causes leading to the Great Schism. He recounts the complex historical events that have made the Catholic and Orthodox churches so different despite the fact that they share the same sacraments (called mysteries in Eastern terminology) and that dogmatically they agree on so much, as indeed they must, since each grew from the same apostolic tradition. We mention this complex history so that readers will not make the mistake of regarding Orthodoxy as Catholicism without the Pope. Those unfamiliar with the nature and history of the Orthodox Church will perhaps realize the confusion that existed with two incidents mentioned by Bishop Kallistos (Ware). In the 1830s an Englishman in the Near East was amazed to find that the Patriarch of Constantinople had never heard of the Archbishop of Canterbury![3] Almost equally astonishing is that certain Orthodox entered into union with the Catholic Church at the Council of Brest-Litovsk (1596) at a time when uneducated people in Little Russia celebrated the fact that the Pope had joined the Orthodox Church.[4] Obviously these represent extreme misunderstandings and lack of knowledge, but they point out that often the real issues were not then or even now well understood.

Bishop Kallistos identifies the two principal matters about which Eastern and Western bishops quarreled—the papal claims and the *filioque* clause of the Nicene Creed. As is well known, the latter dispute was concerned with whether the Holy Spirit proceeds from the Father alone (Orthodox position) or from the Father and the Son (Catholic position). The bishop makes this important point: "Long before there

---

[1] Alexander Schmemann, *The Historical Road of Eastern Orthodoxy*, trans. Lydia W. Kesich (New York: Holt, Rinehart and Winston, 1963), v.

[2] Ibid., 241.

[3] Timothy Ware (Bishop Kallistos of Diokleia), *The Orthodox Church* (London: Penguin Books, 1997), 10.

[4] Ibid., 105.

was any open and formal schism between East and West the two sides had become strangers to one another."[5]

We must recall that Eastern and Western Christianity grew apart for reasons that often were not theological, although theology was eventually used to express them.[6] Perhaps the greatest problem was the difference between the Greek and Roman minds and the way in which the two looked at life and dealt with its challenges. We see this in the differences in emphases and style between East and West after the persecutions ended. Augustine was practical and realistic and yet with a mysticism of humility and charity. His Eastern contemporary, Gregory of Nyssa, was equally interested in the spiritual life, yet he was far more given to symbolism, poetry, and scriptural analogies and far less practical in his mysticism. As bishops, both labored tirelessly for their flocks. Both were spiritual writers of great originality, who left us treatises on similar subjects, although they apparently never read each other's works.

With so much in common, why were they so different? Augustine disliked the Greek language, and Gregory probably never learned Latin. As the centuries went on, the Greek mind took on the work of the dogmatic definition of the mystery of Christ at the great councils, and the Latins, including the bishops of Rome, happily went along. Yet when the crisis arose at Chalcedon (451), the Greeks did not hesitate to accept the explanation of Pope Leo the Great, in spite of the fact that ecumenical councils were often acrimonious. Matters largely continued that way, with Greeks and Latins agreeing on important things, until after the seventh ecumenical council in 787.

By then, the Turks in the East and the barbarian invasions in the West had caused the history of the two wings of Christianity to diverge. In the West, as the Dark Ages ended, the barbarian invaders, having converted and settled down, began to build the civilization that would flower into medieval Christian Europe, a civilization with little knowledge of ancient Eastern Christianity. In the East at this time Christians were forcibly converted to Islam, but Turks rarely converted to Christianity. The Christian populations who resisted, therefore, remained much the same as they had been in the postapostolic era. Thus a new genetically heterogeneous Christian population arose in the West but a traditional ancient Christian people remained in the East.

History and time have driven wedges between Eastern and Western Christianity. They include different concepts of ecclesiastical and civil government, the impact of Aristotelian thought and the development of Scholasticism with its use of logic along with transcendent mystery, the influence of the Renaissance, the development of

[5] Ibid., 52.

[6] See Fr. Nicolas Afanasiev, "Una Sancta", and Sergius Bulgakov, "By Jacob's Well", in *Tradition Alive*, ed. Michael Plekon (Lanham, Md.: Rowman and Littlefield, 2003).

the natural sciences, the rise of nationalism, the Protestant Reformation, and the Enlightenment. In the East, the life of the Church was deeply affected by the isolation caused by Muslim domination, the Bolshevik Revolution, the rise of violent atheistic materialism in Russia, and the imposition of ideas of the Western Enlightenment by governments, beginning in the eighteenth century with Peter the Great. In considering all these historical developments and their effects, we can see why the two ancient wings of Christianity perceive things differently. In these cases and many more, devout clergy and laity did their best to adjust and persevere in the faith. If we examine history, we should not be astonished that East and West are now so different, yet remain essentially so similar.

Such a history makes it is understandable that the first Slav pope should wish to enter into dialogue with the East, as it is understandable that such an overture would cause hesitancy and fear on both sides. Yet Greek and Russian Orthodox friends, clergy and laity, expressed regrets to me that Pope John Paul had not been received more warmly. On the other hand, Pope Benedict's visit with Ecumenical Patriarch Batholomew in Istanbul in 2006, which brought with it some real danger to the Holy Father, profoundly moved observers on all sides.

Anyone who wishes to review the history of Eastern and Western Christianity will find it fascinating and at times horrifying, tragic and yet filled with a mysterious presence, the presence of Jesus Christ in the worship, prayer, and especially in the hearts of those who seek to love Him.

Eastern Devotion After the Seven Councils[7]

In Chapter 5 above we left off our consideration of Christology in the East after St. Maximus the Confessor (580–662) and, later, the tapering off of the iconoclast controversy in the ninth century. We now again focus on the Christian East and its development, and so turn our attention to Constantinople and Greece, and the lands under the retreating Byzantine Empire before the conversion of the Slavs in the Balkans and what is now Russia. A word must be said about the Slavs and their conversion by SS. Cyril (d. 869) and Methodius (d. 885). Although these saints are a link between East and West and are honored by Orthodox and Catholics alike, they brought the Byzantine liturgy to the Slavic people. They were clearly supported by the Pope in their conflict with the Germanic bishops, and they, in turn, greatly honored the Pope. Cyril died in Rome, and Methodius was ordained a bishop, his jurisdiction over Moravia and Pannonia bestowed by the Pope.

[7] The Church both East and West recognizes the first seven councils, up to and including Nicaea II in 787, as ecumenical. The controversial eighth council (Constantinople IV), held in 869–870, is considered ecumenical by Western canonists but not by the Eastern Church.

The use of a language other than Hebrew, Greek, or Latin (the three languages used for the inscription on the Cross) was the source of a heresy charge brought by Germanic bishops, against Cyril and Methodius, but Popes Adrian II and John VII supported the Slavic missionaries. Eventually Old Slavonic would take its place as the liturgical language of Russia and many of the Slavic nations.[8]

While the southern areas of the Eastern Church—the Holy Land, Greece, Asia Minor (Turkey), and North Africa—were trying to cope with the incredibly rapid spread of Islam, the Byzantine Empire in its final two or three centuries gave rise to a number of remarkable spiritual and cultural movements. Many of these involved monasticism at the same time that the Celtic and Benedictine monks were preserving spirituality and human values in the West. Christian monasticism grew out of the early experiences of hermits and communities of ascetics in the eastern Mediterranean world, especially Egypt. As the life of monks and nuns flourished in East and West, however, it took on different forms. In the West, St. Benedict established a specific community and rule. From then on there was a proliferation of orders and lifestyles, ranging from hermits and cloistered nuns to teachers and medical personnel. In the East there was only one order—or, really, only one religious life—encompassing hermits, monks, and nuns, with larger monasteries having a good deal of independence and varying styles.

Mount Athos

Since the tenth century the center of Eastern monasticism has been a raggedly beautiful peninsula jutting into the Aegean Sea in northern Greece. Mount Athos, the holy mount, boasts twenty major monasteries, many smaller ones, and numerous hermit cells. At times it has been a center of scholarship, and hundreds of monks have left this hallowed spot to become bishops and patriarchs.[9]

Almost all the inhabitants, except for a few servants, are monastics, and no women are permitted in this semi-independent Greek republic. In all of Christendom, Mount Athos has no parallel. Along with giving rise to some fascinating spiritual movements, it is the great repository of liturgical and artistic treasures of Eastern Orthodoxy.

Hesychasm: To Pray Always

As we focus on Orthodox devotion to Christ, we must consider some important theological considerations and historical developments. None of these is more significant than what is called hesychasm, or the hesychast controversy. This term comes from the Greek word *hesychia*, which simply means "quietude". The Catholic Church in the West has always had an eremitical tradition, saints who were solitaries, and religious orders

---

[8] See Nicolas Zernov, *Eastern Christendom* (New York: G.P. Putnam's Sons, 1961), 91ff., for a very good historical summary.

[9] Ware, *Orthodox Church*, 42.

given to the eremitical life, like the Carthusians and the Camaldolese. The Eastern monastic tradition, however, has made the seeking of solitude a greater priority. In addition, particularly in Slavic nations, the figure of the hermit, the silent itinerant holy man, became an essential part of the religious landscape.

The word "hesychasm" has come to mean a specific form of quietude, centered on the Jesus prayer.[10] In this prayer, the words "Lord Jesus Christ, Son of God, have mercy on me, a sinner" are first repeatedly whispered in an atmosphere of silence. Then the prayer is repeated silently and more and more frequently day and night. Finally it is incorporated into the person's biorhythms, linked with the beating of the heart. Some, who are familiar only with the externals of prayer, have erroneously seen in this a yogalike practice.[11]

Bishop Kallistos succinctly identifies the misunderstandings surrounding this kind of prayer. He reminds us that all involved in authentic hesychast practice also make use of other forms of prayer—liturgical worship, Scripture reading, and the sacraments.[12] The truly Christological meaning of the prayer, he points out, is that the prayer begins with divinity, which Christ shares equally with the Father and the Holy Spirit (Lord). Then it acknowledges His humanity in the Incarnate Word (Jesus). Next it signifies God's grace in having mercy on us, and finally it acknowledges our total dependence as sinners (have mercy). It is, in fact, a tiny Christian catechism.[13]

An important aspect of this prayer is the avoidance of mental images of anything material while saying it. (Paradoxically, this is happening in the Church of the icons.) One should concentrate only on the meaning of the words. The obvious question, however, is: How does such prayer fit in with a real devotion to Jesus? We will learn the answer from the man who made this kind of prayer well known: St. Gregory Palamas.

St. Gregory Palamas (1296–1359)

Fascinating doctoral dissertations have been written on the spiritual insights of the Orthodox saint Gregory Palamas.[14] The quality and originality of his thought remain a subject for research and new appreciation. In the Gregory Palamas volume of the Classics of Western Spirituality series, Professor Pelikan writes, "The rehabilitation of Gregory Palamas in the Western Church during the twentieth century is a

[10] For an excellent introduction to the spirituality of the Jesus prayer, see Fr. Lev Gillet, *In Thy Presence* (Crestwood, N.Y.: St. Vladimir's Seminary Press, 1998).

[11] Bishop Ignatius Brianchaninov, *On the Prayer of Jesus*, trans. Fr. Lazarus (Rockport, Mass.: Element, 1993). See introduction by Alexander d'Agapeyeff, which sheds a great deal of light on the prayer.

[12] Bishop Kallistos Ware, *The Orthodox Way* (Crestwood, N.Y.: St. Vladimir's Seminary Press, 1979), 122.

[13] Ibid., 68ff.

[14] Fr. John Meyendorff's work is outstanding. Along with Fr. Alexander Schmemann, he was a leader in the impressive Orthodox-Catholic dialogue of the 1970s and 1980s.

remarkable event in the history of scholarship."[15] He goes on to cite an article by Fr. Daniel Honorius Hunter:

> Palamite doctrine on the divine nature of the light of Mt. Tabor and the visible presence of uncreated grace in the pure of heart has been an obstacle for Western theologians in accepting Palamas as a teacher of orthodoxy. On the other hand, Palamas's insistence that the whole man is engraced, body and soul, and the stress that he placed on the role of the body in prayer has been adopted in the West by recent theologians.[16]

Gregory, a young nobleman from Constantinople, had entered the Great Lavra (monastery) of St. Athanasius at Mount Athos. After about ten years, during which he practiced hesychast spirituality, Turkish raids forced the monks to leave, and he found a home in ancient Thessalonica. An ordained priest, he lived as a hermit for five days a week, reciting the Jesus prayer. On Saturday and Sunday he participated in the liturgy and the monastic community life. Eventually he returned to Mount Athos, serving as abbot for a year.[17]

The controversy that marked Gregory's life can be traced to the early origins of the Jesus prayer and the fourth-century writer Pseudo-Macarius. He had borrowed ideas from Evagrius Ponticus (345–399), who was criticized for errors borrowed ultimately from the third-century ecclesiastical writer Origen. Despite Origen's many contributions to Christian thought, he was enmeshed in some of the more esoteric ideas of Neoplatonism. Origen and Evagrius saw the human mind "as naturally divine and as having originally existed without matter, so that the present material world is nothing but a consequence of the Fall".[18] Barlaam the Calabrian, another representative of Eastern theology, attacked Gregory, claiming that his use of Neoplatonic ideas and Macarius led to a heresy called Messalianism. The Messalians followed a form of Manicheism, a heresy revived as Albigensianism in the West shortly before the time Gregory wrote. A whiff of anything Albigensian, however undeserved, was enough to cause Gregory Palamas to be written off in the Western Church.

The Dominicans, who led the struggle against Albigensianism in the thirteenth century, were trying to cope a century later with the writings of their own confrere, the brilliant and deeply mystical but esoteric Meister Eckhart, who spoke in strange terms about union with God. Gregory Palamas, Eckhart's close contemporary, was teaching that by a special grace a very advanced spiritual soul could come into the divine light that enveloped Christ and the apostles on Mount Tabor. Macarius, a favorite of John Wesley, was so important for Gregory and the foundation of

[15] Preface, *Gregory Palamas*, ed. John Meyendorff (New York: Paulist Press, 1983), xi.

[16] *New Catholic Encyclopedia* (New York: McGraw-Hill, 1967), 10:872–74, s.v. "Palamas, Gregory", cited in ibid., xii.

[17] Meyendorff, introduction to *Gregory Palamas*, 5–6.

[18] Ibid., 2.

his Christocentric mysticism that it may be helpful to have the following summary.

> In the late fourth century, this evolution of hesychast spirituality in the direction of Christocentrism was greatly influenced by the writings of an unknown author who used the pseudonym St. Macarius the Great. The writings of Ps. Macarius, very often quoted by Palamas, are rather different from the Neoplatonic intellectualism of Evagrius: The center of human consciousness and of divine presence in man is seen as occurring not in the "mind", but in the "heart". On this point Macarius uses a vocabulary closer to the language of the Psalms (and of Jewish anthropology in general) than of Neoplatonism. In Christianity, one tastes the grace of God, he writes, and sees that the Lord is sweet (Ps. 34:9). This tasting is the dynamic power of the Spirit manifesting itself in full certitude in the heart. The sons of light, ministers of the New Covenant in the Holy Spirit, have nothing to learn from men; they are "taught by God" (Isa. 54:13; Jn. 6:45). Grace itself engraves the laws of the Spirit on their hearts. . . . In fact, "the heart is master and King of the whole bodily organism, and when grace takes possession of the pasture-land of the heart, it rules over all its members and all its thoughts; for it is in the heart that the mind dwells, and there dwell all the soul's thoughts; it finds all its goods in the heart. That is why grace penetrates all the members of the body." [19]

We see in this beautiful writing the danger of subjectivism and Gnosticism. The dogmatic structure of the Orthodox Church and of the ancient united Church, however, were strong enough to keep this Macarian teaching from becoming purely subjective and protect it from Gnostic influences. Had there been no central Church authority or strong adherence to tradition, this trend of thought could have threatened the unity of religious congregations. This indeed would occur when the religion of the heart became predominant, not in the East but in the West, after the Reformation, affecting Protestants and Catholics alike.

Deification in Christ

The idea of deification (*theosis*) of the Christian by the grace of Christ was another important theme in early Christian spirituality. God had become man so that men might become God, a statement of St. Augustine that has often been repeated in East and West.[20] Obviously the early Church Fathers were not pantheists, although the term "deification" may strike Protestant Christians as pantheistic or perhaps as leading to a loss of the sense of original sin. At the very least they will think it is Pelagian. Nevertheless, this idea has solid patristic foundations. Bishop Kallistos cites St. Athanasius: "He is outside all things

[19] Ibid., 3. Quotation from Macarius' *Hom.* 15, 20, in *Patrologia Græca* (hereinafter PG), 34, col. 589AB.

[20] St. Augustine, Sermon 13 de temp.

according to His essence, but He is in all things through His acts of power."[21] St. Basil teaches: "We know the essence through the energy. No one has ever seen the essence of God, but we believe in the essence because we experience the energy."[22]

To avoid pantheism, two points of the Fathers must be kept in mind. First, we do not know God in His essence but in His actions and self-manifestation. Second, the energy of God is not something distinct from Himself; it is not a part of God, but rather the energy signifies God in His action. For a discussion of this truth from a more Western, even Thomistic, point of view one might read Matthias Scheeben's *The Glories of Divine Grace*[23] or Dom Columba Marmion's *Christ, the Life of the Soul*.[24]

These ideas coming from the Church Fathers were held more widely than people realize today. Bishop Kallistos makes a thesaurus of them and includes quotations mostly from the post-Nicaean Fathers of the East.[25] The ideas relating to deification, woven together by Gregory Palamas, focused on Christ and the process of salvation and sanctification through His grace. He made it clear that the Jesus prayer was not simply a use of the name of our Lord as a rhythmic chant, like a Hindu mantra. Rather it was an expression of the process of sanctification that goes on in the Christian soul. It is not a union in person, a hypostatic union like that of the divine and human natures in the person of the Incarnate Word, but a union according to the operation of the energies of God.[26]

A brief consideration of the analogy of light and darkness might be helpful to understand what Palamas was attempting to teach. Bishop Kallistos writes:

> The primary basis for "light" language is the sentence of St. John, "God is light, and in Him is no darkness at all" (1 John 1:5). God is revealed as light above all at the Transfiguration of Christ on Mount Tabor, when "his face shone as the sun, and his raiment was white as the light" (Matt. 17:2). This divine light, seen by the three disciples on the mountain—seen also by many of the saints during prayer—is nothing else than the uncreated energies of God. The light of Tabor, that is to say, is neither a physical and created light, nor yet a purely metaphorical "light of the intellect". Although nonmaterial, it is nevertheless an objectively existent reality. Being divine, the uncreated energies surpass all our human powers of description.[27]

[21] Ware, *Orthodox Way*, 22.
[22] Ibid.
[23] Tan Books, 2001.
[24] For a fuller discussion of Abbot Marmion and his works, see Chapter 26.
[25] Ware, *Orthodox Way*, 23ff.
[26] Ibid., 125.
[27] Ibid., 127.

Bishop Kallistos then makes a startling point, which almost no one in the West ever thinks about. "Although non-physical, the divine light can be seen by a man through his physical eyes, provided that his senses have been transformed by divine grace. His eyes do not behold the light by the natural powers of perception, but through the power of the Holy Spirit acting within him."[28]

Bishop Kallistos uses the following quotation from *The Homilies of Saint Macarius* about the divine light.

> Just as the Lord's body was glorified, when he went up the mountain and was transfigured into the glory of God and into infinite light, so the saints' bodies also are glorified and shine as lightning.... "The glory which thou hast given to me I have given to them" (John 17:22): just as many lamps are lit from one flame, so the bodies of the saints, being members of Christ, must needs be what Christ is, and nothing else.... Our human nature is transformed into the power of God, and it is kindled into fire and light.[29]

While we cannot go into the various defenses Palamas made against Barlaam and others who attacked the hesychast movement, we can meditate on the following quotation of St. Gregory, which represents one of the highest expressions of Christian mysticism. The reference to the Eucharist (His Body) is essential and should be seen in the light of Eucharistic teachings of Western Christians as different as Aquinas and Wesley, as St. Francis and Luther.

> Since the Son of God, in his incomparable love for man, did not only unite His divine Hypostasis with our nature, by clothing Himself in a living body and a soul gifted with intelligence ... but also united himself ... with the human hypostases themselves, in mingling himself with each of the faithful by communion with his Holy Body, and since he becomes one single body with us (cf. Eph. 3:6), and makes us a temple of the undivided Divinity, for in the very body of Christ dwelleth the fulness of the Godhead bodily (Col. 2:9), how should he not illuminate those who commune worthily with the divine ray of His Body which is within us, lightening their souls, as He illumined the very bodies of the disciples on Mount Tabor? For, on the day of the Transfiguration, that Body, source of the light of grace, was not yet united with our bodies; it illuminated from outside those who worthily approached it, and sent the illumination into the soul by the intermediary of the physical eyes; but now, since it is mingled with us and exists in us, it illuminates the soul from within.[30]

---

[28] Ibid.

[29] Quoted by Ware, *Orthodox Way*, 127. The man called St. Macarius of Alexandria was a fourth-century monk. The works originally attributed to him are now thought not to be his, but written somewhat after his time, possibly in Syria.

[30] Gregory Palamas, *Triads*, I, 3, 38, quoted by Meyendorff, in *Gregory Palamas*, 19.

Fr. Meyendorff sums up the ideas of communion with Christ.

> The real communion, the fellowship and—one can almost say—the familiarity with the "One Who is" is, for Palamas, the very content of the Christian experience, made possible because the One Who is became man. It is this familiarity with and immediate communion with God that was at stake, according to Palamas, in his debate with Barlaam. . . . "Did He not deign to make His dwelling in man", asks Palamas, "to appear to him and speak to him without intermediary, so that man should be not only pious, but sanctified and purified in advance in soul and body by keeping the divine commandments, and so be transformed into a vehicle worthy to receive the all-powerful Spirit?"
>
> So, communion with God in Christ is real and immediate. It is not pantheistic absorption into the Divine, however: Man, being "in God", or rather "in Christ", preserves his full humanity, his freedom (he is required to "keep the commandments"), and he participates in a process that knows no end, because God, in His transcendent essence, is always "above" any given experience of Him.[31]

The Jesus prayer, or simply a concentration on the divine presence or indwelling of Christ in the soul (an accepted practice in Western spirituality) may not be the spiritual road for everyone, even in the Orthodox tradition. But these ideas are a very sublime expression of devotion to Christ. Orthodox writers sometimes observe that this high level of Christocentric devotion is lacking in the West. It is my impression that it is there but in different ways. It is almost impossible to read a serious book about the Jesus prayer and not find reference to *The Unseen Warfare*, an edition by Nicodemus of the Holy Mountain of the *Spiritual Combat* by the Italian Theatine priest Lorenzo Scupoli.

Beyond that, it is my observation that devout souls with a reasonably high level of spirituality are aware of Christ's presence in them in a variety of subtle ways. Not only have I known older Catholic religious and laypeople who are constantly aware of His presence but I have also often seen the same realization in humble African Americans who have lived their lives in the light of the Gospel. I think it is best to see the Jesus prayer and the hesychast spirituality as a uniquely Orthodox expression of what is a wider Christian experience. Obviously, if we take Gregory Palamas seriously, we can understand what he is trying to say.

St. Augustine, in his arguments with the Pelagians, stressed the complex effects of original sin, relying on St. Paul's writings and his own tough North African point of view. He is often blamed for not having a hesychast-type spirituality, or at least an illuminated sense of spirituality. I am ready to admit that his approach to spirituality is different, more down to earth and realistic. Augustine was never a hermit;

[31] Meyendorff, *Gregory Palamas*, 21–22.

Gregory was. Once Gregory became a diocesan bishop with pastoral responsibilities, he apparently did not speak again of these controversial issues. Augustine is the grandfather of the friars, who live among the people, not of the monks and hermits. The friars have their holy mountains too. The description of the stigmatization of St. Francis, an Augustinian Christian if there ever was one, would make complete sense to Gregory Palamas, divine light and all. The following quotation from St. Augustine may surprise Eastern Christians who find him too pessimistic. It may also cause Western Christians to realize that Gregory Palamas "deserves attention as something more than a museum piece from Mount Athos".[32]

> Late have I loved Thee, O beauty so ancient and so new; late have I loved Thee! For behold Thou wert within me, and I outside; and I sought Thee outside and in my unloveliness fell upon those lovely things that Thou hast made. Thou wert with me and I was not with Thee. I was kept from Thee by those things, yet had they not been in Thee, they would not have been at all. Thou didst call and cry to me and break open my deafness: and Thou didst send forth Thy beams and shine upon me and chase away my blindness: Thou didst breathe fragrance upon me, and I drew in my breath and do now pant for Thee: I tasted Thee, and now hunger and thirst for Thee: Thou didst touch me, and I have burned for Thy peace.[33]

The De Sales of the East—Nicolas Cabasilas (ca. 1322–ca. 1390)

Were Nicolas Cabasilas better known, I might legitimately have called St. Francis de Sales "the Cabasilas of the West". Indeed this remarkable man, only now becoming known in the Orthodox world and effectively introduced to the West in 1995 by Cardinal Schönborn (see Chapter 5 above) in the *Catechism of the Catholic Church*, preceded the Bishop of Geneva by two hundred years. Why do I compare them? Because they opened up the richest vein of Christian spirituality and most beautiful and fervent love for Christ to multitudes of Christians who were not monks, nuns, hermits, or members of the clergy or religious institutes. It is paradoxical that Cabasilas, a disciple and defender of Gregory Palamas, should bring Orthodox spirituality down to earth. But he did.

So little is known about this uncanonized spiritual writer that it is still debated whether he ended his days as a monk and a priest.[34] He has been confused with his uncle, Nilus Cabasilas, who succeeded Gregory Palamas in 1351 as Archbishop of Thessalonica. Nicholas entered the imperial service as a young man and retired from public life only when his friend, the emperor John VI Cantacuzenus, was

[32] Pelikan in preface to *Gregory Palamas*, xii.

[33] Augustine, *Confessions*, trans. F.J. Sheed (New York: Sheed and Ward, 1965), bk. 10, chap. 27, p. 236.

[34] It is worth mentioning that Bishop Kallistos (*Orthodox Way*) refers to him as St. Nicholas.

deposed in 1354. From then on Cabasilas wrote with a beauty and originality that is possible only in the deeply spiritual. He became a monk at Manganon monastery, near Constantinople, and although the date of his death is unknown, he seems to have lived beyond the fall of Thessalonica to the Turks in 1387.[35]

The relationship between the mystical theology of Gregory Palamas and Cabasilas is fascinating. While the hesychast controversy was still raging, Nicholas wrote a treatise against Gregorius, an opponent of his bishop. Yet he makes no references in his own spiritual writings to Palamas' distinctions between God's essence and energy. He makes no appeal for the stark discipline of the Jesus prayer, the essence of hesychasm.

Did Cabasilas reject Gregory? No. Once Gregory left the holy mountain to become a bishop he never put his own controversial mystical teachings into his sermons at all.[36] Furthermore, the Athonite monks were hostile to secular knowledge, cutting themselves off from the world. On the other hand, Cabasilas espoused a pure, holy Christian humanism, one that Fénelon, de Sales, and the devout humanists of the West would have applauded. "By his nature, his will and his mind, man is drawn to Christ.... Christ is the centre of all human aspirations and becomes the delight of the mind. That any thought or loving aspiration be set on aught but him is to turn from the one thing necessary, is to betray the original likeness impressed on our nature."[37]

Cabasilas profoundly emphasized a Christocentric sacramentalism. This was no contradiction of Palamas, who spent his weekends at a monastery participating in the liturgy and the Office. However, Cabasilas changed the focus from silence and the exercise of the Jesus prayer to the importance of participation in the Eucharistic sacrifice and the frequent reception of Holy Communion. Fr. Bobrinskoy sums up the difference between Cabasilas and Palamas well:

> The mysticism of hesychasm, the interior recollection and the drawing of the mind into the heart, presupposes a particular kind of vocation, intelligible to those who have been called to follow it, a life of asceticism, renunciation of the world and discipline of the will in monastic solitude, and in the spirit of obedience. On the contrary, the sacramental vision, the participation in the universal mysteries of the Church, is the royal way open to all and obligatory not only for ascetics but for all Christian people.[38]

---

[35] Ibid., 9–10.

[36] Ibid., 12.

[37] Nicolas Cabasilas, *The Life in Christ*, bk. 6, cited by Bobrinskoy in his introduction to *The Life in Christ*, trans. Carmino J. Catanzaro (Crestwood, N.Y.: St. Vladimir's Seminary Press, 1998), 19.

[38] Bobrinskoy, op. cit., 19.

Cabasilas refers to his spiritual teaching as the law of love, and its contents remind us very much of the *Treatise on the Love of God* by St. Francis de Sales. He wrote:

> This law demands no arduous nor afflicting work, nor loss of money; it does not involve shame, nor any dishonor, nor anything worse; it puts no obstacle in the pursuit of any art or profession. The general keeps the power to command, the laborer can work the ground, the artisan can carry on with his occupation. There is no reason to retire into solitude, to eat unusual food, to be inadequately clothed, or endanger one's health, or to resort to any other special endeavor; it suffices to give oneself wholly to meditation and to remain always within oneself without depriving the world of one's talents.[39]

The Holy Name and the Sacred Heart of Christ in the Orthodox Church

St. Gregory Palamas taught that the Christian spiritual life should be centered not only on the Jesus prayer and ascetical practices but also on the sacraments. "Come, said Christ, eat of my flesh and drink of my blood . . . not only that you may be made after God's image, but that you may become kings and gods, eternal and heavenly, by putting on me, thy King and God."[40] Cabasilas teaches the same thing: "God comes down to earth and in so doing ennobles man. He becomes man and he deifies man. . . . For as it was impossible for us to rise up to him and to share in his heavenly treasures, so he comes down to us to share our life. . . . He gives himself to us, for by communicating of his body and blood we receive God into ourselves."[41]

However, Cabasilas goes beyond his teacher and shows his originality by his doctrine of the Sacred Heart of Christ. In East and West, the heart, signifying the will and desire and even charity, has been seen as the place from which the most intimate and profound desires arise. The whole Augustinian and Franciscan tradition agree with the Orthodox spiritual teachers as early as the *Homilies of Saint Macarius* in seeing the heart as the center of our being. They also teach the "primacy of love". Cabasilas' teaching may not strike older Catholics as original until they recall that he lived in the fourteenth century, long before St. Margaret Mary.

The true originality of Nicholas Cabasilas was to introduce the traditional theme of the heart into his exposition of sacramental spirituality in that Christocentric perspective which was so dear to him. The first mention that Cabasilas makes of the image of the heart is in connection with the theme of frequent communion.

> It is surely through this blessed Heart that the virtue which flows from the holy table brings forth in us the true life. . . . The Bread of

[39] From *The Life in Christ*, quoted in ibid., 22.

[40] Gregory Palamas, Homily 56, quoted by Bobrinskoy, in introduction to *Life in Christ*, 24.

[41] From *Life in Christ*, quoted by Bobrinskoy, in introduction, 24.

> Life much more than any other rite transforms us into the body of Christ. For as it is by the head and the heart that the members live, 'so he that eats of me even he shall live by me' (Jn. 6:58).... In conformity with what is the usual role of the head and heart we are changed and live, even as Christ himself lives.... As he is Life, he breathes it into us through his own Spirit. He communicates life to us even as the heart and the head to the members of the body.[42]

He goes on to state that the Heart of Christ is the source of grace in the Eucharist. "It is his own blood that he pours into the heart of communicants, so that his own life may be born in us.... This is how he exercised his royalty in purity and truth over men ... for he is more gracious to us than a friend, more impartial than a sovereign, more gentle than a father, closer to us than our own self, more vital to us than our own heart." [43]

It is unfortunate that Bobrinskoy, one of the rediscoverers of Cabasilas, makes a derogatory comparison between his teachings and the devotion to the Sacred Heart in the Catholic Church, which he sees as "individual and pietistic".[44] He obviously made his remarks based on popular images and customs and was unaware of the teachings on the Sacred Heart of Jesus, which present this devotion as extending to the obligation of restoring justice in the social order. Two twentieth-century popes have written on this devotion to the Sacred Heart of Jesus as repairing the social order and our acts of reparation being obligatory in this sense.[45] Cabasilas would have applauded, although his thinking about the responsibility for other people was not expressed in the same modern terms.

> It is Christ himself who invites us to this sacred banquet, who is our companion in this fight.... By the Eucharist he dwells within us and helps us to gain the prize.... When there is need for courage and constancy to gain the victory, Jesus Christ takes it upon himself to provide us with all that we need through the grace of baptism and chrismation.[46]

It is interesting that for all his interest in hesychasm, Cabasilas departs again from one of the basic principles of that movement. He encourages the use of imagination and mental images to recall with gratitude the various incidents in our Savior's life, especially His Passion. Myrrha Lot-Borodine sums this up well by saying, "The Byzantine Master

[42] Bobrinskoy, introduction to *Life in Christ*, 26.

[43] Ibid., 27.

[44] It is worth noting that there is a movement in the Ukrainian and Ruthenian Catholic churches to begin to honor the Heart of Christ as the *Philanthropos*, or lover of mankind.

[45] See the encyclicals *Miserentissimus Redemptor* (1928) of Pope Pius XI and *Haurietis Aquas* (1956) of Pope Pius XII.

[46] From *The Life in Christ*, quoted by Bobrinskoy, 29.

urges us with an authority and verve, rare if not unique in the Christian East, to use our imagination to reconstruct and to see, as though we had been present, the living and inspiring realities which are incarnate in the Person of the Savior."[47]

Finally—and this is astounding to Roman Catholics—Cabasilas encourages the veneration and invocation of the Holy Name of Jesus, but not in the context of the Jesus prayer. Indeed, he is returning to the basic idea of the Jesus prayer, but he does so without requiring the strict regimen of the hesychasts. In the light of Christ, he writes: "We invoke the Name of God with our lips and also in our desires and thoughts in order that in everything we have done amiss we may apply the only health-giving remedy: for there is no other Name under heaven whereby we may be saved (Acts 4:12)."[48]

Before we leave the topic of devotion to the Heart and Holy Name of Jesus taught by Cabasilas, we should recall that far away in Siena the Franciscan reformer St. Bernardine was a boy of ten at the time of Nicholas' death. In a few decades he would be a great preacher of devotion to the Holy Name of Jesus as a means of reforming the Church. The themes of love of Christ, of union with His Sacred Heart, of His indwelling by grace in the soul and welcomed by love will become the basic formulas of Counter-Reformation piety. Did these two worlds, so distant from each other and divided by schism, affect each other even in the fourteenth and fifteenth centuries? This is a great topic for research.

A Final Look at Cabasilas

I cannot leave this almost unknown spiritual giant without one more consideration, namely, his idea of personal friendship with Jesus. In a way that would have thrilled SS. Francis and Catherine of Siena, Cabasilas sees Christ's love for us magnificently as the central mystery of reality, beyond creation itself—the incredible, incomprehensible fact that through Christ we learn of God's love for the inconsistent and sinful members of our fallen race.

The following glorious passage expresses theological truths with an incredible freshness, giving them the glowing reality that caused St. Francis to call out, "Love is not loved". Like St. John of the Cross, Cabasilas compares Christ to a lover.

> Just as human affection, when it abounds, overpowers those who love and causes them to be beside themselves, so God's love for men emptied God (Phil. 2:7). He does not stay in His own place and call the slave, He seeks him in person by coming down to him. He who is rich reaches the pauper's hovel, and He displays His love by approaching in person. He seeks love in return and does not withdraw when

[47] M. Lot-Borodine, *Un maître de la spiritualité byzantine: Nicolas Cabasilas* (Paris: Éditions de l'Orante, 1958), 130, quoted by Bobrinskoy, 31.

[48] From *Life in Christ*, quoted by Bobrinskoy, 32.

He is treated with disdain. He is not angry over ill treatment, but even when He has been repulsed, He sits by the door (Rev. 3:20) and does everything to show us that He loves, even enduring suffering and death to prove it.

Two things reveal him who loves and cause him to prevail—the one, that he in every possible way does good to the object of his love; the other, that he is willing, if need be, to endure terrible things for him and suffer pain. Of the two the latter would seem to be a far greater proof of friendship than the former. Yet it was not possible for God since He is incapable of suffering harm. Since He loves man it was possible for Him to confer benefits on him, yet it was not possible at all for the divine nature to suffer blows. While His affection was exceeding great, yet the sign by which He might make it plain was not available.

It was necessary, then, that the greatness of His love should not remain hidden, but that He should give the proof of the greatest love and by loving display the utmost measure of love. So He devised this self-emptying and carried it out, and made the instrument [that is, Christ's human nature] by which He might be able to endure terrible things and to suffer pain. When He had thus proved by the things which He endured that He indeed loves exceedingly, He turned man, who had fled from the Good One because he had believed himself to be the object of hate, towards Himself.[49]

Cabasilas makes a point that as far as I know is totally original. I do not recall ever reading this particular motive for returning love to Christ in any other writer.

This is the most astounding thing of all. Not only did He endure the most terrible pains and die from His wounds, but also, after He came to life and raised up His body from corruption, He still retained those wounds. He bears the scars upon His body and with them appears to the eyes of the angels; He regards them as an ornament and rejoices to show how He suffered terrible things.... He saw fit to cherish them because of His affection for man, because by means of them He found him who was lost, and by being wounded, he laid hold on him whom He loved. How else would it have been fitting for an immortal body to retain the traces of wounds which art and nature have sometimes eliminated even in mortal and corruptible bodies? As it appears, He had the desire to suffer pain for us many times over.[50]

This remarkable passage reveals a true Christian mystic. In Chapter 14 above a gentle mystic nun, Margaret Mary Alacoque, told us that the thorn-crowned and wounded Heart of Christ burned like a

[49] *Life of Christ,* bk. 6, quoted by Bobrinskoy, 162–63.

[50] Ibid., 163–64.

furnace of love for human beings. We have seen Wesley the Anglican and Johann Arndt the Lutheran rejoice gratefully in the wounds of Christ as signs of His supreme love for souls. Cabasilas demonstrates as well as anyone can that profound devotion to Jesus Christ exists in all Christian traditions and that in East and West we find those who are drawn to holiness by the same spiritual realities which manifest again and again that God so loved the world that He gave His only Son.

Getting to Know Russian Spirituality

In 1453 the army of Mohammed II sacked Constantinople, and the ancient Byzantine civilization went into eclipse. The emperor, patriarch, and papal legate perished, but the Greek Church survived. The sultans now appointed patriarchs and bishops, who kept the Christian faith alive despite centuries of Muslim domination—an atmosphere not conducive to producing great spiritual writers. From 1453 to the establishment of the Greek state in the twentieth century, the Greek people, guided by their bishops, clung to their spiritual identity. All this made it inevitable that the focus of Eastern Christian life and spirituality turned to the Slavic nations, especially to Russia and its distinct but not contradictory devotion to Christ, which evolved in ways that are attractive yet often puzzling to Christians of the West.

The Roots of Holy Russia

The conversion of the Slavs began when the two brothers SS. Cyril and Methodius were commissioned by Pope Adrian II and, in 860, given the papal blessing to translate the liturgy into Old Slavonic.[51] They introduced the Byzantine liturgy into Moravia and to the western Slavs.

A hundred years later St. Vladimir (d. 1015), prince of Kiev, and his grandmother St. Olga organized with great perseverance the conversion of the Slavic tribes and people farther east. These two saints were penitents who openly admitted their sins—Vladimir, who owned up to having lived a dissolute life, and Olga to being rather despotic. The idea of the penitential saint would become an integral part of the Russian spiritual motif. So would suffering and martyrdom, accompanied by resignation and humility. This was at least partially because Vladimir's two sons, SS. Boris and Gleb, were murdered by agents of their elder brother. The young men were not eager to die, but when their appeals for mercy went unheard, they humbly submitted to suffering and death after the example of Christ. They are known in Russia as the "Passion-bearers".

In the nineteenth century, a movement celebrating Russian identity filled Russia with poets and writers called Slavophiles, who fought on two fronts. On one hand, they opposed the nihilists and anarchists who promoted atheism; on the other hand, they disputed the

[51] Ware, *Orthodox Church*, 75.

Westernizers, who attempted to introduce into Russia the ideas of Western Europe. The champion of the Westernizers was Peter the Great (1672–1725). The Slavophiles, however, despised him, regarding him as a heavy-handed Westernizer of the Enlightenment era. It often puzzles Western Christians why the papacy and the Catholic Church are lumped together in the Slavophile mind with rationalism and forms of Enlightenment that were in fact deeply anti-Catholic and opposed to theism in general. Although nihilism in its Bolshevik form has gone into eclipse in the past two decades, Slavophile ideas are still alive. Western Christians, especially Catholics used to decades of ecumenism, were puzzled and even offended by the negative reaction to Pope John Paul's attempts to open dialogue with the Russian Orthodox Church. The lasting effects of Slavophile thought are at least part of the explanation. Msgr. Romano Guardini and many other Dostoievsky fans have had to cope with these anti-Catholic sentiments in the writings of their favorite author, who was deeply anti-Catholic and anti-Western, noticeably in his parable of the Grand Inquisitor.[52]

From the early Russian Christian experience the Slavophiles developed a devotion to the humility of Christ that was called by some a kenotic feature, that is, an emphasis on the emptying, or *kenosis*, of Christ related to St. Paul's words that He "emptied himself, taking the form of a servant, being born in the likeness of men" (Phil 2:7). The distinguished twentieth-century Russian writer Nadejda Gorodetzky has examined the "acceptance of humiliation as a national ideal" by the Slavophiles.[53] In line with this theology Dostoievsky wrote:

> I affirm that our ("people") peasants were already enlightened a long time ago, by accepting Christ and His teaching.... The man of the people knows everything, though he would not pass an examination in the Catechism. He learned in the Churches where during centuries he heard prayers and songs which are better than any sermons ... and he knows by heart "O Lord and Master of my life": all the essence of Christianity is contained in this prayer. But his chief school of Christianity was the ages of endless suffering he endured in the course of history when, abandoned by all, oppressed by all, working for all, he remained all alone with Christ, the Comforter, whom he received then in his soul and who saved this soul from despair.[54]

The prayer that Dostoievsky refers to comes from St. Ephraem of Syria long before the novelist's time and is used in the Byzantine liturgy during Lent. Although it is not obvious in the text, the prayer is

[52] It is interesting and encouraging to note that Pope Benedict XVI's friendly gestures are greeted with more enthusiasm in Russia and in the whole of Eastern Christianity.

[53] Nadejda Gorodetzky, *The Humiliated Christ in Modern Russian Thought* (London: SPCK, 1938).

[54] Dostoievsky, Speech on Pushkin, quoted in ibid., 8.

directed to Christ: "O Lord and Master of my life, give me not a spirit of sloth, of despondency, of lust or of vain talking; but bestow on me, Thy servant, the spirit of chastity, of humility, of patience and love. Yea, O Lord and King, grant to me to see my own errors and not to judge my brother, for blessed art Thou unto ages of ages."[55]

The Slavophiles emphasized the humility of Christ but also tended to idealize the past, seeing in the Russian Church the innocent victim of oppression by a hostile people: the Tartars. It is easy for a persecuted people to see themselves without faults. This idealized view can be seen in the writings of A. S. Khomyakov. "There is no stain of conquest on our early history. Blood and enmity did not serve as the foundation of the Russian state. . . . The Church, having limited the field of her activity, never lost the purity of her inward life and did not preach to her children injustice and violence."[56]

Among the most eloquent Slavophiles was Vladimir Soloviev, who, even though he became a Catholic, never lost his dedication to the ideal of the Russian people and to the hope that ecumenism would lead to reunion. He writes: "[T]he lofty power which the Russian nation has to reveal to humanity is a power not of this world, and exterior wealth or order in relation to it have no value whatever. . . . It is a religious vocation."[57]

While this early Russian emphasis on accepting humiliation in imitation of Christ is romanticized by the Slavophiles, *kenosis* is nonetheless an important, lasting element in Russian devotion to Christ. The honoring of Christ in His humility, the veneration of Christ Crucified and of His wounds, and the call to imitate Him—all had many parallels in the Western Church. A century or so after this development of Russian spirituality, St. Francis and his followers represented the same emphasis in the West. The saint's devotion to Christ's Passion, his mysterious stigmata, and his celebration of patient suffering are similar to early Russian spirituality, particularly to that of the monks, especially, as we shall see, to St. Theodosius.

The Monks of the Caves

Although there were monks in Russia before St. Vladimir, the most influential element in these early days, sponsored by the Kievan royalty, was the Petcherskaya Lavra, or the Monastery of the Caves. This was founded by a monk of Mount Athos, St. Anthony (died ca. 1073), who was inspired by the great penitential asceticism of the Syrian monks, which Bouyer sees as almost inhuman.[58] Anthony began as an extreme ascetic and recluse, but he accepted around himself, perhaps reluctantly, as did St. Benedict, a community of followers. His place was

[55] St. Ephraem's prayer quoted by Gorodetzky, *Humiliated Christ*, 8.

[56] Quoted in Gorodetzky, *Humiliated Christ*, 9.

[57] Quoted in ibid., 12–13.

[58] Louis Bouyer, *Orthodox Spirituality and Protestant and Anglican Spirituality* (New York: Seabury Press, 1982), 7. Hereinafter cited as *Spirituality*.

taken by St. Theodosius (d. 1074), a much more moderate and down-to-earth person who became Russia's third canonized saint, after Boris and Gleb. Modeling himself after the monks of Constantinople, Theodosius supervised the move out of the caves and the establishment of a more monastic rule. He followed the rule of life of the monks of the studium in Constantinople (they were called Studites), and Bouyer compares their way of life to the Rule of St. Benedict. Theodosius came from a well-to-do family but gave away his clothing to the poor, fended off his mother's opposition to his monastic vocation, and even cajoled this imperious lady into becoming a nun.[59] Theodosius was also aware of the social responsibilities of Christians. Bishop Kallistos writes: "Theodosius was conscious of the social consequences of Christianity, and applied them in a radical fashion, identifying himself closely with the poor, much as St. Francis of Assisi did in the west."[60]

Other comparisons have been drawn between St. Theodosius and St. Francis, who lived a century and a half later.[61] (The parallels are more striking when we consider their devotion to Christ in His suffering and humiliation, although none of the authors seemed to notice this.) St. Theodosius was fascinated by the Holy Land, which he never saw. St. Francis is believed to have visited the holy places in Palestine, and his devotion to this land was so strong that since his day the shrines there have been cared for by his friars. Both these saints encouraged a genuine biblical spirituality, especially love of the Gospels. As Fedotov points out, Theodosius is really the founder of this evangelical ideal in monastic life, whereas St. Francis was the "fulfiller" of a movement in the West that had begun at least a century before with souls like St. Bernard and the first Cistercians.[62] St. Francis' special contribution to religious life is that he and St. Dominic began the life of the friars, religious with some monastic traditions who lived among the people. Friars as such are unknown in the Orthodox world, but monks living among the people, like Archbishop Anthony Bloom, are not.

Above all, the devotion of Theodosius and Francis was powerfully focused on the Passion, or kenosis, of Christ. Both were deeply devoted to the Eucharist, and their lives were striking examples of evangelical poverty. It is obvious from Nestor's life of St. Theodosius and Celano's life of St. Francis that Christ as a personal presence was very real to both. I doubt that Francis ever heard of Theodosius, but it is not difficult to imagine them embracing in friendship, like the painting showing the Poverello and St. Dominic embracing. That embrace is meant to express a common ideal, a shared devotion and goal of life. There are things about Theodosius that remind us of Benedict,

[59] Ibid., 8.

[60] Ware, *Orthodox Church*, 79–80.

[61] See George P. Fedotov, *The Russian Religious Mind* (Cambridge, Mass.: Harvard University Press, 1946), 1:129–30.

[62] Ibid.

Francis, and Dominic, who were dramatically devoted to personal poverty and evangelical life. Is this the common thread, the connection that binds the monk or friar—the Christian soul—namely, the desire to follow Christ and seek to imitate His earthly life, even embracing His kenosis, or emptying of self?

Bouyer points out that a "monk in Russia was not so much someone who had a vocation apart as someone who had a particularly intense vocation to fulfill the simple basic Christian requirements. This was also probably why the layman saw monastic life less as an ideal life impossible of attainment than as a positive incentive to transpose into his own conditions the aspiration to be found there at the height of its purity."[63] We see a similar phenomenon in the West with members of third orders (tertiaries), laity affiliated with the mendicant orders, like Catherine of Siena and King Louis IX of France, who wore the Franciscan habit under his royal robes and wrote letters to his son calling the young prince to a holy life.

Prince Vladimir Monomach and the Admonition

The *Admonition* of Prince Vladimir Monomach (d. 1125), calling for a simple evangelical life, could be applied at that time to all with governmental or professional responsibilities. The *Admonition* represented a whole genre of penitential literature. The spirituality of laymen often tended to be quite penitential in East and West, perhaps because these men had experienced a strong conversion after a prodigal youth. Vladimir stresses repentance and God's protection of the just even in this life, but he also bitterly weeps with Christ in His sufferings. The prince was known for weeping copiously at prayer. In his obituary it was noted: "[H]e received such a gift from God, that when he came to a church and heard the singing he instantly shed tears and thus he offered his prayers to the Lord Christ with tears."[64]

Like the tertiaries of the West, Vladimir loved the poor, and his *Admonition* reads like those of St. Francis, which have been popularized in the prayer "Lord, make me an instrument of Your peace": "First of all, do not forget the poor; but in the measure of your possibilities feed them and make presents to the orphan; give justice to the widow and do not permit the mighty to ruin any man.... Visit the sick, walk behind the dead, for we all are mortal; do not pass a man without greeting, say a kind word to him."[65]

Vladimir opposed capital punishment, as well as physical mutilation, which was accepted at that time as a punishment for criminals who were spared execution. Explaining that the psalms and the books of the prophets were Vladimir's preferred biblical reading, Fedotov gives the following summary of the prince's approach to life. "Vladimir's

---

[63] Bouyer, *Spirituality*, 14.

[64] Quoted in Fedotov, *Russian Religious Mind*, 1:251.

[65] Quoted in ibid., 255.

religious ethics moves just at the border line between the Old and New Testament. It is always illuminated by some softened rays falling from the Gospel; and in rare, sublime moments he dares see Christ, the humiliated Lord, face to face."[66]

St. Abraham and Apocalyptic Spirituality

As a distinct Russian spirituality developed, another element emerged which was similar to what was happening in Western Europe at the same time. The fascinating figure of St. Abraham of Smolensk (d. 1221), a monk and perhaps the first great preacher of Russia, reminds us of the first friar preachers in Italy and France. His spirituality was strongly centered on the Bible, popular apocalyptic writings, and the Church Fathers. As with the first Franciscan and Dominican preachers, apocalyptic themes were common in Abraham's writings, as was the figure of the suffering Christ.[67] Fedotov compares him to the Dominican Girolamo Savonarola (1452–1498). However, he is also very similar to the apocalyptic preachers called the Franciscan Spirituals, who latched on to the Eternal Gospel of Joachim of Fiore, as we saw in Chapter 8 above. In a departure from accepted custom, he offered the Eucharist every day, during which he apparently suffered himself, reminding us of the sacrificial piety of St. Padre Pio. Like the twentieth-century stigmatic friar, Abraham was loved and hated at the same time; he spent years under suspicion and was at one time forbidden to offer the Eucharist.

An artist, Abraham left startling images, one of the Last Judgment and the Second Coming. Friars in the West, especially St. Francis, were often preoccupied with the idea of Purgatory and of making amends for life's transgressions on the way to eternal bliss. Although it is not quite the same idea as the Catholic understanding of Purgatory, St. Abraham revived the notion of "tollhouses" along the way to judgment, and this was the subject of another of his icons. He borrowed themes from St. Ephraem the Syrian, as well as from the life of St. Basil the Younger with its "visions of Theodora".[68] So remarkable are the parallels between East and West at this time that we even find the same heresy in each place with different names. The revival of Manicheism, called Albigensianism or Catharism in the West, was called Bogomilism in the East. It was to combat this heresy in France and Italy that St. Dominic founded the Friars Preachers at the beginning of the thirteenth century.

In East and West the figure of the suffering Christ and its opposite—the glorious and victorious Savior and Judge—are used to bring out by contrast the pains of judgment and glory of resurrection. The description of the Last Judgment by St. Abraham is ultimately sound

[66] Ibid., 260.

[67] Ibid., 158–75.

[68] Ibid., 165–66.

theology, a warning to sinners to repent, a reminder of the last reckoning (the tollhouses), the experience of angels and devils after death, and the final great victory of the Lord in the transfigured world. Not only do we find such themes in popular preaching in Western Europe but hymns like the *Dies Irae*, written about seven decades after Abraham and Francis, led to the whole apocalyptic spirituality characterized by Savonarola.[69]

The Apocalypse Comes

Seeking to be objective, historians rarely point out that apocalyptic writings of monks and friars in the thirteenth century in East and West were quite prophetic. The Tartar sack of Kiev in 1227, only six years after the death of St. Abraham, led to the invasion and occupation of most of Russia. This led to a general collapse of political, economic, and cultural life. Although there was no similar invasion in Western Europe, the fourteenth century was one of terrible catastrophes brought about by the Black Death, political turmoil, and endless military conflicts, especially the Hundred Years' War. The Church was racked by the Great Schism of the West, and even the See of Peter was held by several antipopes, that is, by multiple contenders all claiming legitimacy.

When the apocalypse hit Russia in 1237, a century earlier than it hit the West, the Church and its faithful kept the identity of the Russian people alive. What happened in Russia was similar to the fate of the Greeks under the Turks in the fifteenth century. In modern times we saw the identity of the Polish people preserved by their faith during almost a century of military occupation and then surviving for seventy years under the Communists. The history of the Irish under England is another example of national identity preserved by religious faith. The center of Russian life moved to the principality of Moscow, and its Grand Duke inspired resistance to the Mongol hordes, who gradually lost power, especially after the battle of Kulikovo in 1380.[70] As Mongol hegemony slowly declined, the principality of Moscow and the Russian Orthodox Church began to flourish.

St. Sergius of Radonezh (ca. 1314–1392)

The symbol of the spiritual rebirth of Russia and to this day its greatest national saint was a hermit who became a monk and abbot: St. Sergius of Radonezh. His incalculable influence on Russian life can be compared only with that of St. John Chrysostom in the East. No single figure in the West has been so influential. We would have to think of the combined influences of SS. Gregory the Great, Bernard, and Francis, but even then the analogy limps. Despite his great influence, we have no writings of St. Sergius. We learn about him from his

[69] For more on this, see *Apocalyptic Spirituality*, ed. and trans. Bernard McGinn. Classics of Western Spirituality (New York: Paulist Press, 1979).

[70] See Ware, *Orthodox Church*, 82–86.

life and accomplishments. He began his religious life like the hermit St. Anthony of Egypt but moved into the great forests rather than the desert. His hermitage of the Holy Trinity, not far from Moscow, was in his lifetime the greatest religious house in Russia.[71] He kept the tradition of identity with the poor Christ, wearing the poorest clothes, like Theodosius of the Caves before him.

Having been drawn out of the eremitical life, he was not afraid to lead the dukes of Moscow in a renewal of Russian life and even political identity. He blessed Prince Dmitry Donskoi before the crucial battle of Kulikovo. Perhaps his greatest national accomplishment was to begin the colonization of the immense forests in northern Russia with monks, after the manner of St. Benedict several hundred years before. "[A] vast network of religious houses spread quickly across the whole of north Russia as far as the White Sea and the Arctic Circle."[72] But perhaps the least recognized of his accomplishments is that he brought a tradition of mystical prayer to Russian spirituality, an element that scholars say was previously missing. He translated the mystical reflection of the other world into effective action in our own.

In his beautiful evaluation of St. Sergius, Fr. Schmemann points out the most important thing about him: "the absolutism of his Christianity, the image of complete transformation of man by the Holy Spirit and his aspiration to 'life in God'".[73]

Since St. Sergius left no writings, how can we know the nature of his devotion to Christ? The startling answer is to be found in the icons he inspired, especially those of St. Andrei Rublev, one of the world's great iconographers and a monk at Holy Trinity shortly after St. Sergius' death.[74] Fr. Schmemann writes: "His 'Trinity' is a most perfect work of religious art, an actual 'meditation in color.' "[75] I recall visiting the national art gallery in Moscow to see its wonderful collection of icons. After a long wait I entered a very large room filled from floor to ceiling with the most incredible collection of icons I could imagine. A number were by Rublev, but all in the room were of a piece. In the center was Our Lady of Vladimir, before which I knelt and prayed. I realize now that in that room I met the spirit of a great saint—Sergius. He was not the artist, but he embodied the spirit radiating from those paintings.

St. Sergius resisted the entreaties of the Grand Duke Dimitri to become Archbishop of Moscow, saying: "Pardon me, my lord, from my youth I never was a wearer of gold, and in my old age all the more do I wish to live in poverty."[76]

---

[71] Ibid., 84.

[72] Ibid., 85.

[73] Schmemann, *Historical Road*, 307.

[74] Fedotov, *Russian Religious Mind* (Cambridge, Mass.: Harvard University Press, 1966), 2:365–68.

[75] Schmemann, *Historical Road*, 307.

[76] Fedotov, *Russian Religious Mind*, 2:212.

The most obvious characteristic of the Russian national saint is his humility and kenotic spirituality. As we have seen, this is a persistent theme in Russian spiritual history. A story is told that demonstrates this humble man's identification with Christ. A rather simple-minded peasant had come with others to see St. Sergius at a time when the saint had reached the summit of his fame. When the guests arrived, the holy abbot was at work in the monastery garden, and the man was asked to wait. "I came to see the prophet, and you show me a peasant" was the visitor's remark. The monks were going to throw the impudent fellow out, but Sergius "prostrated himself before him and greeted him with the true love of Christ". This account makes the point that "as the proud rejoice in honors and praises, so the humble rejoice in their dishonor and reprobation".[77]

The Monastic Controversies and Their Consequences

After St. Sergius the history of Russian spirituality records a controversy over private ownership of monasteries. The problem finds echoes in the West both in the conflicts of the Franciscan Order over corporate ownership and the position of John Wycliffe and the Lollards that the Church itself should own no property. In Russia St. Nil Sorsky (Nilus of Sora) (1433–1508) and St. Joseph of Volok (or Volokolamsk) (1439–1515), both edifying monks and men of prayer, found themselves at loggerheads over monastic ownership and, eventually, about the whole function of monasticism.[78]

At times the memory of St. Nilus (canonized only in 1903) has been invoked and liberally interpreted in order to present him as a kind of an antiestablishment bohemian, whereas St. Joseph has been shown as a knave who sold out to the establishment. This is a manipulation. Bouyer presents both Nilus and Joseph positively.[79] Nilus' disciples remind us of the early Franciscans and of the Camaldolese and Carthusian hermits, who, like them, live separately in cells around a church, an arrangement called a skete. The life of St. Nilus is as edifying as that of St. Sergius, although the former left a terrifying testament requesting that after death his body be thrown to wild beasts or, if the monks were disinclined to do this, he should be buried without a funeral. St. Joseph, on the other hand, died at the divine liturgy, in a monastery under the patronage of the nobility.

These two men, so very different, were loyal followers of Christ and left a legacy of conflict in Russian spirituality. One side identified with the poor Christ and promised the greatest personal freedom through detachment; the other side preached dedication to obedience and proper monastic order crowned by liturgical splendor. Since neither saint left

[77] Ibid., 2:211.

[78] See ibid., 2:265–84, for an excellent summary of St. Nilus. See also Bouyer, *Spirituality*, 19–32.

[79] Bouyer, *Spirituality*, 19–32.

any literary work of devotion to Christ, we record them and their emphases only because it is necessary to understand the schism that was about to divide the Russian Church. The conflict was based on lifestyle, not belief. One side favored a free-flowing observance, highly individualistic and focused on personal prayer, asceticism, and at least an aspiration for mystical experience. The other side saw the greatest virtue in liturgical prayer and common observance of monastic life.

In 1551 the Council of the Hundred Chapters gave the victory to the followers of St. Joseph by legislating almost every detail of religious life. An unforeseen result of this was that it prepared the way for the schism of Old Believers a century later by focusing too much attention on small liturgical details. On the other hand, the tradition of St. Nilus continued underground, and as Fedotov points out, the sketes and the little clusters of monks ensured a real survival of the spiritual life, while the larger monasteries became sclerotic and ritualized, even becoming the venue of serious moral abuses.[80]

The "ceremonial confessionalism" of St. Joseph's followers left them prey to the effect of too close a dependence on the civil government with all the dangers such a relationship brings. But as Fedotov sums up so well, even in the most dissolute monasteries "a small forest retreat or a recluse's cell might sometimes be found where prayer never stopped".[81] This tradition can be traced to St. Nilus and, before him, to St. Sergius.

During the sixteenth and seventeenth centuries the Russian Church became very ritualized and linked more and more to the evermore authoritarian Tsars. The Russian government, like many in the West, was becoming de-Christianized. There was an inevitable escalation of the conflict. As often happens, the spark that ignited this conflict was nothing of great theological significance. The patriarch Nikhon, who was actually Finnish and a man of iron, led an effort to open the windows of the Church to the influence of the Greek Church to recover some of the original Byzantine customs and rites.[82]

Paradoxically, Bouyer points out that the Greek customs that Nikhon attempted to bring to Russia were actually less authentic than the old Russian customs, which preserved a more ancient aspect of Orthodoxy. Another paradox is that the disciples of St. Joseph, often dependent on the government, were horrified by Nikhon's attempts to go back to a past they did not know. They formed a schism known as the Raskol, or Russian nonconformity, reminding us of the English nonjuror movement.[83]

The government became more oppressive, using the tight liturgical customs to extend its own influence. Despots like Ivan the Terrible

[80] Fedotov, *Russian Religious Mind*, 2:393.

[81] Ibid.

[82] Sergius Bolshakoff, *Russian Mystics* (Kalamazoo, Mich.: Cistercian Publications, 1980), 51.

[83] Ibid.

(1530–1584) "found the most zealous ceremonial piety compatible with refined cruelty.... In Russia as a whole, cruelty, dissoluteness, and sensuality accompanied strict ceremonial piety without strain."[84] Fedotov goes so far as to say that spirituality survived better under the Tartars than under the tsars. Monasteries, once the center of Russian spirituality, became involved with economics. They controlled almost one-third of the population who lived on Church lands.[85]

The reaction came in the form of a schism, resulting in the breakaway group called the Old Believers. It is unfortunate that time does not permit us to investigate the Old Believers here or the multitude of sects that eventually rose out of Russian nonconformity. Since they made their rallying cry the observance of old liturgical rites, little of their personal literature is available at all.

St. Tikhon of Zadonsk (1724–1783)

Having worked with the poor, I have always been involved with those whom the world calls sinners, and my attitude has been affected by the words that Dostoievsky put in the mouth of Fr. Zossima in *The Brothers Karamazov*, a figure inspired largely by St. Tikhon. I did not know that only a few years before my first encounter with Fr. Zossima, which occurred while I was a Capuchin seminarian, Nadejda Gorodetzky had written her fascinating book on St. Tikhon, whom she calls the inspirer of Dostoievsky.[86]

Of course, the portrait of Fr. Zossima is not simply a fictionalized version of St. Tikhon. As Gorodetzky makes clear, there are many influences. There are even some fundamental differences between the fictional character and the saint.[87] Some of Zossima's issues reflect Dostoievsky's concerns regarding his own time, whereas the quiet retired bishop lived a hundred years before the author. Moreover, Tikhon's concerns were almost exclusively spiritual after his retirement from the episcopate after only four years, although he always remained deeply involved in direct care of the poor on a relatively large scale.

As I read the writings of St. Tikhon, I realized that they possess a singularly direct quality and demonstrate the mystical style of Dostoievsky's Fr. Zossima. The only person I know who spoke as directly about the world around us seen in a way that it is transfigured by the presence of God, and especially of Christ, was Mother Teresa. The following quotation from St. Tikhon and then from Fr. Zossima will illustrate how well Dostoievsky captured the spirit of this holy man.

On the subject of not judging others and of forgiving we read these words of St. Tikhon:

---

[84] Fedotov, *Russian Religious Mind*, 2:391.

[85] Bolshakoff, *Russian Mystics*, 51.

[86] Nadejda Gorodetzky, *Saint Tikhon of Zadonsk: Inspirer of Dostoevsky* (Crestwood, N.Y.: St. Vladimir's Seminary Press, 1976; first published by SPCK, London, 1951).

[87] Ibid., 225ff.

> Do not judge others, for you cannot know what is inside the other man. Do not condemn, for he may still rise whilst you may fall. Beware of even talking about others, lest you start judging them. Enquiring into other people's sin is a curiosity hateful to God and man....
>
> It is wrong to judge at all, for both inward righteousness and secret sin are hidden from us, whilst rumors and reports about others are too often unfounded and untruthful. The commandment of Christ expressly forbids it (Matt. 7:1).... Above all, when judging another, we cannot know whether perchance he has not already repented and been forgiven by God.[88]

Compare this with the words Dostoievsky put into the mouth of Fr. Zossima:

> Remember particularly that you cannot be a judge of anyone. For no one can judge a criminal until he recognizes that he is just such a criminal as the man standing before him, and that he perhaps is more than all men to blame for that crime. When he understands that, he will be able to be a judge. Though that sounds absurd, it is true. If I had been righteous myself, perhaps there would have been no criminal standing before me. If you can take upon yourself the crime of the criminal your heart is judging, take it at once, suffer for him yourself, and let him go without reproach. And even if the law itself makes you his judge, act in the same spirit so far as possible, for he will go away and condemn himself more bitterly than you have done. If, after your kiss, he goes away untouched, mocking at you, do not let that be a stumbling-block to you. It shows his time has not yet come, but it will come in due course. And if it come not, no matter; if not he, then another in his place will understand and suffer, and judge and condemn himself, and the truth will be fulfilled. Believe that, believe it without doubt; for in that lies all the hope and faith of the saints.[89]

With the life of St. Tikhon we move from the old form of hagiography to the new. We begin to see our saint from a modern perspective; he is not simply an iconic figure. It may be some consolation to readers to recognize that St. Tikhon, like modern Catholic saints—for example, SS. John Neumann and Thérèse—can be seen with their own personal neuroses admitted. With the unique exception of St. Augustine, who is so psychologically revealing in his *Confessions*, the saints before the seventeenth century tend to be portrayed without warts. Like many of his admirers—Dostoievsky and myself included—St. Tikhon was quite neurotic and took no pains to conceal the fact.

---

[88] From St. Tikhon, *Works*, vol. 1, quoted in ibid., 180–81.

[89] From Fyodor Dostoievsky, *The Brothers Karamazov*, trans. Constance Garnett, bk. 6, chap. 3.

The facts of Tikon's life read like a novel.[90] He was born to a poor family at Korotsk in the diocese of Novgorod at a turbulent period in both religious and civil history. His father, a church sexton, died when Tikhon was a small child, leaving the family of six children nearly destitute. At the age of fourteen he entered the seminary for Novgorod, which was run explicitly along Jesuit lines.[91] In fact, some of the classes were in Latin, and the students studied St. Thomas Aquinas, along with patristics and Old Slavonic. Every effort was made to open Russia to ideas from the West. No doubt this explains why in St. Tikhon's later writings there are obvious influences from Catholic and even Protestant thought.[92] The Novgorod seminary was modeled on one in Kiev opened by Metropolitan Peter Moghila, where Scholastic Latin ideas had first been introduced.[93]

Although he was often mocked because of his piety and poor clothing, Tikhon was respected by the faculty. During these days a brief mystical event took place, which he told to his attendants after he retired. He was on a flight of steps one May evening, he recalled, when the following incident occurred.

> I came out, and was standing there, thinking about eternal bliss. All of sudden the heavens seemed to open and there was such a shining, such a brilliance of light, as mortal tongue cannot describe nor reason understand. This gleam was brief, scarcely a minute, and again the sky appeared in its usual form. From this marvellous sight I conceived a more burning desire for solitary life, and long after this wonderful phenomenon I felt a rapture of mind, and even now, as I recall it, my heart is filled with gladness and joy.[94]

In 1758 Tikhon became a monk and priest and was appointed vice-rector of the seminary; the following year he was named superior of a nearby monastery. The poor young man who had been mocked for his unworldly ways was quickly made rector of Tver Seminary and then, at the incredibly early age of thirty-seven, named Bishop of Keksholm and Ladoga and suffragan, or auxiliary, to the Archbishop of Novgorod. Two years later, by order of Tsarina Catherine II, he was transferred to the see of Voronezh.

This was a dramatic time for the Church because Catherine had gone to war on monastic possessions with the express goal of helping the poor and the serfs.[95] In the process Bishop Tikhon got caught in the whirlwind. On the way to take possession of his new diocese at

---

[90] Gorodetzky's book contains an excellent biography of the saint, to which we will refer throughout.

[91] Bolshakoff, *Russian Mystics*, 62.

[92] Bouyer, *Spirituality*, 37–38.

[93] Ibid., 35.

[94] Gorodetzky, *Saint Tikhon of Zadonsk*, 35.

[95] Ibid., 40–41.

Voronezh, he was obliged, again by order of the tsarina, to stop at Moscow to participate in the formal unfrocking of a bishop, Arseny Matzeevich, who had taken Catherine on. At Voronezh, Tikhon was faced with a difficult border land, considered to be one of the most difficult dioceses in the country to administer. It was dominated by the Cossacks, who operated aggressively and almost independently of the Russian government. The northern bishop was regarded as an outsider, and the city with its cathedral had recently been burned. Tikhon was already showing signs of a serious nervous disorder, which included "shaking hands, giddiness, and fainting spells".[96]

St. Tikhon attempted to restore order and devotion in the diocese, and Gorodetzky gives an account of the difficulties he encountered. Finally in the fall of 1767 he was so ill that he could not function and retired for health reasons to a monastery in the diocese, where he wrote several letters of resignation. His resignation was accepted by Catherine on December 17 and a successor was immediately appointed. His last act as bishop was to send substantial funds to help a poor family whose home had burned. His very last concern was the opening of an almshouse for the poor before winter came.[97]

Thus did a very promising career come to an end, and a deeply spiritual bishop, desperately needed by the Church, was apparently withdrawn from the care of souls. It is yet another lesson in the story of Divine Providence writing straight with crooked lines. St. Tikhon's humiliations were not to end with his retirement. The monks at the Monastery of the Transfiguration were so deeply affected by the Old Believers that they were very ritualistic, but the religious life was very lax. Bishop Tikhon was thought to be in disgrace. His successor apparently did not even invite him to the consecration of the new cathedral, which he had begun after a fire had destroyed the original one. Because of ill health he had to change his place of retirement and moved to an obscure monastery named for the Virgin Mary in Zadonsk, a name that he would now make famous throughout the world.

Although he had a little apartment in the monastery and two faithful attendants who stayed with him until he died fourteen years later, he distributed his pension to the poor. He appears to have gone through a nervous breakdown from the symptoms described, which included irritability and great doubt about the future. Finally, deciding to stay where he was and live a holy Christian life, he sold his bishop's insignia and personal possessions, giving the money to the poor. His rooms became the destination of the poor. He attended the monastic Office faithfully but never again presided at the liturgy, preferring simply to receive the Eucharist. As a bishop, he would have had to preside if he had concelebrated.

---

[96] Ibid., 41.
[97] Ibid., 62.

Tikhon spent endless hours with the poor and especially with poor children. He wrote books that would become part of the treasury of Russian spiritual writing and the riches of all Christendom. He worked in the garden and often chopped firewood. He had an old horse to help with the chores whom he loved and called by the affectionate name "the old man". He even dug a well. Becoming acquainted with Mount Athos, he received monk visitors from there.[98] In a word, through sickness, sorrow, rejection, and failure, Tikhon lived the life to which he had been called so long before, when on that spring evening he saw the light from the sky.

One of his first writings after his retirement was a beautiful meditation, "The Waters which Flow By". Gorodetzky sees in this work the influence of *The Imitation of Christ*, which Tikhon is known to have read. The meditation ends with devotional soliloquies that reveal his spirituality at the beginning of his life as a hermit.

> We see the water of a river flowing uninterruptedly and passing away, and all that floats on its surface, rubbish or beams of trees, all pass by. Christian! So does our life.... I was an infant, and that time has gone. I was an adolescent, and that too has passed. I was a young man, and that too is far behind me. The strong and mature man that I was is no more. My hair turns white, I succumb to age, but that too passes; I approach the end and will go the way of all flesh. I was born in order to die. I die that I may live. Remember me, O Lord, in thy Kingdom! ... I have known gladness and sorrow, I have rejoiced and I have wept; the same happens to me now but, as the days go by, sorrow and gladness, joy and tears go with them. I have been praised and exalted, I have been criticized and abused; and the same who praised me, have cursed; and those who abused have turned to praise me.... Such is our existence in this world. Not thus will be the life to come, of what the Word of God and our faith assure us. Once begun, that life will never end. No illness, age, decrepitude, death or corruption will assail our body; it will become a spiritual, incorruptible, immortal body, whole, light and healthy. There will be peace, joy, comfort and bliss without end. The elect will see God face to face and will reign with Christ as members with the Head.[99]

We turn now to the writings of this holy man that relate to devotion to Christ. It is easy, since his spirituality is founded on two things alone: the Bible and prayer. He seemed little influenced by hesychast methods. The predominant patristic element in his writings seems to be St. John Chrysostom.[100] Surprisingly, there are noticeable echoes of St. Augustine (especially the *Soliloquies*), of *The Imitation of Christ*,

[98] Bolshakoff, *Russian Mystics*, 68.

[99] Quoted in Gorodetzky, *Saint Tikhon of Zadonsk*, 72–73.

[100] Gorodetzky, *Saint Tikhon of Zadonsk*, 118.

and of Arndt's *True Christianity*. The center of Tikhon's life was devotion to and the following of Christ. Bishop Kallistos sums up his spirituality: "Whenever you read the Gospel, Christ Himself is speaking to you. And while you read, you are praying and talking with Him."[101]

Teachings about Charity

The following statement, which could have been written by Mother Teresa or Dorothy Day, captures the simple charity of St. Tikhon. Of course, the voice of reason tells us that this idealistic vision is not always practical. However, even the most practical of us cannot deny that Tikhon's statement sums up beautifully the essence of Christian charity:

> Every man is our brother, created in the image and likeness of God, redeemed by the Blood of Christ, a member of the one Church, called to eternal salvation. To love is to dwell in God—union with God is a great thing. He who loves is Christ's disciple. All other gifts are nothing without love. One cannot love God without it. He who loves his brother remains in the light, he who hates him is a murderer. Love is the foretaste of eternal life, where there will be nothing but love of one another, consolation and joy in one another. Love of one's neighbor is assimilation to God and the approach to him. General welfare derives from mutual love. O happy would all be if they could love one another! ... The courts of law would not be overburdened with complaints; starving brethren would not wander in the streets and markets; half-naked members of Christ would not shiver from cold and frost.... [T]here would be no beggars or paupers but everything would be dangerless, restful, peaceful; all would be equal. O love, bond of perfection, love![102]

Despite these words, St. Tikhon was not unrealistic. He counseled against giving money to drunks. He spoke in defense of women, who were much abused in Russia at that time, and he did the same for the serfs. He confronted the rich in the name of Christ. Repeatedly, he told them to follow the Gospel and to serve Christ in the poor, warning the well-off not to send Christ away empty-handed.

> You believe the Gospels which teach us that Christ imputes to himself anything given in his holy name to a poor man or a beggar. Why, then, do you not feed the hungry? A buffoon who entertains you, a flatterer who shamelessly flatters you, departs from you well satisfied. Christ, the giver of the heavenly kingdom, you send away empty-handed. Liberal is your hand to squander in banqueting; but you would not lose a penny to save a poor peasant from selling the last of his cattle to pay you his rent. The hounds, your pleasure, feed from your

[101] Ware, *Orthodox Way*, 111.

[102] From Tikhon, *Works*, vols. 2 and 3, quoted in Gorodetzky, *Saint Tikhon of Zadonsk*, 124–25.

> table, while your servant does not always have bread for his need.... Such, then, is your faith, such its fruit![103]

He encouraged the serfs, telling them that Christ was their leader and model, alluding to Philippians 2:7, in which St. Paul reminds us that in becoming man, Christ took the form of a servant, or slave. The same passage, as we have already seen, is the *locus classicus* for the idea of kenotic spirituality, of Christ's "emptying himself" of divine majesty and glory to become incarnate. St. Tikhon probably also had in mind the passage from Galatians (3:28), in which the apostle tells us that among the baptized "there is neither Jew nor Greek, neither slave nor free ... you are all one in Christ Jesus".

> Though you are called slaves, you are freemen of Christ; in your body you work for men, but your souls are free from the works of sin; you have no freedom and nobility like your masters, but your souls are bejewelled with Christian freedom and nobility. Rejoice, for the inheritance of the sons of God awaits you also.... They will leave all they possess. Remember the poverty of Christ! Poor people, you beloved sufferers, do not faint in your hearts; here you suffer with Lazarus, but together with him you will dwell in the bosom of Abraham![104]

The retired bishop was dependent on the government for his pension, which he gave away. He had good reason to recall the total disgrace of Archbishop Arseny Matzeevich, who had taken issue with the tsarina. Nonetheless Tikhon himself took on even royalty. "Christian treasure is seldom found in the crowns, titles or great names of the world, in purple and fine linen, or within beautiful and rich walls, but mostly in rags and mangers.... Happy the crown adorned with charity and justice—these jewels are indeed different from the jewels of this world." [105]

He admonishes rulers: "Whosoever wishes to rule others must strive to become the ruler of his own passions—this should be a Christian's desire. Those who are in Christ have crucified their flesh with its lusts—there you are, my lords the Tsars, may God have mercy upon us!" [106] For St. Tikhon the real king was Christ, and the Gospels were His words to us.

Meditation on the Life of Christ

The center of this holy bishop's thoughts was the life of Christ. The following quotations sum up a life of complete devotion to Jesus Christ.

---

[103] Ibid., 131–32.

[104] Ibid., 132.

[105] Tikhon, *Works*, vols. 11, 9, quoted in ibid., 138.

[106] Tikhon, *Works*, vol. 10, quoted in ibid., 138.

> Strive to obtain sincere awe and tenderness of heart by meditating upon the economy of salvation. Reflect how the Son of God and the Lord of all assumed the form of a servant; how the Unbegotten was conceived in the womb of the pure Virgin; how the eternal God became an infant.... He who feeds all flesh, himself hungered and thirsted. The Invisible appeared on earth and lived among men. Reflect that when he was only an infant he was persecuted by Herod ... that he who is sinless was baptized by his servant; that, having himself been tempted by Satan, he helps those in temptation.[107]

The Eucharist, of course, is the principal expression of devotion to Christ. Although frequent Communion was not common in Russia, it was encouraged by Tikhon. At the same time, as the Catholic saints in the West were encouraging worthy Communion, so was he. The following very devout practical advice puts it all very well.

> It is dreadful to approach Communion without being purified by true repentance; dreadful, too, if one who has approached the Eucharist is again soiled by the lusts of the world. Therefore meditation is necessary before and after Communion, and mindfulness of this celestial gift. Before Communion we must have hearty repentance and humility, we must put aside malice, anger and the caprices of the flesh. Be reconciled with your neighbor, have a firm intention and will to lead a new and devout life in Christ Jesus. After Communion some manifestation of amendment of life is necessary; the reality of such amendment is testified by our love of God and of our neighbor, by gratitude, by a sustained effort towards a new, blameless, saintly life.[108]

The effects of worthy reception of the Eucharist are spelled out beautifully by St. Tikhon in words that remind us of Fr. Zossima.

> Man is more beautiful than any other creature since he is in the image of God. Through the incarnation he is justified and is no more under wrath. He has become a member of the body of which the heavenly head is Jesus Christ. He mysteriously partakes of the lifegiving Body and divine Blood. He is made worthy to become the habitation of God and the temple of the Holy Ghost. He is in communion with the Father and his Son Jesus Christ. Through faith in Jesus he becomes a son, an heir, a co-heir with Christ. Read the Acts of the Apostles and you will see that all these titles are ascribed to man by the Holy Ghost.... And what will it be in the future life, according to the unfailing promise of God! What goodness, bliss, honor and glory! The uninterrupted flow of eternal blessedness will be like a river, incomprehensible to the present mind and inexpressible by the tongue,

[107] Tikhon, *Works*, vol. 1, quoted in ibid., 159.
[108] Quoted in ibid., 160.

> the blessedness which "eye hath not seen" spoken of in 1 Cor. 2:9. The children of God will shine like the sun in the kingdom of the heavenly Father, they will be as angels, like other gods. Glory be to the Trinity for having so honored and magnified our kind![109]

The Love of the Suffering Christ

St. Tikhon often focused on the Passion of Christ, and Bouyer says that he had representations of Christ's sufferings in his cell, something almost unique in the history of Orthodoxy.[110] He advises others to do the same. "Keep in your house a picture of the passion of Christ, look at it often and with reverence: it will be to you a substitute for continual reading and visible history. Throw away those masquerading pictures which weaken and tempt and burn your flesh; paint instead the tribulations and victories of Christ; the whole deepest content of the gospel is portrayed in the passion of Christ and incites us to imitation."[111]

Personal participation in Christ's suffering reminds us of St. Margaret Mary's words calling people to make reparation to Christ for the sins of the world. "Many Christians who desire to be glorified with the Lord but who do not wish to be with him in dishonor, to carry the cross, to suffer in the world, show by this that their heart is wrong, that they do not truly love Christ and, to be frank, that they love themselves more than they love Christ. Love of God is shown in the love of our neighbor."[112]

No adequate Christian spirituality ends with the Passion, and for St. Tikhon, Christ's Passion always points to the Resurrection. Tikhon urged the Christian to look forward with great hope to what awaits him. "[T]he resurrection of our bodies; the angels who carry our souls to God; the beginning of a new and better life, where we shall see God, where there will be the amiable society of the Queen of Heaven and of the saints; where we shall become free from this world into which we were born with a cry—for a devout soul feels always like a stranger till it reaches its homeland of heaven. There will it rest from strife and labor—and it will be in eternal rest."[113]

Eternal Life

Some have thought that the desire and goal of eternal life was unworthy of the Christian. St. Tikhon, like St. Francis, would not have understood such an objection.

> Meditate more often, O Christian, on eternity, that you may the better escape sin. One cannot think of eternity without sighing and fear. Meditation upon eternity makes weeping and tears sweet, it lightens every toil, it teaches us to accept with thanksgiving any temporal

---

[109] St. Tikhon, *Private Letters*, quoted in Gorodetzky, 172–73.

[110] Bouyer, *Spirituality*, 37.

[111] St. Tikhon, *The Spiritual Treasure*, quoted in Gorodetzky, *Saint Tikhon of Zadonsk*, 192.

[112] St. Tikhon, *Works*, vol. 3, quoted in Gorodetzky, *Saint Tikhon of Zadonsk*, 196.

[113] Quoted in Gorodetzky, *Saint Tikhon of Zadonsk*, 198–99.

> punishment, sorrow, offence, dishonor, banishment and death itself; it prevents us from falling into the snare of lawlessness. He who thinks of eternity will seek the word of God and instruction to salvation more than he seeks his daily food.[114]

St. Tikhon died very quietly, having requested (but not received) the Holy Eucharist at the hour of death, which took place on Sunday, August 13, 1783. The local bishop put this inscription on his tomb: "[H]e appeared as the image of virtue by his word, life, love, spirit, faith and purity."[115] With these quotations we must move on, but with regret. We live at a time when the world inevitably grows smaller. East and West grow ever closer. On all sides many factors reduce the divide left by the schisms and mistakes of the past. St. Tikhon, so human and so profoundly spiritual, so genuinely Orthodox and yet open to the spirituality of Western Christianity, offers us a marvelous bridge.

That fervent Slavophile, Dostoievsky, found in this saint a model. Yet Tikhon explicitly prayed for all Christians—for all human beings. The anger and hurt feelings characteristic of the Slavophile are not found in him. For those of us on the other side of the gap between East and West he is a remarkably saintly soul helping us to appreciate the best of Russian spirituality.

[114] Quoted in ibid., 200.

[115] Gorodetzky, *Saint Tikhon of Zadonsk*, 90.

18 The Orthodox Renaissance in Greece and Russia in the Eighteenth and Nineteenth Centuries

Geography deeply affects history. Nowhere is this more apparent than in the development of the Orthodox East. The geography of Russia has defeated many invaders; even when some, like the Tartars, managed to conquer, the huge plains and mountain forests made it difficult to maintain long-term control. The opposite situation prevailed for the Greeks. The placid Mediterranean made passage by sea easy, allowing the Turks to maintain tight control over Greece and subjugated people from the Balkans to North Africa. Consequently, the life and development of the Greek Church under the Turks were much more difficult than was the case for the Russian Church under the Tartars. As a result, the Greek Orthodox Church fell behind the Russian Church in certain ways. Nonetheless, despite incredible difficulties Greek-speaking Christians maintained their faith and the memory of their ancient civilization.

After the fall of Constantinople and Greece, the sultans maintained the Christian clergy as a way of governing a subjected people. They treated the Jews and other minority groups in much the same way. However, the Ottoman abuse of the Patriarchate of Constantinople was incredible. Patriarchs were removed at whim, only to be reinstated—sometimes more than once. Each time an appointment or reappointment to the patriarchate was made, a very heavy tax was demanded, which had to be paid by the faithful. In such an atmosphere, intrigue, simony, and the decline of discipline had to be expected.[1] Along with that, patriarchs, bishops, and priests were often killed. That the Ecumenical Patriarchate of Constantinople survived can only be seen as a sign of Divine Providence and protection.

The great stabilizing spiritual force at this time was the monastic peninsula of Mount Athos. As the Benedictines in the West had preserved

[1] George S. Bebis, introduction to *Nicodemos of the Holy Mountain*, trans. Peter A. Chamberas, Classics of Western Spirituality (New York: Paulist Press, 1989), 7.

Scripture, theology, spirituality, culture, and learning during the Dark Ages, so the monks of the Greek-speaking world did in these later dark ages of the Hellenic people, which extended from the fall of Constantinople in 1453 to the struggle for Greek independence, which began in 1821. Like the Dark Ages in the West, this was a period of "dynamic spiritual strength, resourcefulness, and genuine piety grounded in a living theological tradition".[2]

During this lengthy period, the Greeks clung tenaciously to their church in the face of a hostile invader. There was an almost universal resistance to Turkish blandishments offered to potential converts. There were schools and even academies. Many young Greeks studied in Western Europe, bringing back the very learning that had been preserved by the monks of the West, some of it from the Hellenic tradition. In *The Great Church in Captivity*, Sir Steven Runciman assesses Greek culture and life during that period, acknowledging not only that the Orthodox Church kept the nation together but also that the Hellenic tradition of philosophy and history was an important ingredient.

> The importance of the Greek tradition in the survival of Orthodoxy during the Ottoman period must not be forgotten. Throughout all its vicissitudes the Church was determined to keep its flock conscious of the Greek heritage.... Everyone who called himself a Greek, whatever his actual racial origins might be, was proud to think that he was of the same nation of Homer and Plato and Aristotle, as well as of the Eastern Fathers of the Church. This faith of the Greek genius kept hope alive; and without hope few institutions can survive.[3]

St. Nicodemus of the Holy Mountain (1749–1809)

Into this difficult world St. Nicodemus[4] (Nicholas Kallivourtsis) was born in 1749 on the Aegean island of Naxos. Although he inhabited the devout Greek Orthodox world we have described, he came into contact with a Latin-Rite Catholic minority left by the Crusaders and that still survives today. He was both an intellectual genius and a devout candidate for monastic life. It was said of him that "it was enough for him to read a book once and remember it throughout his life".[5] Despite the turbulence of his time, he received an excellent education. He fell under the influence of a group of monks of Mount Athos who were severely criticized over some liturgical issues (beyond most of us) and for encouraging frequent reception of the Holy Eucharist. They were also influential in a movement to return to the Church Fathers. Hostility to these monks, pejoratively called the *Kollyvades* (sweet cakes),

[2] Ibid., 5.

[3] Steven Runciman, *The Great Church in Captivity* (Cambridge: Cambridge University Press, 1968), 410, quoted in ibid, 9.

[4] Some authors use the Hellenic spelling "Nicodemos", but most Western writers prefer the Latinized version that we follow here.

[5] Theokletos Dionysiatis, *Agios Nicodemos, O Hagioretis: O Bios Kai Ta Erga Tou*, ed. Papademetriou (Athens, 1959), quoted in Bebis, introduction to *Nicodemos*, 10.

caused them to be dispersed all over the Greek world, thus becoming the foundation for a renaissance in Orthodox spirituality and life.

Dr. Bebis sees this renaissance as one of the miracles of Church history.[6] The greatest of the *Kollyvades*, St. Macarius of Corinth, became a refugee, and with the permission of the ecumenical patriarch he was named a traveling bishop, a kind of missionary. Macarius met the young Nicholas Kallivourtsis, and no doubt their meeting influenced the latter's decision to enter Mount Athos at the age of twenty-six. His talents were quickly recognized, and he went to work in the library of one of the lavras. He was joined two years later by St. Macarius himself, and they began the publication of the *Philokalia*, the monumental work we have already described. Published originally in Greek in 1782, it was later translated into Slavonic by the Ukrainian monk of Mount Athos, Païssy Velitchkhovsky (1722–1794), whom we shall consider later.[7] The book became the basis of monastic revival throughout the Orthodox world. We must mention that the *Philokalia* also revived the hesychast tradition and spread knowledge and use of the Jesus prayer among modern Russians.[8]

Nicodemus led an ascetical life centered on study. Although one Catholic writer describes him as anti-Western, his biographer Fr. Dionysiatis records that he participated in dialogues with Western Catholic theologians. He dressed very poorly, like the great monastic saints before him, and the descriptions of his life indicate that the kenotic tradition of Russian Orthodox monasticism was very well represented in this very Greek saint. Various delegations who came to see him "were amazed to see a man dressed in rags—he had only one cassock—with plain sandals". In his later years he was "old, without teeth, exhausted from the fasting and the hardships of his strict monastic life".[9] Nicodemus died a holy death on Mount Athos on July 14, 1809. Euthymios, his spiritual brother and earliest biographer, notes that "the rays of his teaching are with us and they illuminate us and they illuminate the Church forever".[10]

Although Nicodemus was considered a saint even before his death (he became known by the encomium the Hagiorite, that is, someone representing the spiritual tradition of Mount Athos), it was not until 1955 that he was canonized by the holy synod of the ecumenical patriarchate and the following year by the Church in Russia. It is remarkable that although he was totally loyal to the Orthodox tradition, his

[6] Bebis, introduction to *Nicodemos*, 12–13.

[7] Bouyer, *Orthodox Spirituality and Protestant and Anglican Spirituality* (Seabury Press, 1981) 44–46. See also ibid., 20–24. The first English translation appeared in the 1950s.

[8] Ted A. Campbell, *The Religion of the Heart: A Study of European Religious Life in the Seventeenth and Eighteenth Centuries* (Columbia: University of South Carolina Press, 1991), 143–44.

[9] Bebis, introduction to *Nicodemos*, 15.

[10] Quoted in ibid.

contacts with Catholics and his extended paraphrases of two Catholic books, *The Unseen Warfare* and the *Spiritual Exercises*, caused him to be criticized for leading the Orthodox faithful astray. He was also ridiculed for his poverty and ascetical ways. Such criticisms tell us more about the narrow-mindedness of his detractors than about this holy man.

St. Nicodemus was among the most prolific writers of all times and produced more than one hundred volumes. His works are almost always pastoral and practical and, consequently, related to devotion. Writing about saints and martyrs, he exhorts the people to remain faithful to Christ and resist the pressures to apostatize to Islam. "Your treasure is Jesus Christ. Your glory is Jesus. Your pleasure is Jesus. Your whole life is Jesus. Because by suffering for Jesus, you have Jesus. And by having Jesus, you have gained all earthly and heavenly things, you have gained everything—everything." [11]

St. Nicodemus' great anthology, the *Philokalia*, was published in Venice in 1782, and this five-volume work was "destined to have an immense impact on the spiritual life of the Russian people".[12] Along with Slavonic, parts of it were published in French and Romanian. The first English translation of the Greek text began to appear only in 1979. Two Russian spiritual writers of the nineteenth century, Ignatius Brianchaninov and St. Theophan the Recluse, both published Russian translations of the *Philokalia*. Their editions, however, were selective and incomplete. In his own introduction to the book, St. Nicodemus refers to his anthology in this way: "A book which is the excellent pattern of the practical virtue and the infallible directive of contemplation, the paradise of the Fathers, the golden series of virtues. A book which is the dense teaching of Christ, the trumpet which recalls back the grace, in two words, it is the instrument itself of deification."[13]

The influence of hesychasm is also noticeable in the invitation that St. Nicodemus extends to the readers of the *Philokalia*: "Being freed from the imprisonment of this world and the wandering of the mind, with your heart purified from the passions, with the awesome unceasing invocation of our Lord Jesus Christ together with the collaborating virtues, which this book teaches, you will be united among yourselves, and united this way, you will all be united with God, according to the prayer of our Lord to his Father, who said, 'So they may be one, as we are one' (Jn 17:11)." [14]

[11] From Nomikos Vaporis, "The Price of Faith: Some Reflections on Nicodemos Hagiorites and His Struggle against Islam, Together with a Translation of the 'Introduction' to His 'New Martyrologion'", *The Greek Orthodox Theological Review* 23(1978): 208, quoted in ibid., 19.

[12] Bebis, introduction to *Nicodemos*, 21.

[13] From *Philokalia ton Ieron Neptikon*, quoted in ibid., 23.

[14] Ibid.

The Special Devotion to the Holy Eucharist

It is interesting that in both Orthodox and Catholic Christianity there has been regular tension over the frequency of receiving the Holy Eucharist although there has been almost universal support for frequent Communion by the very people we have encountered in this study—those who were especially devoted to Jesus Christ. St. Nicodemus, following SS. Tikhon and Sergius in Russia, and St. Gregory Palamas and Nicolas Cabasilas in Greece, encouraged frequent Communion, which was unpopular in their day. Although St. Basil the Great speaks of receiving Communion at least four times a week,[15] this practice had long since been discontinued, with people receiving Communion only three times a year. St. Nicodemus took up a book by an earlier Hagiorite monk, Neophytos, which he expanded from 173 to 343 pages, thus making it largely his own work, called *Concerning Continual Communion of the Divine Mysteries*. (Later he did the same with books of Catholic spiritual writers.) In the book we read this passage.

> The sacred and Most Holy Body of our Lord, when properly and worthily received, becomes a weapon for those who fight the good fight, it becomes the cause of returning back to God for those who went astray; it strengthens the sick, it delights the healthy, it heals illnesses, it preserves health; with the Holy Communion, it is easier to correct ourselves, to become more forbearing and more patient in the pains and the sorrows, more warm in love, more sensitive to knowledge, more willing to obedience, more sensitive and more responsive to the energy of the [divine] charismata.[16]

The Unseen Warfare *and the* Spiritual Exercises

Much has been made of the fact that St. Nicodemus used two very Catholic books. As we mentioned, his critics among the Orthodox have attacked him for this. That the two books were very Catholic no one can deny. As a young man on Naxos, where many Catholics lived, he had read Fr. Lorenzo Scupoli's book *Spiritual Combat*.[17] It was one of the most popular books of post-Reformation piety, and many people, including saints, relied on it.

In trying to bring Scupoli's work into agreement with the Orthodox views of his readers, Nicodemus made a number of changes. He excluded all references to the Sacred Heart and to Purgatory, for example, and introduced the Jesus prayer as well as hesychast ideas into

[15] *St. Basil: Letters: Volume 1*, The Fathers of the Church series, vol. 13 (Washington, D.C.: Catholic University of America Press, 1965), 208–9, quoted in Bebis, introduction to *Nicodemos*, 25.

[16] Constantine Doukakis and Antonio Georgiou, eds., *Peri tes synechous metalepseos ton Theion Mysterion* (Athens, 1887), 103ff., quoted in Bebis, introduction to *Nicodemos* 25–26.

[17] Fr. Scupoli originally published his work as *Combattimento Spirituale* in 1589. Ten years later a second, much expanded edition appeared, and it was this version that St. Nicodemus reworked in Greek. The title *Unseen Warfare* was given to the first English translation, done from a Russian edition of Theophan the Recluse, and published in the 1950s.

Scupoli's discussion of prayer. A discussion of spiritual communion in the original, that is, receiving Christ spiritually when it is not possible to receive the Eucharist, was complemented by Nicodemus with his own teaching on the reception of Holy Communion. Fr. Dionysiatis refers to the book as "a true hymn of the mystical spirit of the Orthodox Fathers, and a clear mirror of the heart and the soul" of the saint.[18] Most Catholics are delighted that an Orthodox saint was able to make use of a Catholic book and are not at all offended that he made Orthodox adaptations to it. Another Orthodox writer has this to say about Nicodemus' achievement: "It is a remarkable feat to have produced two editions of considerable 'Western' works within a fundamentally anti-Latin milieu, and, while respecting the schema and basic contents of them, to have put them in the rediscovered perspective of the experience of prayer, in the most authentic Orthodox tradition."[19]

Nicodemus also took another book, the *Spiritual Exercises* of an Italian Jesuit, Father Pinamonti, and transformed this thirty-page work of meditations, the *Esercizii Spirituali*, into a book of more than six hundred pages. However, the expanded work follows "the order and method of the Ignatian exercises".[20] Understandably, this use of St. Ignatius is troubling to some Orthodox because historically, the Society of Jesus, which was active in Russia and Ukraine, has been seen as inimical to the Orthodox tradition. In more recent times Jesuits have had better relations with the Eastern world, having established the Russian Institute in Rome (and for a while in New York), at which a number of Eastern Orthodox clergy have received degrees.

Fr. Dionysiatis writes that "St. Nicodemos emptied all his wisdom and love into this book".[21] Unfortunately, the book's size has kept it from taking its rightful place as "a masterpiece of Orthodox spirituality".[22] It has not been translated into English. St. Nicodemus returns to principal Christological themes. This is not surprising, since these are the themes of the *Spiritual Exercises* of Ignatius Loyola.

> In precise christological language he speaks about Christ's role on earth. He develops the importance of receiving holy communion. He also stresses the importance of the pentecostal event through which the Holy Spirit completely changed the language, the mind, and the heart of the apostles. He also emphasizes God's love toward humanity. Meditation 17 is a flaming hymn of God's love for humankind.[23]

[18] Dionysiatis, *Agios Nicodemos*, quoted in Bebis, introduction to *Nicodemos*, 27.

[19] Boris Bobrinskoy, "Encounter of Traditions in Greece: St. Nicodemus of the Holy Mountain", in *Christian Spirituality: Post-Reformation and Modern*, ed. Louis Dupré and Don E. Saliers (New York: Crossroad, 1996), 456.

[20] Bouyer, *Spirituality*, 41.

[21] Agios Nidocemos, quoted in Bebis, introduction to *Nicodemos*, 28.

[22] Ibid.

[23] Bebis, introduction to *Nicodemos*, 29

The eternal Father, in order to liberate you from infinite misery which you have in Hades, and in order to make you a communicant of an infinite happiness in paradise, gave to you as a gift his divine Son: "For God so loved the world that He gave His only-begotten Son."[24]

The Works of St. Nicodemus

The same Christological spirit and love of Christ fill the many other volumes written by St. Nicodemus. His monumental work, *The Rudder* (*Pedalion*), which fills 1034 pages in English translation,[25] is a collection and review of Orthodox canons. He uses the analogue of the Church as a ship and says that "its beams and planks [are] the dogmas and traditions of the faith. Its mast represents the Cross; its sail and rigging represent Hope and Love. The master of the vessel is our Lord Jesus Christ, whose hand is on the helm."[26] Another of Nicodemus' works, *A Handbook of Spiritual Counsel*, has been translated by Peter Chamberas and is available in the Classics of Western Spirituality volume on St. Nicodemus. Here Nicodemus moves into a world of theological anthropology, attempting to locate man in the order of creation. Here he sees the human body as a palace and the mind as a king dwelling in it, leading to the recognition of two components of human existence, the spiritual and the physical. The senses serve the body as windows to the world around us; through them man can receive spiritual nurture and even pleasure. Nevertheless the senses can also lead to bondage, which the mind overcomes by spiritual nourishment, especially Sacred Scripture, the doing of virtuous acts, following the commandments of God, and the practice of prayer.[27]

One finds in the *Handbook of Spiritual Counsel* a noticeable absence of the preoccupation with original sin that is often found in Western writings. This is perhaps best understood when we remember that Pelagianism was historically a Western problem. Many Western writers like Augustine and Thomas, and later Luther and Calvin, militated against the human idolatry of Pelagianism. This problem was not obvious in the Orthodox world. The lasting effects of the Fall of the human race are certainly not denied in the East, but they are usually not specifically identified as results of the Fall. For this reason Eastern writers see the possibility of a level of spiritual purification that is not characteristic of Western writers. For our purposes we can gain a good insight into the *Handbook of Spiritual Counsel* from the following summary. If we wish to enjoy the spiritual fruits of grace, our senses must be cleansed, lest the pollution directly touch our hearts and the whole person be polluted. This would happen through sin. Nicodemus admits that the heart is the root of all

[24] St. Nicodemus, from his introduction to the *Spiritual Exercises*, quoted in ibid.

[25] Bebis, introduction to *Nicodemos*, 43.

[26] *The Rudder*, trans. D. Cummings (Chicago: Orthodox Christian Educational Society, 1957), vi., quoted in ibid., 45.

[27] See Bebis, introduction to *Nicodemos*, 47–52, for a precise analysis of the profound concepts of this book, which in many ways was way ahead of its time.

things good and evil. Constant vigilance is required, therefore, to keep the inner self a temple and dwelling place of the Holy Spirit, so that our hearts will be an altar, a sacred sanctuary of our Lord Jesus Christ. The following quotation taken from *A Handbook of Spiritual Counsel* sums up the Christological insights of this remarkable man. He asks the question, How do we make our minds and souls temples worthy of being inhabited by the Holy Spirit? "Through inner attention and the return of the mind to the heart, followed by the practice of sacred mental prayer in the heart saying, 'Lord Jesus Christ, Son of God, have mercy upon me.' When you prepare your heart, my beloved, then the all-holy, all-good, and most man-loving Spirit comes and dwells in you perceptibly, actively, manifestly. Then, my brother, you receive from the Holy Spirit whatever you longed for." [28]

Nicodemus teaches that these gifts come to individuals because they have centered their lives on Christ through the recitation of the Jesus prayer. It is not surprising that even in the last moments of his earthly life St. Nicodemus was reciting this prayer.

Russian Monasticism Survives and Flourishes

Because the monks have been so influential and because Orthodox bishops are drawn from their ranks, Western Christians assume that their numbers were large in Russia and Greece. The fact is that as waves of secularization spread over Europe, East and West, in the eighteenth and nineteenth centuries, most ecclesiastical property was confiscated, including farms and other holdings of monasteries and convents. Whether it was the violent suppression of the French Revolution or the more peaceful consolidation and confiscation of the Austro-Hungarian and Russian imperial governments, the numbers of religious were significantly reduced. This happened especially in Russia, where under Peter the Great, Empress Anne, and Catherine the Great many monasteries were suppressed, the property secularized, and the religious given a meager annual allotment.[29] In 1764, despite the confiscations, there remained over a thousand monasteries, of which one-fourth were convents of nuns. Suppressions continued, however, until only 224 monasteries were allowed to continue with state subsidy and a further 161 without subsidy but with strict controls. In 1762 there were about 12,450 religious; under new laws only 5,100 were permitted. (To understand how small a number this represented, we should remember that there are at least five thousand Catholic religious in the greater New York City area.) The promised state support for monks and nuns was sporadic and meager, and religious houses continued to decline. By 1800 only 452 remained.[30]

[28] Quoted in Constantine Cavarnos, *St. Nicodemos the Hagiorite* (Belmont, Mass.: Institute for Byzantine and Modern Greek Studies, 1974), 145. Also, see ibid., 53.

[29] Sergius Bolshakoff, *Russian Mystics* (Kalamazoo, Mich.: Cistercian Publications, 1980), 57.

[30] Ibid., 58.

St. Demetrius of Rostov (1651–1709)

As often happens in Church history, things begin to get better when they are at their worst. St. Demetrius of Rostov, a Ukrainian monk and abbot, came to the attention of Peter the Great, generally seen as the archenemy of orthodoxy with his Westernizing efforts and his sympathy for Enlightenment Protestantism.[31] Demetrius became Metropolitan of Rostov, and his work was instrumental in keeping the Orthodox Church intact under Peter and his successors long after the bishop's death. Having attended the seminary in Kiev, which, as we saw, was influenced by Western Latin ideas, Demetrius was influenced by Counter-Reformation devotions and even translated St. Ignatius' favorite prayer to Christ, *Anima Christi*. The theme of the Sacred Heart of Jesus was prominent in his writings. Demetrius died long before the approval of this devotion by the Catholic Church in 1765. His death came nearly thirty years after that of St. John Eudes and some twenty years after the death of St. Margaret Mary, the popularizers of this devotion. One wonders about their influence on his own devotion. We may also wonder whether he was influenced by Nicolas Cabasilas, who wrote eloquently in Greek about the Heart of Jesus in the fourteenth century. The following quotation from St. Demetrius is extremely significant. "His heart which was the source and the beginning of every love was wounded ... heart compassionate, charitable! How enflamed was the heart of Christ! It was enflamed by an immense love for man! In order to reduce this heat he received into his heart the cold iron!"[32]

St. Demetrius was completely loyal to the Orthodox Church not only in his convictions but also in his preaching. Unlike St. Tikhon, who lived a generation after him, Demetrius used the Jesus prayer and wrote about it but was not as exclusively involved in it as the early hesychast saints and writers.[33]

The Holy Fools and the Recluses

We must now say a word about some unusual souls and devout eccentrics, whom the Western mind associates with Eastern monasticism, largely because of their place in literature, although some of them actually had nothing to do with monastic life except that monks occasionally fed or housed them. Others were recluses living at the edge of the monastic community after being formed by the monasteries. Religious life in the East is more fluid than in the West. Monks can more easily move from one monastery to another, or to

---

[31] Ibid., 58–60.

[32] Quoted in Bolshakoff, *Russian Mystics*, 58–59. In order to illustrate the influence of Catholicism on Demetrius, Bolshakoff gives the following quotation from a hymn to our Lady: "I venerate your Immaculate Conception and your Nativity from your holy progenitors, Joachim and Anne." The use of the Catholic term "Immaculate Conception" to describe the origins of unique privileges the Orthodox also attribute to Mary is quite remarkable. The term and its specific explanation come from the Franciscan writer Blessed John Duns Scotus in the fourteenth century.

[33] Ibid., 59.

a small monastic settlement called a skete. They can also become recluses. Some monasteries had tight structures, while in others monks could move in and out and still retain the religious habit, identity, and rank. The life of St. Nicodemus illustrates this fluidity and reminds us that it could be put to productive service of the Church. Such a structure gave rise to a group of itinerant religious, some of whom may have tried monastic life and failed, often because of obvious psychological difficulties. The Russian Orthodox tendency toward kenotic spirituality easily identifies the person who has nothing with Christ, even when the individual may have brought his misfortunes on himself.

Since these Holy Fools rarely left writings, we must look to their more respectable colleagues, the monastic recluses, to understand their devotion to Christ. George Mashurin (1789–1827) was a devout officer in the Russian cavalry who entered the monastery at Zadonsk, made famous by St. Tikhon. He soon became a recluse, living in an underground cell and then in a specially built house, where he followed a regime of prayer, night vigils, fasts, and mortification.[34] His life was specifically focused on the sufferings of Christ. Bolshakoff compares his spirituality to that of Madame Acarie and Armand de Rancé, abbot and reformer of La Trappe. Yet with all of this stark unworldliness and penance we find a beautiful devotion to Jesus. In fact, the devotion of George the Recluse to Jesus may have kept him from going into a complete schizophrenic withdrawal. The following selection from George's writings given by Bolshakoff shows Christ's importance to this mysterious figure.

> Those who want to penetrate the Kingdom of God must know the commandments of the Lord Jesus Christ, live accordingly and remember that it is impossible to enter the Kingdom of God except by many sorrows. This kingdom is not found in something external and visible but in our heart after many labors and frequent prayers to Jesus Christ. You will find the way, if you read with attention the lives of the saints glorified by God, Jesus Christ, and by the Orthodox Church. These saints truly found the Kingdom of God within themselves, by faith, hope and love. This is possible for you too in the Lord.[35]

In another letter George writes: "Only prayer to the most sweet Jesus may sweeten your sorrowful heart and raise your soul to the rapture of heavenly joy. . . . All the worries of the sea of life are merely vanity. . . . He who is today on the throne, is tomorrow in the grave. . . . Such is our life." [36]

[34] Bolshakoff, *Russian Mystics*, 108.

[35] Quoted in ibid., 109.

[36] Quoted in ibid., 108–9.

Bolshakoff continues:

> The recluse recommended frequent Communion and meditation on death. The poems of George the Recluse remind us of the wonderful poems of St. John of the Cross. George often experienced the dark night of the soul. In one place he writes: "Heavenly sadness overwhelmed me. I ask myself from where this dark cloud came to my soul. . . . Thought hardly moves in my heart. Life, however, encourages and strengthens me to the continuous endurance of things to come, whispering: 'Be patient a little while and the Omniscient will have compassion on you and will console you with eternal salvation. Pray with the heart. The repentant heart is a true sacrifice.' "[37]

Contemporary Christians tend to evaluate people according to categories of mental health. These categories themselves are really assumptions gathered from a variety of people, some of whom have very little sympathy for the spiritual life. Obviously people like George the Recluse were struggling with deep psychological difficulties. On the other hand, we must admire the greatness of heart and soul and the work of grace in such people, who despite their problems rise to an altruism in which they give themselves totally to God. It is interesting to note that this recluse was known for his concern for people and for his willingness to speak about Christ and heavenly things to those who came into his silent world. George was willing to break his seclusion to give spiritual direction or to speak to the troubled. It is perhaps a fault of our oversanitized and middle-class Christianity that we find it difficult to fit eccentrics into the fold of Christ. It is fortunate for us that God is not a psychologist.

Paissy Velitchkhovsky (1722–1794)

The man to whom the greatest credit is given for the restoration of Russian monasticism in the eighteenth century was a Ukrainian who lived most of his life outside Russia.[38] He brought the reforming spirit of St. Nicodemus from Mount Athos, where he was a monk, to Russia, the Slavic nations, and especially to Romania. Païssy Velitchkhovsky was a great inspirer of others. He once led his 350 disciples, mostly Slavonic monks, in a flight from the Catholic Hapsburgs to Romania, where he increased their number to five hundred.[39] By 1778 Païssy's community numbered a thousand, many of them Russians who were to return joyfully to their motherland, where they became instruments in the revival of monasticism during the nineteenth century.

Païssy was a restless spirit even early in life, moving from one monastery to another, at Athos and beyond, searching for the best possible monastic observance. He usually slept three hours a night and used his

[37] Bolshakoff, *Russian Mystics*, 110.
[38] Ibid., 79ff.
[39] Ibid., 86–87.

private time to translate selections from St. Nicodemus' *Philokalia* (along with many other books) into Slavonic. Bolshakoff speaks of several editions of the Slavonic *Philokalia* (called the *Dobrotolyubie*), saying that their "influence on Russian monks was astonishing. All the Russian contemplatives and mystics of the nineteenth and twentieth centuries were brought up either on the ... *Dobrotolyubie* or its Russian version prepared by the greatest Russian mystic of the nineteenth century, Bishop Theophan the Recluse." [40]

Unfortunately, his support of the revival of the Jesus prayer is the sole example in his writings of his personal devotion to Jesus Christ. "[W]hatever distracting thoughts may come, before they can produce any impression, the appeal to Jesus Christ will expel and destroy them." [41] These words are actually a quotation from St. Simeon the New Theologian.

The work and spirit of Païssy were enshrined at the Optina monastery, which was reformed by one of his novices, Theophanes, at the beginning of the nineteenth century. Optina became a thriving center of Orthodox monasticism, spirituality, and publication of vital translations into Russian, including the works of Païssy.[42] By the time of his death his followers included a thousand professed monks.

Many writers would visit Optina as a great center of Russian spiritual literature. These included Gogol, Soloviev, Tolstoy, and especially Dostoievsky, who is said to have described the monastery in *The Brothers Karamazov*.[43] A Catholic who reads the life of this outstanding monk and leader is likely to think of Dom Prosper Guéranger, who revived Benedictine monasticism in France in the nineteenth century. At Solesmes, the first French Benedictine house to be established after the Revolution, Dom Guéranger built a monastic center of liturgical prayer and study, the fruits of which have spread throughout the world.

St. Seraphim of Sarov (1759–1833)

Like St. Francis of Assisi, to whom he is often compared, Seraphim was the son of a merchant. Although he entered the monastery of Sarov at the age of eighteen, it was nine years before he professed because of the antimonastic laws of the time.[44] By the time he was ordained a priest at the age of thirty-four, he was already known for his holiness and mystical visions. He lived in the difficult time for Russian monasticism we have described above. In fact, he was ordained only a year before the death of Païssy Velitchkhovsky. Seraphim requested

[40] Ibid., 90.

[41] Quoted in ibid., 91.

[42] Bolshakoff, *Russian Mystics*, 92–93.

[43] Bouyer, *Spirituality*, 47.

[44] See Valentine Zander, *St. Seraphim of Sarov*, trans. Sr. Gabriel Anne, S.S.C. (Crestwood, N.Y.: St. Vladimir's Seminary Press, 1999). See also Julia de Beausobre, *Flame in the Snow* (Springfield, Ill.: Templegate Publishers, 1996).

to live as a solitary several miles from the monastery, to which he returned only on Saturdays to observe the liturgy and receive the Holy Eucharist.[45] No one thought that he would ever be known for anything. Later when he moved with permission into complete seclusion, not speaking to anyone for two years, living a life of extreme mortification, he suffered from what he described as diabolical attacks.[46] We get the impression from the attitude of the abbot, Nifont, that some thought Seraphim very odd. After being attacked by robbers at his hermitage, Seraphim returned to his monastery in 1810, where he continued to live a solitary life in his cell. Finally, in 1815, he began to receive people in response, it is said, to an order from our Lady in a vision. Ten years later, in response to another of our Lady's commands, he returned to living in a hut by himself, but because of his infirmities, one was built for him closer to Sarov. Here he received countless visitors. One might expect that such a withdrawn man would greet visitors in a cold, distant way. This was not the case. He called every visitor "my mother" or "my father", or most frequently "my joy".[47]

Bouyer compares St. Seraphim with St. John Vianney, the Curé of Ars, in that as many as five thousand people on a single day came to see the Curé and to hear his words.[48] Bouyer compares St. Seraphim with St. Francis, as well, in that both saints radiated joy and a mysterious friendliness with all creatures. Perhaps such comparisons with Catholic saints help Western readers appreciate Seraphim more easily, but all such comparisons limp. As Bouyer is careful to add, Seraphim was very much a monk and *staretz*, a kind of spiritual director, in the Russian tradition. Still, the similarities are undeniable: Seraphim and John Vianney both attracted huge crowds and were Christians of great biblical simplicity, winning souls to Christ by their uncompromising spirituality and loving kindness. As for St. Francis, the comparison may be even more apt: Francis had his wolf and the birds to whom he preached, and Seraphim had for his friend a bear, which he fed from his meager supplies. Both loved poverty and the folly of the Cross. As is true with Francis, many stories of the miraculous bejeweled Seraphim's reputation.

Unlike many of the Orthodox saints we have considered, St. Seraphim was not a writer or scholar. To gain insight into his devotion to Christ, we must rely on the words of others. Briefly put, his life was one of absolute consecration to God through the gifts of the Holy Spirit. He lived transfigured by grace, in union with the humble Christ

[45] The daily celebration of the divine liturgy was not the custom in the Eastern Church, even for priests. Daily Mass in the West originated at Cluny in the eleventh century and did not have any relationship to the East.

[46] Bolshakoff, *Russian Mystics*, 124–25.

[47] Ibid., 126–27.

[48] Bouyer, *Spirituality*, 48ff.

and His Mother. The best testimony of this seraphic spirituality is found in the notes of Nicholas Motovilov, written during Seraphim's life but not published until 1903, the year of his canonization.[49] Bolshakoff calls the notes the summit of Russian mysticism.

Motovilov, a nobleman, had come like "a decaying corpse" to see the *staretz* of Sarov in 1832 and was challenged by him to say whether he believed that Christ was God incarnate and that His Mother was ever a virgin. He was then asked whether he believed that Christ could heal him through the Virgin's intercession. The man said yes, and St. Seraphim told him he had been healed. At that moment he was.[50]

It is also noted that St. Seraphim had a gift for discerning the origins of people's illnesses, whether psychological or physical. In this respect, it might be said that his divine gifts made him one of the earliest psychotherapists.

The following selection, taken from Motovilov's notes, illustrates Seraphim's devotion, which is linked to his vision of spirituality being the indwelling of the Holy Spirit. In order to understand his Christology, it is important to remember the patristic teaching that after the Ascension, Christ sends the Holy Spirit to everyone who is saved. The Holy Spirit, up until the death of Christ, has given the Son to the world; now Christ gives the Holy Spirit to those who follow Him.[51] Previously we have not seen so explicit a link between devotion to Christ and the Holy Spirit.

> The true goal of Christian life consists in the acquisition of the Holy Spirit. . . . [O]nly the good deed which is performed for Christ's sake brings us the fruits of the Holy Spirit. Everything which is not done for Christ's sake, however good, fails to win compensation in the future life.
>
> The true aim of our Christian life consists in the acquisition of the Divine Spirit; prayer, vigils, fasting, alms, and other virtues practiced for Christ are merely means to the acquisition of that Divine Spirit.
>
> We have become so indifferent to the work of our salvation that we understand many passages of Scripture only in a weak and watered-down sense. The reason is that we do not seek divine grace, do not allow it to enter our souls because of our pride. Therefore, we are not truly enlightened by the Lord. The Spirit is sent into the hearts of those people who hunger and thirst for truth.
>
> When our Lord Jesus Christ accomplished the work of our salvation, after his resurrection, he breathed on the Apostles, renewing

[49] Bolshakoff, *Russian Mystics*, 130–40.

[50] Ibid., 130.

[51] See *Catechism of the Catholic Church*, nos. 690, 703, 725. See also Jn 7:39; 17:22; 16:14; the encyclical *Dominum et Vivificantem*, no. 23; and *St. Basil the Great on the Holy Spirit* (Crestwood, N.Y.: St. Vladimir's Seminary Press, 1980), 60–67.

> the breath of life lost by Adam. He gave to the Apostles Adam's sonship, the grace of the All-Holy Divine Spirit. On the day of Pentecost he solemnly sent to the Apostles the Holy Spirit in storm and tongues of fire. The Spirit descended on every one of them and filled them with the strength of flaming divine grace, which breathes like dew and makes joyful those who participate in its strength and actions. This same firelike grace of the Holy Spirit is given to all of us, the faithful of Christ, in the sacrament of Holy Baptism.
>
> When a sinner is converted to the way of repentance, this light of Christ destroys altogether the very traces of committed crimes and clothes the former criminal once more with the garment of incorruption woven by the grace of the Holy Spirit.[52]

A remarkable event took place when Motovilov asked Seraphim how he could be sure that he was in the grace of the Holy Spirit. The saint took him by the shoulders and said: "We are both now in the Divine Spirit. Why do you not look at me?" Motovilov responded: "I cannot look at you, Father, because lightenings stream from your eyes. Your face has become more brilliant than the sun and my eyes cannot bear it." The *staretz* answered:

> Do not be afraid, Lover of God, because you are now shining just as brightly as I am. You are now in the fullness of the Divine Spirit because, otherwise, you could not see me in that state.... You see, the Lord granted at once the humble request of the poor Seraphim. How much we must thank him for his indescribable gift to both of us. Rarely the Lord God manifests himself in this way, even to the greatest hermits. Divine grace has condescended to console your sorrowful heart, like a fond mother, at the prayer of the Mother of God herself. Why do you not look me in the eyes? Look simply and be not afraid; the Lord is with us.[53]

"After these words", Motovilov continues in his notes, "I looked at his face and even greater respectful fear overcame me. Picture in the midst of the sun at its noon-day brightest the face of the man who talks to you." When Fr. Seraphim asked how he felt, Motovilov said: "I feel such a stillness and peace in my soul that I cannot express them in words."

Seraphim told his friend that his peace was the "peace of which the Lord spoke to his disciples, saying: 'I give you my peace but not as the world gives do I give to you.' " At the end of this startling account he says: "Even more wonderful is that which our Lord Jesus Christ says of those who believe in him: 'He who believes in me, the works which I do, he shall do as well and he shall do much more because I go to

---

[52] Bolshakoff, *Russian Mystics*, 130–35.

[53] Ibid., 135–36.

my Father and will pray to him for you that your joy may be full. You have asked nothing in my Name until now; ask now and you shall receive.' Therefore ... everything you ask the Lord God, you shall receive, but this should be for the glory of God or for the benefit of your neighbor, because everything done on behalf of the latter he relates to himself, saying: 'Everything you did to any one of these little ones, you did for me.' "[54]

On the evening of January 1, 1833, Seraphim visited the infirmary chapel, where he received Communion and said farewell to his community with the words: "Be saved, be courageous and watchful. Today crowns are ready for us." He received visitors and spent his last hours singing Easter hymns. The next day, he was found dead kneeling before an icon of our Lady.

St. Seraphim was canonized in July 1903. The last tsar, Nicholas II, with the grand dukes carried his coffin. There were still voices among the intelligentsia and clergy speaking against his canonization because of the great number of accounts of extraordinary phenomena ranging from healing and levitations to a time of profound prayer that lasted five days and nights. Fortunately, they did not prevail, and as we have seen, the Providence of God used the same agents to preserve his relics as those who had attempted to destroy Christianity in Russia.

St. Theophan the Recluse (1815–1894)

It is appropriate that we bring our survey of the Orthodox world to a close with a very sophisticated, urbane saint (canonized by the Russian Orthodox Church in 1988) who has the intriguing name of Theophan (Feofan) the Recluse. Born the son of a devout priest, a dean of the clergy in his own area, Theophan grew up in a happy and pious home.[55] He attended the Kiev Ecclesiastical Academy and became a monk at the ancient laura of Kiev, making rapid progress up the ecclesiastical ladder because of his intellectual abilities and obvious spirituality. He became seminary rector at Kiev and finally at St. Petersburg. The Russian government sent him as part of a delegation to Palestine. He took the opportunity to visit important centers of monastic spirituality like St. Catherine's monastery in Mount Sinai, and he became familiar with Catholic and Protestant missions in the Holy Land. He learned French, Greek, Arabic, and Hebrew.

The delegation returned to Russia by way of Italy, where they were received by Pope Pius IX. Shortly after, he was to be made Bishop of Tambov and was then transferred to the prestigious and wealthy diocese of Vladimir. As bishop, he did a number of innovative things, opening parishes, schools, girls' academies, and even beginning a diocesan magazine. He was known as a first-class preacher and a fatherly

[54] Ibid., 140.

[55] See ibid., chap 10. See also Sergei Hackel, "Trial and Victory: The Spiritual Tradition of Modern Russia", in Dupré and Saliers, *Christian Spirituality*, 458ff.

bishop whose personal life was ascetic. Even as bishop, he ate only one meal a day. Nonetheless, it was a surprise to many when at the age of fifty, he asked to resign his see to become a contemplative monk. He entered the monastery of Vysha, remaining there until his death at the age of eighty. At first he participated in the Offices of the liturgy, but in 1872 he formally became a recluse, never leaving his small house and receiving no visitors. He offered the liturgy alone, and for the last eleven years of his life he offered it daily. This would not be common among the Orthodox as it is among the hermits of the Catholic Church.

Theophan was not entirely cut off from the world, however. He kept up his correspondence with clergy, religious, and others who sought advice and spiritual direction. He received between twenty and forty letters a day. His literary output was enormous and influential. We have already mentioned that he published a Russian translation of the *Philokalia*. He also translated and edited for Orthodox readers Fr. Scupoli's *Spiritual Combat*, one of the most popular books of post-Reformation piety, and wrote many books on the spiritual life.

Bolshakoff, who calls Theophan "the greatest Russian writer on mystical subjects not only in the nineteenth century but throughout Russian history",[56] provides us with a summary of his most important work, *Way of Salvation*.[57] Since a translation is not available, we will make use of Bolshakoff's summary and occasional direct quotations. Theophan gives a strong Christological description of the spiritual life, one that seems to be influenced by the thought and experience of St. Seraphim.

> Christian faith is not a doctrinal system but a way of restoration of fallen man through the death of the God-Man and the grace of the Holy Spirit. Take anyone who has followed the Lord and you will see that little by little he grows in spirit and becomes great in spite of all his insignificance. Fr. Seraphim is an example. He was a simple, unlearned man and yet to what heights he attained!
>
> God brings about the salvation of everyone in this way. Those who are disposed he attracts to the Son. The Son accepts each as he comes, and each is then transfigured by the grace of the Holy Spirit. This is the first, preliminary period. It lasts from the initial conversion until the time when the voice in the heart says: "God does everything in all." Complete abandonment to Divine Providence then comes to birth and God begins to act in man but through man's own forces. This is the second period—God-manhood. The third period is rest

---

[56] Ibid., 196.

[57] Mention should also be made of Bishop Ignatius Brianchaninov, who had stressed a rather dark view of the world and an aggressive spirituality. Although strongly dedicated to the Jesus prayer, he seemed to have little regard for other forms of spirituality. He was critical of all Western spiritual leaders, including SS. Francis and Ignatius Loyola, as well as of *The Imitation of Christ*. See also ibid., 144–63; 216.

> in God. The true place for this rest is in the world to come, but the beginning of it we have here.[58]

This is a particularly Orthodox summary of the doctrine of the three ways and hearkens back to the fourth-century writings of St. Gregory of Nyssa.[59]

The concept of light, as we have seen, is an important analogue in spiritual writing and is used by both Eastern and Western Fathers, as well as by St. Theophan.

> All heaven is boundless light. The Tri-hypostatic, Tri-illuminated Deity is hidden by the impassable divine light which can only be mentally contemplated. But God the Incarnate Word, although he shines with light of an intensity which created light never possessed, yet his light is accessible to the created eyes and is received according to the perfection of the creature who looks on him. Our Lady, the Theotokos, is nearest. Farther away are the Apostles and the Prophets, who were God-enlightened even here on earth. . . . Then all the saints in their various degrees: martyrs, ascetics, just men from all states and conditions of life. All are inundated with light coming out from the Face of our Lord and Savior, a light beyond all description. Below the saints are those who repented but had no time to purify themselves and who are purified by the action of the grace of penance and the prayer of the Church of the saints perfected and glorified in heaven. The light here is received according to the degree of purification, from a hardly noticeable twilight to the full light.[60]

In elaborating on the spiritual life, Theophan places it entirely as an experience of Christ, particularly related to the Eucharist. This summary is given by Bolshakoff.

> The first thing to do is to repent truly, so strive for the fullest possible confession. This purification is to be followed by Holy Communion which strengthens a man for a new life. Conversion is a pledge of new life, confession and absolution are the assertion of it, Communion is union with Christ. From the moment it is received grace begins to flow. As food is necessary to preserve the body, so Communion is necessary for spiritual life. Offering to God our freedom, we return to him as runaway slaves. In order that God would receive us, we must acknowledge our sins, repent and promise to sin no more. We must imitate the prodigal son who on his return to the father asked to be received as a servant. Sin leaves its traces

---

[58] Quoted in Bolshakoff, *Russian Mystics*, 218–19.

[59] See *From Glory to Glory: Texts from Gregory of Nyssa's Mystical Writings*, trans. and ed. Fr. Herbert Musurillo, S.J. (New York: Charles Scribner's Sons, 1961).

[60] Quoted in Bolshakoff, *Russian Mystics*, 220–21.

> everywhere in us and around us. To live in Christ is to have an intense Eucharistic life.[61]

Theophan of course sees Christ as the supreme spiritual teacher and His words in the Gospels as the highest possible teaching. Bolshakoff again reviews his doctrine:

> The Kingdom of God is within us, and in order to find it we must, according to the Savior, enter into the room of our heart. He who enters the heart and gathers there all his forces is a flaming spirit.
>
> He who enters into his heart is on the threshold of the new world and life. He must impress the structure of the spiritual world on his consciousness and receive it in his feelings. The bishop describes the structure of this invisible and spiritual world in these words: "The one God, worshipped in Trinity, who created and maintains everything, guides all of us in our Lord Jesus Christ through the Holy Ghost, who acts in the Holy Church and translates the faithful, when they are perfect, into another world. This will continue until the time of fulfillment or the end of the world comes. Then, after resurrection and judgment, everyone shall receive according to his deeds. Some will fall into hell while others will go to paradise and God will be all in all."[62]

Bishop Theophan's letters "give deep insight in his spirituality and are full of precious counsels and instructions".[63] The following quotation says a great deal.

> The Savior commanded us to enter into our inner room and there to pray to God the Father in secret. According to St. Demetrius of Rostov, the room means the heart. Consequently, the commandment of the Lord obliges us to pray mentally in our heart to God. This commandment extends to all Christians. The Apostle Paul commands the same, saying that we must pray in spirit always [Eph 6:18]. He commands mental or spiritual prayer to all Christians without exception. He also orders all Christians to pray unceasingly [1 Thes 5:17]. To pray unceasingly is possible only in the heart. Therefore it is impossible to contest the fact that mental prayer is compulsory for all Christians, and if it is obligatory, it is also possible because God does not command the impossible.[64]

Although the spiritual writing of St. Theophan the Recluse is very Orthodox, it is nonetheless in keeping with the development of this whole age in Christianity. In some ways he reminds us of his contemporary, John Henry Newman, which is not surprising since Newman was not

[61] *Russian Mystics*, 205–6.
[62] Ibid., 207.
[63] Ibid., 210.
[64] Quoted in ibid., 210–11.

only a man of his age but also deeply imbued with the spirit of the Church Fathers. Another writer who bears a surprising similarity to Theophan is the recently beatified Irish Benedictine abbot, Dom Columba Marmion (1858–1923).

Later we will return to the writings of Abbot Marmion, one of the most significant Catholic spiritual writers of the twentieth century. In the meantime we see perhaps much more than a similarity between the spiritual experiences of people in different traditions and the various branches of Christianity, all being drawn by the Holy Spirit, who is sent by Christ to open the great vistas of the spiritual life. Catholics and Protestants would do well to learn how the grace of Christ has worked in the East and in the experience of Orthodox Christians extending from Constantinople to Siberian Russia.

19 The Ancient Apostolic Churches

There are very ancient churches that do not fit the description of Orthodox churches; neither are they in union with the Holy See. These churches, often called Oriental Orthodox churches, such as the Armenian Apostolic Church, the Syrian Church of the East, the Coptic Church, the Ethiopian Church, and the Mar Thomas Church of India, represent ancient Christian traditions.[1] Their liturgies often are developments of the liturgy of Jerusalem, called the liturgy of St. James, rather than the Byzantine liturgy of St. John Chrysostom or the Latin liturgy of the West.

Their independent existence is largely traceable to geographic and historical factors that isolated these churches early on, as well as to differences in the understanding of the unity of Christianity and how this unity is to be accomplished. At times, some of these churches became involved in heretical doctrines, namely, the Nestorian understanding of the Incarnation. In recent years, however, these positions have often been reexamined and altered with careful theological study. Joint declarations of their patriarchs with Pope John Paul II have clarified some of the ancient controversies.

Our summary of Christian devotion would be incomplete without a consideration of these churches and their unique approach to Christ, which is often expressed in ancient and unusual terms. Yet, in their sacramental structure and their acceptance of the Scriptures and ancient traditions they are almost identical with the Catholic and Orthodox traditions.

The Armenian Church

For the sake of brevity, we will describe only one of these churches, the Armenian Church. The first Christian nation, Armenia was converted by St. Gregory the Illuminator (or Enlightener, ca. 257–ca. 339) seventeen hundred years ago (A.D. 301), about ten years before the official end of the Roman persecutions. The history of this church and its people is fascinating and includes the tradition that two of the

[1] In context here the term *apostolic* refers to those churches that claim to trace their establishment, usually in the Near East, to one of the original apostles. They are commonly called the Oriental Orthodox churches.

apostles, Bartholomew and Thaddeus, brought the faith to this nation. According to tradition the first saint of the Armenian Church was Princess Sanatruck, converted by Thaddeus and martyred at her father's order. There are good arguments for maintaining that there were Christian bishops in Armenia in the second century, and Tertullian says that Armenians were among those assembled at the first Pentecost. During the persecution by the emperor Diocletian (284–305), a group of nuns from Rome took refuge in Armenia but were eventually martyred, giving Armenia its first saints: Gaiana, Hripsime, and their companions. Since then, the Christian history of Armenia has been frequently anointed with martyrs' blood, a fact sadly repeated even in the twentieth century during the Armenian Holocaust.

The traditional account of the nation's conversion by St. Gregory the Illuminator, although steeped in legend, appears in its basic outline to be credible. He was an Armenian nobleman who as a child escaped the execution that was meted out to the rest of his family as the result of a failed conspiracy against the king. He grew up in Caesarea in Cappadocia, was converted there, and later lived in pre-Christian Rome.

Soon after he returned to Armenia, King Drtad demanded that he worship pagan gods. Gregory refused; he was severely tortured then imprisoned—almost entombed—for nearly thirteen years in a pit, which can still be seen. Shortly after this the king suffered a severe illness, causing him to rave and grunt like an animal. Whatever this illness was, it spread to the ranks of nobility and the army, and then to the general population. At this point, the king's sister reported a vision in which she was told that relief could only be obtained from Gregory, the imprisoned Christian, a man whom no one realized was still alive. When drawn from his pit, he was black as coal; friends cleaned him up before he was sent to see the king.

For the next two months, the king and his attendants, who were still ill, listened to Gregory's instructions. Although he instructed the king, he did not baptize him. Gregory was still a layman, and although he could have performed a valid baptism, he thought the king was not yet ready. Moreover, he knew the necessity of having a properly ordained bishop—something he would have learned living with the Christian community at Caesarea and Rome.

At this point, something of immense importance happened that from then on would shape the spiritual identity of the Armenian people. While the king and his nobles were being instructed and doing penance and fasting in sackcloth, Gregory had a vision. Although the account may be dramatized by legend and myth, the report of this remarkable vision of Christ has given a special identity to the Armenian people. To dismiss it as legend would be to misunderstand this nation. Nor is there any reason to doubt it, since it bears a notable resemblance to certain visions of the Old Testament and to those of the Acts of the Apostles. In Agathangelos' *History*, written probably in the fifth century, we have this account of Gregory's vision:

> One night I heard a fearful thunderous sound like roaring sea waves. The firmament of heaven opened, and a man descended in the form of light. He called my name; I looked up and saw him and fell to the ground, struck by terror. But he commanded me to look up and see great wonders.
>
> I did look up, and saw the firmament opened with the waters above it divided as is the firmament itself. The waters were like valleys and mountaintops, with infinite expanses that went far out of sight. Light flowed down to the earth, and the light was filled with shining two-winged creatures, human in appearance and with wings like fire. Their leader was a tall and fearful man who carried a golden hammer. He flew down near the ground in the middle of the city, and struck the earth. The rumbling sounded even in the depths of hell, and as far as the eye could see the earth was struck as level as a plain.
>
> I saw him in the middle of the city, near the palace, a circular base of gold as big as a hill, with a column of fire on it. On top of the column was a capital of clouds, and above that a cross of light. There were three other bases at the sites where St. Gayane and St. Hripsime were martyred, and one near the wine press where the nuns lived. These bases were blood-red, and they had columns of cloud and capitals of fire. From the columns, marvelous vaults fitted into one another and above this was [a] dome-shaped canopy of clouds. Under the canopy were thirty-seven holy martyrs in shining light—I cannot even describe them.
>
> At the summit of all this was a wonderful throne of fire with the Lord's cross above it. Light spread out in every direction from it. And an abundant spring gushed forth, flowing over and filling the plains as far as one could see. They made a vast bluish sea, the color of heaven. There were numerous fiery altars shining like stars, with a column on each altar and a cross on each column.
>
> There were herds of black goats, which when they passed through the water became sparkling white sheep. They gave birth to more sheep, filling the land. But some of these crossed to the other side of the water and became brown wolves which attacked the flocks. But the flocks grew wings and flew up to join the shining host, and a torrent of fire carried away the wolves.[2]

The heavenly visitor explained the vision to Gregory:

> The light filling the land is the preaching of the Gospel, and the fearsome man is the providence of God, who looks on the earth and

[2] Valerie Goekjian Zahirsky, *The Conversion of Armenia to Christianity: A Retelling of Agathangelos' History* (New York: Diocese of the Armenian Church of America, 2001), 18–20.

> it trembles. . . . The golden base is God's true Church, gathering all His people, and the shining cross above it is Christ Himself. The three-blood-red bases are the martyrs' torments. . . . And the crosses show that they are fellow sufferers with their lord Christ. . . .
>
> The herds of goats are sinners, washed clean by God's mercy, and worthy of His Kingdom. . . . [B]ut the flocks that became wolves are like those who depart from the truth.[3]

Gregory was told to build a temple to God where the golden base had been shown to him. He told the king that the time had come for him and his nobles to be freed from their tormenting demons. Kneeling by the caskets of the martyred nuns, Gregory prayed for Drtad and the others. He then turned to the king and "by Christ's grace cured his hands and feet enough so that he was able with his own hands to dig graves and bury the caskets in them".

Chapels were later built to house the remains of the martyrs. Gregory received the king's permission to destroy all pagan shrines in the country. Then Gregory set crosses on those sites where he wished churches to be constructed. Drtad wanted Gregory to be the people's pastor but he demurred. The king insisted, however, and sent Gregory with an edict to Bishop Leontius at Caesarea, in which he explained the history and miraculous conversion of Armenia to Christianity. Gregory was duly ordained priest and bishop by Bishop Leontius, who would be among the Council Fathers at Nicaea nearly twenty-five years later. According to *The Catholic Encyclopedia*, Gregory's son, Aristakes, was also a bishop and represented the Armenian Church at Nicaea in 325. It is he who brought the Nicene teachings to Armenia, where they have been safely held all these centuries.

Gregory was careful not to baptize people immediately. Instead he began a series of vigils, with periods of repentance and preaching. About a month later he baptized the entire royal family, and great omens and signs, including illuminated crosses, were seen. Holy Communion was distributed in one of the chapels Gregory had built in honor of the martyrs. Gregory saw to the education of candidates for the priesthood, whom he later ordained, and also appointed bishops.

Early accounts of the Armenian Church show that the faith and the power of secular royalty were closely linked. This was, in fact, typical of the nations that became Christian at that time. The early bishops in such countries were almost all noblemen and selected by the rulers. In Armenia the person who gave the church its independence, the one who corrected abuses and gave a powerful example of Gospel values including hands-on work with the poor and sick, was a young nobleman who had first resisted being a bishop out of humility and who finally accepted this role with complete personal commitment. This

[3] Ibid., 21.

was St. Nerses. After becoming chief Bishop of Armenia in 353, he initiated widespread reforms. When the Roman emperor Constantius forcefully attempted to introduce Arianism into the Christian churches, even exiling the Bishop of Rome, Liberius, St. Nerses stood firm in this conflict. King Bab, who went along with Emperor Constantius, was in open conflict with Nerses and other bishops who held an orthodox interpretation of Nicaea. Nerses was poisoned at the king's command, continuing the line of Armenian martyrs. After the rise of Islam, Armenia became an island of orthodox Christianity in a hostile world, suffering much right up to the tragic Armenian Holocaust of 1916. After surviving the Turkish government and the Bolsheviks, Armenia, which is always united to its large and loyal diaspora, continues as a faithful Christian nation to this day.

Karekin I (1932–1999)

I am tempted to plunge into the spiritual history of the modern Armenian martyrs of the Holocaust, for this is a history that should be more widely known. I have chosen, however, an outstanding Armenian of our time to illustrate the devotion of these people to Christ, namely, Karekin I. Born in Kessab, a place to which many Armenians had fled since the eleventh century to escape the Seljuk Turkish dynasty, Karekin I was the 131st Catholicos of all Armenians. Kessab was made famous by the resistance of the Armenians to the Holocaust in World War I and by Franz Werfel's book *The Forty Days of Musa Dagh*.[4] It is worth noting that Archbishop Karekin is sometimes referred to as Karekin II. This was his title when he was Catholicos of Cilicia. When he became Catholicos of All Armenians, his name changed to Karekin I.

Under the name of Karekin II, he is the author of an anthology called *In Search of Spiritual Life*.[5] Speaking of his own relationship with Christ when being interviewed, he responded to the question, "What is your relationship with the Lord today after so many years of following him?"

> The relationship has stayed the same in terms of my attachment to Him; but it has also become stronger, and has matured with my forty-five years of priesthood. In the beginning, there was enthusiasm, the vigor of a young man being called by the Lord. I perceived that call through the need of my people, particularly in the Near East, and then everywhere in the world that I have been. Now, after all these years, I can say that this relationship has become existential. That means that I cannot think of myself without referring to Him, to the Lord. My existence is filled by His presence, and each time that I think of doing such or such a thing, I ask myself what Jesus would

[4] See Giovanni Guaïta, *Between Heaven and Earth, A Conversation with His Holiness Karekin I* (New York: St. Vartan's Press, 2000).

[5] Karekin II, *In Search of Spiritual Life* (New York: Armenian Apostolic Church of America, 1994).

> do in my place. He is my model. Of course, I cannot say that I have followed Him perfectly, but I try to see my life and my work through His eyes. For me, the Gospel is not a book. It is the look of love that Jesus casts upon us. I think that today my relationship with the Lord has become a complete part of my existence.[6]

On the subject of disagreements between the Armenian teaching and the teaching of the Catholic Church on Christ, we must be brief. Put simply, the disagreements are about the nature of the Council of Chalcedon, which was not accepted as an ecumenical council by some of the Oriental churches. The Armenian, Coptic, Syrian and Ethiopian churches see it as a particular council rather than as a general ecumenical council. In December 1996, the Catholicos Karekin I and a number of Armenian bishops visited Pope John Paul II. Together they made a common declaration on Christology by affirming that "Jesus Christ is perfect God and perfect man and that his divinity is one with his humanity in a real and perfect union."[7] The Catholicos pointed out that many of the formulations of Chalcedon expressed what the church believed before the council but that there were other aspects that were adopted as norms of faith which had not been previously accepted, "particularly in Pope Leo's letter to Flavian where he describes the two natures as each having their own operations".[8] Karekin sums up the meeting with the Pope in this way: "So what we said with Pope John Paul II is not really anything new. Our theologians have recognized that we have different formulations but the same Christology."[9]

One of the most significant teachings of Karekin I concerns suffering and its relationship to the Cross. This should surprise no one when we consider the sufferings of the Armenian people. His words represent a very interesting point of view:

> Suffering has to be fought. We cannot accept it with a defeatist approach; we have to revolt against it and try to reduce and conquer it. This means first that we have to assume it voluntarily and courageously, to share it in order to assess personally its tragic nature and its destructive impact. Unless we know it by personal experience we cannot fight it efficiently. We need to taste its bitterness. To escape it seems at first instance the easiest way out. But when suffering has become a common evil we cannot avoid it because we are part of a community. Very simply, the individual human person, by his or her very nature, is a communal being and cannot be unaffected or disinterested. . . .

[6] Guaïta, *Between Heaven and Earth*, 3.
[7] Ibid., 101.
[8] Guaïta, 102.
[9] Ibid.

> Indeed, there is a particular way of conquering human suffering; that is what I would call the *sacrificial way*. It consists in assuming the suffering of others through love, compassion, fellowship, solidarity. That is what we all, as Christians, understand by the word Cross. Suffering ceases to be painful when it is assumed by a personal choice, voluntary action and loving spirit. Cross, above all, means personal engagement. And personal engagement implies faith, hope and love. And these three generate the courage that can defy even death. Today most Christians have turned the Cross into an ornament or a purely formal symbol. Therein lies the whole crisis in our Christian life all over the world. We all speak of the cross and, indeed, very proudly, but seldom accept personal crucifixion.[10]

It is important in understanding the Armenian mind to put suffering and its relationship to Christ in perspective. We need to remember first of all that this is a totally Christian nation. In 1975 in Madison Square Garden in New York, a memorial was held for the one and one half million martyrs of the Armenian Holocaust. At that time Karekin said:

> A sacred legacy has been transmitted to us through the sacrifice of the martyrs sealed by their own blood as the supreme manifestation of their love for and dedication to the highest values and ideals of our Christian faith, national identity and dignity... Such a life of dedication is a costly affair. It requires a sacrificial spirit, a courageous stand, living heroism. Here is where the Cross finds its proper meaning in our national life. For those who believe in the Resurrection, as had been the case of our people in the past, their belief can be recognized as authentic only it is vindicated by a life with the spirit of the cross occupying its center.[11]

Tragedy, martyrdom, and violent death have all been part of the history of the Armenian people though the ages. The accounts that I have heard of the martyrdom of the faithful during the Armenian Holocaust are shocking and devastating. There is a story of two priests, father and son, each being tortured and told that he could save the other by apostasy. They both died defending their faith. In the face of all of this the message of the Resurrection is crucial. The joyful cry "Christ is risen!" particularly echoes through the Eastern churches, both Orthodox and Catholic, at Easter time. Catholicos Karekin writes:

> Christ is risen! That shocking, extraordinary announcement is the only sentence that I would address to someone facing death....
>
> If a person does not believe in the Resurrection, death is truly the end of everything, the annihilation of a human person. The

[10] Karekin II, *In Search of Spiritual Life*, 137.

[11] Ibid., 154.

> Christian believes that man can go beyond death because Christ has already defeated it. . . .
>
> Faith in the Resurrection has been a vital force of our people. That same faith still operates today and always will remain for those who wish to follow Christ.[12]

It should come as a surprise to no one that devotion to Christ as Lord of Life and Death is the devotion of a people so badly treated throughout human history.

[12] Guaïta, *Between Heaven and Earth*, 266–67.

20 The Early American Protestants

The United States is a remarkable mix of peoples, races, and religions struggling together to form one nation. In no aspect of the country's development is this diversity more obvious than in its religious history. Not without struggle did this new nation make room for Catholics, who suffered greatly from prejudice generated by the hostility of the British government. It struggled a bit less to make room for Jews. In more recent times the United States has welcomed Buddhists, Hindus, and Muslims. All this diversity, however, should not obscure the fact that from its foundation the United States was essentially a Protestant nation. Our question is: How did the early American Protestants relate to Jesus Christ? What kind of devotion did they express? Clearly our answer must be complex. There are so many competing trends and ideas that we can summarize only the most important ones.

At the beginning of the Revolutionary War there were about three thousand places of worship in the thirteen colonies. They ranged from the largest denominations—the Congregationalists (749) and Presbyterians (485)—to the smaller ones like the Lutherans (240) and the Quakers, who had about two hundred meetinghouses. The Baptists had 457 churches; Anglicans had 400, and the Dutch and German Reform groups together had 328. This is all the more remarkable since the Church of England was the established church in the colonies. Catholics had only fifty-six churches, and Jews only five synagogues.[1] Most Catholic and Jewish places of worship were in areas where Quakers had extended religious liberty.

What can we say about devotion to Jesus in the New World? As we have seen, such devotion is shaped in part by theological opinion. However, the way in which people even within the same denomination relate to Christ can vary significantly. These variations are part of the drama of religious experience.

Pilgrims and Puritans

The influence of the Protestant Reformation on English-speaking people was considerable and led eventually to dissatisfaction even with

[1] James P. Moore, Jr., *One Nation under God: The History of Prayer in America* (New York: Doubleday, 2005), 55.

the Anglican Church. Anglicans who fled England after the restoration of Catholicism under Queen Mary (1553–1558) returned with ideas taken from Calvinism, Reform Protestantism, and Anabaptist teachings. We will see that the anti-Anglican Protestants had already developed their own approach to Christian life. Protestant writers like William Perkins and William Ames (see Chapter 13 above) developed the theological notion of covenant, and union with Christ in that covenant. The meditative piety of Richard Baxter, John Bunyan, and others mixed with the mystical spirituality of Francis Rous, which was not unlike that of John of the Cross. There was the devotion to the Heart of Jesus, preached by Thomas Goodwin. Many of the anti-Anglican Puritans had lived in Holland, where several competing ideas, including Catholic devotions, found a home. The popularity of *The Imitation of Christ* and the writings of such Catholics as St. Francis de Sales and Fénelon appear also to have influenced them subtly.

Before we can study Puritan devotion, we must recognize that these early colonists were so convinced of their own position that they were intolerant of others. Even though they had suffered persecution and prejudice, they often returned the same to those who disagreed with them, something the Quakers soon found out. However, the lives and attitudes of the Puritans were far more complex than we realize. They saw themselves on the "plain man's pathway to heaven", to borrow the title of one of their favorite books by the English Calvinist Arthur Dent.[2]

The complexity of the Puritan world, beginning with the establishment of the Bay Colony after 1620 and lasting into the nineteenth century, has been admirably explored by Perry Miller in his celebrated study, *The New England Mind*.[3] Before Miller's work, the New England Puritans were seen largely as simplistic and difficult fanatics with a cruel religiosity that came to a head in the Salem witch trials, during which some twenty women became victims of a terrible religious paranoia. Critics of the Puritans, however, rarely know that the principal judge in these trials, Samuel Sewall, Chief Justice of Massachusetts, spent much of the rest of his long life in public acts of penance and remorse for his judgments in these cases. Moore describes the confession Sewall made in 1697 before the congregation of his church, during which his statement was read by the minister. In it Sewall acknowledges his guilt and his willingness to "take the Blame and shame of it". He asks "pardon of men ... desiring prayers that God, who has an unlimited Authority, would pardon that sin and all other sins".[4]

[2] Louis Bouyer, *Orthodox Spirituality and Protestant and Anglican Spirituality*, vol. 3, *A History of Christian Spirituality* (New York: The Seabury Press, 1982), 155.

[3] *The New England Mind: The Seventeenth Century* (New York: Macmillan, 1939) and *The New England Mind: From Colony to Province* (Cambridge, Mass.: Harvard University Press, 1953).

[4] Moore, *One Nation under God*, 40. See also Horton Davies, *The Worship of the American Puritans 1629–1730* (New York: Peter Lang, 1990); *The Puritans in America*, ed. Alan Heimert and Andrew Delbanco (Cambridge, Mass.: Harvard University Press, 1985), 284.

Puritan piety was highly socialized and very related to the congregation. The word "congregation", in fact, was adopted as the name of their church.[5] Puritans spent many hours together at prayer on Sunday, and the sermon often lasted as long as the prayers. They established friendly relationships with the native population and tried to win them over to Christianity. Puritans considered themselves a people given entirely to God, and baptism was reserved for those who made a total commitment or came from totally committed families. As the community grew, however, a kind of half commitment was established, causing considerable debate; this became known as the Half-Way Covenant controversy.[6] Isolation made this kind of insular, completely committed society possible for a time. The Puritans tried to bring into being what Ames and others in England had developed in covenant theology a half century before. However, the isolation of the early Puritans eventually came to an end, forcing them to adjustment to a larger social reality.

The towns and villages, where everyone belonged to the church and participated in its services and activities, would eventually surrender to what the early Puritans saw as the influences of an evil world. The description of early Puritan congregations would lead us to believe that in some ways they resembled what Catholics once knew as settlements for lay members of religious orders (tertiaries), or oblates.

Staunchly opposed to formal liturgy, the Puritans left few written prayers. Those that do exist are often similar to sermons. They are almost all directed to God the Father, or perhaps to the Holy Trinity, addressed as "Almighty God". These prayers are often devotional and express a wide range of personal needs and experiences. They often acknowledge Jesus Christ as the sole author of our salvation, as the Incarnate Son of God, and our final judge. Although examples of Puritan devotion in America are rarer than those of seventeenth-century Catholics, they are rich and of a surprisingly warm and personal quality.

A number of similarities between Puritan and Catholic piety have been recognized by Protestant scholars, and one author portrays Puritan piety as "having many crucial linkages with the medieval Catholic Church, some of its best features being traceable directly to inheritance from Rome".[7]

In analyzing Puritan piety, it is important to know that although Christ is infrequently directly invoked, Puritans saw the whole growth

---

[5] Charles Hambrick-Stowe, ed., "Puritan Spirituality in America", in *Christian Spirituality: Post-Reformation and Modern*, ed. Louis Dupré and Don E. Saliers (New York: Crossroad, 1996), 338.

[6] Heimert and Delbanco, in *Puritans in America*, 218–19, 229, 230, provide a summary of this conflict and who took part in it.

[7] Richard C. Lovelace, "Puritan Spirituality: The Search for a Rightly Reformed Church", in Dupré and Saliers, *Christian Spirituality*, 318.

in the Christian life as an implantation in Christ.[8] This meant that after a profound confrontation with their own sinfulness, involving repentance, contrition, and humiliation (the realization that they could not save themselves), they gradually moved through the grace of Christ and by God's "effectual calling" to "full union with God".[9] Protestant scholars like Hambrick-Stowe note that Puritan spirituality offered union with God, and in this they see a difference from Catholic spirituality. They forget, or perhaps did not know, that Francis de Sales, de Montfort, Fénelon, and many other Catholics were making the same appeal to Catholic laity at the same time.[10]

With all these similarities and differences many Puritan writers were as personally devoted to Christ as were Catholics. Several examples of Puritan devotion given here in chronological order will prove this point.

Thomas Hooker (1586–1647)

Among the earliest Puritan ministers, Thomas Hooker led his congregation from England to settle in the Connecticut River valley.[11] He shows an interesting devotion to the suffering Christ, which had become popular in the Middle Ages, especially with the influence of St. Francis.

> Nay, if yet thou thinkest to lift up thyself above all creatures, and to bear more than they all, then set before thine eyes the sufferings of the Lord Jesus Christ, he that creates the heavens, and upholds the whole frame thereof. When the wrath of God came upon him, only as a surety, he cries out with his eyes full of tears and his heart full of sorrow, and the heavens full of lamentation, "My God, my God, why has thou forsaken me?" Oh thou poor creature, if thou hast the heart of a man, gird up the loins of thy mind, and see what thou canst do! Dost thou think to bear that which the Lord Jesus Christ could not bear without so much sorrow? Yet he did endure it without any sin or weakness; he had three sips of the cup, and every one of them did sink his soul; and art thou a poor sinful wretch, able to bear the wrath of God forever?[12]

He ends this picture of Christ suffering to take away the wrath of God with an appeal "to confess your sins to some faithful minister".[13] Here we are reminded of the call to repentance and sacramental confession that Catholic writers were making in France at the same time.

John Cotton (1584–1652)

Originally an Anglican priest, Cotton preached the farewell sermon when John Winthrop left England in 1630 with a group of Puritans to

[8] See ibid., 340–43.
[9] Hambrick-Stowe, "Puritan Spirituality in America", 340–41.
[10] Ibid., 341.
[11] Heimert and Delbanco, *The Puritans in America*, 22–23.
[12] Thomas Hooker, *The Soul's Preparation for Christ*, quoted in ibid., 25.
[13] Ibid., 26.

establish the Massachusetts Bay Colony. Cotton followed in 1633. By then, he was a Protestant minister and quickly became influential in Boston. In a series of sermons published as *The Way of Life*, he succinctly sums up the doctrine of implantation in Christ.

> A Christian man principally seeks Christ above and before the world (Matt. 6:33). He doth first look for spirituall things, he had rather have his part in Christ, then in all the blessings of this life, he would first order his heart to Christ, his principall care is about that. . . .
>
> Secondly, as he first and principally seeks Christ, so all the good things he hath, he looks for them from Christ, he goes not about his buisnesse in his owne strength, but what he wants he seeks it from Christ, and what he hath he receives it from Christ (Gen. 33:5, 11).
>
> Thirdly, a Christian man, as he receives the world from Christ, so he enjoyes them all in Christ; I meane he enjoyes it not in the sense of his owne desert, but he looks at himselfe less than the least of them all. . . . This is to enjoy all in Christ, not in his own worth, but in the merit of Christ. . . .
>
> Fourthly, he useth and imployeth all for Christ. . . . When he hath many blessings, he considers what he shall doe with them. This is the frame of a living Christian, one whose heart is given to Christ. . . . That God may be glorified in Jesus Christ . . . this is the upshot of all, this is all for Christ.[14]

Anne Bradstreet (1612–1672)

America's first woman poet, Anne Bradstreet is a startlingly original writer who has had an array of interpreters and critics, most of them puzzled by her obvious sensitivity and human qualities. Because of this, it has been suggested that she was a subversive in her society. But those who hold this opinion believe the stereotype of the Puritan as a "black-robed prude". Actually, Bradstreet was not only an authentic member of her society (her husband became governor of Massachusetts) but she was also a devoted disciple of Christ, whom she addresses in a very personal way.

The following poem describing a spiritually intimate experience on a sleepless night expresses, in fact, a universal Christian doctrine.

> I sought him whom my Soul did love,
> With tears I sought him earnestly;
> He bow'd his ear down from Above,
> In vain I did not seek or cry.
>
> My hungry Soul he fill'd with good,
> He in his Bottle putt my teares,
> My smarting wounds washt in his blood,
> And banisht thence my Doubts and feares.

[14] From John Cotton, *Way of Life*, cited in *American Sermons* (New York: Literary Classics of the United States, 1999), 46–47. Spelling slightly modernized.

What to my Saviour shall I give,
Who freely hath done this for me?
I'le serve him here whilst I shall live,
And Love him to Eternity.[15]

Many of Anne Bradstreet's poems refer to domestic life. Some are about praying for her husband and son when they are away; others lament the deaths of children and other relatives. They cover the range of things encountered by anyone trying to lead a Christian life and are marked by a pervasive sensitivity, which contradicts the impression of Puritans as cold and repressed. For all that, the poet was very much a Puritan. Her work is infused with unworldliness and a sense of the vanity of earthly things. More than anything else, she looks toward eternal life, hoping in Christ. Writing of death, she says the following, which is tinged with the Puritan's severe view of God.

What tho my flesh shall there consume
  it is the bed Christ did perfume
And when a few yeares shall be gone
  this mortall shall be cloth'd upon
A Corrupt Carcasse downe it lyes
  a glorious body it shall rise
In weakness and dishonour sowne
  in power 'tis rais'd by Christ alone
Then soule and body shall unite
  and of their maker have the sight
Such lasting joyes shall there behold
  as eare ne'r heard nor tongue e'er told
Lord make me ready for that day
  then Come deare bridegroom Come away.[16]

Anne Bradstreet was remarkably gifted, yet we may assume that she represents in many ways the thinking of ordinary Puritan women throughout those times.

Puritan Challenges

It lies outside our scope to discuss the history of the Puritan struggle to come to grips with a larger society, to deal with people not completely converted to Christ (the Half-Way Covenant) and even to deal with a non-Puritan society, as they were forced to do after the restoration of the Stuarts in England in 1660. The struggle was termed "God's Controversy with New England" by Michael Wigglesworth.

[15] Anne Bradstreet, "By Night When Others Soundly Slept", quoted in *Early New England Meditative Poetry*, ed. Charles E. Hambrick-Stowe (New York: Paulist Press, 1988), 77–78.

[16] Anne Bradstreet, "As Weary Pilgrim, Now at Rest", quoted in ibid., 96.

Increase Mather (1639–1723)

A graduate of Harvard who also studied at Trinity College, Dublin, Increase Mather walked into a controversy on his return to America in 1661. The following year he married John Cotton's daughter and in 1664 was named minister of the Second Church in Boston (the Old North Church), where he remained until his death. He preached against the Indians in King Philip's War in 1676, an uprising by Native Americans who felt that their openness to the Puritans had been abused. He served as president of Harvard from 1685 to 1701. Mather believed that the millennium, the thousand-year rule of Christ, was about to begin. Following his removal from the Harvard presidency, he grew disgusted with the factions among Puritans and wrote bitterly that "in the glorious times promised to the Church on earth, *America* will be hell".[17] Although he looks strange to us, he was a man of his time and a diligent pastor.

The execution in 1685 of James Morgan for murder occasioned one of the most interesting of Puritan religious documents, a sermon by Mather. Morgan had repented of his sins, confessed them publicly, and willingly accepted his punishment even as he warned others to learn from his sad fate. His last words were, "O Lord, receive my spirit, I come unto thee. O Lord.... I come, I come, I come."[18] Mather had no doubt that with sincere repentance this murderer could be saved, yet the words of his sermon are strong and frighteningly Calvinist. At the same time they show an absolute faith in the mercy of Christ. "In this way of sincere repentance, betake yourself to the City of Refuge; go to Christ for life.... They that have a real sight of their sins, and flie from the Avenger of Blood, unto Christ for Life, he is ready to succour them.... Look unto the Lord Jesus, that you may live and not die for ever. Build your hopes of Salvation on Christ and his Righteousness alone: Do not think you shall be saved, only because good men have prayed for you, or for the confession of your sins, which you have now made; or for the sake of any thing but Christ."[19]

Cotton Mather (1663–1728)

The son of Increase, Cotton Mather felt the weight of his inheritance early. He entered Harvard at eleven and at twenty-two was his father's assistant at the Second Church. Increase tried to stop the Salem witch trials, but Cotton objected, despite serious misgivings concerning the trials. He was volatile and, judging from our perspective, may have been bipolar. He became rather meditative in his later years and, indeed, almost mystical. He wrote in 1702, "Without the imitation of Christ all thy Christianity is a meer nonentity."[20] He studied *The Imitation of*

[17] Quoted in Heimert and Delbanco, *Puritans in America*, 239. Mather was equally condemnatory of Catholics, as we read in *American Sermons*.

[18] *American Sermons*, 194.

[19] From "Sermon Occasioned by the Execution of a Man Found Guilty of Murder", in ibid., 193.

[20] Quoted in Heimert and Delbanco, *Puritans in America*, 318.

Christ and corresponded with the German Pietist August Hermann Francke.

Cotton Mather was often preoccupied with what he saw as the works of Satan in the world. No wonder he was conflicted about the Salem witch trials. But even though he saw the Puritan dream of a holy nation disintegrate, his devotion to Jesus remained. That Cotton Mather had some of the less desirable traits of the Puritan stereotype cannot be denied. Nonetheless, he had a great personal devotion to Jesus Christ.

> With a Great Zeal, we should lay hold on the Covenant of God, that we may secure Us and Ours from the Great Wrath, with which the Devil Rages. Let us come into the Covenant of Grace, and then we shall not be hook'd into a Covenant with the Devil. . . . The way to come under the saving influences of the New Covenant is to close with the Lord Jesus Christ, who is the All-sufficient Mediator of it: Let us therefore do that, by Resigning up ourselves unto the Saving, Teaching, and Ruling Hands of this Blessed Mediator. Then we shall be what we read in Jude 1, Preserved in Christ Jesus. . . . Thus the Blood of the Lord Jesus Christ, sprinkled on our Souls, will preserve us from the Devil.[21]

This stern figure in American history had a surprisingly beautiful death, which brings out the positive side of Puritan piety. The day before he died, Cotton said to his son: "I am going to eat the bread of life and drink freely the water of life." He told his wife: "I am going where all tears shall be wiped from my eyes." And again, "Why should I not smile, when everything looks smiling upon me?"[22]

Edward Taylor (1642–1729)

Taylor, with Anne Bradstreet, is among America's earliest poets. Like Bradstreet, his startling emotional imagery and deep sensitivities represent a dramatic exception to the Puritan stereotype. Yet he was very much a Puritan, serving more than fifty years as a minister in Westfield, Connecticut (now Massachusetts).[23] His poems were discovered only in 1937 and are—surprisingly—often meditations on the Eucharist. We must recall that although Calvin and his followers rejected the concept of transubstantiation, they struggled with what to put in its place. Neither Calvin nor Luther could accept Zwingli's symbolic interpretation. Writing about the presence of Christ in the communion supper, Calvin said, "I shall not be ashamed to acknowledge that it is a mystery too sublime for me to be able to express."[24]

[21] From "The Wonders of the Invisible World", in *American Sermons*, 210–11.

[22] C. Bernard Ruffin, *Last Words: A Dictionary of Deathbed Quotations* (Jefferson, N.C.: McFarland, 1995), 132.

[23] Heimert and Delbanco, *Puritans in America*, 294.

[24] Ibid.

The Puritans had already settled the matter of the Half-Way Covenant in the 1660s: the less committed could be baptized but communion remained reserved for the completely converted. Taylor saw his role not only in keeping the unworthy from communion but also in preparing those who were fully converted to receive with great fervor. "Not to prepare is a contempt of the invitation", he said.[25] His poems are really prayers composed as personal notes. With their publication from 1943 to 1960 scholars were able to reexamine the Puritans "from the perspective of a man who for 43 years regularly meditated in a manner traditionally thought of as Catholic in preparation for administering Holy Communion".[26] This becomes even more fascinating when we discover that Oliver Cromwell, sworn enemy of all things Catholic, was a hero of Taylor's.

For those interested in the psychology of religious experience Edward Taylor's writings are a gold mine. Early in life he began writing occasional poems, but it was when he endured the profound sorrow of watching many of his children die in childhood, that his poetry turned to the mystical expression of the saving blood of Christ in the Eucharist. When his beloved wife, Elizabeth, died at the age of thirty-nine following the birth of their eighth child, he wrote an elegy for her that includes these beautiful lines:

> Some deem Death doth the True Love Knot unty:
> But I do finde it harder tide [tied] thereby.
> My heart is in't and will be squeez'd therefore
> To pieces if thou draw the Ends much more.[27]

Taylor hoped that "some Angell may my Poem sing / To thee in Glory". This Puritan minister was a man of great loves. He remarried at fifty, and his second wife, Ruth Wyllys, bore him six more children, the last when he was sixty-six years old. It is not surprising that such a man would use images from the language of eroticism and love in religious poetry. Like some celebrated Catholic mystics and the English Puritan Francis Rous, Taylor could speak of his relationship with Christ as "Thy Person mine, Mine thine, even weddenwise".[28]

As with all Puritans and, ultimately, all real Christians, the mystery of Christ's love for the fallen individual and human race became a theme of wonder and gratitude for Taylor. Meditating on the words "my spouse" in the Song of Songs (4:8), he writes:

---

[25] Ibid., 295.

[26] Hambrick-Stowe, *Early New England Meditative Poetry*, 39.

[27] From Taylor's elegy, entitled "A Funerall Poem Upon the Death of my ever Endeared, and Tender Wife Mrs. Elizabeth Taylor, Who fell asleep in Christ the 7th day of July at night about two hours after Sun setting 1689 and in the 39 yeare of her Life", quoted in ibid., 47.

[28] Quoted in Hambrick-Stowe, *Early New England Meditative Poetry*, 49.

I am to Christ more base, than to a King
A Mite, Fly, Worm, Ant, Serpent, Divell is,
Or Can be, being tumbled all in Sin,
And shall I be his Spouse? How good is this?
It is too good to be declar'de to thee.
But not too good to be believ'de by mee.[29]

Taylor's Eucharistic poems seem to have been written as he contemplated the bread and wine to be used for communion the next day. Unlike Catholics, who approach Christ's presence on the altar after the consecration of the elements, he anticipates this presence in what is called—contrary to popular misconceptions of Congregationalists themselves—"a real spiritual presence". The following lines from his meditation on John 6:51, "I am the bread of life", could have been written by Thomas Aquinas.

The Purest Wheate in Heaven, his deare-dear Son
Grinds, and kneads up into this Bread of Life.
Which Bread of Life from Heaven down came and stands
Disht on thy Table up by Angells Hands.[30]

The poetry of Edward Taylor is filled with biblical and classical imagery. However austere his life may have been, he deserves the title of devout humanist as much as do de Sales and Fénelon. In our final selection from Taylor we also see a different aspect of his poetry, one in which the language is more familiar to us and his use of words closer to our own. Here the poet emphasizes not only that Christ is present in the Eucharist but also that the sacrament fills the individual's spiritual life with graces that are symbolized by nutritious food, just as Christ Himself uses the metaphor of food in chapter 6 of St. John's Gospel.

A Deity of Love Incorporate
My Lord, lies in thy Flesh, in Dishes stable
Ten thousand times more rich than golden Plate
In golden Services upon thy Table,
To feast thy People with. What Feast is this!
Where richest Love lies Cookt in e'ry Dish?

A Feast, a Feast, a Feast of Spiced Wine
Of Wines upon the Lees, refined well
Of Fat things full of Marrow, things Divine
Of Heavens blest Cookery which doth excell.
The Smell of Lebanon, and Carmell sweet
Are Earthly damps unto this Heavenly reech.

[29] "Meditation on Canticle 4:8", quoted in Hambrick-Stowe, *Early New England Meditative Poetry*, 191.

[30] "Meditation on John 6:51: I Am the Living Bread", quoted in Hambrick-Stowe, *Early New England Meditative Poetry*, 171.

Oh! what a feast is here? This Table might
Make brightest Angells blush to sit before.
Then pain my Soule! Why wantst thou appitite?
Oh! blush to thinke thou hunger dost no more.
There never was a feast more rich than this:
The Guests that Come hereto shall swim in bliss.

Hunger, and Thirst my Soule, goe Fasting Pray,
Untill thou hast an Appitite afresh:
And then come here; here is a feast will pay
Thee for the same with all Deliciousness.
Untap Loves Golden Cask, Love run apace:
And o're this Feast Continually say Grace.[31]

The End of the Puritan World

It was inevitable that the closed homogeneous society of the Puritans would come to an end, and it was predictable that as it did so, people would seek an explanation for it all. The Puritan world vision was based on the Bible and their conviction that they had been chosen by God to establish a new Zion on a virgin continent (despite the fact that Native Americans were there long before them). Their first brush with reality came with the Half-Way Covenant controversy a scant forty years after the founding of the Massachusetts Bay Colony. When that compromise did not work out, the Puritans came to the conclusion that the world was about to end, that Christ was about to return in glory to establish His Kingdom. They looked to the mysterious words and symbols of the Book of Revelation, to the prophets Isaiah and Zeccariah, and to Christ's own prediction of the destruction of Jerusalem (in A.D. 70) and the end of the world. Through these things they found hope in the belief that the world they knew would end. For this reason we find people as different as the emotional Cotton Mather and the brilliant and intellectual Jonathan Edwards expecting the end of their world and the coming of the Kingdom of Christ on earth—the millennium. Despite this apocalyptic belief, the latter part of the seventeenth century and the beginning of the eighteenth were a relatively tranquil period. Puritan numbers increased from fewer than twenty thousand in 1640 to more than a hundred thousand in 1700. Other Protestant congregations also continued to grow, and we will soon consider them, especially the Quakers and the Baptists.

But then came "a phenomenon as wondrous as it was inexplicable". Suddenly there was an outpouring of religious fervor, of spirituality and conversion.[32] Actually, the first of these phenomenal periods

[31] "Meditation on Isaiah 25:6: A Feast of Fat Things", quoted in Hambrick-Stowe, *Early New England Meditative Poetry*, 174–75.

[32] Edwin Scott Gaustad, *The Great Awakening in New England* (Chicago: Quadrangle Books, 1968), 16ff.

of conversion began in 1680 and continued through the early eighteenth century in New England, so that in the words of Jonathan Edwards, "the greater part of the young people in the town seemed to be mainly concerned for their eternal salvation".[33] The great revivalist minister who led these "harvests" was Solomon Stoddard (1643–1729), who preached an absolute sovereign God and a miserable eternity to those God did not choose to save. Though Stoddard is not well remembered, one of his descendants would become the most impressive minister of the century.

Jonathan Edwards (1703–1758)

Stoddard's tall and handsome grandson, Jonathan Edwards, left his post as tutor at Yale to come to Northampton, Massachusetts, in 1727 to assist his aging grandfather as minister of the most famous church outside Boston. He was appalled by the "licentiousness ... among the youth of the town". By 1733, however, a remarkable change was taking place.

> This work of God, as it was carried on, and the number of true saints multiplied, soon made a glorious alteration in the town; so that in the spring and summer following, anno 1735, the town seemed to be full of the presence of God: it never was so full of love, nor so full of joy; and yet so full of distress as it was then. There were remarkable tokens of God's presence in almost every house. It was a time of joy in families on the account of salvation's being brought unto them; parents rejoicing over their children as new born, and husbands over their wives, and wives over their husbands.[34]

The fervor spread to many towns in Massachusetts and Connecticut. "There was a general awakening", according to the Reverend Benjamin Lord of Preston, Connecticut, the minister who put a name to this historic reality. Then a natural disaster struck, a serious epidemic of "throat distemper" that lasted more than four years. Great numbers, especially children, died of what may have been diphtheria. Because the awakening and the timing of the epidemic were different and occurred in different places, one could say that the awakening "does not seem to have taken its rise from any sudden and distressing calamity".[35]

Edwards was in the midst of it all. Unlike the Puritans we have already encountered, he was an ordained Presbyterian minister. A brilliant intellect who possessed a remarkably high level of mental energy, he was America's first real psychologist and wrote extensively about his inner experiences in much the same way Augustine had done in the *Confessions* thirteen hundred years before.

---

[33] Cited in ibid., 16.

[34] *The Works of President Edwards in Four Volumes* (New York, 1843), 3, 235, quoted in Gaustad, *Great Awakening*, 18.

[35] Gaustad, *Great Awakening*, 21.

At the age of twenty-seven, Edwards was asked to deliver the famous "Thursday Lecture" in Boston. The concepts he expressed therein seem to embody in embryonic form the most important ideas of his later life. The paper was published as "God Glorified in the Work of Redemption, by the Greatness of Man's Dependence upon him, in the Whole of it".[36] Morimoto, a Japanese Protestant scholar, in a work based on his doctoral dissertation at Princeton Theological Seminary, sees Edwards' view of salvation as closely parallel to Catholic doctrine. This is a real departure especially from the views of Luther, who saw grace and salvation as extrinsic to the saved individual. Morimoto makes the remarkable case for Edwards' having the view of salvation and redemption found among Catholic and Orthodox theologians.

> Edwards's soteriology uniquely accents the inherent good that redeemed persons have by salvation. Grace transforms human beings so that they may have "spiritual excellency and joy by a kind of participation [in] God". They are not only *counted* as righteous, but are themselves *made* excellent "by a communication of God's excellency" and *made* holy "by being made partakers of God's holiness". For Edwards, salvation means a palpable reality of regeneration. To be saved is to participate in the fullness of God by the communication of God's own nature to humanity. God "communicates" himself to human beings, and human beings "participate" in the nature of God. This vision of salvation is attested to in Scripture (2 Peter 1:4) and is shared by the Roman Catholic and Eastern Orthodox churches. According to Thomas Aquinas, the end of grace is to make human beings "partakers of the divine nature", while the Eastern Orthodox term for this vision is "divinization" or "deification" (*theosis*).[37]

When we read this remarkable statement, we should recall that Perry Miller has said, "Puritanism is the essence of Protestantism, and Jonathan Edwards is the quintessence of Puritanism." Yet, building on Calvin's recognition of the possibility of personal sanctification, Edwards came to conclusions that are close to the teachings of the Catholic Church, a fact he would have found astonishing. Unlike his Protestant contemporaries in Europe, Edwards would have had no familiarity with such writers as Francis de Sales or Fénelon. In fact, serious Protestant scholars writing about Edwards' "Catholic concern" emphasize that he did not even think to compare his teaching with Catholic doctrine. Morimoto sums this up: "On Edwards's theological horizon, Roman Catholicism did not present itself as something to be confronted or to be reconciled with."[38] Whatever similarity there may

[36] Anri Morimoto, *Jonathan Edwards and the Catholic Vision of Salvation* (University Park, Penn.: Pennsylvania State University Press, 1995), 4.

[37] Ibid., 5.

[38] Ibid., 9.

have been in doctrinal areas, Edwards could scarcely be accused of having conscious Catholic leanings. Accepting the standard Protestant rhetoric of the day, he classified Catholics as "heathens or atheists". His knowledge of Catholic theology did not go beyond the conventional literature of the time, and he would hardly have been aware of Eastern Orthodox theology.[39]

Edwards did not produce devotional prayers to Christ. However, his sermons are filled with powerful and intellectual devotional sentiments. His devotion is not pietistic or sentimental but is filled with a solemn sense of adoration and gratitude. Of his early years he wrote:

> Since I came to this town [Northampton], I have often had sweet complacency in God, in views of his glorious perfections and the excellency of Jesus Christ. God has appeared to me a glorious and lovely Being, chiefly on account of his holiness. The holiness of God has always appeared to me the most lovely of all his attributes....
>
> I have loved the doctrines of the Gospel; they have been to my soul like green pastures. The Gospel has seemed to me the richest treasure, the treasure I have most desired, and longed that it might dwell richly in me....
>
> It has often appeared to me delightful to be united to Christ, to have Him for my head, and to be a member of His body; also to have Christ for my teacher and prophet. I very often think with sweetness and longings and pantings of soul of being a little child, taking hold of Christ, to be led by Him through the wilderness of this world.... I love to think of coming to Christ, to receive salvation of Him, poor in spirit, and quite empty of self, humbly exalting Him alone; cut off entirely from my own root, in order to grow into and out of Christ; to have God in Christ to be all in all; and to live by faith on the Son of God, a life of humble, unfeigned confidence in Him.[40]

Edwards and Puritan Controversies

The Great Awakening of the 1730s owes much to Edwards, its most eloquent exponent. He was, however, critical of some of its expression, especially of what might be called ecstatic gesturing and hyper-enthusiasm. George Whitefield, an Anglican clergyman we have already met, arrived in New England in September 1740 and added fire and discordant criticism to the awakening with powerful preaching and blunt condemnation of the clergy, who for the most part "do not experimentally know Christ".[41] Of the Puritan colleges, Harvard and Yale, Whitefield said that "their Light is become Darkness". He was suspended for liturgical improprieties by the Episcopal Court in July

[39] Readers interested in Edwards' agreement with Catholic theology on Christ and salvation would do well to study Morimoto's systematic comparison in ibid., chap. 5.

[40] Jonathan Edwards, "Personal Narrative", in *Selected Writings of Jonathan Edwards*, ed. Harold P. Simonson (New York: Frederick Ungar, 1970), 38–40.

[41] George Whitefield, *Seventh Journal*, cited in Gaustad, *Great Awakening*, 30.

1740. Although Whitefield brought great sparkle and notoriety to the awakening, he left America, and it fell to Edwards and the clergy who agreed with him to defend their cause, which came to be identified as the New Light. The Old Lights, the more traditional Calvinists, led by Edwards' former friend Charles Chauncy, became more and more critical of the awakening. The latter group received their nickname to distinguish them from the New Lights.

Eventually Edwards became involved in the old Half-Way Covenant controversy and maintained that only those who had experienced conversion could receive the Eucharist. This caused him to leave Northampton and work as a missionary among Native Americans in western Massachusetts. He also continued to write and study from 1750 to 1757. With all the interest in the awakening, it should be no surprise that Jonathan Edwards was appointed president of the College of New Jersey (now Princeton). Sadly, he died only a year later. Some have called him the greatest intellect in America up to 1900, although he has also often been popularly maligned. His sermon "Sinners in the Hands of an Angry God" is unrepresentative yet is the selection that most students read in anthologies. His beautiful sermon "On the Excellencies of Christ" is rarely quoted.

> How much Christ appears as the Lamb of God in his invitations to you to come to him and trust in him. With what sweet grace and kindness does he from time to time call and invite you.... How graciously is he here inviting everyone that thirsts, and in so repeating his invitation over and over: "Come ye to the waters; come, buy and eat, yea, come!" ...
>
> And how much like a lamb does Christ appear in Matt. xi., 28–30: "Come unto me, all ye that labor, and are heavy laden, and I will give you rest. Take my yoke upon you, and learn of me, for I am meek and lowly in heart; and ye shall find rest to your souls. For my yoke is easy, and my burden is light." O thou poor distressed soul, whoever thou art, that art afraid that you never shall be saved, consider that this that Christ mentions is your very case, when he calls to them that labor, and are heavy laden![42]

The New Light Presbyterians in the middle colonies kept the awakening alive for some time. The College of New Jersey had been opened by the pro-revivalist Presbyterian Synod of New York at Elizabethtown, New Jersey, in 1747. It served as a "nursery of piety" not only for the middle-colony Presbyterians but also for New Light Congregationalists and Baptists.[43]

[42] Jonathan Edwards, "The Excellency of Christ", in *Selected Writings*, 122–23.
[43] Gaustad, *Great Awakening*, 108.

The Puritans and the Catholics

When Catholic immigrants came to New England after the American Revolution had extended religious freedom to all, they found themselves unwelcome and misunderstood. Few colonists had any familiarity with Catholics, and those who did usually had met only a few of the French or Polish officers who had assisted in the war against England.

The New England Puritans had no experience of Catholic worship. Yet Protestant scholars stress the similarities and even the relationships between their ancestors' Protestant piety and that of the Catholic mystics and saints of the time. Hambrick-Stowe, a Protestant scholar, sums up these similarities very well.

> Similarities between Puritan and Catholic encounters with the divine may be explained by the considerable amount of Christian theology they shared. American Puritan diary accounts of self-examination and meditation on sin differ little from the sentiment of the Ignatian *Spiritual Exercises*. Both Teresa of Avila and Cotton Mather recounted angelic visitations and the flight of their souls heavenward. Puritans and Catholics in meditation on the cross or the Sacred Heart experienced the presence of Christ.[44]
>
> The use of physical objects and pictures as means of meditation is commonly associated with Catholic spirituality, but American Puritans made use of them as well. Ministers like the poet Edward Taylor sat before the communion elements and vessels in meditation on Saturday nights prior to administering Holy Communion. Diaries and private poetry suggest that New Englanders used the traditional *memento mori* (symbols of death) in their devotional mortification, confession of sin, and preparation for death.... Scholars have pointed to the similarity between the Roman Catholic confessional and the Puritan diary.[45]

As we leave the Puritans, we realize that they have been negatively stereotyped by many, including the descendants of the Catholic immigrants who had been treated so inhospitably by them. We hope that this book may dispel some of those stereotypes.

The Churches of the Free Spirit

There are at least three traditions in the modern English-speaking world that are ideologically similar in their initial goals but which would appear to be unrelated. Picture a huge Baptist church in a southern American city with several ministers, a staff of fifty, classrooms, a food court, and a sanctuary that holds two thousand worshippers. Then think of a Quaker meetinghouse in the Northeast with a congregation made up of people with at least a master's degree who are quite sophisticated in a modest way. Then move to Lancaster County, Pennsylvania, to a simple Gospel

[44] Hambrick-Stowe, "Puritan Spirituality in America", 339.

[45] Ibid., 351.

service held in an Old Order Amish home, since there are no formal church buildings. The minister of the big Baptist church is an executive; there is no minister at all in the Hicksite (Quaker) Friends Meeting, but one of the farmers in his black Amish suit goes by the title of bishop and exercises more authority over his flock than any Catholic bishop would dream of. What did they have in common when they began, and what makes them so different now? We will look briefly at the similarities and differences before we discuss their devotion to Christ.

First of all the Baptists and the Amish, along with the Mennonites and many smaller churches, like the Dunkers and the Swiss and German Brethren, trace their roots to Anabaptist movements at the time of the Reformation. The Quakers, on the other hand, began with an almost informal collection of devout souls in England during the Protectorate of Oliver Cromwell in the mid-seventeenth century. They were seeking a more intuitive and personal expression of the Christian life than what they found in the churches of the Anglican, Calvinist, or Baptist traditions. The person who brought these people together in a spiritual movement that eventually became a religious denomination was George Fox (1624–1691), a leather-worker and shepherd with little formal education. Although not all of the Friends referred to Fox as founder, an authoritative Quaker writer, Geoffrey Nuttall, wrote: "Nothing can rob him of the glory of having founded Quakerism, and of having done it alone by the sheer force of his personality and of faith in his mission."[46]

If the Baptists and the Quakers have different roots, expressions, and ideas about baptism, why do scholars tend to study them and their spirituality together? The answer is simple and revealing. Baptists and Quakers were in essential agreement that the key for the individual to enter the Kingdom of God was holy obedience to the experiential confession of faith and to holiness of the heart, a holiness that was family centered and founded on personal conversion. This was the message preached in books like *Pilgrim's Progress*, a work that profoundly affected English-speaking Christians. Interior personal inspiration was of supreme importance to Baptists, and they were also deeply influenced by the idea that anyone reading the Scriptures with a pure heart would interpret them correctly. An important Anabaptist writer, Max Göbel, wrote the following illuminating description of Baptist spirituality in 1848. It is cited in the authoritative statement "The Anabaptist Vision", an address given by Harold S. Bender (1943) before the American Society of Church History.

> The essential and distinguishing characteristic of this church is its great emphasis upon the actual personal conversion and regeneration of every Christian through the Holy Spirit.... They aimed

[46] Quoted in Douglas V. Steere, ed., *Quaker Spirituality: Selected Writings*, Classics of Western Spirituality (New York: Paulist Press, 1984), 8.

> with special emphasis at carrying out and realizing the Christian doctrine and faith in the heart and life of every Christian in the whole Christian church. Their aim was the bringing together of all the true believers out of the great degenerated national churches into a true Christian church. That which the Reformation was originally intended to accomplish they aimed to bring into full immediate realization.[47]

Because of the requirement of total dedication similar to the full covenant concept of the Puritans, Baptists on all sides (and there are many denominations) insist that candidates for baptism must give at least "credible testimonies of authentic conversion".[48] There is a difference of opinion as to the minimum age at which this is possible; however, in the last hundred years, according to E. Glenn Hinson, the usual age for baptism has dropped in the various Baptist denominations from twenty to seven or eight years.

The Quaker tradition, of course, avoids sacraments. In place of visible signs, modeling, or good behavior, became an important part of the expression of obedience to the Holy Spirit. William Penn, a personal disciple of George Fox's, remembered him as having a "clear and wonderful depth", capable of bringing out the best in people. Penn recalled his "awful, living, reverent frame" in prayer, "a new and heavenly-minded man".[49] Some Quakers in the Midwestern United States apparently saw this very individual approach as less productive, and they established what are called pastoral Quakers, that is, Friends with their own trained clergy.

Both Quakers and Baptists show concern for the spiritual life and growth of those who have accepted the Holy Spirit. Hinson says that the Baptists have paid less attention to spiritual growth because they have been locked in to a conventional model of parish life and have neglected what others call the need for ongoing conversion, or spiritual development. Eminent Quaker writers like Rufus Jones and, more recently, Douglas Steere have called Quakers to an ongoing spiritual development and have made ample use of Catholic spiritual writers in this endeavor. This remarkable fact is less appreciated than it should be.

Unaware of the fact that Catholic sources were often used in Quaker writings, and even of some mutual local sharing as a result of the Second Vatican Council (at which Steere was the Quaker observer), I recall my astonishment when the daughter of Rufus Jones, arguably the most eminent Quaker spiritual writer of his time, once said to me, "Quakers and Catholics have a great deal in common." She then

[47] Max Göbel, *Geschichte des Christlichen Lebens*, etc., 1, 134, quoted in Harold S. Bender, *The Anabaptist Vision* (Scottdale, Penn.: Herald Press, 1944), 13–14.

[48] E. Glenn Hinson, "Baptist and Quaker Spirituality", in Dupré and Saliers, *Christian Spirituality*, 329.

[49] Ibid.

told me she had attended the installation of Pope John XXIII in 1958 and that her father had given her permission to kiss the foot of the statue of St. Peter at the entrance of St. Peter's Basilica.

This brings me to a surprising fact. Many early Anabaptists and Quakers wanted to form communities made up of those totally obedient to God and enlightened by the Holy Spirit. A number of writers, some of them recognized Baptist scholars, believed this impulse stemmed from the Catholic religious orders and contemplative tradition of the Middle Ages.[50] Particularly because of the persecution endured by Anabaptists at the hands of Catholics, Lutherans, Reform Protestants, Calvinists, and Anglicans, the early pioneers of the spirit did not recognize "the rock from whence they were hewn".[51] Bender quotes Albrecht Ritschl, who sees in Anabaptism "an ascetic semi-monastic continuation of the medieval Franciscan tertiaries and locates the seventeenth-century Pietists in the same line".[52] He prefers to see the movement as an attempt to bring the Reformation to its full expression, rejecting the Lutheran, Calvinist, and Zwinglian approaches.

There is no doubt that both the English Baptists and the early Quakers received much from Puritan spirituality. These movements were also influenced by medieval spirituality and its mystical tradition, as in their use of St. Augustine, Thomas à Kempis, Tauler, and even the post-Reformation Francis de Sales and Fénelon.

The idea of the Church and its relationship to the state presents an important area of difference between medieval Catholics on one hand and Anabaptists and Quakers on the other. Catholics and Orthodox believe the Church was established by Christ and that everyone is obliged to belong to it. In varying degrees many mainstream Reformation traditions have held similar views. Church members who did not lead good Christian lives were supposed to reform, and those who were seriously out of line could be excommunicated. This penalty, however, was meant to be medicinal rather than vindictive and was lifted as soon as repentance was demonstrated. No one expected that this understanding would lead to a church without sinners or weak souls. From Ignatius of Antioch on, the Church was seen as "a field sown with wheat and weeds", to use St. Augustine's analogy borrowed from the Gospel parable. The religious orders and the lay movements attached to them (Benedictine oblates, Franciscan, Dominican, and Carmelite tertiaries, etc.) were the place for those who strove for perfection. Members of these communities were understood to have sins and faults, but they were to engage in a type of spiritual warfare, which would help them to be open to God and obedient to the Gospel. Diocesan

[50] Hinson, 324.

[51] Ibid., 324.

[52] Albrecht Ritschl, *Geshichte des Pietismus*. Cf. R. Friedman, "Conception of the Anabaptist", *Church History* (December 1940) 9:351, quoted in Bender, *Anabaptist Vision*, 12.

priests were still expected to live more devoutly than the laity and to embrace chaste celibacy and obedience to their bishops.

Medieval civilization collapsed in the fifteenth century for many reasons. Thousands of people, including great minds like Dante, found spiritual homes in third-order communities, which emphasized Gospel living, an ascetical or at least a frugal life, charitable works, and the serious practice of prayer and contemplation. In considering the decline of the Catholic Church, we must also recall that bishops during the late medieval period were generally appointed by kings and there was great misuse of the Church's patrimony. Reformers like Wycliffe initially found support among the ranks of the friars until he rejected the concept that Christ established the Catholic Church for all people.

When the first Protestants rejected the visible Church because of many of these issues, the idea of lay communities living a common life (like the Hutterites) or of devout rural societies given to a simple Gospel life gave rise to the Anabaptist movements. Along with the Anabaptists, the reforming friars of the fifteenth century ran into opposition from the hierarchy. The Dominican Girolamo Savonarola (1452–1498) was burned at the stake by the scandalous pope Alexander VI. A century later the Capuchin reformers had to flee papal authority by hiding in the mountains. Great mystics like John of the Cross carried to the grave the scars of flogging by their own confreres for seeking reform within their orders.

When devout people rejected the institutional Church in large numbers, they were often seeking the goals that monks, friars, and nuns had embraced. A Catholic writer of that time, Franz Agricola, wrote of the Anabaptists:

> Among the existing heretical sects there is none which in appearance leads a more modest or pious life than the Anabaptist. As concerns their outward public life they are irreproachable. No lying, deception, swearing, strife, harsh language, no intemperate eating and drinking, no outward personal display, is found among them, but humility, patience, uprightness, neatness, honesty, temperance, straightforwardness in such measure that one would suppose that they had the Holy Spirit of God.[53]

The emphasis of the friars, especially St. Francis, on identification with the suffering Christ had many echoes in Anabaptist spirituality. As the persecutions led by Catholics or Protestants were beginning to pick up steam in 1524, Conrad Grebel (1498–1526), who organized the Swiss Brethren branch of the Anabaptists, wrote: "True Christian believers are sheep among wolves, sheep for the slaughter; they must be baptized in anguish and affliction, tribulation, persecution, suffering, and death; they

[53] Karl Rembert, *Die Wiedertäufer im Herzogtum jülich* (Berlin, 1899), 564, quoted in Bender, *Anabaptist Vision*, 24.

must be tried with fire and must reach the fatherland of eternal rest not by killing them bodily, but by mortifying their spiritual enemies."[54]

The Anabaptists and the Quakers were evangelical pacifists, refusing to bear arms. Some continue that tradition to this day. Seldom do they realize that the lay tertiaries of the major Catholic orders were exempt from military service for similar reasons, and this exemption led to a real decline in the European land wars. Although Catholics never held the absolute pacifism of the Anabaptists and the Quakers, they accepted the Augustinian teaching that only a defensive war could be just and that no Christian prince could rejoice at having to fight.

Quakers and Baptists believed in absolute religious freedom and held that the state had no part in religious functions. In this, they differed considerably from Catholics and most Protestants. Anabaptists generally looked on civil government as evil, although this attitude changed in places like the southern United States, where Baptists came to form a majority of the population and were often elected to public office. Quakers had an even more remarkable experience. They actually established civil governments, like Pennsylvania under William Penn. True to their beliefs, Quakers extended religious freedom even to Catholics and Jews.

The Baptists spread like wildfire in the United States, becoming the largest Protestant denomination in the country. Retaining a simple denominational structure, they have always emphasized personal conversion and the importance of the individual. Pride of place has been given to the Bible, even to the exclusion of other traditional Christian elements like the sacraments and the study of theology and history. Baptism is seen less as a sacrament than a total commitment to Christ, much as religious orders see final vows. In fact, the Anabaptist idea of confessional baptism (adults and older adolescents) may have grown from the profession of third-order lay members. All these things made the Baptists an ideal denomination for the frontier. Enslaved Africans were also drawn to the simplicity of the Baptist observance, its individualism, and the absence of the need for a single church with apostolic succession.

The Quakers, on the other hand, had moved toward a quite respectable, often upper-middle-class membership. Although their body of beliefs was the simplest imaginable, their very silence required a cultured and sophisticated soul. As a friend remarked after attending a Quaker meeting, "It's never going to go over in Puerto Rico". As a result, the Quakers are a very small group, but their influence exceeds their numbers.

A word must be said about the smaller churches coming from Anabaptist roots. Some, like the Hutterites or the Bruderhof, a twentieth-century movement modeled on them, have attracted members not

[54] *Thomas Müntzers Briefwechsel*, ed. H. Böhmer and P. Kirn, 97, quoted in Bender, *Anabaptist Vision*, 28.

born into that way of life. The desire for an authentic and unworldly Christianity with a strong emphasis on nonviolence inspired a number of people to embrace this tradition. They often found that they had an affinity to similar Catholic movements for peace and justice and a sensitivity to nature like that of the Catholic Worker movement, founded by Dorothy Day, and Madonna House, established by Baroness Catherine de Hueck. Others, like the Amish and the Mennonites, held tightly to their own ethnic tradition as a means of retaining their way of life. As we might expect, such groups still lose some of their young people. Their insularity nevertheless preserves their way of life, especially in countries committed to religious freedom, like the United States and Canada.

Although at first the Anabaptists wrote prayers and even used primers, their antiritual bent led them to avoid written prayers almost completely. In recent years the Historical Committee of the Mennonite Church has republished a three-centuries-old German prayer book called the *Prayer Book for Earnest Christians*. About fifty years ago Edward Yoder, a Mennonite elder, used this classical devotional book and was truly inspired "in tone and thought. He lamented that his generation of Mennonites, adopting English, had 'cut themselves off so completely ... from the rich treasures of their heritage'".[55] The following prayer, written to be recited by the whole assembly at the observance of the supper of the Lord, is revealing both in its unexpected Eucharistic content and its medieval-sounding devotion to Jesus Christ.

A Short Unison Prayer

O Lord! almighty, merciful God and dear Father! at this time we are assembled in your presence to keep the blessed memorial of the broken body and shed blood of your Son, Jesus Christ, and to enjoy this blessed communion.

We also sincerely and willingly confess our sins, our unworthiness and nothingness. We come before you stripped of all righteousness, and seek to console ourselves with the righteousness which Christ, your Son, obtained for us with his bitter death, suffering, and shed blood.

O Lord! through your grace and the gift of the Holy Spirit, grant that our hungering souls may in this meal be fed with the body and blood of your beloved Son. May he remain in us and we in him, so that his bitter suffering for us may not have been in vain. May our hope be strengthened thereby, and may we have the assurance in our hearts that through the breaking of the bread we are partakers in all his suffering and merits.

[55] *Prayer Book for Earnest Christians*, trans. and ed. Leonard Gross (Scottdale, Penn.: Herald Press, 1997), 9.

> May we henceforth continue to grow and increase in faith, in love, in patience, in the willingness to bear your Son's cross, and in all the Christian virtues. And may we, with a renewed, temperate, righteous, and devout life, serve you for the rest of our lives.[56]

Following in the medieval tradition, Anabaptists also prayed directly to Jesus Christ and showed a personal devotion to Him. The following prayer to Christ the Savior reminds us to some degree of the words of Martin Luther's hymn *A Mighty Fortress Is Our God*.

> Lord Jesus Christ! . . . I thank you . . . from my heart that you have made me able to share in the inheritance of the saints in the light, and have rescued me from the power of darkness, and transferred me into your kingdom, in which I have salvation through your blood, the forgiveness of sins. . . .
>
> Oh! King of grace, come into my heart. Come softly, and gently shield my heart from all unrest. You came to this world in poverty; come and make me humble and poor in spirit. Thus may I bear suffering for the sake of my sins, and hunger and thirst after your righteousness, that I may be eternally rich in you. . . .
>
> Come, King of Mercies! fill me here in this life with your mercy, so that you may fill me there with your eternal glory. In this, your kingdom of grace, rule over me with your Holy Spirit. Indeed, establish your kingdom in me, which is righteousness, peace, and joy in the Holy Spirit.[57]

The Quaker Experience of God

George Fox

To understand Quaker devotion to Christ, we must begin with the founder of the movement, George Fox. His spiritual search led him to reject both Anglicanism and the Puritan dissenters. In a quandary, he writes:

> I heard a voice which said, "There is one, even Christ Jesus, that can speak to thy condition," and when I heard it my heart did leap for joy. Then the Lord did let me see why there was none upon the earth that could speak to my condition, namely, that I might give him all the glory; for all are concluded under sin, and shut up in unbelief as I had been, that Jesus Christ might have the preeminence, who enlightens, and gives grace, and faith and power. Thus, when God doth work who shall let [prevent] it? And this I knew experimentally.[58]

Fox was imprisoned in 1651 by Cromwell's government and had many conflicts with civil authority and the Puritan Church, whose clergy he refers to as priests, even "Baptist priests", no doubt an insult. He refers to church buildings as steeplehouses. Unlike the Friends of

[56] Ibid., 101–2.

[57] Ibid., 71–72.

[58] From *The Journal of George Fox* (1647), quoted in Steere, *Quaker Spirituality*, 65–66.

today, he was not bashful about telling his critics that they were "reprobates",[59] deceivers, and hirelings. Fox was finally given liberty when King Charles II was restored, apparently because the king was convinced that Fox was opposed to the use of arms.

Although the Friends were apprehensive about the restoration of the monarchy, the situation fluctuated between the king's kindness to them and the injustice of his ministers.[60] Fox was imprisoned and released often. The following touching passage, which he wrote seven years before his death, tells of his trustful reliance on the mystical presence of Christ to protect the Friends. "If it please the Lord and be his will to try you in stinking prisons and dungeons, Brideswells, houses of correction, and suffer you to be put in such places ... I say the Lord can sanctifie such places ... his people are all in the hand, and under the wings of Christ."[61]

Although the Christological decrees of the early ecumenical councils were far from Fox's thoughts, his writings leave little doubt that his starting point was the Christ of the ancient Church. His goal of being led by a purely subjective experience of God, however, now appears naïve, and like many people of his time, he did not recognize the rock from which he was hewn. Modern Quaker writers like Rufus Jones and Douglas Steere see George Fox as part of the mainstream of Christian mystics. It is interesting to speculate what this intrepid spiritual individualist would think of my observations now. I suspect that many Catholic mystics, who clearly adhered to the authority of Scripture, tradition, and the Church and who would never accept a totally subjective interpretation of the life of grace, would still get along with Fox. Perhaps that is what Ruth Jones meant when she surprised me with the remark that Quakers and Catholics have so much in common.

One of the problems facing Christians who are not Quakers as they try to understand the Society of Friends is that such words as "church" and even "Bible" convey similar, though not identical, meanings. When Catholics, Orthodox Christians, Calvinists, and Lutherans speak about "the Church", their meanings are very similar. If we refer to the Society of Friends as a "church", however, we must make some distinctions. Similarly, words like "inspiration", "revelation", and even the proper name of the Holy Spirit may have different connotations. Since Quakers are rooted in personal experience, members of churches with highly articulated statements of belief may feel at sea. Nonetheless, when we review Quaker writings, especially those of the early ones, there can be little doubt that when Fox and his followers speak of Christ, they mean the mystical Christ who is now in eternal glory,

---

[59] Ibid., 78.

[60] See *Journal of George Fox*, quoted in ibid., 122–23, for the king's kindness to Fox's wife and attempts to pardon Fox.

[61] Epistle 398 (1684), *The Epistles of George Fox*, quoted in Steere, *Quaker Spirituality*, 136.

the same Christ confessed by other Christians. The mystical Christ that Fox evoked is also the same Christ "in his death and sufferings".[62] The same Christ comes to them in meetings and elsewhere, so that He "may reign in you".

When George Fox died in 1691, there were thousands of Quakers in England, many of whom had been imprisoned for not participating in the worship of the Established Church. He had spread the movement to the Continent with visits in 1677 and 1684, establishing Yearly Meetings (similar to church conventions) in Holland and Germany. William Penn had been granted a large tract of land by King Charles II, and he set up a colony (Pennsylvania), to which many Quakers went to practice their religion in peace. The growth of religious tolerance in England after the bloodless revolution of 1688, which helped Baptists, Jews, and other religious minorities, is ascribed by some to a "sizable influence exerted by the unflinching, nonviolent Quaker willingness to suffer for full religious freedom to worship God".[63]

Isaac Penington (1616–1679)

Although not an educated man, George Fox was so compelling a preacher that he needed no one to put him on the map. Nevertheless, the Quaker movement found in Isaac Penington someone who could provide it with a serious hearing during some of the most turbulent years of English history. Penington was born into the top echelon of Puritan society. His father was one of the leading Puritan statesmen, a member of Parliament, twice Lord Mayor of London, and a very wealthy man. Penington attended Cambridge, the center of Puritan learning, and married Mary Springett, the wealthy widow of a colonel in Cromwell's army. Penington's stepdaughter, Guli, would become the wife of William Penn.

A few years after their marriage Isaac and Mary heard George Fox preach and were deeply moved by his search for God. They turned their backs on the powerful Puritan establishment, embracing Fox's teaching. It was the custom of the early Quakers to refer to Christ as the "Seed of the Father", the seed that takes root in the grace-filled soul. Penington movingly discusses his conversion: "I have met with my God; I have met with my Saviour; and he hath not been present with me without his salvation. But I have felt the healings drop upon my soul from under his wings. I have met with the true knowledge,

[62] Epistle 230 (1663), *The Epistles of George Fox*, quoted in Steere, *Quaker Spirituality*, 133.

[63] Steere, *Quaker Spirituality*, 125. It is important to note that the revolution of 1688 considerably worsened the Catholic position in England, as it was intended to do. James II was exiled, and the Protestant William and Mary, invited by Parliament to take the throne, continued the anti-Catholic policies of the government. In the colonies, what religious freedom Catholics had gained in places like Maryland was revoked. Catholicism became illegal, and in the eighteenth century additional laws were passed that denied Catholics the franchise and the holding of government posts. Double taxation was imposed on Catholics, and any property held by a priest was confiscated.

the knowledge of life ... which my soul hath rejoiced in, in the presence of the Lord. I have met the Seed's Father, in the Seed I have felt him my Father."[64]

As a result of their total involvement with the Quaker movement, the Peningtons lost most of their fortune. They could not defend themselves in court, because they would not take the oath—something that is a discipline of Friends to this day. Isaac spent a total of five years in prison for the crime of praying in his own house. Despite reversal of fortune and even loss of freedom, nothing deterred the Peningtons from joining the Quaker movement. William Penn, writing at the time of his father-in-law's death, said of Penington: "But to the glory of the living God and praise of this man's memory, let me say neither his worldly station (the most considerable of any that closed in with this way of religion) nor the contradictions it gave to former conceptions, nor the debasement it brought upon his learning or wisdom, nor yet the reproach and loss of all that attended his public espousal of it did deter him from embracing it."[65]

A few selections from Penington's letters will make clear that he saw the center of his spiritual experience as Christ, seen both from His historical distance and from His presence in the soul by grace. "It is not enough to hear of Christ, or read of Christ; but this is the thing, to feel him my root, my life, my foundation; and my soul engrafted into him, by him who hath power to engraft."[66]

Penington's experience of Christ in the soul corresponds with St. Paul's words: "It is no longer I who live, but Christ who lives in me" (Gal 2:20). Pennington's experience of Christ within is very similar to that of contemporary Catholic writers in France, especially Cardinal de Bérulle and St. John Eudes. But we should note that the presence of Christ, or the Seed, does not refer only to a mystical experience. He is always a real historical person. The Quakers were quick to respond to the charge that Christ for them was only an inner experience: "That charge of thine on us, that we deny the person of Christ, and make him nothing but a light or notion, a principle in the heart of man, is very unjust and untrue; for we own that appearance of him in his body of flesh, his sufferings and death, and his sitting at the Father's right hand in glory: but then we affirm, that there is no true knowledge of him, or union with him, but in the seed or principle of his life in the heart, and that *therein* he appears, subdues sin, and reigns over it, in those that understand and submit to the teaching and government of his Spirit."[67]

We cannot read the writings of Penington or of the other early Quakers and fail to be moved by the intensity of their devotion. Those

---

[64] Quoted in ibid., 140.

[65] Quoted in Steere, *Quaker Spirituality*, 140–41.

[66] Letter to Thomas Walmsley, 1670, quoted in Steere, *Quaker Spirituality*, 143.

[67] Penington, Letter (unknown recipient, undated), cited in Steere, *Quaker Spirituality*, 144.

who are familiar with medieval spiritual writers will see how the Quakers take up a tradition of Christ's mystical presence in the soul that runs through the piety of the Middle Ages, in East and West, and is also echoed in German Pietism in the eighteenth century.

John Woolman's Journal*—A Window in Time*

John Woolman (1720–1772), an orchard man and tailor, as well as a devout member of the Quaker community of southern New Jersey, left a journal so remarkable that it is included in the famous Harvard Five-Foot Book Shelf of classics. Woolman's restrained and proper prose describes his journey to visit meetings of Friends up and down the east coast of what is now the United States. His abiding concern was the freeing of slaves and the amelioration of the state in which enslaved Africans were held. His firm but gentle ways in pursuing this cause, as well as his resisting any involvement in military activities, have provided a model for Friends to follow as they try to live their ideals in a world that does not share them.

Woolman's *Journal* is anything but preachy. Only toward the end of his life does he reveal an awareness of Christ's presence similar to the one so movingly recorded by Penington.

> Does mankind walking in uprightness delight in each other's happiness? And do these creatures, capable of this attainment, by giving way to an evil spirit employ their wit and strength to afflict and destroy one another? Remember then—O my soul!—the quietude of those in whom Christ governs, and in all thy proceedings feel after it.
>
> Does he condescend to bless thee with his presence? To move and influence to action? To dwell in thee and walk in thee? Remember then thy station as a being sacred to God, accept of the strength freely offered thee, and take heed that no weakness in conforming to expensive, unwise, and hard-hearted customs, gendering to discord and strife, be given way to. Does he claim my body as his temple and graciously grant that I may be sacred to him? Oh! that I may prize this favour and that my whole life may be conformable to this character.
>
> Remember, O my soul, that the Prince of Peace is thy Lord, that he communicates his unmixed wisdom to his family, that they, living in perfect simplicity, may give no just cause of offense to any creature, but may walk as he walked.[68]

Most Christians place the religious Society of Friends within the context of Protestantism. Although George Fox grew up in the Church of England, and although Quakers are usually counted among Protestants for statistical reasons, there are some real differences between the two bodies, which Douglas Steere sums up this way: "It is important to note that the Quaker movement as a third force never sought

[68] John Woolman, *Journal*, chap. 9, quoted in Steere, *Quaker Spirituality*, 216–17.

to replace the infallible authority of the Church by the infallible authority of the Bible as classical Protestantism had done. Nevertheless, the Bible played, and must always play, a considerable role in helping them to keep within the Christian stream and to cross their inward experience with its searching power and witness."[69]

Along with this difference between the Quaker and the Evangelical Protestant approaches to Scripture, there are, as Ruth Jones revealed to me, a number of things that Quakers and Catholics have in common. Throughout Quaker history, there has been an openness to several Catholic authors, including St. John of the Cross, Thomas à Kempis, St. Francis de Sales, Augustine Baker, and Fénelon.[70]

At various times, Quakers have employed a method of examining their consciences, known as the queries, which was very popular with Catholics. The public nature of this examination of conscience calls to mind the monastic practice of the *culpa*, at which religious recited aloud their faults—usually infractions against the rule—but not their sins, which were always reserved for sacramental confession. Perhaps the most striking similarity between Quaker and Catholic devotions is the awareness of Christ's real presence at the meeting. Thomas R. Kelly (1893–1941), a much-revered twentieth-century Quaker spiritual writer, wrote the following startling paragraph:

> I believe that the group mysticism of the gathered meeting rests upon the Real Presence of God in our midst. Quakers generally hold to a belief in [the] Real Presence, as firm and solid as the belief of Roman Catholics in the Real Presence in the host, the bread and wine of the Mass. In the host the Roman Catholic is convinced that the literal, substantial Body of Christ is present. For him the Mass is not a mere symbol, a dramatizing of some figurative relationship of man to God. It rests upon the persuasion that an Existence, a Life, the Body of Christ, is really present and entering into the body of man. Here the Quaker is very near the Roman Catholic. For the Real Presence of the gathered meeting is an existential fact. To use philosophical language, it is an ontological matter, not merely a psychological matter. The bond of union in divine fellowship is existential and real, not figurative. It is the life of God himself, within whose life we live and move and have our being. And the gathered meeting is a special case of holy fellowship of the blessed community.[71]

Perhaps even more astonishing is Steere's statement relating the Quakers to the Eastern Orthodox Church, in which he compares the most free-form worship in Christianity with the most highly ritualized and structured. Although many may not agree with Steere's point of view,

[69] Steere, *Quaker Spirituality*, 21.

[70] Ibid., 25.

[71] Thomas R. Kelly, "The Gathered Meeting", quoted in ibid., 313.

it is worth citing: "It is interesting that both the Eastern Orthodox and the Quakers look on the experience of the whole worshiping community gathered in corporate prayer as the truest organ for the operation of the Holy Spirit. Isaac Penington writes of the early Quaker groups, 'They are like a heap of fresh and living coals, warming one another as a great strength, freshness, and vigor of life flows into all.'"[72]

A Dutch Reformed Christian Mystic

In earlier accounts of the Reform piety, we cited scholars of this tradition saying that spirituality was a rather elusive concept for them. Zwingli's Christianity focused very much on this world. However, the powerful currents of Christian devotion in other Protestant traditions, as well as the roots of medieval Catholic piety, eventually brought to flower in the reform tradition a true spirituality focused on the presence and love of Christ. The occasion for this was the flight to Holland of many nonconformist refugees from England, as well as the influence of the French Calvinists, who fled to the Netherlands because of the revocation of the Edict of Nantes (1685), which had assured them of religious freedom.

The writings of Archbishop Fénelon and *The Imitation of Christ* were both influential in the Netherlands. Bouyer states that at the end of the seventeenth century in Holland there was "an official Protestantism having a substantial thread of pure and holy evangelical spirituality".[73] Out of the world of Dutch domestic piety, which we are familiar with in the paintings of Protestants like Van Steen and Catholics like Vermeer, there grew a man whom Bouyer calls "perhaps the greatest and most complete spiritual writer that Protestantism has produced"—Gerhard Tersteegen.

Gerhard Tersteegen (1697–1769), the brilliant son of a Protestant weaver, consecrated himself to Christ on Ash Wednesday at the age of twenty-seven, writing his testament in his own blood. His tender love of Christ, joined to great compassion for His sufferings, comes to expression in a complete giving of self.

> O my Jesus, I consecrate myself to thee, my only Saviour, my Spouse, Jesus Christ, so as to belong entirely to thee for all eternity. With all my heart and from today I renounce all the rights and all the power that Satan unjustly gave me over myself, for thou hast ransomed me by thy agony, thy struggles and thy sweating of blood in Gethsemane, thou hast shattered the gates of hell for me and hast opened the heart of thy Father, full of charity. . . . I give thee all power over me and I promise thee with time and help to shed the last drop of my blood rather than willingly disobey thee or be unfaithful to thee. I give all of myself to thee, sweet friend of my soul, and I want to belong to

[72] Steere, *Quaker Spirituality*, 28–29.
[73] Bouyer, *Spirituality*, 198.

thee for ever. May thy Spirit ... seal what here thou art promised in all simplicity by thy unworldly slave, Gerhard Tersteegen.[74]

It goes without saying that Tersteegen's spirituality was rooted in the Bible, especially in John and Paul. As Bouyer points out, there are also similarities with Catholic mystics who preceded him. Tersteegen wrote that God should be found in the depths of the soul, an idea popularized by the Dominican mystic Meister Eckhart, whose works were influential in Lutheran preaching. This is similar also to St. Francis de Sales' expression that we meet God in the fine point of our soul. It is from the soul that the spiritual person moves to "consideration" of the Word of God living within us. This is the *complaisance* of St. Francis de Sales and similar to the elevations of Cardinal de Bérulle. At times Tersteegen sounds like St. John of the Cross when he speaks of pure faith, rather than extraordinary experiences: "It must be admitted that the way of pure faith—the way by which the soul, following the commitment of the spirit of Jesus, lets itself be led outside itself and all created being so as to attach itself to God in spirit and in truth and serve him and partake of his communion—this is the surest way, the truest and most indispensable way; whereas the way by which souls experience extraordinary gifts, visions, ecstasies, and revelations or other supernatural communications is subject to many pitfalls and misunderstandings."[75]

Bouyer maintains that Tersteegen's emphasis on truth marks the first time in Protestantism that "a really lucid critique of faith in one's faith, of faith in one's justification, [becomes] the object of faith".[76] Tersteegen was strong in his emphasis that faith must translate into effective fulfillment of God's will.

> But he who loves him will keep his word (John 14:23). So we must be attentive to his word, and keep it, not externally in Scripture, but we must hear it in our hearts and obey its operation and direction ... He who believes in his heart that a living and omniscient God is in heaven, and that his Word is the truth, according to which he will be judged, he is the man with saving faith. "All right," someone may say, "and nothing else is necessary to faith; then the matter is settled, because I have believed all that since my childhood and I believe it still." But look, do you believe in this huge business with your whole heart? The faith of the heart is the work of the Holy Spirit. So prove this faith in your works. "What works?" you will say. "Works count for nothing." Answer: Certainly it is not works that will earn us heaven, but faith and works go together and follow one another step by step,

[74] Quoted in ibid., 199.

[75] From the *Geistliches Blumengärtlein*, quoted in Bouyer, *Spirituality*, 201.

[76] Bouyer, *Spirituality*, 201.

> or else one doesn't really believe what one says, but only thinks one believes it.[77]

The spiritual road that Tersteegen marks out in his many books and poetry was a way that all Christians are familiar with—the way of complete trust in God. His teaching on trust directly challenged the idea of complete assurance of personal salvation, which had become a popular feature of Reformation spirituality. He advises the Christian to put himself "unreservedly and trustingly in God's hands, follow him faithfully in grace and try to cling to him for today".[78]

> Justification by faith is not the belief that I am justified, it cannot give me the assurance that my sins have been forgiven me. Though God sometimes provides such assurance, it is all the same false and dangerous to make faith and justification coincide absolutely. Faith that justifies consists in this, that a poor and humble sinner believes he finds forgiveness, help and salvation in Christ alone, that he draws near him with all the strength of his heart (John 6:5) and gives himself over entirely to him (2 Cor. 8:5).[79]

Speaking of justification, Tersteegen says: "We ought to believe not only once, but always, and we should be anchored in faith and tested in it, in this way our justification will be the stronger and the higher.... Show me thy faith in thy works (James 2:18). Justifying faith unites us to Christ our Head and is the foundation of a new life. This should show itself. He who is justified should prove it outwardly with evidence, always seeking to become more just (Apoc. 22:11)."[80]

The last words of this humble weaver exerted such influence on his contemporaries that we are reminded of the death of St. John Vianney, the Curé of Ars, who lived a century after Tersteegen and said he went before God with empty hands. As Tersteegen lay dying on April 3, 1769, these words were on his lips: "Poor wretched Lazarus that you are! And yet the angels do not disdain to bear you away."[81]

---

[77] *Geistliches Blumengärtlein*, cited in ibid., 201–2.

[78] Ibid., 201.

[79] Ibid., 202.

[80] Ibid.

[81] Ibid., 203.

21 Catholics in the Eighteenth Century

The eighteenth century was a time of more turbulence than triumph for the Catholic Church. For the most part, northern Europe, including England and Holland, was lost, and Catholic monarchs attempted to reduce the Church to a function of the state, making it in effect an established church. The same thing was occurring simultaneously in Protestant Europe.[1]

The most obvious feature of Catholic spirituality in the eighteenth century, the age of Baroque piety, was a devotion to Jesus Christ in His humanity, suffering, and in His eternal glory, expressed chiefly in the Holy Eucharist. Because of the very strong commitment to the Bible in Protestant countries, Catholics were more inclined to use the Scriptures selectively, as they were expressed in the various liturgical feast days and seasons that celebrated the events of Christ's life. The Rosary with its meditations on the life of Jesus was a popular tool in teaching Christ's mysteries to the faithful.[2]

As Catholics became more literate, there was also a real change of emphasis from the processions and pilgrimages of the earlier days to individual forms of spirituality based on meditation, Scripture reading, examination of conscience, and devotional literature.

Devotional preaching became important in Catholic life and was led by the Jesuits, who catered to the intelligentsia and nobility, and by the friars, who preached to the common people. Among the friars the Capuchin Franciscans stand out. They were counseled to preach, as St. Francis had instructed, with force and fervor, of vices and virtue, of punishment and glory.[3] Towns and cities were called

---

[1] *The Medieval and Reformation Church: An Abridgement of History of the Church*, vols. 4 to 6, ed. Herbert Jedin, trans. John Dolan (New York: Crossroad, 1993), 884ff. See also Henri Daniel-Rops, *The Church in the Eighteenth Century*, trans. John Warrington (New York: E. P. Dutton, 1964).

[2] See Keith P. Luria, "The Counter-Reformation and Popular Spirituality", in *Christian Spirituality: Post-Reformation and Modern*, ed. Louis Dupré and Don E. Saliers (New York: Crossroad, 1996), 93ff. It should be noted that much Baroque piety was a conscious reaction against that of the late Middle Ages, which was seen to be tinged with a superstition that was strongly rejected by Trent.

[3] Capuchin constitutions; see also ibid., 98.

together for missions, or week-long revivals, with every kind of religious experience. There were dramatic sermons on Christ's Passion, preached by thorn-crowned friars in town squares, as well as endless lines of silent penitents receiving the sacrament of reconciliation before Mass. In the eighteenth century, the newly founded Redemptorist congregation took up this work of missions, and in the Italian city of Sarno, taverns are said to have remained empty for ten years following one of the Redemptorists' more successful efforts.[4]

Just as advances in printing caused primers to spread throughout Protestant Europe, so catechisms went everywhere throughout Catholic Europe and in the mission lands. These books called forth a whole religious culture of meditation and good works, following the model of St. Francis de Sales: complacence (*complaisance*) and benevolence, as we saw in Chapter 14 above. We could mention a whole list of great preachers from this period, but we must narrow our focus to two Italians who were outstanding for their devotion to Christ: SS. Alphonsus Liguori (1696–1787) and Paul of the Cross (1694–1775).

St. Paul of the Cross—Mystic of the Passion of Christ

Paul Danei was born to a family of struggling businesspeople, in the geat port city of Genoa. He and his brother, John Baptist, were very devout and early on began to lead an ascetic life. Paul spent several years living almost as a contemplative hermit, and at the age of twenty-six his life changed as a result of a vivid mystical experience. He saw a black religious habit, with an emblem bearing the name JESUS in white letters surmounted by a cross. He heard the Blessed Virgin tell him to found a congregation whose members would wear such a habit and mourn continually for the Passion and death of her Son. Paul's bishop received a written description of this vision. With the recommendation of Paul's Capuchin spiritual director, the Bishop of Alessandria invited the young man to wear the black habit but without the emblem until papal approval could be obtained.[5]

Paul retired to a hermit's cell for forty days and wrote the constitutions for his new congregation, the Congregation of the Passion. Eventually he and his brother, John Baptist, were ordained and received novices, but none of these early novices survived the austerity of their life. Soon the two brothers were preaching missions, focused on the gratitude one must have for the sufferings Christ underwent for our salvation. They also cared for the sick and the dying, a dangerous work in a time of great epidemics. Paul of the Cross became a well-known spiritual director and founded a second religious congregation, the enclosed contemplative Passionist nuns.

---

[4] Luria, "Counter-Reformation and Popular Spirituality", 97, 100.

[5] *Butler's Lives of the Saints*, ed. Herbert Thurston, S.J., and Donald Attwater, rev. ed. (New York: P.J. Kenedy and Sons, 1956), 2:178–79.

He felt a special call to pray for the conversion of England and is reported to have said: "That country is always before my eyes. If England again becomes Catholic, immeasurable will be the benefits to Holy Church."[6] Perhaps some of his concern for England was passed on to his spiritual sons, for a century later Fr. (now Blessed) Dominic Barberi, C.P., received John Henry Newman into the Catholic Church at Littlemore. As we know, "immeasurable benefits" for the Church in England have resulted from that conversion.

While all this was going on, Paul entered a forty-five-year period of spiritual darkness—the dark night described by St. John of the Cross.[7] He was a man of extraordinary gifts, such as prophecy and healing the sick; he was also a man of extraordinary success: by the time he reached old age his religious congregation was spreading far and wide. Much of his personal devotion is revealed in his letters and spiritual direction.

> Love is a unitive virtue, and it makes one's own the sufferings of the Beloved. Do not work with the imagination—this is not the time—but, in pure and holy faith, make a bouquet of the sufferings of Jesus and carry it on the bosom of your soul; or, indeed, remain entirely immersed in God in pure faith, and by means of some loving word recall to Him how much He has done for us, and then let yourself be entirely penetrated by those sufferings, through that love . . . remaining in holy silence, in that sacred wonderment; for you will be enamored of God the more.[8]

In trying to communicate the spiritual importance of Christ's Passion, Paul of the Cross used visual imagery and pictures, which created a false impression of this great mystic's prayer life. People assumed he was given to dramatic sentimentality. The following quotation of his bears much resemblance to the teaching of Tersteegen, his Reform Protestant contemporary, and both echo the teaching of St. John of the Cross.

> Always go to prayer with some mystery of the sacred passion of Jesus Christ; and, devoid of images, your understanding cleared of every other thought, enter the interior temple of your soul. By a sweet soliloquy on the mystery—in pure faith, of course—lose yourself completely in the boundless sea of divine charity. Repose there purely in God, in a sacred silence of faith and holy love, keeping the superior part of your spirit amorously attentive to the sovereign Beloved. But do not revert to yourself; on the contrary, rest peacefully on the bosom of God.[9]

---

[6] Ibid., 179.

[7] *New Catholic Encyclopedia*, (New York: McGraw-Hill, 1967), 11:24.

[8] Quoted in Fr. Brice, C.P., *In Spirit and in Truth: The Spiritual Doctrine of Saint Paul of the Cross* (New York: Frederick Pustet, 1948), 251–52.

[9] Ibid., 253.

Modern Christians may have trouble appreciating a spirituality focused on Christ's suffering and Passion. It is enough to recall that such a devotion, like many we have reviewed, arose from powerful and even mystical experiences. St. Paul of the Cross stands with George Fox, John Wesley, and St. Margaret Mary, all of whom gave themselves completely to the summons of divine grace as they experienced it. They responded to Christ in ways that were surprisingly similar despite sharp denominational lines. Paul of the Cross' unique piety may not find the same appeal among people of our time as it did with his contemporaries. (Let us not assume there is a flaw in his piety; the fault—if fault there is—may lie with us.) At the time of his death crowds thronged the streets of Rome to venerate the saint who would be canonized in ninety-three years.

St. Alphonsus Liguori (1696–1787)

The towering genius of the Catholic Church in the eighteenth century was St. Alphonsus Liguori, founder of the Congregation of the Most Holy Redeemer (Redemptorists). Bishop, missionary, prodigious writer, moral theologian, mystic, and Doctor of the Church, Alphonsus Liguori was a man of profound devotion to Jesus Christ and His Blessed Mother. During the last twenty years of his life he was handicapped by a serious illness of the spine that kept him confined to a wheelchair and caused him to resign as bishop in 1775. The vast bulk of his writing was done before his illness.

Alphonsus witnessed the battle between the Holy See and the secular authorities, who wanted to control the Church as part of the government of the kingdom of Naples. The congregation of missionary priests and brothers he founded in 1732 to teach and preach to the peasants of the mountain villages ran into many disappointing obstacles in its early years. All his first recruits left him, but he went on and eventually the congregation flourished. Later the Holy See removed from his authority a large section of his successful congregation located in the papal states.

His work in moral theology is considered most important and led to his being named patron saint of confessors[10] and moralists. His writings contain 70,000 citations from more than 800 authors, although most of his quotations are from Sacred Scripture. Aphonsus published nearly 120 books, which ranged from daunting theological works to beautiful devotional prayers, poetry, and hymns, including "*Tu scende dalle stelle*", still the most popular Italian Christmas carol. His letters reveal him as a profoundly mystical soul flourishing amid the many duties of a bishop and religious founder.

Several of St. Alphonsus' works brought him the condemnation of Jansenists, whose influence the books diminished. Even his devotional works were dismissed as "'worthless little books of stupid piety' (*ses*

[10] That is, of priests when they are hearing confessions and giving absolution to penitents.

méchants petits livres de piété inepte)".[11] Perhaps no work roused their ire more than his *Novena to the Sacred Heart of Jesus* (1758), a devotion they opposed (see Chapter 14 above). Alphonsus preached often on this devotion and was convinced of the truth of the revelations given to Margaret Mary Alacoque, but his *Novena* enraged the Jansenists, who attempted to stamp out this devotion, which they denounced as "outlandish, incoherent, pharisaical, false . . . and nestorian".[12] In 1765, one of Alphonsus' first acts as Bishop of Sant' Agata dei Gotti was to establish the newly approved feast of the Sacred Heart in his diocese.

The devotional writings of St. Alphonsus Liguori were intended for the growing literate Catholic public and are focused on Christ, His saving grace as Redeemer, His Passion and death, and His presence in the Holy Eucharist. In them he calls the reader to a deeply personal response to biblical words and events, especially those in the Gospel. The following moving passage is from *The Passion and the Death of Jesus Christ.*

> He is dead! O God! who is it that is dead? The author of life, the only-begotten Son of God, the Lord of the world—he is dead. O death! thou wert the amazement of heaven and of all nature. O infinite love! A God to sacrifice his blood and his life! And for whom? For his ungrateful creatures; dying in an ocean of sufferings and shame, in order to pay the penalty due to their sins. Ah, infinite goodness! O infinite love!
>
> O my Jesus! Thou art, then, dead, on account of the love which Thou hast borne me! Oh, let me never again live, even for a single moment, without loving Thee! I love Thee, my chief and only good; I love Thee, my Jesus—dead for me! O my sorrowing Mother Mary! do thou help a servant of thine, who desires to love Jesus.[13]

Many older Catholics remember St. Alphonsus' moving meditations, which nourished generations of the faithful during the Stations of the Cross. Beautifully rendered in English, each meditation could move even the hard-hearted to contrition and sorrow. As the penitent moves along the via dolorosa with Christ, he is invited to "consider" each aspect of the Passion and recall how his sins have brought our Savior to this misery. On "this sorrowful journey" St. Alphonsus evokes in us deep personal sorrow for sins and stirs up a love for Christ that will bring about a truly converted life. Who can forget the haunting refrain with which he ends each meditation: "I love thee, Jesus, my love. I repent of ever having offended thee. Never permit me to offend

[11] Frederick M. Jones, C.Ss.R., *Alphonsus de Liguori: The Saint of Bourbon Naples 1696–1787* (Westminster, Md.: Christian Classics, 1992), 293–94.

[12] Ibid., 295.

[13] Meditation 13 for Holy Thursday, and Meditation 14 for Good Friday, in *The Passion and the Death of Jesus Christ*, vol. 5, *The Complete Works of Saint Alphonsus de Liguori*, ed. Rev. Eugene Grimm, C.Ss.R. (Brooklyn, N.Y.: Redemptorist Fathers, 1927), 454, 455.

thee again. Grant that I may love thee always, and then do with me what thou wilt."

The devotion to the Eucharistic Christ, as we have seen, was popularized by St. Francis of Assisi. After the Reformation it became an ever more important part of Catholic life, one that clearly differentiated Catholics from Protestants. The following excerpt from *The Holy Eucharist* emphasizes the hunger for Christ's presence and the privilege it is for the faithful to rejoice in that presence. In this passage Alphonsus illustrates his love for St. Augustine, whose works he knew so well that he was able to challenge the Jansenists on their selective use of the writings of the ancient Church Father.

> O foolish ones of the world, says St. Augustine, miserable creatures, where are you going to satisfy your hearts? Come to Jesus; for by him alone can that pleasure which you seek be bestowed. "Unhappy creatures, whither are you going? The good you seek for comes from him." My soul, be not of the number of these foolish ones; seek God alone: "seek for that one good in which are all good things." And if thou desirest soon to find him, behold, he is close to thee; tell him what thou desirest, since for this end it is that he is in the ciborium, to console thee, and to grant thy prayer.[14]

Like SS. Ignatius Loyola and Francis de Sales, Alphonsus is concerned with showing the individual Christian the most efficient method of growing in the love of Christ.

> A person will become perfectly holy by loving Jesus Christ, our God, our chief good, and our Savior. He himself says that anyone who loves him will be loved by the eternal Father (John 16:27)....
>
> St. Paul, the great lover of Jesus Christ, could say "the love of Christ impels us" (2 Cor. 5:14). He meant that it was not so much what Jesus Christ has suffered for us as the love he has shown in suffering for us which obliges us, and indeed forces us, to love him. Commenting on this text, St. Francis de Sales asks, "Is knowing that Jesus, true God, has loved us to the extent of suffering death on a cross for us, not like having our heart put into a wine-press, and feeling it wrenched, until love is pressed from it by a force as strong as it is loving?"[15]

Writing to Catholics, St. Alphonsus stresses the unique importance of personal devotion to Christ. Even though he wrote prolifically and beautifully on devotion to the Blessed Virgin, he proclaimed that personal devotion to Jesus was the essential and primary Christian devotion.

[14] Alphonsusde Liguori, *The Holy Eucharist*, vol. 6, *Complete Works*, ed. Rev. Eugene Grimm, C.Ss.R. (1934), 149–50.

[15] St. Alphonsus Liguori, *The Practice of the Love of Jesus Christ*, chap. 1, trans. Brendan McConvery, C.Ss.R., in *Alphonsus de Liguori: Selected Writings*, ed. Frederick M. Jones, C.Ss.R. Classics of Western Spirituality (New York: Paulist Press, 1999), 112–15.

> Devotion to Jesus Christ in which we concentrate on the love our Redeemer has shown, and continues to show us, is the devotion which surpasses all others. A spiritual writer has recently lamented the fact that there are many who practice a variety of other devotions but neglect this. Many preachers and confessors, too, are eloquent about many subjects but speak very little about love for Jesus Christ, when, in point of fact, love for Jesus Christ should be the principal, not to say the only, devotion of a Christian. Consequently, the principal object and effort, both of preachers and confessors, should be to awaken and increase in their audience and penitents this love for Jesus Christ. Negligence in this matter is the fundamental reason why souls make such little progress in virtue.[16]

The following prayer, had it been known to the Protestants of his time, would, I suspect, have summed up their own personal devotion.

> Compassionate heart of Jesus, have mercy on me. Even before I offended you, my Redeemer, I did not deserve the great graces you have given me. You created me, gave me so many inspirations and all totally undeserved on my part. But having offended you, not only did I not deserve your favors, I certainly deserved to be abandoned by you for all eternity. But you, in your great mercy, have waited for me and preserved my life even when I was at enmity with you. Your mercy allowed me to see my misery and you called me to conversion; you gave me sorrow for my sins and a desire to love you. Now, I hope that with your grace I am in your friendship once again.[17]

To make a thorough study of Alphonsus Liguori's spirituality would require much time—because of its volume and scope, rather than because of its complexity. His is a straightforward spirituality that springs from Gospel events and their interpretation by the early Church. Except for the Catholic allusions to the Eucharistic Presence and the Virgin Mary, many of St. Alphonsus' spiritual themes find parallels in Protestant writings, especially in England and particularly in those of Richard Baxter. Apart from specifically Catholic references, many evangelical Protestants would find themselves at home with the spirituality of Alphonsus Liguori.

St. Elizabeth Seton (1774–1821)

There are a number of Catholic devotional writers at the end of the eighteenth century, but now we will consider someone who is not primarily a writer but the foundress of a religious community. We will draw from her limited writings and correspondence an estimate of the influence of Protestant converts on Catholic life. We have already seen several examples of the unrecognized influence of Catholicism

[16] From the *Novena to the Sacred Heart of Jesus* in *Selected Writings*, 220.

[17] *Selected Writings*, 232.

on Protestant and Orthodox piety. Elizabeth Seton represents an influence in the opposite direction. To the present day there are significant examples of converts to the Catholic Church who brought with them ways of being Christ's disciples, that had their origins in the piety of the Orthodox or Protestant world. We have only to mention the name of Vladimir Soloviev (1853–1900), an example of a Catholic writer who brought with him many influences of Eastern Orthodoxy. Later, we will look at John Henry Newman and his Anglican evangelical piety. In him there is a clear recognition that Catholicism has something to receive as well as give in the interchange of people whose convictions and experience bring them out of the Christian milieu in which they were raised. Even today some of the Catholic Church's best apologists learned the Bible and its teachings as Evangelical Protestants.

Elizabeth Ann Bayley was the daughter of a prominent Episcopalian physician in New York and a member of Trinity Church, which a few years after her birth became one of the charter Protestant Episcopal churches of the new republic. At the age of nineteen, she married William Seton, and the couple had five children. By 1800 William's business ventures had failed, the family lost their home, and he was forced to declare bankruptcy. He also contracted tuberculosis, which progressed rapidly. In a few years he was close to death.

The young couple, with their oldest child, Anna Maria, sailed for Leghorn (Livorno) in October 1803, hoping that the voyage and the Italian climate would speed his recovery. William, however, died shortly after they reached Italy, and the young widow and her child were received into the home of the Filicchis, business associates and friends of the Setons. During her stay of several months with the Filicchis, Elizabeth was introduced to Catholicism, especially to its devotional life. The following excerpt, taken from a journal Elizabeth kept, is addressed to Rebecca Seton (1780–1804), her sister-in-law, friend, and confidante, in which she speaks of her growing attraction to two key elements in the life of her Catholic friends—devotion to the Holy Eucharist and to the Blessed Virgin Mary.

> My sister dear how happy would we be if we believed what these dear souls believe, that they *possess* God in the Sacrament and that he remains in their churches and is carried to them when they are sick, oh my—when they carry the Blessed Sacrament under my window while I face the full loneliness and sadness of my case I cannot stop the tears at the thought my God how happy would I be even so far away from all so dear, if I could find you in the church as they do (for there is a chapel in the very house of Mr. F.) how many things I would say to you of the sorrows of my heart and the sins of my life—the other day in a moment of excessive distress I fell on my knees without thinking when the Blessed Sacrament passed by and

> cried in an agony to God *to bless me* if he was there, that my whole soul desired only him—a little prayer book of Mrs. F.'s was on the table and I opened a little prayer of St. Bernard to the Blessed Virgin begging her to be *our Mother*, and I said it to her with such a certainty that God would surely refuse nothing to *his Mother*, and that she could not help loving and pitying the poor souls he died for, that I felt really I had a Mother, which you know my foolish heart so often laments to have lost in early days[18]—from the first remembrance of infancy I have looked in all the plays of childhood and wildness of youth to the clouds for my Mother, and at that moment it seemed as if I had found more than her, even in tenderness and pity of a Mother—so I cried myself to sleep on her heart—[19]

Shortly after Elizabeth's return to New York in 1804, Rebecca Seton died. The depth of their spiritual friendship is reflected in these lines, which also show their deep devotion to Christ. Anyone familiar with Anglican liturgy of that period will recognize the words and phrases filled with biblical allusions and firm hope.

> This is my Rebecca's Birth day in heaven—no more watching now, my darling Sister—No more agonizing sufferings—the hourly prayers interrupted by pains and tears are now exchanged for the eternal Hallelujah. The blessed angels who have so often witnessed our feeble efforts, now teach your Soul the Songs of Sion.—dear dear Soul, we shall no more watch the setting sun on our knees, and sigh our soul to the Sun of Righteousness, for he has recieved [sic] you to his everlasting light—no more sing praises gazing on the moon—for you have awakened to eternal day—that dear voice that soothed the widows heart, admonished the forgetful Soul, inspired the love of God, and only uttered sounds of love and Peace to all shall now be heard no more among us, but the reward of those who lead others to Righteousness now crowns his promise who has said, "they shall shine as the stars forever"—[20]

The young widow's friends, including the Reverend John Henry Hobart, rector of Trinity Church and future Episcopal Bishop of New York, expressed the expected opposition to her intention to convert, since they firmly believed that the Catholic Church was the work of the Antichrist.

In a journal she kept for her friend Amabilia Filicchi, Elizabeth wrote: "[T]he controversies on it [the Catholic Church] I am quite incapable of deciding, and as the strictest Protestant allows Salvation

[18] Elizabeth's mother died when Elizabeth was three years old.

[19] From "The Italian Journal, Part 4", Feb. 24, 1804, quoted in *Elizabeth Seton: Selected Writings*, ed. Ellin Kelly and Annabelle Melville (New York: Paulist Press, 1987), 133–34.

[20] "The Italian Journal, Part 5", July 8, 1804, quoted in *Selected Writings*, 137.

to a good Catholick, to the Catholicks I will go, and try to be a good one."[21]

She was received into the Catholic Church by Fr. Matthew O'Brien on March 14, 1805, at St. Peter's Church on Barclay Street. After that, Elizabeth relied on the same influences she had known as an Episcopalian: Scripture, sermons, and counseling by the clergy. These were the source of her spiritual strength for her remaining sixteen years. Her prayer life left her with a desire for "entire abandonment to His will". Within three years of her conversion, she, her children, and a few helpers moved to Baltimore. There she opened a girls' academy and began the Sisters of Charity of St. Joseph under the direction of John Carroll, first Catholic bishop in the United States. In 1809 Elizabeth, now known as Mother Seton, moved her family, school, and followers to Emmitsburg, a rural area in southwest Maryland and the site of the newly established seminary at Mount St. Mary. Over the years various Sulpician Fathers oversaw the new community, of which Mother Seton was superior; she also served as principal of the school. Mother Seton's Sisters of Charity followed an adaptation of St. Vincent de Paul's rule for the Daughters of Charity.

Death and her response to it unfortunately would provide the theme for Elizabeth's life at Emmitsburg. The death of her beloved Anna Maria in 1812 at the age of sixteen was a severe trial for the young mother and nun. At a time before the nature of infection was known, tuberculosis made its deadly way through the little isolated community at Emmitsburg. One by one she saw the first sisters of her community die, as well as some of her own children.

Mother Seton's writings, letters, and talks to the sisters tell of her faith during these difficult years. Death caused her to turn increasingly to Christ, and her devotion to the Eucharist flowered into a profound awareness of His saving grace. The following prayer shows both her loving devotion to Christ and her acceptance of His will. "O Our Lord Jesus Christ how great is the merit of that blood which abundantly redeems the whole world—and would redeem a million more—and would redeem the demons themselves if they were capable of penitence and salvation as I am—Yes Lord though your thunders should crush me and a deluge overwhelm me, I will yet hope while you destroy my body, you will save my soul."[22]

As one might expect in a devout person surrounded by death, Elizabeth Seton developed a profound trust in God. One of the several priests who directed her over the years was Simon Gabriel Bruté, who encouraged her in such complete trust. But when he received an assignment to care for St. Mary's College, Baltimore, and put the

---

[21] "Journal for Amabilia Filicchi", Jan. 1805, in *Selected Writings*, 165.

[22] Quoted in Annabelle M. Melville, *Elizabeth Bayley Seton* (New York: Charles Scribner's Sons, 1951), 289.

Sisters of Charity under the care of another priest, he chafed and even spoke of going abroad as a missionary. Mother Seton kindly but firmly rebuked Bruté, to whom she wrote: "I see a zealous driving man without experience put in a seminary where he will save none because he cannot wait to gain a heart or unfold a temper, and his zeal instead of bedewing the plant in the thirsty ground crushes it under foot."[23] Since Bruté had taught her to embrace the graces of the moment, she admonished him directly: "[Y]our restless thoughts strike me to the soul. You made the lesson of the grace of the moment so very plain to me I owe you perhaps my very salvation by the faults and sins it has saved me from, yet Physician, you will not heal yourself."[24]

In the last years of her short life, struggling with her own physical decline and the death of so many dear to her, Mother Seton clung to Christ in the Eucharist and to the ideal of complete abandonment to God's will. One may ask how these two spiritual ideals, which sound so Catholic, could be related to her Protestant background. We must recall that Protestants at that time were deeply devoted to Christ in a personal way. This devotion expressed itself by reading the Scriptures and in devout conversations. This was true of Anglicans and Puritan Protestants, as well as Baptists and Methodists. They were all explicitly devoted to Christ. In the Catholic belief in Christ's physical presence in the Blessed Sacrament, Elizabeth Seton found a more intense expression of the devotion she obviously had as an Episcopalian. The evangelical idea of the assurance of salvation, while different, is similar in many practical ways to the popular Catholic spiritual principle of complete trust in the divine will. They are both expressions of St. Paul's assurances that nothing shall separate us from the love of Christ (see Rom 8:35) and that for those who love God all things work together for the good (see Rom 8:28).

Theologically, there were differences that we have already explored. In practice the Protestant who believes he is irrevocably saved and the Catholic who puts complete trust in God, despite whatever is going on, end up in similar psychological states, although they arrive there by different roads. It is worth recalling that the idea of total abandonment to or trust in God had very ancient roots and was particularly dear to seventeenth-century French saints, as we saw in Chapter 14 above. De Caussade's *Abandonment to Divine Providence*, a series of conferences and letters, had been written before Elizabeth Seton's time, although it was not put into book form until after her death. She would have been familiar with these ideas, however, from her reading of St. Francis de Sales and other French spiritual writers who were popular with the Sulpicians at Mount Saint Mary's.

[23] Quoted in ibid.

[24] Quoted in ibid.

Mother Seton died, trusting completely in Christ's gift of eternal life, and putting her little community in the hands of God. She had no idea that her foundation would eventually educate millions in the faith and for life, and care for hundreds of thousands of orphans as well as millions of hospital patients. Her last days were filled with devotion and spirituality.

The canonization of Elizabeth Seton in 1976 forged another link between Protestant and Catholic piety, which few recognize. Catholics tended to emphasize that she was a convert, and Protestants understandably felt ill at ease because she had left them, despite their recognition of how much good her spiritual daughters had done through the many congregations of Sisters of Charity. Through this book and its thesis I hope that all authentic Christian groups will be seen to have much in common when it comes to devotion to Christ, and that Christians will learn to have more esteem for one another. This could be a new beginning coming from Mother Seton's work, another grace coming from her firm discipleship. Catholics especially should recognize that a number of the most effective members of the Church in modern times, like Newman and Mother Seton, received their Christian formation and initial devotion as Protestant Christians.

22 Protestants in the Nineteenth Century

The nineteenth century began badly for Christians in most countries as a result of the rationalism and skepticism that had been nurtured by the Enlightenment and spread by the French Revolution. Nonetheless, the next one hundred years saw a powerful surge of Christian devotion among Protestants in the United States and Canada. In fact, for the followers of John Wesley it proved to be their great century, and Methodists became the largest religious denomination in the United States, with the Baptists right behind them. They were finally overtaken by the huge Catholic immigration from Europe at the end of the century.

When we add to this the flowering of an independent African American Christianity—often called Protestant but, as we shall see, *sui generis* in its origins and expressions—it might be said that the nineteenth century was the Protestant century. Nevertheless, in large cities Catholicism grew to impressive proportions, and a smaller, Jewish community became established as well.

Because of the great diversity among Protestants in the nineteenth century, we will consider only the most important themes of the time and the figures who best illustrate those themes. Although our selection shows some remarkable examples of Christian devotion, I regret that I cannot include even all the larger churches. Fortunately, many small Protestant denominations are very similar to the larger ones, especially in their devotion to Jesus Christ. Shakers and Episcopalians, Covenanters and the earliest Pentecostalists, all shared a common and often unrecognized thread: a heartfelt devotion to Jesus Christ—the same thread of devotion that runs through the Orthodox and Catholic traditions.

In cases like those of Phoebe Palmer, Phillis Wheatley, and Sojourner Truth, our selection was made to illustrate more than one element in the Protestant century. All three of these evangelists, one white and two black, illustrate the new role of women in the Protestant world. This change, a very significant trend in nineteenth-century Protestantism, should be seen as an important element in the struggle for equal rights for women and in the feminist movement. We can see, as well, the opposition to slavery growing as a result of the remarkable development of African American Christianity.

Poets are no longer the spokesmen for Christian devotion they once were, but in the nineteenth century, religious poetry was a significant force in shaping public opinion. In Europe and the United States many great poets displayed a devotion to Christ that has disappeared in our banal and ugly age. Along with poets were religious philosophers, several of whom, despite the abstractness of their profession, expressed a strong devotion to Christ.

We will begin with the great Protestant preachers and evangelists, a group so large that it is difficult to make a selection. We will try at least to explore the devotion of the best known and remembered.

Phoebe Palmer and the Methodists

Only recently have historians of religion understood the significance of Phoebe Palmer (1807–1874), one of the primary figures in the immense success of nineteenth-century Methodism. The distinguished Methodist theologian Thomas Oden does not hesitate to place her on a plane with Teresa of Avila[1] and identifies her as the most influential woman theologian in Protestantism in her time.

Born into a devout New York Methodist family sixteen years after the death of John Wesley, Palmer reflected in her writings the influence of the Greek and Latin Church Fathers. We recall that the group of fervent young men with whom Wesley identified himself at Oxford were also deeply devoted to the Fathers. Of course Palmer also owed much to the classic Protestant writers from the Reformation onward, including Richard Baxter, Johann Arndt, and William Law. She and the Holiness Movement of her time had a "profound spiritual affinity" with SS. Francis of Assisi, Bonaventure, Catherine of Genoa, and Thomas à Kempis, "evidenced in her hunger for undiminished life in Christ".[2] In the introduction to Oden's volume, John Farina finds many similarities between the teaching of St. Catherine of Genoa and Phoebe Palmer. In fact, Thomas Upham, a professor at Bowdoin College who had converted at one of the Palmer prayer group meetings on holiness, published a life of Catherine long before Catholics in the United States did.[3]

Phoebe Palmer was a theologian who ardently opposed slavery. She founded both a powerful spiritual movement (Holiness) and the first inner-city mission to the poor—the Five Points Mission on the Bowery. Her movement influenced the selection of many dedicated Methodist bishops and at least twenty college presidents. Although she was against women preaching during services, she was, by reason of her powerful speaking, a model for women taking decisive roles in the life

[1] Forword to *Phoebe Palmer: Selected Writings*, ed. Thomas C. Oden (New York: Paulist Press, 1988), 14.

[2] Ibid., 16.

[3] Farina, introduction to *Palmer: Selected Writings*, x.

of Christianity. She also had a significant, if less direct, effect on the beginning of the cause for women's rights. Oden lists more than a dozen denominations that find in Phoebe Palmer and her teaching the main stem linking them to the greater Protestant world.

Her *Guide to Holiness*, founded in 1839, was among the most popular religious publications of its day. Ultimately, Phoebe Palmer's importance rests on the fact that she brought the idea of sanctification—the body of concepts that Catholics and Orthodox refer to as the spiritual life—into mainstream Protestant thought. This ideal was already central to the thought of Calvinists like Jonathan Edwards, but through the Methodists' engagement with the poor, the marginal, and the unchurched, Palmer made the spiritual life, along with good works, a vital part of the lives of ordinary Christians. She made the awareness of the Holy Spirit in the Christian soul the spiritual focus for millions, an emphasis that continues today.

Phoebe Palmer's views differed in an essential way from those of John Wesley. Following the classical model of Christian spirituality, with its roots in patristic and medieval literature, Wesley, in his *Plain Account of Christian Perfection*, saw sanctification as a lifetime process. Palmer, however, was inspired by Charles Finney (1792–1876), whose influence was felt by many in the nineteenth-century American Holiness Movement and, later, Pentecostalism. Following him, she taught a "shorter way", by which a person could make a complete commitment to God at a single moment of grace. Then, she thought, by claiming the powers of the Holy Spirit, the person could be sanctified in a short time and live a life of perfection, which had been attained at the time of conversion. This teaching found an enthusiastic audience, as can be seen by the tremendous success of her journal, *Guide to Holiness*, which was in print for more than sixty years. Through her inspiration, summer camp meetings became events of great fervor. At some, sermons went on throughout the day and night. What became known as the Holiness Movement was ultimately the source of many Pentecostal Christian denominations.

Early in her career Phoebe Palmer stepped back from her religious commitments to work on what she called her sanctification, or total consecration to God. Charles Edward White gives a fascinating description of her experiences at this time. Catholics familiar with the biographies of such saints as Francis, Ignatius, Francis de Sales, Catherine of Genoa, and even Mother Teresa of Calcutta will recognize the sign of a special grace and calling. Palmer responded with a desire for total sanctification, a total gift of self to God. Catholics and Orthodox Christians will feel at home with the following passage from her diary.

> I felt that the Spirit was leading into a solemn, most sacred, and inviolable compact between God and the soul that came forth from

> Him, by which, in the sight of God, angels, and men, I was to be united in eternal oneness with the Lord my redeemer, requiring unquestioning allegiance on my part, and infinite love, and everlasting salvation, guidance, and protection, on the part of Him who had loved and redeemed me, so that from henceforth He might say to me, "I will betroth thee unto me for ever" (Hos. 2:19).[4]

Phoebe Palmer knew few Catholics and may never have met an Orthodox Christian, but she was linked through Wesley to the patristic and medieval traditions. As we turn our attention specifically to her devotion to Christ, we realize that it is part of a whole integrated Christian experience, which followed from the action of the Holy Spirit and made her a totally dedicated disciple of Jesus Christ.

Describing what holiness is, Palmer writes:

> Gospel holiness is that state which is attained by the believer when, through faith in the infinite merit of the Saviour, body and soul, with every ransomed faculty, are ceaselessly presented, a living sacrifice, to God; the purpose of the soul being steadily bent to know nothing among men, save Christ and Him crucified, and the eye of faith fixed on "the Lamb of God which taketh away the sin of the world" (John 1:29). In obedience to the requirement of God, the sacrifice is presented through Christ, and the soul at once proves that "He is able to save them to the uttermost that come unto God by Him" (Heb. 7:25).[5]

In a passage that has obvious echoes of the Church Fathers,[6] Palmer speaks of a loving devotional attitude to Christ in ways that would be very familiar to Catholics.

> If Christ were present in the flesh, and I were called, with Martha, to minister to the temporal wants of my Saviour and His disciples, it seems to me I should feel as if I were as engaged in His service; and that the affections prompting to this service were as truly pure and spiritual, as though I were with Mary a wholly unencumbered worshiper at His feet. Or, if I were with devoted Mary, and chanced to cast my eye upon the unprepared table, my listenings to His holy teachings would be broken, by a sympathetic, yet invisible cord, leading from the Saviour's heart of pure love, and drawing aside the thoughts and affections of His waiting one, to the performance of the other service.[7]

[4] Diary, July 27, 1837, quoted in Charles Edward White, *The Beauty of Holiness* (Grand Rapids, Mich.: Francis Asbury Press, 1986), 16.

[5] From *Entire Devotion to God*, in *Palmer: Selected Writings*, 187–88.

[6] See the sermon of St. Augustine currently assigned to the hour of Matins in the Divine Office for the feast of St. Martha (July 29).

[7] From her Diary (1847), quoted in *Palmer: Selected Writings*, 219.

The allusion to the Heart of Christ is a recurring theme in Palmer's writing. About the same time, she wrote the following poem to her friends Bishop Leonidas Hamline and his wife:

> This bliss is ours; *we are in Christ, made one.*
> He is our life, and on His bleeding Heart
> We rest: He is our Shield—our Sun.
> In fellowship we walk, no more to part.
> The blood of Jesus cleanseth from all sin;
> And now *through Christ*, with blended sympathies,
> We'll work out our salvation, whilst He works within;
> When called from earth, we'll meet in paradise.[8]

In her later years, her health declining, Phoebe Palmer continued to travel with her devoted husband. She wrote him a devoutly romantic poem on the forty-fourth anniversary of their wedding, in 1871. She continued to speak at camp meetings as long as her strength held out. A few months before her death, losing her hearing, she wrote to Mrs. Hamline:

> While at the Tuesday meeting, last week, not able to hear much that was said, and suffering with the gathering in my ear, it was suggested, "Can you now say,
> "Thankful, I take the cup from Thee,
> Prepared and mingled by Thy skill."
> All praise to the Great Physician of souls, who has so long had my case in hand, that I was enabled to answer, "Yes, thankful, I take the cup. Infinite love has prepared it. Surely I shall not be permitted to suffer one pang too much."...
> I do not wish you to think that I am in anticipation of immediate dissolution, but I do feel that this earthly house of my tabernacle is being dissolved, and unless I improve soon there remains but little hope of doing much more. But whatever the result may be, I know all will be right. The Lord will not call me till my work is done.[9]

This brief review of a remarkable life and profound religious devotion should make it clear that a high degree of holiness is possible in every denomination sincerely dedicated to Christ and the spreading of His Gospel, providing that there is a real acceptance of His divinity and His humanity and of the necessity of His grace. Phoebe Palmer provides us with insight into a profoundly spiritual life.

Other Great Christians of the Time

All the significant leaders of the spiritual revival of the Protestant century were deeply devoted to Jesus Christ as their personal Savior and illustrate the conviction of a personal relationship with Jesus. Usually their experience was attributed directly to the action of the Holy Spirit.

[8] From "That They All May Be One", in *Palmer: Selected Writings*, 218.

[9] Letter, Feb. 18, 1874, in *Palmer: Selected Writings*, 312–13.

John Farina has brought out quite correctly the relationship of Isaac Hecker and the Protestant perfectionist, or Holiness, Movement. Along with Phoebe Palmer, Asa Mahan was the chief spokesperson of the perfectionist movement at Oberlin College and wrote a foundational work for the movement, *The Baptism of the Holy Ghost*.[10] Thomas Upham, professor at Bowdoin College, was the other leader of the movement. He published (1845) a book about the life of St. Catherine of Genoa, known in Protestant circles as Madame Adorna. The book was aptly titled *The Life of Catherine Adorna*. He used Catherine's experience to illustrate the doctrine of holiness, and his book went through numerous editions. It would be almost thirty years before the first Catholic edition of her life was published in the United States. What made Catherine popular with both Protestants and Catholics was that as a laywoman, her "practical orientation in the world made her an apt model for those seeking perfection in the context of everyday life".[11] The emphasis on the sanctifying work of the Holy Spirit in the soul of the baptized Christian (often referred to as the baptism of the Holy Spirit) was an important teaching for the perfectionists, who saw the work of sanctification continuing after the first conversion of baptism. This is the very doctrine of Wesley and his followers and was a source of contention with the English Calvinists.

The other great evangelists who preached the perfectionist doctrine were Charles G. Finney (1792–1875) and Dwight L. Moody (1837–1899) and the prolific hymn writer Fanny Crosby (1820–1915). All three believed in a second spiritual awakening for those who were already practicing Christians. They felt called to a complete, or perfect, giving of self, not unlike the experiences of SS. Francis, Tikhon, and the other Catholic and Orthodox saints. Finney presented this understanding of the doctrine of perfection in his *Lectures to Professing Christians* (1837):

> Christian perfection is perfect obedience to the law of God. The law of God requires perfect, disinterested, impartial benevolence—love to God and love to our neighbour. It requires that we be motivated by the same feeling, and act on the same principles upon which God acts. It requires us to leave self out of the question as uniformly as he does, to be as much separated from selfishness as he is—in a word, to be in our measure as perfect as God is.[12]

While the perfectionism of these evangelists may leave us with an impression of a good deal of psychological naïveté and even self-righteousness, we can see from the quotations alone the influence of

[10] John Farina, *An American Experience of God: The Spirituality of Isaac Hecker* (New York: Paulist Press, 1981), 168.

[11] Ibid., 170.

[12] Quoted in *The Story of Christian Spirituality*, ed. Gordon Mursell (Minneapolis, Minn.: Fortress Press, 2001), 288–89.

Catholic spiritual writers, including the terminology of St. Francis de Sales in his *Treatise on the Love of God*. Perhaps the natural American optimism of the nineteenth century is also an element. After all, Finney started reading the Bible as part of his law studies, in an effort to trace the origins of English law in the Scriptures.

Personal devotion to Jesus is seen in the hymns of the movement, especially those of Fanny Crosby. Even the titles speak of deep devotion to Christ: "Pass Me Not, O Gentle Saviour"; "Jesus Keep Me Near the Cross"; "Tell Me the Story of Jesus"; and "All the Way My Saviour Leads Me".[13] The Perfectionist revival began to fade early in the twentieth century, although some revival centers lasted for decades after that. The tradition of preaching twenty-four hours a day in prayer halls, more suited to an age of leisure than to the fast-paced twentieth century, was eventually discontinued. The spirit of this revival, Methodist in its roots, would live on in the tradition of Pentecostalism in both the white and African American churches. But the development of Pentecostalism must wait until we move into the twentieth century.

African American Christianity

Related to the American Protestant experience yet distinct from it is the development of a unique expression of Christianity among African Americans, most of whom received their knowledge of Christ from white Protestants. Smaller numbers of African Americans in Louisiana and along the Gulf coast received the Good News from French and Spanish Catholics, and others from Catholic evangelists in the large cities of the North. In either case—Protestant or Catholic—African Americans put their ways of thinking and praying and their African roots into a warm and moving acceptance of Jesus Christ, the suffering Deliverer of the poor. I consider this simple and loving acceptance of Jesus Christ by black people, whose forebears were slaves, to be among the most moving and significant elements of my own efforts to follow the Lord. Moreover, I can't imagine any serious Christian being aware of this remarkable history and not being deeply moved.

Slavery was condemned, with the penalty of automatic excommunication, by Pope Eugene IV in 1435 in his Bull *Sicut Dudum*.[14] However, despite the efforts of friars like Bartolomé de las Casas, slavery and serfdom spread throughout the New World. The Protestant clergy who saw its evil were no more successful in stemming it than were the Catholics, who at least were in conflict with more lenient slave laws in the Spanish colonies.

The New Israel

The New England Puritans saw themselves as God's people opening a "promised land", complete with a covenant. We recall the difficulties of staunch Puritans like Jonathan Edwards with those who went only

[13] Mursell, *Story of Christian Spirituality*.

[14] See Joel S. Panzer, *The Popes and Slavery* (New York: Alba House, 1996), 7ff.

halfway in living the covenant and especially with those who considered themselves Protestants but who never even started living the covenant. In a similar way, as African Americans came to know the Bible, they too saw themselves as God's people and regarded their slave masters as the Egyptians of the Old Testament. Jesus had a special place in their thinking. He was the Suffering Servant (Is 53:1–3). They saw Him as their "companion, friend, fellow sufferer, of humble birth, mistreated; in all ways able to identify with their plight".[15]

Like all oppressed Christian people, they emphasized the redemptive aspect of suffering. Like the early Christians who celebrated the Cross—the sign of slavery and shame transformed into the promise of victory over evil—they celebrated the suffering and victory of Christ. The slaves developed their own music, making possible the survival of some African cultural forms in a society that largely forbade them any remembrance of their homeland.

In *The Spirituals and the Blues*, James Cone gives us an insight into this spiritual music: "The basic idea of the spirituals is that slavery contradicts God; it is a denial of his will. To be enslaved is to be declared nobody, and that form of existence contradicts God's creation of people to be his children."[16] Sometimes the spirituals contain a double meaning, as is shown in this excerpt from one composed when Northern abolitionists were leading slaves to freedom by the Underground Railroad. "Steal away, steal away, steal away to Jesus. I ain't got long to stay here."[17]

The following poem, which could easily be sung, was written by the African American bishop Daniel Alexander Payne in 1837, almost thirty years before the Emancipation Proclamation. It demonstrates a profound but simple devotion to Jesus and reminds us of the twelfth-century Latin hymn *Jesu Dulcis Memoria*.

Now is come the hour of prayer—
Lovely, precious Jesus, hear:
Stoop thou from thy throne above—
Bless me, bless me, Son of God!
Shed thou in my heart, abroad,
Thy saving grace, thy dying love.
O, time of prayer! O, hour divine!—
Ecstatic joys and peace are thine!

O, Jesus, thou my portion art:—
Sun of my life—joy of my heart.
O, raptures! bliss—O, God of love!
Exalt my thoughts, my hopes, my soul,

[15] Ibid., 290.
[16] Quoted in Mursell, *Story of Christian Spirituality*, 291.
[17] Ibid.

Higher than where the planets roll—
Up to thy dazzling throne of love.
O, time of prayer! O, hour divine!—
Ecstatic joys and peace are thine![18]

Among both Protestants and Catholics there was a preponderance of women pioneers in black Christianity. This can be explained partly by the fact that African American women were often better treated than men. They worked in the family as nannies and housekeepers and were regarded as persons, whereas the men were kept in the fields and treated little better than beasts of burden. As we know from the history of Christian martyrs of the first century, it was often women who led the way with intrepid faith and unwavering devotion. It is not surprising that the first outstanding black Christians we will meet are women born in slavery.

Phillis Wheatley (1753–1784)

In a short life, this brilliant woman was recognized as a child prodigy, and her owner, a Boston merchant, treated her like a daughter. The Countess of Huntingdon, George Whitefield's friend whom we met in Chapter 16 above, was so impressed at meeting Phillis Wheatley that she published her poetry. The following letter, written when Wheatley was nineteen, captures in a few lines the devotion to the suffering Redeemer so thematic in black spirituality.

> Inexpressibly happy should we be could we have a due sense of the beauties and excellence of the crucified Saviour. In his Crucifixion may be seen marvellous displays of Grace and Love, sufficient to draw and invite us to the rich and endless treasures of his mercy; let us rejoice in and adore the wonders of God's infinite Love in bringing us from a land semblant of darkness itself, and where the divine light of revelation (being obscur'd) is as darkness....
>
> It gives me very great pleasure to hear of so many of my nation, seeking with eagerness the way of true felicity. O may we all meet at length in that happy mansion.... Till we meet in the regions of consummate blessedness, let us endeavor by the assistance of divine grace, to live the life, and we shall die the death of the Righteous.[19]

Sojourner Truth (Isabella Baumfree, 1797–1883)

This slave girl, born on a Dutch plantation in Ulster County, New York, was separated from her family and sold twice before the age of twelve. Although slavery was illegal in New York State, she and many others were, nonetheless, kept in servitude against the law. At the age

[18] Daniel Alexander Payne, "The Hour of Prayer", in *Conversations with God: Two Centuries of Prayers by African Americans*, ed. James Melvin Washington, Ph.D. (New York: HarperPerennial, 1995), 34–35.

[19] Letter, May 19, 1772, quoted in *In Our Own Voices: Four Centuries of American Women's Religious Writing*, ed. Rosemary Skinner Keller and Rosemary Radford Ruether (San Francisco: Harper San Francisco, 1995), 169–70.

of thirty, after she was given her freedom, she had a vision in which she believed God told her to "travel up an' down the land showin' the people their sins an' bein' a sign unto them".[20] She believed that God Himself gave her the new name by which she was known as an itinerant preacher, abolitionist, advocate for the poor, and promoter of women's rights.

The account of her conversion experience is reminiscent of St. Teresa of Avila in several ways: her familiar relationship with God, her personal awareness of Jesus' presence, and her awareness of her need for conversion. St. Teresa had prayed to Christ: "Oh, who will cry out for You, to tell everyone how faithful You are to Your friends!"[21] Sojourner Truth did exactly that, going up and down the land proclaiming the faithfulness of Christ.

The following passage, written in 1850 by Olive Gilbert, describes an event that took place when Sojourner Truth was in her twenties.

> She ... walked into the house, and made an effort to resume her work. But the workings of the inward man were too absorbing to admit of much attention to her avocations. She desired to talk to God, but her vileness utterly forbade it, and she was not able to prefer a petition. "What!" said she, "shall I lie again to God? I have told him nothing but lies; and shall I speak again, and tell another lie to God?" She could not; and now she began to wish for someone to speak to God for her. Then a space seemed opening between her and God, and she felt that if someone, who was worthy in the sight of heaven, would but plead *for* her in their own name, and not let God know it came from *her*, who was so unworthy, God might grant it. At length a friend appeared to stand between herself and an insulted Deity; and she felt as sensibly refreshed as when, on a hot day, an umbrella had been interposed between her scorching head and a burning sun. But who was this friend? ...
>
> "Who *are* you?" she exclaimed, as the vision brightened into a form distinct, beaming with the beauty of holiness, and radiant with love. She then said, audibly addressing the mysterious visitant—"I *know* you, and I *don't* know you." Meaning, "You seem perfectly familiar; I feel that you not only love me, but that you *always* have loved me—yet I know you not—I cannot call you by name." ... So while she repeated without intermission, "I know you, I know you," that the vision might remain—"Who are you?" was the cry of her heart, and her whole soul was in one deep prayer that this heavenly personage might be revealed to her, and remain with her. At length, after bending both soul and body with the intensity of this desire, till

[20] Mursell, *Story of Christian Spirituality*, 291.

[21] *Life*, chap. 25, in *The Collected Works of St. Teresa of Avila*, trans. and ed. Kieran Kavanaugh, O.C.D., and Otilio Rodriguez O.C.D., (Washington, D.C.: ICS Publications, 1976), 1:221.

> breath and strength seemed failing, and she could maintain her position no longer, an answer came to her, saying distinctly, "It is Jesus." "Yes," she responded, "it is *Jesus*."[22]

This remarkable passage speaks of a true mystical experience and represents the highest form of Christian devotion. Since its origin is not found in the one who experiences Jesus, but is the gracious gift of God, it must be called mystical and not simply religious. The word "religious" describes that by which men reach up to God; mystical refers to the unseen, to God's wonderful invitation to His children. On the basis of her life, work, and experience, it would seem that if she had been a Catholic, Sojourner Truth would be a canonized saint of the Church.

Christ in the Black Churches

The earliest organized churches serving African Americans were mostly in the North before the Civil War, in Philadelphia, New York, and Boston, where there were many freed slaves and their descendants, but the roots of original black Christianity date from long before these. It is amazing that the first continuing black congregation was founded in Aiken County, South Carolina, about 1774 and later established as the Springfield Baptist Church in Augusta, Georgia.[23] Many plantation owners saw to it that their slaves sat through long Sunday morning services, almost always in a segregated area such as the choir loft. Since these services were rather sedate and, except for the Baptists and Methodists, somewhat heady, slaves met on their own in the woods on Sunday evenings. This was done in secret: often discovery resulted in a beating. They mixed Bible reading and exhortation with African modalities of worship: ceremonial dance, and wordless songs similar to the yodeling or madrigal singing of European peasants. The rather loose organizational structure of the Baptist Church fitted in well with the secret congregations. The services were often called "shouts" because of the ecstatic prayer.[24] It was not unusual for the participants to hold large cooking pots over their heads so that they would not be heard by the slave owners. The emergence of black Christianity coincided with the first great awakening sparked by Whitefield and Wesley in the 1740s. Thus revivalism and conversion, as well as an emphasis on moral and even physical healing, became hallmarks of black Christianity in America.

Lemuel Haynes (1753–1834), a veteran of the War for Independence, was ordained a Congregational minister in 1785, becoming the first black clergyman in a white congregation. It was not an easy road for the black ministers in the well-established white churches, so independent black congregations came into existence.

---

[22] Quoted in Keller and Ruether, *In Our Own Voices*, 173–74.

[23] Mark A. Noll, *A History of Christianity in the United States and Canada* (Grand Rapids, Mich.: William B. Eerdmans, 1992), 108.

[24] Ibid., 199ff.

Richard Allen (1760–1831) was born a slave and began preaching after joining the Methodist Church at age seventeen. As a freed slave he often preached in Philadelphia four or five times a day.[25] Along with his friend Absalom Jones, he founded the Free African Society, the first black organization in the United States, and they won wide recognition for their heroic work with the sick and dying during the 1793 yellow fever epidemic in Philadelphia. Eventually Jones became minister at St. Thomas Episcopal Church in Philadelphia. Allen was ordained a Methodist deacon in 1799, six years after establishing the Bethel Church for Negro Methodists.

Conflicts with white leadership continued, and in 1814 Allen and other black clergy founded the African Methodist Episcopal Church. Black Christianity then moved into the mainstream of American life, although the great prejudice against African Americans continued, at times growing virulent, until the civil rights movement of the 1960s, which was led largely by black clergy backed up by a fervent army of black Christian women.

James Weldon Johnson (1871–1938), a black lawyer, editor, writer, and an organizer of the National Association for the Advancement of Colored People (NAACP), summed up the contribution of the spirituals and their composers, and indirectly that of the black clergy, in the following stanzas of "O Black and Unknown Bards".

> Heart of what slave poured out such melody
> As "Steal away to Jesus"? On its strains
> His spirit must have nightly floated free,
> Though still about his hands he felt his chains.
> Who heard great "Jordan roll"? Whose starward eye
> Saw chariot "swing low"? And who was he
> That breathed that comforting, melodic sigh,
> "Nobody knows de trouble I see"?
>
> You sang far better than you knew; the songs
> That for your listeners' hungry hearts sufficed
> Still live—but more than this to you belongs:
> You sang a race from wood to stone to Christ.[26]

It is one of the many paradoxes of history that during the nineteenth century, the faith of white liberal Protestants in Europe and America was deeply eroded by the skepticism of certain European biblical scholars. At the same time, black Christians in the United States, the Caribbean, and Canada were looking toward the "sweet Lord Jesus" as their Savior. Although some of the intelligentsia look disparagingly on devotion, it represents one of the most admirable

[25] Ibid., 201.
[26] Ibid., 335.

aspects of American history and has become one of the most productive forms of American religious culture. It is regrettable that most American Christians know little about Christ's deeply penetrating presence in the black history of the United States.

The following sampler of spirituals and poems will show just how real Jesus' presence was to Christians in a number of congregations: the Church of God in Christ, the Apostolic Faith, the various black Pentecostal denominations, as well as the better known Baptist, Methodist, and African Methodist Episcopal Church, and the smaller Zion churches that came from these.

> Did ever you see the like before?
> Jesus preaching to the poor.
>
> I know the Lord has laid his hands on me.
>
> Oh, wasn't that a happy day
> Jesus washed my sins away?
>
> I know the Lord has laid his hands on me, When
> I know the Lord has laid his hands on me.[27]

Poetry is often the fervent expression of an oppressed people, as it can be committed to memory if paper is unavailable. Poetry is often the best medium to express the highest religious sentiments without becoming maudlin, and we see examples of this with Francis of Assisi, John of the Cross, John Milton, and Thérèse of Lisieux. There is a rich treasure of such poetry of the spirit in black Christianity.

The following is a prayer written in 1906 by Charles Price Jones (1865–1949), founder and first bishop of the Church of Christ (Holiness). Jones' hymnal, *His Fullness*, is considered one of the significant contributions to African American spirituality. This poem can remind Catholics of the poetry and hymns of English Catholics, especially Fr. Faber.

> Jesus, Jesus, I would be
> Consecrated all to Thee;
> In Thee wholly sanctified,
> Free from selfishness and pride.
>
> Jesus, I am very sure
> Thou canst ev'ry weakness cure;
> In my feeble heart believe
> All Thy fullness Thou wilt give.
>
> Jesus, I am satisfied
> If in Thee I may abide;

[27] "I Know the Lord Has Laid His Hands on Me", Negro Spiritual, from the *African American Heritage Hymnal* (Chicago: GIA Publications, 2001), no. 360.

Cause all thoughts of earth to flee,
Set my mind alone on Thee.

Jesus, fix me just as Thou
Wouldst delight to have me now;
Nothing would I have but Thee,
Be Thou all in all to me.[28]

One of the most interesting families in the American black experience were the Tanners of Philadelphia. Henry Ossawa Tanner (1859–1937) is black America's first world-class painter. His works usually focus on biblical scenes, but they avoid the sentimentality of so many religious paintings of the time. His *Annunciation* and *Mary Teaching Christ to Read* are among the most moving paintings I have ever seen. Filled with mysticism and dignity, they show no trace of sentimentality. His father, Benjamin Tucker Tanner (1835–1923), a bishop in the African Methodist Episcopal Church, was a cartographer of such merit that his maps, like his son's paintings, are on view in the Philadelphia Museum of Art.

Bishop Tanner, reputed to be the first African American who could read and write Latin, composed the following poem entitled "Who?" as a kind of commentary on Romans 8:28, 34. The King James translation, which Tanner would have used, reads: "And we know that all things work together for good to them that love God, to them who are the called according to his purpose.... Who is he that condemneth? It is Christ that died, yea rather, that is risen again, who is even at the right hand of God, who also maketh intercession for us."

Quis est qui condemnet

If Jesu, Lord, I come to thee,
And freely thou receivedst me,
    Who shall say, nay?
Who shall bring up the days of sin,
When earthly passions raged within?

If Jesu, Lord, I should profess
Thy name—Thy boundless love confess,
    Who shall deny?
That thou thyself hast made me bold
To claim the blessings long foretold?

If Jesu, in the throng I raise
My voice in notes of praise,
    Who say, be still?
Who chide me for the words I speak
And tell me I should be more meek?

[28] "Prayer for Consecration", in Washington, *Conversations with God*, 78.

Dear Jesu, 'tis thy precious Name
That doth alone my heart inflame—
    My heart inspire.
And makes me fearless of the world—
Thy children—of the arrows hurled.[29]

In this poem we discover much of the strength that enabled the descendants of the first African Americans, so unjustly enslaved, mercilessly treated, and burdened with poverty, injustice, and brutality, to survive and to prosper despite "the arrows hurled".

The Social Gospel Movement

We will look next at the Social Gospel movement, even though it is really a phenomenon of the late nineteenth and early twentieth centuries, because its founders received their inspiration from the person of Christ as He was known to the evangelists of that time. Unfortunately, few Protestants are now aware of the movement and its personal devotion to Christ, confusing it with the more liberal theological ideas and preachers of the mid-twentieth century. The movement's characteristic devotion to Christ derived from the poor and was a response to Jesus' words in Matthew 25: "I was hungry and you gave me food." We have seen that even in the patristic era, Christianity produced many saints with a strong sense of social responsibility. Preachers like St. John Chrysostom were followed, in medieval times, by Francis of Assisi, who worked with lepers, and John of Martha, who freed the slaves. Later came Vincent de Paul and Martin de Porres, whose heroic acts of charity are celebrated to this day. All these have served to remind Christians that we cannot pray to Jesus in church if we have just walked by Him disguised as a beggar in the street.

It is not surprising that a spiritual evangelical interest in the poor began with the Baptists in the early nineteenth century. Although the name Walter Rauschenbusch (1861–1918) has become synonymous with the Social Gospel movement, it had its roots in the preaching of William R. Williams, a minister for fifty-three years at Amity Baptist Church in New York City. Williams was one of the most respected voices in Baptist history, recognized for "undoubted piety, unexampled humility ... unusual attainment in literature ... and rare genius as a writer".[30] In 1838 Williams gave a lecture at Brown University to the Society of Missionary Inquiry. His topic, "The Jesuits as a Missionary Order", was an attempt to show "what a few resolute hearts may accomplish".

If this reference to the Jesuits seems somewhat shocking, it is even more astonishing to note Williams' comment to that gathering of earnest young Protestants, some of whom had never seen a Catholic, much less a Jesuit.

---

[29] "Who?" in Washington, *Conversations with God*, 81.

[30] *Walter Rauschenbusch: Selected Writings*, ed. Winthrop S. Hudson (New York: Paulist Press, 1984), 10, n. 14.

> When Ignatius [of Loyola] with his first companions bound themselves by a midnight vow ... some three centuries ago, to renounce the world for the purpose of preaching the gospel wherever the supreme pontiff might send them, the engagement was one most momentous to the interests of our entire race. That company of seven poor students, with but zeal, talent, and stout hearts, and a burning enthusiasm, formed then a bond far more important to the after history of mankind than most of the leagues made by kings at the head of embattled squadrons.[31]

Williams' son, Leighton, who was heir to a remarkable family tradition of ministers in New York, joined the newly assigned minister of the second German Baptist Church, Walter Rauschenbusch, on West 45th Street in Manhattan, and Nathaniel Schmidt, recently ordained minister at the Swedish Baptist Church. Williams was older and initially the leader of the group. Schmidt was the scholar and would later be professor of Semitic studies at Cornell. Rauschenbusch came from a long line of Lutheran pastors, but influenced by Charles Finney and Dwight Moody, he had become an evangelical Baptist.

These fervent young ministers bound themselves together in 1887, fifty years after Leighton Williams' father gave his lecture at Brown, to be "a true society of Jesus in which individual ambitions should be subordinated to a common and lofty aim". In Williams' words, it was to be "a new society of Jesus, of the union and combination of Catholic devotion with Protestant faith in the service of Jesus as Lord and Master".[32]

In later years, Rauschenbusch would remember the Communion services of this period "with special joy", adding that "a tranquil spirit of reverence and contemplation, a deep reverence toward our Lord, a sense of his real presence, and unusual joy in Christian fellowship invited the soul to rest and true prayer".[33]

The little society of Jesus often met at the Williams farm near Marlboro, New York, sixty miles from the city. The Holy Spirit was obviously working in this little group. In September 1890 Rauschenbusch wrote in the farm's guest book: "Only an afternoon and evening, yet enough talk to turn over the world and enough love to make any heart happy".[34]

At the time Rauschenbusch became pastor in Manhattan, New York was a city of tenements; dimly lit, foul-smelling, five-story buildings housed three-quarters of the population. The high mortality rate among

---

[31] Quoted in ibid., 11.

[32] Leighton Williams, *The Brotherhood of the Kingdom and Its Work*, quoted in Rauschenbusch, *Selected Writings*, 13.

[33] Quoted in Rauschenbusch, *Selected Writings*, 12.

[34] Paul M. Minus, *Walter Rauschenbusch: American Reformer* (New York: Macmillan, 1988), 58. Of the society the author comments: "It was an association reminiscent of those enjoyed by Francis, Ignatius, Wesley, and other Christian pioneers early in their ministries."

children deeply disturbed Rauschenbusch. About this time the little "society of Jesus" came to an end when Schmidt moved on to become a teacher, and Rauschenbusch became depressed by the conditions of the poor and the working classes. In 1889 he told a Baptist congregation that after living among the poor for three years, "by reason of the pity and sympathy which the Lord Jesus Christ has implanted in my heart, I have not been able to look on the things I see about me unmoved, or without thinking on the causes of those sad appearances".[35]

In 1886, Rauschenbusch launched into the turbulent waters of social problems by supporting Henry George, a crusading journalist, in his campaign for the mayoralty of New York. George, who today would seem a moderate socialist and even a supporter of competition, was thought by his contemporaries to be a radical. Rauschenbusch, uninformed about politics and economics in his early days, learned a great deal from George and testified later in life: "I owe my own first awakening to the world of social problems to the agitation of Henry George in 1886 and ... record my lifelong debt to this single-minded apostle of a great truth." Any doubts Rauschenbusch might have had about supporting George were dispelled by Fr. Edward McGlynn, a Catholic pastor in New York, whose fervent oratory convinced Rauschenbusch of the righteousness of George's cause.[36]

Leighton Williams then introduced Rauschenbusch to an Episcopalian layman, Richard Ely, a professor at Johns Hopkins. Profoundly influenced by Ely's book *Social Aspects of Christianity*, which urged Christians to recognize that the truth of the Gospel was both individual and social, Rauschenbusch became deeply, even entirely, involved in a Christianity that called for the conversion not only of the inner person but also of society itself. For the rest of his life he would work and preach for both these goals. Although the three members of the "society of Jesus" were separated, they remained in constant contact and did little without prior consultation.[37]

It is important to understand that Rauschenbusch and his associates never separated the Gospel message from their work to reform society. The following passage from an article by Rauschenbusch on foreign missions was published in 1892.

> First of all and above everything comes evangelical Christianity. And what do I mean by that? I mean by that, not any particular type of doctrine, but the extension of faith in the crucified and risen Christ, who imparts his Spirit to those who believe in him, and thereby redeems them from the dominion of the flesh and the world and their corruption, and transforms them into spiritual beings, conformed to his likeness and partaking of his life. That is the primary

[35] Ibid., 61.

[36] Ibid., 61–62.

[37] Rauschenbusch, *Selected Writings*, 21.

aim of Christian missions, first in the order of importance, first in the order of time.[38]

Rauschenbusch preached a "new evangelism" that must "appeal to motives which powerfully seize men", and "must hold up a moral standard so high above their actual lives that it will smite them with conviction of sin".[39] Despite his insistence on real conversion, Rauschenbusch realized that the providence of God also operated through social forces, which could be directed by men of Christian values. This same realization gave rise a decade or two later to the Christian democratic movement in Catholic Europe and provided the Continent with leaders, such as Adenauer and de Gasperi, who would lead Europe out of the ashes of war.

There is even a parallel (with one important exception) between the papal writings of *Rerum Novarum* (1891) and *Quadragesimo Anno* (1931) and the ideas of Rauschenbusch and associates: Popes Leo XIII and Pius XI never espoused socialism. After twenty years of preaching the Social Gospel, Rauschenbusch published his important work *Christianity and the Social Crisis* in 1907. Widely read, it provoked much comment. Leighton Williams had a mild, but important, criticism—one of emphasis—that is very interesting. He reminds Rauschenbusch of the essential spiritual nature of social reform. "The heart of our movement is a deep, personal experience, mystical in its nature, which forever makes us different men from what we were before we received it, and puts a gulf between us and the world that has it not.... All our opinions were verified for us by this inner light."[40] Leo XIII and Pius XI would have agreed with Williams' reminder of the link between spirituality and social concern. In a later work, *Christianizing the Social Order* (1912), Rauschenbusch reemphasized the spiritual element that had been important early on: "Spiritual regeneration is the most important fact of any life history. A living experience of God is the crowning knowledge attainable to a human mind."[41]

Times and issues have changed in the decades since Rauschenbusch's death in 1918. However, the necessity of linking devotion to Christ with responsibility for others, especially for the needs of society, remains as important as ever. The failure of socialism as an economic system makes Rauschenbusch's answer, like that of many in earlier times, little more than a historical curiosity. It is almost embarrassing. Christians as different as the liberation theologians of South

---

[38] "Conceptions of Missions", *The Watchman* (November 24/December 1, 1892), quoted in Rauschenbusch, *Selected Writings*, 67.

[39] "The New Evangelism", *The Independent* (Jan.–June 1904), quoted in Rauschenbusch, *Selected Writings*, 139.

[40] Rauschenbusch, *Selected Writings*, 38.

[41] Ibid., 39.

America, Dorothy Day, and Mother Teresa made the same message clear in the last decades of the twentieth century. The most lasting aspect of Rauschenbusch's work is a book of devotion, *For God and the People: Prayers of the Social Awakening*. The response to the book was "astonishing". Newspapers printed the prayers, and hundreds of thousands of copies were printed in several languages. Rauschenbusch really meant to formulate a new prayer style or kind of devotion.[42] He had obviously grown impatient with irrelevant and merely sentimental Christian devotion.

There are prayers for children who work and children of the street, artisans and men of business, artists and judges, writers and newspapermen, and even prayers of wrath against war and the seeking of mammon. The following prayer for the Kingdom of God represents the best of Social Gospel spirituality and devotion to Jesus Christ. The assumptions of this prayer may seem obvious to us, but that is because the Social Gospel movement, although it did not survive as Rauschenbusch intended, left a lasting mark on the way modern followers of Christ see the world and recognize what it means to be a Christian.

> O Christ, thou hast bidden us pray for the coming of thy Father's kingdom, in which his righteous will shall be done on earth. We have treasured thy words, but we have forgotten their meaning, and thy great hope has grown dim in thy Church. We bless thee for the inspired souls of all ages who saw afar the shining city of God, and by faith left the profit of the present to follow their vision.... Help us, O Lord, in the courage of faith to seize what has now come so near, that the glad day of God may dawn at last. As we have mastered Nature that we might gain wealth, help us now to master the social relations of mankind that we may gain justice and a world of brothers. For what shall it profit our nation if it gain numbers and riches, and lose the sense of the living God and the joy of human brotherhood? ...
>
> Help us to make the welfare of all the supreme law of our land, that so our commonwealth may be built strong and secure on the love of all its citizens. Cast down the throne of Mammon who ever grinds the life of men, and set up thy throne, O Christ, for thou didst die that men might live.... Our Master, once more we make thy faith our prayer: "Thy kingdom come! Thy will be done on earth!"[43]

[42] Ibid., 207ff.

[43] Walter Rauschenbusch, *Prayers of the Social Awakening* (New York: Pilgrim Press, 1910), 107–8; see also Rauschenbusch, *Selected Writings*, 228–29.

23 Catholics in the Nineteenth Century

Catholic Immigrants in America

During the nineteenth century, the Catholic Church in the United States was a church of transplanted faith from many diverse sources. Although the experience of faith in Europe varied considerably, even among people of the same language and within the same nation, the immigrants brought with them a firm faith, which colored every aspect of their lives. In the fascinating immigration museum at Ellis Island in New York harbor, there is a display of very plain but meaningful religious objects: Jewish prayer shawls, Lutheran Bibles, Protestant hymnals, rosaries, and statues of Christ and the Blessed Virgin from Poland. The sign at this exhibit tells us that almost all the immigrants brought with them a strong religious faith, which stood them in good stead in the New World. The number of immigrants was immense. Through Castle Garden and, later, Ellis Island, sixteen million immigrants passed during the period from the Civil War to shortly after World War I. More than one hundred million Americans today are descended from those immigrants. Among the newly arrived were canonized and uncanonized saints, scientific geniuses, actors and writers, construction workers, salesmen, and innumerable farmers. The farmers' wives would soon work in the deplorable conditions of the great factories of the New World.

Almost all brought their clergy, who were often cast in the role of patriarchs because they could read, write, and deal with the often hostile and unwelcoming local population. With a unanimity that was not always obvious because of their different experiences and beliefs, they all prayed to God and relied on His protection. The majority of nineteenth-century immigrants to America were Christian—Catholic, Orthodox, and Protestant—but there was also a vast influx of Jews at the beginning of the twentieth century. Although these people did not know the word "ecumenism", they did respect one another's religious values.

It is difficult to choose a single Catholic of outstanding qualities among the immigrants because there are so many. Women of incredible vision and dedication started numerous congregations of sisters, to perform every conceivable Christian work. Benedictine monks, and friars of the mendicant orders, as well as Clerks Regular (Jesuits,

Redemptorists, Passionists, to mention a few) chose exile in a new country, sometimes fleeing persecution in their homeland, to care for immigrants in the United States. The clergy served their fellow immigrants who had come from very specific locations in Europe. Whole Catholic and Protestant parishes often served people who had come from the same area overseas. The Irish were accompanied by an army of diocesan priests. Religious orders in Ireland had been forced underground by the British persecution of the Catholic Church, and when they were emancipated, the Church flourished, ordaining more priests than Ireland needed.

During the same period another aspect of the Church's life was being established in the United States, coming as a silent army whose only weapons were the Gospel counsels of prayer and fasting. The contemplative orders have been a powerful yet hidden influence and a powerful aid to Catholic devotional life and the sanctification of the people. If the priests and religious in this country have achieved—*Spiritu Sancto cooperantes*—astonishing results in their apostolic works, we may look to the lives of prayer and sacrifice of the contemplative religious for at least part of the explanation.

By 1848 the Cistercian monks of the Strict Observance (Trappists) settled in Kentucky. By mid-century, they were in Iowa as well. The first community of religious women to be established in the United States was the Discalced Carmelite nuns, who founded a monastery at Port Tobacco, Maryland, in 1790. A few years later Visitation nuns settled at Georgetown. Poor Clares and Dominican nuns began arriving in the United States in the 1870s, and other contemplative communities were established in the decades that followed.[1] The monastic orders flourished, especially in the twentieth century, once the tide of vocations set in. All these groups were of European origin, and like many of the émigré priests and active religious, some of the contemplatives were fleeing persecution or revolution at home. All, however, were eager to establish foundations in an immigrant land, where many of their compatriots would begin new lives.

St. John Neumann (1811–1860)

While the difficulty of choosing one example of holiness from so many is very real, none is better suited to our purposes here in terms of devotion to Jesus Christ that is pure, simple, and profound than the Redemptorist Bishop of Philadelphia and Bohemian immigrant John Neumann. He came from a devout middle-class family and was a brilliant student, especially in science.

"I cannot say that I felt a decided inclination for the priesthood when I was a child", he tells us in his autobiography. The "idea of the

[1] A foundation of Carthusians would not take place until the middle of the twentieth century (Camaldolese hermits followed a few years later), when, it may be said, the Catholic Church in the United States had come of age.

priesthood was so exalted that it seemed beyond my reach".[2] Throughout his life, he would consistently underestimate his worth and capabilities. As he grew older, he thought of a vocation, though he was far from committed to the idea even during his university studies. When it came time to make a choice of career, his inclinations lay with medicine or law rather than the Church. His mother's influence, however, led him to begin theological studies at the Budweis diocesan seminary, in 1831. After two years, he transferred to the seminary in Prague and completed his studies in 1835. Ordination was delayed, however, owing to an abundance of priests in his diocese. Hearing of appeals from bishops in the United States who sought priests to work with German-speaking people in America, Neumann resolved to go. The following year he sailed for New York, where he hoped to be ordained. Although his parents knew of his decision to go to America, he did not inform them of his exact date of departure and in the end decided to leave "without taking a formal farewell".[3] As he said in a letter written during his journey, he wanted "to lessen the pain of separating from you".[4]

Because of his university education, John Neumann was ordained by Bishop Dubois almost immediately on arriving in New York in 1836 and for the next four years he labored among the German-speaking immigrants in upstate New York. He received little money and wrote to a priest in Europe: "If you want to be a missionary, you have to love poverty and be entirely disinterested"—advice he followed for the rest of his life.

In 1840 he joined the Redemptorist congregation, which St. Alphonsus had founded a century before and which had been established in the United States only eight years earlier. A man of intense humility and modesty who preferred to remain in the background, Neumann was known for his outstanding abilities and total dedication. As a result, he became provincial of the Redemptorists and in 1852 Bishop of Philadelphia. It was at this time that the anti-Catholic Know-Nothing riots were in full swing. During his first eight years as bishop seventy-two churches and chapels opened in his diocese, and almost ten thousand children entered Catholic schools. He founded a community of Franciscan teaching sisters, and he finished building the diocesan cathedral begun by his predecessor.

SS. Francis de Sales and Alphonsus Liguori were Neumann's guides in the life of prayer and mortification, but "no one's life story inflamed him more with a desire of God's love than that of St. Teresa of Avila",[5] to whom, like his Redemptorist founder, he was devoted. In

[2] *The Autobiography of St. John Neumann*, trans. Alfred C. Rush, C.Ss.R. (Boston: St. Paul Editions, 1977), 23.

[3] Ibid., 30.

[4] Michael J. Curley, C.Ss.R., *Bishop John Neumann, C.Ss.R.* (Philadelphia: Bishop Neumann Center, 1952), 41.

[5] Ibid., 76.

addition to his spirit of poverty and ascetical life, Bishop Neumann was known for his humility, which, as Fr. Curley points out, runs throughout his diary. "Neumann knew that of himself he was nothing and could do nothing. This was no superficial sentiment that might cloak a hidden pride. It was absolute sincerity before God which distinguished him all the days of his life."[6] He never felt himself worthy of or equal to the challenges of the episcopacy. During his years as bishop, "he did not hesitate to open the doors of the church at 4:00 A.M. during a mission, to light the lamps, to prepare the altars and perform such menial tasks as clearing stray bits of litter from the church floor."[7]

Despite his prodigious work and many accomplishments, he saw himself as a failure, unable to deal with the sophisticated people of Philadelphia. He requested the Holy See to accept his resignation from the episcopate or to place him among the mines and farms, where he could serve simple people. When he died at the age of forty-nine, the following was written in the Philadelphia *Evening Bulletin* and tells a great deal about this remarkable man and the public attitude toward the Catholic Church in the City of Brotherly Love. "Two thousand people were present at St. Peter's Church for interment ceremonies. The broad aisles were dense, the chances of pickpockets were superior, had the pickings been desirable, but the ragged outcasts and very humble citizens, with an infusion of colored little ones, who made up the motley crowd, offered no tempting inducements to the light-fingered."[8]

Bishop Neumann had a special love for the poor. Often his colleagues would reproach him for what they considered his excessive generosity. When he ran out of money, he would give away clothing, linens, or shoes. "Some of those who sought alms at the episcopal residence were shrewd. Knowing that when Bishop Neumann was at home they would get more, they accordingly watched for his coming."[9] He was always careful not to hurt their feelings. On one occasion a poor man came to the residence and, despite his poverty, was determined to make a small contribution to the cathedral building fund. The bishop accepted and, after the man left, turned to a woman and handed her some money, asking her to follow the man and give it to him. "I knew he could not afford to offer me anything, but I could not hurt his feelings by refusing his gift", the bishop explained.[10]

The prayers of St. John Neumann, drawn from his diary and personal papers, reveal an intense love for Christ as his Savior, strength, and friend, as we see in the following prayer for holiness.

---

[6] Ibid., 373.

[7] Ibid., 374.

[8] Quoted in "John Neumann, C.Ss.R.: The Immigrant Shepherd" (pamphlet—no author, publishing data), 28.

[9] Curley, *Bishop John Neumann*, 366.

[10] Ibid., 367.

> Help me, dear Jesus, to grow in virtue, since I dwell so near to the fountain of living water. Help me to advance on the road to surrender, the road that leads to You, my dearly beloved Savior and my only Treasure. O my Jesus, the very thought of You fills me with a longing desire for Your love. Delay no longer to shower upon my parched soul the consolations of Your love. St. Teresa, you whose heart was so inflamed with love of Your Divine Spouse, pray for me that God may purify, justify, and sanctify me. Behold, O Jesus, my desire to love You and to give myself to You.[11]

John Neumann's life was not an easy one. He was often misunderstood and criticized because he demanded so much of himself. Like many saintly people, he failed to see that others had not yet arrived at his level of devotion and holiness. As a result, he had severe critics, whom he often did not recognize as such. This excerpt from one of his prayers shows a man of very human feelings but one relying totally on Christ to guide and assist him.

> My Jesus, relieve me of my discouragement. My devotion has vanished; spiritual thoughts no longer soothe my troubled soul. Even the remembrances of Your passion and of Your Blessed Mother grow dim before my vision. O Jesus, do not forsake me. Help me, help me! I am resolved not to omit a single one of my devotions. Hear me, O my God, strengthen and increase my faith.[12]

Neumann's death was as humble as his life. On his way to retrieve a chalice for a priest in a remote part of his diocese, he collapsed on a Philadelphia street with what seems to have been a heart attack. He was carried to a nearby house, where he died almost immediately.

John Henry Newman (1801–1890)

John Henry Newman, popularly known as Cardinal Newman, is the towering figure of nineteenth-century English-speaking Catholicism. He is also the most famous and gifted convert to the Catholic Church in modern times. His writings display a deep commitment to the Church, although his orthodoxy was frequently but unjustifiably questioned by the extreme pro-papal party known as the ultramontanes and led by another Anglican convert, Henry Edward (later Cardinal) Manning.

Before his conversion, Newman was an Oxford don, a world-class patristic scholar, and, at his request, pastor of a poor Anglican parish of farmers at Littlemore, a few miles outside the university town. He served the people of Littlemore with zeal and supported the parish in many ways, raising money from his friends to build the beautiful Gothic church that still serves the village.

---

[11] "Prayer for Holiness", in "Saint John Neumann's Favorite Prayers Taken from His Diary" (Philadelphia: Saint John Neumann Shrine, n.d.), 24–25.

[12] "Prayer in Discouragement", in "Neumann's Favorite Prayers", 36–38.

From his mother, Newman inherited a vibrant evangelical Anglican piety, and like Wesley before him, was part of a fervent Oxford student group who read the Church Fathers and practiced a deeply sacramental piety. This circle of friends later formed the nucleus of the Oxford movement, which profoundly influenced many Christian denominations, giving them a sense of the ancient Church as well as respect for the spirituality of medieval Catholicism.

A great preacher, Newman is also considered by many to be the greatest English prose stylist of his time—not an easy distinction to achieve when placed among a galaxy of great men of letters in an eloquent and scholarly age. His books and sermons are still widely read, and in traditional Catholic circles he is enjoying a revival. His life and sanctity have been thoroughly examined, and in 2010 he received the title Blessed, taking him a step closer to canonization.

Newman's years as a Catholic priest were very fruitful, but to use his own expression, he was "under a cloud".[13] He founded the English branch of the Oratory of St. Philip Neri, in a poor section of Birmingham, where his congregation consisted largely of Irish immigrants. His conversion to the Catholic Church in 1845 occurred during one of the many periods of anti-Catholicism in England. It might therefore have been supposed that he would languish in a permanent limbo. However, he continued to write, and his books, often produced in controversy, kept his name a household word in England. During his Catholic period—roughly the second half of his life—he published his *Essay on the Development of Christian Doctrine* (1845, though this was written before his conversion); the *Apologia pro Vita Sua* (1864), and *the Dream of Gerontius* (1865), a dramatic poem on Purgatory, perhaps the most widely read of Newman's works at that time and later beautifully set to music by Sir Edward Elgar. These works, as well as his earlier patristic studies, hymns, and the volumes of his *Parochial and Plain Sermons*, ensured his reputation as a major Victorian literary figure. Shortly after the election of Pope Leo XIII, Newman received the red hat of a cardinal at a consistory in May 1879.

Newman's devotion to God the Father, Son, and Holy Spirit, and to the saints, was an integral part of his life, yet few biographers take into account this aspect of his search for holiness. In the introduction to Newman's *Meditations and Devotions*, the late Meriol Trevor, an excellent Newman scholar, pointed out that he never wrote devotional works.

[13] At the time of his elevation to the Sacred College in 1879 Newman wrote: "One naturally likes the good opinion of one's Catholic brethren and it was hard to receive letters to the effect that I was under a cloud." He clearly regarded the unexpected honor of the red hat as something of a vindication of his life and work, which had often been the object of suspicion and attack. His celebrated quotation "The cloud is lifted from me forever", referring to this mark of papal approbation, is recorded only in a secondary source—a letter from Bishop Ullathorne (Newman's Ordinary at Birmingham) to Cardinal Manning—but is certainly indicative of Newman's feelings at the time.

This is unusual in an age that produced devotional writers like Fr. Faber, who was also part of the Oxford movement and a member of the English Oratory. After Newman's death his dedicated secretary, Fr. William Neville, published a collection of works entitled *Meditations and Devotions*. This anthology gives us a window into Newman's devotional life, especially its flowering in his old age. In defense of Newman biographers, it must be admitted that his devotional life, though rich, was largely private, which made "some emotional Catholics regard him as cold and half-hearted".[14] Newman did not nourish his spiritual life on the sixteenth- and seventeenth-century mystics, but rather on the Church Fathers. In this he resembled his spiritual father, St. Philip Neri, to whom he referred as a "man of primitive times".[15]

Newman's spiritual writings present, to my mind, the paradigm of Christian devotion we offered at the beginning of this study. It is helpful to review the elements of that analysis of devotion in Newman's works and keep them in mind as we approach the end of this long history. He is one of the best subjects to do this with because, although a Roman Catholic during the second half of his life, his spiritual roots are in Evangelical Anglican piety, which formed and nourished him as a young student and priest at Oxford. Moreover, his personal interest and object of special study lay with the ancient Church Fathers, thus linking him with the Orthodox tradition.

Newman's Concept of God and the Individual

Newman's sermons, delivered while he was vicar at the university Church of St. Mary's at Oxford, emphasized the intimate and absolute relationship between God and the individual. Newman was fascinated by the fact that every person who once lived is still alive. The realization of the permanence and individuality of every soul is the foundation of devotion, that is, the vibrant conviction that Christ in eternal glory knows me as an individual.

This understanding and existential relationship with God is used by Newman in a way that may seem shocking in our time, which is inclined to be so socially oriented. The following text may be jarring to modern sensibilities and requires some pondering.

> To understand that we have souls, is to feel our separation from things visible, our independence of them, our distinct existence in ourselves, our individuality, our power of acting for ourselves this way or that way, our accountableness for what we do. These are the great truths which lie wrapped up indeed even in a child's mind, and which God's grace can unfold there in spite of the influence of the external world; but at first this outward world prevails. We look off from self to the things around us and forget ourselves in them.... We still

[14] John Henry Newman, *Meditations and Devotions*, introduction by Meriol Trevor (London: Burns and Oates, 1964), v.

[15] Ibid., ix.

> crave for something, we do not well know what; but we are sure it is something which the world has not given us. And then its changes are so many, so sudden, so silent, so continual.... And should it so happen that misfortunes come upon us (as they often do), then still more are we led to understand the nothingness of this world; then still more are we led to distrust it, and are weaned from the love of it, till at length it floats before our eyes merely as some idle veil, which, notwithstanding its many tints, cannot hide the view of what is beyond it—and we begin, by degrees, to perceive that there are but two beings in the whole universe, our own soul and the God who made it....
>
> And as to those others nearer to us, who are not to be classed with the vain world, I mean our friends and relations, whom we are right in loving, these, too, after all, are nothing to us here. They cannot really help or profit us; we see them, and they act upon us, only (as it were) at a distance, through the medium of sense; they cannot get at our souls; they cannot enter into our thoughts or really be companions to us. In the next world it will, through God's mercy, be otherwise; but here we enjoy, not their presence, but the anticipation of what one day shall be; so that, after all, they vanish before the clear vision we have, first, of our own existence, next of the presence of the great God in us and over us, as our Governor and Judge, who dwells in us by our conscience, which is His representative.[16]

If all this sounds very severe, it must also be said that Newman maintained that his greatest blessing in life was having good friends. He loved and served many, from his friends in the Oxford movement to the poor at Littlemore, the Oratorians, and the innumerable souls he included as his friends later in life. First in his life always was his supreme and absolute relationship with God, and then all others in God.

We move to Newman's concept of devotion to Christ, which is by no means a saccharine dependency, although many of Christ's simple disciples present their devotion in this way. For Newman, Christ was first of all the high priest who mysteriously brings about the justification and sanctification of the world. His devotion is absolutely founded on Scripture.

> Christ, we are told, has gone up on high "to present Himself before the face of God for us." He has "entered by His own blood once for all into the holy place, having effected eternal redemption." "He ever liveth to make intercession for those who come unto God by Him; He hath a priesthood which will not pass from Him." "We have such a High Priest who is set on the right hand of the throne of the

[16] John Henry Newman, "The Immortality of the Soul", in *Parochial and Plain Sermons*, (San Francisco: Ignatius Press, 1997), 1:16–18.

Majesty in the heavens; a Minister of the Sanctuary and of the true Tabernacle, which the Lord pitched and not man."[17]

Newman is convinced that the processes of our salvation are mysterious, but he avoids the error, so common today, of ignoring what one cannot understand. He clearly saw that such a procedure was, in his words, liberalism, which he fought against all his life. Bouyer quotes Paul Lobstein, a liberal theological writer who described the liberalism of the time as "justified by faith independently of beliefs".[18] Newman railed repeatedly against this procedure, saying it would end in heresy.

The magnificence of Christ's role as Savior presented in Christian doctrine is reflected in these glowing words.

> Shall we therefore explain away its language as merely figurative, which (as the word is now commonly understood) is next to saying it has no meaning at all? Far from it. Clouds and darkness are round about Him. We are not given to see into the secret shrine in which God dwells. Before Him stand the Seraphim, veiling their faces. Christ is within the veil. We must not search curiously what is His present office, what is meant by His pleading His sacrifice and by His perpetual intercession for us. And since we do not know, we will studiously keep to the figure given us in Scripture: we will not attempt to interpret it or change the wording of it, being wise above what is written. We will not neglect it because we do not understand it. We will hold it as a mystery, or (what was anciently called) a Truth Sacramental; that is, a high invisible grace lodged in an outward form, a precious possession to be piously and thankfully guarded for the sake of the heavenly reality contained in it.[19]

The words he wrote as an Anglican find an echo in later writings during his Catholic years. He continued to struggle with the mystery of God's preknowledge of the saved and the lost, a struggle that in our own time is avoided like the plague. In the following passage, as with so many of his prayers, we see Newman's emotional and intellectual sides.

> I cannot penetrate Thy secret decrees, O Lord! I know Thou didst die for all men really; but since Thou hast not effectually willed the salvation of all, and since Thou mightest have done so, it is certain that Thou doest for one what Thou dost not do for another. I cannot tell what has been Thy everlasting purpose about myself, but if I go by all the signs which Thou hast lavished upon me, I may hope that I am one of those whose names are written in Thy book....

[17] "Mysteries in Religion", in *Parochial and Plain Sermons*, 2:360.

[18] Louis Bouyer, *Newman's Vision of Faith* (San Francisco: Ignatius Press, 1986), 47.

[19] "Mysteries in Religion", 361.

> Thou hast led me on by ten thousand merciful providences; Thou hast brought me near to Thee in the most intimate of ways; Thou hast brought me into Thy house and chamber; Thou hast fed me with Thyself. Dost Thou not love me?[20]

Doing the Will of Christ

An integral part of real devotion is the awareness that Christ has required certain things of us and that we must take these commands seriously. Any failure to do so requires contrition, penance, and an appeal for forgiveness. Faith requires us to recognize that we are God's creatures, that we must surrender ourselves to Him, placing all things in the hands of Him who is all good. Obedience to God's law is the natural response of those who fear their Maker and acknowledge their sinfulness. In Newman's writings there are many examples of a deep moral sense of the requirements of faith and devotion.

> [F]rom the beginning to the end of Scripture, the one voice of inspiration consistently maintains, not a uniform contrast between faith and obedience, but this *one* doctrine, that the only way of salvation open to us is the surrender of ourselves to our Maker in all things—supreme devotion, resignation of our will, the turning with all our heart to God.[21]

Newman gives us many instances of the powerful conviction of repentance, which is so necessary for true devotion. Only a few decades ago serious Christians on all sides were convinced that their sins added mysteriously to the sufferings of Christ's Passion. A strong realization of our part in Jesus' suffering is essential in the Christian spiritual life. The following prayer of Newman's, written after his conversion, expresses the deep motivation for Christian repentance and sorrow for sin.

> My dear Lord and Saviour, how can I make light of that which has had such consequences! Henceforth I will, through Thy grace, have deeper views of sin than before. Fools make jest of sin, but I will view things in their true light. My suffering Lord, I have made Thee suffer. Thou art most beautiful in Thy eternal nature, O my Lord; Thou art most beautiful in Thy sufferings! Thy adorable attributes are not dimmed, but increased to us as we gaze on Thy humiliation. Thou art more beautiful to us than before. But still I will never forget that it was man's sin, my sin, which made that humiliation necessary. *Amor meus crucifixus est*—"my Love is crucified," but by none other than me. I have crucified Thee, my sin has crucified Thee. O my Saviour, what a dreadful thought—but I cannot undo it; all I can do is to hate that which made Thee suffer.[22]

---

[20] *Meditations and Devotions*, 73–74.

[21] "Faith and Obedience", *Parochial and Plain Sermons*, 3:537.

[22] *Meditations and Devotions*, 37.

Trust in Christ

Trust is an essential component in Christian devotion, and trust in God was a key element in Newman's spiritual life. The following famous paragraph illustrates this very well. These words were written about the time Newman was setting up the Oratory, his community. From the beginning, Newman had critics even in the ranks of Catholics.

> God has created me to do Him some definite service; He has committed some work to me which He has not committed to another. I have my mission—I never may know it in this life, but I shall be told it in the next. Somehow I am necessary for His purposes, as necessary in my place as an Archangel in his—if, indeed, I fail, He can raise another, as He could make the stones children of Abraham. Yet I have a part in this great work: I am a link in a chain, a bond of connection between persons. He has not created me for naught. I shall do good, I shall do His work; I shall be an angel of peace, a preacher of truth in my own place, while not intending it, if I do but keep His commandments and serve Him in my calling.
>
> Therefore I will trust Him. Whatever, wherever I am, I can never be thrown away. If I am in sickness, my sickness may serve Him; in perplexity, my perplexity may serve Him; if I am in sorrow, my sorrow may serve Him. My sickness, or perplexity, or sorrow may be necessary causes of some great end, which is quite beyond us. He does nothing in vain; He may prolong my life, He may shorten it; He knows what He is about. He may take away my friends, He may throw me among strangers, He may make me feel desolate, make my spirits sink, hide the future from me—still He knows what He is about.[23]

Hope of Salvation

The final element of Christian devotion is the hope and trust that as we go through the doors of death, we enter the presence of Christ, who will be merciful in His judgment. This attitude is part of a life guided by faith and trust. Christians of all persuasions should be able to relate to this prayer of Newman's found among his meditations. He was obviously thinking about the mystery of death.

> O my Lord and Saviour, in Thy arms I am safe; keep me and I have nothing to fear; give me up and I have nothing to hope for. I know not what will come upon me before I die. I know nothing about the future, but I rely upon Thee. I pray Thee to give me what is good for me; I pray Thee to take from me whatever may imperil my salvation; I pray Thee not to make me rich, I pray Thee not to make me very poor; but I leave it all to Thee, because Thou knowest and I do not. If Thou bringest pain or sorrow on me, give me grace to bear it well—keep me from fretfulness and selfishness. If Thou givest

[23] Ibid., 6–7.

me health and strength and success in this world, keep me ever on my guard lest these great gifts carry me away from Thee.

O Thou who didst die on the Cross for me, even for me, sinner as I am, give me to know Thee, to believe in Thee, to love Thee, to serve Thee; ever to aim at setting forth Thy glory; to live to and for Thee; to set a good example to all around me; give me to die just at that time and in that way which is most for Thy glory, and best for my salvation.[24]

Christian Apostolic Charity

A necessary response to devotion is an apostolic charity for souls, a reflection of the charity and love that Christ has for us and a grateful response to His love. We saw this in the lives of SS. Francis and Vincent de Paul and the early Methodists. The following prayer written by Newman, which was a favorite of Mother Teresa of Calcutta, brings devotion to its fullness, allowing the life of Christ to live in us (see Gal 2:20). It also brings to a fitting conclusion our study of the very rich evangelical, patristic, and Catholic devotion of one who has been called the last of the Church Fathers.

> Stay with me, and then I shall begin to shine as Thou shinest: so to shine as to be light to others. The light, O Jesus, will be all from Thee. None of it will be mine. No merit to me. It will be Thou who shinest through me upon others. O let me thus praise Thee, in the way which Thou dost love best, by shining on all those around me. Give light to them as well as to me; light them with me, through me. Teach me to show forth Thy praise, Thy truth, Thy will. Make me preach Thee without preaching—not by words, but by my example and by the catching force, the sympathetic influence, of what I do—by my visible resemblance to Thy saints, and the evident fulness of the love which my heart bears to Thee.[25]

St. Thérèse of Lisieux (1873–1897)

No survey of Catholic devotion to Christ in the nineteenth century would be complete without a consideration of the twenty-four-year-old Carmelite nun Thérèse Martin. We often call her St. Thérèse of Lisieux; in the past she was usually referred to by her Carmelite name, St. Thérèse of the Child Jesus, or, frequently in English-speaking countries, by a popular designation based on her own self-reference, the Little Flower.

Born at Alençon, where her mother, Zélie, was a lacemaker and her father, Louis, a successful watchmaker, Thérèse was the last of nine children, of whom five lived to maturity. At the age of four and a half, she moved with her family to the Norman market town of Lisieux after the death of her mother. Throughout her life Thérèse's acquaintances were limited to her devout middle-class family, a tiny

---

[24] Ibid., 221.

[25] Ibid., 54.

circle of friends, and the small community of some twenty nuns at the Carmel (three of whom were her blood sisters). She lived her brief life intensely but with almost no extraordinary phenomena, yet she was canonized a saint in 1925. A century ago such a short span of time between death and canonization was very unusual.

Pope Pius XI, who canonized St. Thérèse, said that in her we see confirmed "the solemn and celebrated command of Uncreated Wisdom: 'Except you are converted and become as little children, you shall not enter the Kingdom of Heaven.' It is in this precisely that the special character of this sanctity to which God called Thérèse consists."[26] Forever after, the term "the way of spiritual childhood" has been inextricably linked with the saint, although she never used it in her writings. There are several references in her autobiographical work to the "little way", a phrase she often used in her conversation, but it was only in her final weeks of life that she spelled out her meaning. "I feel that my mission is about to begin", she said to Mother Agnes of Jesus (her sister Pauline) in July 1897, "my mission of making God loved as I love Him, of giving my little way to souls".[27]

Later she elaborated on the little way she wanted to teach others: "Mother, it's the way of spiritual childhood, it's the way of confidence and total abandon. I want to teach them the little means that have so perfectly succeeded with me, to tell them there is only one thing to do here on earth: to cast at Jesus the flowers of little sacrifices."[28]

Without exception her writings are personal documents, including the *Story of a Soul*, an autobiographical account written at the request of others. There is also a collection of letters written mostly to family members, with some to priests and two seminarians, whom she accepted, at the request of her superiors, as brothers in prayer. The incredible impact of her autobiography led to her canonization and later to her being named Doctor of the Church (1997), so that she has joined the ranks of theologians like Thomas Aquinas and Bonaventure, and spiritual writers like Teresa of Ávila and Catherine of Siena. She has also been named, along with St. Joan of Arc, secondary patron of France, and (with St. Francis Xavier) patron of the missions. Her intercession with God is invoked by millions every day, and her statue or portrait can be seen throughout the world.

When we ask how this could happen, the answer seems obvious: it is a work of God. But the means that Providence used—the brief autobiography—had an original printing of only two thousand copies and was circulated simply as an obituary notice, according to

[26] John Beevers, *Storm of Glory* (Garden City, N.Y.: Image Books, 1955), 150–51. This work, though originally published more than fifty years ago, remains one of the best introductions to the saint.

[27] *St. Thérèse of Lisieux: Her Last Conversations*, trans. John Clarke, O.C.D. (Washington, D.C.: ICS Publications, 1977), 102.

[28] Ibid., 257.

Carmelite custom, to a very limited group of people. John Beevers, one of the English translators of the work, wrote in 1957:

> When we pick up *The Story of a Soul*, we are handling something akin to a miracle. We have a book which was never written as a book. It was scribbled very quickly and produced in three parts, each addressed to a different person. Much of it was written when its author knew she was dying and was suffering all the pain and distress of a fatal illness. Now it is the most widely read book of spirituality in the world and is acclaimed by popes for the sureness of its teaching.[29]

Thérèse's teaching is far from original; it is basic New Testament spirituality, put in a very personal and affirmative way, expressing unshakable confidence in God's love and mercy for each of us. St. Thérèse was a realist with a very sensitive and, in her early life, a scrupulous conscience. However, she never let sin obfuscate the fact that God loves us. Her goal each day was to offer every act, however trivial, to God in worship and to accept every event as a possible source of grace. It would be a serious mistake to dismiss her message because it is couched in the flowery rhetoric of the late-nineteenth-century bourgeoisie. It is deeply rooted in the Gospel, especially in the "new commandment" of the Lord, and is presented with a freshness that makes sanctity seem attractive and possible to people of every station—hence, the universality of her appeal, which has been seen only rarely since the time of St. Francis.

The *Story of a Soul* is easily divided into three parts, or manuscripts—A, B, and C. Thérèse did not do this by design, nor did she write in chapters. All of that was done later by others. She simply wrote as she was told to do.

Manuscript A—the first eight chapters—was written in 1895 under obedience to Mother Agnes of Jesus, who requested a memoir of Thérèse's childhood years. They contain all the hurts, misunderstandings, and illnesses of childhood, as well as an account of the many graces she received and the flowering of her vocation in Carmel. Manuscript B, a letter written the following year to her sister Marie of the Sacred Heart, is perhaps the most beautiful of all her writings and contains the revelation of her vocation: "My vocation is love!" It is the summation of her life and her reason for being—"In the heart of the Church I will be love"—and includes every other vocation to which she feels drawn: apostle, missionary, priest, Doctor, martyr. Her very weakness and powerlessness, she admits, are the wellspring of her boundless confidence in God and His mercy.

The last two chapters of the autobiography—manuscript C—were written during June and July of 1897, while she was in the final stages

[29] Introduction to *Story of a Soul: The Autobiography of St. Thérèse of Lisieux*, trans. John Beevers (Garden City, N.Y.: Image Books, 1957), 16.

of terminal tuberculosis.[30] They are addressed to and written under obedience to Mother Marie de Gonzague, the difficult and mercurial prioress who succeeded Mother Agnes in 1896. Mother Marie in fact was Thérèse's superior for most of her religious life and played an essential role in Thérèse's sanctification during her years in Carmel.[31] In these chapters Thérèse discusses the depths of her trial of faith, which at that point had lasted well over a year and would continue until her death. Drawing on her nine years of religious life and her work with the novices, she also gives us some of the finest insights on fraternal charity.

The work reveals Thérèse's profound yet simple approach to spirituality—the little way of love, in which every event is offered to God in union with Christ. Any Christian will be deeply impressed by St. Thérèse's Christocentric spirituality. In her remarkable examination of charity to God and neighbor she is entirely guided by the Gospel.

> The Lord, in the Gospel, explains in what His new commandment consists. He says in St. Matthew: "You have heard that it was said, 'You shall love your neighbor and hate your enemy.' But I say to you, love your enemies ... pray for those who persecute you." No doubt we don't have any enemies in Carmel, but there are feelings. One feels attracted to this Sister, whereas with regard to another, one would make a long detour in order to avoid meeting her. And so, without even knowing it, she becomes the subject of persecution. Well, Jesus is telling me that it is this Sister who must be loved, she must be prayed for even though her conduct would lead me to believe that she doesn't love me....
>
> It is only charity that can expand my heart. O Jesus, since this sweet flame consumes it, I run with joy in the way of *Your new commandment*. I want to run in it until that blessed day when, joining the virginal procession, I shall be able to follow You in the heavenly courts, singing Your New *canticle*, which must be *Love*.[32]

---

[30] Thérèse often spoke of her desire to "die of love", by which she understood a death conformed to that of Jesus on the Cross. Not only did she suffer the slow ravages of tuberculosis consuming her lungs and intestines without drugs or palliatives of any kind, but for the last eighteen months of her life she endured a profound night of faith reserved to those who walk in the mystic way.

[31] See Ida Friederike Görres, *The Hidden Face*, trans. Richard and Clara Winston (New York: Pantheon Books, 1959) for an interesting study of the saint. The author has many insights into the formative influences on Thérèse, including the Church in the nineteenth century and the *raison d'être* of the Carmelite reform of St. Teresa. She also gives a keen analysis of the odd personality of Mother Marie de Gonzague. Some of the saint's perceptive biographers agree that while Marie de Gonzague was ill-suited to be either prioress or Carmelite, she alone of the saint's contemporaries estimated the heroic nature of Thérèse's character and desire for sanctity, which even her own sisters, as close as they were, failed to recognize.

[32] *Story of a Soul: The Autobiography of St. Thérèse of Lisieux*, trans. John Clarke, O.C.D. (Washington, D.C.: ICS Publications, 1996), 224–26.

As a Carmelite, Thérèse was bidden by her rule to "meditate on the law of the Lord day and night". We see from her writings how deeply she penetrated the meaning of God's word in Scripture and what fruit it bore in her relationships with others in her community. Commenting on John 15:13 ("Greater love has no man than this, that a man lay down his life for his friends"), she has this to say:

> [W]hen meditating on these words of Jesus, I understood how imperfect was my love for my Sisters. I saw I didn't love them as God loves them. Ah! I understand now that charity consists in bearing with the faults of others, in not being surprised at their weakness, in being edified by the smallest acts of virtue we see them practice. But I understood above all that charity must not remain hidden in the bottom of the heart. Jesus has said: "No one lights a lamp and puts it under a bushel basket, but upon the lampstand, so as to give light to ALL in the house." It seems to me that this lamp represents charity which must enlighten and rejoice not only those who are dearest to us but "ALL who are in the house" without distinction.[33]

Chapter 9 of her autobiography, addressed to Sr. Marie of the Sacred Heart, is really a spiritual commentary on Christ's words in the New Testament concerning love. Those who know and love the Gospels will feel very much at home with St. Thérèse, but they may also find that in their previous study of Christ's words they have missed the greatest depths of meaning. The following well-known passage must be read in light of Thérèse's complete immersion in the Gospels. Commenting on St. Paul's words "earnestly desire the higher gifts" (1 Cor 12:31), she writes of her vocation, not as an isolated contemplative mystic but very much as one centered in the Church.

> Considering the mystical body of the Church, I had not recognized myself in any of the members described by St. Paul, or rather I desired to see myself in them all. Charity gave me the key to my vocation. I understood that if the Church had a body composed of different members, the most necessary and most noble of all could not be lacking to it, and so I understood that the Church had a Heart and that this Heart was *burning with love.* I understood it was Love alone that made the Church's members act, that if Love ever became extinct, apostles would not preach the Gospel and martyrs would not shed their blood. I understood that Love comprised all vocations, that love was everything, that it embraced all times and place ... in a word, that it was eternal!
>
> Then in the excess of my delirious joy, I cried out: "Jesus, my Love ... my vocation, at last I have found it. My vocation is Love![34]

---

[33] Ibid., 220.

[34] Ibid., 194. Years before, Thérèse had taken as a kind of motto the words of St. John of the Cross: "Love is repaid by love alone" (*Spiritual Canticle*, st. 9, no. 7).

These lines have caused many of Thérèse's devotees to overlook the depth of her darkness and suffering. Msgr. Guy Gaucher, a Carmelite bishop, has written an intriguing study of her spiritual and physical sufferings and her attitudes toward them.[35] Without hesitation, suffering is turned into love. Thérèse lived at a time of philosophical nihilism, which holds that there is no purpose or reason to life, no God, no hereafter. She experienced this nihilism in her own person. To Mother Marie de Gonzague, she writes:

> When I want to rest my heart fatigued by the darkness that surrounds it by the memory of the luminous country after which I aspire, my torment redoubles; it seems to me that the darkness, borrowing the voice of sinners, says mockingly to me: "You are dreaming about the light, about a fatherland embalmed in the sweetest perfumes; you are dreaming about the eternal possession of the Creator of all these marvels; you believe that one day you will walk out of this fog that surrounds you! Advance, advance; rejoice in death which will give you not what you hope for, but a night still more profound, the night of nothingness!"[36]

She even went further:

> If you are judging according to the sentiments I express in my little poems composed this year, I must appear to you as a soul filled with consolations and one for whom the veil of faith is almost torn aside; and yet it is no longer a veil for me, it is a wall which reaches right up to the heavens and covers the starry firmament. When I sing of the happiness of heaven and of the eternal possession of God, I feel no joy in this, for I sing simply what I *want to believe*. It is true that at times a very small ray of the sun comes to illumine my darkness, and then the trial ceases for an instant, but afterward the memory of this ray, instead of causing me joy, makes my darkness even more dense.[37]

Cardinal Cahal Daly, retired Primate of Ireland and a recognized philosopher, once commented that many in the nineteenth century have expressed their experience of nihilism, but none so powerfully as Thérèse of Lisieux, precisely because she was a believer.

When St. Thérèse said her vocation was to be love, she meant it. With great devotion, she prayed for the two spiritual brother seminarians assigned to her by her superiors. Her correspondence with them is always loving, without in any way reflecting a natural affection. Bishop Patrick Ahern has written a beautiful book on her spiritual friendship with one of them, Maurice Bellière.[38] Her final letter

[35] Guy Gaucher, *The Passion of Thérèse of Lisieux* (New York: Crossroad, 1989).

[36] Clarke, *Story of a Soul*, 213.

[37] Ibid., 214.

[38] *Maurice and Thérèse: The Story of a Love* (New York: Doubleday, 1998).

to him discusses her impending death and informs him that he will be a beneficiary under her will. Touchingly human, the letter, dated August 10, 1897, illustrates how someone can have great love without what is usually called affection. It is a love without self-indulgence and yet it is very moving—in short, a relationship most people are totally unfamiliar with.

> I have to tell you, little brother, that we don't understand heaven in the same way. You think that once I share in the justice and holiness of God, I won't be able to excuse your faults as I did when I was on earth. Are you then forgetting that I shall also share in the infinite mercy of the Lord? I believe that the Blessed in heaven have great compassion for our miseries. They remember that when they were weak and mortal like us, they committed the same faults themselves and went through the same struggles, and their fraternal tenderness becomes still greater than it ever was on earth. It's on account of this that they never stop watching over us.[39]

It cannot be stressed too much that the spiritual message of St. Thérèse is pure New Testament. Her autobiography makes it clear that the Gospels and St. Paul are the basis of her whole life. The groundwork for the transforming power of Christ's word in the New Testament was well laid when, as a young child, she had memorized the entire *Imitation of Christ*. She tells us also that at the ages of seventeen and eighteen, all her spiritual nourishment came from the writings of St. John of the Cross. The *Story of a Soul* contains many allusions to, if not outright quotations from, his works, especially the *Spiritual Canticle*. Later, spiritual books gave her no help, and only Sacred Scripture, "above all the Gospel", sustained her during her hours of prayer. In the Gospel, she says, "I find everything my poor soul needs. . . . I am forever discovering new lights, mysterious and hidden meanings".[40]

I would encourage Christians of all denominations to read the *Story of a Soul* and witness from within a complete and heroic love for Christ, and for God in Christ, on the part of a young woman of our time.

Isaac Hecker (1819–1888)

Few Catholics in modern times have entered into dialogue with other Christians more intensely than Isaac Hecker. If Bouyer could call Count Zinzendorf, the great light of the Moravians, "an astonishing person" (Chapter 15 above), we can easily apply the same words to Fr. Hecker, founder of the Paulists. Born in New York, the last of five children of German immigrant parents, Isaac Hecker was raised a Methodist, the religion of his mother, and was drawn by an interest in mysticism to the American transcendentalist movement with such luminaries as Henry David Thoreau and Ralph Waldo Emerson. Hecker was also influenced

[39] Ibid., 209–11.

[40] *Story of a Soul*, chap. 8 (author translation).

by the American philosopher Orestes Brownson and the German romantics like Schiller. Eventually his journey led to his unpredictable entrance into the Catholic Church. Hecker's life represents the American effort to make a synthesis of the many elements that came to this new land and to harmonize many experiences, ways of thinking, and even philosophies of life.

At a time when Catholics were excluded from the major intellectual currents of American society, Hecker was in touch with the important people in these movements, and they, in turn, were interested in what he had to say.[41] His biographer, John Farina, sums up Hecker's unique Catholicism: "His life bridged forces that others saw as totally distinct: American Protestantism and Catholicism, liberal democracy and the Church, contemplation and action, and personal holiness and social reform. And he did it all with an openness to experimentation and innovation and a concern for the practical that were typically American."[42]

Throughout his searching, even with the transcendentalists who tended toward a vague natural mysticism that was Unitarian, at best, Hecker was deeply devoted to Jesus Christ. He retained this devotion, rooted in a Protestant experience (in his case, Methodist Evangelicalism), throughout his years as a Catholic priest and widely respected religious leader. Despite his Evangelical traits, he was invited to attend the Third Plenary Council in Baltimore and was a *peritus*, or theological adviser, at the First Vatican Council.

Hecker was in his early twenties when, in January 1843 at the suggestion of Orestes Brownson, he began an eight-month stay at Brook Farm, near Boston, a transcendentalist community founded by George and Sarah Ripley to elevate the dignity of manual labor by combining it with intellectual and spiritual goals. The community, which had once included Nathaniel Hawthorne, numbered about ninety at the time of Hecker's arrival. Farina emphasizes that even though the young Hecker, no longer a Methodist, delighted in the airy speculation of the transcendentalists, "he could not abandon Christ for the nebulous gods of the New England Romantics". Farina sums up the place of Christ in the life of the young Hecker:

> Christ was seen as more than a model for leading a spiritual life. He was seen, rather, as a living person whose life could be shared by those who believed in him. This sharing was a communing, a partaking of Christ's Spirit. Christ's Spirit was not merely conceived of as the sense or significance of Christ. It was instead the very principle of life that animated him. In this manner Hecker again reflected

[41] See John Farina, ed., *Hecker Studies: Essays on the Thought of Isaac Hecker* (New York: Paulist Press, 1983); John Farina, *An American Experience of God: The Spirituality of Isaac Hecker* (New York: Paulist Press, 1981); *Isaac T. Hecker: The Diary*, ed. John Farina (New York: Paulist Press, 1988).

[42] Farina, *Hecker Studies*, 3.

the influence of the Methodists who placed a considerable emphasis on the person of the Holy Ghost as the Spirit of Jesus—God in us and with us. The concept of real participation in the divine, or divinization, was one of the things that most attracted Wesley to the Church Fathers, especially Gregory of Nyssa.[43]

The following passage from his diary is dated January 10, 1843, the day he arrived at Brook Farm.

> My love of all worldly things are gone. They are past without gratification. My mind has been clear and why now this state of lonliness I labored for Riches but renounced them Friendship is gone Love in its accustomed sense is gone and here I am left alone and I would cry with all my soul and heart what shall I do? Who will be unto me now a friend a Comforter? Will it be said Christ? Alas in this I drink too deeply. . . . Neither can I go forwards hence I would be glad if I was taken from this life in my present state as I am. O Lord receive me Yet would I do my duty here establish thy Kingdom here and which I pray O Lord open thou my eyes to see the path thou wouldst have me to walk in.[44]

The very next day he is more composed and writes:

> Who can fathom the blessings of God? It is infinite in its source and its kind. . . . The peace of God passeth all understanding. Oh how full of it were the apostles but to God I raise my feeble voice for all that he is done and that even now in these days he has brought to light the Gospel again. This does my soul confess to itself. Who can measure the depths of Christs suffering? . . . Oh how sweet must it have been to his soul when he found even one who received even a portion of that precious gift which he came to the world to bestow. Well could he say Father forgive them they know not what they do? He would give them life but they would not receive. He would save them but they rejected him. He love them and they despised him alas alas.[45]

Clearly, although Hecker was at Brook Farm only a short time, he was confronted with an atmosphere that did not permit him to place Christ at the center of the spiritual quest. In fact, for Hecker, Christ was at the center of everything, and he asks the question: "Who has measured in a small degree the Love of Christ and yet denies his superiority over Man His Love Goodness mercy are unbounded Oh Lord

---

[43] Farina, *American Experience of God*, 58.

[44] Hecker, *The Diary*, 89. Excerpts are given here *verbatim*, with all of Hecker's ungrammatical English usage, including lack of punctuation. At this point in his life, he had little facility in the written word, a result of the lack of formal schooling in his early years.

[45] Ibid., 90.

may I daily come in closer & closer communion with Thy son Jesus Christ." [46]

After eight months at Brook Farm and a short stay at a similar community called Fruitlands and a visit to the Shaker community at Harvard, Hecker returned to New York, where he came into contact with the Oxford movement in its American form; however, along with Brownson, he found himself moving ever closer to Rome.

During the period before his entrance into the Catholic Church, Hecker filled his diary with the reasons for his making the move that seemed so strange to his many friends. All the reasons related to Christ and to the ancient faith of the Church, which he had learned first as a Methodist. We must understand that many liberal intellectuals of Hecker's time called themselves secular Christians but were, in fact, Arians or, worse, adoptionists, thinking of Jesus only as a very poor man whom God had taken to be His Son. Hecker completely rejected such theories.

> We say Jesus was the Christ not that he yielded himself to the Christ Spirit as Pythagoras Socrates Plato Zeno etc. as many nowadays do contend. Jesus was the Christ, the Word made flesh, sent from heaven, not one of the human species, born of the Immaculate Virgin, conceived by the Holy Ghost.[47]

Hecker met with Bishop John McCloskey of New York and arranged to take instruction preparatory to entering the Catholic Church. He was baptized a Catholic on August 1, 1844.

Later, in the fifth volume of his diaries, written in the first six months of 1845, Hecker faces the predictable result of a powerful conversion—a deep awareness of his own sins and faults.

> This week and the week past I have felt more the necessity of my giving up more and of greater self denial if I would continue to increase in the love of Jesus. Oh that I would give myself wholly up to Jesus how much more should Jesus be to me. I see in Jesus more than all the wisdom of the world and power omnipotent....
>
> In to Thy hands oh Lord I commend my spirit. Oh may I be a brave & valiant soldier in thy cause. Oh Jesus take pity on me. Thou knowest our human frailties. Forgive and bless me oh Jesus. The enemy lies always in watch of us. Jesus. Jesus. Jesus.[48]

Hecker became a priest of the Redemptorist congregation but left this order in 1857 to begin the Congregation of Missionary Priests of St. Paul the Apostle, better known as the Paulists. Two years later he was permitted to open a church on West 59 Street in Manhattan. His

[46] Ibid.

[47] Ibid. (July 14, 1844), 220.

[48] Ibid. (Jan. 22, 1845), 302–3.

religious congregation grew, becoming involved in Catholic publications, as well as missionary preaching and the care of Catholic students at secular universities. The Church of St. Paul, a cathedral-like structure, stands today just south of Lincoln Center.

Like the Methodists from whom he came, Hecker was deeply involved in the search for social justice. Professor David O'Brien has examined the relationship between Hecker's Evangelical and Catholic views of the essential involvement of the believing Christian in social justice and the care of the poor.[49]

In our times, many have apparently thought that the effort to bring Christian denominations together, especially under the mantle of an ever more secularized approach to theology, requires a complete uprooting of devotion, even devotion to Christ. These antidevotional trends are seen often among the intelligentsia. Hecker, in touch with many different intellectual trends and familiar with the leading intellects of his time, illustrates that this way of action is uncalled for and may signal an unintentional distortion of the Christian life.

Summary

The four people we have chosen as examples of Christian devotion in this chapter do not adequately represent all the Catholics of the nineteenth century. The devotional lives of so many people from so many nations and cultures are simply too diverse. From the missionary martyrs of the Orient to the apostles of charity like Frédéric Ozanam, founder of the St. Vincent de Paul Society, from the armies of religious sisters who taught, nursed, and cared for the multitudes to the many devout laypeople, Catholic piety was thriving at a time when governments were attempting to suppress and even destroy the churches.

The nineteenth century was a time of turmoil and upheaval. There were repeated attacks on the Church in France, in other European countries, and often in Latin America. The papal states were lost, while secularism and agnosticism seemed to triumph. Consequently, many historians have seen the period as a time of Church decline. But when we look at the faith and strength of devotion to Christ on the part of Catholics, another picture emerges. Christ was very real to the vast population in Europe and to the great number of Catholic immigrants. Despite their ethnic and national differences, all were united in a fervent love and devotion to the Son of God.

---

[49] See *Hecker Studies*, 87ff.

24 Protestants in the Twentieth Century

The Pentecostal Experience

Without doubt Pentecostalism, in terms of the number of people it has affected, is the most significant experience of Protestant devotion in the twentieth century. Protestant Pentecostalism, together with its Catholic equivalent, the charismatic movement, has arguably been the expression of a powerful religious experience for more than one hundred million people. Because of its simple theological foundation and its appeal to less educated Christians, however, its importance is sometimes overlooked or denied.

Protestant Pentecostalism sprang from the holiness movement, which, in turn, owed its origins to Wesley and the early Methodists. This expression of spiritual renewal has been carefully documented by Vinson Synan, an insightful historian who has written on many of the individual movements that comprise Pentecostalism.[1] The popularity and expansion of the Pentecostal renewal have apparently waned in the English-speaking world, but it is now vibrant in Latin America, Asia, and Africa in both Protestant and Catholic expressions.

There have been many expressions of Pentecostalism and varying theological positions among those who claim to have received the baptism of the Holy Spirit, making it difficult to give an accurate definition. This movement, therefore, is best approached through historical description.

Charles Parham, a former Methodist minister, began a home for spiritual healing and Bible study in Topeka, Kansas, in 1898. By that time the basic teachings of the holiness movement had moved from Wesley's patristic Anglican theology to more traditional Protestant ideas: justification by faith, personal sanctification as a special and second grace for the individual, divine healing of soul and body, and a belief in a premillennial second coming of Christ.[2]

---

[1] Vinson Synan, *The Century of the Holy Spirit* (Nashville, Tenn.: Thomas Nelson Publishers, 2001).

[2] Vinson Synan, introduction to *Azusa Street* by Frank Bartleman (Plainfield, N.J.: Logos International, 1980), ix. The premillennial coming refers to an establishment of God's Kingdom on earth before the end of the ages.

In the first months of the twentieth century an eighteen-year-old girl, Agnes Ozman, was baptized in the Holy Spirit and for the next three days spoke and wrote in a tongue at first unrecognizable but later believed to be Chinese.[3] Parham concluded from this that the evidence for baptism of the Spirit was glossolalia, speaking in tongues.[4] This term properly refers to someone's speaking a recognized language he does not know. In the next ten years, Parham attracted twenty-five thousand followers to his Apostolic Faith missions. One of these was a Southern African American holiness preacher named William J. Seymour, who moved to Los Angeles in 1906. At that time the city had a number of Evangelical movements, one led by Phineas Bresee, who founded the Pentecostal Church of the Nazarene in 1895 as a reform of the Methodist Church. The Nazarene Church by this time was becoming the largest Holiness church. Seymour preached in a humble chapel on Azusa Street in Los Angeles, and his work is seen as the origin of modern Pentecostalism.

Controversy and scorn greeted Seymour's preaching and the idea that speaking in tongues was evidence of baptism in the spirit. This claim led to a rift with other Pentecostals. Seymour was forced out of the Nazarene Church, and his followers were branded a "sect of fanatics" by the *Los Angeles Times*. Praying in tongues, although obviously part of New Testament experience, was called "weird babel".[5] It is interesting to note that this phenomenon so ridiculed by the media became part of the faith of more than one hundred million people in less than a century.

The Remarkable Growth of Pentecostalism

Because of the Pentecostals' overwhelming emphasis on individual experience and their concept of the Church as simply a fellowship of those who had accepted Christ as Savior, it was inevitable that many Pentecostal denominations would emerge. In fact, many such denominations or free churches included no more than a minister and congregation. In the past, these were often storefront churches, but at present some are great temples seating thousands.

Some of the largest Pentecostal churches include the Church of God in Christ, founded by two African American preachers, C. H. Mason and C. P. Jones, both of whom were born shortly after their parents were emancipated from slavery.[6] This church, which represents African American Christianity in a pure form, is the fastest-growing religious denomination in the United States. Other important movements included the

[3] Synan, *Century of the Holy Spirit*, 44.

[4] For anyone not familiar with glossolalia, it is important to know that this phenomenon is not the same as what is termed "praying in tongues". In the latter, which is much more common than glossolalia, the person utters sounds of no known human language. The best-known demonstration of glossolalia, which must be considered a supernatural phenomenon, was on the day of Pentecost (Acts 2:1–11; see also 1 Cor 14:1–33).

[5] Ibid., xvii.

[6] Synan, *Century of the Holy Spirit*, 100ff.

Pentecostal Holiness Church, which is very large in the rural South and is expanding to other parts of the country and to foreign missions.[7]

A theological controversy, concerning whether immediate sanctification by baptism of the Holy Spirit was possible or whether sanctification was a gradual process, divided Pentecostalism in the early part of the twentieth century. The latter position was defended by William H. Durham (1873–1912) and is referred to as the "finished work" theory of salvation.[8] It taught that Christ had finished the work of salvation on Calvary, that people gradually grew into acceptance of the grace that this work provided, being transformed into Christ's image. From this controversy, and following Durham's thought, came the Assemblies of God Church in 1914, which developed rapidly, as did many other Pentecostal denominations in the second half of the twentieth century. The Assemblies of God now have extensive foreign missions, and in 2000 claimed to be making ten thousand converts a day.[9]

The Assemblies of God experienced a serious theological crisis, which is relevant to our study. Eudorus Bell, the church's first general superintendent, within a year of its founding joined a group within the church known as the "Jesus name" movement. Incredible as it may seem, this group denied the doctrine of the Trinity and claimed that baptism had to be given only in Jesus' name. This radical departure from Christian tradition was defeated at the fourth general assembly of the Assemblies of God in 1916.[10] The Oneness Movement, as the "Jesus name" movement came to be called, appears to be a form of an ancient heretical teaching condemned by the Council of Nicaea called Modalism, or Sabellianism. This maintains that the Persons of the Trinity are distinct only in their mode of operation. The Oneness Movement considered the doctrine of the Trinity, proclaimed at Nicaea, to be both an invention of the Roman Catholic Church and a corruption. It is interesting that Oneness Pentecostalism retained belief in Christ's two natures, a dogma of the Councils of Ephesus and Chalcedon. The Oneness Pentecostals left the Assemblies of God to form new churches called Pentecostal Assemblies of the World. These churches insist that those baptized with the Trinitarian formula (Mt 28:19) must be rebaptized in Jesus' name. Eventually the Pentecostal Assemblies of the World divided according to racial lines, and a new predominantly white church came into existence as the United Pentecostal Church.[11]

Pentecostalism Grows and Spreads to Other Churches

After World War II, Pentecostalism became an accepted part of the Protestant world. Television brought Pentecostal preachers like Oral Roberts into people's living rooms. The civil rights movement brought

[7] Ibid., 107ff.
[8] Ibid., 123ff.
[9] Ibid., 131.
[10] Ibid., 129.
[11] Ibid., 146.

wider interest in and respect for the African-American segment of American society, including the black churches, many of which were Pentecostal.

A number of ministers from mainline Protestant denominations, including Episcopalian, Lutheran, Reformed, and Methodist, called people to pray in tongues with a variety of results.[12] In 1956, Richard Winkler, rector of Trinity Episcopal Church in Wheaton, Illinois, appears to have been the first Episcopalian pastor in America to embrace Pentecostalism. He drew criticism from various sources, including Bishop James A. Pike, who later became involved with spiritualism, the attempt to contact the dead through a medium.[13] Another Episcopalian rector, Dennis Bennett, carried on a successful Pentecostal ministry in an Episcopal church in Seattle for several decades after being removed from his original diocese in California for praying in tongues. Finally, with the approval of the Episcopal Church's General Convention, the Pentecostal experience spread through American Anglicanism and from there throughout the Anglican Communion, with Bennett's Holy Trinity Society becoming the first organized charismatic society in a mainstream American denomination.[14] The Anglican charismatic experience came to a rather dramatic crescendo in 1978, when two thousand worshippers, led by Archbishop William Burnett of Capetown, prayed in Canterbury Cathedral with all the charismatic gifts after having been warmly received by Archbishop Donald Coggan of Canterbury.[15]

When Pentecostal elements entered the mainstream churches, some feared being identified with the early Pentecostals—popularly considered Holy Rollers. Soon the word "neo-Pentecostal" came into being. When Catholics began to accept the movement, they chose the term "charismatic renewal". Fr. Edward O'Connor, C.S.C., a well-recognized writer of the Catholic Charismatic Renewal, notes that the use of this term indicates the belief that the whole Pentecostal experience "is to be regarded fundamentally not as an original interpretation of Christianity or a new school of spirituality, but as a reemergence of certain authentic aspects of Christian life which have fallen somewhat into neglect".[16] He makes the point that there is only one way to be a Christian and ultimately only one form of Christian spirituality: this "consists in being conformed to the image of Jesus Christ by His Spirit dwelling within us".[17] As we noted, Catholics and many mainline Protestant denominations hold the conviction that the Church, however they define it, goes back to the Church of the New Testament;

[12] Ibid., 149ff.

[13] Ibid., 154–55.

[14] Ibid., 156–57.

[15] Ibid., 157–58.

[16] Edward D. O'Connor, C.S.C., *The Pentecostal Movement in the Catholic Church* (Notre Dame, Ind.: Ave Maria Press, 1971), 30.

[17] Ibid.

therefore, the word "renewal" is important. The early Anabaptists believed they were starting Christianity anew in the fifteenth and sixteenth centuries. The Reformation churches did not see themselves that way, nor did Wesley and the early Methodists. The term "renewal" reflects the belief that the Holy Spirit has always been present in the Church. Hence both Catholics and many older Protestant denominations are more comfortable with the term "charismatic renewal" than with the term "Pentecostal".

Vinson Synan gives a thorough account of the charismatic renewal in the Lutheran, Presbyterian, Methodist, Baptist, United, Wesleyan, and Nazarene churches. Eventually even Eastern Orthodoxy felt the effects of this movement. While Synan maintains that "no major body of Christians in the world has been less affected by the charismatic movement" and that there has been strong resistance to it from many Church leaders, "several Orthodox priests and laymen have personally struggled to plant the seeds of renewal".[18] The reaction of Orthodox bishops is related to the fact that Orthodoxy has always claimed to be charismatic in its worship. It has never accepted the idea, common in Western Christianity, that the gifts of the Holy Spirit ceased after the Church was well established in the early centuries. The Catholic tradition has always focused more on the gifts indicated in Isaiah 11:2—wisdom, understanding, counsel, fortitude, knowledge, piety (which is loyalty), and fear of the Lord, or reverence. They are related to Christ's identifying Himself with Isaiah's words quoted in St. Luke's Gospel (4:18–19). The Orthodox Church has said that prophecy, healing, gifts, and signs have been an important part of its tradition.[19]

The Catholic Charismatic Renewal

Although for the sake of clarity we have divided our chapters between Protestants, Catholics, and Orthodox, we will include a discussion of the Catholic charismatic movement in this chapter for the sake of continuity of topic. In fact, as Synan points out, "This is the first time in Christian history that a movement of Protestant provenance had not only entered the Roman Catholic Church, but had also been received and accepted by church authority. This remarkable fact alone suggests that the Catholic expression of the charismatic movement has a major significance and a vast potential."[20] Synan and O'Connor see the movement's acceptance in traditional Catholic circles to be rooted in a revival of devotion to the Holy Spirit begun by Pope Leo XIII. In an 1897 encyclical, the Holy Father called for a novena to the Holy Spirit to be held in every parish during the nine days preceding Pentecost. It is worth pointing out that the year almost coincides with the beginning of Pentecostalism in the United States. No one at the time

---

[18] Synan, *Century of the Holy Spirit*, 199.

[19] Ibid.

[20] Ibid., 211.

would have been likely to see a connection between the little church on Azusa Street and the publication of a papal encyclical on the Holy Spirit, but they certainly seem to be related events.

The actual beginning of the Catholic Charismatic Renewal (CCR) can be dated to 1967 at Duquesne University in Pittsburgh, where a small number of laypeople, faculty and students, began to pray fervently and experience what they believed to be a real and personal contact with the living Christ.[21] Four faculty members had attended a charismatic group led by a Presbyterian woman, Flo Dodge. Some had received the baptism of the Holy Spirit.[22] In February 1967, what has come to be known as "the Duquesne weekend" took place at the Ark and Dove retreat house with twenty professors and students, including those who had been prayed over by Dodge. Patty Gallagher Mansfield, who became an important leader in the movement, writes:

> That night the Lord brought the whole group into the chapel.... The professors then laid hands on some of the students but most of us received the baptism of the Spirit while kneeling before the Blessed Sacrament in prayer. Some of us started speaking in tongues; others received gifts of discernment, prophecy and wisdom.
>
> But the most important gift was the fruit of love which bound the whole community together. In the Lord's Spirit we found a unity we had long tried to achieve on our own.[23]

David Mangan, another Duquesne student, describes his experience. "I cried harder than I ever cried in my life, but I did not shed one tear. All of a sudden Jesus Christ was so real and so present that I could feel him all around. I was overcome with such a feeling of love that I cannot describe it."[24]

Reports of this meeting and the events that followed spread quickly and were received enthusiastically at Notre Dame and Michigan State universities. Soon Notre Dame and Ann Arbor became centers of the burgeoning CCR. With amazing rapidity the movement, focused primarily on prayer groups, spread through the English-speaking Catholic Church. In a few dioceses some parishes became identified as spiritual centers for the CCR. Because of the leadership of Fr. Michael Scanlan, T.O.R., a quiet little Franciscan college in Steubenville, Ohio, became a thriving university with a strong charismatic identity. Several thousand students and adults continue to participate each year in a variety of summer conferences focused on the charismatic movement and various faith concerns.

[21] O'Connor, *Pentecostal Movement in the Catholic Church*, 15.

[22] Synan, *Century of the Holy Spirit*, 211.

[23] Patti Gallagher Mansfield, *As by a New Pentecost* (Steubenville, Ohio: Franciscan University Press, 1992), as quoted in ibid., 209–10.

[24] Vinson Synan, *In the Latter Days* (Ann Arbor, Mich.: Servant Publications, 1984), 110.

The CCR spread throughout the world, with bishops and cardinals supporting and sometimes joining it. To the amazement of many Protestant Pentecostals, Catholic charismatics prayed in tongues in St. Peter's in Rome and were warmly welcomed by Popes Paul VI and John Paul II. In 1987 the Pope welcomed CCR leaders and thousands of worshippers with these words:

> The vigor and fruitfulness of the Renewal certainly attest to the powerful presence of the Holy Spirit at work in the Church in these years after the Second Vatican Council. Of course, the Spirit has guided the Church in every age, producing a great variety of gifts among the faithful. Because of the Spirit, the Church preserves a continual youthful vitality. And the Charismatic Renewal is an eloquent manifestation of this vitality today, a bold statement of what "the Spirit is saying to the churches" (Rev. 2:7) as we approach the close of the second millennium.[25]

In the United States, Pentecostalism and the Catholic Charismatic Renewal reached a crescendo in the 1980s. The number of leaders, preachers, clergy, and prelates involved makes a summary difficult. Synan has done this as well as possible, considering the complexity of this phenomenon. The growth and enthusiasm of the movement, however, has leveled off in recent years, and the number of people involved has declined noticeably. While this may be disappointing to some, it suggests that a form of Christian spirituality that is personal, spontaneous, engaging, and founded on the Scriptures has entered the mainstream of many Christian denominations. It is worth noting that the greatest interest in Pentecostalism and the CCR in the United States is currently among new immigrants and people of humble means. Did Christ not foretell that when He said, "Blessed are the poor in spirit, for theirs is the kingdom of heaven"?

Christ in Pentecostalism and in the Charismatic Renewal

Much attention in Pentecostalism and CCR is paid to the gifts of the Holy Spirit, including deliverance from evil spirits and physical healing. As a result, those unfamiliar with the charismatic renewal may not be aware that Christ, experienced as a personal presence, is the pivotal center of the movement. This is best brought out by Fr. O'Connor, who analyzes the unity that is expressed in a charismatic prayer meeting or assembly. He writes:

> [T]he unity comes from Christ, who is present and actively leading the meeting through his Spirit. Without any doubt, the principal inspiration of these meetings is the Lord's promise, "Where two or three are gathered together in my name, there am I in the midst of

[25] Pope John Paul II, from a 1987 address in Rome, quoted in Synan, *Century of the Holy Spirit*, 222.

> them" (Matt. 18:20). It is very consciously in order to enter into and participate in this presence of Christ that the community assembles. . . .
>
> Christ is not in the prayer meetings merely as a presence; he is there as sovereign Lord, who wills to lead the meeting actively by the inspirations of his Spirit. Hence, while all are given the freedom to say or do what they will, this is not a license to "do as they please." It is their grave obligation, in virtue of the very sense and meaning of the prayer meeting, to follow, to the best of their ability, the gentle leading of the Holy Spirit. Where this really occurs, the prayer meeting becomes a beautiful realization of the body of Christ, in which each member carries on a function assigned and consecrated by the Spirit of Christ.[26]

Those unfamiliar with Pentecostal or charismatic religious experience will be unable to appreciate how Christ-centered this form of prayer is. As previously noted, spontaneous prayers are rarely written down, and even when they are, the ambience of the prayer experience cannot be duplicated. Simply reading the prayers of others falls short of communicating the sense of Christ's presence.

A familiarity with any type of charismatic or Pentecostal service would make it clear that Christ is experienced as present, completely in control, and the center of worship. This is not to say that the Father and the Holy Spirit are ignored or not addressed. The other Persons of the Trinity are acknowledged, but Christ's humanity make these experiences acts of devotion to Him in an all-encompassing way.

Voices of the Mainstream Protestant Experience

Dag Hammarskjöld (1905–1961): A Modern Skeptic Finds His Way to Christ

In stark contrast to the Pentecostals, we come to the spiritual journey of Dag Hammarskjöld, one of the great interior dramas of the century. Protestant Pentecostals and Catholics in the charismatic movement might at first show little appreciation of a man like Hammarskjöld, whose journey from skepticism to a deeply experienced belief in Christ followed a very intellectual path. A close examination, however, reveals surprising similarities between the emotional expression of the charismatics and the calm, cautious intellectual belief of Hammarskjöld, not in the mode of expression but in devotion to Christ as the personal source of salvation.

This fascinating traveler on the spiritual road spent his most productive years as secretary-general of the United Nations. His death, which was tragic and untimely, occurred in a plane crash in Africa, while he was on a U.N. mission. Sometime later it became known that he left behind a notebook of spiritual thoughts, questions, quotations, and poetry. This book, *Markings*, is essentially an account of milestones on a spiritual journey.

When *Markings* was published, many were astonished that this extraordinarily capable man of intense and dedicated public service had such

[26] O'Connor, *Pentecostal Movement in the Catholic Church*, 113–14.

a deep level of spirituality, one that had developed after decades of searching and struggle. Gustaf Aulén, a theologian and bishop of the Swedish Lutheran Church, points out, however, that in a radio interview with Edward R. Murrow in 1953, Hammarskjöld endorsed "his Christian belief 'without any compromise with the demands of the intellectual honesty which is the very key to maturity of mind'".[27]

Hammarskjöld was raised in an affluent and culturally rich environment. His father was prime minister of Sweden (1914–1917) and governor in Uppsala, a city which was a religious and cultural center but also much influenced by the antireligious philosophy of Axel Hägerström.[28] His father was a formidable figure, very conservative and regarded by some as one of the most hated men in Sweden.[29] During his youth, Dag enjoyed the friendship of the family of Archbishop Nathan Söderblom, one of the founders of the ecumenical movement. Söderblom was dedicated to keeping the Christian faith relevant in a Europe that was becoming increasingly secular.

According to Aulén, Hammarskjöld received from his father the idea that "no life was more satisfactory than one of selfless service to your country—or humanity". From his mother, who had a devout and traditional faith, he received "a belief that, in the very radical sense of the Gospels, all men were equals as children of God, and should be met and treated by us as our masters in God".[30] For Hammarskjöld, these beliefs gave "life direction even when my intellect still challenged their validity".[31]

Markings demonstrates an intensity of devotion comparable intellectually to Newman's, but coming from one who was educated in an atmosphere of skepticism and hopelessness. For this reason Hammarskjöld is one of the most interesting and spiritually relevant pilgrims of our time. While other biographies have stressed the absence of Christian religious conviction in his early life, Sven Stolpe, a Catholic Swedish writer who knew Hammarskjöld, recalls many incidents indicating that Dag's mother's devout Lutheran Christianity shaped his moral attitudes profoundly.[32] One of the best ways to understand Hammarskjöld's spiritual journey is to go through its phases as outlined in *Markings*.

Skepticism and Hopeless Determination

The Swedish edition of *Markings* begins with four pages dated 1925 to 1930, four dated 1941 and 1942, thirteen dated 1945 to 1949, and then many entries dated by year. In 1956, Hammarskjöld wrote that

[27] Gustaf Aulén, *Dag Hammarskjöld's White Book: An Analysis of Markings* (Philadelphia: Fortress Press, 1969), 2.

[28] Ibid., 15.

[29] Sven Stolpe, *Dag Hammarskjöld, A Spiritual Portrait*, trans. Naomi Walford (New York: Scribner, 1966), 12.

[30] Aulén, *Hammarskjöld's White Book*, 6.

[31] Ibid.

[32] Stolpe, *Hammarskjöld, A Spiritual Portrait*, 27–29, 66.

the notes were "signposts" of his journey. The first years of *Markings*, 1925 to 1929, speak of a powerful determination in the face of an apparently meaningless existence, although there are frequent, if tentative, expressions of prayer. The opening lines of the book suggest a journey but one without the certitude of ever arriving at a destination.

> I am being driven forward
> Into an unknown land.
> The pass grows steeper,
> The air colder and sharper.
> A wind from my unknown goal
> Stirs the strings
> Of expectation.
> Still the question:
> Shall I ever get there?[33]

There is an air of hopelessness, possibly resulting from the tension between his high moral values and determination and his lack of certitude about faith.

> Tomorrow we shall meet
> Death and I—
> And he shall thrust his sword
> Into one who is wide awake.
> But in the meantime how grievous the memory
> Of hours frittered away.[34]

Hammarskjöld's writings display a yearning to purify his motives, and this is a desire central to his thinking. He is deeply aware that he cannot achieve moral righteousness without help from outside himself—from God—yet remains unsure if God exists or cares. He can see no solution to this problem. The temptation to self-importance, so serious for a gifted, successful man, is clearly recognized: "There is only one path out of the steamy dense jungle where the battle is fought over glory and power and advantage—one escape from the snares and obstacles you yourself have set up. And that is—to accept death."[35]

The idea of God comes to light again and again, although tentatively, or only as the symbol of a terrifying judgment. "On the bookshelf of life, God is a useful work of reference, always at hand but seldom consulted. In the whitewashed hour of birth, He is a jubilation and a refreshing wind, too immediate for memory to catch. But when we are compelled to look ourselves in the face—then He rises

[33] "Thus it was", in Dag Hammarskjöld, *Markings*, trans. Leif Sjöberg and W.H. Auden (New York: Alfred A. Knopf, 1964), 5.

[34] Ibid., 6.

[35] *Markings*, 13.

above us in terrifying reality, beyond all argument and 'feeling,' stronger than all self-defensive forgetfulness." [36]

After twenty-five years of painful searching, Hammarskjöld, was extremely self-critical. His mother's faith, which he did not explicitly share, helped him to continue.

> At least he knew this much about himself—I know what man is—his vulgarity, lust, pride, envy—and longing. Longing—among other things, for the Cross. . . .
>
> Never let success hide its emptiness from you, achievement its nothingness, toil its desolation. And so keep alive the incentive to push on further, that pain in the soul which drives us beyond ourselves.[37]

As we move to the second phase of Hammarskjöld's journey, the one that leads to Christ, we are reminded of his dark state of mind and sense of self: "The ride on the Witches' Sabbath to the Dark Tower where we meet only ourselves, ourselves, ourselves." [38]

If Hammarskjöld had a spiritual guide in his early life, it was Albert Schweitzer. This man of genius and generosity was very popular in Sweden during Hammarskjöld's youth, and his medical work in Africa received much support. Physician, world-class musician and interpreter of Bach, medical missionary, and pioneer in the modernist historical-critical interpretation of Scripture, Schweitzer was also the spiritual leader of a generation of intelligentsia who wanted to hold on to some aspects of Christianity with little attention to its theological contents. He was a renowned representative of the new "liberated Christianity", which believed *in* Jesus Christ but could not define *what* it believed about Him except for His moral and ethical teachings, which it valued highly.

Hammarskjöld stated that his own inherited ideals had been "harmonized and adjusted to the demands of our world today" by Schweitzer. He also found Schweitzer's rationalistic approach to the Bible "a key for modern man to the world of the Gospels".[39] Hammarskjöld was already intrigued by the figure of Jesus of Nazareth, whom he had come to see as a "superhero", because he thought that the highest achievement was to sacrifice oneself for the good without personal gain.

We come abruptly to a long and important passage in *Markings*. It signals a change in Hammarskjöld's spiritual life, the first stirrings of personal devotion to Christ. The influence of Schweitzer's thought is still obvious, yet Hammarskjöld moves beyond this, seeing Jesus as the Lamb of God.

---

[36] Ibid., 16.

[37] Ibid., 55.

[38] Ibid., 63.

[39] Aulén, *Hammarskjöld's White Book*, 6.

> A young man, adamant in his committed life. The one who was nearest to him relates how, on the last evening, he arose from supper, laid aside his garments, and washed the feet of his friends and disciples—an adamant young man, alone as he confronted his final destiny. . . .
>
> He had assented to a possibility in his being, of which he had had his first inkling when he returned from the desert. If God required anything of him, he would not fail. Only recently, he thought, had he begun to see more clearly, and to realize that the road of possibility might lead to the Cross. He knew, though, that he had to follow it, still uncertain as to whether he was indeed "the one who shall bring it to pass," but certain that the answer could only be learned by following the road to the end. The end *might* be a death without significance—as well as being the end of the road of possibility. . . .
>
> Is the hero of this immortal, brutally simple drama in truth "the Lamb of God that taketh away the sins of the world"? Absolutely faithful to a divined possibility—in that sense the Son of God, in that sense the sacrificial Lamb, in that sense the Redeemer. A young man, adamant in his commitment, who walks the road of possibility to the end without self-pity or demand for sympathy, fulfilling the destiny he has chosen—even sacrificing affection and fellowship when the others are unready to follow him—into a new fellowship.[40]

After this the tone of *Markings* continues to change; darkness and indecision give way to descriptions of positive and bright experiences of prayer. Hammarskjöld is moving toward believing in Christ as man and God.

> Now you know. When the worries over your work loosen their grip, then this experience of light, warmth, and power. From without—a sustaining element, like air to the glider or water to the swimmer. An intellectual hesitation which demands proofs and logical demonstration prevents me from "believing"—in this, too. Prevents me from expressing and interpreting this reality in intellectual terms. Yet, through me there flashes this vision of a magnetic field in the soul, created in a timeless present by unknown multitudes, living in holy obedience, whose words and actions are a timeless prayer.
>
> —"The Communion of Saints"—and—within it—an eternal life.[41]

A Believing Christian and Secretary-General

Sven Stolpe calls the next step a decisive one for Hammarskjöld. *Markings* records a quotation attributed to Thomas Aquinas, but Stolpe points out that it is actually from Thomas à Kempis, author of *The Imitation of Christ*, an important work in Hammarskjöld's life. April 7, 1953, the day

[40] Ibid., 68–69.
[41] Ibid., 84.

of his nomination as secretary-general, was of great significance in Hammarskjöld's spiritual life. The entry for that day reads, quoting Kempis,

> "Their lives grounded in and sustained by God, they are incapable of any kind of pride; because they give back to God all the benefits He has bestowed on them, they do not glorify each other, but do all things to the Glory of God alone." [42]

Hammarskjöld continues with thoughts on the doctrine of the Cross. He applies this to his own life—personal sacrifice with no gain:

> In the last analysis, what does the word "sacrifice" mean? Or even the word "gift"? He who has nothing can give nothing. The gift is God's—to God.
>
> He who has surrendered himself to it knows that the Way ends on the Cross—even when it is leading him through the jubilation of Gennesaret or the triumphant entry into Jerusalem.[43]

Bishop Aulén says of this quotation: "This is a meditation in the presence of Christ—a meditation concerning the significance of the discipleship which follows Him on the way of self-surrender. To follow Him means to be prepared to pay the cost." [44] Aulén also points out that the next marking is an absolute acceptance of God's will and providence: "To be free, to be able to stand up and leave *everything* behind—without looking back. To say Yes—".[45]

The bishop comments: "All of these pronouncements from the spring of 1953, now considered, reveal the meaning which his yes, once said in secret, had for him in the time of his life's momentous change." [46] Aulén stresses that Hammarskjöld's conversion was not sudden. He never abandoned the effort "to build up a personal belief in the light of experience and honest thinking".[47] Aulén notes that "the relevant passages [in *Markings*] make it clear that his yes had been a *slowly growing yes*".[48] Although at times, in 1952, Hammarskjöld "dared not believe", he was a Christian believer from the following year onward. By September 1957 he could write:

> The best and most wonderful thing that can happen to you in this life is that you should be silent and let God work and speak.
>
> Long ago you gripped me, Slinger. *Now* into the storm. *Now* towards your target.[49]

[42] Ibid., 91.
[43] Ibid.
[44] Aulén, *Hammarskjöld's White Book*, 12.
[45] *Markings*, 91.
[46] Aulén, *Hammarskjöld's White Book*, 12.
[47] Dag Hammarskjöld, "Old Creeds in a New World", as cited in ibid., 13.
[48] Aulén, *Hammarskjöld's White Book*, 13.
[49] *Markings*, 156.

Once Hammarskjöld made his act of faith, he turned his attention to pride, which he considered his greatest fault, one he struggled with all his life. Most would not have seen him as a proud man, but he saw himself as such. He made the discovery that faith leads from pride to humility.

> Except in faith, nobody is humble. The mask of weakness or of Phariseeism is not the naked face of humility.
>
> Except in faith, nobody is proud. The vanity displayed in all its varieties by the spiritually immature is not pride.
>
> To be, in faith, both humble and proud: that is, to *live*, to know that in God I am nothing, but that God is in me.[50]

Events moved rapidly in Hammarskjöld's spiritual life. His writings, especially after 1953, increasingly reflect the typical experiences of the Christian spiritual traveler. Several key passages demonstrate that he was following the steps often outlined by Christian spiritual masters. Following conversion, the next step is the darkness of faith. During his first year as secretary-general he recorded a significant marking based on the writings of St. John of the Cross:

> Faith is the marriage of God and the soul.
>
> Faith *is*: it cannot, therefore, be comprehended, far less identified with, the formulae in which we paraphrase what is.
>
> —*"en una noche oscura."* The Dark Night of the Soul—so dark that we may not even look for faith. The night in Gethsemane when the last friends left you have fallen asleep, all the others are seeking your downfall, and *God is silent*, as the marriage is consummated.[51]

Bishop Aulén takes exception to one aspect of the English translation of *Markings*, which is by the poet W. H. Auden. Aulén calls Auden's use of the word "marriage" here a "notable and serious mistranslation" of the Swedish and states that the proper translation is "Faith is God's union with the soul".[52] He sees this exact translation of the Swedish as "perfectly in accord" with a statement that Hammarskjöld made in 1953: "Faith is a state of the mind and the soul. In this sense we can understand the words of the Spanish mystic, Saint John of the Cross: 'Faith is the union of God with the soul.' "[53]

Aulén points out that despite his use of such phrases as "the union of God with the soul", Hammarskjöld never speaks in terms of the "bride-mysticism" of the Middle Ages, which we saw represented by St. Bernard. Aulén's summary of Hammarskjöld's approach to mysticism is based on his observation on Hammarskjöld's own statement

[50] Ibid., 92.
[51] Ibid., 97.
[52] Aulén, *Hammarskjöld, A Spiritual Portrait*, 41–42.
[53] Hammarskjöld, "Old Creeds in a New World", 23, quoted in ibid., 42.

(quoted above). Yet Hammarskjöld states in *Markings* that he found the help he was seeking "in the writings of those great medieval mystics for whom 'self-surrender' had been the way to self-realization, and who in 'singleness of mind' and 'inwardness' had found strength to say yes to every demand which the needs of their neighbors made them face."[54] He was of the opinion that for the mystics the word "love", "much misused and misinterpreted", was "simply an overflowing of the strength with which they felt themselves filled when living in true self-oblivion. And this love found natural expressions in an unhesitant fulfillment of duty and an unreserved acceptance of life, whatever it brought them personally of toil, suffering—or happiness."[55]

Like many deeply religious people, Hammarskjöld discovered that there is a mysticism that leads to community and self-giving to others. In this he made a synthesis of his father's ideal of service and his mother's strong faith. Hammarskjöld's genius, as well as his intense, sincere spiritual striving, make *Markings* a unique spiritual testimony. He brings the love of God and neighbor together in terms comprehensible to those who come from nonreligious or even antireligious backgrounds.

Several entries in *Markings* demonstrate Hammarskjöld's personal devotion to Christ and are quite different from both his earlier admiration of Christ as a superhero and his understanding of "the historical Jesus" based on Schweitzer's scholarship. The following prayer from 1954 is an example of traditional Christian devotion to the suffering Christ.

> Thou who has created us free, Who seest all that happens—yet art confident of victory,
> Thou who at this time art the one among us who suffereth the uttermost loneliness,
> Thou—who art also in me,
> May I bear Thy burden, when my hour comes,
> May I—[56]

This quotation reminds us of the justification of devotion to Christ Crucified given by Cardinal Bérulle. Hammarskjöld's following beautiful prayer of consecration is obviously directed to Christ.

> Thou who art over us,
> Thou who art one of us,
> Thou who *art*—
> Also within us,
> May all see Thee—in me also,
> May I prepare the way for Thee,
> May I thank Thee for all that shall fall to my lot,
> May I also not forget the needs of others,

[54] Ibid., 24, 43.
[55] Ibid.
[56] *Markings*, 98.

Keep me in Thy love
As Thou wouldest that all should be kept in mine.
May everything in this my being be directed to Thy glory
And may I never despair.
For I am under Thy hand,
And in Thee is all power and goodness.
Give me a pure heart—that I may see Thee,
A humble heart—that I may hear Thee,
A heart of love—that I may serve Thee,
A heart of faith—that I may abide in Thee.[57]

Because of statements about the absolute incomprehensibility of God, some may question whether Hammarskjöld was really a Christian. The following doxology to the Trinity, however, makes his commitment to Christian dogma clear and precise.

Before Thee, Father,
In righteousness and humility,
With Thee, Brother,
In faith and courage,
In Thee, Spirit,
In stillness.[58]

Hammarskjöld consistently returns to Christ's suffering and to the idea, very popular in the devotion of Catholics, that He continues to suffer in His members until the end of the world. The times Hammarskjöld refers to in the following excerpt are the sequence of events given in the Gospel accounts of Christ's Passion and death.

> The third hour. And the ninth.—They are *here*. And *now*. They *are* now!
>
> "Jesus will be in agony even to the end of the world. We must not sleep during that time." (Pascal)
>
> We must not—And for the watcher is the far-off present—also present in his contact with mankind among whom, at every moment, Jesus dies in someone who has followed the trail marks of the inner road to the end:
> love and patience,
> righteousness and humility,
> faith and courage,
> stillness.[59]

We must not think that after Hammarskjöld's conversion in 1953 he no longer faced the dark struggles that had been so much a part of his life before that point. It is simple realism to state that no one on the

[57] Ibid., 100.
[58] Ibid., 123.
[59] Ibid., 126.

spiritual journey can make constant progress without periods of darkness. A marking from 1957, which was written during continuing controversies at the United Nations, when Khrushchev and others were attacking Hammarskjöld, is particularly revealing. Stolpe recalls that the Soviet delegation at the U.N. reviled Hammarskjöld for being corrupt and dishonest. They also accused him of being an accomplice to the murder of Patrice Lumumba in the Congo. Hammarskjöld, however, remained polite, despite the cruelty of the attack and the pain he must have felt because of it.[60] In the following words we see Hammarskjöld's conscious attempt to carry the cross behind his Savior.

> For the sacrificed—in the hour of sacrifice—only one thing counts: faith—alone among enemies and skeptics. Faith, in spite of the humiliation which is both the necessary precondition and the consequence of faith, faith without any hope of compensation other than he can find in a faith which reality seems so thoroughly to refute.
>
> Would the Crucifixion have had any sublimity or meaning if Jesus had seen Himself crowned with the halo of martyrdom? What we have later added was not there for Him. And we must forget all about it if we are to hear His commands.[61]

In Hammarskjöld's last years his notes consist mostly of poetry, some of his own, often in haiku form, and some from Swedish literature. Stolpe believes that this change from the very expressive years 1957 and 1958 reflects Hammarskjöld's exhaustion because of his work during bitter conflicts in Africa, especially in the Congo. In the midst of the controversy and conflict he was trying to remain detached from earthly desires. Such detachment is not easy when standing at the center of world conflict. We get a glimpse of his peace and resolution from a marking in 1959:

> To be nothing in the self-effacement of humility, yet, for the sake of the task, to embody *its* whole weight and importance in your bearing, as the one who has been called to undertake it. To give to people, works, poetry, art, what the self can contribute, and to take, simply and freely, what belongs to it by reason of its identity. Praise and blame, the winds of success and adversity blow over such a life without leaving a trace or upsetting its balance.
> Towards this, so help me, God—[62]

It is interesting to note that W. H. Auden recalls that when Hammarskjöld was working in Paris, he often travelled many miles to visit the beautiful basilica at Vézelay in Burgundy, with its marvelous statuary, especially the triumphant Christ over the main portal. When

[60] Stolpe, *Hammarskjöld, A Spiritual Portrait*, 121.
[61] *Markings*, 151.
[62] Ibid., 174.

Hammarskjöld visited Nepal, he wrote a haiku recalling this great church at Easter:

> Himalayan ice cliffs
> Beyond the hills
> Of Vézelay at Easter.[63]

In a 1959 haiku he writes of the beauty of the natural world but then turns to the suffering Christ.

> God took the form of man
> In the victim
> Who chose to be sacrificed.[64]

To understand the poetry of his last two years of life (1959–1961), we must realize that Hammarskjöld, for whatever reasons, was anticipating his death. I do not suggest that he had a mystical revelation of impending death; but his poems of that period are filled with memories of childhood, perhaps the first signs of approaching age. Often, as the years pass, people's thoughts turn increasingly to the past. His constant theme in *Markings*, expressed in several New Year's entries, is that "Night is drawing nigh!"[65]

An oft-repeated theme of his last years is the struggle to forgive. This reflects, I am sure, his own attempts to grow in charity (not merely kindness or generosity), which requires us to love our enemies: "Love your enemies and pray for those who persecute you" (Mt 5:44). This is the acid test for those who enter the second, or illuminative, stage of the spiritual life.[66] The entry for Easter 1960 renews the struggle to forgive and the atmosphere of death. "Forgiveness breaks the chain of causality because he who 'forgives' you—out of love—takes upon himself the consequences of what *you* have done. Forgiveness, therefore, always entails a sacrifice. . . . When I think of those who will come after—or survive me—I feel as if I were taking part in the preparations for a feast, the joys of which I shall not share."[67] In his entry for Christmas Eve that year the theme of Christ's sacrificial death and our imitation of Him is still central to his thought. "How proper it is that Christmas should follow Advent.—For him who looks towards the future, the Manger is situated on Golgotha, and the Cross has already been raised in Bethlehem."[68] These words could have been written by St. Francis of Assisi.

---

[63] Ibid., 186–87.

[64] Ibid., 190.

[65] See, for example, *Markings*, 37 (and Auden's note), 61, 81, 89, etc.

[66] See Benedict Groeschel, *Spiritual Passages: The Psychology of Spiritual Development* (New York: Crossroad, 1983), 149–51.

[67] *Markings*, 197.

[68] Ibid., 198.

On Pentecost Sunday 1961 there is another clear allusion to death and sacrifice united to Christ's. "As I continued along the Way, I learned, step by step, word by word, that behind every saying in the Gospels stands *one* man and *one* man's experience. Also behind the prayer that the cup might pass from him and his promise to drink it. Also behind each of the words from the Cross."[69] Here Hammarskjöld makes an extremely important observation about learning. Those on the spiritual journey are learners. They do not simply achieve a fixed idea or accomplish something, in the sense that one learns mathematics or studies literature. Instead one learns "step by step, word by word" the meaning of the Gospel and Christ's own personal summons to him.

Other Persons of Note

Grace Reaches Out to a Skeptic

Markings reflects the mysterious action of grace at work in a soul. Grace, like sunlight, takes on the contours, texture, and color of the life into which it comes. In the life of so complex a man, grace must appear subtly. It may operate in ways less obvious than it might in the life of a simple believer struggling with a heavy cross or in the life of an addict who turns to God for deliverance. As we come to the end of *Markings*, however, it is difficult to imagine how an unbiased person can read the passages written in the months before Hammarskjöld's death and not find there a premonition of his end. They also contain a strong suggestion of his linking his own death to that of those who gave their lives for the Gospel or, in a broader context, for the cause of good. Skeptics will cry, "Paranoia!" at the identification with Christ, the martyrs, and the mystics, but the words are there, written by a man fully engaged in the service of peace and human dignity. The allusions in the following selections obviously relate to martyrdom.

Asked if I have courage
To go on to the end,
I answer Yes without
A second thought.

The gate opens: dazzled,
I see the arena,
Then I walk out naked
To meet my death. . . .

I have watched the others:
Now I am the victim,
Strapped fast to the altar
For sacrifice.

[69] Ibid., 205.

Dumb, my naked body
Endures the stoning, dumb
When slit up and the live
Heart is plucked out.[70]

One of the last entries of *Markings* is a prayer for forgiveness that is reminiscent of prayers of the Christians mystics. The call for grace and salvation and the recognition of God's majesty are clear:

Have mercy
Upon us.
Have mercy
Upon our efforts,
That we
Before Thee,
In love and in faith,
Righteousness and humility,
May follow Thee,
With self-denial, steadfastness, and courage,
And meet Thee
In the silence.

Give us
A pure heart
That we may see Thee.
A humble heart
That we may hear Thee,
A heart of love
That we may serve Thee,
A heart of faith
That we may live Thee,

Thou
Whom I do not know
But Whose I am.
Thou
Whom I do not comprehend
But Who hast dedicated me
To my fate.
Thou—[71]

There is no doubt that the person of Christ is the moving and integrating force in Hammarskjöld's later life: the Christ known in Scripture, encountered in the depths of the soul, present among us in every human suffering and need, and teacher of the parable of the

[70] Ibid., 206–7.
[71] Ibid., 214–15.

Last Judgment (Mt 25). It is significant that when Hammarskjöld's body was examined after the fatal plane crash, rescuers found in his pocket a copy of *The Imitation of Christ*, for this is what his life was about all the years he served as secretary-general of the United Nations.

Arthur Michael Ramsey (1904–1988)

In our review of Christian devotion since the Protestant Reformation, no small part has been played by Anglicans. Beginning with Richard Hooker, we have seen the development of a distinct Anglican spirituality, which, although related to and dependent on historical Catholicism, is not simply the "Catholic Church without the Pope", as some superficially conclude. Anglicanism not only takes; it also gives. Evangelical Anglicanism provided the foundation and spiritual outlook of Methodism with John Wesley. Another less recognized influence is seen in the spiritual perspective of Cardinal Newman. Liturgical Anglicanism with its strong academic interest in Church history and tradition has affected the liturgical movement not only in the Catholic Church but also in the emergence of liturgical practice in Calvinism. I saw this when I visited the mother church of Presbyterianism, St. Giles in Edinburgh. Along with a life-size statue of John Knox in the church, I noticed that the communion table was so well prepared liturgically that I could have offered Mass there. There were even some statuettes of Catholic saints, including St. Francis, who stood there alongside statues of the great reformers. Catholic influences in Presbyterianism without doubt came through Anglicanism and not through direct contact with Catholicism, which would be considered very foreign to Calvinists. Say what you will, Anglicanism has always served as a bridge between the Catholic and Protestant worlds.

We will focus on a man who can be considered the most representative Anglican of the twentieth century: Arthur Michael Ramsey, who was successively Archbishop of York and of Canterbury. In the latter post he was spiritual head of the worldwide Anglican Communion. Archbishop Ramsey was also, in my estimation, one of the most powerful Christological writers of the century, a time when scriptural and traditional belief in the divinity of Christ was under severe attack from parts of academia.

Although he was not a full-time biblical scholar, Ramsey was as informed and engaged in the presentation of Christian biblical theology and its effective pastoral application as anyone of his time. He was well prepared for this task, having been Regius Professor of Divinity at Cambridge and having studied under many renowned English Scripture scholars.

Archbishop Ramsey was also an important ecumenical figure during and after the Second Vatican Council. He wrote a scholarly analysis of trends in the Church of England, published as *An Era in Anglican Theology*, in which he took up what was then termed liberalism. He identified the Anglican position as one based on Scripture, tradition, and reason, but he also stressed the importance of sacraments, liturgy, and order in the church.[72] For many who question the nature of the Anglican position because of the wide range of views found in that communion of churches, it might be helpful to read Archbishop Ramsey's analysis.

Following the patristic tradition, Ramsey based his New Testament interpretations on the core of Christian belief—the Incarnation as defined by early Church councils. His theology never strayed from this tradition. Ramsey emphatically preached that the Incarnate Son of God is revealed first and foremost in the Crucifixion-Resurrection event, by which the glory of God is revealed in its fullness so that we may enter that glory in union with Christ. The divine nature is revealed ultimately as love—God's love for us, Christ's love for the Father, and His totally unselfish love for us.

The importance of Ramsey's teaching does not lie in its being new or groundbreaking; in fact, it is deeply traditional. Its important contribution is that it confronts an age when Christian writers of many persuasions attempted to defend Christianity by using methods that all but ignored early Church tradition, which, after all, is the best interpretation of what the early Church believed and taught.

Beginning with Mark's Gospel (assumed by many to be the earliest) and going on to those portions common to Luke and Matthew, Ramsey identified a few of the claims that Christ made, although he tells us there are plenty of others. He makes clear that these claims were not made in any egotistical way but were rather "in the context of Jesus's own self-effacement": "His message is not about himself. He is absorbed in the sovereignty, the purpose, and the presence of God. Yet the implied claims recur. It is Jesus who will accept or reject men in the future judgement (Matt. 7:21–22). It is for Jesus that the renunciations of discipleship are made (Mark 8:35–37). It is Jesus's death that will bring deliverance (Mark 10:45) and be the ground of a new covenant (Mark 14:24)."[73]

In many contemporary schools of theology, the faith has been all but emptied of meaning and the trustworthiness of Scripture and the early Church regularly discounted. The Christian faith is reduced to little more than a system of symbols used to represent a God that can never be directly encountered. It is in his eloquent opposition to this that we find the importance of Archbishop Ramsey's forceful and biblically founded popular theology and preaching. He was a truly pastoral, biblical scholar.

Beneath his solid scholarship there is a rich devotion to Christ, founded on Ramsey's understanding of the Resurrection. He asserts

---

[72] *An Era in Anglican Theology* (New York: Charles Scribner's Sons, 1960). See also *To Believe Is to Pray: Readings from Michael Ramsey*, ed. James E. Griffiss (Boston: Cowley Publications, 1996), xiii–xv.

[73] Michael Ramsey, *Canterbury Pilgrim* (New York: Seabury Press, 1974), 35.

that all of Christianity, including the teachings and the death of Jesus, finds meaning in the Resurrection, which was not a teaching of the apostles but something they experienced personally. They recognized their Master raised from the dead. The tomb was empty, and the risen Christ had flesh and blood. The Resurrection was not only a spiritual return of Jesus, but a physical and, therefore, cosmic event. It was in every sense a miracle, "an event wrought by God which does not fit into the hitherto observable laws of nature".[74]

Taking on the scholars and preachers who say that the Gospel message stands on its own without the Resurrection, Ramsey states:

> Jesus Christ had, it is true, taught and done great things, but He did not allow the disciples to rest in these things. He led them on to paradox, perplexity, and darkness; and there He left them. There too they would have remained, had He not been raised from death. But His Resurrection threw its own light backwards upon the death and the ministry that went before; it illuminated the paradoxes and disclosed the unity of His words and deeds.[75]

Ramsey calls it a "desperate procedure" to try to build a Christian Gospel on Jesus' words apart from the climax of Calvary, Easter, and Pentecost. He attacks the contemporary biblical scholars who claim that Jesus had no intention of saving the world and uses as his focus for this the importance of Jesus' complete freedom. Along with Romano Guardini, his contemporary, he sees that because of His complete freedom in fulfilling His vocation, "the figure of Jesus goes on haunting the thoughts and consciences of people".[76] Jesus' freedom brings Him to accept the complete self-effacement of His death, by which He glorifies the Father and knows that the Father glorifies Him. Glory is one of the central biblical themes of Ramsey's theology. God's glory is revealed as Jesus predicted at the beginning of the Passion (Jn 12:23–36). Jesus' self-effacement reveals "the character of eternal deity, love, glory, freedom. In Jesus we see not only what it means for men and women to be free but also what it means for God to be God."[77]

Archbishop Ramsey stresses that Christ's divinity is revealed in His dereliction and death:

> It was darkness, destruction, and apparent defeat. But St. John shows that because it was self-giving love, it was also glory and victory. The self-giving love of Calvary discloses not the abolition of deity but the essence of deity in its eternity and perfection. God is Christlike, and

[74] Arthur Michael Ramsey, *The Resurrection of Christ* (London: Geoffrey Bles: Centenary Press, 1946), 35.

[75] Ibid., 7. See also N. T. Wright, *The Resurrection of the Son of God* (Minneapolis, Minn.: Augsburg Fortress Press, 2003).

[76] Griffiss, *To Believe Is To Pray*, 87.

[77] Ibid., 88.

> in him is no un-Christlikeness at all, and the glory of God in all eternity is that ceaseless self-giving love of which Calvary is the measure.... Love and omnipotence are one.[78]

Ramsey's blending of patristic theology and contemporary scholarship, particularly Scripture studies, leads to the question: What does he say about personal devotion to Jesus? Ramsey, always a man of prayer, held that to believe is to pray. He sees the Gospel, especially that of St. John, calling the individual by His self-giving to a relationship that has no parallel. "I am the vine, you are the branches." "Abide in me and I in you" (Jn 15:5, 4). Linking this relationship with Christ to the Eucharist, Ramsey tells us that the sacrament of Holy Communion "is *broken* body, blood *poured* or *offered* that we receive as the food of our souls".[79]

Archbishop Ramsey's writings, although centered on preserving the truth of the Gospel in skeptical times, are strongly theological and rich in personal devotion and awareness of Christ's presence. The Christ-centered thought of this devoted shepherd is seen in the following prayerful meditation.

> The tears of Jesus unite our world and show us how bound in a bundle we are. Jesus would have us share in his grief, and if we are his followers we shall not wish it otherwise. But those who share in the grief of Jesus are admitted to a share in his joy: his joy over one sinner who mends his ways, his joy over every cup of cold water given to a child who is in need, his joy over every act of true service to his heavenly Father and to mankind. We shall not ask, "Who is my neighbour?" My neighbour is Christ and Christ is everywhere.[80]

Dietrich Bonhoeffer (1906–1945)

Although he left behind no collection of devotional writings, Dietrich Bonhoeffer's popular books (in contrast to his scholarly theological works) are modern classics of devotion to Christ. They have been immensely important in the lives of innumerable Christians in the second half of the twentieth century. Bonhoeffer opened a way for Christians not only in his own time—one dominated by the most sinister of paganisms—but also for many living after his death. He proclaimed a powerful confession of the traditional devotion based on gratitude for salvation and redemption by Christ the Lord. He was also deeply aware of Christ's presence in everyday life.

Dietrich Bonhoeffer, who was a pastor of the German Lutheran Church, was favored with a childhood that was as bright as his last

---

[78] Arthur Michael Ramsey, *God, Christ and the World* (London: SCM Press, 1969), 41.

[79] Arthur Michael Ramsey, *Introducing the Christian Faith* (London: SCM Press, 1961), 44.

[80] Ramsey, *Canterbury Pilgrim*, 159.

years were dark.[81] He was born into a prominent and sophisticated family that was more or less Christian in what was then called the liberal and humanitarian tradition. His father was a distinguished professor of psychiatry in Breslau and later in Berlin.[82]

He came from a line of distinguished Lutheran pastors, and his grandfather had been chaplain to the emperor. At fourteen, Dietrich decided to study theology and was taught by a list of famous theologians at Tübingen, where he enjoyed the high opinion of teachers and students alike. In 1930, at the age of twenty-four, he began to lecture in systematic theology at the University of Berlin. He also went to Union Theological Seminary in New York, where Reinhold Niebuhr called him "a brilliant and theologically sophisticated young man".[83] His book *The Cost of Discipleship* (1937) spread his reputation in the theological world. After his death, this book took on the aspect of a very powerful affirmation of the Christian faith in the face of modern neopaganism and totalitarianism.

Following the rise of the Nazis, Bonhoeffer led an illegal training college for church workers, which functioned somewhat like a religious community. Bonhoeffer described the ideals of this community in his book *Life Together*. In 1934 he said that when war came, he would "pray to Christ to give me the power not to take up arms". While abroad he was counseled not to return to Germany. On his trip to America, Bonhoeffer wrote to Niebuhr:

> I shall have no right to participate in the reconstruction of Christian life in Germany after the war if I do not share the trials of this time with my people.... Christians in Germany will face the terrible alternative of either willing the defeat of their nation in order that Christian civilization may survive, or willing the victory of their nation and thereby destroying our civilization. I know which of these alternatives I must choose, but I cannot make this choice in security.[84]

Through friends he managed to avoid being called up for military service, and he continued to work for the Confessing Lutheran Church and his underground anti-Nazi activity. As the war turned against the Nazis, they became more vicious and visited their vengeance on those who made the slightest criticism or showed reluctance to support their cause. On April 5, 1943, Bonhoeffer, his sister, and brother-in-law were arrested. He so inspired his fellow prisoners and even his guards that they smuggled his papers and book on ethics out of the prison. He survived several bombings, and when the Gestapo prison in Berlin

[81] A summary of Bonhoeffer's life, "Memoir", is given by G. Leibholz in Bonhoeffer's *The Cost of Discipleship* (New York: Macmillan, 1963).

[82] It is interesting to note that the equally devout Edith Stein also was born at Breslau and met her death at the hands of the Nazis.

[83] Leibholz, "Memoir", 13.

[84] Ibid., 16.

was destroyed, he went to Büchenwald concentration camp and then to Flossenburg, where on April 9, 1945, a few weeks before the end of the war, he was executed on Himmler's orders. Other relatives were executed at the same time in other places.[85]

The central thesis of *The Cost of Discipleship* is the nature of the true Christian discipleship and the inescapable intense struggle between the world and the Gospel. The book is best known for Bonhoeffer's distinction between costly and cheap grace. His definition of costly grace can be seen as prophetic of his martyrdom.

> Costly grace is the Gospel which must be sought again and again, the gift which must be asked for, the door at which a man must knock.
>
> Such grace is costly because it calls us to follow, and it is grace because it calls us to follow Jesus Christ. It is costly because it costs a man his life, and it is grace because it gives a man the only true life. It is costly because it condemns sin, and grace because it justifies the sinner. Above all, it is costly because it cost God the life of His Son: "ye were bought at a price," and what has cost God much cannot be cheap for us. Above all, it is grace because God did not reckon His Son too dear a price to pay for our life, but delivered Him up for us. Costly grace is the Incarnation of God.[86]

We get the best insight into Bonhoeffer's personal relationship with Christ and his devotion from his little book *Life Together*, which was written in 1938, during the time he led the undercover Christian training school for anti-Nazi pastors. Community will thrive in any idealistic group of people endangered because of a threat by a common enemy. This will be all the more true when the members are bound together by a personal loyalty to Jesus. Despite all the skepticism generated by the search for the historical Jesus, Bonhoeffer saw Christ as the center of reality. In strangely prophetic words he writes:

> It is not in our life that God's help and presence must still be proved, but rather God's presence and help have been demonstrated for us in the life of Jesus Christ. It is in fact more important for us to know what God did to Israel, to His Son Jesus Christ, than to seek what God intends for us today. The fact that Jesus Christ died is more important than the fact that *I* shall die, and the fact that Jesus Christ rose from the dead is the sole ground of my hope that I, too, shall be raised on the Last Day. . . .
>
> In this light the whole devotional reading of the Scriptures becomes daily more meaningful and salutary. What we call our life, our troubles, our guilt, is by no means all of reality; there in the Scriptures is

[85] Ibid., 21.

[86] Bonhoeffer, *The Cost of Discipleship*, 47–48.

> our life, our need, our guilt, and our salvation. Because it pleased God to act for us there, it is only there that we shall be saved. Only in the Holy Scriptures do we learn to know our own history.[87]

For Bonhoeffer and presumably for his group of fervent students, praying together became an inspired experience. His writings on community and prayer are marked by a beautiful awareness of Christ's presence, an awareness that remained with him throughout his imprisonment, causing his fellow prisoners also to be aware of God's presence.[88]

Bonhoeffer examines the deepest Christian meaning of prayer and of confession and Communion. He begins with a profound sense that we are sinners who need confession, that we need to accept our sinfulness because Christ has accepted and taken our sins on Himself.

> It was none other than Jesus Himself who suffered the scandalous, public death of a sinner in our stead. He was not ashamed to be crucified for us as an evildoer. It is nothing else but our fellowship with Jesus Christ that leads us to the ignominious dying that comes in confession, in order that we may in truth share in his Cross. The Cross of Jesus Christ destroys all pride. We cannot find the Cross of Jesus if we shrink from going to the place where it is to be found, namely, the public death of the sinner. And we refuse to bear the Cross when we are ashamed to take upon ourselves the shameful death of the sinner in confession. In confession we break through to the true fellowship of the Cross of Jesus Christ, in confession we affirm and accept our cross.[89]

Bonhoeffer is of great interest because he courageously went directly against the political correctness of his generation. He would make absolutely no compromise with evil. I don't think any Christians in Germany really agreed with Hitler, but many went along. No matter what the personal cost, however, Bonhoeffer would not. According to a close friend of his, Bonhoeffer believed that "the sin of respectable people reveals itself in flight from responsibility".[90] This is a sin in which Bonhoeffer would have no part.

Bonhoeffer's greatness was to offer a new and radical look at the faith convictions of the church, at life together, prayer, work, and the experience of Christ in the sacrament of His presence and forgiveness. All this was done in community. It was also done under the worst of circumstances, in the face of monumental evil and incredible peril. His example of vital and fervent personal devotion may have more meaning for Christians in the years to come than it has at present. If

[87] *Life Together*, trans. John W. Doberstein (New York: Harper and Row, 1976), 54.
[88] Ibid., 12–13.
[89] Ibid., 114.
[90] Ibid., 11.

that is true, he is still in the same prophetic role he assumed in his brief life.

Peter Marshall (1902–1949)

One of the most respected Protestant ministers of twentieth-century America was the Scottish-born Peter Marshall. Despite his short life of forty-seven years, he had a very successful career as a fervent, down-to-earth preacher, and he became chaplain to the United States Senate two years before his death. His devoted wife, Catherine, wrote his engaging biography, *A Man Called Peter*, and edited a book of his sermons, *Mr. Jones, Meet the Master.*[91]

In several ways, Peter Marshall departed from the profile of a mainline Protestant minister of his time. He grew up in Scotland amid poverty with an abusive, alcoholic stepfather. He came to the United States almost penniless and worked as a laborer. He was adopted by members of a church in Birmingham, Alabama, and through their generosity was able to attend the seminary. He was distinguished by his Scottish accent, keen wit, and, more important, by his personal friendship and familiarity with our Savior. The latter qualities eventually brought him to the pulpit of the prestigious New York Avenue Presbyterian Church, in Washington, D.C., and to the daily responsibility of opening the United States Senate meetings. At the time of his death the Washington *Evening Star* wrote: "Living and working in Washington only eleven years, the Reverend Dr. Peter Marshall nevertheless has left his mark upon the whole city. He was a man of contagious spirit, eager and alert, quick to see opportunities of service and to meet their challenge.... In classic language, he was a builder of the kingdom of God on this earth."

In the 1930s he was pastor at the Westminster Presbyterian Church in Atlanta. In the preface to *The Prayers of Peter Marshall*, Catherine Marshall writes: "Peter *knew* Christ was there, and he was somehow able to transmit that knowledge to the waiting congregation bowed before him. That was why hungry-hearted people would make almost any sacrifice to get to Westminster Church."[92]

Catherine Marshall also pointed out that her husband's great concern was for the homespun virtues of honesty, integrity, and goodness. This led to his eagerness for the United States to follow a righteous course in its dealings with the world. He was opposed to an understanding of American freedom that some would now consider simply as moral autonomy, and he repeatedly called Americans back to the basic realities of moral responsibility. The following prayer illustrates in Marshall's thinking the second important ingredient in devotion, which is the willingness to follow God's law.

---

[91] Both books have gone through many editions.

[92] *The Prayers of Peter Marshall*, ed. Catherine Marshall (New York: McGraw-Hill, 1954), 4.

> O Lord Jesus, I remember that Thou hast said, "Lay not up for yourselves treasures upon earth, where moth and rust doth corrupt...." O God, deliver me from falling in love with things. Help me rather to love people, to love principles, to love righteousness, to love Thee.... Help me to believe this. Help me to practice it, that I may find for myself that the promise is true, that all my needs shall be met....
>
> Help me to live the Christian life in daring faith and humble trust, that there may be worked out in me, even in me, Thy righteousness and goodness. With a sense of adventure, I make this prayer. Amen.[93]

The last component of devotion, which is trust, is illustrated by many of Peter Marshall's prayers. We assume that in the hours between his heart attack and death, these prayers of trust were with him as he consciously faced the possibility of death. The following brings his trust in Christ clearly into focus.

The Cry of the Human Heart

> Lord Jesus, Thou knowest the things that are trembling upon our lips, stirring in our hearts and along the corridors of our souls ... conforming to the distant pealing of an angelus, looking expectantly upward, making prayers without words.
>
> Hear us, we pray Thee, as we call upon Thee for help, for strength, for peace; for grace, for reassurance, for companionship; for love, pardon, for health, for salvation—for joy. Hear us, Lord Jesus. Amen.[94]

It is interesting to note that decades later the secularization of Western society and the idea of moral autonomy—life without moral responsibility—were frequently criticized by Popes John Paul II and Benedict XVI. Peter Marshall saw the paths that were open to the American people long before and expressed the challenge this way:

> The choice before us is plain: Christ or chaos, conviction or compromise, discipline or disintegration. I am rather tired of hearing about our rights and privileges as American citizens. The time is come, it is now, when we ought to hear about the duties and responsibilities of our citizenship. America's future depends on her accepting and demonstrating God's government.[95]

Elisabeth Elliot

One of the best-known twentieth-century Evangelical writers, whose twenty books seemed to grow more devotional over the decades, is Elisabeth Elliot. Apparently she did not set out to be a spiritual writer but was content with being the wife and co-missionary of her husband, James Elliot. As part of a group of young, zealous evangelical missionaries, they went to Ecuador to preach to the jungle tribes.

[93] Ibid., 17.
[94] Ibid., 67.
[95] Ibid.

Their carefully planned and courageous attempts to contact a hostile tribe, the Aucas, however, went terribly wrong and led to all five men of their group being killed in January 1955, leaving their wives and children grieving but faithful, not far away.

Elisabeth wrote a fascinating account of this experience in her book *Through Gates of Splendor*. She ends with descriptions of her winning the confidence of the Aucas and of her friendship with those who had killed her husband and the other missionaries, whom the natives believed to be cannibals intending to kill them. Biblical references abound in this moving account, as do quotations from the King James Bible, but there are only indirect references to personal devotion, which the reader must infer from her writings. There are, however, a number of revealing quotations from the writings of the young men as they prepared for their mission. For example, one, Roger Youderian, was struggling with a "dark night of the soul". His wife, Barbara, has written: "He was cleansed through the Spirit for the task that lay ahead of him and went with a happy, expectant mind and his heart full of joy."[96] He wrote in his diary: "I will die to self. I will begin to ask God to put me in a service of constant circumstances where to live Christ I must die to self. I will be alive unto God. That I may learn to love Him with my heart, mind, soul, and body."[97]

Just before he joined the others, Youderian wrote the following revealing verses.

> There is a seeking of honest love
> Drawn from a soul storm-tossed,
> A seeking for the gain of Christ,
> To bless the blinded, the beaten, the lost.
>
> Those who sought found Heavenly Love
> And were filled with joy divine,
> They walk today with Christ above
> ....[98]

He told his wife that he would finish the poem when he returned home.

On learning of her husband's death, Barbara Youderian wrote in her diary:

> God gave me this verse two days ago, Psalm 48:14, "For this God is our God for ever and ever; He will be our Guide even unto death." As I came face to face with the news of Roj's death, my heart filled

[96] Quoted in Elisabeth Elliot, *Through Gates of Splendor* (Carol Stream, Ill.: Tyndale House Publishers, 1996), 149.

[97] Quoted in ibid., 150.

[98] Quoted in ibid., 150.

> with praise. He was worthy of his home-going. Help me, Lord, to be both mummy and daddy. "To know wisdom and instruction."[99]

Elisabeth Elliot offers several glimpses of her husband's devotion, the devotion of a missionary intent on bringing the saving Gospel of Christ to those in darkness—a zeal reminiscent of St. Paul.

> Oh, the fullness, pleasure, sheer excitement of knowing God on earth! I care not if I never raise my voice again for Him, if only I may love Him, please Him. Mayhap in mercy He shall give me a host of children that I may lead them through the vast star fields to explore His delicacies whose finger ends set them to burning. But if not, if only I may see Him, touch His garments, and smile into His eyes—ah, then, not stars nor children shall matter, only Himself.
>
> O Jesus, Master and Center and End of all, how long before that Glory is thine, which has so long waited Thee? Now there is not thought of Thee among men; then there shall be thought for nothing else. Now other men are praised; then none shall care for any other's merits. Hasten, hasten, Glory of Heaven, take Thy crown, subdue Thy Kingdom, enthrall Thy creatures.[100]

We must look now at the faith experience of Elisabeth Elliot herself in light of all that happened. She is the only person written of in this book who is still alive at the time of my writing. With admirable spiritual realism she pondered the death of her husband and the other missionaries. After briefly mentioning the tension and misunderstanding among those who were "picking up the pieces", she moves on to the theme that is central to her Christian experience—the absolute will and goodness of God and our need to accept this mystery.[101] Although her experience of faith is expressed in biblical terms it is not presented in a particularly devotional way. The following lines express a profound realistic faith, but not in devotional terms.

> It is not the level of our spirituality that we can depend on. It is God and nothing less than God, for the work is God's and the call is God's and everything is summoned by Him and to His purposes, the whole scene, the whole mess, the whole package—our bravery and our cowardice, our love and our selfishness, our strengths and our weaknesses. . . .
>
> We are not always sure where the horizon is. We would not know which end is up were it not for the shimmering pathway of light falling on the white sea. The One who laid earth's foundations and settled its dimensions knows where the lines are drawn. He gives all the light we need for trust and for obedience.[102]

---

[99] Quoted in ibid., 231.

[100] Quoted in Elliot, *Through Gates of Splendor*, 250–51.

[101] Elliot, *Through Gates of Splendor*, 266.

[102] Ibid., 267–68.

Elisabeth gives us an even more explicit insight into her own spiritual experience of the missionaries' deaths. Although it was a tragedy by any human reckoning, she sees by faith an entrance into eternal life through "gates of splendor". Writing of the native people, she says:

> Their story, at the time of the deaths of the men, later when I lived with the Indians themselves, and during all the years since as I have recounted it and reflected on it in the light of my own subsequent experience, has pointed to one thing: God is God. If He is God, He is worthy of my worship and my service. I will find rest nowhere but in His will, and that will is infinitely, immeasurably, unspeakably beyond my largest notions of what He is up to....
>
> God is the God of human history, and He is at work continuously, mysteriously, accomplishing His eternal purposes in us, through us, for us, and in spite of us.[103]

Elisabeth Elliot does not accept easy answers, and she is down to earth when she cites the words of Job in struggling to come to a resolution. However, she moves on from Job to cite a Catholic mystic we have met earlier: Julian of Norwich, with her signature quotation. Julian believed that the Lord said to her, "All shall be well, and all shall be well, and every manner of thing shall be well."

It is worth noting that in her earliest account of the five young martyrs Elisabeth does not do what Christian mystical writers from St. Francis to Dag Hammarskjöld have done: to see their suffering through the prism of the Passion and death of Christ. While there are many references to Christ as Son of God and Savior, this account of a brave and deeply believing Christian does not reveal an ostensible impulse to find meaning and solace in this traditional way. There is no indication of identification with the Crucified.

It is only fair, then, to see how she has developed her thought over the years, when she lived through the death of her second husband, who was a devout Evangelical like Jim. Writing in 1989, she gave her more developed reflections on trust in God in a collection of informal essays with the thought-provoking title *On Asking God Why*. She begins with the powerful statements of faith we found at the end of her first book thirty years before: "God does many things that we do not understand".[104] Elisabeth writes much more about the experienced presence of God in her later books. As her second husband, Addison Leitch, began the long painful road of death by cancer, Elisabeth could write:

> My questions were not answered, but I wanted to "see" God, to know Him. So I kept on reading the Book, kept trying to apply it to my life,

[103] Ibid., 263.

[104] Elisabeth Elliot, *On Asking God Why* (Grand Rapdis, Mich.: Revell, 1989), 11.

> kept bringing my own thinking and conduct under its authority, seeking God's meaning in every event that touched me, including Jim's death and other crises. As God had promised, his Word proved true. He instructed me. He kept me. He held me. He showed me all I *needed* to know for life and godliness, although he did not unfold all I *wanted* to know for understanding.[105]

Elisabeth then looks at various aspects of the problem of evil. Her thinking very much parallels St. Augustine's statement: "God does not cause evil, but He causes that evil should not become the worst." She struggles with the idea of evil, as any Christian might, and finds great meaning, as one would expect, in Christ's words about evil on the eve of His Passion and death (Jn 14:30–31ff.). The mystery of evil is summed up well in these words: "The world's prince has power. That power does not nullify the will of the Father (it is still in effect), or defeat the obedience of the Son (he will go straight into the jaws of death). Nevertheless, the will of the Father, plus the obedience of the Son, plus the power of evil equaled the crucifixion. *The world must be shown.* Through that hideous punishment the world would be shown two things: the Son's love and his absolute obedience." She then revealingly concludes. "The powers of hell can never prevail against the soul that takes its stand on God and on His Word. This kind of faith overcomes the world. . . . We (you and I) must show them what Jesus showed the world on that dark day so long ago—that we love the Father and will do what he says."[106]

We have repeatedly mentioned that the most appropriate reaction to the experience of God's love is to trust Him completely. Along with an awareness of God's presence and a willingness to obey His commandments, we must trust Him. Elliot brings that out very well in the last lines of this passage: "Letting go of what the world calls safety and surrendering to the Lord is our insurance of fulfillment. Christ knew his Father and offered himself unreservedly into his hands. If we let ourselves be lost for his sake, trusting the same God as Lord of all, we shall find safety where Christ found his, in the bosom of the Father."[107]

In keeping with our description of devotion, we can see that over the years and amid many struggles Elisabeth came to a profound awareness not only of the divine presence but also of Christ's love for humanity. It was not that she ever doubted that, but this emphasis on love and trust is the key element in understanding devotion. She writes:

> Whatever dark tunnel we may be called upon to travel through, God has been there. . . . Faith is not merely "feeling good about God" but

[105] Ibid., 140–41.
[106] Ibid., 142–43.
[107] Ibid., 143.

a conscious choice, even in the utter absence of feelings or external encouragements, to obey his Word when he says, "Trust me."...

Does he love us? *No, no, no* is what our circumstances seem to say. We cannot deduce the fact of His unchanging love from the evidence we see around us. Things are a mess. Yet to turn our eyes back to the cross of Calvary is to see the irrefutable proof that has stood all the tests of the ages: "It is by this that we know what love is: that Christ laid down his life for us" (John 3:16 NEB).[108]

The three elements of Christian devotion are obviously found in Elisabeth's experience—a deep awareness of Christ's presence, obedience (especially as acceptance of God's mysterious will), and trust. In a conversation with Dr. Timothy George, I mentioned that in some Evangelical preaching there is a lack of the strong affective (emotional, if you will) expression we find in writers from St. Augustine and St. Francis to contemporary African-American Protestants. He suggested that this may reflect a certain historical holdover, a reaction typical of the old austere Calvinist approach. There is much evidence that this is true. Perhaps the real differences are not based on theology but on cultural and national personality traits and how different groups experience life and relationships. Elisabeth Elliot demonstrates that the Christian experience is essentially the same for all: presence, obedience, and trust.

Christ Found in Diversity

The amazing diversity of those who are called Protestants has been illustrated by this selection of remarkable spiritual people in the twentieth century. From Pentecostals like the Reverend Seymour to the Archbishop of Canterbury, we find a common thread of personal devotion to Christ. Sometimes this is expressed sentimentally and at others with great erudition and willpower; it is found consistently in the best and most effective Protestant writings. As we move on to the Catholics of the twentieth century, we will again see that there are parallels and similarities that cannot be overlooked. It is unfortunate that historians of Protestantism like Sydney Ahlstrom and Mark Noll generally have avoided an assessment of the devotional aspects of Protestantism. Because Catholics tend to identify their most representative members from among canonized saints, there is more emphasis on devotion in Catholic historical studies.

James Moore's recent book (see Chapter 20 above) illustrates the importance of prayerful devotion in the history of our country. Although he does not confine his book to Protestants, they are most frequently cited because they have been the dominant religious group in American history almost up to the present time.

[108] Elliot, *On Asking God Why*, 149.

25 The Twentieth-Century Orthodox Experience of Christ

The twentieth century brought momentous changes and challenges to the Orthodox Church and the churches that comprise Eastern Christianity, including the ancient Oriental Orthodox churches and the churches in communion with Rome. In the first decades of the century, the Ottoman Empire, under which the churches in the East had struggled to survive for centuries, was dismantled by the victorious allies of World War I. At almost the same time, Bolshevik Communism came to power, aiming its militant atheism directly at the Russian Orthodox Church.

The enormous struggle of the Orthodox Church to survive in Soviet Russia is yet to be fully told. The struggles of other churches in Eastern Europe, having more communication outside the Soviet empire, are historically better known. However, a relatively small community of Russian émigrés—about a hundred thousand people—have provided a fascinating example of the survival and triumph of the Christian faith over the appalling onslaught of militant atheism. In an interesting series of short biographies of important Russian Orthodox émigrés, Michael Plekon gives us a kaleidoscope of devout Christians who lived through "the greatest turmoil of the twentieth century: the Russian Revolution, emigration forced and voluntary, the Great Depression, the death and terror of World War II . . . the Iron Curtain, the cold war, and the bomb".[1]

One of the most interesting people in this group is Mother Maria Skobtsova, canonized by the Holy Synod of the Ecumenical Patriarchate in 2004, along with her son, George Skobtsov, and Fr. Dimitri Klepinine, all of whom died together at the hands of the Nazis.

Mother Maria Skobtsova (1891–1945)

Mother Maria (Elizabeth Pilenko), who lived a life of great charity and love for the poor, had an intense spirituality and died in the Nazi gas chambers at the end of the war. In her youth she was an aspiring poet, a gifted iconographer and craftswoman, and a theological student at a

[1] Michael Plekon, *Living Icons* (Notre Dame, Ind.: University of Notre Dame Press, 2002), 1.

time when that was a rarity for women. She was also put on trial during the revolution by the imperial White Army for being a Communist sympathizer. Later she was nearly executed by the Bolsheviks as a counterrevolutionary. She married young and impulsively but later divorced. On her way into exile, she married again—this time to the judge who had tried her as a Communist sympathizer. After the death of her second husband she lived in poverty in Paris, where she came under the influence of Orthodox scholars who had gathered at the St. Sergius Theological Institute.

In 1932, she obtained the permission of Metropolitan Evlogy to become a nun without a cloister while working for the poor, and she founded several small residences for the needy. Her writings were in some ways similar to those of Dorothy Day and Catherine Doherty. She saw our lives in the sharp perspective of the Gospel, based on love of God and realistic love of neighbor, especially the poor. Having become a nun she saw the life of love of God and service to neighbor as a singular Christian vocation.[2] "At the Last Judgment I will not be asked whether I satisfactorily practiced asceticism, nor how many prostrations and bows I have made before the holy table. I will be asked whether I fed the hungry, clothed the naked, visited the sick and the prisoner in jail. That is all I will be asked."[3]

It may be said that Mother Maria had a phobia about unearthly piety. She saw the Church as Christ at work in the world.

> Christ, in ascending into heaven, did not raise with himself the Church on earth. He did not halt the course of history. Christ left the Church in the world and the Church has remained as a small portion of the yeast which makes the entire dough rise. Put differently, within the limits of history, Christ has given the whole world to the Church and she has no right to refuse to spiritually lift the world, to transfigure it. And for this, the Church needs a powerful army, and this is monasticism.[4]

A Church reformer in the tradition of St. Catherine of Siena, Mother Maria left in her unpublished writings a penetrating analysis of the problems of Christians. Plekon gives an insightful summary of her criticisms of deficient types of religious life. They included synodal piety or mere observance of rubrics in vogue in the Orthodox Church before the Russian Revolution. Many felt that the Bolshevik opposition to religion was due in large part to this kind of cold mechanical piety, which did little for one's neighbor.

---

[2] Ibid., 60.

[3] T. Stratton Smith, *Rebel Nun* (Springfield, Ill.: Templegate, 1965), 135, quoted in ibid., 60.

[4] Hélène Arjakovsky-Klépinine, *Le Sacrement du frère* (Paris: Cerf, 1995), 126, quoted in Plekon, *Living Icons*, 61.

She was also critical of what she called ritualism, an excessive attention to the details of rubrics without sufficient attention to the meaning of the Eucharist. She calls this "liturgy ripped out of life". She writes: "Instead of the living God, instead of Christ crucified and risen, do we not have here a new idol, a new form of paganism which is manifested in arguments over calendars, rubrics, rules, prohibitions and the Sabbath which triumphs over the Son of Man.".[5]

She also had some tough words for those who were involved in aesthetic Christianity, religion concerned only with a beautiful presentation of faith. This criticism was from someone who even in the Ravensbruck concentration camp was able to paint a beautiful icon. She was by no means against the appreciation of beauty, but she was against beauty becoming an idol. She was also critical of ascetics, who see religion largely as a collection of penitential practices and who tend to compete with one another.

Deeply devoted to Jesus Christ, Mother Maria saw the whole of life's purpose to be His disciple. In Eastern Christianity, there is an explicit emphasis, but it is not so obvious in the West: this is the process of Christification, or becoming one with Christ. Generally, in Protestantism and Catholicism it is seen as a most earnest form of discipleship, based on St. Paul's words "[I]t is no longer I who live, but Christ who lives in me" (Gal 2:20). Christification in the Eastern tradition is a more dramatic and explicit expression of this process. It probably refers to the unitive way and to the transforming union. About this true goal of Christian life Mother Maria says:

> "Christification" is based on the words, "It is no longer I who live, but Christ who lives in me." The image of God, the icon of Christ which truly is my real and actual essence is the only measure of things, the only way given to me.... Christ gave us two commandments: to love God and to love our fellow man. Everything else, even the Beatitudes, are merely elaborations of the two commandments which contain within themselves the totality of Christ's Good News.[6]

Mother Maria's attempt to form a monastic community was not successful. The exception was Fr. Klepinine, her chaplain, who died with her in the concentration camp. Archbishop Anthony Bloom, who will be our next subject, wrote of her: "Mother Maria is a saint of our day and for our day, a woman of flesh and blood possessed by the love of God, who stood fearlessly face-to-face with the problems of our century."[7]

---

[5] *Sourozh* 75:15, quoted in Plekon, *Living Icons*, 68.

[6] Ibid., 76:26–27, 74.

[7] Fr. Sergei Hackel, *Pearl of Great Price* (Crestwood, N.Y.: St. Vladimir's Seminary Press, 1981), xi–xii, quoted in *Living Icons*, 80.

St. Maria Skobtsova joins the great Christian women of the twentieth century—Elisabeth Elliot, Dorothy Day, Catherine Doherty, and Mother Teresa of Calcutta. It is easy to draw parallels between this exuberant extroverted nun who loved solitude and the quiet, gentle Mother Teresa, whose vocation brought her before the world. They were very different personalities, but they were both touched by the same profound love of Christ, whom they served in their fellow human beings even in times of great darkness.

Archbishop Anthony Bloom

Into the chaos of cultural uprooting, religious persecution, and philosophical skepticism André Borisovich Bloom (Metropolitan Anthony) was born in Switzerland in 1914.[8] On his mother's side of the family, he was related to the famous Russian composer Aleksandr Scriabin. His maternal grandfather, Nikolai Scriabin, was in the diplomatic service, which took him and his wife, Olga, to various foreign posts. Their daughter, Xenia, was Archbishop Anthony's mother. His father, Boris Edwardovich Bloom, son of a distinguished physician with Dutch and Scottish ancestry, was a diplomat in Persia when the revolution of 1917 ended the Russian imperial government. A strange footnote to this brief family history is that André was a distant relative of Vyacheslav Mikhailovich Scriabin, an infamous Bolshevik who became known by his revolutionary name of "The Hammer"—Molotov. He signed the Nazi-Soviet alliance that brought together the two evil empires in the years before World War II.[9]

In 1920, after the Russian Revolution, André, his mother, and grandmother tried to make their way to England but ended up, providentially, in Vienna and later in Paris, where they became part of the destitute Russian émigré community. The greatest of their sufferings was that all three lived separately, wedged into the only quarters they could obtain with their meager means. Young and impressionable, André suffered much. A deplorable incident took place when he was refused admission to a Catholic boarding school because he was not willing to convert to Catholicism. This unfortunately colored his view of the Catholic Church for the rest of his life. Gradually as the Blooms' circumstances improved, he was able to go to better schools and his family found an apartment, in which he had a precious private room. Although he had no memory of life in Russia, he remained an outsider to the French and gravitated toward the many cultural and political currents sponsored by the émigré community, beginning with Russian-speaking Boy Scouts. A brilliant student, he eventually decided to study medicine.

The Blooms were only marginally involved with the Russian Orthodox Church as it sought to establish itself in Paris, and André resisted

[8] See Gillian Crow, *'This Holy Man'* (London: Darton, Longman and Todd, 2005), chap. 1.

[9] Ibid., 10.

any involvement or attendance, even at Good Friday services. By the time he was fourteen, he considered himself an atheist, but then a fascinating event took place that would alter his life forever. The Russian youth group he belonged to held a lecture by a priest from the recently founded St. Sergius Institute, in Paris.[10] André was completely repulsed by the talk and came home angry at having wasted his time. He asked his mother for a book of the Gospels so that he might verify in its pages what the priest had said and thereby dismiss Christianity forever as a worthless pursuit. He read the Gospel of St. Mark because it is the shortest, and his account of what followed makes a fascinating contribution to the history of Christian religious experience. He has given it several times, always with the same details.

> While I was reading the beginning of St. Mark's Gospel, before I reached the third chapter, I suddenly became aware that on the other side of my desk there was a presence. And the certainty was so strong that it was Christ standing there that it has never left me. This was the real turning point. Because Christ was alive and I had been in his presence I could say with certainty that what the Gospel said about the crucifixion of the Prophet of Galilee was true, and the centurion was right when he said, "Truly he is the Son of God." It was in the light of the Resurrection that I could read with certainty the story of the Gospel, knowing that everything was true in it because the impossible event of the Resurrection was to me more certain than any event of history. History I had to believe, the Resurrection I knew for a fact. I did not discover, as you see, the Gospel beginning with its first message of the Annunciation, and it did not unfold for me as a story which one can believe or disbelieve. It began an as event that left all problems of disbelief behind because it was a direct and personal experience.[11]

A different description of this event stressed God's personal love.

> Another thing that struck him from his first reading of the gospels was that God's love was so limitless that in Christ he was prepared to share every part of the human condition in order to redeem it—even that most terrible consequence of human sin: the loss of God from which humanity dies. In his cry from the cross, "My God, my God, why hast thou forsaken me?" Christ himself had experienced the terrifying separation from the divine presence that is the common lot of fallen humanity, and he had descended into hell.[12]

When asked whether his conviction of faith remained or whether he was troubled with doubts, he answered:

---

[10] Ibid., 40ff.

[11] Archbishop Anthony Bloom, *Beginning to Pray* (New York: Paulist Press, 1970), 10.

[12] Crow, *'This Holy Man'*, 42.

> I became absolutely certain within myself that Christ is alive and that certain things existed. I didn't have all the answers, but having touched that experience, I was certain that ahead of me there were answers, visions, possibilities. This is what I mean by faith—not doubting in the sense of being in confusion and perplexity, but doubting in order to discover the reality of the life, the kind of doubt that makes you want to question and discover more, that makes you want to explore.[13]

Archbishop Anthony kept his experience secret, but people could see that he had changed. He began to go to church, do good deeds, read the Gospels, and pray. No one took notice of this, as he was still a teenager. He examined various churches, and his study confirmed him in Orthodoxy because "its teaching and experience accorded most closely with the truth and beauty of the Gospel as he understood it".[14] When he was seventeen, he met Archimandrite Afanasy, a monk exiled from the monastery of Valaamo, whom he chose as his spiritual director. Fr. Afanasy was perfect for that role, having himself been converted initially by a Salvation Army officer, and later finding his vocation as an Orthodox monk.[15]

We must remember that one can be an Orthodox monk without belonging to a specific monastery. Such a man must be prepared by a spiritual director to embrace monastic vows and to live the Gospel life. It is always the initial intention of monks to live together in a monastery in relative seclusion and prayer. However, because of the pastoral needs of Orthodox Christians after the 1917 revolution, the vast majority of monks have been ordained to the priesthood and taken on pastoral responsibilities.[16]

The ecclesiastical situation for Russian Orthodox Christians in exile was confused and problematic following the revolution. Few wanted to be affiliated with the Moscow patriarchate, which they felt was controlled by the Soviet government. The position of Orthodox bishops within Russia was sometimes described as that of birds in a gilded cage. They had to endure great humiliation and subjugation in order to keep the Orthodox Church alive under Communism. Many clergy and laity, however, believed that their bishops had betrayed Orthodoxy. Metropolitan Evlogy, the Russian bishop in Paris before 1917, left the jurisdiction of the Moscow patriarchate, placing himself under the Ecumenical Patriarch of Constantinople. He returned to the Moscow patriarchate with part of his flock in 1945. Only one parish in Western Europe—the one to which Fr. Afanasy belonged—remained loyal to the Moscow patriarchate. Among its members was Vladimir Lossky, who believed that Christian unity could be achieved only

[13] Bloom, *Beginning to Pray*, 10–11.
[14] Crow, *'This Holy Man'*, 44.
[15] See Plekon, *Living Icons*, pp. 149ff.
[16] Ibid., 46.

through the Orthodox faith and its growth in the West. Along with others of similar views, therefore, he was eager to see Orthodoxy shed its Russian or Greek appearance and become known to Westerners in ways comprehensible to them. Eventually the liturgy was celebrated in French in the Church of the Three Hierarchs, in Paris.

Into this group Fr. Afanasy introduced the young André Bloom, who would thrive in its atmosphere. Many years later Archbishop Anthony described Fr. Afanasy: "He was luminous, reflecting the glory of God; a profound yet very simple man, not a saint, just a man of our times—but a man who was free, with that incomparable, sovereign freedom of which Christ speaks."[17]

André received his medical degree, becoming a general practitioner, and at the same time became increasingly responsible for the support of his mother and grandmother. Despite all this, he looked into studying for the priesthood at St. Sergius Institute, hoping to manage both responsibilities simultaneously. While at the Sorbonne he had read the Church Fathers and was particularly moved by St. Theophan the Recluse (see Chapter 18 above). Dostoievsky and Maurice Curie, nephew of Madame Curie, also influenced him. From the latter he learned to see physics as "deep and vast, a harmony full of meaning and beauty".[18]

During the war years André Bloom struggled to be a monk, living in Nazi-occupied Paris and working in a military hospital. His early encounter with Christ in his room while reading the Gospel continued to lead him on his way.

Many years later, Archbishop Anthony summed up his spiritual insights and beliefs, which are rooted deeply in the Gospel. He had asked himself: "If God is all-powerful, if he is the Lord of all, I can indeed worship him. I can fear him. Perhaps I can even love him. But can I respect him, can I see in him someone who is worthy of being respected?"

His answer came from his reading of the Gospel:

> Yes, I can respect a God who has not created us irresponsibly. This God, having created a world that it might be in glory and partake in his own life, such that one day all creatures should be united to him and he should be all in all, has not created us with the dread gift of freedom and then left us to perish and to come one day to be judged. But he has entered into history and carried in his human life the cross of the whole created world that had fallen away, and he has paid the cost of his act of creation and the cost of his giving us freedom. And I felt therefore that I could love him with veneration and respect, and not simply because of an impulsive movement of my heart.[19]

[17] Ibid., 49.

[18] Ibid., 55.

[19] Ibid., 42–43.

It is important to remember that André, having lived privately as a monk for some time, was ordained a priest of the Orthodox Church without completing seminary studies. In modern times this is unusual. However, the fact that he had never been a seminarian makes much of his life and career as a bishop more comprehensible. During his years as metropolitan in England, many of his attitudes suggest that he was more monk than priest. It seems to have been his monastic convictions rather than his priestly virtues that engendered most of the criticisms levelled at him. A good priest, well honed by seminary life, is like Cardinal Newman's "gentleman"—someone who does not cause pain or embarrassment to others. A cleric, even a tough one, has to be careful not to hurt the feelings of others. After all, he is not only a servant of God but a servant of the people.

These qualities—relatively unimportant for a monk—sometimes seem to be lacking in Archbishop Bloom. As Archbishop of England, he dutifully fulfilled his responsibilities in creative and determined ways. He often failed, however, to show the polish and deference that clergy learn in any worthwhile seminary.

Fr. Anthony's Priesthood

After the war, André continued his medical work, becoming well known for his kind treatment of the dying, often sitting vigil with them through the night. He had not, however, forgotten his early desire to be a priest. A number of friends urged him to pursue the priesthood, and the shortage of priests was acute in the postwar years. Others felt he ought to stay where he was, including his mother, who was opposed to his exchanging a promising medical career for the low status of a priest. Eventually he was ordained a deacon, which precipitated his entrance into the priesthood in an almost comical manner. Deacons in the Orthodox Church need musical ability and good singing voices. André had neither. The bishop asked the parish priest how long he wanted André to remain a deacon. "As short a time as possible", the priest answered. "He's ruining the choir every time he opens his mouth!"[20]

He was duly ordained to the priesthood, his monastic vows became public, and he assumed his monastic name of Anthony. He was assigned to celebrate the Liturgy at a home for elderly Russians.[21] Because of his linguistic skills he was able to do so in both French and Slavonic, which endeared him to many.

In 1949, he and his mother moved to England, where there was a great need for Orthodox priests who belonged to the Moscow patriarchate. Early on he established a warm, positive relationship with the Anglican Church, which continued for the rest of his life. Unfortunately, his relations with the Catholic Church remained poor, but he

[20] Ibid., 89.

[21] In the Orthodox Church, "Liturgy" is used as the equivalent of the Western term "holy Mass".

learned that he had something in common with Evangelical Protestants. It is surprising that he got on badly with Catholics at that time, since relations between the two churches in the United States during those years improved greatly.

His relationship with the Russian Orthodox Church in England was also difficult. The Anglicans required both the Patriarchal Church and the Church-in-Exile to share one building, St. Philip's. The pastor of the Church in Exile, Fr. Vitaly, would rebless the church after it had been used by Fr. Anthony. One evening Fr. Anthony asked him how he saw him as a priest of the Moscow patriarchate. Fr. Vitaly is alleged to have answered: "I think you are an honest man, so I will be straight with you. If I wanted to be polite, I would say you are no priest. But as I want to be truthful, I will tell you what I think: you are a priest of Satan." [22]

This must have been very painful for Fr. Anthony, since his reasons for being loyal to the Moscow patriarchate did not involve any regard for the Bolsheviks. He believed, along with many others, that this was the historical and original jurisdiction and that those responsible for it were doing their best to keep the faith alive under very trying circumstances.

Archbishop of England

Metropolitan Anthony's career as Russian Orthodox Archbishop of England lasted for more than three decades, during which he oversaw a growing community of Russian immigrants to England and a steady trickle of English converts to the Orthodox Church. He was particularly active in ecumenical affairs with the Church of England and in many respects became the voice of Orthodoxy in Britain. His BBC broadcasts were well received, at home, in Eastern Europe and in Russia. His background as a physician and a monk prepared him for his role, and he was a gifted spontaneous speaker.

He was nonetheless a man of contradictions: an Orthodox bishop who could not sing, a monk who had never lived in a monastery, a man of kindness and charity who was impatient and abrupt, a man who charmed people as regularly as he hurt their feelings. Someone once remarked that there were two Archbishop Anthonys, to which someone else responded that there are "at least five!" [23]

How can all this be reconciled? At the center of his life was his early encounter with Christ. He consistently tried to see life as God's calling to each one through Christ. For him each human being was loved by God. There was no question that Christ was the center of his life.

> When the Lord Christ spoke to his disciples and to the crowds that surrounded him, he did not deliver a general teaching to be received

[22] Crow, *'This Holy Man'*, 103.

[23] Ibid., 243.

> by all in the terms he was using. Part of his teaching had a universal meaning, but part of those words of Christ which are recorded in the Gospel were spoken to one particular man in one particular situation. This man had to receive them as the word of God, because they were addressed to him. Others in the crowd might not have found in them an answer to their question. We must be attentive, when we read the Gospels, to those passages which first of all apply to us directly, in order to become doers of the will of God. There are passages in the Gospel which we understand intellectually; other passages which we do not understand. There are passages against which we rebel; there are passages which, in the words of St. Luke, "make our hearts burn within us". These words ... are spoken to us directly. We may assume that here the Lord Christ and we are of the same mind, understand one another, that these words of Christ tell us of what we already know from experience of life, and those are absolute commandments. Those words we must never forget. We must apply those words in our life at every moment. Whenever we fail to do so, we break our relationship with Christ, we turn away, we refuse the burden, the yoke of his discipleship.[24]

In considering the personality and life of Archbishop Anthony, it can be said that they come together and make sense in the light of Christ, who he knew "with certainty" had come to him and whom he worshipped with all his being. His life was one of sacrifice and success, of embracing contradictions that others could not understand. His inability to overcome his prejudice against the Roman Catholic Church is lamentable. An event that is in many ways unworthy of him occurred during Pope John Paul II's visit to England in 1982. At an ecumenical gathering, which Metropolitan Anthony attended reluctantly owing to his antipathy to the papacy, the Pope embraced him in a gesture of fraternal goodwill. Later the archbishop brushed off his sleeve, as if dismissing the Pope's embrace.[25]

Had Metropolitan Anthony known Pope John Paul II personally, perhaps the two might have got on well together. They were both larger than life and wholly dedicated to Christ. They both refused to make compromises with the Gospel message, and each was quite capable of admitting his faults. It is tragic that Archbishop Anthony did not get to know Pope John Paul II, himself a Slav and a pope who apologized to many people, including the Orthodox.

St. Maria and Archbishop Bloom are among many modern Orthodox writers and scholars who are dedicated to a theology and spirituality centered on Christ. Those familiar with the expressions of Eastern Christianity will be aware of this Christological emphasis. It

[24] Archbishop Anthony Bloom, *Meditations: A Spiritual Journey* (Denville, N.J.: Dimension Books, 1971), 17–18.

[25] Crow, *'This Holy Man'*, 176.

is interesting that in the early days of Christianity the eastern part of the empire was much more aware of its philosophical foundations, particularly concerning Plato and Aristotle. The ideas of both philosophers profoundly influenced the Church East and West, but they were certainly not Christological, nor could they have been. Without disparaging devotion to Christ in the West, it is nonetheless true that there exists an obvious strain of Christification in the Orthodox and Eastern traditions that is both profound and unique.

26 Catholics in the Twentieth Century

As the nineteenth century drew to a close, Catholics in Europe and America entered the middle class. The old world of peasants and aristocrats was dying, and increasing numbers of Catholic peasantry moved into towns and cities. It is one of the largely unrecognized accomplishments of the nineteenth century that most Catholic farmers and tradesmen kept their faith in London, New York, Boston, Philadelphia, and other urban areas. From these, they migrated to smaller cities and towns, and finally to the farms of the New World, becoming property owners and entrepreneurs. Everywhere the clergy as well as religious brothers and sisters encouraged education at every level. This immense change in the world of Catholics profoundly affected the way they expressed their devotion to Christ and the saints.

The most notable change was in the intellectual quality of devotion. Beginning with Newman, and even more with his confrere and fellow Oratorian Frederick William Faber, Catholic devotion became more intellectual but no less fervent and personal. Fr. Faber's thoughtful, deeply devotional works, especially *All For Jesus*, set the stage for twentieth-century piety. As we did with Protestant writers, we will do with Catholics and present a few select representatives to illustrate the various strands of Catholic devotion.

Two Great Catholic Thinkers of the Early Twentieth Century

Blessed Columba Marmion (1858–1923)

The revival of a strong Christocentric Catholicism, after the turbulence of the early nineteenth century, owes much to Faber in England, to the incredibly erudite and energetic Fr. Matthias Joseph Scheeben in Germany, and to Bishop Charles Gay in France. Above all, however, the greatest debt is owed to Dom Columba Marmion, abbot of Maredsous, in Belgium.[1]

Son of an Irish father and French mother, Joseph Marmion studied for the diocesan priesthood at Clonliffe in Dublin and later at Rome, where he was ordained in 1881 at the early age of twenty-three. Returning to Ireland that summer, he visited a friend who had just entered

[1] M. M. Philipon, O.P., *The Spiritual Doctrine of Dom Marmion*, trans. Dom Matthew Dillon, O.S.B. (Westminster, Md.: Newman Press, 1956), 11.

the recently founded Benedictine monastery at Maredsous in Belgium.[2] It was a decisive event for the young priest, in whom was awakened the call to monastic life. It was only in 1886, having served as parish priest and professor at Clonliffe, that Marmion, with the approval of the Archbishop of Dublin, was able to follow his vocation to Benedictine life and begin his novitiate at Maredsous.

Although half French, Marmion had to learn the language after entering the monastery.[3] Years later, when he came to publish books, they appeared first in French, since they were based largely on conferences and retreats given to his monks and others. He relied on the Benedictine nuns of Tyburn Convent to translate his works into English, which, thus available in the two principal languages of Europe, enjoyed a wide distribution and influence. His oft-quoted statement, "For me Jesus is everything", sums up his monumental spiritual works, the titles of which tell us much about the man and his thought. They read like a litany: *Christ, the Life of the Soul*; *Christ in His Mysteries*; *Christ, the Ideal of the Priest*; *Christ, the Ideal of the Monk*.[4]

Dom Columba's spiritual doctrine rests completely on the Bible, especially the New Testament, particularly the Gospels and St. Paul. He was imbued with the scriptural interpretations of the Church Fathers and the early councils, and these found expression in his own goal: "to live as a child of the heavenly Father".[5] In fact, to be a child of God in union with Christ and to live in a way expressive of that salvation encapsulates Marmion's spiritual doctrine.

Completely centered on Christ, he was concerned always, in his teaching, conferences, retreat work, and spiritual correspondence, to bring others to a Christocentric fidelity and devotion: "The more I read Holy Scripture, the more I live the liturgy, the more clearly I see that one thought reigns supreme: Christ is the very centre of Creation."[6]

This was no mere pious thought. His monumental books, conferences, and spiritual correspondence are all centered on the goal of becoming a true child of God by adoption through the grace of baptism. He notes that baptism initiates us into the dead and risen Christ and leads us to the double character of the Christian life: death to sin and life for God. "According to [St. Paul], baptism represents the death and resurrection of Christ Jesus, and it produces

---

[2] Maredsous had been founded in 1872 from the German abbey of Beuron.

[3] Mark Tierney, O.S.B., *Dom Columba Marmion: A Biography* (Dublin: Columba Press, 1994), 56.

[4] In addition to individual titles mentioned in this chapter, some of which are no longer in print, see Dom Columba Marmion, O.S.B., *Spiritual Writings* (Paris: P. Lethielleux, 1998), which contains in one volume *Christ, the Life of the Soul*; *Christ in His Mysteries*; *Christ, the Ideal of the Monk;* and a selection of his English letters.

[5] Dom Raymund Thibaut, *Abbot Columba Marmion: A Master of the Spiritual Life*, trans. Mother Mary St. Thomas (London: Sands, 1932), 386.

[6] Marmion, Conference to the Benedictine nuns of Maredret (Apr. 22, 1914), quoted in Philipon, *Spiritual Doctrine*, 18.

that which it represents: it makes us die to sin, and grants us to live in Jesus Christ."[7]

In addition to being baptized into the life and death of Christ, the Christian is reconciled to the Father, becomes co-heir with Christ of eternal life, and participates in the life of the Trinity. For this reason Marmion's life was centered on the New Testament. As a seminary student he had learned by heart all the Pauline epistles and retained them in memory all his life. Apart from St. Paul, he quoted St. John most often. He had little interest in the critical approach to the Bible, which was coming into vogue during his youth. His later study of the theology of St. Thomas Aquinas did not overshadow his original biblically based study of the Christian spiritual life. He used the Latin Vulgate of St. Jerome and continued to memorize long passages of the Old as well as the New Testaments. He generally cites the Scriptures in Latin, which makes reading his books a bit awkward today, since most readers must keep a Bible translation at hand.

In 1893, the young monk made several notes on the conferences during the community retreat. He recorded that the retreat's "chief fruit was a great desire to make Jesus my only love". His early biographer, Dom Raymund Thibaut, comments: "[T]his fruit of the retreat was to ripen. The thought of Jesus took greater and greater hold of him; it was little by little to take full possession of the monk's soul so generously given up to the divine action. At this period of his monastic life, the 'lights' that visited him were more and more directed towards the thought that Jesus is the Alpha and Omega of all spiritual life."[8]

In *Christ and His Mysteries*, Marmion presents a theological doctrine of the spiritual life. Not only do Christians, when reading his works, readily agree with and accept his teachings, but his articulation of the truths of faith is so well developed that his words provide food for many years' meditation.

> [L]ove for His Father was the underlying motive power of every act in the life of the Incarnate Word. At the moment of completing His work, Christ declares to His Apostles that it is because He loves His Father that He is about to deliver Himself up: *Ut cognoscat mundus quia diligo Patrem* [that the world may know that I love the Father] (John 14:31). In that wonderful prayer which He then makes, Jesus says that He has accomplished His work which was to glorify His Father upon earth: *Ego te clarificavi super terram; opus consummavi quod dedisti mihi ut faciam* [I glorified thee on earth, having accomplished the work which thou gavest me to do] (John 17:4)....
>
> But His love for the Father is not the only love with which Christ's Heart beats. He loves us too and in an infinite manner. It was veritably

[7] *Christ, the Life of the Soul*, trans. Alan Bancroft (Bethesda, Md.: Zaccheus Press, 2005), 205.

[8] Thibaut, *Abbot Columba Marmion*, 94.

> for us that He came down from heaven, in order to redeem us and save us from death.... For us He became incarnate, was born at Bethlehem, and lived in the obscurity of a life of toil. For us He preached and worked miracles, died and rose again. For us He ascended into heaven and sent the Holy Spirit. He still remains in the Eucharist for us, for love of us. Christ, says St. Paul, loved the Church and delivered Himself up for her that He might purify and sanctify her and win her to Himself (Ephesians 5:27).
>
> So then, Jesus lived all His mysteries for us, in order to give us to be one day where He is, by right, in the glory of His Father.... His immolation was but the crowning point of the mysteries of His earthly life. It was for me, because He loved me, that He accomplished all things.[9]

It is important to note that even with his exalted emphasis on Christ in union with the Father and the Trinity, Marmion never loses sight of Christ's humanity. He writes:

> Christ has passed through divers states. He has been a Child, a Youth, a Doctor of the truth, a Victim upon the Cross, He has been glorious in His Resurrection and His Ascension: in thus traversing all the successive stages of His earthly existence, He has sanctified all human life.
>
> But there is one essential state which He never leaves: He is always "the Only-begotten Son Who is in the bosom of the Father" [Jn 1:18].[10]

The high and beautiful spiritual doctrine of Blessed Columba is summed up in his great act of consecration to the Holy Trinity.

Consecration to the Blessed Trinity

Eternal Father,
prostrate in humble adoration at your feet,
we consecrate our whole being
to the glory of your Son Jesus, the Incarnate Word.
You have established him King of our souls.
Bring our souls, our hearts, our bodies
into submission to him;
and let nothing in us move
without his orders, without his inspiration.
United with him
may we be brought into communion with you,
and perfected in the unity of your Love.

[9] *Christ in His Mysteries*, trans. Mother M. St. Thomas (St. Louis: B. Herder, 1939), 11–12.

[10] Ibid., 35.

Jesus,
Unite us to you in your life of perfect holiness,
wholly consecrated to your Father and to souls.
Be "our wisdom, our justice, our sanctification, our redemption,"
our *all.*
Sanctify us in the truth.
Holy Spirit,
Love of the Father and the Son,
establish yourself as a furnace of love in the center of our hearts,
and bear constantly upwards, like burning flames,
our thoughts, our affections, our actions, to communion *on high*
with the Father.
May our whole life be
a *Gloria Patri et Filio et Spiritui Sancto.*

Mary, Mother of Christ, Mother of holy love,
form us
according to the heart of your Son.

Dom Marmion's knowledge of the spiritual life and his wide experience of souls were the fruit of long years of prayer and fidelity to Christ—in Pauline terms, knowing Christ Jesus—as seminarian, priest, and monk. It is no surprise, therefore, that he was in demand as a retreat master, and he traveled frequently through Belgium, France, England, and Ireland for that purpose.

In 1909, at a little past fifty, he was elected abbot of Maredsous, becoming responsible for a community of well over a hundred monks, and two thriving schools. By then his spiritual reputation was set, and his election was taken almost for granted. "The community recognized that they had in Marmion a man who was a master of the spiritual life, and capable of providing them with a spiritual leadership." [11] His years as abbot were not easy. In addition to the heavy responsibilities mentioned, there were several trips to Rome on business for the Benedictines, and his health was frequently poor. During the war years monastic as well as civilian life was disrupted in occupied Belgium. Seventeen monks of Maredsous who were German nationals were forced from the monastery and returned to Germany in 1914.[12] Maredsous received crowds of refugees, and the schools were converted into hospitals for the wounded. Marmion was obliged to relocate part of his community elsewhere, deciding eventually for a temporary foundation at Edermine House, in Ireland. The separation, while necessary, was not a happy resolution and caused at least as many problems as it solved.[13]

[11] Tierney, *Marmion: A Biography*, 264.

[12] Ibid., 229.

[13] See ibid., especially chap. 8.

After the war, Marmion faced a number of difficult tasks, including the repatriation of several of his monks, the reintegration of the religious community, and stabilization of monastic life. Also, since anti-German feeling in Belgium understandably ran high, it was impossible for Maredsous to remain any longer in the Beuron (German) Benedictine Congregation. It fell to Abbot Columba to secure the necessary permissions and undertake all the work to separate from Beuron and set up a new Belgian Congregation within the Order of St. Benedict. In addition, Maredsous was requested to send monks to act as custodians of Dormition Abbey in Jerusalem,[14] the German monks of Dormition having been expelled by Allied forces in 1918. In all these weighty matters Marmion demonstrated great tact and diplomacy, making every effort to avoid offending anyone, including his confreres of Beuron or the abbot primate, also a German.

Christ was always the Rock on whom Marmion depended, and he strove to unite his own will with Christ's and, like Him, to give glory in all things to the heavenly Father. He believed firmly in St. Benedict's injunction that "the abbot holds the place of Christ in the monastery",[15] but any kind of self-promotion or arbitrary use of authority was alien to him. He made no important decisions without prayer and counsel, consulting his monks and his superiors in the order and even in Rome before proceeding with major projects. He wrote: "His [the abbot's] duty is then to try to learn at every moment what God wills of him. And to this end he ought to live a life of prayer and union with God.... [H]e ought to strive 'to abide in the sublimity of prayer and of the Divine Presence'."[16]

In October 1922, Maredsous kept its golden jubilee, which turned out to be Dom Columba's last public ceremony. Just after Christmas he came down with his final illness, which began as influenza. By a special mark of Divine Providence, he offered his last Mass on January 25, 1923, feast of the conversion of St. Paul, to whom he had been so devoted. The next day he was diagnosed with bronchial pneumonia and received the sacrament of the anointing of the sick. In those preantibiotic days the *dénouement* was swift. On the twenty-seventh he received Holy Communion, still fully alert. When the monk who offered him the Eucharist mistakenly said: "*Ecce Agnus Dei*", Marmion corrected him, saying: "Ecce Viaticum" [Behold the Food for the journey].[17] Three days later, at ten o'clock in the evening, he returned to Christ as his monks recited the *De Profundis* and the *Subvenite*. Dom Columba Marmion had entered the eternal contemplation of Christ in His mysteries.

---

[14] The Abbey and Basilica of Our Lady of Mount Sion, built on the site of our Lady's death, or dormition, had since 1906 been staffed by monks of Beuron.

[15] *Rule of St. Benedict*, chap. 2.

[16] Conference to the nuns of Maredret (Nov. 1916), quoted in Thibaut, *Abbot Columba Marmion*, 198.

[17] Ibid., 257.

It is difficult to summarize Abbot Marmion because his brilliant mind and sanctity caused him to see the vast dimensions and complexities of life in Christ. On the other hand, his Christology placed everything within the context of the divine Sonship of Jesus Christ, and he put in one sentence the fundamental axiom of his teaching: "All our sanctity consists in becoming by grace what Jesus Christ is by nature, the Child of God."[18]

I urge my readers to enjoy the treasures in all Marmion's works and here provide what I hope will be a few enticing samples.

Marmion on prayer:

> The essential element of prayer is the supernatural contact of the soul with God, in which the soul draws upon that Divine life which is the source of all holiness.... Prayer is ... the flowering, under the action of the gifts of the Holy Spirit, of the feelings that result from our divine adoption in Jesus Christ; and that is why it has to be accessible to every baptized soul of good will.[19]

Marmion on Holy Communion:

> [T]his heavenly bread ... is the food of the soul that maintains, mends, increases, and gladdens the life of grace in the soul, because it gives to it the very Author of grace. The divine life can enter into us by other doors, but it is by Holy Communion that it inundates our souls like a river in flood.[20]

Marmion on liturgy:

> Around the Sacrifice of the Mass, the center of our whole religion, the Church organizes the public worship which she alone has the right to offer in the name of Christ, her Spouse.... All year long, she arranges a celebration of the mysteries of her Divine Spouse, in such wise that her children shall be able, each year, to re-live these mysteries, to give thanks to Christ Jesus and His Father for them, and to draw forth from them the divine life that these mysteries, lived in the first place by Jesus, have merited for us.[21]

Marmion on the Sacred Heart:

> [T]he Heart which we honor, which we adore in this Humanity united to the Person of the Word, serves here as a symbol of what? Of love. When God says to us in the Scriptures: "My son, give Me Thy heart," [Prov 23:26] we understand that the heart here signifies love.... In

[18] Retreat conference to the Canonesses of St. Augustine (Hayward's Heath, Aug. 1905) quoted in Philipon, *Spiritual Doctrine*, 98.

[19] Bancroft, *Christ, the Life of the Soul*, 422–23.

[20] Ibid., 360.

[21] Ibid., 113–14.

> the devotion to the Sacred Heart of Jesus we then honor the love that the Incarnate Word bears towards us....
>
> This contemplation of the benefits of Jesus towards us ought to become the source of our practical devotion to the Sacred Heart. Love alone can respond to love.... It is then by love, by the gift of the heart that we should respond to Christ Jesus.[22]

Few Catholics and even fewer Protestant and Orthodox Christians know much about the spiritual dimensions of this most Christocentric of spiritual writers. It is my hope that the republication of Marmion's works, which is currently underway, will open the rich treasures of Christ as they were communicated to this holy monk through Scripture, tradition, and grace.

Archbishop Alban Goodier, S.J. (1869–1939)

Like Abbot Marmion, the English Jesuit missionary Alban Goodier did much to refocus Catholic spiritual writing on Jesus Christ, His life, and His influence on the spiritual growth of His disciples. Alban Goodier joined the Society of Jesus in his late teens and was ordained in 1903. While he was superior of the Jesuit students in London in 1915, he was sent to India to deal with a crisis caused by the withdrawal of the German Jesuits from Bombay University because of World War I. In 1920, he was made Archbishop of Bombay. After six difficult years, during which he distinguished himself by his work for the poor, he resigned and returned to England, where he became a popular spiritual writer, preacher, and retreat master.

Goodier is best known for his meditations on the life of Christ. These approach the Gospels in an informed spiritual way but without any particular reference to the new critical method of biblical studies. Like Marmion, who was his friend by correspondence, Goodier was intensely focused on the obvious meaning of the Gospels. Although he lacked Marmion's profound theological depth, Goodier had a great gift for bringing home to the average reader both the teachings of Christ and His real, compelling, and consoling presence in the lives of those who seek Him.

It was not that Goodier, a learned man, was unaware of biblical criticism. He recognized that as a mere intellectual enterprise, it could not go far enough. The following passages from *Jesus Christ, the Son of God* demonstrate the error of simply relying on biblical criticism without taking into account what Christ means to the believer, who has the gift of faith, or to the unbeliever, who, although he is without faith, is aware of Jesus of Nazareth but does not know how to find Him.

> This Jesus Christ ... must have been more than man; in Himself, in His personality, in His influence, in His effects, there is that about Him which is more than human; in some sense He is divine....

[22] Thomas, *Christ in His Mysteries*, 369, 373.

> And ... deep down in the heart of every man there is a wistful longing to which this fact of Christ, truly Man and truly God, appeals with superhuman force. In the heart of everyone of us, if we will listen to it, there is a voice crying out: "Oh! that it might be so! That God might come to man, in order that man might be one with God!" It is not St. Paul alone that pities man for this unceasing craving; nor St. Augustine alone that, on this very account, declares man to be "naturally Christian"; there is something in us all which confesses that this fact of Jesus Christ, Son of Man and Son of God, at once human and divine, uniting God and Man in Himself, wholly above nature and above comprehension as it is, is also wholly consonant with human nature.[23]

Having affirmed the divinity of Christ, Archbishop Goodier also consistently stressed His true humanity. He stated unambiguously that the Incarnate Word of God, in His humanity, suffered much as we do. The Gospels make this an inescapable conclusion. He notes that before the Incarnation, God had often revealed Himself to man: to Moses in the burning bush and on Mount Sinai, and by His presence in the Ark and in the Temple. "Might God-made-man", Goodier asks, "be no more than God appearing as man, as He had appeared in other ways before?" He continues: "He knew that this doubt might be; indeed, He knew that it would be. Since He passed from the earth, the difficulty of mankind has been to keep its balance. Either it becomes too learned in the signs of His human nature, and so fails to see that He is God, or it is overwhelmed with the proofs of His divinity, and hence doubts—in practice, at least—the evident fact that He is man."[24]

Goodier was concerned with those who might doubt or diminish Christ's humanity, like the disciples of Eutyches, whose mischief we encountered between the Councils of Ephesus and Chalcedon. He therefore emphasized this humanity in startling and significant ways. Writing of those who might deny His humanity, Goodier says of Jesus Christ:

> He must not let them doubt His relationship with them. He must not let them think He was removed from them, that He belonged wholly to another sphere, another order of creation; that their experiences were not His own; that He did not know and understand and feel whatever they endured; that they were called upon to carry a burden that was not also His own. At whatever risk, this must not be permitted. Neither the greatness of His teaching, nor the wonder of His miracles, nor the confession of devils, of men, of angels,

[23] Alban Goodier, S.J., *Jesus Christ the Son of God* (London: Burns, Oates and Washbourne, 1920), 6–7.

[24] Alban Goodier, S.J., *The Meaning of Life: The Catholic Answer* (Manchester, N.H.: Sophia Institute Press, 2002), 128.

> and of the Father Himself, should so exalt Him as to make His children think that He was not one of their own household.[25]

Goodier also saw Christ's humanity as the most significant expression of the divine love: "From the beginning He lay at the mercy of men, at the mercy of His parents, at the mercy of Herod, helpless in the shriveled hands of Simeon and Anna, and never raised a finger as a sign of His power."[26]

Goodier was also a man of great personal sensitivities, who projected into the Gospels his knowledge of psychology. While we may dispute his interpretations, we cannot fail to recognize that his observations are backed up by the descriptions of Christ we find in the Gospel.

> When he meets a poor widow wailing for the loss of her only son, He is "moved with pity" [Lk 7:13] and He cannot contain Himself. When people do not thank Him, He is hurt; when they do, He overflows with gratitude. He has a tender place for children, and no less tender a place for wistful, half-despairing sinners—for Zachaeus and Levi and Magdalene and Peter. He is roused when His friends are abused, enthusiastic when they are praised, compassionate when they are suffering or in want, indulgent as a mother when they are being tried. And, to crown all, He breaks into tears—cries because a dear friend is dead, cries again at the thought that His own Jerusalem had failed Him.
>
> Then there is the story of the Passion—a story of human weakness without a parallel. The Evangelists strain to find words that will adequately describe Him as He enters upon it. "He began to be sorrowful, and to be very troubled." "He began to be dumbfounded." "My soul is sorrowful, even to death" [Mt 26:38; Jn 13:21].[27]

With an eloquence beyond Marmion's and with a sensitivity most writers would envy, Goodier teaches convincingly that Christ, the Son of God, "emptied himself, taking the form of a servant" (Phil 2:7). His central message is that Christ is present here and now to each person, and it is He who gives meaning to human existence. The following passage is a testimony to the meaning of Christ to the believer. I read these words when I was a young teenager, and they directed my life for good. They continue to direct the best part of my energy and intention when I escape from my own self-centeredness.

> What is Jesus Christ to me? "Christ loved me and gave himself to me and for me"; that is what He means to me. Christ loved me, and asked me for my love; that is what He means to me. Christ loved me,

[25] Ibid., 129.
[26] Ibid.
[27] Ibid., 132–33.

> and came down the lane of life looking for me, and became a child with me, and exchanged His confidences with me, and listened while I told Him my heart's desire, and told me His heart's desire in return, and gave Himself to me, and taught me how to love in a way I had never known before, nor could anyone else have taught me. Christ loved me, and let me see a little of His Heart; and I felt its trembling weakness yet leaned upon its strength; I pitied its littleness yet gloried in its greatness; I ached for its sadness yet triumphed in its glory; all within me was a turmoil of joy and anguish, and when I turned to go away I found my heart had been stolen from me. He had stolen my heart from me, and it was an agony; but an agony so sweet that I trust to have it till my dying day.[28]

Archbishop Goodier challenges the unbelieving soul to open itself to the possibilities of divine love. He invites those with a superficial or lukewarm faith to look at the Gospels and see into the light of Christ. He continues:

> His proof of love takes my breath away and I cannot speak; His condescension almost makes me doubt; so human is He that many even of His friends will not believe it is all true. They say He is God; and they will not feel His throbbing Heart beside their own. They say He is too far away, and they will not believe that His hand lies between theirs. They say He is too great to need a love like theirs, too perfect for a sinful soul like theirs, too almighty, too faultless, to need their comfort, and they will not see the price He has paid, the self He has annihilated, the eyes welling with hot tears, that He might be wholly one with them, that He might both give human love and receive it.
>
> What is Jesus Christ to me? He is my love in the deepest human sense of which my human heart is capable; do I need to say anymore? He is my satisfaction, pressed down deep and flowing over, is not that enough? He is my inspiration: in Him, and for Him, and from Him, and with Him is my life and all that it contains: let Him take it and do with it exactly what He pleases. He is my strength and my support; when I fail He lifts me up, when I suffer He is my companion, when I am alone and despairing, He is at my side. And He is my crown; I ask for nothing more; with Him, come what may, I know I shall have enough, here in this life and for all eternity.[29]

Goodier is among the best examples of a spiritual writer and Christian humanist. His humanism is always enlightened by the love of Christ. It was Goodier's opinion, which he shared with many other spiritual writers, that we cannot be fully human without embracing

[28] *Jesus Christ the Son of God*, 139–40.

[29] Ibid., 141–42.

Christ in His fullness. Goodier disposes of a superficial form of Christianity by pointing out that Christ expands the human heart and its capacity to love with His transforming love.

> That is the wonder of it: while He loves you, He loves me no less, while He loves you and me with all the love we creatures can receive, He loves all the world with an infinite love. Let a man learn that and it will suffice; but love Jesus Christ and you will discover all the rest. You will learn in very truth what love means; not the cramped, limping, narrowed, self-indulgent thing that men often fancy it, but the great, noble, self-sacrificing, all-embracing thing that makes a man close akin to the loving God Himself.[30]

Despite their immense popularity during the early part of the twentieth century, Marmion and Goodier were rather forgotten figures until recently. Yet in their once very popular writings we find the roots of a significant era of Catholic theology that came into vogue during the period immediately before World War II and lasting up to the Second Vatican Council. Their contributions to spirituality influenced the devotion of millions of educated Catholics during the middle decades of the century. Now, from our perspective, we can see that Abbot Marmion's classic Scripture-based writings and Archbishop Goodier's bold attempts to engage the Christian in a psychologically rich approach to the Gospel opened the way for a *ressourcement*, or rediscovery of the riches of the whole of the Church's two thousand year tradition,[31] which had been partially lost during the conflicts and persecution of the nineteenth century.

Devout Catholic Intellectuals

Among the many great minds of the productive first half of the century are also poets like Charles Péguy and Paul Claudel, liturgists from the abbey of Maria Laach like Dom Ildefons Herwegen and Dom Odo Casel, and scholars whose scope of knowledge is difficult to categorize. They are philosophers, theologians, students of culture and history, like Karl Adam and Romano Guardini—a whole crop of theologians with broad backgrounds in patristics, history, and culture who filled the Church with fascinating, refreshing insights while often conflicting with one another. Coming into prominence a few years later were such names as Henri de Lubac, Jean Daniélou, Yves Congar, Hans Urs von Balthasar, Louis Bouyer, Dietrich von Hildebrand, and Karl Rahner. We also should not forget the creative poetic genius Léon Bloy or the philosopher Jacques Maritain. The single-minded evangelism of Dorothy Day and Catherine Doherty brought Christ to numerous people during this period, and the witty and

[30] Ibid., 143.

[31] Aiden Nichols, introduction to *Mysterium Paschale: The Mystery of Easter*, by Hans Urs von Balthasar, trans. Aidan Nichols, O.P. (San Francisco: Ignatius Press, 2005), see p. 2.

erudite apologetics of Frank Sheed and his wife, Maisie Ward, did the same in a very different way. These names should be familiar to Catholics, although those educated during the last two decades of the twentieth century may never have heard of them at all. The proportion of educated and disciplined readers has declined, as has the ability of contemporary Catholic culture to produce writers of genius, such as those we have mentioned.

The outstanding writers of this period, which spanned the first part of the century, are different from one another but united in the presupposition stated by de Lubac: "The renewal of Christian vitality is linked at least partially to a renewed exploration of the periods and the works where the Christian tradition is expressed with particular intensity."[32] As we review this era of extraordinary theological vitality, it becomes clear that all these writers focused on the person of Jesus Christ and His centrality to any valid understanding of Christianity, His meaning for mankind in all its struggles, and His care for the individual human soul. They also urged the importance of devotion to Him, although they rarely used this word, because for some it had saccharine, emotional connotations.

This focus on Christ is, of course, no surprise. Despite their differences, these writers were united in a common need to respond to the secularism and skepticism of their time. They were also in reaction to the ultimate inhumanity of European thought as it passed from prewar nihilism to philosophical and cultural skepticism, which found expression in much of the period's art and literature and continues now on its melancholy way as deconstructionism.

We cannot hope to review the Christology of all the leading Catholics of this period, which included the preparation for and unfolding of Vatican II. Instead we select a few who represent different schools of thought and approached their subject in ways especially meaningful to the believers of their time.

Romano Guardini (1885–1968)

Few Catholic intellectuals have enjoyed the influence of Romano Guardini, a priest of Italian birth, but a German citizen, whose life and work embraced philosophy, culture, theology, and liturgy. He also had an influential career in youth leadership, which was brought to an end by the Nazis, who held him under virtual house arrest. Early on, Guardini, as the rare Catholic professor in the University of Berlin, brought to intellectual German Protestants an appreciation of Catholic teaching and culture. In his engaging biography of Guardini, Robert Krieg has shown him to be one of the important precursors of Vatican II, a scholar whose intellectual vision was not limited to the strict Thomist method of the Neo-Scholastics of his time. He reawakened in Catholicism the vision of Augustine and Bonaventure, whose

[32] Quoted in ibid.

theory of knowledge was the subject of his doctoral dissertation at Freiburg.[33] Throughout his works, there is the constantly expressed assumption that the Christian life is founded on the experience of Christ. His definition of revelation as essentially *God at work in the world* guided many through murky debates on the nature of revelation during the decades following Vatican II.

Few would think of this powerful intellect as a devotional writer, yet his very devout and individualized approach to the personal experience of Christ made him the theologian with the widest readership between World War II and the council. The fact that he had his reservations about some of the directions taken after the council make him a very respectable spokesman for those who have second thoughts of their own. A largely unexpected revival of interest in Guardini has led to a republication of a number of his works.

Guardini's best-known and most appreciated work is *The Lord*, a series of short sermons (of three or four pages each) on Christ's life and teachings, given between 1932 and 1936 to a student congregation in Berlin. In an introduction for a recent edition of this work, then Cardinal Ratzinger wrote: "[T]he essence of Christianity is not an idea, not a system of thought, not a plan of action. The essence of Christianity is a Person: Jesus Christ Himself. That which is essential is the One who is essential. To become truly real means to come to know Jesus Christ and to learn from Him what it means to be human."[34]

In his preface, Guardini recognizes the "limitations" imposed by his subject matter.

> [T]hough Christ . . . lived in a specific historical milieu, and though knowledge of the forces at work in it does further an understanding of him, a biography of Christ is practicable only within the narrowest confines. Neither his personality nor his works are immediately traceable to the conditions of the times, for he came to us out of the fullness of time contained in the mystery of God, and it was to this mystery that he returned after he had "moved among us" (Acts 1:22).[35]

Having read and reread this masterpiece for many years, I must say that I see Christ the Savior mostly through the prism of Guardini's thought. All my knowledge of Christ has come to me from the New Testament through SS. Augustine and Bonaventure and Romano Guardini. They have taught me much about Christ: His absolute mystery, power, pathos, and glory; the union of His humanity and divinity in the depth of the Passion and the bright light of the Resurrection;

---

[33] Robert A. Krieg, C.S.C., *Romano Guardini: A Precursor of Vatican II* (Notre Dame, Ind.: University of Notre Dame Press, 1997), 6.

[34] Joseph Ratzinger, introduction to *The Lord*, by Romano Guardini, trans. Elinor Castendyk Briefs (Washington, D.C.: Regnery, 2002), xiv.

[35] Guardini, *The Lord*, xvi.

and, finally, the glorious hope of directly knowing my Redeemer. Guardini immerses us in the Gospel, and we experience God operating in the world of time and in the present moment.

The following brief quotation on Christ's Nativity has guided me in a time when many tried to tell us what the God-Man knew or did not know, or at least, to my way of thinking, introduced an intellectually offensive skepticism into the understanding of the mystery of the Incarnation. After quoting the Gospel account of Christ's birth from St. Luke, Guardini says:

> What we have just attempted to grasp in the obscurity of divine action now presents itself to us in visible form. At first a child like any other, it cries, is hungry, sleeps, and yet is "the Word ... become flesh." It cannot be said that God "inhabits" this infant, however gloriously; or that heaven has set its seal upon him, so that he must pursue it, suffer for it in a manner sublimely excelling all other contacts between God and man; this child *is* God in essence and in being.
>
> If an inner protest should arise here, give it room. It is not good to suppress anything; if we try to, it only goes underground, becomes toxic, and reappears later in far more obnoxious form. Does anyone object to the whole idea of God-become-man? Is he willing to accept the Incarnation only as a profound and beautiful allegory, never as literal truth? If doubt can establish a foothold anywhere in our faith, it is here. Then we must be patient and reverent, approaching this central mystery of Christianity with calm, expectant, prayerful attention; one day its sense will be revealed to us. In the meantime, let us remember the directive "But love does such things!" [36]

Guardini was well aware that he was taking on various establishments in Christian thought, especially German Protestant Scripture scholars. The following words from the conclusion of *The Lord* have much to say to those who have been told that Sacred Scripture and the tradition of the Church cannot be considered trustworthy in telling us who Jesus really was and what He did. Guardini attempts to state the position of the Christological skeptics this way:

> Can such a being as the Jesus Christ sketched in these pages exist? The answer is contained in the question. It runs: In history only that is possible which is humanly possible. If we accept only the human in Jesus Christ, then naturally, the greater part of the New Testament becomes a mere web of speculations and pious legends woven about the figure of the historic Nazarene. It may have its sense in the religious needs of the individual, or even of a church or of an age; but it cannot be called truth. The truth of Christ reaches only as far as

[36] Ibid., 18–19.

> human possibility, and it is the task of science to discover where this lies.[37]

Guardini had no patience with ideas about the Christ of faith as contrasted with the historical construct of Jesus of Nazareth presented by those who claimed to discover the "real Jesus". He describes this very popular and supposedly scientific point of view in these words:

> Christian faith must reject both the Jesus of historical research and the pseudo faith which such a Jesus would imply. There is only one true Jesus Christ: the God-man of full uncrippled Christian belief. And faith is as essential to our understanding of him as the eye is to color and the ear to sound. From the start Jesus demanded of all would-be followers a clear Yes! or No! to the demands of faith he made upon them—affirmation or rejection, not a little of each. This point is essential and needs no further illumination, though it is interesting to call attention to the complete nullity of the figure known as "the historical Jesus." When we measure it with the necessary objectiveness and by its own standards, we can only be amazed that human intelligence can possibly contribute such a person with the effects that Jesus actually produced.[38]

This last sentence is borne out by many of the most skeptical writers on the New Testament who say that the only mystery about the historical Jesus is that anyone believes in Him after two thousand years. Coming from the opposite perspective, Guardini agrees that no one could believe in their characterization of Jesus Christ, which is that of "an undistinguished peasant who became clothed with the 'symbols' of the church's faith in 'the Christ event' ".[39] Guardini was uncompromising with any intellectual reduction of Christ, any Christology "from below", a phrase as absurd as it is confusing.

> Christ came to redeem us. To do this, he had to inform us who God is, and what man is in the sight of God; and this in such a way that the doors to our conversion are flung open, and we are given the strength to enter into the new. He who succeeds in this cannot be substantially judged by men. The moment man assumes the right to decide how his redeemer is or is not to be, that redeemer is reduced to human limitations, and the given conditions of human existence, as well as the whole sense of redemption, is lost. If redemption exists at all, it necessarily demands that the competence of human judgment halt before him who announces and accomplishes it. And not only relatively, with the "special consideration" due to greatness or

[37] Ibid., 627.

[38] Ibid., 628.

[39] H. D. McDonald, "The Symbolistic Christology of Paul Tillich", *Vox Evangelica* 18 (1988): 75.

> genius, but fundamentally, because he is the Redeemer. A "savior" with human limitations is hardly worth believing in. Anyone with the least idea of what Christian life demands in the way of conversion and sacrifice knows this. If the genuine Jesus Christ were no more than the greatest of men, it would be better to hack our way alone through existence.
>
> For Christ there is no norm; he himself is the Establisher of all norms. Once we meet him the only way he can be met, in faith; once we renounce all personal judgment, letting Scripture speak with the full weight of its authority, every line of the New Testament suddenly comes alive. The Son of God and man escapes all categories—also those of the genius or religious founder. He steps out of eternity, the unknown, an immeasurable Being revealed to us bit by bit through the word of his messengers or through some personal trait. He himself surpasses all description, though so many have attempted to tell us of him—the synoptics, Saints Paul and John and James and Jude—all speak stammeringly. And if the portraits they trace are not identical, then only because Jesus Christ can never be intellectually unified. Faith alone senses the incomprehensible oneness of his many-faceted reality with its beatific promise of eternity.[40]

Romano Guardini was recognized as one of the great Christian geniuses of his time. It is widely believed that he declined the cardinalate in his old age. He was praised by Karl Rahner, who succeeded him at Ludwig Maximilian University of Munich, at a scholarly presentation in his honor. He challenged many of the great minds of his time.

It is worth noting that Guardini moved in the rarefied atmosphere of European intellectualism. His mind, his originality, his singular dedication to Christ were recognized explicitly by Pope John Paul II.[41] Yet his message of the absolute need for conversion of heart, will, and mind would be appreciated by the simplest prayerful reader of the Bible.

St. Teresa Benedicta of the Cross (Edith Stein, 1891–1942)

Much publicity and discussion swirled around the canonization of a Carmelite nun who died in Auschwitz because she was a Jew. Opinion pro and con focused on whether in these times of religious understanding it was right for the Catholic Church to canonize a Jew, even one who had never been a practicing member of the Jewish community. All the rhetoric could be reduced to one question: Did St. Teresa Benedicta merit the highest honor of the Catholic Church, or was the title bestowed as part of a Vatican public relations stunt? I was puzzled by the discussion until I realized that very few on either side of the issue seemed to appreciate the extraordinary, heroic holiness of this remarkable woman.

[40] *The Lord*, 628–29.

[41] Krieg, *Romano Guardini*, 193.

Born at Breslau, part of Silesia,[42] in the last decade of the nineteenth century, Edith Stein came from a devout Jewish home, though she herself lost her faith as a young woman. She studied at the University of Breslau and later at Göttingen. In 1916, having served as a nurse with the Red Cross for a period, she moved on to the University of Freiburg, where she received her doctorate and was assistant to Edmund Husserl, the distinguished philosopher and founder of the phenomenology movement. Like Romano Guardini, she was part of the heady intellectual atmosphere of Europe between the two world wars.

By the summer of 1921, Edith Stein was seriously considering the claims of Christianity when, seemingly by chance, she read the autobiography of St. Teresa of Avila, a book that changed her life. She began taking instruction in the faith and was received into the Catholic Church in January 1922. Almost immediately she felt the call to religious life, but her spiritual director advised her to wait. She might have pursued a university career, but with Nazism in the ascendant it became impossible for Jews to secure university positions. She did, however, write and lecture, and she taught for several years at Catholic institutions until that also became too dangerous. Finally, in 1933, shortly after Hitler's fateful election, she received permission to enter the Carmel at Cologne-Lindenthal, taking the name Sr. Teresa Benedicta of the Cross.

Her Gospel-centered faith and the influence of the Carmelite writers led her to study Christian mysticism even before she became a religious. Her sisters in Carmel remembered her for her silence and spirit of prayer, not as a well-known philosopher, lecturer, and writer. She reveals a Christ-centered absorption that can only be called mystical and devotional and reminds us of her two Carmelite models, St. Teresa of Avila and St. John of the Cross.

The following Christmas meditation, written as the Nazis were removing religious symbols, including crucifixes throughout Germany, provides a glimpse of her piety, intense sensitivity, and her humble acceptance of faith.

> The Star of Bethlehem is a star in a dark night, even today.... Where is now the jubilation of the heavenly hosts? Where the silent bliss of the Holy Night? Where is the peace on earth? Peace on earth to men of good will. But not all are of good will. Therefore the Son of the Eternal Father had to descend from the glory of Heaven, because the mystery of iniquity had wrapped the earth in night. Darkness covered the earth, and He came as the light.... To those who received Him He brought light and peace ... but not peace with the children of darkness. To them the Prince of Peace does not bring peace but the sword.... This is a heavy and serious truth which must not be suffered to be concealed by the Child in

[42] Once German, since 1945, the city has been called Wroclaw and been part of Poland.

the manger. The mystery of the Incarnation and the mystery of iniquity are closely related.[43]

Sr. Teresa Benedicta's piety was deeply colored by Christ's suffering and Passion. At every stage of her life, there was the shadow of the Cross.[44] In that, we see not only the Carmelite appreciation of the experience of spiritual darkness but also the simple gratitude of St. Francis for the Incarnation, for the life and death of Christ. This selection from her poem "I Will Remain with You" reveals much about the devotion of this German Jewish intellectual and reminds us of St. Gertrude and other medieval German mystics.

You reign at the Father's right hand
In the kingdom of his eternal glory
As God's Word from the beginning.

You reign on the Almighty's throne
Also in transfigured human form,
Ever since the completion of your work on earth.

I believe this because your word teaches me so,
And because I believe, I know it gives me joy,
And blessed hope blooms forth from it.

For where you are, there also are your own,
Heaven is my glorious homeland,
I share with you the Father's throne.

The Eternal who made all creatures,
Who, thrice holy, encompasses all being,
In addition has a silent, special kingdom of his own.

The innermost chamber of the human soul
Is the Trinity's favorite place to be,
His heavenly throne on earth.

To deliver this heavenly kingdom from the hand of the enemy,
The Son of God has come as Son of Man,
He gave his blood as the price of deliverance.

In the heart of Jesus, which was pierced,
The kingdom of heaven and the land of earth are bound together.
Here is for us the source of life.[45]

---

[43] *The Mystery of Christmas*, quoted in Hilda C. Graef, *The Scholar and the Cross* (Westminster, Md.: Newman Press, 1955), 128.

[44] Her conversion to Catholicism was regarded as an act of great disloyalty to her heritage and family, especially by her religious mother. Edith was painfully aware that in deciding to embrace monastic life in Carmel, she was causing her mother even greater sorrow.

[45] Edith Stein, "I Will Remain with You" (*"Ich bleibe bei euch"*), in *The Hidden Life: Hagiographic Essays, Meditations, Spiritual Texts*, trans. Waltraut Stein, vol. 4, *The Collected Works of Edith Stein*. (Washington, D.C.: ICS Publications, 1992), 135–39.

In 1938, persecution of Jews in Germany escalated, and fearing that her presence in the monastery was a threat to all the nuns, Sr. Teresa Benedicta transferred to the Carmel at Echt, Holland, which had been founded from Cologne during the previous century. Divine Providence had given her a spirituality of the Cross for reasons that became obvious as the end of her life approached. When the Dutch bishops protested the deportation of Jews in 1942, the Nazi overlord Arthur Seyss-Inquart responded by ordering the deportation of all Jews who were Christians by conversion or by partial parentage. Within a matter of days, the saint and her sister Rosa were arrested.[46] Three days later they arrived at the concentration camp of Westerbork, where they were lodged in a hut with ten other nuns. A Jewish businessman who escaped deportation met Sr. Teresa Benedicta and has left the following account:

> Among the prisoners who arrived on 5 August Sister Benedicta made a striking impression by her great calm and composure. The misery in the camp and the excitement among the newcomers were indescribable. Sister Benedicta walked about among the women, comforting, helping, soothing like an angel. Many mothers were almost demented and had for days not been looking after their children, but had been sitting brooding in listless despair. Sister Benedicta at once took care of the poor little ones, washed and combed them, and saw to it that they got food and attention. As long as she was in the camp she made washing and cleaning one of her principal charitable activities, so that everyone was amazed.[47]

Another survivor of those days, the mother of a future Dominican, gives us her impression of Sr. Teresa Benedicta among the other nuns who had been deported.

> The great difference between Edith Stein and the other sisters lay in her silence. My personal impression is that she was most deeply sorrowful, but without anxiety. . . . She hardly ever spoke, but she often looked at her sister Rosa with indescribable sadness. . . . She was thinking of the sorrow she foresaw, not her own sorrow, for that she was far too calm, she thought of the sorrow that awaited the others. Her whole appearance, as I picture her in my memory sitting in that hut, suggested only one thought to me: a Pietà without Christ.[48]

From Westerbork, Sr. Teresa Benedicta and Rosa were transported to Auschwitz, Poland, where they were killed on August 9.

[46] Rosa had also converted to the Catholic faith and was living at the Carmel of Echt, outside the enclosure.

[47] Quoted in Graef, *Scholar and the Cross*, 229.

[48] Ibid.

SS. Teresa Benedicta and Maximilian Kolbe and others who died in the Second World War remind us that Christ's Cross must always be at the center of our world, especially in troubled times. An ancient motto of the Carthusian Order says *Stat crux dum volvitur orbis* (the Cross stands firm while the world turns).

Theologians, Visionaries, and Servants of the Poor

Dietrich von Hildebrand (1889–1977)

Of all the Catholics in modern times whom we are studying, perhaps none had a more favored youth than Dietrich von Hildebrand. At the same time, none had to move further from his roots to find the Catholic faith. His father, Adolf, a celebrated sculptor, raised his family in Italy among the secularized, nonreligious upper classes. The family were acquainted with such luminaries as Franz Liszt, Richard Wagner, Henry James, and Rainer Maria Rilke. Von Hildebrand and his sisters were raised in an agnostic, humanistic atmosphere, one not hostile to religion but completely uninformed about it. They knew nothing of the Church beyond Catholic contributions to European culture in the past.

In personal letters to me, von Hildebrand's widow, Alice, has described her husband's family home as "a noble pagan world of beauty, in which religion had no place". Romano Guardini speaks of European high society in similar terms in *The End of the Modern World*, and he saw the catastrophe of the world wars and the rise of the Nazis and Communists as the bitter fruit of this "noble pagan world".

An early sign that von Hildebrand was different from the other members of his family came when he was fourteen during a discussion with his older sister Nini, in which he vigorously defended the objectivity of moral values and the need to come to terms with the question of the immortality of the soul. After reading the *Dialogues* of Plato at the age of fifteen, he became convinced that philosophy was to be his vocation. At the University of Munich, he met the philosopher Max Scheler, an intellectually convinced Catholic but a man whose life was morally disordered. Nonetheless, he introduced the young von Hildebrand to the "new world of Christianity" and told him that the Catholic Church had the truth. When von Hildebrand asked what he meant by that statement, Scheler said that the Church produced saints and then proceeded to outline the true essence of holiness as exemplified in Francis of Assisi. The young man was on his way. On Holy Saturday of 1914, von Hildebrand and his first wife, Gretchen, were received into the Catholic Church.

In the *putsch* of 1923, Hitler and the National Socialists attempted to gain control of Bavaria. When Hitler came to power in 1933, von Hildebrand, vigorously opposing them, abandoned his professorship in Munich, going to Vienna. He subsequently produced an anti-Nazi, anti-Communist newspaper, but the Nazis pursued him in Austria, where at first he was able to lecture only with police protection. In 1938, on the day the Germans seized Austria, von Hildebrand escaped to Switzerland and later went to France. When the Germans invaded France, he fled again, this time to the United States, where he remained until his death. He became professor of philosophy at Fordham University in New York and wrote a series of powerful books defending Christian ethics from situation ethics. He also wrote about love, marriage, celibacy, religious experience, and devotion. His work *The Sacred Heart: An Analysis of Human and Divine Affectivity* gives a unique and important insight into philosophical and psychological considerations of Christian devotion. Although some readers may not be able to appreciate the importance of this analysis of affectivity, it is crucial in order to understand the deepest roots of Christian devotion, for without that understanding, it may be dismissed by its critics as simple emotion. We will examine von Hildebrand's ideas briefly.

After an incisive philosophical and psychological analysis of affectivity, the action of the heart, he points out that although "we find the true self primarily in the will . . . it is the *heart* which is the most intimate part of the person, the core, the real self, rather than the will or the intellect."[49] It is the heart that supports the closest relationships. "When we love a person and long for a return of our love, it is the heart of the other person which we want to call ours." Freedom of will, especially "cooperative freedom", that is, human freedom working with the unmerited gift of grace, is often thought to be the highest expression of the true self. Cooperative freedom simply means the freedom operating in cooperation with the divine will with divine grace. The perfect example of cooperative freedom is the Blessed Virgin's consent at the Annunciation: "Be it done unto me according to thy word." Von Hildebrand explains: "Man is greater and deeper than the range of things he can control with his free will. . . . Nothing expresses this fact more adequately perhaps than the truth that God is nearer to us than we are to ourselves. . . . It now becomes more intelligible why in certain domains the heart is more the true self than the will."[50]

It has often been noted that there is more to man than the analysis of memory, intelligence, and will. The simple Aristotelian analysis of man is inadequate. The idea of affectivity and cooperative freedom opens up understandings of other domains of human freedom and operation. When we do something from the depth of our being, cooperating completely with divine grace, it seems that we have gone beyond intellect and will. They are operative, but there is something beneath this which is sometimes called the heart, which can go on when all rational arguments call for giving up, when the will is drawn in other directions but nonetheless stays on course, and when there is no other

[49] Dietrich von Hildebrand, *The Sacred Heart: An Analysis of Human and Divine Affectivity* (Baltimore: Helicon Press, 1965), 109. This work was reprinted as *The Heart* in 1977 by Franciscan Herald Press.

[50] Ibid., 113.

good reason for doing something except what speaks to a human being from the depth of his heart, or inner being. This is where divine grace may be operative.

If it is difficult to grasp the idea of affectivity and its possibilities of going beyond mind and will, the expression "The heart has its reasons" is good to keep in mind. A bit of reflection on our own behavior, especially our very best and very worst, will give some idea of affectivity. A person may be said to have a good heart or an evil heart. Such expressions refer to something beyond the concept of the will.

As regards the best of human behavior, we can cite *The Imitation of Christ*: "Nothing is stronger than love."

> Love is ever on the watch; it rests, but does not slumber, is wearied but not spent, alarmed but not dismayed; like a living flame, a blazing torch, it shoots upward, fearlessly passing through aught that bars its path. If anyone has this love, he will know what I mean. A loud cry in the ears of God is that burning love for him in the soul which says: "My God, my love, you are all mine and I all yours." [51]

And the worst of affectivity can be summed up in the old pagan saying "Those whom the gods would destroy, they first make mad with love."

With this insight, we can approach the figure of Jesus Christ, who, although divine, "has taken upon Himself a true human body and a true human soul", as the Council of Ephesus tells us. To this, we can add the teaching of the Third Council of Constantinople that He also had a true human will. It is vital to recognize that Jesus Christ, the Incarnate Word, is God's revelation of Himself. Von Hildebrand is careful in speaking of the higher affectivity of Christ: "We must guard ourselves from reverting to a familiar natural affectivity and from interpreting the life of the Sacred Heart by merely natural and even trite categories. Only by lifting up our hearts can we hope to catch a glimpse of the holy life of the Heart of the God-Man".[52]

Von Hildebrand cites the Beatitudes, many of the parables and miracles, and the events of the Passion, showing how they reveal the kindness and mercy of God in the human life of Jesus Christ. This beautiful and meditative review of the Gospel is quite original. It gives us a new insight into the Heart of Christ, which is even beyond His human memory, intellect, and will. Why do we use the word "heart" referring to Christ? Why does He use it of Himself? It seems that by limiting ourselves to the Aristotelian/Thomistic analysis of the human personality, we may fail to appreciate Christ's full meaning when He speaks of His Heart: "Indeed, in the face of this overwhelming mercy,

---

[51] Thomas à Kempis, *The Imitation of Christ*, trans. Ronald Knox and Michael Oakley (San Francisco: Ignatius Press, 2005), bk. 3, chap. 5, no. 5, p. 116.

[52] *Sacred Heart*, 118.

this tender indulgence, this divine patience dwelling in the Heart of Jesus, we fall on our knees and pray: *Cor Jesu, patiens et multae misericordiae, miserere nobis*, 'Heart of Jesus, patient and abounding in mercy, have mercy on us.'"[53]

Von Hildebrand states that the affectivity and mercy of Christ are unlimited and directly related to our human need for forgiveness and mercy and concludes: "This superabundant affectivity of Christ, his boundless charity, his unlimited humility, his inexhaustible mercy, his glorious divine majesty, all reveal the pulsation of the Sacred Heart of Jesus."[54] This gives rise to an unavoidable question: What response must we now make to such divine love?

At this point, von Hildebrand makes an important distinction: Can the will and the heart be moved in different directions and have different responses to God's call? In making his distinction, he evokes the figure of Abraham. The holy patriarch's will was certainly to do God's will, even to the point of sacrificing his son, because the command to offer Isaac came from the Lord (see Gen 22). But what of Abraham's heart? Did it simply go along with his will? Did he stoically and without feeling take all the steps leading up to the sacrifice of his son? Such an idea is monstrous. Did Christ not weep for Lazarus? Did He not pray in the garden that the chalice of suffering might pass Him by?

Von Hildebrand refers to the process of spiritual development as the Christian's transformation in Christ.[55] He distinguishes between the Christian approach and a kind of Oriental stoicism, which allows no creature to be "the object of our love or joy". He points out that a "certain tendency in this direction is to be found in the early writings of St. Augustine—theses which he later modified greatly—in which he claims that no created good should ever be the object of *frui* (enjoying) but only of an *uti* (using)."[56] We can see this struggle in the *Confessions*, in which Augustine, describing his grief at the death of his beloved mother, Monica, fears that he grieves too much.[57]

Von Hildebrand then makes his own the later statement of St. Augustine: "I am not saying that you should not love your wife, but that you should love Christ more." All Christians would agree that our love for the Lord should have absolute priority. If we wish to imitate Christ, however, we must be free from hard-heartedness. There can be no indifference in us to God, to others, or to any of creation. We must struggle to free our hearts from all corruption or absorption with lesser goods, which would block or enfeeble our activity. Von Hildebrand

[53] Ibid., 133.

[54] Ibid., 143.

[55] Dietrich von Hildebrand, *Transformation in Christ* (Manchester, N.H.: Sophia Institute Press, 1998).

[56] *Sacred Heart*, 171.

[57] See *Confessions*, trans. Frank Sheed (New York: Sheed and Ward, 1965), bk. 9.

cites another of his works (*Not as the World Gives*) to acknowledge the priority of importance among natural goods and how one's affectivity toward them must be prioritized. We must be grateful to God and others for all good gifts. Some goods show the goodness, truth, and beauty of God more than others. To enjoy these legitimately in themselves but in due proportion and with moral responsibility does not mean that we always have to think of them directly and explicitly in some relationship to God or Christ. For the believer, the relationship is often obvious, like listening to great music or seeing a beautiful painting. God's part is not obvious when we enjoy a needed night's sleep, but we can be nonetheless grateful to Him for providing it. The person striving to please God may often be operating on a habitual intention, frequently strengthened by explicit acts of devotion.

The greatest devotion to Jesus consists in making a genuine attempt throughout life to follow the Gospel, having in us that mind which is in Christ Jesus (see Phil 2:5), treating others as we think Christ would treat them, and having a prayerful attraction of the will and heart. "If you love me, you will keep my commandments" (Jn 14:15). Von Hildebrand's analysis of this affectivity and of the development of the various stages and dangers of mediocrity can provide substantial help for those seeking to love Christ with ever maturing devotion.

Hans Urs von Balthasar (1905–1988)

In attempting to examine the devotion to Christ of a great theological mind like Balthasar, I may have bitten off more than I can chew. As I approach his monumental works, I am deeply aware of this challenge, so I have chosen to use another writer to introduce him: Fr. Aidan Nichols, O.P., an English Dominican whose own works have a consistent quality, clarity, orthodoxy, and brevity. He presents a clear, Christ-centered understanding of Balthasar's incredible mind, which combined orthodoxy, tradition, creativity, and a mesmerizing sense of beauty. I have relied on Nichols' introduction to Balthasar's *Mysterium Paschale*, which should be read in its entirety.

Balthasar was born in Lucerne, then the center of Catholic Switzerland, a city of singular natural beauty, immediately adjacent to the snow-covered Mt. Pilatus. He was educated at several universities, including Berlin, where he was taught by Guardini. Although his education and intellectual training were similar to Guardini's in many ways (he has been called the most cultivated man of his age[58]), he was influenced by the brilliant German Jesuit Erich Przywara toward Neo-Scholastic rather than Augustinian studies. Now nearly forgotten, Fr. Przywara compiled anthologies of Augustine and Newman but was nevertheless a loyal Neo-Scholastic. For all his creativity Balthasar remained faithful to a historical Scholasticism, which Nichols characterizes as "repristinated", that is, Thomistic theology brought back to

[58] Nichols, introduction to *Mysterium Paschale*, 1n; see note 31 above.

its pristine form. He also retained an enthusiasm for patristics, especially the more speculative writings of the Fathers.[59]

The Society of Jesus, which he entered in 1929, was another formative influence. As a Jesuit, he made the Ignatian Spiritual Exercises, which left him with an uncompromising faithfulness to Christ the Word in the midst of the secular world. During his years with the Society, he was influenced especially by two Jesuits of the "New Theology", Henri de Lubac and Jean Daniélou, who, like himself, were later nominated as cardinals.[60] Balthasar spent the war years in Switzerland as chaplain at the University of Basel, where he met Adrienne von Speyr, a brilliant, if unusual, convert. He was influenced by her mystical experiences and her commentaries on the Gospel of John and other New Testament books. Von Speyr died in 1967, but even after her death, he continued to derive inspiration from her writings.

Two years later, Pope Paul VI appointed Balthasar to the International Theological Commission. He continued to write, adding to his great corpus, and in 1972 founded *Communio*, an international Catholic review. He died in Basel in June of 1988, just three days before his scheduled investiture as a cardinal.[61]

One of the fascinating complexities of Balthasar's career is that such a Catholic theologian, explicitly and clearly dedicated to the primacy of Peter and the hierarchical structure of the Church, could be deeply influenced by the Christology of Karl Barth, the monumental Protestant mind of his time. Nichols tells us that Balthasar's book on Barth is regarded by some of the latter's disciples as the best book on him ever written.[62] Balthasar believed strongly that some of the trends in theology in the years after the council would "dilute Christocentrism", whether because of German Idealism (Karl Rahner), evolutionism (Teilhard de Chardin), or Marxism (liberation theology).[63] He also understood that an overemphasis on contemporary psychological theory and other pastoral issues could likewise distract from the mystery of Christ.

Like Guardini, Balthasar made little effort to incorporate modern biblical studies into his understanding of Christ. According to Nichols, he ignored much contemporary exegetical study because he was convinced that "the identification of ever more sub-structures, redactional frameworks, 'traditions', *perikopai*, binary correspondences, and other methodological items in the paraphernalia of gospel criticism,

[59] Ibid., 2.

[60] Following a dispute over the establishment of a secular institute, Balthasar left the Jesuits in 1950 and became a diocesan priest.

[61] Nichols, introduction to *Mysterium Paschale*, 3. It is one of my great personal disappointments that Balthasar was unable to come to New York to lecture at the request of Msgr. Michael Wrenn, who had arranged for him to stay for six weeks as our guest at Trinity Retreat House.

[62] Ibid, 5.

[63] Ibid.

tears into fragments what is an obvious unity."[64] By the time these various exegetical teachings—or simply their unchallenged conclusions—are filtered down into the Sunday sermon, they come across as statements that have become detatched from both the plain meaning of the text and the mystery of Christ. It does not take too much imagination to justify the reactions of men like Balthasar, Guardini, or Barth to such efforts. Their disdain can be explained by the fact that the statements of contemporary biblical critics are presented as unassailable truth rather then the interpretations they really are. Both Guardini and Balthasar agreed that faith in Christ is best described as a personal relationship with Christ and an ongoing conversion. Balthasar clearly saw that "only the contemplative reading of the New Testament is adequate to the glory of God in Jesus Christ".[65]

One of the Balthasar's central creative ideas in *Mysterium Paschale* is based to some degree on the mystical insights of Adrienne von Speyr. It concerns his understanding of *kenosis*, or the emptying of Christ, seen in the mystery of His death and descent into hell. Christ empties Himself to the very depths during His Passion, death, and descent into the underworld with unconditional, gracious, sacrificial love, which reflects the Trinity itself. Simply put, the mystery of the Father is seen in the total expression of Himself in His Word; the Word then gives Himself completely by death and descent for our salvation, and only the Holy Spirit can relate as a bond of love between Father and Son. The Father's acceptance of Christ's sacrifice is the mystery of redemption. Balthasar bases this rather unusual description of the descent on Gregory the Great: "Christ went down into the deepest abysses of the sea, when he went into the Lowest Hell, to fetch forth the souls of his elect. Before the redemption, the depth of the sea was a prison, not a way.... But God made of this abyss a road.... It is also called "the deepest abyss" on the grounds that, just as the depths of the sea cannot be fathomed by any human gaze, so too the secret of Hell is impenetrable to all human knowledge."[66]

The heads of many readers are probably spinning as they read this. They may well say that they would rather stick with the simpler, traditional explanations of salvation. Balthasar never denied those explanations. He tried to go beyond them, looking into what we may yet learn about the mystery of redemption.

We might ask why he follows trails into this mystical forest. For two reasons. The first is that Western European thought has been preoccupied for a century with evil—the evil resulting from the Enlightenment and leading to technological accomplishment without moral guidance or restraint. The results stretch from the battle of Verdun (at

---

[64] Ibid., 6.

[65] Nichols, introduction to *Mysterium Paschale*, 6.

[66] Balthasar, *Mysterium Paschale*, 175–76.

the time the bloodiest in history) to World War II, with its holocausts, atom bombs, and the possibility of total annihilation. Now a new evil, the specter of biological warfare, rises in our minds. Confronted with all this evil, those who believe in the Christian God find a place of refuge in the suffering of that Person who is both divine and yet mysteriously human. Jesus is the suffering God. For Balthasar this suffering is not simply an accident of history. It is the constantly repeated drama of the expression of absolute divine love, giving itself completely, only to be rejected by men.

Balthasar's second original concept, which we can only mention here, is his explanation of beauty, the forgotten fourth transcendental quality of being (the others being unity, truth, and goodness). The beauty of beings is the reflection of God's glory. This study is called theological aesthetics, or the consideration of the principle of beauty coming from God.

I have chosen Balthasar's most poetic and mystical book, *Heart of the World*, to illustrate his appreciation of divine things. In his introduction to this work, the translator, Erasmo Leiva, sums up in a few lines what Fr. Nichols was able to analyze so well. In the light of that analysis we can appreciate the evaluation of the translator.

> [T]he vibrant christological poetry before us is the epiphany of a lively faith that issues from the depths of the experience of God, a faith that cannot help but sing in a music of image, surprise, color, movement. These poetic elements go to shape a breathless hymn of praise whose continual invention and variety witness to the infinite richness of the object in question: the human Heart of God. The lyrical form of this theology, then, is no personal whim of the author; its perfect pattern crystallizes in lucid obedience to the nature of his material.[67]

The following quotation is from Balthasar's meditation for Holy Saturday. The words are those of a lost soul, someone who, like Judas, believes that he has betrayed the love of Christ.

> I have used up your Cross and your mercy. Everything has been consumed, to the very last drop—even the return of the lost son and the lamb caught among the thorns and the lost drachma. Everything used up and worn out. One can play this scene twenty times over, fifty perhaps, but then it turns stale and loses its salt. Once again I hear your Apostle saying: When we sin intentionally with full knowledge of the truth, then there no longer is any sacrifice for our sins. Rather a horrible judgment and the blast of the fire await us which will destroy the adversaries. Whoever violates the law of Moses will be

[67] Hans Urs von Balthasar, *Heart of the World*, trans. Erasmo S. Leiva (San Francisco: Ignatius Press, 1979), 8.

killed without mercy upon the testimony of two or three witnesses. How much heavier a punishment will overtake the one who tramples on the Son of God with his feet, who holds the blood of the Covenant, with which he has been sanctified, to be base, who scoffs at Grace. . . .

Leave me alone. Neither let your Mother touch me. I am no sight for you two. Do not waste your compassion on me: it would be misplaced. Let the inevitable come down upon me. To the one on your right up there you promised Paradise. I heartily concede it to him. He has earned it. He did not know what he was doing. Be happy together in your eternal garden! But don't torture yourself over me. I'll always be the one on your left. And stop torturing me too with your torture. Try to forget me.

WAS THAT LIGHTNING? Was the fruit on the Cross visible in the darkness for a flash as the sky was rent—motionless, stiff as death itself, with fixed, vacant eyes, pale as a maggot, probably already dead? That was indeed his body, but where is his soul? In what shoreless beaches, in what waterless depths of the sea, on the bottom of what dark flames does it drift about? Suddenly all of them standing around the gallows know it: he is gone. Immeasurable emptiness (not solitude) streams forth from the hanging body. Nothing but this fantastic emptiness is any longer at work here. The world with its shape has perished; it tore like a curtain from top to bottom, without making a sound. It fainted away, turned to dust, burst like a bubble. There is nothing more but nothingness itself. The world is dead. Love is dead. God is dead. Everything that was, was a dream dreamt by no one. The present is all past. The future is nothing. The hand has disappeared from the clock's face. No more struggle between love and hate, between life and death.[68]

In vibrant, poetic ways Balthasar describes the nothingness of Holy Saturday. He was perhaps inspired by or reflecting on the ancient homily of the Holy Saturday Office of Readings, which tell us that everything is silent. And then very faintly, out of the mist, life begins; it is seen almost as a drop of water emerging from the chaos.

Hold the breath of your thoughts! It's still much too early in the day to think of hope. The seed is still much too weak to start whispering about love. But look there: it is indeed moving, a weak, viscous flow. It's still much too early to speak of a wellspring. It trickles, lost in the chaos, directionless, without gravity. But more copiously now. A wellspring in the chaos. It leaps out of pure nothingness, it leaps out of itself. It is not the beginning of God, who eternally and mightily brings himself into existence as Life and Love and triune Bliss. It is not the beginning of creation, which gently and in slumber slips out

[68] Ibid., 147–50.

of the Creator's hands. It is a beginning without parallel, as if Life were arising from Death, as if weariness (already such weariness as no amount of sleep could ever dispel) and the uttermost decay of power were melting at creation's outer edge, were beginning to flow, because flowing is perhaps a sign and a likeness of weariness which can no longer contain itself, because everything that is strong and solid must in the end dissolve into water. But hadn't it—in the beginning—also been born from water? And is this wellspring in the chaos, this trickling weariness, not the beginning of a new creation? ...

Only the wound is there: gaping, the great open gate, the chaos, the nothingness out of which the wellspring leaps forth. Never again will this gate be shut. Just as the first creation arose ever anew out of sheer nothingness, so, too, this second world—still unborn, still caught up in its first rising—will have its sole origin in this wound, which is never to close again. In the future, all shape must arise out of this gaping void, all wholeness must draw its strength from the creating wound. High-vaulted triumphal Gate of Life! Armored in gold, armies of graces stream out of you with fiery lances. Deep-dug Fountain of Life! Wave upon wave gushes out of you inexhaustible, ever-flowing, billows of water and blood baptizing the heathen hearts, comforting the yearning souls, rushing over the deserts of guilt, enriching over-abundantly, overflowing every heart that receives it, far surpassing every desire.[69]

This incredibly poetic imagery, like the entire work, must be contemplated in quiet. It will slowly open up mysteries in the Gospel narrative of the Passion for those who take the time to pray with it. It is work of an incredible mind mining the gold of the Gospel narrative.

St. Faustina Kowalska (1905–1938)

As we continue our journey through the twentieth century, we come to the private revelation of the simple peasant nun St. Faustina. Though Balthasar's contemporary, she could not have been more unlike him. She recorded what she believed to be the revelation of the Divine Mercy and described a conversation of Christ with a despairing soul. Recorded by a woman with three years' formal education, Faustina's revelations were written twenty years before Balthasar wrote his meditations. Yet the two writings have something in common: the experience of Christ as the God of infinite mercy—mercy coming from the Father.

Devotion to the Divine Mercy has, in our day, become inseparably linked with the name of this saint. Her writings are voluminous, and they are written in a manner typical of private revelations. They show no attempt at literary composition and were not intended for publication. Consequently, the writer in a naïve way is unable to separate what were inspired words, called locations or sequential words, from

[69] Ibid., 151–53.

her ordinary thoughts and imagination. When first published in an inaccurate French edition, her revelations were novel enough to be condemned by the Church. However, when Karol Wojtyła (Pope John Paul II) became Archbishop of Krakow, the city where this humble nun lived and died, he set a theologian to make a careful study and publish an accurate edition of her diary. Subsequently, the Church's condemnation was reversed. The Church can never give absolute approval to private revelations, even to those that stand the test of time. What it sometimes does—as with the apparitions and revelations at Lourdes and Fatima—is to give qualified approval by advising the faithful that they may give credence to a particular private revelation and a certain devotional message that may flow from it.[70] The Divine Mercy devotion became the most popular Catholic devotion to Christ by the end of the twentieth century, and Sr. Faustina became the first saint to be canonized in the third millennium.

According to Faustina, devotion to the Divine Mercy is an aspect of devotion to the Sacred Heart of Jesus. In her vision of the merciful Savior, she saw rays of divine mercy coming from the area of His Heart, which is invisible. The message she explains in her writings is actually the same as St. Margaret Mary's: Christ now in eternal glory is concerned for and reaches out to every soul that will respond to Him. This revelation is obviously another expression of the words of Christ that are the foundation of all Christian devotion: "Come to me, all who labor and are heavy laden, and I will give you rest" (Mt 11:28).

Nothing in St. Faustina's experience is new to Christians, and this is as it should be with any authentic private revelation. In one area, however, her writings give an insight, which, while not contradicting revelation or tradition, adds an interesting dimension to our thinking on the possible salvation of those who have lived far from God. She recorded several dialogues with Christ, in which she believed He revealed His infinite love for the human soul in the hour of death. The dialogues included His words to the devout soul, the suffering soul, and the despairing soul. At first, this private revelation seemed to go against the words of the Gospel, namely, that at the end of the world Christ will "repay every man for what he has done" (Mt 16:27). After reading these words of Christ, some may conclude that however devout this humble peasant nun was, she was deluded in this experience of revelation. On further examination, the words can easily be seen as a spiritual commentary on one of the most surprising events in the New Testament—the promise of salvation to the good thief on the cross found in the Gospel of St. Luke.[71]

[70] See Fr. Benedict J. Groeschel, *A Still, Small Voice* (San Francisco: Ignatius Press, 1993), 27–29.

[71] See Lk 23:39–43.

Those who are put off by the merciful Savior's conversation with the despairing soul, as recorded in Faustina's diary, should recall that the good thief had not entered by the narrow gate or walked on the straight path. We know nothing about him except that he said he deserved the punishment he was receiving. Yet Christ promised that wretched man salvation that very day. Salvation is gratuitous, a gift offered to all.

There is an even more subtle theological idea here. Christ's dialogue with the despairing soul as recorded by Faustina makes clear that the soul's first impulse to repentance and hope is purely an act of grace; it is unearned (as is all grace) and does not originate with the dying person. This reflects an early Church teaching against Pelagius, who made salvation primarily dependent on the individual's willingness to follow Christ's teachings. As the Church taught long ago, before anyone can turn to God or do an act of Christian virtue, as distinct from a naturally good act, there must be an initial, or prevenient, grace from God in order for the individual to accept the grace to act.[72] This ancient teaching was especially important to the early Protestant reformers, who accused Catholics of their time of being Pelagian, despite the Church's repeated condemnation of Pelagius through the centuries. I doubt that St. Faustina ever heard of prevenient grace, although the doctrine would have been implied in much of the preaching and teaching to which she was exposed.

Her revelations also opened her to another possible error or heretical idea, one which is almost the opposite of Pelagianism, namely, that the final decision of the soul to accept grace is not necessary. Faustina is clear that the soul must consent to receive God's grace and also that the individual's salvation depends completely on the grace of Christ. We could wish that the humble young woman had lived just before the Protestant Reformation. The popular devotion she revealed might have answered many of the most controversial questions in a way that both scholars and laypeople could have understood.

Although St. Faustina has not attracted much attention from professional theologians, a modest estimate of the number of those influenced by this devotion would indicate that at least one hundred million people now look more lovingly on the merciful Savior. The following prayer of St. Faustina illustrates her very personal and yet profound devotion to Christ as the Savior of the world.

In the terrible desert of life,
O my sweetest Jesus,
Protect souls from disaster,
For You are the Fountain of Mercy.

---

[72] "Prevenient grace" refers to a grace that comes before another grace.

Let the resplendence of Your rays,
O sweet Commander of our souls,
Let mercy change the world.
And you who have received this grace, serve Jesus.

Steep is the great highway I must travel,
But I fear nothing,
For the pure font of mercy is flowing for my sake,
And, with it, strength for the humble soul.[73]

Rose Hawthorne (Mother Alphonsa, O.P., 1851–1926)

No survey of Catholic devotion during the period between the Civil War and the Second Vatican Council would be complete without a representative of the army of Catholic nuns and sisters who dedicated themselves to loving service of Christ and the souls He had come to save. It is said that there were more women religious in the United States in the first half of the twentieth century than there were in Europe during the entire medieval period. The Catholic countries of Europe and even in the missions and Australia saw a similar remarkable growth of religious life of priests and brothers, but especially of sisters. The heart of these communities was devotion to Christ and His Mother. It is difficult to choose one representative of this army of great souls. Among them are a number of canonized saints who lived after the time of Mother Seton, including Mothers Frances Xavier Cabrini, Rose Philippine Duchesne, and Katherine Drexel. Others are candidates for beatification like the two African American sisters Mother Henriette de Lisle and Mother Mary Elizabeth Lange.

I have chosen another woman religious whose cause for beatification has been introduced—Rose Hawthorne, foundress of the Dominican Sisters, Servants of Relief for Incurable Cancer.[74] Many readers will be intrigued by the fact that she was the daughter of the American novelist Nathaniel Hawthorne, who was a Unitarian and, like Isaac Hecker, a member of the transcendentalist movement. Although her father died when Rose was only thirteen, her published memoirs about him are very beautiful and depict him in a noble light:

> His companionship was exquisitely restful, since it was instinctively sympathetic. He did not need to exert himself to know you deeply, and he saw all the good in you there was to know.... As for his spirit, it was always arousing mine, or any one's, and acting towards one's spiritual being invisibly and silently, but with gentle earnestness. He evinced by it either a sternly sweet dignity of tolerance, or an approbation generous as a broad meadow, or a sadly glanced, adverse comment that lashed one's inner consciousness with remorse. He was

[73] Ibid., 383.

[74] For much information about Rose Hawthorne and her family, I have relied on the private manuscript *Rose Hawthorne (Mother Mary Alphonsa, O.P.) 1851–1926*, so generously supplied by the Rose Hawthorne Guild, to which I acknowledge a debt of gratitude.

> meditative, as all those are who care that the world is full of sorrow and sin, but cheerful, as those are who have the character and genius to see the finite beauty and perfection in the world, which are sent to the true-hearted as indications of heaven.[75]

Nathaniel Hawthorne and his wife, Sophia Peabody, belonged to prominent New England families descended from the original Massachusetts Bay colonists. After her husband died in 1864, Sophia found herself in difficult financial circumstances. Wanting to maintain a high level of education and social life for her children, the young widow, for business reasons, moved her family to Dresden, Germany, in 1868. There Rose met George Lathrop, also of a prominent New England family. They all moved to England at the time of the Franco-Prussian War, and after Sophia died there in 1871, Rose married George. The marriage caused a good deal of apprehension to her family, who thought George immature and financially insecure. Their only child, Francis, died in 1881, at the age of four. They both pursued literary careers, and Rose became friends with several writers, particularly Emma Lazarus, who wrote the famous poem inscribed on the Statue of Liberty.

Rose and George were received into the Catholic Church at St. Paul the Apostle, in New York, on March 19, 1891, by Fr. Alfred Young, C.S.P., a student of Fr. Hecker. The couple were part of a group of blue-blooded Protestant converts, and they worked hard to begin a Catholic summer school movement. Unfortunately, George's instability led to a serious alcohol problem, and Rose, with ecclesiastical permission, obtained a permanent separation in 1895.

Rose continued to focus her life on Christ and on charitable works, and the following year, at the age of forty-five, she enrolled in a training course for nurses at the New York Cancer Hospital. She was inspired to undertake such work when she heard from Fr. Young the story of an indigent seamstress dying of cancer who, because she could not pay the rent, was put out of her residence and sent to die at a city-run almshouse without medical facilities. In the closing years of the nineteenth century, New York was a city of extreme economic contrasts: the rich lived in palatial townhouses while the poor struggled in disease-ridden tenements and hovels.

Rose completed the training course, her thoughts constantly focused on how the sick poor were to receive the help they desperately needed. Afterwards, she wrote: "A fire was then lighted in my heart, where it still burns.... I set my whole being to endeavor to bring consolation to the cancerous poor".[76] She rented a cold-water flat in lower Manhattan and, having obtained permission from the city health commissioner, began

---

[75] Rose Hawthorne Lathrop, *Memories of Hawthorne* (Boston: Houghton Mifflin, 1897), 214–15.

[76] Maurice Francis Egan, "A Legacy of Hawthorne", *New York Times Book Review and Magazine*, Apr. 16, 1922, quoted in *Rose Hawthorne.*

to minister to the poor who suffered from cancer. Soon her work expanded to include the poor with other needs, and she decided to "take the lowest class both in poverty and suffering and put them in such a condition that if our Lord knocked at the door we would not be ashamed to show what we had done".[77]

No doubt using her own contacts and her family name, Rose made appeals for alms in the newspapers and drew the attention of Alice Huber, an art student and daughter of a Kentucky physician, who joined Rose in her work. They attended daily Mass, said prayers in common, and obtained spiritual direction.

In February 1899 Fr. Clement Thuente, O.P., of the Church of St. Vincent Ferrer in Manhattan, visited Rose, who was then nursing one of his parishioners. A few days later he wrote: "The great self-sacrificing work of charity I witnessed last Monday when visiting your humble home has made a great and lasting impression on me. I was encouraged and edified by it and thanked God that His example and precept of charity are still imitated and observed."[78] Seeing a statue of St. Rose of Lima at Rose's apartment, he was prompted to suggest that the two women affiliate their work with the Order of Preachers, by becoming Dominican tertiaries. Rose and Alice were moved by Fr. Clement's affirmation and promise of guidance, and on the feast of the Exaltation of the Holy Cross, September 14, they were received as Dominican tertiaries.

In May of that year, with help from generous friends and benefactors, they opened a more spacious house on Cherry Street, where they lived and cared for fifteen poor women with cancer. St. Rose's Free Home, dedicated to the saint of Lima, was thus established. As Dominican tertiaries, they took religious names: Rose became Sr. Alphonsa, and Alice Huber, Sr. Rose.[79] In 1900 they received permission from the Archbishop of New York to form a religious community, and on the feast of the Immaculate Conception they were clothed in the Dominican habit and made first vows as religious. Their community was known as the Servants of Relief for Incurable Cancer, or the Dominican Congregation of St. Rose of Lima.

Within a year, they acquired an old hotel located about an hour's train ride north of the city. There was some conflict at the time about what to call the place. The neighborhood was known as Sherman Park, but the railway station and post office went under other names. Finally Dr. Clendenin, Episcopal rector in nearby Chappaqua, proposed that the

[77] Mother Mary Alphonsa, "Comments upon the East Side, Made in 1897", in *Christ's Poor* 1 (July 1902), 15, quoted in *Rose Hawthorne*.

[78] Letter Feb. 1899 to Rose Hawthorne Lathrop. Archives, Rosary Hill Home.

[79] Some confusion ensued years later between Sister Rose (Huber), who later as superior general of the congregation was Mother Rose, and Rose Hawthorne—Sister (later Mother) Alphonsa, who was never designated Mother Rose. However, when her cause for beatification was opened in 2003, her official name was given as Mother Rose Hawthorne.

village be named Hawthorne. At first Sr. Alphonsa thought the suggestion was made in jest, but it came to be. Unfortunately, it was rumored that she had paid to have the place named after her father. The fact is that it is one of only three towns in the United States named after a nun.

After beginning religious life, Sr. Alphonsa's writing was confined to *Christ's Poor*, "a monthly report of work for incurables among the destitute, nursed by the Dominican Sisters". In the little periodical, published for a few years, she informed the public of the need for her work, communicated news of the community and its mission, made appeals for financial help, and encouraged vocations. To this day, the sisters' finances are inspiring. They accept no payment, not even government or health benefits, for any patient. If a patient's relative sends the sisters a check, it is immediately returned. Even though they have six homes for cancer patients in the eastern United States, they accept donations from a patient's family only after that patient is deceased. Each patient is directly cared for by a sister, which puts considerable strain on the members. Despite the confusion and decline that characterizes many religious communities today, the Dominican Sisters of Hawthorne (as they are popularly called) continue to thrive and do their quiet work with joy and love.

Mother Alphonsa died in her sleep on July 9, 1926. Her cause for beatification was introduced in February 2003. There is no doubt from her writings that Christ was the center of her life. In her Office book was found a prayer of St. Catherine of Siena that she had copied out.

> O Holy Ghost, O Deity Eternal, Christ-Love, come into my heart. By Thy power allure me to Thee, my God, and grant me charity with fear. Guard me, O Love unspeakable, from every evil thought; warm me and fire me with Thy sweetest love, that every pain seem slight to me! My Holy Father, my dearest Lord. Help me now in my every service.
>
> Christ-Love! Christ-Love! Amen.[80]

We get a glimpse of Mother Alphonsa's personal devotion and her familiarity with Jesus in a letter of March 6, 1903, when adoration of the Holy Eucharist began for the community at Rosary Hill, the name given to the sisters' home for cancer patients at Hawthorne, New York.

> This is a wonderful day. Our Blessed Lord has for the first time granted to this community the greatest of blessings to its hours, to its visible offerings, and the greatest dignity to its outward observance. As I knelt during the first adoration, I could not but feel the difference to our whole being as a work, a group of enchained laborers, now that this glorious privilege has been given to us.

[80] From the archives of Rosary Hill Home.

> You must come, and let successively your women come, on First Fridays to this chapel, or else manage to have the privilege at St. Rose's Home. There is no describing the difference it makes. Our Lord is so much more mercifully simple than anyone else; when on earth He was the only one who never made difficulties, showing how friendly God is, and He is ready to be worshipped under the most adverse conditions, if only true veneration springs up like His own fountain in our heart.[81]

Mother Alphonsa's responsibilities for her new religious family, her work with the poor and ill, and the need to raise funds to support both, left her little time for writing or anything else. There are several photographs of Rose Hawthorne taken during her earlier life, but as a religious, she avoided the camera. As incredible as it may seem, there is but one photo of her during the quarter century before her death—a casual picture, not one for which she posed. Among her personal notes we find the following, which shows a soul turning more and more to God, beginning to model the words of St. Paul: "Have this mind among yourselves, which was in Christ Jesus" (Phil 2:5). Unfortunately, these notes are not dated.

> If there are any lovely flowers left in the garden of our lives, of selfish enjoyment, let us gather them as a gift to Jesus Christ, although he does not beg for them. We say that there is a whole army of human occupations and interests which are all due of our personal comfort; but every one of these detracts somewhat from the comfort of the divine joy of our Lord. Which is the most deserving of our care—our Lord's comfort or our own?
>
> Those for whom we have some respect and admiration in the world are apt to be so deformed when we compare them with the beautiful proportions and freshness of complexion of the saints, that we turn in the greatest repugnance from their bestiality or disease of mind—their futility of energy, which struggles in space, detached from all order and immortality.
>
> When tempted to remember any wrongs done to one's self, or to brood over one's trials, think clearly of the Face of our Lord as He walked among his disciples; picture to one's self the emaciated hands with which he healed the wretched objects brought to Him in their sin and sickness, and which he raised in exhortation above the heads of the multitude of poor and unintelligent whom He called to the Light. Picture the sacred feet which trod among the erring footsteps around Him, feet weary and torn, and robes so filled with His holy purity that to touch them was to receive life. But more than all, picture the Holy Face.[82]

[81] Letter to unknown correspondent, Mar. 6, 1903, in ibid.

[82] Mother Alphonsa, Spiritual Maxims, Archives, Rosary Hill Home.

The few notes and memos that have come down to us from Mother Alphonsa reveal a soul totally dedicated to Christ in the poorest of the poor—the terminally ill, who would otherwise have no one to give them adequate care.

Other Catholics of the Twentieth Century

Because of the number of people of outstanding devotion in our times, it is necessary to discuss a few briefly and in pairs because their personalities or positions make an interesting complementarity. One pair are American bishops, who have been proposed for beatification: Archbishop Fulton Sheen and Terence Cardinal Cooke. Another pair are two humble Capuchins whose lives were filled with supernatural phenomena and who in some ways are similar: St. Pio of Pietrelcina and the Venerable Solanus Casey.

Archbishop Fulton J. Sheen (1895–1980) and Terence Cardinal Cooke (1921–1983)

These two men were both auxiliaries, or assistant bishops, to Cardinal Spellman of New York. It would be difficult to find two clerics who had more in common in terms of devotion to Christ but who were completely different in so many other ways. They shared the modest beginnings common to descendants of immigrants: Archbishop Sheen's father ran a hardware store in rural Illinois, and Cardinal Cooke's father, an immigrant from Ireland, was a chauffeur and tile setter in the Bronx. Both men showed real promise as seminarians; the brilliant Sheen was sent abroad to obtain a doctorate in philosophy, whereas Cooke had to discontinue doctoral studies in history at the University of Chicago because of ill health. Eventually, though, he earned a Master's degree in social work at Catholic University in Washington. Fr. Sheen was someone who would not be overlooked, even in a crowd. Fr. Cooke, on the other hand, might be passed by unnoticed; but if you needed something, this quiet gentle priest would be there to help you.

Fulton Sheen was the greatest Catholic preacher of the twentieth century. The notable thing about his writings and sermons, heard on television for years, was that they were dominated by the image of Jesus Christ, especially the suffering Christ. His Good Friday sermons and especially his *Life of Christ*, a monumental meditation book, are mesmerizing for the reader who wishes "to know Christ Jesus", crucified, risen, and coming again. Sheen had adopted the position that Christ's sole purpose in becoming man was to die on the Cross, to accept lovingly that terrible fate so as to atone for the sins of the world, which He redeemed by His holy death. This is a clear acceptance of the *felix culpa*—the happy fault that merited for us such a Redeemer. Sheen ignored the more Franciscan idea that if mankind had not fallen, Christ would have come as king of creation. As he often said with great fervor, Jesus Christ is the only person ever born to die and not to live. In the following quotation Sheen comments on Christ's last instruction to His disciples before His Resurrection.

> Several times Our Lord told His own autobiography, and in each instance without exception it referred to the atonement He would make between God and man. He now summarized His life for the last time, repeating that the Old Testament referred to Him as the Suffering but Conquering Servant.
>
> So it was written, and so it was fitting
> That Christ should suffer,
> And should rise again from the dead on the third day.
> (Luke 24:46)
>
> It is not His Sermon on the Mount that He would have remembered, but His Cross. There would have been no Gospel had there been no Cross; and the death on the Cross would have been useless for the removal of human guilt, if He had not risen from the dead. He said it behooved Him to suffer because He had to show the evil of sin, and evil is most manifest in the Crucifixion of Goodness. No greater darkness would ever descend upon the earth than that which fell upon Him on Calvary. In all other wars, there is generally a gray, or a mixture of good and evil, on both sides; but in the Crucifixion, there was black on one side and white on the other. Evil would never be stronger than it was on that particular day. For the worst thing that evil can do is not to bomb cities and to kill children and to wage wars; the worst thing that evil can do is to kill Goodness. Having been defeated in that, it could never be victorious again.
>
> Goodness in the face of evil must suffer, for when love meets sin, it will be crucified. A God Who wears His Sacred Heart upon His sleeve, as Our Lord did when He became man, must be prepared to have human daws peck at it. But at the same time, Goodness used that very suffering as a condition of overcoming evil. Goodness took all the anger, wrath, and hate, and pleaded: "Forgive"; it took life and offered it for another. Hence to Him it was expedient that He suffer in order to enter glory. Evil, conquered in its full armor and in the moment of its monumental momentum, might in the future win some battles, but it would never win the war.[83]

Bishop Sheen's theology of atonement and of the necessity of good destroying evil is one of his most profound insights. Although it may not be original, his presentation of this truth certainly captured the mind and imagination of millions of Christians, Catholic and non-Catholic.

He was a very devout man, spending a continuous hour each day in prayer before the Holy Eucharist. As national director of the Society for the Propagation of the Faith, he worked unceasingly to raise funds for evangelization and for the care of the poor in the Third World. He suffered much. The kind of popularity and fame that accompanied

[83] Fulton J. Sheen, *Life of Christ* (New York: McGraw-Hill, 1958), 521–22.

his preaching and writing were certain to excite some jealousy and misunderstanding. Although in his later years he was in poor physical health, he carried his cross without complaint. He openly confessed that he had many faults, vanity among them. It is hard to know whether someone's negative assessment of self is really accurate, but when he failed in his role as Bishop of Rochester, he accepted the humiliation peacefully. Sister Mary Aloysius McBride, a member of the Carmelite Sisters for the Aged and Infirm, who interviewed him for admission to their home for the elderly a few days before his death, described him as a simple, humble man with no airs of importance.

Sheen's cause for beatification was opened by the Bishop of Peoria, his home diocese, and it remains to be seen what the result will be. Whatever the Church's judgment on his cause, there can be no doubt that Fulton Sheen lived a consistent and fervent life of devotion to the One he usually referred to as "Our Blessed Lord".

Terence Cardinal Cooke, who suffered from ill health for much of his life and from terminal metastasized cancer for his last nine years, believed a priest must be a servant, listener, victim, and friend.[84] Those who knew him would agree that such noble characteristics applied to him, although he was unaware of it. His appointment as Archbishop of New York, in 1968, came as a complete surprise to almost everyone and seemed to be a recognition of his zealous and diligent fidelity to duty. Despite his unusual practical intelligence even in business and financial matters, he was best known for his extraordinarily kind and deferential personality. His years as archbishop in New York were filled with turbulence and postconciliar unrest. His first duty as archbishop was to attend the funeral of the Rev. Martin Luther King, Jr., who was assassinated on the day of Archbishop Cooke's installation. He was only a mediocre preacher, and he made no pretense of being a scholar. On the other hand, he was an excellent administrator, succeeding in the very tasks that brought Bishop Sheen to failure. He had a tremendous gift for friendship, and the city of New York went into mourning when he died. About a quarter of a million people participated in some aspect of his obsequies, and a great number identified themselves as his friends.

Devotion to Christ was the center of his life. He never entered or left a church without genuflecting and kneeling in adoration for a short time, even if he was late for an appointment. His prayer book contained many prayers to Christ, some of which were his own compositions, and all of which typify his spiritual outlook and attitude.

> Teach me, my Lord, to be sweet and gentle in all the events of life—in disappointments, in the thoughtlessness of others, in the insincerity of those I trusted, in the unfaithfulness of those on whom I relied.

[84] See Benedict J. Groeschel, C.F.R., and Terrence L. Weber, *Thy Will Be Done: A Spiritual Portrait of Terence Cardinal Cooke* (New York: Alba House, 1990), 193.

> Let me put myself aside to think of the happiness of others, and to hide my little pains and heartaches, so that I may be the only one to suffer from them....
>
> May no one be less good for having come within my influence—no one less pure, less true, less kind, less noble for having been a fellow traveler in our journey toward eternal life....
>
> Lord Jesus, I unite myself to your perpetual, unceasing sacrifice. I offer myself to you every day of my life and every moment of every day, according to your most holy and adorable will.... Accept my desire, take my offering, graciously hear my prayer. Let me live for love of you; let me die for love of you; let my last heartbeat be an act of perfect love. Amen.[85]

Cardinal Cooke disguised his terminal illness for nine years; in addition, he kept to himself the fact that he had had cancer for a number of years before that. His physicians assured me that he should have died about five years after he received the diagnosis of terminal illness, and that he should have been very limited in his activity toward the end. He actually worked until a few weeks before he died. His death was ultimately caused not by cancer, but by the damaging effects of prolonged chemotherapy. He spent his last six weeks in prayer, often in adoration of his beloved Lord when the Holy Eucharist was brought to his sick room.

Unlike Bishop Sheen, Cardinal Cooke's most obvious fault was a dislike of controversy. Bishop Sheen continually attacked the Freudian theories of psychoanalysis as materialistic and un-Christian and relentlessly attacked Communism, predicting its final fall. Cardinal Cooke, however, with reason, persuasion, and appeals to mercy and justice tried to oppose abortion legislation, which was then coming before state and federal legislative bodies. When forced to disagree publicly with politicians and their positions, he did it much as Martin Luther King had done: he attacked the evil, not the person responsible for it. Throughout his episcopate, Cardinal Cooke remained a tireless defender of life. By the end of his life, the scope of the attack on human life had taken on much greater proportions than anyone could have foreseen fifteen years earlier. This was uppermost in his mind, and his last pastoral to his people was a plea for respect for all life at every stage of development.

There is a real significance in Cardinal Cooke's deference to Bishop Sheen in his later years in extending the exceptional honor of having Sheen's body entombed in St. Patrick's Cathedral crypt, something usually reserved for the deceased archbishops of New York. Today they lie side by side: one, an eloquent preacher of the Gospel of Christ; the other, a gifted administrator and model of the humility and charity that Jesus

---

[85] Terence Cardinal Cooke, *Prayers for Today* (New York: Alba House, 1991), 82–83.

preached by word and example. Both have been declared Servants of God by the Church.

St. Pio of Pietrelcina (1887–1968) and Ven. Solanus Casey (1870–1957)

Padre Pio, the Italian stigmatist, and Fr. Solanus Casey, the American miracle-worker, were both Capuchin Franciscan friars with much in common, including an incredibly deep devotion to Christ, especially to Christ Crucified. The lives of both humble men were filled with extraordinary, even miraculous, phenomena. Both had their critics and were ridiculed even by those close to them. They endured much misunderstanding because of their miraculous gifts, over which they had no direct control. Padre Pio bore the stigmata, the wounds of Christ. The miraculous origin of the wounds and the fact that although always open, they were never infected, made Padre Pio's life very confined and penitential. He had a robust, peasant sense of humor, and when asked whether the wounds hurt, he answered, "Do you think I got them for an ornament?"

For decades hundreds of thousands of people confessed to and conversed with Padre Pio. His priestly ministry was filled with mysterious phenomena, like the ability to tell penitents their own sins. The supernatural phenomena surrounding Padre Pio's life are well described by a Lutheran pastor, Reverend Bernard Ruffin, in his fascinating biography, *Padre Pio: The True Story*.[86] Padre Pio's devotion to Christ in His Passion was a lifelong act of loving gratitude. He regularly fell into ecstatic prayer during Mass. The following brief selection from his letters to his spiritual director give an insight into this man whose Christ-centered life was similar to that of St. Francis, the first person we know to have received the stigmata.

> I am suffering, and suffering very much, but thanks to our good Jesus I still feel a little strength, and when aided by Jesus what is the creature not capable of doing? I don't desire by any means to have my cross lightened, since I am happy to suffer with Jesus. In contemplating the Cross on His shoulders, I feel more and more fortified and I exult with a holy joy.
>
> * * *
>
> When Jesus wants to make me understand that he loves me, he permits me to relish the wounds, the thorns, the anguish of his Passion. When he wants me to rejoice, he fills my heart with that spirit which is all fire and he speaks to me of his delights. But when he wants to be delighted, he speaks to me of his sufferings, he invites me in a tone which is both a request and a command, to offer my body that his sufferings may be alleviated.[87]

---

[86] Huntington, Ind: Our Sunday Visitor, 1991.

[87] Padre Pio of Pietrelcina, *Letters, Vol. 1: Correspondence with His Spiritual Directors (1910–1922)*, ed. Fr. Gerardo Di Flumeri, O.F.M. Cap. (San Giovanni Rotondo: Editions "*Voce di Padre Pio*", 1980), 342–43, 377–78.

Fr. Solanus spent a humble life as a priest with limited duties. Because he had failed theological studies given in German, he could offer Mass but was restricted from other pastoral activities such as preaching and hearing confessions. His extraordinary piety and humility, as well as his humor and compassion, endeared him to vast numbers of people who besieged St. Bonaventure Friary in Detroit to receive his counsel and especially to ask his prayers for the sick. As with similar accounts we read in the Gospel, Fr. Solanus' prayers could, with obvious divine intervention, cure even the dying. In my youth I knew people who had been cured of serious, even terminal, illnesses by Fr. Solanus' prayers. Even in his eighties he had the incredible strength to spend long hours in prayer through the night and in constant work for those who sought his help. He was also very interested in the care of the poor and opened a free soup kitchen in Detroit, which has served millions of meals up to this day.

Fr. Solanus wrote little. His few writings, which were not intended for publication, show a simple and all-encompassing faith. In a letter he wrote: "There is such a thing as getting a 'taste of heaven' in this world, as we see in the lives of the saints. But it is up to each of us to strive for—inasmuch as our virtue of hope is inspired by faith in God and strengthened—sweetened—in confidence of His great merciful goodness." [88] His simple and direct approach to the Christian life is evident in the following:

> We do well to remember how very short, after all, it is till our suffering and our time of merit, too, will be over. Let us offer everything, therefore, to the divine Spouse of our souls, that He may accept it as helping Him to save immortal souls—our own included.
>
> Let us thank God ahead of time for whatever He foresees is pleasing to Him, leaving everything at His divine disposal, including—with all its circumstances—when, where, and how He may be pleased to dispose the events of our death.[89]

The adoration of Christ in the Holy Eucharist was the center of his life. I recall an incident long ago when I came upon him as he knelt in ecstasy before the tabernacle in the monastery chapel. It was late at night, and the chapel was in darkness. When I switched on the light, there was no movement or reaction from Fr. Solanus. It seemed he had no idea I was there. His eyes were half open but riveted on the tabernacle, just a few feet away, since he was kneeling, with arms extended, on the top step of the altar platform. Although this happened more than fifty years ago, I can still sense the mystery and awe

[88] Letter to Sister Mary Joseph, May 21,1945, quoted in Br. Leo Wollenweber, O.F.M. Cap., *Meet Solanus Casey: Spiritual Counselor and Wonder Worker* (Ann Arbor, Mich.: Servant Books, 2002), 58.

[89] Quoted in Wollenweber, *Meet Solanus Casey*, 125, 127.

I experienced as I watched this holy man for several minutes in silent communication with the Lord.

These two men, who never had any ecclesiastical position of importance, were totally imbued with the love of Christ. Neither was a great preacher or writer, yet each gave to thousands an experience of Christ operating in another person.

Spiritual Giants of the Late Twentieth Century

As the twentieth century drew to a close, the number of great Catholic theologians and philosphers seemed sadly reduced. At this time the Church seemed beset by a confusion and uncertainty that was all but absent in the early years of the century. Yet giants remained. Here we will examine the two greatest among them: a pope who was also a great philosopher and theologian and a humble nun whose total devotion to Christ made her known throughout the world.

Blessed Teresa of Calcutta (1910–1997)

We come to a towering figure, one who died shortly before the end of the twentieth century and was beatified in October 2003. At the time of her death I had known Mother Teresa for more than three decades—half my life—and therefore I feel a responsibility to attempt to shed some light on her life of dedication to Christ and the souls He loves. In her, we see a reflection not only of the love between Christ and the individual but also of His divine love for all.

As part of the beatification process, a collection of letters was assembled, which Mother Teresa had written to her spiritual directors in the years following the establishment of her community, the Missionaries of Charity. Except for these letters, excerpts from which were printed in articles in Indian Catholic publications, Mother Teresa's spiritual life might have remained a mystery to most of us. These heartrending documents, which reveal her great spiritual trials during that period, left many of her friends, including myself, completely astonished. Almost everyone who had known Mother Teresa assumed that she experienced God's presence and in some way felt His love, which motivated her words and example. Although the letters are testimonies to her devotion, it was a devotion in the midst of darkness for many years. For forty years she seems to have lived through what the mystics refer to as the "dark night of the soul".

Mother Teresa was born to devout Catholic parents and grew up in a middle-class home in Macedonia, although the family was ethnically Albanian. Early in childhood she experienced a great devotion to Christ and a desire to serve Him. "From childhood the Heart of Jesus has been my first love.... From the age of 5½ years, when first I received Him, the love for souls has been within. It grew with the years."[90]

[90] Brian Kolodiejchuk, M.C., "The Soul of Mother Teresa: Hidden Aspects of Her Interior Life", pt. 1, unpublished manuscript by the postulator of her cause.

It is no surprise to friends and family that this serious young woman, whose deep eyes look out at you from a photograph taken when she was eighteen, entered the convent of the Loreto Sisters in Ireland and was eventually sent as a missionary to India. After spending several years as a teacher and headmistress of a school for both indigent and wealthy girls, Mother Teresa, who had already made a private vow of total dedication to Christ in 1942, experienced a powerful call, or inspiration, to begin a new community dedicated to free, hands-on service to the poor.[91] The members of the community would follow Indian customs and lifestyle and wear the sari, the traditional dress for Indian women. The whole purpose was to serve Christ in the poorest of the poor and especially to share in their suffering and deprivation.

After a year's delay and prayerful consideration, the Archbishop of Calcutta gave his approval, and Mother Teresa went for some months to train as a nurse with the Little Sisters of the Poor. With about eight cents in her pocket, she moved into a borrowed room to begin her work. In the street, she found a dying man, covered with maggots, and brought him in to care for him. From small beginnings, the Missionaries of Charity grew to more than four thousand sisters at the time of Mother Teresa's death. There is also a contemplative branch of the Congregation and two parallel communities of priests and brothers.

I first met Mother Teresa in 1967 in the crowded Manhattan apartment of Eileen Egan, one of her biographers. As we spoke, it seemed to me that I was all alone with her. The roomful of people seemed to disappear, and I became mesmerized by her gentle voice and simple yet profound words. Those few minutes were a unique experience in my life. In 1974 Cardinal Cooke asked me to be his liaison with the Missionaries of Charity, and over the years I was privileged to know this dedicated soul very well. I was also privileged to offer Mass for her and her contemplative sisters the day before she left New York for India, eight weeks before her death.

Mother Teresa's great mystical devotion to Christ, especially present in the Holy Eucharist and in the poor, was apparent to anyone who knew her even superficially. It could be summed up in the words "I thirst" (Jn 19:28). These words of Christ from the Cross are placed on the wall behind the altar in each of the chapels of the Missionaries of Charity. They are a unique expression of Christian devotion, one that we have not considered during this long account. Mother Teresa explored the significance of the words of the suffering Jesus as He hung on the Cross.

> The time has come for me to speak openly on the gift God gave me on Sept. 10th, to explain as fully as I can what means to me the thirst

[91] Ibid.

of Jesus. For me the thirst of Jesus is something so intimate, so I have felt shy until now to speak to you about September 10th.... Everything in MC exists only to satiate Jesus. His words on the wall of every MC chapel are not from the past only, but alive here and now, spoken to you.... Jesus Himself must be the one to say to you "I thirst." Hear your own name, not just once, every day.... "I thirst" is something much deeper than Jesus just saying "I love you." Unless you know deeply inside that Jesus thirsts for you, you cannot begin to know what He wants to be for you and what He wants you to be for Him.[92]

The thirst for Jesus in the individual soul has been recognized by several mystics in this study, especially SS. Margaret Mary and Francis de Sales in the seventeenth century. It was the center of Mother Teresa's whole devotion to Jesus. Amid all her trials she never lost sight of our Lord's thirst and love for those He came to save. Mother Teresa's unusual experience was her own deep thirst for the presence of Christ and some sign of His affection. It extended over forty years of painful spiritual aridity and darkness. Not since the writings of St. John of the Cross in the sixteenth century has anyone revealed the depth of darkness, spiritual hunger and thirst, and sense of abandonment by God that Mother Teresa describes to her spiritual directors, who must have been puzzled by this revelation.

In the darkness ... Lord, my God, who am I that you should forsake me? The child of your love—and now become as the most hated one. The one You have thrown away as unwanted—unloved. I call, I cling, I want, and there is no one to answer.... Where I try to raise my thoughts to heaven, there is such convicting emptiness that those very thoughts return like sharp knives and hurt my very soul....

The whole time smiling—Sisters and people pass such remarks—they think my faith, trust and love are filling my very being & that the intimacy with God and union to His will must be absorbing my heart. Could they but know ... how my cheerfulness is the cloak by which I cover the emptiness and misery. In spite of all, this darkness and emptiness is not as painful as the longing for God.

* * *

Pray for me, Father. Inside of me there is so much of suffering—pray for me that I may not refuse God in this hour—I don't want to do it, but I am afraid I may do it. Pray for me.

* * *

[92] Letter, Mar. 25, 1993, to all members of the Missionaries of Charity, cited in J. Neuner, S.J., "Mother Teresa's Charism", in *Vidyajyoti Journal of Theological Reflection*, March 2001, 180. September 10, 1946, the founding day of the Missionaries of Charity (MC).

> I must have been so very full of self all this year—Since God is taking so long to empty me. I hope one day when I am fully empty He comes. Pray for me.[93]

In the midst of the many decades of aridity, Mother Teresa held on to two things: the belief that Christ was present to her and the need to "smile back" at Him, to suffer in silence, that is, "to give something beautiful to God". In giving the following advice to a priest in 1974, she revealed how she viewed her own suffering.

> You have said "yes" to Jesus and He has taken you at your word. The Word of God became Jesus the poor one. And so this terrible emptiness you experience. God cannot fill what is full. He can only fill emptiness—deep poverty—and your "yes" is the beginning of being or becoming empty. It is not how much we really "have" to give, but how empty we are, so that we can receive fully in our life and let Him live His life in us. In you today He wants to relive His complete submission to His Father—allow Him to do so. It does not matter what you feel but what He feels in you. Take away your eyes from yourself and rejoice that you have nothing—that you are nothing—that you can do nothing. Give Jesus a big smile each time your nothingness frightens you. This is the poverty of Jesus. You and I must let Him live in us and through us in the world. Cling to Our Lady, for she too—before she could become full of grace—full of Jesus—had to go through that darkness.[94]

In her darkness, Mother Teresa clung firmly to the Christian doctrine of redemption as an explanation of the suffering she endured. It is important to note that this quotation reveals how she identified her own sufferings with those of the poor.

> Try to increase your knowledge of the mystery of redemption. This knowledge will lead you to love, and love will make you share through your sacrifice in the passion of Christ. My dear children, without suffering our work would just be social work—very good and helpful, but it would not be the work of Jesus Christ, not part of the redemption. Jesus wanted to help us by sharing our life, our loneliness, our agony and death. All that He has taken upon Himself and has carried it in the darkest night. Only by being one with us has He redeemed us. We are able to do the same. All the desolation of the poor people, not only their material poverty but their spiritual destitution, must be redeemed, and we must have our share in it. Pray thus when you find it hard: I wish to live in this world which is so

[93] Letters to Lawrence Picachy, S.J., undated; Dec. 13, 1959; Feb. 13, 1963, quoted in Albert Huart, S.J., "Mother Teresa: Joy in Darkness", *Vidyajyoti Journal of Theological Reflection* (Sept. 2000): 656–57.

[94] Letter, Feb. 7, 1974, quoted in Huart, "Joy in Darkness", 658.

> far from God, which has turned so much from the light of Jesus, to help them—to take upon myself something of their suffering. Yes, my dear children, let us share the sufferings of the poor, for only by being one with them can we redeem them; that is bringing God into their lives and bringing them to God.[95]

The center of Mother Teresa's life was the presence of Christ in the Holy Eucharist. She began each day with a holy hour at four in the morning, an hour before the other sisters awakened. She made an additional holy hour in the afternoon with the rest of the community. Often she was exhausted after a strenuous day, and I have had the humbling experience of seeing her fall asleep on her knees as I tried to give a few spiritual thoughts to the community at their convent in the South Bronx on a hot summer afternoon.

Mother Teresa often spoke of Jesus as someone with whom she was very familiar. On one occasion, an earthy New York radio raconteur asked her, "What do you think of abortion?" Without hesitation, she replied by asking what he thought Jesus thought of abortion. He was speechless. Despite her darkness and sense of abandonment by God, Mother Teresa never betrayed any loss of zeal or ability to follow her beloved Master. Even as an old woman, with many illnesses, she traveled the world establishing homes to serve the poor. She referred to her convents as tabernacles because of Christ's presence in the Eucharist. When she received the Nobel Prize in 1979 and again when she gave a commencement address at Harvard in 1982, she quietly presented the Gospel teaching in unflinching words, defending the unborn in Sweden and praising the beauty of virginity and chastity in Cambridge. Her sincerity in confessing Christ before these unbelieving audiences brought them at first to absolute silence and then, especially at Harvard, moved them to thunderous applause.

I am convinced that during the last weeks of her life Mother Teresa experienced the darkness lifting. When Fr. Andrew Apostoli, my confrere, and I offered Mass for her eight weeks before her death, she was a different person. She was filled with joy, enthusiasm, and gratitude that her community was established in 115 countries and had more than five hundred convents. I knew some great change had taken place in her. There had always been a certain gravity about Mother Teresa, which I took to be a sorrow and preoccupation with the sufferings of the poor. That was gone. As we left her, I said to Fr. Andrew that we would never see her again. She was already approaching the gates of the Kingdom promised to the merciful, the pure of heart, the peacemakers, and the poor in spirit. Without any equivocation, I can say that I never knew anyone who tried to please Christ more, to live for

[95] Address to the Sisters of the Missionaries of Charity (July 16, 1993), quoted in Neuner, "Mother Teresa's Charism", 181.

Him more, and who hungered and thirsted more with Him for justice and mercy.

Those familiar with the great library of writings on the spiritual life will not be surprised that the Lord used darkness to prepare this chosen soul for an ever closer union with Him. The postulator of her cause has summed up the place of darkness in her life.

> Progressively Mother Teresa's abandonment and intense and painful longing for God became her way of union and identification with her Beloved in His agony on the Cross. "For my meditation I am using the Passion of Jesus. I am afraid I make no meditation but only look at Jesus suffer and keep repeating: 'Let me share with you His pain.' " She understood that the darkness she experienced was a mystical participation in Jesus' sufferings: "Father, I am alone. I have His darkness. I have His pain." Because it was His, she also had joy: "Today really I felt a deep joy that Jesus can't go anymore through the agony, but that He wants to go through it in me. More than ever I surrender myself to Him. Yes, more than ever I will be at His disposal." [96]

Mother Teresa's spiritual darkness served the additional purpose of uniting her with the poor, and her sense of being rejected gave her a unique ability to understand and feel one with them.

> Very often she was heard to say that the greatest poverty is to be "unwanted, unloved, lonely, uncared for." It is now evident that her extraordinary sensitivity to emotional and spiritual suffering and her capacity for compassion and love had a root in her own interior experience. Even when she was experiencing severe interior pain, her attention was completely focused on others and their particular suffering. By a gentle touch, a kind word, a small service or simply a smile she communicated the truth that "God wants you, God loves you, God is with you, God cares for you." In a word, "God thirsts for you." [97]

For thoughtful people who met her, even in the most formal public settings, Mother Teresa, a little, old bent-over nun, communicated an immense silent strength, as well as utter determination. Once she was convinced that something was God's will, nothing could stand in her way. I believe that this strength was the result of years of suffering. Like tempered steel, the Lord had forged her soul through suffering and spiritual thirst. When she spoke at the United Nations, the secretary-general introduced her by saying, "From this podium have spoken the most powerful men in the world. Today we hear from the most powerful woman in the world".

[96] Kolodiejchuk, "Soul of Mother Teresa", 3–4.

[97] Ibid., 4.

We are reminded of St. Paul's words that "power is made perfect in weakness" (2 Cor 12:9). Mother Teresa also reveals that "the poor things of this world has God chosen" (Jas 2:5).

As liaison with the Missionaries of Charity, I sometimes disagreed with Mother Teresa (I always lost). On one occasion, when we disagreed, she said something revealing. She asked me why I thought Christ had called me to the priesthood. She did not smile when I said I thought it was because of His sense of humor. Instead she answered: "We are chosen by the humility of God. He chooses the weakest, poorest, most inadequate instruments. He chooses us. Father, don't forget that you were chosen by the humility of God." No one has ever said anything more revealing to me. I felt I was walking on a road in Galilee, and Jesus Christ Himself had spoken to me.

Pope John Paul II (1920–2005)

Pope John Paul II's long life and pontificate were marked by deep and unwavering devotion to Christ, His Mother, and the saints, which grew from his strong Polish roots and particularly from the devotion of his father, a widower, who raised his two sons largely on his own. An early photograph of Karol Wojtyła shows him in his First Communion suit just a month after his mother's death. His father was responsible for ensuring that the boy's religious formation went forward despite the family's profound grief.

It can almost be said that the focus of the culture in which John Paul grew up, during the time of Nazi and Communist oppression, was devotion to Jesus Christ. It was a culture filled with liturgy, shrines, and personal prayer. Nowhere was this more obvious than in the many demonstrations of piety toward Christ's presence in the Eucharist.

The facts of Pope John Paul's life are well known, and it is obvious that his decision to follow Christ in the priesthood was based on personal devotion. His rise in the hierarchy does not tell us much about his devotion except that the direction of his labors under Communism was toward making Christ real to the people.

From his early days as pope, it was obvious that John Paul was a man of devotion. His first words to the people gathered in St. Peter's Square were "Praised be Jesus Christ". At his installation he seized the processional cross and held it high with great enthusiasm before a cheering crowd. His first encyclical, *Redemptor Hominis*, stressed the importance of understanding the traditional Christian teaching on Christ's divinity and His significance to each person for salvation and redemption. The new Pope was beginning to counter the declining appreciation of Christology and the denial of Christ's divinity in any orthodox sense and of His unique work as Redeemer of mankind. By the beginning of the new millennium, this trend had become a *cause célèbre* for avant-garde Catholic and Protestant writers.

Following the conciliar teaching in *Gaudium et Spes* on redemption, John Paul wrote:

> [W]e do not forget even for a moment that Jesus Christ, the Son of the living God, became our reconciliation with the Father. He it was, and He alone, who satisfied the Father's eternal love, that fatherhood that from the beginning found expression in creating the world, giving man all the riches of creation, and making him "little less than God".... He and he alone also satisfied that fatherhood of God and that love which man in a way rejected by breaking the first Covenant and the later covenants that God "again and again offered to man." The redemption of the world—this tremendous mystery of love in which creation is renewed—is, at its deepest root, the fullness of justice in a human Heart—the Heart of the first-born Son—in order that it may become justice in the hearts of many human beings, predestined from eternity in the first-born Son to be children of God and called to grace, called to love.[98]

While we cannot review the huge corpus of John Paul's writings on Christ, there are three areas of importance that summarize his personal devotion, which he shared at all times with all Christians who would receive it. They are Christ's saving suffering and its meaning for each person, the mercy of God shown to men by Christ, and the mystery of the Holy Eucharist, which, despite its profound theological and ecclesial significance, ultimately has its full flowering in individual devotion to Christ's person.

In all his theological writings, the individual—Christian or non-Christian, believer or nonbeliever, saint or sinner—is never far away. From his earliest days as a teacher of youth in Communist-dominated Poland, especially at the Catholic University of Lublin, he always began and ended his teaching with individual experience. His philosophical personalism was essential for devotion, as we have defined it. Moreover, the paradigm of devotion that we presented at the beginning of this book found strong echoes in his first encyclical and would be repeated in many other documents. In his apostolic letter *Salvifici Doloris* (1984), after a long analysis of suffering and its significance in Christ's life, we read of a particular power concealed in suffering and drawing us to Christ. The Pope outlines the spiritual steps by which Christ draws the soul to Himself.

> It is He Himself who acts at the heart of human sufferings through His Spirit of truth, through the consoling Spirit. It is He who transforms, in a certain sense, the very substance of the spiritual life, indicating for the person who suffers a place close to Himself. It is He—as the interior Master and Guide—who reveals to the suffering brother and sister this wonderful interchange, situated at the very heart of the mystery of the Redemption. Suffering is, in itself, an experience of evil. But Christ has made suffering the firmest basis of the definitive

[98] Pope John Paul II, *Redemptor Hominis*, 9.1.

> good, namely, the good of eternal salvation. By His suffering on the cross, Christ reached the very roots of evil, of sin and death. He conquered the author of evil, Satan, and his permanent rebellion against the Creator. To the suffering brother or sister, Christ discloses and gradually reveals the horizons of the kingdom of God: the horizons of a world converted to the Creator, of a world free from sin, a world being built on the saving power of love.[99]

The Pope goes on to point out that the suffering person poses the question "Why?" to God and Christ. "He [the sufferer] asks the meaning of his suffering and seeks an answer to this question on the human level. Certainly he often puts this question to God, and to Christ. Furthermore, he cannot help noticing that the One to whom he puts the question is Himself suffering and wishes to answer him from the cross, from the heart of His own suffering."[100] Thus in the eyes of John Paul II, Christian suffering, experienced in faith and love, fulfills all the requirements of true devotion.

In his milestone encyclical *Dives in Misericordia* (1980), inspired in part by the private revelations of St. Faustina, John Paul discusses the need of most believers for God's mercy and forgiveness.[101] After exploring the biblical and theological aspects of Divine Mercy, he focuses on the need for Christians, especially in the Church, to lead a life of mercy, forgiveness, and compassion.

> Everything that I have said in the present document on mercy should therefore be continually transformed into an ardent prayer: into a cry that implores mercy according to the needs of man in the modern world. May this cry be full of that truth about mercy which has found such rich expression in Sacred Scripture and in Tradition, as also in the authentic life of faith of countless generations of the People of God. With this cry let us, like the sacred writers, call upon the God who cannot despise anything that He has made, the God who is faithful to Himself, to His fatherhood and His love.... Let us have recourse to that fatherly love revealed to us by Christ in his messianic mission, a love which reached its culmination in His Cross, in His death and Resurrection. Let us have recourse to God through Christ, mindful of the words of Mary's Magnificat, which proclaim mercy "from generation to generation."[102]

---

[99] Pope John Paul II, *Salvifici Doloris*, 26.

[100] Ibid.

[101] Since Church teaching is always based on Scripture and tradition, and never on private revelation, Faustina Kowalska is not mentioned in the encyclical. (It would be another twenty years before she was canonized—the first person so honored in the new millennium.) An encyclical may be occasioned by a private revelation that emphasizes a theological teaching, such as several papal documents on the Sacred Heart of Jesus.

[102] John Paul II, *Dives in Misericordia*, 15.3.

Toward the end of his life, he focused the attention of the Catholic world on the Holy Eucharist as it is traditionally understood: as sacrifice, the Mass, sacrament, Holy Communion, and presence. He validated again the devotion of the reservation of the Eucharist for prayer in the encyclical *Ecclesia de Eucharistia* as the final, substantial teaching of his pontificate. He proclaimed a Eucharistic year intended to increase devotion to the presence of Christ in the Blessed Sacrament. John Paul died during that year, on the eve of Divine Mercy Sunday, a feast he had assigned to the Sunday after Easter. In a concluding paragraph on understanding this devotion and its contribution to life of the faithful John Paul II wrote: "The mystery of the Eucharist—sacrifice, presence, banquet ... must be experienced and lived in its integrity, both its celebration and in the intimate converse with Jesus which takes place after receiving communion or in a prayerful moment of Eucharistic adoration apart from Mass. These are times when the Church is firmly built up."[103]

Interestingly, after emphasizing the Catholic faith and tradition about the Eucharist, Pope John Paul referred to the Church's path at the beginning of the new millennium as one "of renewed ecumenical commitment".

> The path itself is long and strewn with obstacles greater than our human resources alone can overcome, yet we have the Eucharist, and in its presence we can hear in the depths of our hearts, as if they were addressed to us, the same words heard by the prophet Elijah: "Arise and eat, else the journey will be too great for you" (1 Kings 19:7).
>
> Let us take our place, dear brothers and sisters, at the school of the saints, who are the great interpreters of true Eucharistic piety. In them the theology of the Eucharist takes on all the splendor of a lived reality; it becomes "contagious" and, in a manner of speaking, it "warms our hearts".[104]

It is most appropriate to conclude this lengthy study, which I hope will have an impact on ecumenical relations, with a recognition of Pope John Paul II, a great ecumenical figure who was not confused by the relativism of his times. He has been praised by Orthodox Christians and Protestants of every tradition, but especially Evangelical Protestants.

[103] John Paul II, *Ecclesia de Eucharistia*, 61.

[104] Ibid.

27 An Overview

It should be obvious by now that the history of devotion to Christ is as interesting and varied as the history of the human race. It is a vast panorama that includes the entire sweep of Christian history from east to west and from apostolic times to the present moment. Because of the intense individuality of personal spiritual experience and the many forms that Christian belief has taken, however, it has been impossible to represent this devotion in all its myriad forms or even in every Christian denomination and tradition. The most frustrating part of writing a book such as this is the many things that must be omitted— people, movements, ideas. Some traditions resist depiction: the Anabaptists are reluctant to write about their devotional thoughts, lest such thoughts become ritualized; the essence of Pentecostalism can be experienced far better than it can be described. When it comes to churches with a liturgical life, one must look beyond ritual to discover how personal devotion endows ceremonies with life and relates them to the truths of faith. Both devotion and informed theological conviction are essential so that a person attending a liturgy is not a spectator but a full participant in faith and love. Both solemn liturgical ritual and free-form public worship should lead to the love of God, of Christ, and of neighbor.

Three Goals The goals of this book, as we noted, are threefold. First, to demonstrate that devotion, as defined in the opening chapter, has been an essential component of Christian life: it is the vibrant personal experience that Christ in eternal glory knows us individually, cares for us, expects things from us, hears us, and will meet us when we pass beyond this world. This truth is both a source of loving gratitude and a warning to be ready because "the Son of man is coming at an hour you do not expect" (Mt 24:44).

The second goal was to identify the many ways in which devotion to Jesus crosses denominational lines and to show the deep commonality among all those who seek to know and love our Savior. My long experience with Protestant and Orthodox friends has led me to believe that we often fail to realize how much we share. Until I began this study, I had no idea of the immense number of similarities and the endless interconnections that exist. Although it is true that each tradition strengthens its own identity by emphasizing real, theologically significant differences, in the past, these differences have often been exaggerated because of ignorance and the failure to recognize other believers' love for Christ and the work of the Holy Spirit. Through angry polemics the commonality of Christian experience has been obscured, yet we all read the same Gospels, pray to the same Christ, and have the same hope of experiencing His redemption. These facts have given rise to a similarity of devotion, which few recognize. The profound impact of Eastern Christian writings is often overlooked. The Catholic influence on Protestant devotion is remarkable but often ignored. As we have seen, it was Protestant scholars like E. Glenn Hinson who realized that many do not recognize their own roots (see Chapter 20). We have but to read the sermon of Cromwell's chaplain on the Sacred Heart or the Wesleys' 160 hymns for the holy sacrifice of the Eucharist to be confronted with the crossover influence. On the other hand, we see Protestant influence on Catholics in the evangelical tone of such important figures as Cardinal Newman and Mother Seton and in the Catholic charismatic renewal, which had its start in the Protestant Pentecostalism of a century ago.

If you studied this book by beginning with those parts of Christianity familiar to you and skipping over unfamiliar things, you should go back now and see how Christians interacted to one another during the periods we have indicated. Catholics and Protestants should review the great figures of the Protestant Reformation and the Catholic Counter-Reformation to find similarities and interconnections of which we were unaware. All should strive to understand the depth of the Eastern Orthodox experience, which has been made available to Westerners since the Orthodox Church became free of Muslim and then Communist domination.

Many areas of interconnection deserve greater study. Such study will enrich one's understanding of one's own tradition and increase comprehension of and esteem for others. Devotion to Christ is a non-controversial, positive area for exploration. It is an activity in which there is no place for the arguments and pedantic details so often found in books written to attack of defend various theological positions.

The third and most important goal of this book has been to demonstrate that devotion to our Savior is an essential element of Christian life. The recent decline of devotion among many Christians finds both its causes and effects in worldliness, a loss of the sense of discipleship, skepticism in biblical studies, and moral and theological relativism. It is a crippling symptom of our post-Christian era. The poor and humble, who preserve a vibrant sense of devotion, have much to teach us. Many of the young are so devoid of an experience of devotion that they have easily been drawn into the paganism of our time. When they become aware of the riches and power of devotion to our

Lord Jesus Christ, however, many respond quickly, easily, and joyfully to devotional prayer and meditation.

We have examined the devotion of some of the most impressive figures in Christian history. These lovers of Christ were more disciples than they were church people. By "church people" we mean those who follow the teaching of the churches but whose daily lives do not really spring from the Gospel, those who follow the rules but do not really imitate Christ. This distinction is ambiguous and difficult to apply, since there are Christians of all denominations moving in the same direction. Some are fervent followers of Christ in their youth, often after a conversion, but in later life they may slip into the role of being simply church members. They may focus on the externals of Christianity rather than making the sacrifices required to be fervent disciples. If ever there was a problem ecumenically shared, it is putting the tangible activities of religiosity before spiritual truths.

On the other hand, many start out merely as observant church members. As a result of grace and perhaps the example of some holy people, they move from external church membership to true discipleship. They will often know conflict as the attitudes and activities important to some church members—clergy and religious—gradually appear to be at odds with the following of Christ and devotion to Him.

The great defense of established church members who do not want to change is to belittle devotion as outmoded, irrelevant, and even an obstacle to more efficient operation of their denomination or the professional care of the needy. The example of Mother Teresa of Calcutta reveals the superficiality of these criticisms. If we look carefully in the Christian world, we see those for whom Christ is real. They love to speak to Him in prayer, and speak of Him to others. They base their decisions on His Gospel, and they try constantly to follow Him. They are often the "little people", like the unknown women who followed Christ to Calvary. Sometimes, however, they are great minds with little formal training, like Sojourner Truth or Phoebe Palmer, or nuns and monks, like St. Teresa or St. Tikhon of Zadonsk. Others are bishops like Archbishop Ramsey of Canterbury or Cardinal Cooke, or unknown souls like Thérèse of Lisieux or the devout souls found in any good-sized parish. Still others have been great sinners who struggled to turn to Christ. If you try to give all this a name, you will find that only one name fits: devotion to Jesus Christ, our Savior.

It is my hope that all who have delved into this book will utter a deeply felt amen to the phrase "Christ yesterday, today, and forever." Belief in the absolute centrality of Jesus of Nazareth, the Christ of God, is both the origin and experience of Christian devotion. Reviewing the whole Christian experience from the perspective of personal devotion enables us to grasp what it is that brings Christ's disciples together in something more than goodwill and fellowship. It is shared religious experience of the deepest kind.

An Overview

In 1989 Cardinal Ratzinger in a summer course in Spain was asked to give a final lecture to students who had heard theologians and scholars from several denominations and disciplines discussing controversial issues in Christology. His entire lecture makes fascinating reading, since he confronts so much of the skepticism and confusion in both the academic world and in much of contemporary culture. Although his remarks were not directly related to Christian devotion, his address contains the following passage, which is a fitting way to bring this book to a conclusion:

> The first encounter with Jesus Christ occurs in the present; indeed, one can only encounter him because he is a today for many and therefore has a today. But to ensure that I get close to the whole Christ and not just a piece of him perceived by chance, I must heed the Christ of yesterday as he reveals himself in the sources, especially in Scripture. If, in the process, I listen to him carefully and do not excise essential parts of his appearance because of a dogmatically asserted worldview, I see him open to the future and I see him coming from eternity, which embraces the past, the present, and the future, all at once. Where such a holistic understanding has been sought and lived, there Christ has always completely become "today," for only that which has roots in yesterday and powers of growth for tomorrow and which is in touch with the eternal beyond all time has real power over and in the present. The great periods in the history of faith have each produced its own image of Christ in this way; each period was capable of seeing him anew from the perspective of its own today, and precisely in this way each period recognized "Christ yesterday and today and forever." [1]

[1] Joseph Ratzinger, *A New Song for the Lord* (New York: Crossroad, 1996), 13.

Selected Bibliography

The African American Heritage Hymnal. Chicago: GIA Publications, 2001.

Ahern, Patrick V. *Maurice and Thérèse: The Story of a Love*. New York: Doubleday, 1998.

Alphonsus de Liguori. *Alphonsus de Liguori: Selected Writings*. Edited by Frederick M. Jones, C.Ss.R. Classics of Western Spirituality. New York: Paulist Press, 1999.

———. *Complete Works of Saint Alphonsus de Liguori*. Edited by Eugene Grimm, C.Ss.R. Brooklyn, N.Y.: Redemptorist Fathers, 1927.

American Sermons: The Pilgrims to Martin Luther King, Jr. New York: Literary Classics of the United States, 1999.

Anthony. *Saint Anthony: Herald of the Good News*. Translated and edited by Claude M. Jarmak, O.F.M. Conv. Ellicott City, Md.: Conventual Franciscan Friars, 1995.

Arndt, Johann. *Johann Arndt: True Christianity*, trans. Peter Erb. Classics of Western Spirituality. New York: Paulist Press, 1979.

Atkinson, James, ed. *The Darkness of Faith: Daily Readings with Martin Luther*. London: Darton, Longman and Todd, 1987.

Augustine. *Augustine: Major Writings*. Edited by Benedict J. Groeschel, C.F.R. New York: Crossroad, 1995.

———. *The City of God*. Abridged ed. Translated by Gerard Walsh, S.J., et al. Garden City, N.Y.: Image Books/Doubleday, 1958.

———. *The Confessions of Saint Augustine*. Translated by Frank J. Sheed. New York: Sheed and Ward, 1965.

———. *Saint Augustine: Sermons on the Liturgical Seasons*. Translated by Sr. Mary Sarah Muldowney. New York: Fathers of the Church, 1959.

Aulén, Gustaf. *Dag Hammarskjöld's White Book: An Analysis of Markings*. Philadelphia: Fortress Press, 1969.

Baker, Augustine. *Sancta Sophia*. Edited by Dom Norbert Sweeney, O.S.B. London: Burns and Oates, 1876.

———. *Secretum*. Edited by Abbot Justin McCann. London: Burns, Oates and Washbourne, 1922.

Barnett, Lincoln. *The Universe and Dr. Einstein*, New York: William Morrow and Company, 1948.

Bartleman, Frank. *Azusa Street*. Plainfield, N.J.: Logos International, 1980.

Battles, Ford Lewis, and Stanley Tagg, ed. and trans. *The Piety of John Calvin*. Grand Rapids, Mich.: Baker Book House, 1978.

Beausobre, Julia de. *Flame in the Snow*. Springfield, Ill.: Templegate Publishers, 1996.

Bebis, George S. *Nicodemos of the Holy Mountain*. Translated by Peter A. Chamberas. Classics of Western Spirituality. New York: Paulist Press, 1989.

Bedoyere, Michael de la. *Saint Maker*. Manchester, N.H.: Sophia Institute Press, 1998.

Beevers, John. *Storm of Glory*. Garden City, N.Y.: Image Books, 1955.

Bender, Harold S. *The Anabaptist Vision*. Scottdale, Penn.: Herald Press, 1944.

Bloom, Anthony. *Beginning to Pray*. New York: Paulist Press, 1970.

———. *Meditations: A Spiritual Journey*. Denville, N.J.: Dimension Books, 1971.

Bobrinskoy, Boris. "Encounter of Traditions in Greece: St. Nicodemus of the Holy Mountain". In *Christian Spirituality: Post-Reformation and Modern*. Edited by Louis Dupré and Don E. Saliers. New York: Crossroad, 1996.

Bolshakoff, Sergius. *Russian Mystics*. Kalamazoo, Mich.: Cistercian Publications, 1980.

Bonaventure. *Bonaventure: The Soul's Journey into God*; *The Tree of Life*; *The Life of St. Francis*. Translated and edited by Ewert Cousins, New York: Paulist Press, 1978.

Bonhoeffer, Dietrich. *The Cost of Discipleship*. New York: Macmillan, 1963.

———. *Life Together*. Translated by John W. Doberstein. New York: Harper and Row, 1976.

Bougaud, Emile. *The Life of Saint Margaret Mary Alacoque*. Translated by a Visitandine of Maryland. Rockford, Il.: Tan Books, 1990.

Bourguet, R. P. du, S.J. *Art Paléochrétien*. Paris: Editions Cercle d'Art, 1970.

Bousset, Wilhelm. *Kyrios Christos: A History of the Belief in Christ from the Beginnings of Christianity to Irenaeus*. Nashville: Abingdon, 1970.

Bouyer, Louis. *Newman's Vision of Faith*. San Francisco: Ignatius Press, 1986.

———. *The Spirit and Forms of Protestantism*. Westminster, Md.: Newman Press, 1961.

———. *Orthodox Spirituality and Protestant and Anglican Spirituality*. Vol. 3, *A History of Christian Spirituality*. New York: Seabury Press, 1982.

Bradshaw, Brendan, and Eamon Duffy, eds. *Humanism, Reform and the Reformation: The Career of Bishop John Fisher*. Cambridge: Cambridge University Press, 1989.

Brémond, Henri. *A Literary History of Religious Thought in France*. Vol. 2. London: SPCK, 1930.

Brianchaninov, Ignatius. *On the Prayer of Jesus*. Translated by Father Lazarus. Rockport, Mass.: Element, 1993.

Brice, Father, C.P. *In Spirit and in Truth: The Spiritual Doctrine of Saint Paul of the Cross*. New York: Frederick Pustet, 1948.

Bridgett, T. E. *Life of Blessed John Fisher*. 4th ed. London: Burns, Oates and Washbourne, 1922.

Brousse, Jacques. *The Lives of Ange de Joyeuse and Benet Canfield*. Translated by Robert Rookwood. Edited by T. A. Birrell. London: Sheed and Ward, 1959.

Brown, John. *Puritan Preaching in England*. London: Hodder and Stoughton, 1900.

Buckley, Michael J., S.J. "Seventeenth-Century French Spirituality: Three Figures". In *Christian Spirituality: Post-Reformation and Modern*. Edited by Louis Dupré and Don E. Saliers. New York: Crossroad, 1996.

Büsser, Fritz. "The Spirituality of Zwingli and Bullinger in the Reformation of Zurich", In *Christian Spirituality, High Middle Ages and Reformation*. Edited by Jill Raitt. New York: Crossroad, 1988.

Butler's Lives of the Saints. Edited by Herbert Thurston, S.J., and Donald Attwater. New York: P. J. Kenedy, 1963.

Cabasilas, Nicholas. *The Life in Christ*. Translated by Carmino J. de Catanzaro. Crestwood, N.Y.: St. Vladimir's Seminary Press, 1998.

Cabrol, Fernand, O.S.B. *Liturgical Prayer: Its History and Spirit.* Reprint, Westminster, Md.: Newman Press, 1950.

Campbell, Ted A. *The Religion of the Heart: A Study of European Religious Life in the Seventeenth and Eighteenth Centuries.* Columbia: University of South Carolina Press, 1991.

Carol, Juniper B., O.F.M. *Mariology.* 3 vols. Milwaukee: Bruce, 1954.

Catherine of Siena. *The Prayers of Catherine of Siena.* Translated and edited by Suzanne Noffke. San Jose/New York: Authors Choice Press, 2001.

The Catholic Encyclopedia. New York: Appleton and Company, 1907.

Caussade, J. P. de, S.J. *Self-Abandonment to Divine Providence.* Translated by Algar Thorold. Rockford, Ill.: Tan Books, 1987.

Cavarnos, Constantine. *St. Nicodemos the Hagiorite.* Belmont, Mass.: Institute for Byzantine and Modern Greek Studies, 1974.

Clare of Assisi. *Clare of Assisi: Early Documents.* Edited and translated by Regis J. Armstrong, O.F.M. Cap. New York: Paulist Press, 1988.

The Cloud of Unknowing. Edited by James Walsh, S.J. Classics of Western Spirituality. New York: Paulist Press, 1981.

Colledge, Eric, O.S.A. *The Mediæval Mystics of England.* New York: Charles Scribner's Sons, 1961.

Cooke, Terence. *Prayers for Today.* New York: Alba House, 1991.

Cousins, Ewert. "The Humanity and the Passion of Christ". *Christian Spirituality: High Middle Ages and Reformation.* Edited by Jill Raitt. New York: Crossroad, 1988.

Cranmer, Thomas. *The Collects of Thomas Cranmer.* Edited by C. Frederick Barbee and Paul F. M. Zahl. Grand Rapids, Mich.: William B. Eerdmans, 1999.

Crossan, John Dominic. *Jesus: A Revolutionary Biography.* San Francisco: Harper Collins, 1995.

Crow, Gillian. *'This Holy Man'.* London: Darton, Longman and Todd, 2005.

Cullmann, O. *The Tradition of The Early Church: Studies in Early Christian History.* Philadelphia: Westminster Press, 1956.

Curley, Michael J., C.Ss.R. *Bishop John Neumann, C.Ss.R.* Philadelphia: Bishop Neumann Center, 1952.

Daniel-Rops, Henri. *The Church in the Eighteenth Century.* Translated by John Warrington. New York: E. P. Dutton, 1964.

———. *The Church in the Seventeenth Century.* Translated by J. J. Buckingham. New York: Doubleday, 1964.

Davies, Horton. *The Worship of the American Puritans 1629–1730.* New York: Peter Lang, 1990.

Donne, John. *The Complete English Poems.* London: Everyman's Library, 1991.

Doukakis, Constantine, and Antonio Georgiou, eds. *Peri tes synechous metalepseos ton Theion Mysterion.* Athens, 1887.

Dubois, Elfrieda. "Fénelon and Quietism". In *The Study of Spirituality.* Edited by Cheslyn Jones, Geoffrey Wainwright, and Edward Yarnold, S.J. New York: Oxford University Press, 1986.

Duffy, Eamon. *The Stripping of the Altars: Traditional Religion in England c. 1400–c. 1580.* New Haven: Yale University Press, 1992.

Dulles, Avery, S.J. "Can Philosophy Be Christian?" *First Things* 103, April 2000.

Dupré, Louis. "Jansenism and Quietism", *Christian Spirituality: Post-Reformation and Modern.* Edited by Louis Dupré and Don E. Saliers. New York: Crossroad, 1996.

Edwards, Jonathan. *Selected Writings of Jonathan Edwards*, Edited by Harold P. Simonson. New York: Frederick Ungar, 1970.

Egan, Maurice Francis. "A Legacy of Hawthorne". *New York Times Book Review and Magazine*, April 16, 1922.

Elliot, Elisabeth. *On Asking God Why*. Grand Rapids, Mich.: Revell, 1989.

———. *Through Gates of Splendor*. Carol Stream, Ill.: Tyndale House, 1996.

Emery, Kent, Jr. *Renaissance Dialectic and Renaissance Piety: Benet of Canfield's Rule of Perfection*. Binghamton, N.Y.: Medieval and Renaissance Texts and Studies, 1987.

The Epistle of Privy Counsel. Edited by Abbot Justin McCann. London: Burns and Oates, 1964.

Erb, Peter C., ed. *Pietists: Selected Writings*. Classics of Western Spirituality. New York: Paulist Press, 1983.

Farina, John. *An American Experience of God: The Spirituality of Isaac Hecker*. New York: Paulist Press, 1981.

———, ed. *Hecker Studies: Essays on the Thought of Isaac Hecker*. New York: Paulist Press, 1983.

Fedotov, George P. *The Russian Religious Mind*. Cambridge, Mass.: Harvard University Press, 1946.

Felder, Hilarin. *The Ideals of St. Francis of Assisi*. Translated by Birchmans Bittle. Quincy, Ill.: Franciscan Press, 1982.

Fénelon, Francois. *Fénelon: Letters of Love and Counsel*. Translated and edited by John McEwen. New York: Harcourt, Brace and World, 1964.

Ferguson, Everett, ed. *The Bible in the Early Church*. New York and London: Garland, 1990.

Fortini, Arnaldo, and Helen Moak. *Francis of Assisi*. New York: Crossroad, 1981.

Fox, Charles James. "Liberty Is Order, Liberty Is Strength". *What Is a Man? 3,000 Years of Wisdom on the Art of Manly Virtue*. Edited by Waller R. Newell. New York: Harper, 2001.

Francis de Sales. *Introduction to the Devout Life*. Translated by Michael Day, C.O.. Westminster, Md.: Newman Press, 1956.

———. *On the Love of God*. Translated by John K. Ryan. Rockford, Ill.: Tan Books, 1975.

———. *Treatise on the Love of God*. Edited by Wendy M. Wright. New York: Crossroad, 1993.

Francis de Sales, and Jane de Chantal. *Francis de Sales and Jane de Chantal: Letters of Spiritual Direction*. Translated by Péronne Marie Thibert, V.H.M. New York: Paulist Press, 1988.

Francis of Assisi. *Francis of Assisi: Early Documents*. Edited by Regis J. Armstrong, O.F.M. Cap., et al. New York: New City Press, 1999.

———. *St. Francis of Assisi: Writings for a Gospel Life*. Edited by Regis J. Armstrong, O.F.M. Cap., et al. New York: Crossroad, 1994.

Gamache, Cyprien de. *Memoirs of the Mission in England of the Capuchin Friars of the Province of Paris from the Year 1630 to 1669*. London: Henry Colburn, 1848.

Gaucher, Guy. *The Passion of Thérèse of Lisieux*. New York: Crossroad, 1989.

Gaustad, Edwin Scott. *The Great Awakening in New England*. Chicago: Quadrangle Books, 1968.

Gebhard, H. P. *The World of Icons*. New York: Harper and Row, 1957.

George, A. Raymond. "John Wesley and the Methodist Movement". In *The Study of Spirituality*. Edited by Cheslyn Jones, Geoffrey Wainwright, and Edward Yarnold, S.J. London: SPCK, 1986.

George, Timothy "The Pattern of Christian Thought". In *First Things* 154, June/July 2005.

———. "Southern Baptists after the Revolution". In *First Things* 165, August/September 2006.

Gillet, Lev. *In Thy Presence*. Crestwood, N.Y.: St. Vladimir's Seminary Press, 1998.

Gilley, Sheridan. *Newman and His Age*. London, England: Darton, Longman and Todd, 2002.

Gingras, George, ed. *Egeria: Diary of a Pilgrimage*. New York: Newman Press, 1970.

Glimm, Francis X., et al. *The Fathers of the Church*. New York: Cima, 1947.

Goodier, Alban, S.J. *Jesus Christ the Son of God*. London: Burns, Oates and Washbourne, 1920.

———. *The Meaning of Life: The Catholic Answer*. Manchester, N.H.: Sophia Institute Press, 2002.

Goodwin, Thomas. *The Works of Thomas Goodwin*. Vol. 4. Edinburgh: James Nichol, 1862.

Gorday, Peter, and Thomas C. Oden, eds. *Ancient Christian Commentary on Scripture*. Downers Grove, Ill.: InterVarsity Press, 1995.

Gorodetzky, Nadejda. *The Humiliated Christ in Modern Russian Thought*. London: SPCK, 1938.

———. *Saint Tikhon of Zadonsk: Inspirer of Dostoevsky*. Crestwood, N.Y.: St. Vladimir's Seminary Press, 1976; first published by SPCK, London, 1951.

Görres, Ida Friederike. *The Hidden Face*. Translated by Richard and Clara Winston. New York: Pantheon Books, 1959.

Graef, Hilda. *Mary: A History of Doctrine and Devotion*. London: Sheed and Ward, 1963.

———. *The Scholar and the Cross*. Westminster, Md.: Newman Press, 1955.

Gregory of Nyssa. *From Glory to Glory: Texts from Gregory of Nyssa's Mystical Writings*. Translated and edited by Herbert Musurillo, S.J. New York: Charles Scribner's Sons, 1961.

Grisbrooke, W. Jardine. *Anglican Liturgies of the Seventeenth and Eighteenth Centuries*. London: SPCK, 1958.

Griffis, S., James E., ed. *To Believe Is to Pray: Readings from Michael Ramsey*. Boston: Cowley Publications, 1996.

Groeschel, Benedict J., C.F.R. *The Reform of Renewal*. San Francisco: Ignatius Press, 1990.

———. *A Still, Small Voice: A Practical Guide on Reported Revelations*. San Francisco: Ignatius Press, 1993

———. *Spiritual Passages: The Psychology of Spiritual Development*. New York: Crossroad, 1983.

Groeschel, Benedict J., C.F.R., and James Monti. *In the Presence of Our Lord: The History, Theology, and Psychology of Eucharistic Devotion*. Huntington, Ind.: Our Sunday Visitor, 1997.

Groeschel, Benedict J., C.F.R. with Kevin Perrotta. *The Journey toward God*. Ann Arbor, Mich.: Servant Publications, 2000.

Groeschel, Benedict J., C.F.R., and Terrence L. Weber. *Thy Will Be Done: A Spiritual Portrait of Terence Cardinal Cooke*. New York: Alba House, 1990.

Guaïta, Giovanni. *Between Heaven and Earth, A Conversation with His Holiness Karekin I*. New York, St. Vartan's Press, 2000.

Guardini, Romano. *The End of the Modern World*. New York: Sheed and Ward, 1956.

———. *The Humanity of Christ*. London: Burns and Oates, 1963.

———. *The Lord*. Translated by Elinor Castendyk Briefs. Washington, D.C.: Regnery, 2002.

Habig, Marion, ed. *St. Francis of Assisi: Writings and Early Biographies: English Omnibus of the Sources for the Life of St. Francis*. Chicago, Ill.: Franciscan Herald Press, 1973.

Hackel, Sergei. "Late Medieval Russia: The Possessors and the Non-Possessors". In *Christian Spirituality: High Middle Ages and Reformation*. Edited by Jill Raitt. New York: Crossroad, 1988.

———. *Pearl of Great Price*. Crestwood, N.Y.: St. Vladimir's Seminary Press, 1981.

———. "Trial and Victory: The Spiritual Tradition of Modern Russia". In *Christian Spirituality: Post-Reformation and Modern*. Edited by Louis Dupré and Don E. Saliers. New York: Crossroad, 1996.

Hadewijch of Antwerp. *Hadewijch: The Complete Works*. Translated and edited by Columba Hart, O.S.B. New York: Paulist Press, 1980.

Hall, Christopher A. *Reading Scripture with the Church Fathers*. Downers Grove, Ill.: InterVarsity Press, 1998.

Hall, N. John. *Trollope: A Biography*. Oxford: Clarendon Press, 1991.

Hambrick-Stowe, Charles E., ed. *Early New England Meditative Poetry*. New York: Paulist Press, 1988.

———. "Puritan Spirituality in America". In *Christian Spirituality: Post-Reformation and Modern*. Edited by Louis Dupré and Don E. Saliers. New York: Crossroad, 1996.

Hamman, A., O.F.M., ed. *Early Christian Prayers*. Chicago: Henry Regnery, 1961.

Hammarskjöld, Dag. *Markings*. Translated by Leif Sjöberg and W. H. Auden. New York: Alfred A. Knopf, 1964.

———. "Old Creeds in a New World". *Servants of Peace*. Edited by Wilder Foote. New York: Harper, 1962.

The HarperCollins Book of Prayers. Edited by Robert Van de Wayer. Edison, N.J.: Castle Books, 1993.

Hecker, Isaac T. *Isaac T. Hecker: The Diary*. Edited by John Farina. New York: Paulist Press 1988.

Heimert, Alan, and Andrew Delbanco, eds. *The Puritans in America*. Cambridge, Mass.: Harvard University Press, 1985.

Herambourg, Peter, C.J.M. *Saint John Eudes, a Spiritual Portrait*. Translated by Ruth Hauser. Edited by Wilfrid E. Myatt, C.J.M. Westminster, Md.: Newman Press, 1960.

Hillerbrand, Hans J. *The Reformation*. Grand Rapids, Michigan.: Baker Book House, 1979.

Hinson, E. Glenn. "Baptist and Quaker Spirituality". In *Christian Spirituality: Post-Reformation and Modern*. Edited by Louis Dupré and Don E. Saliers. New York: Crossroad, 1996.

Holwerda, David E., ed. *Exploring the Heritage of John Calvin*, Grand Rapids, Mich.: Baker Book House, 1976.

Honoré, Jean. *The Spiritual Journey of Newman*. New York: Alba House, 1992.

Hooker, Richard. *Tractates and Sermons*. Cambridge, Mass.: Harvard University Press, 1990.

Hughes, Philip. *A Popular History of the Reformation*. New York: Image/Doubleday, 1960.

Hunter, Daniel Honorius, O.P. "Palamas, Gregory", In *New Catholic Encyclopedia*. New York: McGraw-Hill, 1967.

Hurtado, Larry W. *Lord Jesus Christ: Devotion to Jesus in Earliest Christianity*. Grand Rapids, Mich.: William B. Eerdmans, 2003.

———. *One God, One Lord: Early Christian Devotion and Ancient Jewish Monotheism*. 2nd ed. Edinburgh: T. and T. Clark, 1998.

———. *At the Origins of Christian Worship: The Context and Character of Earliest Christian Devotion*. Grand Rapids, Mich.: Eerdmans, 2000.

Ignatius Loyola. *The Spiritual Exercises of St. Ignatius*. Translated by Anthony Mottola. Garden City, N.Y.: Image Books/Doubleday, 1963.

James, M.R. *The Apocryphal New Testament*. Oxford: Clarendon Press, 1924.

Jedin, Herbert, ed. *The Medieval and Reformation Church: An abridgement of History of the Church*. New York: Crossroad, 1993.

Jelly, Frederick, O.P. *Madonna: Mary in the Catholic Tradition*. Huntingdon, Ind.: Our Sunday Visitor, 1986.

John of Damascus. *On the Divine Images*. Translated by David Anderson. Crestwood, N.Y.: St. Vladimir's Seminary Press, 1980.

John of the Cross. *The Collected Works of St. John of the Cross*. Translated and edited by Kieran Kavanaugh, O.C.D., and Otilio Rodriguez, O.C.D. Washington, D.C.: Institute of Carmelite Studies, 1973.

———. *The Poems of St. John of the Cross*. Translated by Ken Krabbenhoft. New York: Harcourt Brace, 1999.

John Paul II. *The Encyclicals of John Paul II*. Edited by J. Michael Miller, C.S.B. Huntington, Ind.: Our Sunday Visitor, 1996.

———. Apostolic Letter of His Holiness John Paul II: *Orientale Lumen*. Boston, St. Paul Editions, Daughters of Saint Paul.

Johnson, Luke Timothy. *The Real Jesus*. San Francisco: Harper Collins, 1996.

Johnston, William. *The Mysticism of* The Cloud of Unknowing. St. Meinrad, Ind.: Abbey Press, 1975.

Jones, Frederick M., C.Ss.R. *Alphonsus de Liguori: The Saint of Bourbon Naples 1696–1787*. Westminster, Md.: Christian Classics, 1992.

Jørgensen, Johannes. *Saint Francis of Assisi: A Biography*. Garden City, New York: Image/Doubleday, 1955.

———. *Saint Catherine of Siena*. New York: Longmans, Green, 1938.

Julian of Norwich. *Julian of Norwich: Showings*. Translated and edited by Edmund Colledge, O.S.A., and James Walsh, S.J. New York: Paulist Press, 1978.

Karekin II. *In Search of Spiritual Life*. New York: Armenian Apostolic Church of America, 1994

Keller, Rosemary Skinner and Rosemary Radford Ruether, eds. *In Our Own Voices: Four Centuries of American Women's Religious Writing*. San Francisco: Harper San Francisco, 1995.

Kempis, Thomas à. *The Imitation of Christ*. Translated by Ronald Knox and Michael Oakley. San Francisco: Ignatius Press, 2005.

Ker, Ian. *John Henry Newman: A Biography*. Oxford University Press, 1988.

Knowles, David. *The English Mystical Tradition*. New York: Harper and Brothers, 1961.

Knox, Ronald A. *Enthusiasm*. New York: Oxford University Press, 1950.

Kolodiéjchuk, Brian. *Mother Teresa: Come Be My Light, the Private Writings of the Saint of Calcutta*. New York: Doublday, 2007.

Kowalska, Maria Faustina. *Diary: Divine Mercy in My Soul*. Stockbridge, Mass.: Marians of the Immaculate Conception, 2000.

Krieg, Robert A., C.S.C. *Romano Guardini: A Precursor of Vatican II*. Notre Dame, Ind.: University of Notre Dame Press, 1997.

Lathrop, Rose Hawthorne. *Memories of Hawthorne*. Boston: Houghton Mifflin, 1897.

Laurentin, René. *Queen of Heaven: A Short Treatise on Marian Theology*. London: Burns, Oates and Washbourne, 1956.

Leclercq, Jean, et al. *A History of Christian Spirituality*. 3 vols. New York: The Seabury Press, 1982.

Leinenweber, John. *Be Friends of God: Spiritual Reading from Gregory the Great*. Cambridge, Mass.: Cowley Publications, 1990.

Lewis, C. S. *The Four Loves*. New York: Harcourt, Brace, 1960.

Lewis, John. *The Life of Dr. John Fisher*. Vol. 1. London: Joseph Lilly, 1855.

Lienhard, Marc. "Luther and the Beginnings of the Reformation". *Christian Spirituality: High Middle Ages and Reformation*. Edited by Jill Raitt. New York: Crossroad, 1988.

The Liturgy of the Hours. 4 vols. New York: Catholic Book Publishing, 1976.

Lot-Borodine, M. *Un maître de la spiritualité byzantine: Nicolas Cabasilas*. Paris: Éditions de l'Orante, 1958.

Lotz, David W. "Continental Pietism". In *The Study of Spirituality*. Edited by Cheslyn Jones, Geoffrey Wainwright, and Edward Yarnold, S.J. London: SPCK, 1986.

Lovelace, Richard C. "Puritan Spirituality: The Search for a Rightly Reformed Church". In *Christian Spirituality: Post-Reformation and Modern*. Edited by Louis Dupré and Don E. Saliers. New York: Crossroad, 1996.

Luddy, Ailbe J., O.Cist. *Life and Teaching of St. Bernard*. Dublin: M. H. Gill and Son, 1927.

Lund, Eric. "Second Age of the Reformation: Lutheran and Reformed Spirituality, 1550–1700" In *Christian Spirituality: Post-Reformation and Modern*. Edited by Louis Dupré and Don E. Saliers. New York: Crossroad, 1996.

Luria, Keith P. "The Counter-Reformation and Popular Spirituality". In *Christian Spirituality: Post-Reformation and Modern*. Edited by Louis Dupré and Don E. Saliers. New York: Crossroad, 1996.

Mansfield, Patti Gallagher. *As By a New Pentecost*. Steubenville, Ohio: Franciscan University Press, 1992.

Marmion, Columba, O.S.B. *Christ, the Life of the Soul*. St. Louis: B. Herder, 1925.

———. *Christ in His Mysteries*. Translated by Mother M. St. Thomas. St. Louis: B. Herder, 1939.

———. *Spiritual Writings*. Paris: P. Lethielleux, 1998.

Marshall, Peter. *The Prayers of Peter Marshal*. Edited by Catherine Marshall. New York: McGraw-Hill, 1954.

Martz, Louis. *The Poetry of Meditation*. New Haven: Yale University Press, 1954.

Marucchi, Orazio. *Manual of Christian Archaeology*. Paterson, N.J.: St. Anthony Guild Press, 1949.

McGinn, Bernard, ed. and trans. by *Apocalyptic Spirituality*. Classics of Western Spirituality. New York: Paulist Press, 1979.

McNabb, Vincent, O.P. *Saint John Fisher*. London: Sheed and Ward, 1935.

Meier, John. *A Marginal Jew: Rethinking the Historical Jesus*. 2 vols. New York: Doubleday, 1991.

Melville, Annabelle M. *Elizabeth Bayley Seton*. New York: Charles Scribner's Sons, 1951.

Merton, Thomas. "Reflections on the Character and Genius of Fénelon". In *Fénelon: Letters of Love and Counsel*. Edited and Translated by John McEwen. New York: Harcourt, Brace and World, 1964.

Meyendorff, John, ed. *Gregory Palamas*. New York: Paulist Press, 1983.

Miller, Perry. *The New England Mind: The Seventeenth Century*. New York: Macmillan, 1939.

Minus, Paul M. *Walter Rauschenbusch: American Reformer*. New York: Macmillan, 1988.

Montfort, Louis Marie de. *God Alone: The Collected Writings of St. Louis Marie de Montfort*. Bay Shore, N.Y.: Montfort Publications, 1997.

Moore, James P., Jr. *One Nation Under God: The History of Prayer in America*. New York: Doubleday, 2005.

Morgan, Derec Llwyd. *The Great Awakening in Wales*. Translated by Dyfnallt Morgan. London: Epworth Press, 1988.

Morimoto, Anri. *Jonathan Edwards and the Catholic Vision of Salvation*. University Park, Penn.: Pennsylvania State University Press, 1995.

Mursell, Gordon, ed. *The Story of Christian Spirituality*. Minneapolis, Minn.: Fortress Press, 2001.

Musurillo, Herbert, S.J. *Acts of the Christian Martyrs*. Oxford: Clarendon Press, 1972.

Neuner, J., S.J. "Mother Teresa's Charism". In *Vidyajyoti Journal of Theological Reflection*. March 2001.

New Catholic Encyclopedia. New York: McGraw-Hill, 1967.

Newman, John Henry. *Meditations and Devotions*. London: Burns and Oates, 1964.

———. *Parochial and Plain Sermons*. San Francisco: Ignatius Press, 1997.

———. *Prayers, Verses, and Devotions: The Devotions of Bishop Andrewes*. San Francisco: Ignatius Press, 1989.

Noll, Mark A. *A History of Christianity in the United States and Canada*. Grand Rapids, Mich.: William B. Eerdmans, 1992.

Nugent, Madeline Pecora. *Saint Anthony: Words of Fire, Life of Light*. Boston: Daughters of St. Paul, 1995.

O'Connor, Edward D., C.S.C. *The Pentecostal Movement in the Catholic Church*. Notre Dame, Ind.: Ave Maria Press, 1971.

O'Connor, James T. *The Father's Son*. Boston: St. Paul Editions, 1984.

———. *The Hidden Manna: A Theology of the Eucharist*. San Francisco: Ignatius Press, 1988.

Olin, John C. *The Catholic Reformation: Savonarola to Ignatius Loyola*. New York: Fordham University Press, 1992.

O Maidin, Uinseann, O.C.R. *The Celtic Monk: Rules and Writings of Early Irish Monks*. Translated by Robin Flower. Kalamazoo, Mich.: Cistercian Publications, 1996.

Panzer, Joel S. *The Popes and Slavery*. New York: Alba House, 1996.

Paor, Máire, and Liam de. *Early Christian Ireland*. New York: Frederick A. Praeger, 1958.

Payne, Daniel Alexander. "The Hour of Prayer". In *Conversations with God: Two Centuries of Prayers by African Americans*. Edited by James Melvin Washington, Ph.D. New York: HarperPerennial, 1995.

Pelikan, Jaroslav. *Jesus through the Centuries*. New Haven: Yale University Press, 1985.

———. *Mary through the Centuries*. New Haven: Yale University Press, 1996.

Pepler, Conrad, O.P. *The English Religious Heritage*. London: Blackfriars Publications, 1958.

Philip, Mary. *A Jesuit at the English Court*. London: Burns, Oates and Washbourne, 1922.

Philipon, M. M., O.P. *The Spiritual Doctrine of Dom Marmion*. Translated by Dom Matthew Dillon, O.S.B. Westminster, Md.: Newman Press, 1956.

The Philokalia. 4 vols. Translated by G.E.H. Palmer, et al. London: Faber and Faber, 1979.

Pieper, Josef. *The Silence of St. Thomas*. Translated by Daniel O'Connor. London: Faber and Faber, 1957.

Pio of Pietrelcina. *Letters*. Vol. 1. *Correspondence with His Spiritual Directors (1910–1922)*. Edited by Fr. Gerardo Di Flumeri, O.F.M. Cap. San Giovanni Rotondo: Editions "Voce di Padre Pio", 1980.

Pius XI. Encyclical Letter of His Holiness Pope Pius XI: *Miserentissimus Redemptor* (1928). Vatican website: http://www.vatican.va.

Pius XII. Encyclical Letter of His Holiness Pope Pius XII: *Haurietis Aquas* (1956). Vatican website: http://www.vatican.va.

Plekon, Michael. *Living Icons*. Notre Dame, Ind.: University of Notre Dame Press, 2002.

———. ed. *Tradition Alive*. Lanham, Md.: Rowman and Littlefield, 2003.

Poulain, A., S.J. *The Graces of Interior Prayer*. Translated by Leonora L. Yorke-Smith. London: Routledge and Kegan Paul, 1957.

Prayer Book for Earnest Christians. Translated and edited by Leonard Gross. Scottdale, Penn.: Herald Press, 1997.

Przywara, Erich, S.J. *The Heart of Newman*. San Francisco: Ignatius Press, 1997.

———. ed. *An Augustine Synthesis*. New York: Sheed and Ward, 1945.

Quenot, Michel. *The Icon: Window on the Kingdom*. Crestwood, N.Y.: St. Vladimir's Seminary Press, 1996.

Ramsey, Arthur Michael. *God, Christ and the World*. London: SCM Press, 1969.

———. *Introducing the Christian Faith*. London: SCM Press, 1961.

———. *The Resurrection of Christ*. London: Geoffrey Bles: Centenary Press, 1946.

Ratcliff, E. C., ed. *The First and Second Prayer Books of Edward VI*. New York: Everyman's Library, 1949.

Rattenbury, J. Ernest. *The Eucharistic Hymns of John and Charles Wesley*. Akron, Ohio: OSL Publications, 1996.

Ratzinger, Joseph. *A New Song for the Lord*. New York: Crossroad, 1996.

———. *Jesus of Nazareth*. Translated by Adrian J. Walker. New York: Doubleday, 2007.

Rauschenbusch, Walter. *Prayers of the Social Awakening*. New York: Pilgrim Press, 1910.

———. *Walter Rauschenbusch: Selected Writings*. Edited by Winthrop S. Hudson. New York: Paulist Press, 1984.

Reinhold, H. A., ed. *The Soul Afire: Revelations of the Mystics*. Garden City, N.Y.: Image Books, Doubleday, 1973.

Reynolds, E. E. *Saint John Fisher*. Rev. edition. Wheathampstead: Anthony Clarke Books, 1972.

Rideman, Peter. *Confession of Faith: Account of Our Religion, Doctrine and Faith*. Rifton, N.Y.: Plough Publishing House, 1970.

The Roman Missal: The Sacramentary. Translated by International Commission on English in the Liturgy. New York: Catholic Book Publishing, 1974.

Ruffin, C. Bernard. *Last Words: A Dictionary of Deathbed Quotations*. Jefferson, N.C.: McFarland, 1995.

Runciman, Steven. *The Great Church in Captivity*. Cambridge: University Press, 1968.

The Sadness of Christ. Edited by Gerard Wegemer. Translated by Clarence Miller. Princeton, N.J.: Scepter Press, 1993

Salmon-Malebranche, A. R. *Madame Acarie*. Translated by Jeanne Dumais, O.C.D.S., and Sister Miriam, O.C.D. Eugene, Ore.: Four Corners Press, 1981.

Saward, John. *Perfect Fools*. Oxford: Oxford University Press, 1980.

Scarisbrick, J.J. *Henry VIII*. 2nd ed. New Haven: Yale University Press, 1997.

Schmemann, Alexander. *The Historical Road of Eastern Orthodoxy*. Translated by Lydia W. Kesich. New York: Holt, Rinehart and Winston, 1963.

Schnackenburg, Rudolf. *The Moral Teaching of the New Testament*. 3rd ed. London: Burns and Oates, 1974.

Schönborn, Christoph, O.P. *God's Human Face: The Christ-Icon*. San Francisco: Ignatius Press, 1994.

Seton, Elizabeth. *Elizabeth Seton: Sèlected Writings*. Edited by Kelly Ellin Kelly and Annabelle Melville. New York: Paulist Press, 1987.

Sheen, Fulton J. *Life of Christ*. New York: McGraw-Hill, 1958.

Skinner, B. F. *A Matter of Consequences*. New York: Alfred A. Knopf, 1983.

Sola Pinto, Vivian de. *Peter Sterry: Platonist and Puritan*. Cambridge: Cambridge University Press, 1934.

Stackpole, Robert A. *Jesus, Mercy Incarnate*. Stockbridge, Mass.: Marians of the Immaculate Conception, 2000.

Stanwood, Paul G., ed. *William Law*. Classics of Western Spirituality. New York: Paulist Press, 1978.

Starbuck, Edwin Diller. *The Psychology of Religion: An Empirical Study of the Growth of Religious Consciousness*. New York: Scribner, 1911.

Steere, Douglas V., ed. *Quaker Spirituality: Selected Writings*. Classics of Western Spirituality. New York: Paulist Press, 1984

Steichen, Donna. *Ungodly Rage*. San Francisco: Ignatius Press, 1991.

Stein, Edith. "I Will Remain With You" (*"Ich bleibe bei euch"*). In *The Hidden Life: Hagiographic Essays, Meditations, Spiritual Texts*. Translated by Waltraut Stein. Vol. 4. *The Collected Works of Edith Stein*. Washington, D.C.: ICS Publications, 1992.

Stolpe, Sven. *Dag Hammarskjöld, A Spiritual Portrait*. Translated by Naomi Walford. New York: Scribner, 1966.

Stopp, Elisabeth. "François de Sales". In *The Study of Spirituality*. Edited by Cheslyn Jones, Geoffrey Wainwright, and Edward Yarnold, S.J. London: SPCK, 1986.

———. "Healing Differences: St. Francis de Sales in Seventeenth-Century England". *The Month* 38 (1967).

Synan,Vinson. *In the Latter Days*. Ann Arbor, Mich.: Servant Publications, 1984.

———. *The Century of the Holy Spirit*. Nashville, Tenn.: Thomas Nelson Publishers, 2001.

Taylor, Jeremy. *Jeremy Taylor: Selected Works*. Edited by Thomas K. Carroll. Classics of Western Spirituality. New York: Paulist Press, 1990.

Teresa of Avila. *The Collected Works of St. Teresa of Avila*. Translated and edited by Kieran Kavanaugh, O.C.D., and Otilio Rodriguez, O.C.D. Washington, D.C.: ICS Publications, vol. 1, rev. ed., 1987; vol. 2, 1980; vol. 3, 1985.

———. *Way of Perfection*. Translated by E. Allison Peers. New York: Image Books, 1991.

Thérèse of Lisieux. *Story of a Soul: The Autobiography of St. Thérèse of Lisieux*, Translated by John Clarke, O.C.D. Washington, D.C.: ICS Publications, 1996.

———. *St. Thérèse of Lisieux: Her Last Conversations*. Translated by John Clarke, O.C.D. Washington, D.C.: ICS Publications, 1977.

The Works of Thomas Goodwin. Vol. 4. Edinburgh: James Nichol, 1862.

Thibaut, Raymund. *Abbot Columba Marmion: A Master of the Spiritual Life*. Translated by Mother Mary St. Thomas. London: Sands, 1932.

Thomas Aquinas. *Devoutly I Adore Thee: The Prayers and Hymns of St. Thomas Aquinas*. Translated and edited by Robert Anderson and Johann Moser. Manchester, N.H.: Sophia Institute Press, 1993.

Thomas More. *The Complete Works of St. Thomas More*. Vol. 14. Translated and edited by Clarence H. Miller. New Haven: Yale University Press, 1976.

Thompson, William M., ed. *Bérulle and the French School: Selected Writings*. Translated by Lowell M. Glendon, S.S. Classics of Western Spirituality. New York: Paulist Press, 1989.

Tierney, Mark, O.S.B. *Dom Columba Marmion: A Biography*. Dublin: Columba Press, 1994.

Tillyard, H.J.W. *Byzantine Music and Hymnography*. London: Faith Press, 1923.

Treatise on the Love of God. Edited by Wendy M. Wright. New York: Crossroad, 1993.

Trevor, Meriol. *Newman: The Pillar of the Cloud*. New York: Doubleday, 1962.

Trollope, Anthony. *The Letters of Anthony Trollope*. Edited by John N. Hall. Stanford, Calif.: Stanford University Press, 1983.

Twentieth Century Encyclopedia of Catholicism. New York: Hawthorn Books, 1963.

Tylenda, Joseph N. "Calvin and Christ's Presence in the Supper—True or Real." *Scottish Journal of Theology* 27 (February 1974): 65–75.

Van de Wayer, Robert, ed. *The HarperCollins Book of Prayers*. Edison, N.J.: Castle Books, 1993.

Van Dusen, Henry Pitney. *Dag Hammarskjöld: The Statesman and His Faith*. New York: Harper, 1967.

Vaporis, Nomikos. "The Price of Faith: Some Reflections on Nicodemos Hagiorites and His Struggle against Islam, Together with a Translation of the 'Introduction' to His 'New Martyrologion'". *The Greek Orthodox Theological Review* 23: 208.

Vaughan, Henry. *Sacred Poems of Henry Vaughan*. New York: Charles Scribner's Sons, 1890.

Von Balthasar, Hans Urs. *Heart of the World*. Translated by Erasmo S. Leiva. San Francisco: Ignatius Press, 1979.

———. *Mysterium Paschale: The Mystery of Easter*. Translated by and with an introduction by Aidan Nichols, O.P. San Francisco: Ignatius Press, 2005.

Vincent de Paul, and Louise de Marillac. *Vincent de Paul and Louise de Marillac: Rules, Conferences, and Writings*. Edited by Frances Ryan, D.C. and John E. Rybolt, C.M. New York: Paulist Press, 1995.

Von Hildebrand, Alice. *The Soul of a Lion: Dietrich von Hildebrand*. San Francisco: Ignatius Press. 2000.

Von Hildebrand, Dietrich. *The Sacred Heart: An Analysis of Human and Divine Affectivity*. Baltimore: Helicon Press, 1965.

———. *Transformation in Christ*. Manchester, N.H.: Sophia Institute Press, 1998.

Von Hügel, Friedrich. *The Mystical Element of Religion*. 2 vols. London: James Clarke, 1909.

Vitz, Paul. *Psychology as Religion*. Grand Rapids, Mich.: Eerdmans, 1975.

Waal, Esther de. *Every Earthly Blessing: Celebrating a Spirituality of Creation*. Ann Arbor, Mich.: Servant, 1991.

Wakefield, Gordon S. "Anglican Spirituality". In *Christian Spirituality: Post-Reformation and Modern*. Edited by Louis Dupré and Don E. Saliers. New York: Crossroad, 1996.

Walsh, John Evangelist. *The Bones of St. Peter: The First Full Account of the Search for the Apostle's Body*. Garden City, N.Y.: Doubleday, 1982.

Ware, Kallistos. *The Orthodox Way*. Crestwood, N.Y.: St. Vladimir's Seminary Press, 1979.

Ware, Timothy. *The Orthodox Church*. London: Penguin Books, 1997.

———, ed. *The Art of Prayer: An Orthodox Anthology*. Translated by E. Kadloubovsky and E. M. Palmer. London: Faber and Faber, 1971.

Watkin, E. I. *Poets and Mystics*. London: Sheed and Ward, 1953.

Wesley, John and Charles. *John and Charles Wesley: Selected Writings and Hymns*. Edited by Frank Whaling. Classics of Western Spirituality. New York: Paulist Press, 1981.

West, Delno C., and Sandra Zimdars-Swartz. *Joachim of Fiore: A Study in Spiritual Perception and History*. Bloomington, Ind.: Indiana University Press, 1983.

White, Charles Edward. *The Beauty of Holiness*. Grand Rapids, Mich.: Francis Asbury Press, 1986.

White, Helen C. *The Tudor Books of Private Devotion*. Madison, Wisc.: University of Wisconsin Press, 1951.

Wright, N. T. *The Resurrection of the Son of God*. Minneapolis, Minn.: Augsburg Fortress Press, 2003.

Zahirsky, Valerie Goekjian. *The Conversion of Armenia to Christianity: A Retelling of Agathangelos' History*. New York: Diocese of the Armenian Church of America, 2001.

Zander, Valentine. *St. Seraphim of Sarov*. Translated by Sister Gabriel Anne, S.S.C. Crestwood, N.Y.: St. Vladimir's Seminary Press, 1999.

Zernov, Nicolas. *Eastern Christendom*. New York: G. P. Putnam's Sons, 1961.

Index